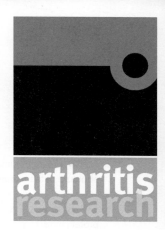

The Scientific Basis of Rheumatology

Editors:
Marc Feldmann, Hideaki Nagase, Jeremy Saklatvala
Kennedy Institute of Rheumatology Division, Faculty of Medicine,
Imperial College of Science, Technology and Medicine

Mark Walport
Division of Medicine, Faculty of Medicine,
Imperial College of Science, Technology and Medicine

Proceedings of a symposium held on 24–26 June 2002 in London, UK

Published as a supplement to *Arthritis Research* (http://arthritis-research.com)

Answers. Accelerated.

Funded by an unrestricted educational
grant from Abbott Immunology

Cover illustrations

Left: Structure of tumor necrosis factor alpha (TNF-α). View from the top of the trimer, showing a transparent molecular surface, with the secondary structure of the subunits represented as ribbons.

The image was created with Swiss-PdbViewer (Guex N, Peitsch MC: SWISS-MODEL and the Swiss-PdbViewer: an environment for comparative protein modeling. *Electrophoresis* 1997, **18**: 2714-2723), using the PDB ID:1TNF coordinates from the Protein Data Bank of the TNF-α structure solved by Eck and Sprang (Eck MJ, Sprang SR: The structure of tumor necrosis factor-alpha at 2.6 Å resolution. Implications for receptor binding. *J Biol Chem* 1989, **264**:17595-17605).

Centre: Structure of the TIMP-1 complex (green) and the MMP-3 catalytic domain (orange) represented as ribbons. Catalytic and structural zinc are shown in purple and calcium ions in orange. Three histidines that coordinate with the catalytic zinc are shown in orange. The N-terminal α-amino group and carbonyl oxygen of Cys 1 in TIMP-1 chelate the zinc atom (see the review article by H Nagase and K Brew in this issue).

The image was created with Swiss-PdbViewer (Guex N, Peitsch MC: SWISS-MODEL and the Swiss-PdbViewer: an environment for comparative protein modeling. *Electrophoresis* 1997, **18**: 2714-2723) and rendered with POV raytrace, using the PDB ID:1UEA coordinates from the Protein Data Bank of the structure solved by Gomis-Rüth *et al.* (Gomis-Rüth FX, Maskos K, Betz M, Bergner A, Huber R, Suzuki K, Yoshida N, Nagase H, Brew K, Bourenkov GP, Bartunik H, Bode W: Mechanism of inhibition of the human matrix metalloproteinase stromelysin-1 by TIMP-1. *Nature* 1997, **389**:77-81). MMP = matrix metalloproteinase; TIMP = tissue inhibitor of metalloproteases.

Right: Expression of von Willebrand factor in RA synovium. Frozen sections were stained using antibodies against von Willebrand factor (vWf). Samples were then incubated with biotinylated anti-mouse or anti-goat immunoglobulin, followed by streptavidin–horseradish peroxidase. Immune complexes were detected using 3,3′-diaminobenzidine. (For more details, see the review article by EM Paleolog in this issue.) RA = rheumatoid arthritis.

Published by BioMed Central Ltd, Middlesex House, 34–42 Cleveland Street, London W1T 4LB, UK.

British Library Cataloguing-in-Publication Data.

A catalogue record for this book is available from the British Library.

ISBN 0-9540278-1-7

This copy of *The Scientific Basis of Rheumatology* is presented as a service to medicine by Abbott Laboratories Inc. Sponsorship of this copy does not imply the sponsor's agreement or otherwise with the views expressed herein.

Although every effort has been made to ensure that drug doses and other information are presented accurately in this publication, the ultimate responsibility rests with the prescribing physician. Neither the publishers nor the authors can be held responsible for errors or for any consequences arising from the use of information contained herein. Any product mentioned in this publication should be used in accordance with the prescribing information prepared by the manufacturers. No claims or endorsements are made for any drug or compound at present under clinical investigation.

Project editor: Suzanne Miller, Wight Scientific, London, UK
Freelance copy-editors: Stella Morris, Oxfordshire, UK, and Helen Morris, Cambridge, UK
Illustrator/Typesetter: Neil Morris, Lincolnshire, UK
Production: Adrienne Hanratty
Printed in the UK by Latimer Trend & Company Ltd, Plymouth, UK

Arthritis Research
http://arthritis-research.com

Vol 4 Suppl 3 2002

Editorial Board of *Arthritis Research*

Arthritis Research Journal Information

http://arthritis-research.com

Arthritis Research (Print ISSN 1465-9905; online ISSN 1465-9913) is published by

BioMed Central Ltd
Middlesex House
34–42 Cleveland Street
London W1T 4LB, UK
Tel +44 (0)20 7631 9131
Fax +44 (0)20 7631 9926
Email info@arthritis-research.com

The electronic version of the journal can be found on the web under the following address: **http://arthritis-research.com**

Electronic and print versions
The complete version of the journal can be found on the World Wide Web (**http://arthritis-research.com**). Not all material available online is included in print. Articles included in the printed version of the journal may refer to supplementary data (eg raw data, additional figures, detailed discussion) which can only be found on the World Wide Web (**http://arthritis-research.com**). The online journal will be updated continuously and will always be up to date.

There will be six printed issues of *Arthritis Research* in each calendar year.

For further information about the journal, please see the description available on the *Arthritis Research* website (**http://arthritis-research.com**).

Article reprints are available.
For information contact:
Arthritis Research Editorial Office (Reprints)
Tel +44 (0)20 7323 0323
Fax +44 (0)20 7631 9923
Email reprints@arthritis-research.com

Advertising information
Advertising is accepted by *Arthritis Research*. Further information regarding advertising, including rate cards, specifications, etc, can be obtained from the Advertising Department:

Tel +44 (0)20 7323 0323
Fax +44 (0)20 7580 1938
Email advertising@arthritis-research.com

Disclaimer: Whilst every effort is made by the publishers and editorial board to see that no inaccurate or misleading data, opinions or statements appear in this publication, they wish to make it clear that the data and opinions appearing in the articles and advertisements herein are the responsibility of the contributor or advertiser concerned. Accordingly, the publishers, the editor and editorial board and their respective employees, officers and agents accept no liability whatsoever for the consequences of any such inaccurate or misleading data, opinion or statement.

Subscription information
Subscriptions are charged on an annual basis, from January to December or from the month the payment is made for a period of 12 months.

Indexing services
Arthritis Research is indexed in Chemical Abstracts Service, EMBASE, Index Medicus/MEDLINE, PubMed, Science Citation Index Expanded/Web of Science, Index to Scientific Reviews, ISI Alerting Services, and Current Contents/Clinical Medicine. Research is also freely available through PubMed Central and BioMed Central.

Typeset by Neil Morris, Lincolnshire, UK and printed by Latimer Trend & Company Ltd, Plymouth, UK

2002 Subscription rates Rates include airspeed delivery (6 issues)

	North/South America[1] US$	Rest of World[2] GB£	€[6]
Personal (online and print)	300	200	330
Personal (online only)	112	75	123
Academic institutional[3] (20–500 full-time employees; online and print)	540	360	594
Corporate institutional[3] (20–500 full-time employees; online and print)	1080	720	1188
Student[4], **nurse**[5] **or doctor-in-training**[4] (online only)	56	38	62

[1]**Canadian** subscribers add GST. [2]**EU** subscribers may be liable to European sales tax. [3]**Academic and corporate** rates for institutions with different numbers of full-time employees are available on request (subscription includes a single print copy for the institution and online access for all employees, all of which may be personalized). [4]**Students** and **doctors-in-training** must provide a letter from the head of department at their institution indicating that they are undergoing full-time education. The student rate is available for a maximum of 2 years per subscriber. [5]**RN** license number or equivalent required. [6]**Euro checks** incur high banking costs and €8 must be added to any check payment under €250: customers are advised to pay by credit/debit card to avoid this charge.

Postage paid at Far Rockaway.

Airfreight and mailing in the USA by
World Net Shipping
254 Henry Street
Inwood
NY 11096
USA

US Postmaster send address corrections to
Arthritis Research
c/o Current Science Inc
400 Market Street
Suite 700
Philadelphia
PA 19106-2514
USA

Subscription orders and enquiries

Any enquiries about subscriptions (new, existing or renewals) should be sent directly to:

Arthritis Research Customer Services
BioMed Central Ltd
Middlesex House
34–42 Cleveland Street
London W1T 4LB, UK
Tel +44 (0)20 7631 9131
Fax +44 (0)20 7631 9926
Email info@arthritis-research.com

Send notices of changes of address at least 8 weeks in advance, including both old and new address. Cancellations on renewed subscriptions will not be accepted after the first issue has been shipped.

In case of particular difficulty, please contact:
Mike Brown
BioMed Central Ltd
Middlesex House
34–42 Cleveland Street
London W1T 4LB, UK
Tel +44 (0)20 7631 9131
Fax +44 (0)20 7631 9926
Email mike@current-science.com

The Scientific Basis of Rheumatology

Arthritis Research Vol 4 Suppl 3 2002 (http://arthritis-research.com)

Contents

The Scientific Basis of Rheumatology
Contents continued

The Scientific Basis of Rheumatology
Contents continued

Preface

Professor Ravinder Maini, known as 'Tiny' to all, has had a most distinguished career as a rheumatologist, a clinical immunologist, a clinical triallist, and the head of a large academic research centre, the Kennedy Institute of Rheumatology. He steered the institute into being one of the world's leading 'translational' research centres in rheumatology and has received international recognition for his many achievements: the American College of Rheumatology awarded him the Distinguished Investigator Award – he was the first non-US citizen to be thus recognised – and the Université René Descartes of Paris awarded him the degree of Doctor *honoris causa*. He has been an enthusiastic teacher and mentor. Many of his trainees, friends, and colleagues, past and present, are participating in this conference and many have travelled long distances to do so.

This volume and the corresponding website are designed to fulfil two goals. First, they provide a summary of the presentations at the conference The Scientific Basis of Rheumatology, held in London on 24–26 June 2002 at the Royal College of Physicians. Secondly, they provide a useful introduction and teaching aid for scientists entering the field of rheumatology research. This multidisciplinary area requires knowledge of a number of research fields, including cytokines, cell signalling, matrix biology, vascular biology, immunology, and inflammation. The website will be continuously developed to enhance its teaching value. We will seek volunteers to flesh it out with further interesting and useful chapters.

When Tiny Maini started his scientific career at the Kennedy Institute of Rheumatology (the flagship research centre of the Arthritis Research Campaign, now at Imperial College) in 1968, his early work examined the activities of supernatants of lymphoid cell cultures. These bioactivities were eventually purified to yield the cytokines. So it is fitting that his best-known scientific contribution has been in establishing that a single cytokine, tumour necrosis factor alpha (TNF-α), is an important therapeutic target in rheumatoid arthritis and that his best-known medical contribution has been in leading the clinical trials that verified that TNF-α blockade, using anti-TNF-α monoclonal antibody, was indeed effective. This work has been recognized by the award of several prizes, most notably the Crafoord Prize awarded by the Royal Swedish Academy in 2000, which was shared with Marc Feldmann and was a fitting testimony to a successful collaboration spanning almost 20 years. This work has led to the approval of two

Marc Feldmann and Tiny Maini receiving the Crafoord Prize from the King of Sweden - September 2000

drugs that are already widely used and two more in the pipeline. At the time of writing, approximately 250,000 patients have been treated with anti-TNF therapy worldwide, with significant benefits for patients who have severe rheumatoid arthritis that does not respond to other treatment.

The National Institute for Clinical Excellence (NICE) in the UK is a government body set up to advise the National Health Service on making new drugs available to patients. It has evaluated anti-TNF therapy for rheumatoid arthritis and appraised it as cost effective in March 2002. It should now be more readily available for patients in the UK, and this will be a source of much personal satisfaction to Tiny, as the culmination of a glittering career.

The scientific meeting reported here was made possible by significant contributions from Schering-Plough, Centocor, and Roche Bioscience, and the publication and website by a contribution from Abbott Laboratories. We are very grateful for their support. The organizers of the meeting, who are also the editors of these proceedings, are long-term friends and admirers of Tiny Maini, and this volume is dedicated to him with the warmest wishes for a productive and enjoyable next stage of life.

Marc Feldmann
Hideaki Nagase
Jeremy Saklatvala
Mark Walport

Clinical therapy

Supplement Review

Immunotherapy of type 1 diabetes: lessons for other autoimmune diseases

Jean-François Bach

INSERM U 25, Hôpital Necker, Paris, France

Correspondence: Jean François Bach, MD, INSERM U 25, Hôpital Necker, 161 rue de Sèvres, 75743 Paris Cedex 15, France.
Tel: +33 (0)1 44 49 53 71; fax: +33 (0)1 43 06 23 88; e-mail: bach@necker.fr

Received: 23 January 2002
Revisions requested: 26 February 2002
Revisions received: 27 February 2002
Accepted: 3 March 2002
Published: 9 May 2002

Arthritis Res 2002, **4 (suppl 3)**:S3-S15

This article may contain supplementary data which can only be found online at http://arthritis-research.com/content/4/S3/S003

Chapter summary

The nonobese diabetic (NOD) mouse is a well-recognised animal model of spontaneous autoimmune insulin-dependent diabetes mellitus. The disease is T-cell mediated, involving both CD4 and CD8 cells. Its progress is controlled by a variety of regulatory T cells. An unprecedented number of immunological treatments have been assessed in this mouse strain. This chapter systematically reviews most of these therapeutic manoeuvres, discussing them in the context of their significance with regard to the underlying mechanisms and the potential clinical applications. The contrast between the surprisingly high rate of success found for a multitude of treatments (more than 160) administered early in the natural history of the disease and the few treatments active at a late stage is discussed in depth. Most of the concepts and strategies derived from this model apply to other autoimmune diseases, for which no such diversified data are available.

Keywords: autoimmune diseases, immunotherapy, insulin-dependent diabetes mellitus

Introduction

Insulin-dependent diabetes mellitus (IDDM), or type 1 diabetes, is a T-cell-mediated autoimmune disease. Much effort has been devoted over the past two decades to establishing an immunological treatment that could substitute for insulin therapy. In this chapter, I provide an update of the noteworthy preclinical data obtained in the spontaneous animal models of the disease and of clinical trials in progress. These data are presented with particular attention to lessons that could benefit the immunotherapy of other autoimmune diseases, notably rheumatoid arthritis.

IDDM as an autoimmune disease

It is now firmly established that in the vast majority of cases, IDDM has an autoimmune origin [1]. This does not preclude the possible aetiological role of a triggering envi-

ronmental factor, notably a pancreatotropic virus, but the fact remains that the β-cell lesion is mediated by β-cell-specific autoreactive T cells.

No consensus has been reached on the nature of the effector T cell(s). Research on the nonobese diabetic (NOD) mouse has shown that both CD4 and CD8 clones could induce the disease separately, but it is likely that the two cell types cooperate in the β-cell lesion. CD8 T cells could act through a direct cytotoxic mechanism, although this has not been proven. CD4 cells could act either as helper T cells or as effector cells through cytokine production.

Increasing importance is given to various subsets of regulatory T cells that have been shown to control the onsets of diabetes in both the NOD mouse and the BioBreeding

A glossary of specialist terms used in this chapter appears at the end of the text section. A list of common abbreviations used in this issue appears just before the indexes.

(BB) rat. Three main types of regulatory T cell have been described [2]: Th2 cells, which appear after administration of soluble β-cell autoantigens, CD4+CD25+ T cells, and natural killer T cells, which probably appear spontaneously during ontogeny. It is not yet clear whether the onset of diabetes results from the decline of T-cell-mediated regulation or, what is more likely, from the overriding of the regulation by activation of β-cell-specific effector T cells. Another major uncertainty relates to the nature of the events that trigger such activation. Antigen mimicry or pancreatic inflammation are the most likely, but not necessarily the only, mechanisms.

Strengths and limitations of the NOD mouse model

More than 100 reports have been published using the NOD mouse to set up new immunotherapeutic strategies. Table 1 presents a nonexhaustive list of the main products or strategies tested so far.

The large number of successful results in this mouse has raised the question of the validation of the model as a preclinical tool for identifying strategies to be applied ultimately to humans. For several substances, the success in the NOD mouse has been confirmed in humans, e.g. cyclosporin A [3,4], heat shock protein (hsp)60 peptide [5], and anti-CD3 antibody (K Herold, unpublished observations). For others, however, such confirmation was not obtained, e.g. nicotinamide [6], oral insulin [7,8], and BCG (bacille Calmette–Guérin) [9]. It is important to realise that, contrary to human diabetes, which is essentially seen in the clinic when the disease is overt, diabetes in the NOD mouse can be studied at all stages of its natural history, including the preclinical stages. It is interesting in this context that the three drugs shown to be effective in human diabetes were still efficient in the NOD mouse at an advanced stage, whereas nicotinamide, BCG, and oral insulin worked only at the preclinical stage.

An intriguing question is whether the preventive effects observed after administration of a drug at a very early stage (e.g. 4–6 weeks of age) are specific. An attractive hypothesis is that early intervention resets the homeostasis of the immune system before the disease starts to progress irreversibly. It could be postulated that there is a checkpoint before which the disease outcome is not yet fixed. An agent that would inhibit the triggering event or boost immunoregulation could then show a long-term effect. Applied after this checkpoint, the agent would not show any significant therapeutic effect. To illustrate this concept, it may be suggested that if a virus causes the initial insult that triggers the onset of the diabetogenic process and that virus can be eliminated, an antiviral treatment could be effective if applied very early but would be ineffective once the initial inflammation had occurred and induced a sustained immune response to β-cell autoantigens.

The NOD mouse is one of the few spontaneous models of T-cell-mediated autoimmune diseases, and as such it is of special interest to all students of autoimmunity. This mouse strain is also of major interest because it has been used to generate many genetically modified models in which various genes have been deleted or overexpressed as transgenes in various tissues including the β cells (using the rat insulin promoter). Such mice provide invaluable help in discerning the mode of action of the various therapeutic strategies shown to operate in wild NOD mice.

A weakness of the NOD mouse model is that the putative target β-cell autoantigen(s) is (are) unknown. Several candidates have been proposed, such as glutamic acid decarboxylase, insulin, hsp60, and IA-2 [1], but no firm evidence has shown any of them to be primary autoantigens. This is not necessarily a major pitfall, since data have been accumulated to indicate that such a primary autoantigen may not exist. Even if it exists, diversification of autoimmune specificities (antigen spreading) occurs so fast that the primary antigen may not be crucial. Additionally, at the level of cytokine-dependent immunoregulation (cytokines are discussed further in section 6 below), the occurrence of bystander suppression [10] allows the suppression initially directed against a given β-cell antigen, whether it is a primary autoantigen or not, to be extended to most β-cell-specific T-cell responses.

Preclinical studies: a unique array of approaches

As mentioned above, a wide spectrum of agents or manipulations has been shown to prevent, and more rarely to cure, IDDM in NOD mice. They are listed here according to the factors postulated to contribute to the development of the disease. The various strategies that have been reported are presented below, and Table 1 lists the reference or references relevant to each product or strategy.

1. T-cell depletion or sequestration/diversion

The most straightforward approach to immunotherapy of a T-cell-mediated autoimmune disease such as IDDM is the removal of T cells, either targeted as a whole or as subsets. This has been accomplished in the NOD mouse using several approaches.

Anti-T-cell depleting antibodies offer the easiest strategy. One may thus delay the onset of diabetes by administration of depleting CD4 antibodies such as GK 1.5 and, to a lesser extent, CD8, CD44, CD45RA, or CD45RB antibodies. However, although the onset of diabetes can be prevented in the best cases, there is no clear effect on overt disease, even when it is only recently established. In recently established disease, besides anti-CD3 antibodies, which essentially act independently of major T-cell depletion (see below), only a mixture of depleting CD4 and CD8 antibodies or polyclonal antilymphocyte antibodies have been

Table 1

Immunotherapeutic agents or other treatments used in NOD mice

1 T-cell depletion or sequestration/diversion
  1.1 Depletion
      Anti-CD3 [28]
      Anti-CD4 [40]
      Anti-CD8 [41]
      Anti-CD44 [42]
      Anti-CD45RA [43]
      Anti-CD45RB [44]
      Anti-Thy I.2 [45]
      Antilymphocyte globulin [11,45]
      Neonatal thymectomy [46]
  1.2 Sequestration/diversion
      Anti-CD43 [47]
      Anti-VLA-I [48]
      Anti-VLA-4 [48,49]
      VLA-4/Ig fusion protein [50]
      Anti-CD62L [49]
2 Blockade of T-cell activation
  2.1 Chemical immunosuppressants
      Cyclosporin A [51]
      FK-506 [52]
      Azathioprine [53]
      Rapamycin [54]
      Deoxyspergualin [55]
  2.2 γ Irradiation [56]
3 Targeting of T-cell receptors
  3.1 TCRαβ antibody [13]
  3.2 CD3 antibody [28]
  3.3 Vβ8 antibody [57]
  3.4 T-cell vaccination
      Polyclonal activated T cells [58]
      Glutaraldehyde-treated T cells [59]
      Activated T cells
      Vβ8 T cells [60]
      Anti-hsp60 T-cell clone [61]
  3.5 Blocking peptides [62]
4 Targeting of MHC molecules
  4.1 Anti-class-I [63]
  4.2 Anti-class-II [64]
  4.3 MHC transgenic mice
      Class I [65]
        I-A [16,66]
        I-E [67]
5 Targeting of costimulation and adhesion molecules
  5.1 Costimulation molecules
      Anti-CD28 [68]
      CTLA-4–Ig fusion protein [69]
      Anti-B7.2 [69]
      Anti-CD40L [70]
  5.2 Adhesion molecules
      Anti-ICAM-1 [71]
      Soluble ICAM-1
        Recombinant protein [72]
        Gene therapy (P Lemarchand, unpublished observations)
      Anti-Mac [73]
      Anti-LFA-I [71]
6 Cytokine blockade
  6.1 IFN-γ
      Anti-IFN-γ [74,75]
      IFN-γR/IgG1 fusion protein [76]
  6.2 IL-2
      Anti-IL-2R [77]
      IL-2R/Ig fusion protein [78]
      IL-2 diphtheria-toxin protein [79]

  6.3 IL-12
      Anti-IL-12 [80]
      IL-12 antagonist (p40)2 [81]
  6.4 IFN-α (oral) [82]
  6.5 IL-1
      IL-1 antibody [83]
      IL-1 antagonist [84]
  6.6 IL-6 [75]
  6.7 Lymphotoxin receptor [85]
7 Pharmacologically active cytokines
  7.1 IL-4 [86]
  7.2 IL-10 [87,88]
  7.3 IL-13 [89]
  7.4 IL-3 [37]
  7.5 G-CSF (F Zavala, unpublished observations)
  7.6 Lymphotoxin [90]
  7.7 IL-11 [91]
  7.8 IL-1α [92]
  7.9 TNF-α [26]
8 Tolerance to soluble β-cell autoantigens
  8.1 Insulin
      Oral [93]
      Oral + IL-10 [94]
      Intranasal [34,95]
      Subcutaneous
        Native protein [96]
        B chain [96]
        Inactive analogue [95,97]
      DNA vaccination [98]
      Gene-transfer delivery [99] (proinsulin gene)
      Cholera-toxin conjugate [100]
  8.2 Glutamic acid decarboxylase (GAD)
      Oral [101]
      Intranasal [102]
      Subcutaneous [103]
      Intrathymic [104]
      DNA vaccination   [105]
      Anti-GAD antibody [106]
  8.3 Heat shock protein 60 (hsp60)
      Subcutaneous or intraperitoneal
        Protein [107]
        P277 peptide [108,109]
      Gene-transfer delivery [110]
  8.4 Pancreatic extracts (oral) [111]
9 Stimulation of regulatory T cells
  9.1 Pathogens
      Bacteria
        Mycobacteria
          Mycobacterium bovis [112]
          M. avium [113]
          Complete Freund's adjuvant [114]
        Lactobacillus casei [115]
        Streptococcal extract [116]
        Klebsiella extract [117]
        Escherichia coli (+ oral insulin) [118]
      Viruses
        Mouse hepatitis virus [119]
        Lactate dehydrogenase virus [120]
        Lymphocytic choriomeningitis virus [121]
      Parasites
        Filariae [122]
        Schistosomes [123]
  9.2 Stimulation of innate immunity
      α-Galactosylceramide [33,124]

Continued overleaf

Table 1 continued

Immunotherapeutic agents or other treatments used in NOD mice

9.3 Nondepleting anti-T-cell antibodies	12 Inhibition of β-cell lesion	
Anti-CD3 [28]	12.1 Nicotinamide [145]	
Anti-CD4 [30]	12.2 Antioxidants	
Superantigens [125]	Vitamin E [146]	
10 Gene therapy	Probucol analog [147]	
10.1 β-cell antigens	Probucol + deflazacort [148]	
DNA vaccination [98,105]	Aminoguanidine [149]	
GAD immunoglobulin [126]	12.3 Anti-inflammatory agents	

9.3 Nondepleting anti-T-cell antibodies
    Anti-CD3 [28]
    Anti-CD4 [30]
    Superantigens [125]
10 Gene therapy
  10.1 β-cell antigens
      DNA vaccination [98,105]
      GAD immunoglobulin [126]
  10.2 IL-4
      Retrovirus (T-cell transfection) [127]
      Biolistic [128]
      Adenovirus [129]
      IL-4/IgG1 fusion protein [130]
  10.3 IL-10
      T-cell transfection [131]
      Local [132]
      Systemic [133]
  10.4 ICAM-1 (P Lemarchand, in preparation)
  10.5 IFN-γR/IgGl fusion protein [76,130]
  10.6 TGF-β [134]
  10.7 Calcitonin [135]
11 Cell therapy
  11.1 Islet or segmental pancreas transplantation
      (+ immunosuppression)
      Syngeneic [12]
      Allogeneic [136] (+ immunosuppression)
  11.2 Intrathymic islet transplantation [38]
  11.3 Bone marrow transplantation
      Allogeneic [137,138]
      Syngeneic [37]
  11.4 Dendritic cells [139,140]
  11.5 Natural killer T cells [141]
  11.6 CD4 cell lines
      Polyclonal [142]
      Anti-Ia^{g7} [143]
  11.7 Allogeneic cells
      Macrophages [144]
      Spleen cells [36]

12 Inhibition of β-cell lesion
  12.1 Nicotinamide [145]
  12.2 Antioxidants
      Vitamin E [146]
      Probucol analog [147]
      Probucol + deflazacort [148]
      Aminoguanidine [149]
  12.3 Anti-inflammatory agents
      Pentoxifylline [150]
      Rolipram [150]
13 Miscellaneous
  13.1 Immunomodulators
      Linomide [151]
      Ling-zhi-8 [152]
      D-Glucan [153]
      Multi-functional protein 14 [154]
      Ciamexon [155]
      Cholera toxin B [156,157]
      Vanadate [158]
      Vitamin D_3 analogue [159]
  13.2 Hormones and related proteins
      Androgens [160]
      IGF-I [153]
  13.3 Immunomanipulation
      Natural antibodies [161,162]
      Lupus idiotype [163]
      Lipopolysaccharide [164,165]
  13.4 Diet
      Casein hydrolysate [166,167]
  13.5 Other
      Sulfatide [168]
      Bee venom [90]
      Kampo formulation [169]
      Silica [170]
      Ganglioside [171]
      Antiasialo GM-1 antibody [172]
      Hyaluronidase [42]
      Concanavalin A [173]

CD45RA(B), CD45 receptor A(B); CDXXL, CDXX ligand; CFA, complete Freund's adjuvant; GAD, glutamic acid decarboxylase; G-CSF, granulocyte-colony-stimulating factor; ICAM-1, intercellular adhesion molecule-1; IFN, interferon; MHC, major histocompatibility complex; TCR, T-cell receptor; V, variable region (of immunoglobulin); VLA, very late antigen.

found to reverse the disease [11]. Immunosuppression is not specific to β-cell antigens and may be prolonged, thus exposing the patient to the hazards of generalised immunosuppression. A more subtle approach, which is probably less hazardous but also less efficient, targets T-cell homing molecules, aiming at diverting pathogenic T cells or their precursors from migrating to the islets. This is the putative mode of action of anti-VLA-1, anti-VLA-4, anti-CD43, and anti-L-selectin (CD62L) antibodies.

2. Blockade of T-cell activation
A less radical but similar approach to the previous one is to reversibly block T-cell activation. At present, this is achieved using chemical immunosuppressants.

Most drugs used in organ transplantation where T cells are also incriminated have been used, and these include, notably, cyclosporin A, azathioprine, rapamycin, FK506, and deoxyspergualin. Again, these drugs essentially worked when given early in the course of the disease as a preventive, but not a curative, treatment. This point is illustrated by results reported by Wang and Lafferty and their coworkers, showing that in diabetic NOD mice transplanted with syngeneic islets, recurrence of diabetes could be prevented by a depleting CD4 antibody (GK 1.5) but not by cyclosporin A [12].

3. Targeting of T-cell receptors
T-cell-receptor(TCR)-mediated recognition of β-cell autoantigens is a central step in the diabetes pathogenesis, at both the triggering and the effector phases. It was thus logical to attempt to block TCRs. This has been successfully achieved using a number of approaches.

Global TCR blockade can be obtained by administering antibodies directed against the constant portion of αβ TCRs or to the CD3 complex with which TCR is tightly associated both physically and functionally. In the case of CD3, though, the blockade effect is only part of the antibody mode of action, which also involves depletion (at least when the entire antibody molecule is used) and especially T-cell activation notably of regulatory T cells (see below). Here again, at least for TCRαβ antibody, immunosuppression is of the global type and works only preventively. Regression of diabetes was observed in mice with recently manifested diabetes [13], which is interesting inasmuch as it provides strong support to the argument that reversible T-cell-mediated inflammation takes place in the islets. However, such regression was inconsistent and transient (at variance with that induced by anti-CD3 as described below).

A more selective approach is to target T-cell subsets using selective TCR Vβ antibodies, on the assumption that pathogenic T cells preferentially use selective Vβ genes. Some encouraging but as yet unconfirmed results have been reported for Vβ8.1 and Vβ6. In fact, the experimental model in which such Vβ gene restrictive usage was initially reported, namely experimental allergic encephalomyelitis [14], has not been confirmed for other experimental autoimmune diseases. When whole myelin antigens are used, no clear Vβ gene restrictive usage has been found in human autoimmune diseases. A special case might be made for human diabetes for Vβ7 (and perhaps Vβ13), which are seemingly preferentially used by T cells present in islet infiltrates [15].

A last and even more specific TCR blockade could be obtained by immunising against idiotypes of pathogenic T cells, ideally T-cell clones. This has been attempted in the NOD mouse either using polyclonal T cells or T-cell clones, notably clones of anti-hsp60 T cells. Some effect was reported, but the results, which were often only partial, require confirmation.

4. Targeting of MHC molecules
Peptides of β cells are presented to T cells in the context of MHC molecules. It was thus logical to attempt to modulate the course of β-cell-specific autoimmunity in NOD mice targeting MHC molecules. Administration of either class-I-specific or class-II-specific monoclonal antibodies in young NOD mice (less than 2 months old) but not older ones prevents the onset of diabetes. The protection afforded by class II antibodies is long lasting and resistant to cyclophosphamide and can be transferred to nonantibody-treated mice by T cells. Its precise mode of action, however, remains elusive. It is noteworthy that NOD transgenic mice overexpressing mutated MHC non-NOD class II genes are protected from diabetes and, again, the protection can be transferred to wild NOD mice by T cells

from transgenic mice [16,17]. Collectively, these data suggest that targeting MHC molecules might lead to stimulation of regulatory class II restricted CD4 T cells, which are as yet uncharacterised.

MHC molecules could also be targeted by blocking peptide binding to those molecules; this possibility is suggested by the prevention of diabetes that is afforded by the administration of Ia^{g7} immunogenic but not tolerated peptide binder. Again, one would have to demonstrate that the Ia^{g7} binder in question does not act as an altered peptide ligand (APL) known to stimulate regulatory T cells in these models.

5. Targeting of costimulation and adhesion molecules
The activation of autoreactive T cells specific to β-cell antigens involves a number of costimulation and adhesion molecules. Thus, antibodies to B7.1 or to CD40L prevent the onset of diabetes. CTLA-4–Ig, a fusion protein of CTLA-4 and IgG Fc, which inhibits the binding of CD28 to B7, also delays the onset of diabetes. A similar preventive effect has been reported for an anti-CD28 antibody, but here the mechanism of action of the antibody probably relates to an agonistic effect leading to signalling of regulatory T cells. In fact, this therapeutic approach is more generally complicated by the dual effect of some of the agents used, depending when they are administered. Thus, CTLA-4–Ig fusion protein prevents the onset of diabetes when administered late but accelerates the progression of the disease when administered early [18].

Note also that CD28$^{-/-}$ and B7$^{-/-}$ NOD mice show fulminant diabetes, probably because of the absence of regulatory T cells [18,19].

Diabetes has also been prevented by blocking adhesion molecules, particularly using antibodies against intercellular adhesion molecule (ICAM)-1 and LFA-1. Workers in this laboratory have recently found that administration of adenovirus-infected cells producing soluble recombinant ICAM-1 also protected NOD mice against diabetes. We have even shown that such gene therapy can reverse recently established diabetes (P Lemarchand, unpublished observations).

6. Cytokine blockade
A wide array of cytokines are involved in the differentiation and activation of the various T-cell subsets contributing to diabetes pathogenesis in NOD mice. All antibodies directed at cytokines or cytokine receptors inhibiting the onset of diabetes relate to Th1 cells. Thus, the onset of diabetes is prevented by antibodies directed against IFN-γ, IL-2 receptor (an association with low-dose cyclosporin A is required), or IL-12. Interestingly, a similar effect was obtained by blocking the cytokine receptor with a receptor/immunoglobulin fusion protein or by destroying the

receptor-bearing cell with a cytokine-toxin conjugate. The preventive effect of orally administered IFN-α is interesting but is difficult to interpret. Also intriguing is the absence of diabetes prevention in NOD mice genetically deficient in IFN-γ, IFN-γ receptor, or IL-12 [20–22], a paradox probably explained by a redundancy of the genes coding for these cytokines and their receptors. Prevention of diabetes has been reported after blockade of proinflammatory cytokines, namely IL-1, IL-6, and tumour necrosis factor (TNF)-α. In the latter case, the effect was observed only when the neutralising antibody was administered at a very young age.

7. Pharmacologically active cytokines

Many of the strategies resulting in stimulation of regulatory cells may be assumed to involve the suppressive effect of cytokines acting either systematically or locally at the islet level. The onset of diabetes may also be prevented by the direct administration of regulatory cytokines.

IL-4

Systemic administration of IL-4 can delay the onset of diabetes. The effect is not as dramatic as that of other procedures described here, but is nevertheless quite significant. In fact, the effect is more clear cut when the cytokine is directly delivered in the islet using either gene therapy or β-cell-targeted transgenesis.

IL-10

Findings similar to those reported for IL-4 have been reported for IL-10 after systemic administration of the recombinant cytokine. Paradoxically, however, the onset of diabetes is accelerated by intra-islet delivery of IL-10 in transgenic mice [23] or by systemic administration of an IL-10–Ig fusion protein [24], possibly due in the latter case to an unexpected Th2 polarization.

IL-13

A modest but significant delay in the onset of diabetes has been reportedly achieved by IL-13, another Th2 cytokine.

G-CSF

Granulocyte-colony-stimulating factor (G-CSF) has been used successfully to protect NOD mice from diabetes, following previous results in this laboratory showing that G-CSF could prevent systemic lupus erythematosus in (NZB × NZW)F$_1$ mice [25]. Data collected in these various models suggest that the effect of G-CSF could involve Th2 polarisation.

TNF

Contrasting results have been reported for TNF. Given in the adult NOD mouse, TNF prevents the onset of diabetes [26] (an observation in keeping with the insulitis acceleration brought about by anti-TNF antibodies). Conversely, given to newborn NOD mice, TNF accelerates disease progression [27].

IL-1

IL-1 has been reported to protect NOD mice from the onset of diabetes. This is a surprising observation, because IL-1 has been shown to be exquisitely toxic to β cells and because an Il-1 antagonist has been reported to protect against diabetes.

IL-12

Again depending on the protocol of administration, IL-12 may accelerate or slow down the progression of diabetes.

Lymphotoxin

Diabetes protection has also been reported for lymphotoxin and lymphotoxin–receptor fusion protein.

8. Tolerance to soluble β-cell autoantigens

Many efforts have been made to induce tolerance to candidate β-cell autoantigens. Prevention of disease (but not cure of established disease) has been obtained with insulin, glutamic acid decarboxylase, and hsp60. In the case of insulin, evidence indicated that the effect was not exclusively linked to the hormone's metabolic activity, since the disease could be prevented with insulin, metabolically inactive B chain, or inactive analogues. In the case of hsp60, the antigen is not, strictly speaking, β-cell-specific, but its overexpression in inflamed β cells leads to some β-cell-selective expression.

With each of these three antigens, diabetes was prevented by using various routes of administration: subcutaneous (+ adjuvant), oral, nasal, intravenous, intrathymic. Tolerance was also induced by vaccination with antigen-specific DNA, as well as by transgenic overexpression of the autoantigen.

At the level of underlying mechanisms, there is no true antigen-specific tolerance, since the downregulation of autoimmunity extends to antigens other than the tolerogen. Accumulated data show that soluble β-cell autoantigens induce a deviation in immunity towards Th2, with bystander suppression probably involving local release of immunosuppressive cytokines [2].

9. Stimulation of regulatory T cells

The diabetogenic autoimmune response is tightly controlled by a variety of regulatory T cells. I have pointed out how the administration of soluble β-cell autoantigens could stimulate Th2 cells and prevent the onset of diabetes if given when the mice are young enough. Many other strategies have been used to prevent the onset of diabetes targeting non-Th2 regulatory T cells. One may assume, a priori, that most of these strategies are not β-cell-specific, since they use non-β-cell-related agents. The possibility cannot be excluded that, at least in some cases, the induced regulation is β-cell-specific at the effector level. One may postulate that a nonspecific stimulation leads to the activation or boosting of β-cell-specific regulatory T cells, whether or not they are of the Th2 type. The strategies for stimulating regulatory T cells may be classified according to whether they make use of nondepleting anti-T-cell monoclonal antibodies, stimulation of innate immunity, or pathogens, as discussed below.

Nondepleting anti-T-cell monoclonal antibodies

Administration of anti-CD3 antibodies to NOD mice with recently manifested IDDM induces long-term remission of the disease. The effect is obtained after brief treatment (5 days) and does not require the use of the mitogenic whole autoantibody molecule (nonactivating F(ab')2 fragments are tolerogenic) [28,29]. My colleagues and I have recently obtained data indicating that the effect is mediated by active tolerance involving TGF-β-dependent CTLA$^+$CD25$^+$ T cells (L Chatenoud, unpublished observations).

Similar, though less well documented, data have been reported for nondepleting anti-CD4 antibodies [30], in keeping with the analogous effect of the same antibodies in transplantation. [31].

Stimulation of innate immunity

NOD mice show an early deficit in NK (natural killer) T cells, both quantitatively and qualitatively (deficient IL-4 production) [32]. It was thus logical to attempt to prevent IDDM in such mice by stimulating the function of NK T cells. This was recently done by administering a selective NK-T-cell ligand, the glycolipid α-galactosylceramide. Interestingly, the protection still applies in some protocols when the glycolipid is given late, and can inhibit the recurrence of disease in diabetic mice with grafts of syngeneic islets [33].

Stimulation of γδ regulatory T cells has been reported after intranasal administration of insulin [34]. It will be interesting to learn whether such T cells that protect against diabetes after nasal administration of insulin are insulin specific.

Pathogens

Bacteria. A whole array of bacteria have been shown to prevent the onset of diabetes in NOD mice. Mycobacteria have been extensively studied, particularly *Mycobacterium bovis* (the source of BCG vaccine) and *M. avium*. The effect is also obtained with mycobacteria extracts (in complete Freund's adjuvant). The role of regulatory T cells in protection induced by complete Freund's adjuvant or vaccination with BCG is demonstrated by the transfer of protection that is achieved when CD4 T cells from protected mice are transferred to naive mice [35]. The nature of the regulatory cells in question is open to speculation (are they Th2 cells? CD25 cells?). Other bacterial-cell extracts have also been shown to prevent the onset of diabetes in NOD mice, notably extracts of streptococcus or klebsiella.

Viruses. The onset of diabetes in NOD mice can be prevented by infection with various viruses, in partucular lymphochoriomeningitis virus (LCMV), murine hepatitis virus (MHV), and lactate dehydrogenase virus (LDHV).

Parasites. Diabetes can also be prevented by deliberate administration of parasites, such as schistosomes or filariae.

10. Gene therapy

Gene therapy may be used in many ways to prevent or cure diabetes in NOD mice. Insulin gene therapy and related strategies are not discussed in this chapter.

Immune-based gene therapy has been developed along several lines. One possibility is to overexpress cytokines or cytokine receptors with the aim of reproducing the pharmacological effect of the particular molecules. Various experimental settings have been considered, including local intra-islet delivery of the cytokine (using transgenic mice or islet-specific T-cell transfection) and systemic delivery. Various vectors (viral and nonviral) have been used. IL-4, IL-4–Ig fusion protein, IL-10, IFN-γ receptor, Ig, and TGF-β all protected the mice from diabetes.

We recently reported that systemic delivery of soluble ICAM-1 using a recombinant adenovirus vector could also be protective and even curative in mice that had recently developed diabetes (P Lemarchand, unpublished observations).

Less expected is the protective effect of calcitonin gene therapy.

11. Cell therapy

Islet transplantation

Syngeneic islet transplantation is really a palliative procedure, not an immunotherapeutic one. However, unlike insulin therapy, it poses the problems of the prevention of disease relapse on the graft and consequently requires associated immunotherapy. Many of the procedures described above have been used to prevent such disease relapse, e.g. anti-CD3 and anti-CD4 antibodies, soluble glutamic acid decarboxylase, α-galactosylceramide, and BCG vaccination. Similar immunological problems will be met with attempts to regenerate islet cells from ductal stem cells, as has been recently described. The problem is even more serious in the case of allogeneic islet transplantation, in which two problems – relapse and allograft rejection – are combined.

Bone marrow transplantation

Allogeneic bone marrow transplantation. Another approach consists in replacing the bone marrow T (and B) cell precursors. This is not an easy approach, because of the associated allogeneic reaction (graft versus host and host versus graft). Such alloimmune response could have a protective effect, probably through the production of immunoregulatory cytokines: this possibility is suggested by the protection afforded by induction of (usually partial) allogeneic tolerance in newborn NOD mice, which also totally protects from diabetes [36].

Syngeneic bone marrow transplantation. More unexpectedly, syngeneic bone marrow transplantation may also afford protection (in conjunction with IL-3), possibly by resetting immunoregulatory mechanisms that override effector ones [37].

Infusion of mononuclear cells
Prevention of diabetes has been reported after infusion of dendritic cells and CD4$^{-/-}$CD8$^{-/-}$ thymocytes presumably enriched in NK T cells. It has also been extensively demonstrated that the onset of diabetes in NOD mice is prevented by administering mature CD4 T cells (either polyclonal, notably of the CD25 type, or monoclonal).

Intrathymic islet transplantation
Diabetes has been prevented in NOD mice upon intrathymic grafting of syngeneic or allogeneic islets, either at birth or within 4 weeks of age. The preventive effect was associated with a complete absence of insulitis in most animals. The observations that spleen cells from tolerant islet-grafted NOD mice did not transfer diabetes into immunoincompetent hosts [38] and that cyclophosphamide did not break the tolerance in one study [39] are compatible with a preferential deletional mechanism.

12. Inhibition of β-cell lesion
Inhibition of the effector mechanisms leading to destruction of β cells has been attempted with limited success.

Nicotinamide has some protective effect but only at relatively high doses and early in the disease history. Nitric oxide (NO) inhibitors have also shown some effects as do antioxidants, pentoxifylline, and rolipram.

Anti-TCR antibodies and CD3 antibodies also deserve mention here. They probably act, at least in part, by inactivating effector T cells, as is suggested by virtually immediate reversal of hyperglycaemia after the first injection of such antibodies [13,28].

13. Miscellaneous
Immunomodulation
Some products known to modulate immune responses (without showing a clear overall suppressor or stimulator pattern of activities) prevent the onset of diabetes in NOD mice. These include linomide, ciamexon, vanadate, vitamin D3, and D-glucan.

Hormones
Some hormones or related compounds can also prevent insulitis and the progression of diabetes in NOD mice.

This has notably been reported for androgens, a finding in keeping with the acceleration of disease seen after castration in males and the high female/male ratio of affected mice. The onset of diabetes is also prevented by IGF-I.

Immunomanipulation
Unexpectedly, immunisation against the lupus-associated idiotype 16/6 protects NOD mice from diabetes. The protective effect of natural antibodies presumably has a similar mode of action. The effect of such antibodies is interesting, but their mode of action is poorly defined.

Diet
Various diets have been shown to slow the progression of diabetes in NOD mice, notably the low-protein diets. It has been reported that casein hydrolysate formula does likewise.

Other products
A number of products listed in Table 1 that have an ill-defined action on the immune system have also been reported to prevent the onset of diabetes in NOD mice.

Concluding remarks
The number and variety of therapeutic interventions capable of preventing diabetes represents an unprecedented observation in immune pathology. The number of interventions that work in mice with advanced disease, and particularly with established diabetes, is much more limited, indicating that the majority of efficacious treatments are active only at the very early stages of a chronic process progressing from insulitis to clinical diabetes. As has been mentioned above, the only products that have been shown to arrest the destruction of β cells in man are those shown to act late in the natural history of the disease in NOD mice. Nevertheless, the early-acting procedures may prove useful in combination with late-acting drugs. One might envision treating patients who have recently diagnosed diabetes with the late-acting drugs, followed by administration of early-acting drugs, which would regain their activity once the immune homeostasis has been reset. Alternatively, these numerous early-acting compounds could be applied in man very early if valid prediction could identify subjects at risk of developing the disease. However, the logistic problems associated with such prediabetes trials should not be overlooked (for example, the number of subjects to be screened and enrolled and the duration of the trial). Lastly, many of the concepts and therapeutic strategies described above for IDDM could probably be extrapolated correctly to other autoimmune diseases, notably rheumatoid arthritis.

Glossary of terms
BB = BioBreeding (rat); BCG = bacille Calmette–Guérin; NOD = nonobese diabetic (mouse).

References

1. Bach JF: **Insulin-dependent diabetes mellitus as an autoimmune disease.** *Endocr Rev* 1994, **15**:516-542. [key review]
2. Bach JF, Chatenoud L: **Tolerance to islet autoantigens and type I diabetes.** *Annu Rev Immunol* 2001, **19**:131-161. [key review]
3. Feutren G, Papoz L, Assan R, Vialettes B, Karsenty G, Vexiau P, Du Rostu H, Rodier M, Sirmai J, Lallemand A, Bach JF: **Cyclosporin increases the rate and length of remissions in insulin-dependent diabetes of recent onset. Results of a multicentre double-blind trial.** *Lancet* 1986, **2**:119-124. [general reference]
4. The Canadian-European Randomized Control Trial Group: **Cyclosporin-induced remission of IDDM after early intervention. Association of 1 yr of cyclosporin treatment with enhanced insulin secretion.** *Diabetes* 1988, **37**:1574-1582. [general reference]
5. Raz I, Elias D, Avron A, Tamir M, Metzger M, Cohen IR: **Beta-cell function in new-onset type 1 diabetes and immunomodulation with a heat-shock protein peptide (DiaPep277): a randomised, double-blind, phase II trial.** *Lancet* 2001, **358**: 1749-1753. [general reference]
6. Lampeter EF, Klinghammer A, Scherbaum WA, Heinze E, Haastert B, Giani G, Kolb H: **The Deutsche Nicotinamide Intervention Study: an attempt to prevent type 1 diabetes. DENIS Group.** *Diabetes* 1998, **47**:980-984. [general reference]
7. Chaillous L, Lefevre H, Thivolet C, Boitard C, Lahlou N, Atlan Gepner C, Bouhanick B, Mogenet A, Nicolino M, Carel JC, Lecomte P, Marechaud R, Bougneres P, Charbonnel B, Sai P: **Oral insulin administration and residual beta-cell function in recent-onset type 1 diabetes: a multicentre randomised controlled trial.** *Lancet* 2000, **356**:545-549. [general reference]
8. Pozzilli P, Pitocco D, Visalli N, Cavallo MG, Buzzetti R, Crino A, Spera S, Suraci C, Multari G, Cervoni M, Bitti MLM, Matteoli MC, Marietti G, Ferrazzoli F, Faldetta MRC, Giordano C, Sbriglia M, Sarugeri E, Ghirlanda G: **No effect of oral insulin on residual beta-cell function in resent-onset Type I diabetes (The IMDIAB VII).** *Diabetologia* 2000, **43**:1000-1004. [general reference]
9. Allen HF, Klingensmith GJ, Jensen P, Simoes E, Hayward A, Chase HP: **Effect of Bacillus Calmette-Guerin vaccination on new-onset type 1 diabetes. A randomized clinical study.** *Diabetes Care* 1999, **22**:1703-1707. [general reference]
10. Weiner HL, Friedman A, Miller A, Khoury SJ, Al-Sabbagh A, Santos L, Sayegh M, Nussenblatt RB, Trentham DE, Hafler DA: **Oral tolerance: immunologic mechanisms and treatment of animal and human organ-specific autoimmune diseases by oral administration of autoantigens.** *Annu Rev Immunol* 1994, **12**:809-837. [key review]
11. Maki T, Ichikawa T, Blanco R, Porter J: **Long-term abrogation of autoimmune diabetes in nonobese diabetic mice by immunotherapy with anti-lymphocyte serum.** *Proc Natl Acad Sci USA* 1992, **89**:3434-3438. [general reference]
12. Wang Y, Hao L, Gill RG, Lafferty KJ: **Autoimmune diabetes in NOD mouse is L3T4 T-lymphocyte dependent.** *Diabetes* 1987, **36**:535-538. [general reference]
13. Sempe P, Bedossa P, Richard MF, Villa MC, Bach JF, Boitard C: **Anti-alpha/beta T cell receptor monoclonal antibody provides an efficient therapy for autoimmune diabetes in nonobese diabetic (NOD) mice.** *Eur J Immunol* 1991, **21**:1163-1169. [general reference]
14. Acha-Orbea H, Mitchell DJ, Timmermann L, Wraith DC, Tausch GS, Waldor MK, Zamvil SS, McDevitt HO, Steinman L: **Limited heterogeneity of T cell receptors from lymphocytes mediating autoimmune encephalomyelitis allows specific immune intervention.** *Cell* 1988, **54**:263-273. [general reference]
15. Conrad B, Weissmahr RN, Boni J, Arcari R, Schupbach J, Mach B: **A human endogenous retroviral superantigen as candidate autoimmune gene in type I diabetes.** *Cell* 1997, **90**:303-313. [general reference]
16. Slattery RM, Kjer-Nielsen L, Allison J, Charlton B, Mandel TE, Miller JF: **Prevention of diabetes in non-obese diabetic I-Ak transgenic mice.** *Nature* 1990, **345**:724-726. [general reference]
17. Singer SM, Tisch R, Yang XD, McDevitt HO: **An Abd transgene prevents diabetes in nonobese diabetic mice by inducing regulatory T cells.** *Proc Natl Acad Sci USA* 1993, **90**:9566-9570. [general reference]
18. Lenschow DJ, Herold KC, Rhee L, Patel B, Koons A, Qin HY, Fuchs E, Singh B, Thompson CB, Bluestone JA: **CD28/B7 regulation of Th1 and Th2 subsets in the development of autoimmune diabetes.** *Immunity* 1996, **5**:285-293. [general reference]
19. Salomon B, Lenschow DJ, Rhee L, Ashourian N, Singh B, Sharpe A, Bluestone JA: **B7/CD28 costimulation is essential for the homeostasis of the CD4+CD25+ immunoregulatory T cells that control autoimmune diabetes.** *Immunity* 2000, **12**:431-440. [general reference]
20. Hultgren B, Huang XJ, Dybdal N, Stewart TA: **Genetic absence of gamma-interferon delays but does not prevent diabetes in NOD mice.** *Diabetes* 1996, **45**:812-817. [general reference]
21. Serreze DV, Post CM, Chapman HD, Johnson EA, Lu BF, Rothman PB: **Interferon-gamma receptor signaling is dispensable in the development of autoimmune type 1 diabetes in NOD mice.** *Diabetes* 2000, **49**:2007-2011. [general reference]
22. Trembleau S, Penna G, Gregori S, Chapman HD, Serreze DV, Magram J, Adorini L: **Pancreas-infiltrating Th1 cells and diabetes develop in IL-12-deficient nonobese diabetic mice.** *J Immunol* 1999, **163**:2960-2968. [general reference]
23. Wogensen L, Lee MS, Sarvetnick N: **Production of interleukin 10 by islet cells accelerates immune-mediated destruction of beta cells in nonobese diabetic mice.** *J Exp Med* 1994, **179**: 1379-1384. [general reference]
24. Zheng XX, Steele AW, Hancock WW, Stevens AC, Nickerson PW, Roy-Chaudhury P, Tian Y, Strom TB: **A noncytolytic IL-10/Fc fusion protein prevents diabetes, blocks autoimmunity, and promotes suppressor phenomena in NOD mice.** *J Immunol* 1997, **158**:4507-4513. [general reference]
25. Zavala F, Masson A, Hadaya K, Ezine S, Schneider E, Babin O, Bach JF: **Granulocyte-colony stimulating factor treatment of lupus autoimmune disease in MRL-lpr/lpr mice.** *J Immunol* 1999, **163**:5125-5132. [general reference]
26. Jacob CO, Aiso S, Michie SA, McDevitt HO, Acha-Orbea H: **Prevention of diabetes in nonobese diabetic mice by tumor necrosis factor (TNF): similarities between TNF-alpha and interleukin 1.** *Proc Natl Acad Sci USA* 1990, **87**:968-972. [general reference]
27. Yang XD, Tisch R, Singer SM, Cao ZA, Liblau RS, Schreiber RD, McDevitt HO: **Effect of tumor necrosis factor alpha on insulin-dependent diabetes mellitus in NOD mice. I. The early development of autoimmunity and the diabetogenic process.** *J Exp Med* 1994, **180**:995-1004. [general reference]
28. Chatenoud L, Thervet E, Primo J, Bach JF: **Anti-CD3 antibody induces long-term remission of overt autoimmunity in nonobese diabetic mice.** *Proc Natl Acad Sci USA* 1994, **91**: 123-127. [general reference]
29. Chatenoud L, Primo J, Bach JF: **CD3 antibody-induced dominant self tolerance in overtly diabetic NOD mice.** *J Immunol* 1997, **158**:2947-2954. [general reference]
30. Hutchings P, O'Reilly L, Parish NM, Waldmann H, Cooke A: **The use of a non-depleting anti-CD4 monoclonal antibody to reestablish tolerance to beta cells in NOD mice.** *Eur J Immunol* 1992, **22**:1913-1918. [general reference]
31. Waldmann H, Cobbold S: **How do monoclonal antibodies induce tolerance? A role for infectious tolerance?** *Annu Rev Immunol* 1998, **16**:619-644. [key review]
32. Gombert JM, Herbelin A, Tancrede-Bohin E, Dy M, Carnaud C, Bach JF: **Early quantitative and functional deficiency of NK1(+)- like thymocytes in the NOD mouse.** *Eur J Immunol* 1996, **26**:2989-2998. [general reference]
33. Sharif S, Arraeza GA, Zucker P, Mi QS, Sondhi J, Naidenko OV, Kronenberg M, Koezuka Y, Delovitch TL, Gombert JM, Leite de Moraes M, Gouarin C, Zhu R, Hameg A, Nakayama T, Taniguchi M, Lepault F, Lehuen A, Bach JF, Herbelin A: **Activation of natural killer T cells by α-galactosylceramide treatment prevents the onset and recurrence of autoimmune Type 1 diabetes.** *Nat Med* 2001, **7**:1057-1062. [general reference]
34. Harrison LC, Dempsey-Collier M, Kramer DR, Takahashi K: **Aerosol insulin induces regulatory CD8 gamma delta T cells that prevent murine insulin-dependent diabetes.** *J Exp Med* 1996, **184**:2167-2174. [general reference]
35. Qin HY, Sadelain MW, Hitchon C, Lauzon J, Singh B: **Complete Freund's adjuvant-induced T cells prevent the development and adoptive transfer of diabetes in nonobese diabetic mice.** *J Immunol* 1993, **150**:2072-2080. [general reference]

36. Bendelac A, Boitard C, Bach JF, Carnaud C: **Neonatal induction of allogeneic tolerance prevents T cell-mediated autoimmunity in NOD mice.** *Eur J Immunol* 1989, **19**:611-616. [general reference]

37. Ito A, Aoyanagi N, Maki T: **Regulation of autoimmune diabetes by interleukin 3-dependent bone marrow-derived cells in NOD mice.** *J Autoimmun* 1997, **10**:331-338. [general reference]

38. Gerling IC, Serreze DV, Christianson SW, Leiter EH: **Intrathymic islet cell transplantation reduces beta-cell autoimmunity and prevents diabetes in NOD/Lt mice.** *Diabetes* 1992, **41**:1672-1676. [general reference]

39. Charlton B, Taylor-Edwards C, Tisch R, Fathman CG: **Prevention of diabetes and insulitis by neonatal intrathymic islet administration in NOD mice.** *J Autoimmun* 1994, **7**:549-560. [general reference]

40. Shizuru JA, Taylor-Edwards C, Banks BA, Gregory AK, Fathman CG: **Immunotherapy of the nonobese diabetic mouse: treatment with an antibody to T-helper lymphocytes.** *Science* 1988, **240**:659-662. [general reference]

41. Hutchings PR, Simpson E, O'Reilly LA, Lund T, Waldmann H, Cooke A: **The involvement of Ly2+ T cells in beta cell destruction.** *J Autoimmun* 1990, **3 (Suppl 1)**:101-109. [general reference]

42. Weiss L, Slavin S, Reich S, Cohen P, Shuster S, Stern R, Kaganovsky E, Okon E, Rubinstein AM, Naor D: **Induction of resistance to diabetes in non-obese diabetic mice by targeting CD44 with a specific monoclonal antibody.** *Proc Natl Acad Sci USA* 2000, **97**:285-290. [general reference]

43. Sempe P, Ezine S, Marvel J, Bedossa P, Richard MF, Bach JF, Boitard C: **Role of CD4+CD45RA+ T cells in the development of autoimmune diabetes in the non-obese diabetic (NOD) mouse.** *Int Immunol* 1993, **5**:479-489. [general reference]

44. Abu-Hadid MM, Lazarovits AI, Madrenas J: **Prevention of diabetes mellitus in the non-obese diabetic mouse strain with monoclonal antibodies against the CD45RB molecule.** *Autoimmunity* 2000, **32**:73-76. [general reference]

45. Harada M, Makino S: **Suppression of overt diabetes in NOD mice by anti-thymocyte serum or anti-Thy 1, 2 antibody.** *Jikken Dobutsu* 1986, **4**:501-504. [general reference]

46. Ogawa M, Maruyama T, Hasegawa T, Kanaya T, Kobayashi F, Tochino Y, Uda H: **The inhibitory effect of neonatal thymectomy on the incidence of insulitis in non-obese diabetic (NOD) mice.** *Biomed Res* 1985, **6**:103-105. [general reference]

47. Johnson GG, Mikulowska A, Butcher EC, McEvoy LM, Michie SA: **Anti-CD43 monoclonal antibody L11 blocks migration of T cells to inflamed pancreatic islets and prevents development of diabetes in nonobese diabetic mice.** *J Immunol* 1999, **163**:5678-5685. [general reference]

48. Tsukamoto K, Yokono K, Amano K, Nagata M, Yagi N, Tominaga Y, Moriyama H, Miki M, Okamoto N, Yoneda R: **Administration of monoclonal antibodies against vascular cell adhesion molecule-1/very late antigen-4 abrogates predisposing autoimmune diabetes in NOD mice.** *Cell Immunol* 1995, **165**:193-201. [general reference]

49. Yang XD, Karin N, Tisch R, Steinman L, McDevitt HO: **Inhibition of insulitis and prevention of diabetes in nonobese diabetic mice by blocking L-selectin and very late antigen 4 adhesion receptors.** *Proc Natl Acad Sci USA* 1993, **90**:10494-10498. [general reference]

50. Jakubowski A, Ehrenfels BN, Pepinsky RB, Burkly LC: **Vascular cell adhesion molecule-Ig fusion protein selectively targets activated alpha 4-integrin receptors in vivo. Inhibition of autoimmune diabetes in an adoptive transfer model in nonobese diabetic mice.** *J Immunol* 1995, **155**:938-946. [general reference]

51. Mori Y, Suko M, Okudaira H, Matsuba I, Tsuruoka A, Sasaki A, Yokoyama H, Tanase T, Shida T, Nishimura M, Terada E, Ikeda Y: **Preventive effects of cyclosporin on diabetes in NOD mice.** *Diabetologia* 1986, **29**:244-247. [general reference]

52. Miyagawa J, Yamamoto K, Hanafusa T, Itoh N, Nakagawa C, Otsuka A, Katsura H, Yamagata K, Miyazaki A, Kono N, Tarui S: **Preventive effect of a new immunosuppressant FK-506 on insulitis and diabetes in non-obese diabetic mice.** *Diabetologia* 1990, **33**:503-505. [general reference]

53. Calafiore R, Basta G, Falorni A, Pietropaolo M, Picchio ML, Calcinaro F, Brunetti P: **Preventive effects of azathioprine (AZA) on the onset of diabetes mellitus in NOD mice.** *J Endocrinol Invest* 1993, **16**:869-873. [general reference]

54. Baeder WL, Sredy J, Sehgal SN, Chang JY, Adams LM: **Rapamycin prevents the onset of insulin-dependent diabetes mellitus (IDDM) in NOD mice.** *Clin Exp Immunol* 1992, **89**:174-178. [general reference]

55. Nicoletti F, Borghi MO, Meroni PL, Barcellini W, Fain C, Di Marco R, Menta R, Schorlemmer HU, Bruno G, Magro G, Grasso S: **Prevention of cyclophosphamide-induced diabetes in the NOD/WEHI mouse with deoxyspergualin.** *Clin Exp Immunol* 1993, **91**:232-236. [general reference]

56. Takahashi M, Kojima S, Yamaoka K, Niki E: **Prevention of type I diabetes by low-dose gamma irradiation in NOD mice.** *Radiat Res* 2000, **154**:680-685. [general reference]

57. Bacelj A, Charlton B, Mandel TE: **Prevention of cyclophosphamide-induced diabetes by anti-V beta 8 T-lymphocyte-receptor monoclonal antibody therapy in NOD/Wehi mice.** *Diabetes* 1989, **38**:1492-1495. [general reference]

58. Gearon CL, Hussain MJ, Vergani D, Peakman M: **Lymphocyte vaccination protects prediabetic non-obese diabetic mice from developing diabetes mellitus.** *Diabetologia* 1997, **40**:1388-1395. [general reference]

59. Smerdon RA, Peakman M, Hussain MJ, Vergani D: **Lymphocyte vaccination prevents spontaneous diabetes in the non-obese diabetic mouse.** *Immunology* 1993, **80**:498-501. [general reference]

60. Formby B, Shao T: **T cell vaccination against autoimmune diabetes in nonobese diabetic mice.** *Ann Clin Lab Sci* 1993, **23**:137-147. [general reference]

61. Feili-Hariri M, Frantz MO, Morel PA: **Prevention of diabetes in the NOD mouse by a Th1 clone specific for a hsp60 peptide.** *J Autoimmun* 2000, **14**:133-142. [general reference]

62. Vaysburd M, Lock C, McDevitt H: **Prevention of insulin-dependent diabetes mellitus in nonobese diabetic mice by immunogenic but not by tolerated peptides.** *J Exp Med* 1995, **182**:897-902. [general reference]

63. Taki T, Nagata M, Ogawa W, Hatamori N, Hayakawa M, Hari J, Shii K, Baba S, Yokono K: **Prevention of cyclophosphamide-induced and spontaneous diabetes in NOD/Shi/Kbe mice by anti-MHC class I Kd monoclonal antibody.** *Diabetes* 1991, **40**:1203-1209. [general reference]

64. Boitard C, Bendelac A, Richard MF, Carnaud C, Bach JF: **Prevention of diabetes in nonobese diabetic mice by anti-I-A monoclonal antibodies: transfer of protection by splenic T cells.** *Proc Natl Acad Sci USA* 1988, **85**:9719-9723. [general reference]

65. Miyazaki T, Matsuda Y, Toyonaga T, Miyazaki J, Yazaki Y, Yamamura K: **Prevention of autoimmune insulitis in nonobese diabetic mice by expression of major histocompatibility complex class I Ld molecules.** *Proc Natl Acad Sci USA* 1992, **89**:9519-9523. [general reference]

66. Singer SM, Tisch R, Yang XD, Sytwu HK, Liblau R, McDevitt HO: **Prevention of diabetes in NOD mice by a mutated I-Ab transgene.** *Diabetes* 1998, **47**:1570-1577. [general reference]

67. Nishimoto H, Kikutani H, Yamamura K, Kishimoto T: **Prevention of autoimmune insulitis by expression of I-E molecules in NOD mice.** *Nature* 1987, **328**:432-434. [general reference]

68. Arreaza GA, Cameron MJ, Jaramillo A, Gill BM, Hardy D, Laupland KB, Rapoport MJ, Zucker P, Chakrabarti S, Chensue SW, Qin HY, Singh B, Delovitch TL: **Neonatal activation of CD28 signaling overcomes T cell anergy and prevents autoimmune diabetes by an IL-4-dependent mechanism.** *J Clin Invest* 1997, **100**:2243-2253. [general reference]

69. Lenschow DJ, Ho SC, Sattar H, Rhee L, Gray G, Nabavi N, Herold KC, Bluestone JA: **Differential effects of anti-B7-1 and anti-B7-2 monoclonal antibody treatment on the development of diabetes in the nonobese diabetic mouse.** *J Exp Med* 1995, **181**:1145-1155. [general reference]

70. Balasa B, Krahl T, Patstone G, Lee J, Tisch R, McDevitt HO, Sarvetnick N: **CD40 ligand-CD40 interactions are necessary for the initiation of insulitis and diabetes in nonobese diabetic mice.** *J Immunol* 1997, **159**:4620-4627. [general reference]

71. Hasegawa Y, Yokono K, Taki T, Amano K, Tominaga Y, Yoneda R, Yagi N, Maeda S, Yagita H, Okumura K, Kasuga M: **Prevention of autoimmune insulin-dependent diabetes in non-obese diabetic mice by anti-LFA-1 and anti-ICAM-1 mAb.** *Int Immunol* 1994, **6**:831-838. [general reference]

72. Martin S, Heidenthal E, Schulte B, Rothe H, Kolb H: **Soluble forms of intercellular adhesion molecule-1 inhibit insulitis and**

onset of autoimmune diabetes. *Diabetologia* 1998, **41**:1298-1303. [general reference]

73. Hutchings P, Rosen H, O'Reilly L, Simpson E, Gordon S, Cooke A: **Transfer of diabetes in mice prevented by blockade of adhesion-promoting receptor on macrophages.** *Nature* 1990, **348**:639-642. [general reference]

74. Debray-Sachs M, Carnaud C, Boitard C, Cohen H, Gresser I, Bedossa P, Bach JF: **Prevention of diabetes in NOD mice treated with antibody to murine IFN gamma.** *J Autoimmun* 1991, **4**:237-248. [general reference]

75. Campbell IL, Kay TW, Oxbrow L, Harrison LC: **Essential role for interferon-gamma and interleukin-6 in autoimmune insulin-dependent diabetes in NOD/Wehi mice.** *J Clin Invest* 1991, **87**:739-742. [general reference]

76. Prudhomme GJ, Chang Y: **Prevention of autoimmune diabetes by intramuscular gene therapy with a nonviral vector encoding an interferon-gamma receptor/IgG1 fusion protein.** *Gene Ther* 1999, **6**:771-777. [general reference]

77. Kelley VE, Gaulton GN, Hattori M, Ikegami H, Eisenbarth G, Strom TB: **Anti-interleukin 2 receptor antibody suppresses murine diabetic insulitis and lupus nephritis.** *J Immunol* 1988, **140**:59-61. [general reference]

78. Zheng XX, Steele AW, Hancock WW, Kawamoto K, Li XC, Nickerson PW, Li Y, Tian Y, Strom TB: **IL-2 receptor-targeted cytolytic IL-2/Fc fusion protein treatment blocks diabetogenic autoimmunity in nonobese diabetic mice.** *J Immunol* 1999, **163**:4041-4048. [general reference]

79. Pacheco-Silva A, Bastos MG, Muggia RA, Pankewycz O, Nichols J, Murphy JR, Strom TB, Rubin-Kelley VE: **Interleukin 2 receptor targeted fusion toxin (DAB486-IL-2) treatment blocks diabetogenic autoimmunity in non-obese diabetic mice.** *Eur J Immunol* 1992, **22**:697-702. [general reference]

80. Fujihira K, Nagata M, Moriyama H, Yasuda H, Arisawa K, Nakayama M, Maeda S, Kasuga M, Okumura K, Yagita H, Yokono K: **Suppression and acceleration of autoimmune diabetes by neutralization of endogenous interleukin-12 in NOD mice.** *Diabetes* 2000, **49**:1998-2006. [general reference]

81. Rothe H, O'Hara RM Jr, Martin S, Kolb H: **Suppression of cyclophosphamide induced diabetes development and pancreatic Th1 reactivity in NOD mice treated with the interleukin (IL)-12 antagonist IL-12(p40)2.** *Diabetologia* 1997, **40**:641-646. [general reference]

82. Brod SA, Malone M, Darcan S, Papolla M, Nelson L: **Ingested interferon alpha suppresses type I diabetes in non-obese diabetic mice.** *Diabetologia* 1998, **41**:1227-1232. [general reference]

83. Cailleau C, Diu-Hercend A, Ruuth E, Westwood R, Carnaud C: **Treatment with neutralizing antibodies specific for IL-1beta prevents cyclophosphamide-induced diabetes in nonobese diabetic mice.** *Diabetes* 1997, **46**:937-940. [general reference]

84. Sandberg JO, Eizirik DL, Sandler S: **IL-1 receptor antagonist inhibits recurrence of disease after syngeneic pancreatic islet transplantation to spontaneously diabetic non-obese diabetic (NOD) mice.** *Clin Exp Immunol* 1997, **108**:314-317. [general reference]

85. Wu Q, Salomon B, Chen M, Wang Y, Hoffman LM, Bluestone JA, Fu YX: **Reversal of spontaneous autoimmune insulitis in nonobese diabetic mice by soluble lymphotoxin receptor.** *J Exp Med* 2001, **193**:1327-1332. [general reference]

86. Rapoport MJ, Jaramillo A, Zipris D, Lazarus AH, Serreze DV, Leiter EH, Cyopick P, Danska JS, Delovitch TL: **Interleukin 4 reverses T cell proliferative unresponsiveness and prevents the onset of diabetes in nonobese diabetic mice.** *J Exp Med* 1993, **178**:87-99. [general reference]

87. Rabinovitch A, Suarez-Pinzon WL, Sorensen O, Bleackley RC, Power RF, Rajotte RV: **Combined therapy with interleukin-4 and interleukin-10 inhibits autoimmune diabetes recurrence in syngeneic islet-transplanted nonobese diabetic mice. Analysis of cytokine mRNA expression in the graft.** *Transplantation* 1995, **60**:368-374. [general reference]

88. Pennline KJ, Roque-Gaffney E, Monahan M: **Recombinant human IL-10 prevents the onset of diabetes in the nonobese diabetic mouse.** *Clin Immunol Immunopathol* 1994, **71**:169-175. [general reference]

89. Zaccone P, Phillips J, Conget I, Gomis R, Haskins K, Minty A, Bendtzen K, Cooke A, Nicoletti F: **Interleukin-13 prevents autoimmune diabetes in NOD mice.** *Diabetes* 1999, **48**:1522-1528. [general reference]

90. Kim JY, Cho SH, Kim YW, Jang EC, Park SY, Kim EJ, Lee SK: **Effects of BCG, lymphotoxin and bee venom on insulitis and development of IDDM in non-obese diabetic mice.** *J Kor Med Sci* 1999, **14**:648-652. [general reference]

91. Nicoletti F, Zaccone P, Conget I, Gomis R, Moller C, Meroni PL, Bendtzen K, Trepicchio W, Sandler S: **Early prophylaxis with recombinant human interleukin-11 prevents spontaneous diabetes in NOD mice.** *Diabetes* 1999, **48**:2333-2339. [general reference]

92. Formby B, Jacobs C, Dubuc P, Shao T: **Exogenous administration of IL-1 alpha inhibits active and adoptive transfer autoimmune diabetes in NOD mice.** *Autoimmunity* 1992, **12**:21-27. [general reference]

93. Zhang ZJ, Davidson L, Eisenbarth G, Weiner HL: **Suppression of diabetes in nonobese diabetic mice by oral administration of porcine insulin.** *Proc Natl Acad Sci USA* 1991, **88**:10252-10256. [general reference]

94. Slavin AJ, Maron R, Weiner HL: **Mucosal administration of IL-10 enhances oral tolerance in autoimmune encephalomyelitis and diabetes.** *Int Immunol* 2001, **13**:825-833. [general reference]

95. Daniel D, Wegmann DR: **Protection of nonobese diabetic mice from diabetes by intranasal or subcutaneous administration of insulin peptide B-(9-23).** *Proc Natl Acad Sci USA* 1996, **93**:956-960. [general reference]

96. Muir A, Peck A, Clare-Salzler M, Song YH, Cornelius J, Luchetta R, Krischer J, MacLaren N: **Insulin immunization of nonobese diabetic mice induces a protective insulitis characterized by diminished intraislet interferon-gamma transcription.** *J Clin Invest* 1995, **95**:628-634. [general reference]

97. Karounos DG, Bryson JS, Cohen DA: **Metabolically inactive insulin analog prevents type I diabetes in prediabetic NOD mice.** *J Clin Invest* 1997, **100**:1344-1348. [general reference]

98. Urbanek-Ruiz I, Ruiz PJ, Paragas V, Garren H, Steinman L, Fathman CG: **Immunization with DNA encoding an immunodominant peptide of insulin prevents diabetes in NOD mice.** *Clin Immunol* 2001, **100**:164-171. [general reference]

99. French MB, Allison J, Cram DS, Thomas HE, Dempsey-Collier M, Silva A, Georgiou HM, Kay TW, Harrison LC, Lew AM: **Transgenic expression of mouse proinsulin II prevents diabetes in nonobese diabetic mice.** *Diabetes* 1997, **46**:34-39. [general reference]

100. Bergerot I, Ploix C, Petersen J, Moulin V, Rask C, Fabien N, Lindblad M, Mayer A, Czerkinsky C, Holmgren J, Thivolet C: **A cholera toxoid-insulin conjugate as an oral vaccine against spontaneous autoimmune diabetes.** *Proc Natl Acad Sci USA* 1997, **94**:4610-4614. [general reference]

101. Ramiya VK, Shang XZ, Wasserfall CH, MacLaren NK: **Effect of oral and intravenous insulin and glutamic acid decarboxylase in NOD mice.** *Autoimmunity* 1997, **26**:139-151. [general reference]

102. Tian J, Atkinson MA, Clare Salzler M, Herschenfeld A, Forsthuber T, Lehmann PV, Kaufman DL: **Nasal administration of glutamate decarboxylase (GAD65) peptides induces Th2 responses and prevents murine insulin-dependent diabetes.** *J Exp Med* 1996, **183**:1561-1567. [general reference]

103. Kaufman DL, Clare-Salzler M, Tian J, Forsthuber T, Ting GSP, Robinson P, Atkinson MA, Sercarz EE, Tobin AJ, Lehmann PV: **Spontaneous loss of T-cell tolerance to glutamic acid decarboxylase in murine insulin-dependent diabetes.** *Nature* 1993, **366**:69-72. [general reference]

104. Tisch R, Yang XD, Singer SM, Liblau RS, Fugger L, McDevitt HO: **Immune response to glutamic acid decarboxylase correlates with insulitis in non-obese diabetic mice.** *Nature* 1993, **366**:72-75. [general reference]

105. Filippova M, Liu J, Escher A: **Effects of plasmid DNA injection on cyclophosphamide-accelerated diabetes in NOD mice.** *DNA Cell Biol* 2001, **20**:175-81. [general reference]

106. Menard V, Jacobs H, Jun HS, Yoon JW, Kim SW: **Anti-GAD monoclonal antibody delays the onset of diabetes mellitus in NOD mice.** *Pharmaceut Res* 1999, **16**:1059-1066. [general reference]

107. Elias D, Markovits D, Reshef T, Van Der Zee R, Cohen IR: **Induction and therapy of autoimmune diabetes in the non-obese diabetic (NOD/Lt) mouse by a 65-kDa heat shock protein.** *Proc Natl Acad Sci USA* 1990, **87**:1576-1580. [general reference]

108. Elias D, Meilin A, Ablamunits V, Birk OS, Carmi P, Konen-Waisman S, Cohen IR: **Hsp60 peptide therapy of NOD mouse diabetes induces a Th2 cytokine burst and downregulates**

autoimmunity to various beta-cell antigens. *Diabetes* 1997, 46:758-764. [general reference]

109. Elias D, Cohen IR: **Peptide therapy for diabetes in NOD mice.** *Lancet* 1994, **343**:704-706. [general reference]

110. Birk OS, Douek DC, Elias D, Takacs K, Dewchand H, Gur SL, Walker MD, Van Der Zee R, Cohen IR, Altmann DM: **A role of hsp60 in autoimmune diabetes: analysis in a transgenic model.** *Proc Natl Acad Sci USA* 1996, **93**:1032-1037. [general reference]

111. Reddy S, Stefanovic N, Karanam M: **Prevention of autoimmune diabetes by oral administration of syngeneic pancreatic extract to young NOD mice.** *Pancreas* 2000, **20**:55-60. [general reference]

112. Yagi H, Matsumoto M, Kishimoto Y, Makino S, Harada M: **Possible mechanism of the preventive effect of BCG against diabetes mellitus in NOD mouse. II. Suppression of pathogenesis by macrophage transfer from BCG-vaccinated mice.** *Cell Immunol* 1991, **138**:142-149. [general reference]

113. Bras A, Aguas AP: **Diabetes-prone NOD mice are resistant to *Mycobacterium avium* and the infection prevents autoimmune disease.** *Immunology* 1996, **89**:20-25. [general reference]

114. Sadelain MW, Qin HY, Lauzon J, Singh B: **Prevention of type I diabetes in NOD mice by adjuvant immunotherapy.** *Diabetes* 1990, **39**:583-589. [general reference]

115. Matsuzaki T, Nagata Y, Kado S, Uchida K, Kato I, Hashimoto S, Yokokura T: **Prevention of onset in an insulin-dependent diabetes mellitus model, NOD mice, by oral feeding of *Lactobacillus casei*.** *APMIS* 1997, **105**:643-649. [general reference]

116. Toyota T, Satoh J, Oya K, Shintani S, Okano T: **Streptococcal preparation (OK-432) inhibits development of type I diabetes in NOD mice.** *Diabetes* 1986, **35**:496-499. [general reference]

117. Sai P, Rivereau AS: **Prevention of diabetes in the nonobese diabetic mouse by oral immunological treatments. Comparative efficiency of human insulin and two bacterial antigens, lipopolysacharide from *Escherichia coli* and glycoprotein extract from *Klebsiella pneumoniae*.** *Diabetes Metab* 1996, **22**:341-348. [general reference]

118. Hartmann B, Bellmann K, Ghiea I, Kleemann R, Kolb H: **Oral insulin for diabetes prevention in NOD mice: potentiation by enhancing Th2 cytokine expression in the gut through bacterial adjuvant.** *Diabetologia* 1997, **40**:902-909. [general reference]

119. Wilberz S, Partke HJ, Dagnaes-Hansen F, Herberg L: **Persistent MHV (mouse hepatitis virus) infection reduces the incidence of diabetes mellitus in non-obese diabetic mice.** *Diabetologia* 1991, **34**:2-5. [general reference]

120. Takei I, Asaba Y, Kasatani T, Maruyama T, Watanabe K, Yanagawa T, Saruta T, Ishii T: **Suppression of development of diabetes in NOD mice by lactate dehydrogenase virus infection.** *J Autoimmun* 1992, **5**:665-673. [general reference]

121. Oldstone MB: **Viruses as therapeutic agents. I. Treatment of nonobese insulin-dependent diabetes mice with virus prevents insulin-dependent diabetes mellitus while maintaining general immune competence.** *J Exp Med* 1990, **171**:2077-2089. [general reference]

122. Imai S, Tezuka H, Fujita K: **A factor of inducing IgE from a filarial parasite prevents insulin-dependent diabetes mellitus in nonobese diabetic mice.** *Biochem Biophys Res Comm* 2001, **286**:1051-1058. [general reference]

123. Cooke A, Tonks P, Jones FM, O'Shea H, Hutchings P, Fulford AJ, Dunne DW: **Infection with *Schistosoma mansoni* prevents insulin dependent diabetes mellitus in non-obese diabetic mice.** *Parasite Immunol* 1999, **21**:169-176. [general reference]

124. Hong S, Wilson MT, Serizawa I, Wu L, Singh N, Naidenko OV, Miura T, Haba T, Scherer DC, Wei J, Kronenberg M, Koezuka Y, Van Kaer L: **The natural killer T-cell ligand alpha-galactosylceramide prevents autoimmune diabetes in non-obese diabetic mice.** *Nat Med* 2001, **7**:1052-1056. [general reference]

125. Kawamura T, Nagata M, Utsugi T, Yoon JW: **Prevention of autoimmune type I diabetes by CD4+ suppressor T cells in superantigen-treated non-obese diabetic mice.** *J Immunol* 1993, **151**:4362-4370. [general reference]

126. Tisch R, Wang B, Weaver DJ, Liu S, Bui T, Arthos J, Serreze DV: **Antigen-specific mediated suppression of beta cell autoimmunity by plasmid DNA vaccination.** *J Immunol* 2001, **166**:2122-2132. [general reference]

127. Yamamoto AM, Chernajovsky Y, Lepault F, Podhajcer O, Feldmann M, Bach JF, Chatenoud L: **The activity of immunoregulatory T cells mediating active tolerance is potentiated in nonobese diabetic mice by an IL4-based retroviral gene therapy.** *J Immunol* 2001, **166**:4973-4980. [general reference]

128. Cameron MJ, Strathdee CA, Holmes KD, Arreaza GA, Dekaban GA, Delovitch TL: **Biolistic-mediated interleukin 4 gene transfer prevents the onset of type 1 diabetes.** *Hum Gene Ther* 2000, **11**:1647-1656. [general reference]

129. Cameron MJ, Arreaza GA, Waldhauser L, Gauldie J, Delovitch TL: **Immunotherapy of spontaneous type I diabetes in nonobese diabetic mice by systemic interleukin-4 treatment employing adenovirus vector-mediated gene transfer.** *Gene Ther* 2000, **7**:1840-1846. [general reference]

130. Chang YG, Prudhomme GJ: **Intramuscular administration of expression plasmids encoding interferon-gamma receptor/IgG1 or IL-4/IgG1 chimeric proteins protects from autoimmunity.** *J Gene Med* 1999, **1**:415-423. [general reference]

131. Moritani M, Yoshimoto K, Ii S, Kondo M, Iwahana H, Yamaoka T, Sano T, Nakano N, Kikutani H, Itakura M: **Prevention of adoptively transferred diabetes in nonobese diabetic mice with IL-10-transduced islet-specific Th1 lymphocytes - A gene therapy model for autoimmune diabetes.** *J Clin Invest* 1996, **98**:1851-1859. [general reference]

132. Kawamoto S, Nitta Y, Tashiro F, Nakano A, Yamato E, Tahara H, Tabayashi K, Miyazaki J: **Suppression of T(h)1 cell activation and prevention of autoimmune diabetes in NOD mice by local expression of viral IL-10.** *Int Immunol* 2001, **13**:685-694. [general reference]

133. Koh JJ, Ko KS, Lee M, Han S, Park JS, Kim SW: **Degradable polymeric carrier for the delivery of IL-10 plasmid DNA to prevent autoimmune insulitis of NOD mice.** *Gene Ther* 2000, **7**:2099-2104. [general reference]

134. Piccirillo CA, Chang YG, Prudhomme GJ: **TGF-beta 1 somatic gene therapy prevents autoimmune disease in nonobese diabetic mice.** *J Immunol* 1998, **161**:3950-3956. [general reference]

135. Khachatryan A, Guerder S, Palluault F, Cote G, Solimena M, Valentijn K, Millet I, Flavell RA, Vignery A: **Targeted expression of the neuropeptide calcitonin gene-related peptide to beta cells prevents diabetes in NOD mice.** *J Immunol* 1997, **158**:1409-1416. [general reference]

136. Mottram PL, Murray-Segal LJ, Han W, Maguire J, Stein-Oakley A, Mandel TE: **Long-term survival of segmental pancreas isografts in NOD/Lt mice treated with anti-CD4 and anti-CD8 monoclonal antibodies.** *Diabetes* 1998, **47**:1399-1405. [general reference]

137. Yasumizu R, Sugiura K, Iwai H, Inaba M, Makino S, Ida T, Imura H, Hamashima Y, Good RA, Ikehara S: **Treatment of type 1 diabetes mellitus in non-obese diabetic mice by transplantation of allogeneic bone marrow and pancreatic tissue.** *Proc Natl Acad Sci USA* 1987, **84**:6555-6557. [general reference]

138. Mathieu C, Casteels K, Bouillon R, Waer M: **Protection against autoimmune diabetes in mixed bone marrow chimeras: mechanisms involved.** *J Immunol* 1997, **158**:1453-1457. [general reference]

139. Feili-Hariri M, Dong X, Alber SM, Watkins SC, Salter RD, Morel PA: **Immunotherapy of NOD mice with bone marrow-derived dendritic cells.** *Diabetes* 1999, **48**:2300-2308. [general reference]

140. Clare-Salzler MJ, Brooks J, Chai A, Van Herle K, Anderson C: **Prevention of diabetes in nonobese diabetic mice by dendritic cell transfer.** *J Clin Invest* 1992, **90**:741-748. [general reference]

141. Hammond KJ, Poulton LD, Palmisano LJ, Silveira PA, Godfrey DI, Baxter AG: **Alpha/beta-T cell receptor (TCR)(+)CD4(-)CD8(-) (NKT) thymocytes prevent insulin-dependent diabetes mellitus in nonobese diabetic (NOD)/Lt mice by the influence of interleukin (IL)-4 and/or IL-10.** *J Exp Med* 1998, **187**:1047-1056. [general reference]

142. Boitard C, Yasunami R, Dardenne M, Bach JF: **T cell-mediated inhibition of the transfer of autoimmune diabetes in NOD mice.** *J Exp Med* 1989, **169**:1669-1680. [general reference]

143. Chosich N, Harrison LC: **Suppression of diabetes mellitus in the non-obese diabetic (NOD) mouse by an autoreactive (anti-I-Ag7) islet-derived CD4+ T-cell line.** *Diabetologia* 1993, **36**:716-721. [general reference]

144. Georgiou HM, Constantinou D, Mandel TE: **Prevention of autoimmunity in nonobese diabetic (NOD) mice by neonatal transfer of allogeneic thymic macrophages.** *Autoimmunity* 1995, **21**:89-97. [general reference]

145. Yamada K, Nonaka K, Hanafusa T, Miyazaki A, Toyoshima H, Tarui S: **Preventive and therapeutic effects of large-dose nicotinamide injections on diabetes associated with insulitis. An observation in nonobese diabetic (NOD) mice.** *Diabetes* 1982, **31**:749-753. [general reference]

146. Hayward AR, Shriber M, Sokol R: **Vitamin E supplementation reduces the incidence of diabetes but not insulitis in NOD mice.** *J Lab Clin Med* 1992, **119**:503-507. [general reference]

147. Heineke EW, Johnson MB, Dillberger JE, Robinson KM: **Antioxidant MDL 29,311 prevents diabetes in nonobese diabetic and multiple low-dose STZ-injected mice.** *Diabetes* 1993, **42**:1721-1730. [general reference]

148. Rabinovitch A, Suarez WL, Power RF: **Combination therapy with an antioxidant and a corticosteroid prevents autoimmune diabetes in NOD mice.** *Life Sci* 1992, **51**:1937-1943. [general reference]

149. Corbett JA, Mikhael A, Shimizu J, Frederick K, Misko TP, McDaniel ML, Kanagawa O, Unanue ER: **Nitric oxide production in islets from nonobese diabetic mice: aminoguanidine-sensitive and -resistant stages in the immunological diabetic process.** *Proc Natl Acad Sci USA* 1993, **90**:8992-8995. [general reference]

150. Liang L, Beshay E, Prud'Homme GJ: **The phosphodiesterase inhibitors pentoxifylline and rolipram prevent diabetes in NOD mice.** *Diabetes* 1998, **47**:570-575. [general reference]

151. Gross DJ, Sidi H, Weiss L, Kalland T, Rosenmann E, Slavin S: **Prevention of diabetes mellitus in non-obese diabetic mice by Linomide, a novel immunomodulating drug.** *Diabetologia* 1994, **37**:1195-1201. [general reference]

152. Kino K, Mizumoto K, Sone T, Yamaji T, Watanabe J, Yamashita A, Yamaoka K, Shimizu K, Ko K, Tsunoo H: **An immunomodulating protein, Ling Zhi-8 (LZ-8) prevents insulitis in non-obese diabetic mice.** *Diabetologia* 1990, **33**:713-718. [general reference]

153. Kida K, Kaino Y, Ito T, Hirai H: **Controversies on the prevention of insulin-dependent diabetes mellitus by immunomodulation: lessons from NOD mice treated with beta-1,6;1,3-D-glucan and rhIGF-I.** *J Pediatr Endocrinol Metab* 1998, **11 (Suppl 2)**:327-333. [general reference]

154. Panerai AE, Nicoletti F, Sacedote P, Arvidsson L, Conget I, Gomis R, Bartorelli A, Sandler S: **MFP14, a multifunctional emerging protein with immunomodulatory properties, prevents spontaneous and recurrent autoimmune diabetes in NOD mice.** *Diabetologia* 2001, **44**:839-47. [general reference]

155. Krug J, Lampeter EF, Williams AJ, Procaccini E, Cartledge C, Signore A, Beales PE, Pozzilli P: **Immunotherapy with ciamexon in the non obese diabetic (NOD) mouse.** *Hormone Metab Res* 1992, **24**:1-4. [general reference]

156. Burkart V, Kim Y, Kauer M, Kolb H: **Induction of tolerance in macrophages by cholera toxin B chain.** *Pathobiology* 1999, **67**:314-317. [general reference]

157. Sobel DO, Yankelevich B, Goyal D, Nelson D, Mazumder A: **The B-subunit of cholera toxin induces immunoregulatory cells and prevents diabetes in the NOD mouse.** *Diabetes* 1998, **47**:186-191. [general reference]

158. Meyerovitch J, Waner T, Sack J, Kopolovic J, Shemer J: **Attempt to prevent the development of diabetes in non-obese diabetic mice by oral vanadate administration.** *Israel Med Assoc J* 2000, **2**:211-214. [general reference]

159. Casteels KM, Mathieu C, Waer M, Valckx D, Overbergh L, Laureys JM, Bouillon R: **Prevention of type I diabetes in nonobese diabetic mice by late intervention with nonhypercalcemic analogs of 1,25-dihydroxyvitamin D-3 in combination with a short induction course of cyclosporin A.** *Endocrinology* 1998, **139**:95-102. [general reference]

160. Fox HS: **Androgen treatment prevents diabetes in nonobese diabetic mice.** *J Exp Med* 1992, **175**:1409-1412. [general reference]

161. Andersson A, Forsgren S, Soderstrom A, Holmberg D: **Monoclonal, natural antibodies prevent development of diabetes in the non-obese diabetic (NOD) mouse.** *J Autoimmun* 1991, **4**:733-742. [general reference]

162. Forsgren S, Andersson A, Hillorn V, Soderstrom A, Holmberg D: **Immunoglobulin-mediated prevention of autoimmune diabetes in the non-obese diabetic (NOD) mouse.** *Scand J Immunol* 1991, **34**:445-451. [general reference]

163. Krause I, Tomer Y, Elias D, Blank M, Gilburd B, Cohen IR, Shoenfeld Y: **Inhibition of diabetes in NOD mice by idiotypic induction of SLE.** *J Autoimmun* 1999, **13**:49-55. [general reference]

164. Tian J, Zekzer D, Hanssen L, Lu Y, Olcott A, Kaufman DL: **Lipopolysaccharide-activated B cells down-regulate Th1 immunity and prevent autoimmune diabetes in nonobese diabetic mice.** *J Immunol* 2001, **167**:1081-1089. [general reference]

165. Iguchi M, Inagawa H, Nishizawa T, Okutomi T, Morikawa A, Soma GI, Mizuno D: **Homeostasis as regulated by activated macrophage. V. Suppression of diabetes mellitus in non-obese diabetic mice by LPSw (a lipopolysaccharide from wheat flour).** *Chem Pharmaceut Bull* 1992, **40**:1004-1006. [general reference]

166. Hermitte L, Atlan-Gepner C, Payan MJ, Mehelleb M, Vialettes B: **Dietary protection against diabetes in NOD mice: lack of a major change in the immune system.** *Diabete Metab* 1995, **21**:261-268. [general reference]

167. Hoorfar J, Buschard K, Dagnaes Hansen F: **Prophylactic nutritional modification of the incidence of diabetes in autoimmune non-obese diabetic (NOD) mice.** *Br J Nutr* 1993, **69**:597-607. [general reference]

168. Buschard K, Hanspers K, Fredman P, Reich EP: **Treatment with sulfatide or its precursor, galactosylceramide, prevents diabetes in NOD mice.** *Autoimmunity* 2001, **34**:9-17. [general reference]

169. Kobayashi T, Song QH, Hong T, Kitamura H, Cyong JC: **Preventive effect of Ninjin-to (Ren-Shen-Tang), a Kampo (Japanese traditional) formulation, on spontaneous autoimmune diabetes in non-obese diabetic (NOD) mice.** *Microbiol Immunol* 2000, **44**:299-305. [general reference]

170. Charlton B, Bacelj A, Mandel TE: **Administration of silica particles or anti-Lyt2 antibody prevents beta-cell destruction in NOD mice given cyclophosphamide.** *Diabetes* 1988, **37**:930-935. [general reference]

171. Wilberz S, Herberg L, Renold AE: **Gangliosides in vivo reduce diabetes incidence in non-obese diabetic mice.** *Diabetologia* 1988, **31**:855-857. [general reference]

172. Maruyama T, Watanabe K, Takei I, Kasuga A, Shimada A, Yanagawa T, Kasatani T, Suzuki Y, Kataoka K, Saruta T: **Anti-asialo GM1 antibody suppression of cyclophosphamide-induced diabetes in NOD mice.** *Diabetes Res* 1991, **17**:37-41. [general reference]

173. Pearce RB, Peterson CM: **Studies of concanavalin A in nonobese diabetic mice. I. Prevention of insulin-dependent diabetes.** *J Pharmacol Exp Ther* 1991, **258**:710-715 [general reference]

Supplement Review
Perspectives for TNF-α-targeting therapies

Hanns-Martin Lorenz and Joachim R Kalden

Institute for Clinical Immunology and Rheumatology, Department of Medicine, University of Erlangen-Nuremberg, Erlangen, Germany

Correspondence: Dr Hanns-Martin Lorenz, Inst. for Clin. Immunology and Rheumatology, Dept of Medicine III, University of Erlangen-Nuremberg, Krankenhausstr. 12, 91054 Erlangen, Germany. Tel: +49 9131 853 6387 or -9107; fax: +49 9131 853 4770; e-mail: Hannes.Lorenz@med3.imed.uni-erlangen.de

Received: 12 March 2002

Revisions requested: 12 March 2002

Revisions received: 13 March 2002

Accepted: 18 March 2002

Published: 9 May 2002

Arthritis Res 2002, **4 (suppl 3)**:S17-S24

This article may contain supplementary data which can only be found online at http://arthritis-research.com/content/4/S3/S017

© 2002 BioMed Central Ltd
(Print ISSN 1465-9905; Online ISSN 1465-9913)

Chapter summary

Rheumatoid arthritis (RA) is the most common chronic autoimmunopathy, clinically leading to joint destruction as a consequence of the chronic inflammatory processes. The pathogenesis of this disabling disease is not well understood, but molecular events leading to tissue inflammation with cartilage and bone destruction are now better defined. Therapy with slow-acting, disease-modifying antirheumatic drugs (DMARDs), such as low-dose methotrexate, which is generally accepted as a standard, leads to a significant amelioration of symptoms but does not stop joint destruction. Due to these disappointing treatment options and the identification of certain inflammatory mediators as therapeutic targets, novel therapeutic agents such as monoclonal antibodies, cytokine-receptor/human-immunoglobulin constructs or recombinant human proteins have been tested in RA with some success. Clinical trials testing anti-TNF-α agents, alone or in combination with methotrexate, have convincingly shown the feasibility and efficacy of these novel approaches to the therapy of RA. A clinical trial testing combination therapy with chimeric (mouse/human) anti-TNF-α monoclonal antibody infliximab and methotrexate showed, for the first time in any RA trial, that there was no median radiological progression in the groups given infliximab plus methotrexate over a 12-month observation period. Similar encouraging results might arise from trials employing other TNF-α-directed agents, such as the fully human monoclonal antibody D2E7, the p75 TNF-α-receptor/Ig construct, etanercept, or others, as discussed in this review. Combination partners other than methotrexate will be established as suitable cotreatment along with anti-TNF-α biologicals. Forthcoming new indications for TNF-α-targeted therapies are discussed.

Keywords: D2E7, etanercept, infliximab, TNF-α, therapy

Introduction

The central role of tumour necrosis factor (TNF-α) in the initiation and/or perpetuation of the inflammatory processes in rheumatoid arthritis (RA), Crohn's disease (CD) and many more chronic inflammatory diseases has been suggested by experimental *in vitro* and *in situ* data. This has been clearly verified by the overwhelming success of TNF-α-targeted therapies. Thus, a lot of enthusiasm has been put into the development of further strategies aimed at blocking TNF-α with new and innovative drugs (immunobiologicals and synthetic inhibitors of TNF-α synthesis or signal transduction). Furthermore, new indications for TNF-α-targeted treatment are forthcoming.

Rheumatoid arthritis and Crohn's disease: future directions
Further studies with immunobiologicals

After TNF-α-targeting immunobiologicals like etanercept and infliximab have been approved for the treatment of Crohn's disease, rheumatoid arthritis and juvenile chronic

---

A glossary of specialist terms used in this chapter appears at the end of the text section. A list of common abbreviations used in this issue appears just before the indexes.

arthritis, further steps will be taken to establish this therapeutic principle for treatment of other chronic inflammatory diseases. These developments may include additional clinical trials with the established agents, or clinical studies with new TNF-α-targeting immunobiologicals, such as the human D2E7 antibody [1]. Other TNF-α blocking agents are also being developed (e.g. polyethylenglycol [PEG]-bound p55 TNF-receptor [PEG-TNFRI] [2] or the PEGylated TNF-α antibody fragments [CDP-870]). A soluble type 1 p55 TNF-receptor (onercept) is currently being tested in CD. Further long-term observations are required concerning side effects and efficacy of these agents, focusing particularly on radiological progression under therapy with anti-TNF agents in combination with methotrexate. This information is required specifically for the combinations of etanercept plus methotrexate and D2E7 plus methotrexate in patients with RA, but needs to be determined for all new agents.

To date, TNF-α blockade is only recommended for therapy-resistant cases. A clinical trial has been initiated testing efficacy in RA patients in an early phase of their disease. This will be especially interesting since one could hypothesize that early and effective blockade of the chronic inflammatory processes in RA will be more efficient. This should lead to the prevention of tissue destruction and disability as well as higher frequencies of long-term remissions, compared to situations where treatment is semi-efficient with perpetuating inflammation over years. These studies might, therefore, help to define criteria that prospectively characterize an RA patient as one with better prognosis (and defensive therapeutic strategy) versus a worse prognosis with a requirement for aggressive treatment from the beginning of his/her disease. Prospective parameters could include HLA type, radiological signs of joint desruction early after disease onset or a high number of involved joints at the beginning of the disease. It is unclear to date whether the presence of TNF-α-promoter polymorphisms can predict the severity of RA, but certain promoter polymorphisms could be another discriminator that might dictate early, aggressive therapy.

Alternative combination partners

Since methotrexate is generally accepted as the standard first line disease-modifying antirheumatic drug (DMARD) in RA, most of the anti-TNF-α trials have been performed with this combination partner. However, not all patients respond to, or tolerate, methotrexate, so alternative combination partners substituting methotrexate are warranted. Leflunomide is currently being tested along with infliximab in RA patients. Azathioprin, cyclosporin A or sulfasalazine might be alternative candidates [3]. This will considerably increase the spectrum of therapeutic modalities affiliated with the TNF-α-targeting drugs.

New indications for TNF-α-targeting therapies
Psoriatic arthritis and psoriasis

The prevalence of psoriasis is reported as 1–3% of adults in the United States, and psoriatic arthritis (PsA) occurs in approximately 6–20% of psoriasis patients [4]. Psoriatic arthritis is an inflammatory arthropathy that may develop before skin involvement. It presents in a symmetric or asymmetric polyarticular form, with or without onycholysis. The current therapeutic approaches for PsA are similar to those for RA and include nonsteroidal anti-inflammatory drugs (NSAIDs), DMARDs and immunosuppressive agents. Only two DMARDs, methotrexate and sulfasalazine, have demonstrated efficacy in the treatment of PsA.

Circulating T lymphocytes and macrophages isolated from PsA patients produce an increased amount of TNF-α compared with macrophages isolated from healthy controls [5]. Furthermore, the levels of TNF-α are elevated in the synovial fluid [6], tissue [6,7] and skin lesions [8,9] in PsA patients, with TNF-α levels correlating with disease activity [10,11].

As a logical consequence, studies with TNF-α-blocking biologicals were initiated. Several open-label studies have investigated the use of anti-TNF-α agents in the treatment of PsA and psoriasis [12–16]. In a single-centre, open-label report on the treatment of spondyloarthropathies, van den Bosch et al. [12] reported that nine PsA patients treated with infliximab (5 mg/kg at weeks 0, 2 and 6) experienced significant improvement in physician's global assessment (PGA), erythrocyte sedimentation rates (ESR), and C-reactive protein (CRP) levels. Of these patients, eight had psoriasis at baseline. After 12 weeks of infliximab treatment, baseline Psoriasis Area and Severity Index (PASI) scores were significantly improved. The clinical improvements in all PsA and psoriasis disease manifestations were maintained over a follow-up period of 1 year [13]. In another open-label study, eight out of 10 heavily pretreated PsA patients experienced improvements in Health Assessment Questionnaire scores and PGA scores after 12 months of treatment with etanercept (25 mg given subcutaneously twice a week). All four patients in this trial with active psoriasis had significant improvement in their psoriatic skin lesions, including complete resolution in three patients [14].

In our open-label experience, infliximab treatment was efficacious and safe in PsA and psoriasis [15,16]. With infliximab treatment (5 mg/kg at weeks 0, 2, and 6), all 10 patients in our study achieved 20% improvement in arthritis according to the American College of Rheumatology response criteria (ACR20) by week 2. After 10 weeks of treatment, eight patients achieved 70% improvement (ACR70), six of whom maintained this improvement to week 54. In addition, magnetic resonance imaging showed an 82% reduction in perfusion of inflamed joints, and mean PASI scores were reduced by 71% at week 10. After 10 weeks of infliximab therapy, six patients experienced nearly complete clearing of erythematous psoriasis plaques. Histopathological analysis of psoriatic plaques showed a reduction in epidermal hyperplasia and inflammation by week 10 [16]. This reduction in hyperplasia was associated with a decrease in plaque size and was evident by the near-normal epidermal structure after infliximab treatment. In a more detailed analysis we recently showed that, besides a decrease of the cellular infiltration (lymphocytes, granulocytes), the protein expression of TNF-α, intercellular adhesion molecule-1 and leukocyte function-associated antigen-1, the mRNA expression of IL-8, IL-20 and TNFR type I were significantly lower in psoriatic plaques after 4 weeks of treatment (Ogilvie et al., submitted). The use of anti-TNF-α agents in treating PsA and psoriasis has also been investigated in a randomized, double-blinded, placebo-controlled study. Mease et al. [17] reported that 87% patients receiving etanercept (25 mg subcutaneously twice a week) achieved PsA response criteria, compared with 23% of placebo patients ($P < 0.0001$). In addition, 73% of etanercept-treated patients achieved ACR20 compared with 13% of placebo-treated patients ($P < 0.0001$). Of 19 patients in each treatment group with active psoriasis, the median improvement in PASI scores was significantly higher in etanercept-treated patients than in placebo-treated patients. Of psoriasis patients treated with etanercept, 26% achieved a 75% improvement, whereas no patients improved when treated with placebo. In an open-label extension study, etanercept continued to effectively reduce clinical signs and symptoms of PsA and psoriasis for up to 36 weeks [18].

Recently, Chaudhari et al. [19] described the first reported placebo-controlled, randomized study designed to investigate the efficacy of an anti-TNF agent in psoriasis patients. In this study, 30 patients ware randomized to receive infliximab (5 or 10 mg/kg) or placebo. Nine of 11 (82%) patients treated with infliximab at 5 mg/kg achieved good, excellent, or clear ratings on PGA, compared with only 2/11 (18%) patients receiving placebo ($P = 0.0089$). In addition, 10/11 (91%) patients treated with infliximab at 10 mg/kg achieved these ratings ($P = 0.0019$ compared to placebo). A significantly higher proportion of patients treated with infliximab obtained a 75% improvement in PASI scores compared with placebo ($P = 0.0089$, infliximab 5 mg/kg versus placebo; $P = 0.03$, infliximab 10 mg/kg versus placebo). The results of these studies suggest that TNF-α plays a pivotal role in the pathogenesis of PsA and psoriasis. In addition, anti-TNF-α therapy offers patients with PsA and psoriasis a new therapeutic option for the control of their disease.

Ankylosing spondylitis

Ankylosing spondylitis (AS) is an inflammatory arthropathy that preferentially affects the axial skeleton, usually manifesting in the sacroiliac joints and then ascending to involve the back bone, frequently accompanied by peripheral arthritis. Treatment for AS includes NSAIDs and sulfasalazine, which is the only DMARD that shows activity in the disease, albeit only for peripheral joints.

Only limited evidence exists to support a role for TNF-α in the pathophysiology of AS. Braun et al. [20] showed that TNF-α mRNA and protein were present in inflamed sacroiliac joints of AS patients. Lange et al. [21] reported significantly increased TNF-α plasma levels in AS patients, with a positive correlation between TNF-α plasma levels and the Bath Ankylosing Spondylitis Disease Activity Index (BASDAI). In addition, the strong link between AS and inflammatory bowel disease, where 20–60% of spondyloarthropathy patients have gastrointestinal lesions resembling those in CD, provides circumstantial evidence for a role of TNF-α in AS [22].

In an open-label study, 11 patients with AS of short duration were treated with infliximab (5 mg/kg at weeks 0, 2, and 6) [23]. Improvements in activity, function and pain scores of $\geq 50\%$ were reported in 9/10 eligible patients. The median CRP level decreased to normal and the median improvement in BASDAI score after 4 weeks was 70%. In another open-label study of patients with different subtypes of spondyloarthropathy, 10 AS patients treated with infliximab at 5 mg/kg every 14 weeks achieved significant improvements in morning stiffness, tender and swollen joint counts, ESR, CRP, BASDAI score, Bath Ankylosing Spondylitis Functional Index score, and Bath Ankylosing Spondylitis Metrology Index score. Improvement in the other endpoints were significant at days 3–14 and were maintained to day 84 or longer [13].

In a larger open-label study, 48 patients with severe AS were treated with infliximab. At week 8, significant improvements in mean disease activity, global pain, BASDAI score, Bath Ankylosing Spondylitis Functional Index score, and CRP levels were observed [24]. The results of the aforementioned open-label studies were recently confirmed in a double-blind, placebo-controlled, phase III clinical trial [25]. A total of 70 patients with active AS were enrolled in the study and randomized to receive placebo ($n = 35$) or infliximab at 5 mg/kg ($n = 35$) at weeks 0, 2 and 6, and then every 6 weeks until week 48. At the time of the report, 66 patients had completed 3 months of treatment. A 50% improvement in BASDAI score was achieved by 53% of patients treated with infliximab, compared with 9% of patients treated with placebo ($P < 0.01$). Interestingly, only patients with elevated serological markers of inflammation responded to anti-TNF-α therapy. Similar data have recently been reported with etanercept in AS patients [26].

Adult-onset Still's disease

Adult-onset Still's disease (AOSD) is a rare systemic inflammatory disorder of unknown etiology. Clinical symptoms of this disease are high spiking fever, arthritis, transient cutaneous rashes, hepatosplenomegaly, leukocytosis and sore throat. A markedly elevated serum ferritin correlates with disease activity and several inflammatory cytokines are elevated in these patients. Furthermore, Hoshino et al. [27] reported elevated serum levels of TNF-α in AOSD patients. Recently, Kawashima et al. [28] demonstrated that the proinflammatory cytokine IL-18 is markedly, and in this quantity rather specifically, elevated in the serum of AOSD patients during the acute phase of their disease. Because it has been shown that TNF-α induces the expression of IL-18 in synovial tissues [29], anti-TNF agents may lead to a reduction of IL-18 in AOSD patients. Bombardieri et al. [30] recently demonstrated that infliximab reduced IL-18 serum levels in RA patients. Therefore, studies to determine if infliximab also reduces IL-18 serum levels in AOSD are warranted.

The current treatment for AOSD is mostly limited to the use of NSAIDs and, in severe cases, prednisone. However, many patients become dependent on high-dose prednisone or are refractory to corticosteroid treatment. In a retrospective analysis of 26 AOSD patients, methotrexate was an effective second-line treatment for patients who had not responded to prednisone. However, controlled studies of methotrexate and other DMARDs in the treatment of AOSD have not been performed. Thalidomide, a known inhibitor of TNF-α, was reported to markedly improve clinical symptoms in a patient with treatment-resistant AOSD [31].

Systematic investigation of anti-TNF-α therapy in AOSD is in its early stages. An open-label trial evaluated the efficacy of infliximab in the treatment of AOSD refractory to conventional therapy [32]. Three patients with chronic and active AOSD who were unresponsive to corticosteroids and methotrexate were administered infliximab at 3 mg/kg at weeks 0, 2, and 6, and then every 8 weeks thereafter, along with concomitant methotrexate (15 mg/week). At 50 weeks of follow up, disease activity improved in all three patients, and two patients experienced reductions in ESR, CRP, prednisone dose and PGA. In a recent pilot study conducted at our institution, six AOSD patients treated with infliximab reported marked improvements in the clinical signs and symptoms of AOSD [33]. Patients were treated with infliximab at 5 mg/kg at weeks 0, 2, and 6, and thereafter at intervals of 6–8 weeks. In all six patients, fever, arthralgias, myalgias, splenomegaly and rash were resolved within the first three courses of infliximab treatment. Although the results of these open-label trials need to be confirmed in randomized, placebo-controlled studies, preliminary results suggest that infliximab is effective in managing relapses in refractory AOSD patients. This has meanwhile been confirmed by another group [34]. Tamesis et al. [35] treated five AOSD patients with etanercept (2 × 25 mg/week, subcutaneously) with good success in all disease parameters up to 12 months. Weinblatt et al. [36] treated 12 patients with etanercept (initial dosage 2 × 25 mg/week, subcutaneously). Of these 12 patients, two withdrew because of disease flares and four had to increase their etanercept dosage to 3 × 25 mg/week. In the three patients with fever and rash, only one improved in these features.

Polymyositis and dermatomyositis
Polymyositis and dermatomyositis are idiopathic inflammatory myopathies that are characterized by proximal muscle weakness, skeletal muscle inflammation and damage, and elevated serum levels of muscle-derived proteins such as creatinine kinase. Polymyositis is associated with lymphocyte invasion of muscle fibres, predominantly cytotoxic CD8+ T lymphocytes, which leads to muscle fibre necrosis, degeneration and fibrosis. The current first-line therapy for polymyositis is prednisone. However, many patients only achieve partial response or do not respond at all to high dose corticosteroids. Because early recognition and treatment of polymyositis is critical to prevent irreversible muscle damage, second-line therapies such as methotrexate or azathioprine should be administered to patients who fail to respond to corticosteroid treatment. Alternatively, or in addition, high dose immunoglobulins have been proven efficacious in refractory cases.

Using monoclonal antibodies to TNF-α, Tateyama et al. [37] demonstrated that TNF-α positive macrophages and lymphocytes invade the endomysium in the muscles of polymyositis patients. In addition, the authors describe a correlation between TNF-α levels in the endomysium and muscle fibre atrophy. Kuru et al. [38] also demonstrated infiltration of TNF-α-positive CD8+ lymphocytes and macrophages into the muscle fibres of polymyositis patients.

The apparent involvement of cytokine-producing T lymphocytes in polymyositis has initiated interest in treating these patients with anti-TNF agents. Saadeh [39] treated four refractory patients with dermatomyositis with satisfying benefit. Hengstman et al. [40] treated two dermatomyositis patients with infliximab (10 mg/kg every second week) with good responses. We recently treated a patient with polymyositis refractory to immunosuppressive regimens with infliximab (4 mg/kg every 6 weeks) and concomitant methotrexate therapy. This patient showed a significant response to infliximab treatment, including a significant improvement in mobility. The skeletal muscle-specific enzymes returned to normal serum levels, indicating a substantial reduction in inflammation. However, this could not be confirmed in another patient. Although this is a single case, it suggests that anti-TNF-α therapy may be a viable treatment alternative for certain patients with refractory polymyositis. Further studies to fully investigate the potential for anti-TNF-α therapy in treating polymyositis are warranted .

Vasculitis (Behçet's disease, Wegener's granulomatosis)

Behçet's disease is a chronic autoimmune disorder characterized by systemic vasculitis. This disease is associated with mucocutaneous, ocular, articular, vascular, gastrointestinal and central nervous system manifestations. Approximately 70% of patients experience relapsing ocular inflammation that can lead to blindness. The etiology of Behçet's disease is unknown, although a genetic association to human leukocyte-associated antigen-B5 has been described [41]. However, some evidence suggests that increased levels of TNF-α and soluble TNF receptors are associated with active disease [42,43]. Thalidomide has been successfully used in the treatment of Behçet's disease, possibly by accelerating the degradation of TNF-α mRNA [44].

Recently, anti-TNF therapy has been used for the treatment of these patients. Travis et al. [45] reported the successful use of infliximab in two Behçet's disease patients with rare gastrointestinal ulcerations; this has been confirmed by others [46]. Within 10 days of infliximab treatment, the ulcers had healed and all extraintestinal manifestations had resolved. Furthermore, five patients with relapsing panuveitis were successfully treated with infliximab. Remission of ocular inflammation was evident within the first 24 hours and complete suppression was observed within 7 days of infliximab therapy [47]. This has been confirmed in case reports by other authors [48,49]; treatment with infliximab (10 mg/kg, twice at week 0 and 4) has resulted in long-term remission over more than 12 months [49]. Clearly, the rapid and effective response of this handful of Behçet's disease patients to infliximab warrants further studies of the use of anti-TNF therapy in treating this disease.

Wegener's granulomatosis (WG) is a chronic necrotizing vasculitis involving small to middle-sized vessels. Virtually every organ can be involved, but typically eyes, lungs, joints and kidneys are affected. It is characterized by the occurrence of cytoplasmic antineutrophil cytoplasmic antigen antibodies directed against proteinase 3. The production of TNF-α in peripheral blood mononuclear cells and CD4+ T cells isolated from patients with WG was elevated, when compared with healthy donors [50]. Moreover, Noronha et al. [51] found expression of TNF-α at active sites of inflammation in kidney biopsies.

Consequently, a clinical study with infliximab in patients with WG was initiated [52]. Six patients who were refractory to therapy with cyclophosphamide were treated with infliximab at 3–5 mg/kg (day 0, weeks 2 and 6, every fourth week thereafter). Three patients had imminent visual loss due to progressive retroorbital granulomas, two patients had progressive glomerulonephritis, and one patient suffered from progressive pulmonary granulomas. Infusion of infliximab resulted in a rapid and significant improvement in

five patients, one patient was withdrawn due to suspected infection. Similar results were reported by Bartolucci et al. in 10 patients (seven with WG, two with RA-associated systemic vasculitis and one with cryoglobulinemic vasculitis) [53]. In a randomized trial with active WG, 20 patients were enrolled for treatment with etanercept (2 × 25 mg/week, subcutaneously) on methotrexate background. All patients could taper their steroid dosage within 6 months. Long-term efficacy data are not available so far [54]. In another study, Stone et al. [55] included 20 active WG patients. Etanercept was added to the standard therapeutic regime including cyclophosphamide in six patients. Nineteen out of the 20 patients remained on the drug over the observation period of 6 months, one patient developed retroorbital granulomas at 4 months. Birmingham Vasculitis Activity Score decreased from 3.6 to 0.6, and the mean daily prednisolone dosage could be reduced from 19 mg to 7.4 mg. However, persistently active disease was common and present in 15/19 patients; one patient developed renal involvement and mesenteric vasculitis while taking etanercept.

New nonbiological TNF-α-targeting agents

Given the high costs associated with immunobiologicals and the need for saving expenses in virtually every health care system worldwide, a specific TNF-α blockade employing synthetic (and therefore less expensive) agents is most desirable. Another advantage would be the possible oral availability of these drugs. In this context, inhibition of TNF-α gene transcription, inhibition of TNF-α mRNA translation or blockade of TNF-α-specific signal transduction could be envisioned. A 10 amino acid peptide could block TNF-α synthesis at the translational level both in vitro and in vivo (rat arthritis model; murine colitis model) through unknown mechanisms. A TNF-α mRNA antisense construct (ISIS 25302) might qualify as a further drug with high specificity. However, both drugs must be evaluated for efficacy and safety in preclinical and clinical trials in both animals and humans.

Insights into signal transduction events associated with TNF-α and/or other proinflammatory cytokines enable targeting of intracellular key molecules, thereby blocking consequences of TNF-α signaling at the subreceptor level. One needs to keep in mind, however, that, so far, there are no chemical signal transduction inhibitors that are 100% specific for one certain kinase; so the side effects might be less favorable than the immunobiologicals. Moreover, many (probably most) intracellular signaling enzymes are not completely specific for one certain signalling cascade, but are redundantly employed by various receptor-associated signalling cascades. This is not necessarily a disadvantage, but bears the risk for a broader spectrum of side effects.

One of the therapeutic target structures involved in the TNF-α associated signalling cascades is p38 mitogen-activated protein kinase (MAPK), which is important for the initiation of TNF-α synthesis [56]. Thus, 'specific' inhibitors of p38 MAPK were developed (SCIO-469; VX-745; BIRB 796), which are currently being evaluated in animal models. At high dosage, BIRB 796 has been shown to effectively inhibit arthritis progression in established collagen-induced arthritis [57].

Thalidomide has TNF-α inhibiting properties which might be centrally mediated through inhibition of phosphodiesterase IV. Disadvantages of this old drug are obviously affiliated to its teratogenicity and sedative properties. Several companies are in the course of developing phosphodiesterase-IV-dependent or -independent thalidomide derivatives with similar TNF-α neutralising efficacy, but lower toxicity. Roflumilast, an orally available selective phosphodiesterase IV inhibitor, has been shown to decrease TNF-α concentrations in a lipopolysaccharide model, both *in vivo* and *in vitro*, and to protect mice in the collagen-induced arthritis model, especially in combination with methotrexate [58].

Nuclear factor (NF)-κB is responsible for both synthesis of TNF-α as well as transmission of TNF-α-mediated effects [56,59]. NF-κB is a p50/p65 heterodimer which is bound to, and inactivated by, its inhibitor, IκB. After activation of the cell, IκB-kinases (IκK) phosphorylate and degrade IκB, enabling NF-κB to translocate into the nucleus and to bind to its specific promoter sites. An inhibition of IκK will thereby indirectly block transmission of TNF-α-associated intracellular signals [60]. Several IκK inhibitors have been developed, but to our knowledge none is yet in preclinical trials in humans. In DBA/1 mice, collagen-induced arthritis was treated with two IκK inhibitors, AS 2868 or AS 2920, at occurrence of first signs of the disease [61]. Disease severity was dose-dependently decreased, particularly by AS 2920. In an adjuvant arthritis model in Lewis rats, the IκK inhibitor, SPC-839, was orally given in various doses once daily. The authors describe a dose-dependent decrease in paw swelling and a near complete inhibition of radiographic damage, associated with improvement of histological features [62].

Another strategy focuses on TNF-α converting enzyme (TACE), a metalloproteinase that is important for cleavage of membrane-bound TNF-α. Inhibitors of TACE could prevent secretion of TNF-α and possibly decrease concentrations of (soluble) TNF-α at the inflammatory site. On the other hand, Kollias and his group have shown that overexpression of only the membrane-bound TNF-α in mice still leads to a chronic destructive arthritis [63]. In addition, TACE is responsible for the cleavage of TNF-α receptors, thereby preventing solubilization of these natural TNF-α binding and neutralizing proteins. Therefore, TACE inhibitors might not only have anti-inflammatory properties.

An orally available TACE inhibitor, DPC 333, has been successfully tested in several mouse and rat models of arthritis. A double-blind, placebo-controlled, phase IIa study in RA patients was initiated, but has been put on hold after the merging of Bristol-Myers Squibb and DuPont Pharmaceuticals.

Concluding remarks
The overwhelming success of TNF-α-targeting therapies in treatment of RA, CD and juvenile chronic arthritis has lead to an avalanche of new therapeutic trials aiming at neutralising TNF-α, including long-term treatment in RA patients, introduction of new anti-TNF-α immunobiologicals, new indications for TNF-α blockade and (yet still quite early in development) orally available inhibitors of TNF-α synthesis or signal transduction. Both patients and physicians can optimistically await the next years, as new agents and study results will considerably broaden the range of improved therapeutic options in chronic inflammatory diseases.

Glossary of terms
ACR 20 (50) (70) = American College of Rheumatology criteria for 20% (50%) (70%) improvement; AOSD = Adult onset Still's disease; AS = ankylosing spondylitis; BASDAI = Bath Ankylosing Spondylitis Disease Activity Index; CD = Crohn's disease; PASI = psoriasis area and severity index; PDE = phosphodiesterase; PGA = physician's global assessment; PsA = psoriatic arthritis; TACE = TNF-α converting enzyme; WG = Wegener's granulomatosis.

References
1. van de Putte LBA, Rau R, Breedveld FC, Kalden JR, Malaise MG, Schattenkirchner M, Emery P, Burmester GR, Zeidler H, Moutsopoulos HH, Compagnone D, Kempeni J, Kupper H: **Efficacy of the fully human anti-TNF antibody D2E7 in rheumatoid arthritis [abstract].** *Arthritis Rheum* 1999, **42**:S400. [general reference]
2. Davis MW, Feige U, Bendele AM, Martin SW, Edwards III CK: **Treatment of rheumatoid arthritis with PEGylated recombinant human soluble tumour necrosis factor type I: a clinical update.** *Ann Rheum Dis* 2000, **59**:i41-i43. [key review]
3. Grünke M, Schiller M, Hieronymus T, Geiler T, Kalden JR, Manger B, Lorenz H-M: **Synergistic effects of combinations of established DMARDs and immunobiological drugs in vitro [abstract].** *Arthritis Rheum* 2000, **43**:S364. [general reference]
4. Boumpas D, Tassiulas IO: **Psoriatic arthritis.** In: *Primer on the Rheumatic Diseases.* Edited by Klippel JH, Weyand CM, Wortmann RL. Atlanta, GA: Arthritis Foundation; 1997:175-179.
5. Austin LM, Ozawa M, Kikuchi T, Walters IB, Krueger JG: **The majority of epidermal T cells in psoriasis vulgaris lesions can produce type 1 cytokines, interferon-gamma, interleukin-2, and tumor necrosis factor-alpha, defining TC1 (cytotoxic T lymphocyte) and TH1 effector populations: a type 1 differentiation bias is also measured in circulating blood T cells in psoriatic patients.** *J Invest Dermatol* 1999, **113**:752-759. [general reference]
6. Ritchlin C, Haas-Smith SA, Hicks D, Cappuccio J, Osterland CK, Looney RJ: **Patterns of cytokine production in psoriatic synovium.** *J Rheumatol* 1998, **25**:1544-1552. [general reference]
7. Danning CL, Illei GG, Hitchon C, Greer MR, Boumpas DT, McInnes IB: **Macrophage-derived cytokine and nuclear factor kappaB p65 expression in synovial membrane and skin of patients with psoriatic arthritis.** *Arthritis Rheum* 2000, **43**:1244-1256. [general reference]

8. Ettehadi P, Greaves MW, Wallach D, Aderka D, Camp RD: Elevated tumour necrosis factor-alpha (TNF-alpha) biological activity in psoriatic skin lesions. *Clin Exp Immunol* 1994, 96: 146-151. [archival reference]

9. Uyemura K, Yamamura M, Fivenson DF, Modlin RL, Nickoloff BJ: The cytokine network in lesional and lesion-free psoriatic skin is characterized by a T-helper type 1 cell-mediated response. *J Invest Dermatol* 1993, 101:701-705. [archival reference]

10. Bonifati C, Carducci M, Cordiali Fei P, Trento E, Sacerdoti G, Fazio M, Ameglio F: Correlated increases of tumour necrosis factor-alpha, interleukin-6 and granulocyte monocyte-colony stimulating factor levels in suction blister fluids and sera of psoriatic patients—relationships with disease severity. *Clin Exp Dermatol* 1994, 19:383-387. [archival reference]

11. Mussi A, Bonifati C, Carducci M, D'Agosto G, Pimpinelli F, D'Urso D, D'Auria L, Fazio M, Ameglio F: Serum TNF-alpha levels correlate with disease severity and are reduced by effective therapy in plaque-type psoriasis. *J Biol Regul Homeost Agents* 1997, 11:115-118. [general reference]

12. van den Bosch F, Kruithof E, Baeten D, De Keyser F, Mielants H, Veys EM: Effects of a loading dose regimen of three infusions of chimeric monoclonal antibody to tumour necrosis factor alpha (infliximab) in spondyloarthropathy: an open pilot study. *Ann Rheum Dis* 2000, 59:428-433. [general reference]

13. Kruithof E, van den Bosch F, Baeten D, De Keyser F, Mielants H, Veys EM: TNF-alpha blockade with infliximab in patients with active spondyloarthropathy: follow-up of one year maintenance regimen [abstract]. *Ann Rheum Dis* 2001, 60:59. [general reference]

14. Yazici Y, Erkan D, Lockshin MD: A prelirninary study of etanercept in the treatment of severe, resistant psoriatic arthritis. *Clin Exp Rheumatol* 2000, 18:732-734. [general reference]

15. Antoni C, Dechant C, Lorenz H-M, Ogilvie A, Kalden-Nemeth D, Kalden JR: Successful treatment of severe psoriatic arthritis with infliximab. *Arthritis Rheum* 1999, 42:S371. [general reference]

16. Ogilvie AL, Antoni C, Dechant C, Manger B, Kalden JR, Schuler G, Luftl M: Treatment of psoriatic arthritis with antitumour necrosis factor-alpha antibody clears skin lesions of psoriasis resistant to treatment with methotrexate. *Br J Dermatol* 2001, 144:587-589. [general reference]

17. Mease PJ, Goffe BS, Metz J, VanderStoep A, Finck B, Burge DJ: Etanercept in the treatment of psoriatic arthritis and psoriasis: a randomised trial. *Lancet* 2000, 356:385-390. [general reference]

18. Mease PJ, Goffe BS, Metz J, van der Stoep A, Burge DJ: Enbrel® (etanercept) in patients with psoriatic arthritis and psoriasis [abstract]. *Ann Rheum Dis* 2001, 60:146. [general reference]

19. Chaudhari U, Rornano P, Mulcahy LD, Dooley LT, Baker DG, Gottlieb AB: Efficacy and safety of infliximab monotherapy for plaque-type psoriasis: a randomised trial. *Lancet* 2001, 357: 1842-1847. [general reference]

20. Braun J, Bollow M, Neure L, Seipelt E, Seyrekbasan F, Herbst H, Eggens U, Distler A, Sieper J: Use of immunohistologic and in situ hybridization techniques in the examination of sacroillac joint biopsy specimens from patients with ankylosing spondylitis. *Arthritis Rheum* 1995, 38:499-505. [archival reference]

21. Lange U, Teichmann J, Stracke H: Correlation between plasma TNF-alpha, IGF-1, biochemical markers of bone metabolism, markers of inflammation/disease activity, and clinical manifestations in ankylosing spondylitis. *Eur J Med Res* 2000, 5: 507-511. [general reference]

22. Mielants H, Veys EM, Cuvelier C, De Vos M: Course of gut inflammation in spondyloarthropathies and therapeutic consequences. *Baillieres Clin Rheumatol* 1996, 10:147-164. [key review]

23. Brandt J, Haibel H, Cornely D, Golder W, Gonzales J, Reddig J, Thriene W, Sieper J, Braun J: Successful treatment of active ankylosing spondylitis with the anti-tumor necrosis factor alpha monoclonal antibody infliximab. *Arthritis Rheum* 2000, 43:1346-1352. [general reference]

24. Breban MA, Vignon E, Claudepierre P, Saraux A, Wendling D, Lespesailles E, Euller-Ziegler L, Sibilia J, Perdringer A, Alexandre C, Dougados M: Efficacy of infliximab in severe refractory ankylosing spondylitis (AS). Results of an open-label study [abstract]. *Ann Rheum Dis* 2001, 59:58. [general reference]

25. Brandt J, Alten R, Burmester G, Gromnica-Ihle E, Kellner H, Schneider M, Sörensen H, Zeidler H, Thriene W, Sieper J, Braun J: Three months results of a double-blind placebo controlled, phase-111 clinical trial of infiiximab in active ankylosing spondylitis [abstract]. *Ann Rheum Dis* 2001, 61:63. [general reference]

26. Gorman JD, Sack KE, Davis JC: A randomized, double-blind, placebo-controlled trial of etanercept in the treatment of ankylosing spondylitis [abstract]. *Arthritis Rheum* 2001, 44: S90. [general reference]

27. Hoshino T, Ohta A, Yang D, Kawamoto M, Kikuchi M, Inoue Y, Kamizono S, Ota T, Itoh K, Oizumi K: Elevated serum interleukin 6, interferon-gamma, and tumor necrosis factor-alpha levels in patients with adult Still's disease. *J Rheumatol* 1998, 25:396-398. [general reference]

28. Kawashima M, Yamamura M, Taniai M, Yamauchi H, Tanimoto T, Kurimoto M, Miyawaki S, Amano T, Takeuchi T, Makino H: Levels of interleukin-18 and its binding inhibitors in the blood circulation of patients with adult-onset Still's disease. *Arthritis Rheum* 2001, 44:550-560. [general reference]

29. Gracie JA, Forsey RJ, Chan WL, Gilmour A, Leung BP, Greer MR, Kennedy K, Carter R, Wei XQ, Xu D, Field M, Foulis A, Liew FY, McInnes IB: A proinflanimatory role for IL-18 in rheumatoid arthritis. *J Clin Invest* 1999, 104:1393-1401. [general reference]

30. Bombardieri M, Pittoni V, Conti F, Spinelli FR, Spadaro A, Riccieri V, Alessandrini C, Scrivo R, Valesini G: Reduction of IL-18 serum levels in rheumatoid arthritis during short term-treatment with infliximab [abstract]. *Ann Rheum Dis* 2001, 99:54. [general reference]

31. Stambe C, Wicks IP: TNF alpha and response of treatment-resistant adult-onset Still's disease to thalidomide. *Lancet* 1998, 352:544-545. [general reference]

32. Cavagna L, Caporali R, Epis O, Bobbio-Pallavicini F, Montecucco C: Infliximab in the treatment of adult Still's disease refractory to conventional therapy. *Clin Exp Rheumatol* 2001, 19:329-332. [general reference]

33. Dechant C, Antoni C, Lorenz H-M, Kalden-Nemeth D, Kalden JR, Manger B: Treatment of severe adult onset Still's disease with infliximab [abstract]. *Ann Rheum Dis* 2000, 59:162. [general reference]

34. Aurrecoechea E, Blanco R, Gonzales S, Martinez-Taboada VM, Rodriguez.Valverde V: Successful therapy with infliximab in refractory Adult Onset Still's Disease [abstract]. *Arthritis Rheum* 2001, 44:S118. [general reference]

35. Tamesis ER, Reginato AM, Hubscher O, Reginato AJ: Etanercept in recalcitrant Adult Onset Still's Disease [abstract]. *Arthritis Rheum* 2001, 43:S229. [general reference]

36. Weinblatt ME, Maier AL, Overman SS, Mease PJ, Fraser PA, Gravallese EM: Etanercept in Still's disease in the adult [abstract]. *Arthritis Rheum* 2000, 43:S391. [general reference]

37. Tateyama M, Nagano I, Yoshioka M, Chida K, Nakamura S, Itoyama Y: Expression of tumor necrosis factor alpha in muscles of polymyositis. *J Neurol Sci* 1997, 146:45-51. [general reference]

38. Kuru S, Inukai A, Liang Y, Doyu M, Takano A, Sobue G: Tumor necrosis factor alpha expression in muscles of polymyositis and dermatomyositis. *Acta Neuropathol* 2000, 99:585-588. [general reference]

39. Saadeh CK: Etanercept is effective in the treatment of polymyositis/dermatomyositis which is refractory to conventional therapy including steroids and other disease-modifying agents [abstract]. *Arthritis Rheum* 2000, 43:S193. [general reference]

40. Hengstman G, van den Hoogen F, van Engelen B, Barrera P, Netea M, van de Putte L: Anti-TNF blockade with infliximab in polymyositis and dermatomyositis [abstract]. *Arthritis Rheum* 2000, 43:S193. [general reference]

41. Paul M, Klein T, Krause I, Molad Y, Narinsky R, Weinberger A: Allelic distribution of HLA-B*5 in HLA-B5-positive Israeli patients with Behçet's disease. *Tissue Antigens* 2001, 58:185-186.

42. Kosar A, Haznedaroglu S, Karaaslan Y, Buyukasik Y, Haznedaroglu IC, Ozath D, Sayinalp N, Ozcebe O, Kirazli S, Dundar S: Effects of interferon-alpha2a treatment on serum levels of tumor necrosis factor-alpha, tumor necrosis factor-alpha2 receptor, interleukin-2, interleukin-2 receptor, and E-selectin in Behcet's disease. *Rheumatol Int* 1999, 19:11-14. [general reference]

43. Turan B, Gallati H, Erdi H, Gurler A, Michel BA, Villiger PM: Systemic levels of the T cell regulatory cytokines IL-10 and IL-12 in Behcet's disease; soluble TNFR-75 as a biological marker

of disease activity. *J Rheumatol* 1997, **24**:128-132. [general reference]

44. Calabrese L, Fleischer AB: **Thalidomide: current and potential clinical applications.** *Am J Med* 2000, **108**:487-495. [general reference]

45. Travis SP, Czajkowski M, McGovern DP, Watson RG, Bell AL: **Treatment of intestinal Behcet's syndrome with chimeric tumour necrosis factor alpha antibody.** *Gut* 2001, **49**:725-728. [general reference]

46. Hassard PV, Binder SW, Nelson V, Vasiliauskas EA: **Anti-tumor necrosis factor monoclonal antibody therapy for gastrointestinal Behcet's disease: a case report.** *Gastroenterology* 2001, **120**:995-999. [general reference]

47. Sfikakis PP, Theodossiadis PG, Katsiari CG, Kaklamanis P, Markomichelakis NN: **Effect of infliximab on sight-threatening panuveitis in Behcet's disease.** *Lancet* 2001, **358**:295-296. [general reference]

48. Robertson LP, Hickling P: **Treatment of recalcitrant orogenital ulceration of Behcet's syndrome with infliximab.** *Rheumatology* 2001, **40**:473-474. [general reference]

49. Goossens PH, Verburg RJ, Breedveld FC: **Remission of Behcet's syndrome with tumour necrosis factor alpha blocking therapy [abstract].** *Ann Rheum Dis* 2001, **60**:637. [general reference]

50. Ludviksson BR, Sneller MC, Chua KS, Talar-Williams C, Langford CA, Ehrhardt RO, Fauci AS, Strober W: **Active Wegener's granulomatosis is associated with HLA-DR+ CD4+ T cells exhibiting an unbalanced Th1-type T cell cytokine pattern: reversal with IL-10.** *J Immunol* 1998, **160**:3602-3609. [general reference]

51. Noronha IL, Kruger C, Andrassy K, Ritz E, Waldherr R: **In situ production of TNF-alpha, IL-1 beta and IL-2R in ANCA-positive glomerulonephritis.** *Kidney Int* 1993, **43**:682-692. [archival reference]

52. Lamprecht P, Voswinkel J, Lilienthal T, Noelle B, Heller M, Gross W, Gross W, Grause A: **Successful treatment of refractory Wegener's granulomatosis with infliximab [abstract].** *Arthritis Rheum* 2001, **44**:S56. [general reference]

53. Bartolucci P, Ramanoelina J, Cohen P, Le Hello C, Guillevin L: **Pilot study on infliximab for 10 patients with systemic vasculitis not responding to steroids and immunosuppressants [abstract].** *Arthritis Rheum* 2001, **44**:S56. [general reference]

54. Langford CA, Talar-Williams C, Barron KS, McCabe KE, Sneller MC: **PhaseI/II trial of etanercept in Wegener's granulomatosis: safety and preliminary experience [abstract].** *Arthritis Rheum* 2000, **43**:S163. [general reference]

55. Stone J, Uhlfelder M, Hellmann D, Crook S, Bedocs N, Hoffman G: **Etanercept in Wegener's granulomatosis: a six month open-label trial to evaluate safety [abstract].** *Arthritis Rheum* 2000, **43**:S404. [general reference]

56. Van den Berghe W, Vermeulen L, De Wilde G, De Bosscher K, Boone E, Haegeman G: **Signal transduction by tumor necrosis factor and gene regulation of the inflammatory cytokine interleukin-6.** *Biochem Pharmacol* 2000, **60**:1185-1195. [general reference]

57. Nabozny G, Souza D, Raymond E, Pargellis C, Regan J: **Inhibition of established collagen-induced arthritis with BIRB 796, a selective inhibitor of p38 MAP kinase [abstract].** *Arthritis Rheum* 2001, **44**:S368. [general reference]

58. Barsig J, Leung BP, Bundschuh DS, Wollin L, Marx D, Beume R, Beume R, Liew FY: **The novel phosphodiesterase-4 inhibitor Roflumilast suppresses TNF-α production and efficiently protects mice against collagen-induced arthritis alone and in combination with methotrexate [abstract].** *Arthritis Rheum* 2001, **44**:S367. [general reference]

59. Umezawa K, Ariga A, Matsumoto N: **Naturally occurring and synthetic inhibitors of NF-kappaB functions.** *Anticancer Drug Des* 2000, **15**:239-244. [general reference]

60. Yamamoto Y, Gaynor RB: **Therapeutic potential of inhibition of the NF-kappaB pathway in the treatment of inflammation and cancer.** *J Clin Invest* 2001, **107**:135-142. [general reference]

61. Sagot Y, Sattonnet-Roche P, Bhagwat SS, Grimshaw CE, Dreano M, Plater-Zyberk C: **Two IκK inhibitors are orally active small molecules decreasing severity of collagen-induced arthritis in DBA/1 mice [abstract].** *Arthritis Rheum* 2001, **44**:S368. [general reference]

62. Bhagwat SS, Bennett BI, Satoh Y, O'Leary EC, Leisten J, Firestein GS, Boyle DS, Dreano M, Anderson DW, Grimshaw CE: **The** small molecule IκK2 inhibitor SPC-839 is efficacious in an animal model of arthritis [abstract].** *Arthritis Rheum* 2001, **44**: S213. [general reference]

63. Alexopoulou L, Pasparakis M, Kollias G: **A murine transmembrane tumor necrosis factor (TNF) transgene induces arthritis by cooperative p55/p75 TNF receptor signaling.** *Eur J Immunol* 1997, **27**:2588-2592. [general reference]

Supplement Review
Therapy of systemic lupus erythematosus: a look into the future
Josef S Smolen

Department of Rheumatology, Internal Medicine III, Vienna General Hospital, University of Vienna, and 2nd Department of Medicine, Lainz Hospital, Vienna, Austria

Correspondence: Josef S Smolen, MD, Department of Rheumatology, Internal Medicine III, Vienna General Hospital, University of Vienna, Waehringer Guertel 18-20, A-1090 Vienna, Austria. Tel: +43 1 40400 4300; fax: +43 1 40400 4331; e-mail:smj@2me.khl.magwien.gv.at

Received: 19 March 2002
Accepted: 23 March 2002
Published: 9 May 2002

Arthritis Res 2002, **4 (suppl 3)**:S25-S30

This article may contain supplementary data which can only be found online at http://arthritis-research.com/content/4/S3/S025

This manuscript is dedicated to Professor Tiny Maini in admiration of his grand mind and great work, in thankful appreciation of the numerous hours of our scientific debates, discussions on the future of rheumatology, and great personal enjoyment over the past 15 years, and with sincere gratitude for his support, guidance, and friendship over so many years

Chapter summary

The prognosis for patients with systemic lupus erythematosus has greatly improved over the past two decades. However, therapies that are more effective and that have fewer sequelae are needed to rescue patients from organ failure and further reduce mortality. Research under way, including that into induction of tolerance to self-antigens, prevention of the consequences of pathogenic autoantibody production, interference with the cytokine network and signal transduction, the identification and treatment of any infectious triggers, and stem cell therapy, offers hope of improved remedies or even of cure. Given the fact that a number of biological therapies for rheumatologic disease are already in use or are in the development stage, such progress may come soon.

Keywords: systemic lupus erythematosus, therapy

Introduction

The prognosis of patients with systemic lupus erythematosus (SLE) has improved significantly over the past two decades [1]. Earlier diagnosis on the basis of better awareness, description of new autoantibody specificities, and improvement of serological techniques may have supported this development. However, the introduction of pulse cyclophosphamide therapy for lupus nephritis [2] as well as advances in hemodialysis techniques were pivotal for this improvement, since it was irreversible renal failure and its consequences that previously had a high impact on mortality [3]. Nevertheless, almost 10% of SLE patients still die within the first 5 years of their disease and their mean life expectancy is significantly shorter than in the general population, due partly to relentlessly progressive lupus in some patients and partly to sequelae of treatment, particularly those of cytotoxic agents and glucocorticoids [4,5]. This situation calls for the search for new therapeutic strategies with higher efficacy and lesser comorbidity.

SLE is the prototype non-organ-specific autoimmune disease. A multisystem disorder, it destroys cells and organs by means of autoantibodies and immune complexes. The mechanisms underlying the hyper-reactivity and autoreactivity of the immune system in SLE are unknown. A setting of genetic susceptibility involving multiple genes [6] in conjunction with environmental triggers constitutes the hypothetical etiopathogenic background. As long as the

---

A glossary of specialist terms used in this chapter appears at the end of the text section. A list of common abbreviations used in this issue appears just before the indexes.

triggers of the disease are unknown, novel therapeutic approaches must be aimed mainly at interference with the generation of autoantibodies and immune complexes or with their consequences, namely cell destruction and inflammation. In this review, some of the many potential future therapeutic approaches are discussed. Further information is included in a recent textbook chapter [7].

Is there a potential for causative treatment?

The role of infectious triggers of autoimmune diseases has been debated for decades. The earliest evidence pointing to such associations stems from acute rheumatic fever induced by streptococcal infections and the subsequent generation of antistreptococcal antibodies, which cross-react with cardiac tissue and lead to rheumatic heart disease in susceptible individuals [8]. Type I diabetes has been often linked to Coxsackie virus infections [9]; some forms of vasculitis appear to be a consequence of infection with hepatitis B or C virus [10]; and peptide sequences of a variety of SLE-related autoantigens are homologous to sequences of various viral proteins [11–14]. In fact, a peptide of the Sm protein, which can elicit a variety of autoantibodies and experimental lupus in an immunized animal, has homologies with a protein present on Epstein–Barr virus (EBV) [15,16].

In contrast to the earlier, unsupported hypotheses, there is at least some recent important epidemiological evidence that SLE may be associated with EBV infection [16]. EBV is a common infection worldwide. In the African regions, EBV infection is commonly associated with a variety of malignancies [17]. In these regions, SLE is rare [18]. On the other hand, in the industrialized world, people of African origin have a high risk of developing SLE [18], while EBV-associated malignancies are rare in those regions. Thus, it is conceivable that under different environmental circumstances EBV may induce different diseases or be, at least, a cofactor in the pathogenesis of different disorders, one of them SLE. Importantly, as EBV is one cause of lymphomas in the industrialized world [17] and is usually contracted during adolescence, one wonders if the design of a vaccine protecting against EBV infection and given in early childhood would reduce the risk not only of such malignancies, but also of SLE.

Induction of tolerance

Autoimmune diseases are often considered to be a consequence of lost tolerance to self-antigens. Whether this is truly the case or there are other pathways responsible for the evolution of a pathogenic autoimmune response, induction of unresponsiveness and reversal of the respective immune response might constitute an interesting and successful therapeutic approach.

Given that some of the presumably most pathogenic types of autoantibodies in SLE are directed to dsDNA, down-

modulation of their production is one important therapeutic aim. In experimental animals, a compound containing four oligonucleotides on a triethylene glycol backbone (LJP 394) is capable of downmodulating anti-dsDNA production, presumably by cross-linking the specific antigen receptor on the surface of the B cell. This approach led to amelioration of disease and higher survival in mice with lupus [19]. Anti-dsDNA was also reduced in patients with SLE who were treated with LJP 394 [20]. Phase II/III randomized controlled trials are now under way.

In patients with autoimmune diseases, autoantibodies are usually of the IgG class and have hypermutated V region genes in comparison with the germ line. This clearly suggests the involvement of T-cell help. In fact, T cells incubated with nucleosomes or histones in both experimental and human SLE support the production of anti-dsDNA by B cells [21,22]. Since autoimmunity directed towards histone H1 appears to be of pivotal importance in SLE [23], induction of tolerance to nucleosomal antigens may be an interesting approach; it has already been successfully applied in experimental models [24]. Moreover, activation of 'suppressor' T cells, which more than two decades ago were found to be defective in SLE [25] and have conceptually re-emerged more recently as 'regulatory' T cells [26], may be an interesting new therapeutic approach for the induction of unresponsiveness. Moreover, since interaction of CTLA-4 with its ligand CD80/86 interrupts the costimulatory pathways needed to activate T cells [27], application of a CTLA-4–IgG fusion protein may interfere with the immunologic processes involved in disease induction in mice and man [28,29] and lead to tolerance. Similar effects may be seen with antibodies to CD80/86 (B7.1 and 2) [30].

Tolerance may also be achieved by active immunization with tolerizing peptides and a reduction of autoantibody production has been observed experimentally when peptides from anti-dsDNA antibodies were used [31].

Prevention of the consequences of pathogenic autoantibody production

The mere presence of autoantibodies is not necessarily associated with disease. On the one hand, nonpathogenic autoimmunity is part of our 'normal' immunologic repertoire [32]; on the other hand, the pathogenicity of autoantibodies and the consequent immune complexes is mostly brought about by the activation of complement and the interaction with cell-membrane-bound Fc receptors. Thus, interference with the complement pathways, as in knockout mice or when specific antibodies are used, can prevent or ameliorate lupus [33,34]. Soluble complement receptors may also be beneficial [35]. Likewise, interference with the IgG Fcγ receptor (FcγR) interaction, as in FcγR I/III knockout mice or when anti-CD16 antibodies are used, can prevent the evolution of clinical manifestations of the disease [36,37]. On the other hand, activation of inhibitory FcγRs which contain an immunoreceptor tyrosine inhibitory motif (ITIM), in contrast with the immunoreceptor tyrosine activation motif (ITAM) of other FcγRs [38], may downmodulate B-cell function when co-cross-linked with the B cell's antigen receptor. Such FcγR-mediated inhibition of B-cell activity may not only be induced by immune complexes that carry an antigen binding to the surface immunoglobulin of the B cell while the immunoglobulin moiety of the immune complex engages the FcγRIIb, but also by intravenous immunoglobulin [39]. There are reports of the efficacy of intravenous immunoglobulin in SLE [40], although further confirmation is awaited. The importance of FcγRs as potential therapeutic targets is also supported by reports on genetic linkage of SLE with a region on chromosome 1 that encodes the FcγRs [41].

The interventions discussed above were all directed at the consequences of immune complex production. However, considering autoantibody production, pathogenicity may also be prevented by interfering with autoantibody binding to the (auto)antigen or by eliminating the already bound autoantigen. The latter approach was not blessed with clinical efficacy, since the application of recombinant DNase, aiming at eliminating DNA from the respective immune complexes, had no clinical effects [42]. In contrast, the application of heparin, which prevents the binding of circulating charged nucleosomal antigens to the glomerular basement membrane, prevented the occurrence of nephritis in experimental lupus and possibly should constitute an adjunctive therapy in patients with lupus nephritis [43]. Another interesting means is to displace the antigen in the pathogenic immune complex with cross-reactive peptides. In one study, such an approach using peptides containing D-amino acids prevented glomerular deposition [44].

Interference with the cytokine network and signal transduction

Although the debate whether SLE is primarily a Th1- or a Th2-mediated disease is still unresolved, cytokines appear to play important roles both in human and murine lupus. Not only has IFN-γ been found to be highly increased in sera of patients with lupus [45], but therapy with this cytokine has led to activation and induction of SLE [46,47]. The value of IFN-γ as a therapeutic target is supported by the fact that IFN-γ knockout lupus-prone mice do not develop the disease; moreover, treatment of experimental SLE with IFN-γ receptors inhibits lupus nephritis [48–51]. All these notions are further supported by the observation of an amelioration of experimental lupus by the prototypic Th2 cytokine IL-4 [52].

While the lymphokines mentioned above play important roles in the generation of the primary immune response and its skewing towards specific reactivity patterns [53],

the proinflammatory cytokines are significantly involved in tissue destruction. The central proinflammatory cytokines, tumor necrosis factor (TNF)-α and IL-1, are increased in SLE and can both be activated by immune complexes [54–56]. Moreover, we have recently observed significant amounts of TNF-α by immunohistochemistry in renal biopsies from patients with lupus nephritis (manuscript in preparation). Nevertheless, the role of TNF-α is currently under intensive discussion. On the one hand, in experimental animals, TNF can induce nephritis and TNF-α deficiency ameliorates nephritis [57,58]; on the other hand, injection of TNF-α can ameliorate murine SLE under certain circumstances [59]. This latter observation in conjunction with an occasional appearance of a lupus-like syndrome in patients with rheumatoid arthritis (RA) who are treated with TNF blockers [60] has led to the suggestion that TNF may be protective in lupus and that inhibition of TNF may therefore be potentially detrimental. However, not only are these events rare and, as of now, no more commonly observed than similar drug-induced lupus syndromes during many other therapies used for RA [61,62], but also the anti-dsDNA autoantibodies observed among patients treated with TNF blocker are not consistently observed and are usually of the IgM rather than a pathogenic IgG isotype [63,64].

To account for all these findings, my colleagues and I have proposed that TNF may play a dual role in SLE. This cytokine could well interfere with the regulation of the immune response and lead to an increase of autoantibody production; however, it may also have a critical role in the final pathway of SLE disease, namely immunologically induced and inflammation-induced tissue destruction. Thus, inhibition of TNF-α may, in fact, be a highly valuable tool in patients with active SLE, while inhibition of a potential autoantibody-enhancing activity could be achieved by concomitant immunosuppressive agents. The rapid interference of TNF blockers with the inflammatory response [65] suggests that they may be very beneficial for patients with active lupus nephritis and possibly other SLE manifestations [66,67]. Support for the efficacy and safety of TNF blockade in connective tissue disease stems from observations in patients with RA/SLE overlap (D Furst, personal communication) and individual cases of patients with mixed connective tissue disease ([68] and unpublished observations). My colleagues and I are currently embarking on a small clinical trial with Ethical Committee approval to address the potential of TNF blockade to ameliorate SLE.

Targeting signal transduction pathways

Proinflammatory cytokines and lymphokines mediate their effects by activating transcription factors via diverse signal transduction mechanisms induced after receptor ligation. Among the most important pathways are those involving mitogen-activated protein kinases (MAPKs) and nuclear factor (NF)-κB as well as the Janus kinases (JAKs). Interference with these pathways can ameliorate inflammatory diseases. One compound already approved for RA, leflunomide, interferes with NFκB activation [69] and also has some beneficial effects on mild SLE [70,71]. Many other drugs are currently in development and may have a potential as future therapeutic agents [72,73].

Stem cell therapy

The use of myeloablative cytotoxic therapy to combat the immunoinflammatory insult, with subsequent stem cell rescue to replenish the hematopoietic system and reconstitute the immune system, may be an attractive way of treating aggressive forms of SLE. Autologous stem cell therapy has been performed in small series of patients in recent years with some success [74], and we ourselves also had successful results in relentlessly progressive, life-threatening SLE [75].

Conclusion

In summary, rescue from organ failure and survival of patients with SLE need to be further improved. Advances in immunology and molecular biology have provided new therapeutic targets and new tools for potential treatment success. It will be important to study such new therapies using thoroughly designed protocols [76], but clearly there is hope for even better remedies than are available today and possibly cure of the disease.

Glossary of terms

CTLA-4 = cytotoxic T-lymphocyte antigen 4.

References

1. Urowitz MB, Gladman DD, Abu-Shakra M, Farewell VT: **Mortality studies in systemic lupus erythematosus. Results from a single centre. III. Improved survival over 24 years.** J Rheumatol 1997, **24**:1061-1065. [general reference]
2. Balow JE, Austin HA, Muenz LR, Joyce KM, Antonovych TT, Klippel JH, Steinberg AD, Plotz PH, Decker JL: **Effect of treatment on the evolution of renal abnormalities in lupus nephritis.** N Engl J Med 1984, **311**:491-495. [archival research]
3. Estes D, Christian CL: **The natural history of systemic lupus erythematosus by prospective analysis.** Medicine 1971, **50**:85-95. [general reference]
4. Urowitz MB, Gladman DD: **How to improve morbidity and mortality in systemic lupus erythematosus.** Rheumatology (Oxford) 2000, **39**:237-243. [general reference]
5. Aringer M, Smolen JS, Graninger WB: **Severe infections in plasmapheresis-treated systemic lupus erythematosus.** Arthritis Rheum 1998, **41**:414-420. [general reference]
6. Wakeland EK, Wandstrat AE, Liu K, Morel L: **Genetic dissection of systemic lupus erythematosus.** Curr Opin Immunol 1999, **11**:701-707. [key review]
7. Smolen JS: **Experimental therapies in systemic lupus erythematosus.** In Dubois' Lupus Erythematosus, 6th edn. Edited by Wallace DJ, Hahn BH. Philadelphia, USA: Lippincott Williams & Wilkins; 2002:1276-1283.
8. Gibofsky A, Kerwar S, Zabriskie JB: **Rheumatic fever. The relationships between host, microbe and genetics.** Rheum Dis Clin North Am 1998, **24**:237-259. [key review]
9. Kukreja A, Maclaren NK: **Current cases in which epitope mimicry is considered as a component cause of autoimmune disease: immune-mediated (type 1) diabetes.** Cell Mol Life Sci 2000, **57**:534-541. [key review]
10. Guillevin L: **Virus-associated vasculitides.** Rheumatology (Oxford) 1999, **38**:588-590. [key review]
11. Guldner HH, Netter HJ, Szostecki C, Jaeger E, Will H: **Human anti-p68 autoantibodies recognize a common epitope of U1 RNA containing small nuclear ribonucleoprotein and influenza B virus.** J Exp Med 1990, **171**:819-829. [general reference]
12. Query CC, Keene JD: **A human autoimmune protein associated with U1 RNA contains a region of homology that is cross-reactive with retroviral p30gag antigen.** Cell 1987, **51**:211-220. [general reference]
13. Scofield RH, Dickey WD, Jackson KW, James JA, Harley JB: **A common autoepitope near the carboxyl terminus of the 60-kD Ro ribonucleoprotein: sequence similarity with a viral protein.** J Clin Immunol 1991, **11**:378-388. [general reference]
14. Smolen JS, Steiner G: **Are autoantibodies active players or epiphenomena?** Curr Opin Rheumatol 1998, **10**:201-206. [key review]
15. James JA, Gross T, Scofield RH, Harley JB: **Immunoglobulin epitope spreading and autoimmune disease after peptide immunization: Sm B/B'-derived PPPGMRPP and PPPGIRGP induce spliceosome autoimmunity.** J Exp Med 1995, **181**:453-461. [general reference]
16. James JA, Neas BR, Moser KL, Hall T, Bruner GR, Sestak AL, Harley JB: **Systemic lupus erythematosus in adults is associated with previous Epstein-Barr virus exposure.** Arthritis Rheum 2001, **44**:1122-1126. [general reference]
17. Murray PG, Young LS: **The role of Epstein-Barr virus in human disease.** Front Biosci 2002, **7**:D519-540. [key review]
18. Hopkinson ND, Doherty M, Powell RJ: **Clinical features and race-specific incidence/prevalence rates of systemic lupus erythematosus in a geographically complete cohort of patients.** Ann Rheum Dis 1994, **153**:675-680. [general reference]
19. Jones DS, Barstad PA, Feild MJ, Hachmann JP, Hayag MS, Hill KW, Iverson GM, Livingston DA, Palanki MS, Tibbetts AR, et al.: **Immunospecific reduction of antioligonucleotide antibody-forming cells with a tetrakis-oligonucleotide conjugate (LJP 394), a therapeutic candidate for the treatment of lupus nephritis.** J Med Chem 1995, **38**:2138-2144. [general reference]
20. Weisman MH, Blustein HG, Berner CM: **Reduction in circulating dsDNA antibody titer after administration of LJP 394.** J Rheumatol 1997, **24**:314-318. [general reference]
21. Lu L, Kaliyaperumal A, Boumpas DT, Datta SK: **Major peptide autoepitopes for nucleosome-specific T cells of human lupus.** J Clin Invest 1999, **104**:345-355. [general reference]
22. Voll RE, Roth EA, Girkotaite I, Fehr H, Herrmann M, Lorenz HM, Kalden JR: **Histone-specific Th0 and Th1 clones derived from systemic lupus erythematosus patients induce double-stranded DNA antibody production.** Arthritis Rheum 1997, **40**:2162-2171. [general reference]
23. Schett G, Rubin RL, Steiner G, Hiesberger H, Muller S, Smolen J: **The lupus erythematosus cell phenomenon: comparative analysis of antichromatin antibody specificity in lupus erythematosus cell-positive and -negative sera.** Arthritis Rheum 2000, **43**:420-428. [general reference]
24. Datta SK, Kaliyaperumal A, Desai-Mehta A: **T cells of lupus and molecular targets for immunotherapy.** J Clin Immunol 1997, **17**:11-20. [general reference]
25. Sakane T, Steinberg AD, Green I: **Studies of immune functions of patients with systemic lupus erythematosus. I. Dysfunction of suppressor T-cell activity related to impaired generation of, rather than response to, suppressor cells.** Arthritis Rheum 1978, **21**:657-664. [general reference]
26. Shevach EM, McHugh RS, Thornton AM, Piccirillo C, Natarajan K, Margulies DH: **Control of autoimmunity by regulatory T cells.** Adv Exp Med Biol 2001, **490**:21-32. [general reference]
27. Bluestone JA: **Is CTLA-4 a master switch for peripheral T cell tolerance?** J Immunol 1997, **158**:1989-1993. [key review]
28. Finck BK, Linsley PS, Wofsy D: **Treatment of murine lupus with CTLA4Ig.** Science 1994, **265**:1225-1227. [general reference]
29. Abrams JR, Lebwohl MG, Guzzo CA, Jegasothy BV, Goldfarb MT, Goffe BS, Menter A, Lowe NJ, Krueger G, Brown MJ, Weiner RS, Birkhofer MJ, Warner GL, Berry KK, Linsley PS, Kreuger JG, Ochs HD, Kelley SL, Kang S: **CTLA4Ig-mediated blockade of T-cell costimulation in patients with psoriasis vulgaris.** J Clin Invest 1999, **103**:1243-1252. [general reference]

30. Daikh DI, Wofsy D: **Effects of anti-B7 monoclonal antibodies on humoral immune responses.** *J Autoimmun* 1999, **12**:101-108. [general reference]

31. Waisman A, Ruiz PJ, Israeli E, Eilat D, Konen-Waisman S, Zinger H, Dayan M, Mozes E: **Modulation of murine systemic lupus erythematosus with peptides based on complementarity determining regions of a pathogenic anti-DNA monoclonal antibody.** *Proc Natl Acad Sci USA* 1997, **94**:4620-4625. [general reference]

32. Rose NR, Bona C: **Defining criteria for autoimmune diseases (Witebsky's postulates revisited).** *Immunol Today* 1993, **14**:426-430. [key review]

33. Monia H, Holers VM, Li B, Fung Y, Mariathasan S, Goellner J, Strauss-Schoenberger J, Karr RW, Chaplin DD: **Markedly impaired humoral immune response in mice deficient in complement receptors 1 and 2.** *Proc Natl Acad Sci USA* 1996, **93**:3357-3361. [general reference]

34. Wang Y, Hu Q, Madre JA: **Amelioration of lupus-like autoimmune disease in NZB/W F1 mice after treatment with a blocking monoclonal antibody specific for complement component C5.** *Proc Natl Acad Sci USA* 1996, **93**:8563-8568. [general reference]

35. Weisman HF, Bartow MK, Leppo MP, Boyle MP, Marsh HC Jr, Carson GR, Roux KH, Weisfeldt ML, Fearon DT: **Recombinant soluble CR1 suppressed complement activation, inflammation and necrosis associated with reperfusion of ischemic myocardium.** *Trans Assoc Am Physicians* 1990, **103**:64-72. [general reference]

36. Clynes R, Dumitru C, Ravetch JV: **Uncoupling of immune complex formation and kidney damage in autoimmune glomerulonephritis.** *Science* 1998, **279**:1052-1054. [general reference]

37. Watanabe H, Sherris D, Gilkeson GS: **Soluble CD16 in the treatment of murine lupus nephritis.** *Clin Immunol Immunopathol* 1998, **88**:91-95. [general reference]

38. Bolland S, Ravetch JV: **Inhibitory pathways triggered by ITIM-containing receptors.** *Adv Immunol* 1999, **72**:149-177. [general reference]

39. Samuelsson A, Towers TL, Ravetch JV: **Anti-inflammatory activity of IVIG mediated through the inhibitory Fc receptor.** *Science* 2001, **291**:445-446. [general reference]

40. Levy Y, Sherer Y, George J, Rovensky J, Lukac J, Rauova L, Poprac P, Langevitz P, Fabbrizzi F, Shoenfeld Y: **Intravenous immunoglobulin treatment of lupus nephritis.** *Semin Arthritis Rheum* 2000, **29**:321-327. [key review]

41. Lehrnbecher T, Foster CB, Zhu S, Leitman SF, Goldin LR, Huppy K, Chanock SJ: **Variant genotypes of low affinity Fcgamma receptors in two control populations and a review of low-affinity Fcgamma receptor polymorphisms in control and disease populations.** *Blood* 1999, **94**:4220-4232. [general reference]

42. Davis JC, Manzi S, Yarboro C, Rairie J, McInnes I, Averthelyi D, Sinicropi D, Hale VG, Balow J, Austin H, Boumpas DT, Klippel JH: **Recombinant human DNaseI (rhDNase) in patients with lupus nephritis.** *Lupus* 1999, **8**:68-76. [general reference]

43. van Bruggen MCJ, Walgreen B, Rijke RPM, Corsius MJAMM, Assmann KJM, Smeenk RJT, van Dedem GWK, Kramers K, Berden JHM: **Heparin and heparinoids prevent the binding of immune complexes containing nucleosomal antigens to the GBM and delay nephritis in MRL/lpr mice.** *Kidney Int* 1996, **50**:1555-1564. [general reference]

44. Gaynor B, Putterman C, Valadon P: **Peptide inhibition of glomerular deposition of an anti-DNA antibody.** *Proc Natl Acad Sci USA* 1997, **94**:1955-1960. [general reference]

45. Hooks JJ, Moutsopoulos HM, Geis SA, Stahl NI, Decker JL, Notkins AL: **Immune interferon in the circulation of patients with autoimmune disease.** *N Engl J Med* 1979, **301**:5-8. [general reference]

46. Machold KP, Smolen JS: **Interferon-gamma induced exacerbation of systemic lupus erythematosus.** *J Rheumatol* 1990, **17**:831-832. [general reference]

47. Graninger WB, Hassfeld W, Pesau BB, Machold KP, Zielinski CC, Smolen JS: **Induction of systemic lupus erythematosus by interferon-gamma in a patient with rheumatoid arthritis.** *J Rheumatol* 1991, **18**:1621-1622. [general reference]

48. Seery JP, Carroll JM, Cattell V, Watt FM: **Antinuclear autoantibodies and lupus nephritis in transgenic mice expressing interferon gamma in the epidermis.** *J Exp Med* 1997, **186**:1451-1459. [general reference]

49. Balomenos D, Rumold R, Theofilopoulos AN: **Interferon-gamma is required for lupus-like disease and lymphoaccumulation in MRL-lpr mice.** *J Clin Invest* 1998, **101**:364-371. [general reference]

50. Ozmen L, Roman D, Fountoulakis M, Schmid G, Ryffel B, Garotta G: **Experimental therapy of systemic lupus erythematosus: the treatment of NZB/W mice with mouse soluble interferon-gamma receptor inhibits the onset of glomerulonephritis.** *Eur J Immunol* 1995, **25**:6-12. [general reference]

51. Lawson BR, Prud'homme GJ, Chang Y, Gardner HA, Kuan J, Kono DH, Theofilopoulos AN: **Treatment of murine lupus with cDNA encoding IFN-gammaR/Fc.** *J Clin Invest* 2000, **106**:207-215. [general reference]

52. Santiago ML, Fossati L, Jacquet C, Muller W, Izui S, Reininger L: **Interleukin-4 protects against a genetically linked lupus-like autoimmune syndrome.** *J Exp Med* 1997, **185**:65-70. [general reference]

53. Romagnani S: **The Th1/Th2 paradigm.** *Immunology Today* 1997, **18**:263-266. [key review]

54. Studnicka-Benke A, Steiner G, Petera P, Smolen JS: **Tumour necrosis factor alpha and its soluble receptors parallel clinical disease and autoimmune activity in systemic lupus erythematosus.** *Br J Rheumatol* 1996, **35**:1067-1074. [general reference]

55. Chouchakova N, Skokowa J, Baumann U, Tschernig T, Philippens KM, Nieswandt B, Schmidt RE, Gessner JS: **Fc gamma RIII-mediated production of TNF-alpha induces immune complex alveolitis independently of CXC chemokine generation.** *J Immunol* 2001, **166**:5193-5200. [general reference]

56. Cobb RR, Molony JL: **Interleukin-1beta expression is induced by adherence and is enhanced by Fc-receptor binding to immune complex in THP-1 cells.** *FEBS Lett* 1996, **394**:241-246. [general reference]

57. Yokoyama H, Kreft B, Kelley VR: **Biphasic increase in circulating and renal TNF-alpha in MRL-lpr mice with differing regulatory mechanisms.** *Kidney Int* 1995, **47**:122-130. [general reference]

58. Le Hir M, Haas C, Marino M, Ryffel B: **Prevention of crescentic glomerulonephritis induced by anti-glomerular membrane antibody in tumor necrosis factor-deficient mice.** *Lab Invest* 1998, **78**:1625-1631. [general reference]

59. Jacob CO, McDevitt HO: **Tumour necrosis factor-alpha in murine autoimmune 'lupus' nephritis.** *Nature* 1988, **331**:356-358. [general reference]

60. Hanauer SB: **Review article: safety of infliximab in clinical trials.** *Aliment Pharmacol Ther* 1999, **13** (Suppl 4):16-22. [key review]

61. Gunnarsson I, Kanerud L, Pettersson E, Lundberg I, Lindblad S, Ringertz B: **Predisposing factors in sulphasalazine-induced systemic lupus erythematosus.** *Br J Rheumatol* 1997, **36**:1089-1094. [general reference]

62. Gough A, Chapman S, Wagstaff K, Emery P, Elias E: **Minocycline induced autoimmune hepatitis and systemic lupus erythematosus-like syndrome.** *BMJ* 1996, **312**:169-172. [key review]

63. Charles PJ, Smeenk RJT, DeJong J, Feldmann M, Maini RN: **Assessment of antibodies to double-stranded DNA induced in rheumatoid arthritis patients following treatment with infliximab, a monoclonal antibody to tumor necrosis factor alpha: findings in open-label and randomized placebo-controlled trials.** *Arthritis Rheum* 2000, **43**:2383-2390. [general reference]

64. Smolen JS, Steiner G, Breedveld FC, Kalden JR, Lipsky PE, Maini RN, St Clair EW, Harriman G, Schaible T: **Anti-TNF alpha therapy and drug-induced lupus-like syndrome.** *Ann Rheum Dis* 1999, **58** (Suppl):S217. [general reference]

65. Elliott MJ, Maini RN, Feldmann M, Kalden JR, Antoni C, Smolen JS, Leeb B, Breedveld FC, Macfarlane JD, Bijl H, Woody JN: **Randomised double-blind comparison of chimeric monoclonal antibody to tumour necrosis factor α (cA2) versus placebo in rheumatoid arthritis.** *Lancet* 1994, **344**:1105-1111. [general reference]

66. Pisetsky DS: **Tumor necrosis factor alpha blockers and the induction of anti-DNA autoantibodies.** *Arthritis Rheum* 2000, **43**:2381-2382. [Editorial]

67. Aringer M, Steiner G, Graninger W, Smolen JS: **Role of tumor necrosis factor alpha and potential benefit of tumor necrosis factor blockade treatment in systemic lupus erythematosus: comment on the editorial by Pisetsky.** *Arthritis Rheum* 2001, **44**:1721-1722. [general reference]

68. Schneeweiss B, Graninger WB: **Treatment of mixed connective tissue disease with infliximab [abstract].** *Clin Exp Rheumatol* in press.

69. Manna SK, Mukhopadhyay A, Aggarwal BB: **Leflunomide suppresses TNF-induced cellular responses: effects on NF-kappa B, activator protein-1, c-Jun N-terminal protein kinase, and apoptosis.** *J Immunol* 2000, **165**:5962-5969. [general reference]

70. Petera P, Manger B, Manger K, Rosenburg R, Smolen JS, Kalden JR: **A pilot study of leflunomide in systemic lupus erythematosus (SLE).** *Arthritis Rheum* 2000, **43(Suppl)**:S241. [general reference]

71. Remer CF, Weisman MH, Wallace DJ: **Benefits of leflunomide in systemic lupus erythematosus: a pilot observational study.** *Lupus* 2001, **10**:480-483. [general reference]

72. Lee JC, Kassis S, Kumar S, Badger A, Adams JL: **p38 mitogen-activated protein kinase inhibitors-mechanisms and therapeutic potentials.** *Pharmacol Ther* 1999, **82**:389-397. [general reference]

73. Firestein GS, Manning AM: **Signal transduction and transcription factors in rheumatic disease.** *Arthritis Rheum* 1999, **42**:609-621. [general reference]

74. Marmont AM: **Stem cell transplantation for severe autoimmune diseases. Progress and problems.** *Haematologia* 1998, **83**:733-743. [general reference]

75. Machold in press. [general reference]

76. Smolen JS, Strand V, Cardiel M, Edworthy S, Furst D, Gladman D, Gordon C, Isenberg DA, Klippel JH, Petri M, Simon L, Tugwell P, Wolfe F: **Randomized clinical trials and longitudinal observational studies in systemic lupus erythematosus: consensus on a preliminary core set of outcome domains.** *J Rheumatol* 1999, **26**:504-507. [general reference]

Supplement Review
Genes and environment in arthritis: can RA be prevented?
Lars Klareskog*, Johnny Lorentzen*, Leonid Padyukov* and Lars Alfredsson†

*Rheumatology Unit, Department of Medicine at Karolinska Hospital, Stockholm, Sweden
†Institute for Environmental Medicine, Karolinska Institutet, Stockholm, Sweden

Correspondence: Lars Klareskog, MD, Rheumatology Unit, Department of Medicine at Karolinska Hospital, S-171 76 Stockholm, Sweden.
Tel: +46 8 51774529; fax: +46 8 51773080; e-mail: lars.klareskog@medks.ki.se

Received: 7 March 2002
Accepted: 17 March 2002
Published: 9 May 2002

Arthritis Res 2002, **4 (suppl 3)**:S31-S36

This article may contain supplementary data which can only be found online at http://arthritis-research.com/content/4/S3/S031

Chapter summary

Understanding of how interactions between genes and environment contribute to the development of arthritis is a central issue in understanding the etiology of rheumatoid arthritis (RA), as well as for eventual subsequent efforts to prevent the disease. In this paper, we review current published data on genes and environment in RA as well as in certain induced animal models of disease, mainly those in which adjuvants only or adjuvants plus organ-specific autoantigens are used to induce arthritis. We refer to some new data on environmental and genetic factors of importance for RA generated from a large case–control study in Sweden (1200 patients, 1200 matched controls). We found an increased risk of seropositive but not of seronegative RA in smokers, and there are indications that this effect may be due to a gene–environment interaction involving MHC class II genes. We also found an increased risk of RA in individuals heavily exposed to mineral oils. This was of particular interest because mineral oils are strong inducers of arthritis in certain rodent strains and because polymorphisms in human genetic regions syntenic with genes predisposing for oil-induced arthritis in rats have now been shown to associate with RA in humans. Taken together, our data support the notion that concepts and data on gene-environment interactions in arthritis can now be taken from induced animal models of arthritis to generate new etiological hypotheses for RA.

Keywords: animal model, environmental factors, genetics, major histocompatibiity complex, rheumatoid arthritis

Introduction and historical background

Rheumatoid arthritis (RA) is a condition that is today defined from a set of rather arbitrarily built criteria; those criteria have been very helpful in identifying an entity for which new therapies can be investigated, and such therapies have lately been amazingly successful [1–4]. Despite the continuing successes in developing therapies, the underlying etiology of the disease, i.e. what eventually triggers it and what genetic context allows it to progress, have remained elusive. Consequently, only vague and often scientifically unproven thoughts have been prevalent in the public as well as in the professional arena when ways of achieving primary or secondary prevention of the disease are being considered.

In parallel, it has often been claimed that the disease is so complicated and multifaceted that it may be an insurmountable task to elucidate the interactions between genes and environment that ultimately determine whether arthritis will occur and persist.

In one way, this situation of rapidly emerging new genetic technologies in genetics but prevalent vague ideas of etiology recalls the situation in the late 1980s, when new knowledge in the field of molecular immunology was paralleled

---

A glossary of specialist terms used in this chapter appears at the end of the text section. A list of common abbreviations used in this issue appears just before the indexes.

by a rather vague understanding of the molecular pathology of RA. It was frequently claimed then that the situation was far too complicated to permit targeted therapy against single components of the immune system, such as tumor necrosis factor.

Taking the dramatic demonstration in recent years that complicated problems such as finding targeted therapies for RA can indeed be resolved by less complicated solutions than hitherto for unravelling the remaining difficult questions, we have contemplated the issue of gene–environment interactions in RA and subsequent preventive strategies towards the disease as being a reasonable research effort to discuss at the current symposium and in this supplement to *Arthritis Research*.

What is currently known about genes and environment in the development of RA?

Knowledge about environmental influences on the development of RA are of two kinds. The first – circumstantial – kind of knowledge is derived from twin and kinship studies, which all indicate that the genetic influence is important but probably less influential than environmental effects. Concordance between monozygotic twins with regard to RA has been reported to be between 10% and 15% [5], or even lower [6]. The second – more direct – kind of knowledge derives from case–control or cohort studies on the influence of distinct agents or events on RA, in which exposure to a number of agents have been reported to be associated with RA. Such agents include smoking, which has been shown to be a risk factor in several studies [7,8], silica [9,10] and blood transfusion [11]. Taken together, the knowledge of environmental agents predisposing to RA remains rudimentary. Virtually no molecular mechanisms have been proposed for how such agents may work, and no work has been presented to show that agents associated with RA in humans cause arthritis in an animal model of RA.

Although genetic influences on RA have been more extensively studied than environmental effects, current knowledge is nevertheless sketchy, even with regard to the most studied genetic region, the major histocompatibility complex (MHC). Thus, it has been shown that different MHC alleles are associated with RA in different populations [12], and also that the degree of association between a certain allele and RA varies depending on which population of RA patients is selected. That the arthritis denoted RA is associated with certain HLA-DR4 alleles in studies on White populations from the USA or Western Europe but with other alleles in Japanese or Jewish populations [12] clearly indicates that other genes interact with the MHC genes in mediating the susceptibility to arthritis.

The demonstration of only a moderate association between HLA-DRB1*0401 in a group of RA patients from a population-based survey [13] but a much higher association in RA populations in hospital settings indicates that HLA-DRB1*0401 may be as much a severity factor as a susceptibility factor. Because the association between MHC class II alleles and RA is the most convincing evidence of a role of HLA-DR restricted T-cell activation in the pathogenesis of RA, these studies also indicate that there is a marked heterogeneity within an RA population as to the role of such T-cell activation, which is smaller in early, mild arthritis.

Other genes contributing to susceptibility to RA have so far been sought mainly in cytokine-associated genes. Several associations have been described between functionally relevant cytokine promotor genes and RA [14–17]. Also, the wide genome scans that have been reported from North America and Europe have suggested that gene regions outside the MHC may be relevant, though the relevant genes within these regions have not yet been identified.

Finally, very few efforts have hitherto been directed towards the investigation of the interactions between genes and environment in the pathogenesis of RA. The rest of this review is concerned with a discussion of how such investigations may be conducted, given the current knowledge of genes and environment and given that leads regarding both potential environmental triggers and genes important for disease may be derived from relevant animal models.

What are relevant animal models for RA, and how can these be used to generate concepts about gene–environment interactions in arthritis?

In the light of the background given above, there are four prerequisites for relevant animal models for RA. First, the disease should be inducible by nonspecific triggers (comparable with cigarette smoking or silica exposure in humans). In addition, the models must be characterized by certain genetic contexts in which MHC class II genes may act as both susceptibility and severity factors. They should also be highly variable in disease course, which should often involve tissue destruction and chronicity. And finally, they should sometimes but not always involve autoimmune reactions towards both cartilage-specific and ubiquitously expressed autoantigens.

Here we restrict ourselves to describing a number of such models in the rat, as that species appears to offer models for several chronic inflammatory diseases that are more similar to the comparable disease in man than is the case in mouse models [18]. Two basic features are critical to the understanding of the arthritis models in the rat. First, triggers can be of several different kinds, including both nonspecific 'nonimmunogenic' substances – such as glucans (from yeast), lipopolysaccharides (from bacteria), squalene (endogenous) or mineral oil (exogenous)

Table 1

Arthritogenic agents

Simple, nonimmunogenic agents	Molecules giving rise to specific immune responses
Glucans	Collagens II, IX, XI
Pristane	Cartilage oligomeric matrix protein (COMP)
Mineral oils	Proteoglycans
Squalene	
Bacterial DNA (CpG)	

[19,20] – and more specific cartilage-derived antigens such as collagen II or cartilage oligomeric matrix protein (COMP) [18,21] (for an overview, see Table 1). In some strains, exposure to one of the nonspecific stimuli (given intracutaneously or sometimes even percutaneously) may by itself cause arthritis [22–24], whereas in others, stimulation with both nonspecific stimuli and cartilage-derived molecules are prerequisites for the development of arthritis [25]. In some typical situations, the addition of anticartilage immunity to the effects of nonspecific stimuli may change the course of the disease from monophasic and nondestructive in character to chronic and destructive.

The second feature of the rat models is the involvement of many polymorphic genes in determining the character of the disease course after a given stimulus. Thus, a nonspecific stimulus may produce a monophasic, nondestructive disease in one strain but a chronic, relapsing–remitting, severely destructive disease in another [26]. Interestingly, it has recently been shown that certain sets of genes may be most instrumental in determining the overall susceptibility to disease, while other sets may preferentially determine the chronicity and still others may determine destructiveness. Taken together, these findings show that there is no single disease phenotype associated with one given triggering agent. Rather, both exposure to simple stimulating adjuvants and combinations of adjuvants and autoantigens can give rise to a highly variable disease course, depending on the overall genetic make-up.

In recent years, polymorphic genes determining the phenotype of arthritis in rats have been studied quite intensively and a number of gene regions have been identified that influence susceptibility to arthritis and the destructiveness and severity of the disease. Further production of inbred strains, congenic for small parts of the identified candidate gene regions, have permitted the identification of smaller gene regions that appear to contain the respective susceptibility or severity genes [20]. An interesting aspect of this work is that the same genetic context that predisposes for development of adju-

vant arthritis induced by single compounds (oil, pristane, squalene) also predisposes to the development of collagen-induced arthritis, in which the additional presence of certain MHC class II genes is mandatory for the development of disease [20,26–28].

It thus appears that a certain set of genes may determine the response of the innate immune system to adjuvants, sometimes resulting in arthritis without the addition of further stimuli. The addition of a specific immunity to self-antigens such as collagen will in these cases make the arthritis more severe and destructive. In other genetic contexts, the combination of immunity to self-antigens and a still strong and genetically determined response to adjuvants is necessary to induce disease. Such a multiple-hit mode would explain why similar sets of 'adjuvant-associated' genes influence development of both adjuvant arthritis and collagen-induced arthritis, and how, in addition, mainly MHC-related genes influence the development of collagen-induced arthritis. So far, no single susceptibility gene has been definitely identified using this method, but research in the field is moving so rapidly that this could happen soon.

Taken together, these animal data indicate that exposure to nonspecific triggers affecting mainly the innate immune system may in certain genetic contexts suffice to induce arthritis, whereas in other genetic contexts participation of the adaptive immune system is mandatory. In addition, it is reasonable to believe that different combinations of these mechanisms may be important in different phases of arthritis development.

Can concepts of mechanisms, potential triggers and potential candidate genes generated in experimental rodent models be meaningfully transferred and tested in humans?

A classic question in research on all inflammatory humans diseases is whether experience from animal models is at all relevant and valuable for the human diseases, in particular when defined triggers are used in animals, and where almost nothing is known about whether there are triggers in humans, and if there are, what they might be. The alternative in human disease, however, would be to be restricted to whole-genome scans in the search for relevant disease genes, and to a very unfocused investigation of environmental factors in the search for potential triggers of disease. In the face of this choice, we have set out to study both candidate genes and environmental factors, taking our lead from the animal experience discussed in the previous section.

Thus, a case–control study has been initiated in Sweden, using an ongoing population-based, multicenter surveillance program for early incident cases of RA as the basis for identification of cases, and a well-established system for identification of controls matched for age, sex and area of residence (P Stolt *et al.*, manuscript submitted for publication). For these individuals, both cases and controls, extensive information has been accumulated about environmental exposure preceding the onset of arthritis for cases and during a comparable period for controls. Also, blood samples for genotyping, serology and other laboratory investigations have been accumulated from cases as well as controls at the time of onset for cases (and the same time for controls). The future strategy is obviously to test potential effects of environmental agents in a conventional case–control setting and simultaneously to try to use information about synteny between rodent (here rat) genes and human genes to identify relevant candidate genes or candidate gene regions for RA. Polymorphisms within these candidate regions should be investigated as to their influence both on susceptibility to RA and on the course of the disease. So far, the research team has accumulated 1200 cases and 1200 controls and has started to test the viability of the approach.

The first environmental exposure we set out to investigate was smoking, which has previously been shown to be a risk factor for RA, although quantification of the risk has been somewhat ambiguous and we do not know whether the risk is in any way confined to individuals with a certain genetic make-up. The first investigation (P Stolt *et al.*, manuscript submitted for publication) thus showed a significantly increased relative risk of RA in ever-smokers compared with never-smokers (RR = 1.5), that this risk was confined to individuals who smoked for a long time, and that smoking was a risk factor only for rheumatoid-factor (RF)-positive RA, but not for RF-negative RA. The latter observations suggested that there might be a sequence of events whereby smoking induces production of RF, which in turn contributes to the development of RA. The other – and not exclusive – possibility would be that RF positivity is merely a marker for a certain genotype, and that mainly individuals with this genotype would have an increased risk of RA after smoking. As RF-positive RA has in several studies been linked to presence of certain HLA-DR allotypes, mainly the 'shared epitope', we thus also stratified our patients according to whether they were shared epitope (SE)-positive. The increased relative risk of developing RA in smokers was restricted to the group of individuals who carried the SE genes (L Padyukov *et al.*, manuscript in preparation). Although still confined to results from a subanalysis of the first 500 patients investigated in our RA cohort, this preliminary finding may be the first documentation of a gene–environment interaction in development of RA, and thereby it may also be of value in supporting the general scope of our research approach.

A second striking finding in our analysis of odds ratios for the development of RA after various environmental exposures relates to mineral oils. An odds ratio of 1.9 was found for individuals exposed to hydraulic oils (almost all men). Because exposure to mineral oil by subcutaneous injection or the percutaneous route was previously shown to induce arthritis in certain rodent strains (see above), this observation in RA suggests that disease mechanisms similar to those in rodents may be involved in some cases of RA. We have not yet been able to investigate to what extent the risk associated with this exposure to oil is restricted to individuals with a certain genetic constitution. However, a recent family study in the UK showed an increased risk of RA in individuals carrying a certain allelic form of a gene region on human chromosome 17, defined by means of synteny with a genetic region that determines susceptibility to oil-induced arthritis in rats [29,30]. This observation is, as far as we know, the first to identify a gene region of importance for the development of RA following leads from animal studies on non-MHC arthritis susceptibility gene regions.

Hopefully, these two observations may pave the way for a future investigation of whether exposure to oil confers an even higher risk of RA in individuals carrying certain alleles of this 17q region, but, more importantly, may also make possible functional studies of how a particular potential trigger of arthritis influences the immune system in individuals carrying a certain set of susceptibility genes (see summary picture of strategy in Fig. 1).

When and in which patients is there a role for organ-specific autoimmunity?

The animal model studies indicate that specific autoimmune reactions to organ-specific antigen, such as collagen II, may contribute to both the onset and the severity of arthritis, but that this phenomenon is restricted to individuals carrying specific MHC class II alleles. Transferred to the human situation, such findings indicate that specific immunity to organ-specific antigens should be performed in the context of genetic characterization of subgroups of patients. So far, this has been done to some extent for collagen II and on a very small scale for other organ-restricted antigens.

However, an immune response to collagen II in both T and B cells has been reported in individuals carrying the SE genes, albeit at a rather low frequency [31–33]. Furthermore, HLA-DRB1*0401 transgenic mice have been shown to be susceptible to collagen-induced arthritis and to mount a strong immune response to collagen II [34]. Taken together, these data thus indicate that collagen autoimmunity may after all contribute to arthritis in a genetically defined subset of RA patients. The identification of this subset by genetic and other means may permit us to investigate further which environmental and genetic factors favor the onset of a collagen immunity, and also to investigate how collagen immunity may add to the effects of other agents, for example adjuvants, in making RA more severe (Fig. 2 presents a hypothetical model of this situation).

Figure 1

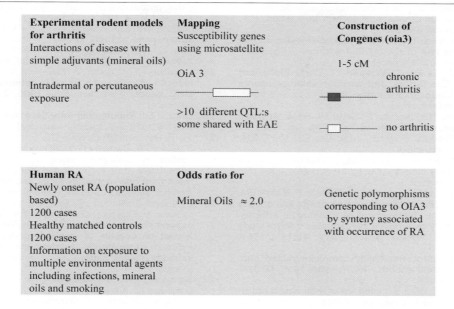

Research strategy for a combined effort in rodents (rats) and in man to define gene–environment interactions of relevance for the onset and course of arthritis

Figure 2

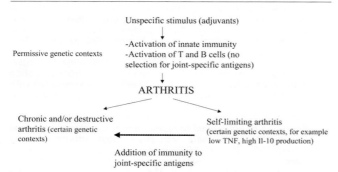

Hypothetical picture of events contributing to development of arthritis and to the course of the disease.

Concluding remarks

We provide arguments for, but not really against, the use of data and ideas generated in induced animal models to generate viable research strategies to study gene–environment interaction of importance for human arthritis. Privileged by the opportunity to contribute to a volume on arthritis research in connotation with one of the most importance breakthroughs in therapy of RA, we have felt it possible to present this unbalanced but hopefully productive view on how to attack still underlying fundamental problems in rheumatology. We believe that the encouragement given to rheumatology from the progress in therapeutics will greatly help us in solving also these further questions about origin and potential future prevention of the disease.

Glossary of terms

RF = rheumatoid factor; SE = shared epitope.

Acknowledgements

Our studies referred to here were financially supported by the Swedish Research Council, the Swedish Rheumatism Association, King Gustaf V:s 80 years Foundation, the insurance company AFA and the Karolinska Institutet. The participants in the EIRA study group, in particular Dr Patrik Stolt, are gratefully acknowledged for generously sharing their data with us.

References

1. Elliott MJ, Maini RN, Feldmann M, Kalden JR, Antoni C, Smolen JS, Leeb B, Breedveld FC, Macfarlane JD, Bijl H, *et al.*: **Randomised double-blind comparison of chimeric monoclonal antibody to tumour necrosis factor alpha (cA2) versus placebo in rheumatoid arthritis.** *Lancet* 1994, **344**:1105-1110. [archival reference]
2. Maini RN, Breedveld FC, Kalden JR, Smolen JS, Davis D, Macfarlane JD, Antoni C, Leeb B, Elliott MJ, Woody JN, Schaible TF, Feldmann M: **Therapeutic efficacy of multiple intravenous infusions of anti-tumor necrosis factor alpha monoclonal antibody combined with low-dose weekly methotrexate in rheumatoid arthritis.** *Arthritis Rheum* 1998, **41**:1552-1563. [general reference]
3. Lipsky PE, van der Heijde DM, St Clair EW, Furst DE, Breedveld FC, Kalden JR, Smolen JS, Weisman M, Emery P, Feldmann M, Harriman GR, Maini RN: **Infliximab and methotrexate in the treatment of rheumatoid arthritis. Anti-Tumor Necrosis Factor Trial in Rheumatoid Arthritis with Concomitant Therapy Study Group.** *N Engl J Med* 2000, **343**:1594-1602. [general reference]
4. Bathon JM, Martin RW, Fleischmann RM, Tesser JR, Schiff MH, Keystone EC, Genovese MC, Wasko MC, Moreland LW, Weaver AL, Markenson J, Finck BK: **A comparison of etanercept and methotrexate in patients with early rheumatoid arthritis.** *N Engl J Med* 2000, **343**:1586-1593. [general reference]
5. MacGregor AJ, Snieder H, Rigby AS, Koskenvuo M, Kaprio J, Aho K, Silman AJ: **Characterizing the quantitative genetic contribution to rheumatoid arthritis using data from twins.** *Arthritis Rheum* 2000, **43**:30-37. [general reference]

6. Svendsen AJ, Holm NV, Kyvik K, Petersen PH, Junker P: **Relative importance of genetic effects in rheumatoid arthritis: historical cohort study of Danish nationwide twin population.** *BMJ* 2002, **324**:264. [general reference]

7. Uhlig T, Hagen KB, Kvien TK: **Current tobacco smoking, formal education, and the risk of rheumatoid arthritis.** *J Rheumatol* 1999, **26**:47-54. [general reference]

8. Reckner Olsson A, Skogh T, Wingren G: **Comorbidity and lifestyle, reproductive factors, and environmental exposures associated with rheumatoid arthritis.** *Ann Rheum Dis* 2001, **60**:934-939. [general reference]

9. Klockars M, Koskela RS, Jarvinen E, Kolari PJ, Rossi A: **Silica exposure and rheumatoid arthritis: a follow up study of granite workers 1940-81.** *Br Med J (Clin Res Ed)* 1987, **294**: 997-1000. [general reference]

10. Turner S, Cherry N: **Rheumatoid arthritis in workers exposed to silica in the pottery industry.** *Occup Environ Med* 2000: **57**: 443-447. [general reference]

11. Symmons DP, Bankhead CR, Harrison BJ, Brennan P, Barrett EM, Scott DG, Silman AJ: **Blood transfusion, smoking, and obesity as risk factors for the development of rheumatoid arthritis: results from a primary care-based incident case-control study in Norfolk, England.** *Arthritis Rheum* 1997, **40**:1955-1961. [general reference]

12. Nepom GT: **Major histocompatibility complex-directed susceptibility to rheumatoid arthritis.** *Adv Immunol* 1998, **68**:315-332. [general reference]

13. Silman AJ, Hennessy E, Ollier B: **Incidence of rheumatoid arthritis in a genetically predisposed population.** *Br J Rheumatol* 1992, **31**:365-368. [archival reference]

14. Cantagrel A, Navaux F, Loubet-Lescoulie P, Nourhashemi F, Enault G, Abbal M, Constantin A, Laroche M, Mazieres B: **Interleukin-1beta, interleukin-1 receptor antagonist, interleukin-4, and interleukin-10 gene polymorphisms: relationship to occurrence and severity of rheumatoid arthritis.** *Arthritis Rheum* 1999, **42**:1093-1100. [general reference]

15. van Krugten MV, Huizinga TW, Kaijzel EL, Zanelli E, Drossaers-Bakker KW, van de Linde P, Hazes JM, Zwinderman AH, Breedveld FC, Verweij CL: **Association of the TNF +489 polymorphism with susceptibility and radiographic damage in rheumatoid arthritis.** *Genes Immun* 1999, 1:91-96. [general reference]

16. Waldron-Lynch F, Adams C, Amos C, Zhu DK, McDermott MF, Shanahan F, Molloy MG, O'Gara F: **Tumour necrosis factor 5' promoter single nucleotide polymorphism influence susceptibility to rheumatoid arthritis (RA) in immunogenetically defined multiplex RA families.** *Genes Immun* 2001, **2**:82-87. [general reference]

17. Yamada R, Tanaka T, Unoki M, Nagai T, Sawada T, Ohnishi Y, Tsunoda T, Yukioka M, Maeda A, Suzuki K, Tateishi H, Ochi T, Nakamura Y, Yamamoto K: **Association between a single-nucleotide polymorphism in the promoter of the human interleukin-3 gene and rheumatoid arthritis in Japanese patients, and maximum-likelihood estimation of combinatorial effect that two genetic loci have on susceptibility to the disease.** *Am J Hum Genet* 2001, **68**:674-685. [general reference]

18. Larsson P, Kleinau S, Holmdahl R, Klareskog L: **Homologous type II collagen-induced arthritis in rats. Characterization of the disease and demonstration of clinically distinct forms of arthritis in two strains of rats after immunization with the same collagen preparation.** *Arthritis Rheum* 1990, **33**:693-701. [archival reference]

19. Lorentzen JC, Erlandsson H, Mussener A, Mattsson L, Kleinau S, Nyman U, Klareskog L: **Specific and long-lasting protection from collagen-induced arthritis and oil-induced arthritis in DA rats by administration of immunogens.** *Scand J Immunol* 1995, **42**:82-89. [archival reference]

20. Holm BC, Xu HW, Jacobsson L, Larsson A, Luthman H, Lorentzen JC: **Rats made congenic for Oia3 on chromosome 10 become susceptible to squalene-induced arthritis.** *Hum Mol Genet* 2001, **10**:565-572. [key reference]

21. Carlsen S, Hansson AS, Olsson H, Heinegard D, Holmdahl R: **Cartilage oligomeric matrix protein (COMP)-induced arthritis in rats.** *Clin Exp Immunol* 1998, **114**:477-484. [general reference]

22. Kleinau S, Erlandsson H, Holmdahl R, Klareskog L: **Adjuvant oils induce arthritis in the DA rat. I. Characterization of the disease and evidence for an immunological involvement.** *J Autoimmun* 1991, **4**:871-880. [archival reference]

23. Sverdrup B, Klareskog L, Kleinau S: **Common commercial cosmetic products induce arthritis in the DA rat.** *Environ Health Perspect* 1998, **106**:27-32. [general reference]

24. Griffiths MM, Cannon GW, Leonard PA, Reese VR: **Induction of autoimmune arthritis in rats by immunization with homologous rat type II collagen is restricted to the RT1av1 haplotype.** *Arthritis Rheum* 1993, **36**:254-258. [archival reference]

25. Lorentzen JC, Olsson T, Klareskog L: **Susceptibility to oil-induced arthritis in the DA rat is determined by MHC and non-MHC genes.** *Transplant Proc* 1995, **27**:1532-1534. [archival reference]

26. Griffiths DJ: **Rheumatoid arthritis: a viral aetiology?** *Hosp Med* 2000, **61**:378-379. [general reference]

27. Joe B, Remmers EF, Dobbins DE, Salstrom JL, Furuya T, Dracheva S, Gulko PS, Cannon GW, Griffiths MM, Wilder RL: **Genetic dissection of collagen-induced arthritis in Chromosome 10 quantitative trait locus speed congenic rats: evidence for more than one regulatory locus and sex influences.** *Immunogenetics* 2000, **51**:930-944. [general reference]

28. Dahlman I, Lorentzen JC, de Graaf KL, Stefferl A, Linington C, Luthman H, Olsson T: **Quantitative trait loci disposing for both experimental arthritis and encephalomyelitis in the DA rat; impact on severity of myelin oligodendrocyte glycoprotein-induced experimental autoimmune encephalomyelitis and antibody isotype pattern.** *Eur J Immunol* 1998, **28**:2188-2196. [general reference]

29. Barton A, Eyre S, Myerscough A, Brintnell B, Ward D, Ollier WE, Lorentzen JC, Klareskog L, Silman A, John S, Worthington J: **High resolution linkage and association mapping identifies a novel rheumatoid arthritis susceptibility locus homologous to one linked to two rat models of inflammatory arthritis.** *Hum Mol Genet* 2001, **10**:1901-1906. [key reference]

30. Lorentzen JC, Glaser A, Jacobsson L, Galli J, Fakhrai-rad H, Klareskog L, Luthman H: **Identification of rat susceptibility loci for adjuvant-oil-induced arthritis.** *Proc Natl Acad Sci USA* 1998, **95**:6383-6387. [key reference]

31. Ronnelid J, Lysholm J, Engstrom-Laurent A, Klareskog L, Heyman B: **Local anti-type II collagen antibody production in rheumatoid arthritis synovial fluid. Evidence for an HLA-DR4-restricted IgG response.** *Arthritis Rheum* 1994, **37**:1023-1029. [archival reference]

32. Berg L, Ronnelid J, Sanjeevi CB, Lampa J, Klareskog L: **Interferon-gamma production in response to in vitro stimulation with collagen type II in rheumatoid arthritis is associated with HLA-DRB1(*)0401 and HLA-DQ8.** *Arthritis Res* 2000, **2**:75-84. [general reference]

33. Tarkowski A, Klareskog L, Carlsten H, Herberts P, Koopman WJ: **Secretion of antibodies to types I and II collagen by synovial tissue cells in patients with rheumatoid arthritis.** *Arthritis Rheum* 1989, **32**:1087-1092. [general reference]

34. Sønderstrup G, Cope AP, Patel S, Congia M, Hain N, Hall FC, Parry SL, Fugger LH, Michie S, McDevitt HO: **HLA class II transgenic mice: models of the human CD4+ T-cell immune response.** *Immunol Rev* 1999, **172**:335-343. [general reference]

Matrix biology

Supplement Review
Matrix metalloproteinases in arthritic disease

Gillian Murphy, Vera Knäuper, Susan Atkinson, George Butler, William English, Mike Hutton, Jan Stracke and Ian Clark

School of Biological Sciences, University of East Anglia, Norwich, UK

Correspondence: Gillian Murphy, School of Biological Sciences, University of East Anglia, Norwich, NR4 7TJ, UK. Tel: +44 (0)1603 593811; fax: +44 (0)1603 592250; e-mail: g.murphy@uea.ac.uk; department website: http://www.bio.uea.ac.uk

Received: 21 January 2002
Revisions requested: 12 March 2002
Revisions received: 15 March 2002
Accepted: 21 March 2002
Published: 9 May 2002

Arthritis Res 2002, **4 (suppl 3)**:S39-S49

This article may contain supplementary data which can only be found online at http://arthritis-research.com/content/4/S3/S039

© 2002 BioMed Central Ltd
(Print ISSN 1465-9905; Online ISSN 1465-9913)

Chapter summary

The role of matrix metalloproteinases in the degradative events invoked in the cartilage and bone of arthritic joints has long been appreciated and attempts at the development of proteinase inhibitors as potential therapeutic agents have been made. However, the spectrum of these enzymes orchestrating connective tissue turnover and general biology is much larger than anticipated. Biochemical studies of the individual members of the matrix metalloproteinase family are now underway, ultimately leading to a more detailed understanding of the function of their domain structures and to defining their specific role in cellular systems and the way that they are regulated. Coupled with a more comprehensive and detailed study of proteinase expression in different cells of joint tissues during the progress of arthritic diseases, it will be possible for the future development and application of highly specific proteinase inhibitors to be directed at specific key cellular events.

Keywords: matrix metalloproteinases, osteoarthritis, proteinase inhibitors, rheumatoid arthritis

Introduction

The past decade has seen major advances in the understanding of the pathogenesis of arthritic diseases and has markedly influenced pharmacological approaches. The development of inflammatory rheumatic diseases, including an initiation phase associated with genetic susceptibilities, the activation of synovial cells and the development of the pannus are well characterised. Subsequent cartilage and bone destruction leads to an irreversible pathology. Osteoarthritis (OA) is far less well understood, but also leads ultimately to joint tissue destruction. Hence, a detailed knowledge of the events underlying these degradative processes is a prerequisite for all arthritic diseases for the development of therapies targeting their prevention. Key to this is an understanding of the proteinases involved in terms of their regulation and specific function.

This review outlines the detailed studies of the background biochemistry of the matrix metalloproteinases (MMPs), which are major players in extracellular matrix (ECM) turnover in both physiology and pathology. Such studies are the basis of specific inhibitor development as potential therapies. The study of metalloproteinase expression in relation to the progress of different forms of arthritis is outlined. It is clear that the latter picture is particularly incomplete, with most studies focused on the MMPs identified some years ago but rarely focused on newer potential contributors to the degradative pathology of arthritic tissues. Future approaches will need to

---

A glossary of specialist terms used in this chapter appears at the end of the text section. A list of common abbreviations used in this issue appears just before the indexes.

look at the overall patterns of proteinase function in joint tissues allowing the most precise targeting of new generations of highly specific inhibitors.

Historical background

Progressive degradation of the ECM that comprises joint tissues, including articular cartilage, bone and even intra-articular ligaments and tendons, is a major feature of the arthritic diseases, leading to permanent loss of function. Although proteinases of all mechanistic classes play a role in the degradation of connective tissue macromolecules, it has long been thought that the major activities involved in this process belong to the family of MMPs. These enzymes are secreted by both the resident cells of joint tissues as well as by invading cells, they are active around neutral values of pH, and they have the combined ability to degrade all the components of the ECM (Table 1). MMPs play significant roles in both developmental and repair processes, and it appears that aberrant regulation, which can occur at many levels (see next section), leads to their hyperactivity in diseases such as rheumatoid arthritis (RA) and OA.

There is now significant evidence for the overexpression of MMPs in tissues derived from patients with arthritic disease. Cultures of cells derived from rheumatoid synovia secreted a collagenolytic activity into the medium [1], and stromelysin-1 [2] and collagenase-1 were detected by immunolocalisation at sites of cartilage erosion in rheumatoid joints [3]. Both of these enzymes, as well as the tissue inhibitor of metalloproteinase (TIMP)-1, were immunolocalised in synovial samples from both RA and OA patients [4].

The finding of stromelysin-1 in all synovial samples from 10 patients with different clinical diagnoses and histories, in contrast to its absence from normal synovia [5], clearly implicated this enzyme in the arthritic process. It was also shown that collagenase-1, gelatinase A and matrilysin may have a role in the synovitis associated with RA, but that they are not a significant feature in osteoarthritic joints. Marked regional variations were found in the synthesis of these MMPs, however, indicating that these diseases are episodic and that the control of enzyme synthesis is focal. This indicates the need for further work to colocalise MMP synthesis with cytokine and matrix expression in synovia from diseased joints in order to explore further the mechanisms that control the synthesis and degradation of ECM components of articular cartilage. Stromelysin-1 and collagenase-1 have also been measured in the synovial fluids from rheumatoid and osteoarthritic knee joints [6–8].

Other studies of MMP expression in normal and diseased cartilage have documented the presence of stromelysin-1, with lower levels of collagenase-1 [9]. Gelatinase B is detected as both mRNA and protein in osteoarthritic cartilage, but not in normal tissue [10], and is detectable in the synovial fluid from rheumatoid joints. Collagenase-2 and

collagenase-3 have more recently been identified in arthritic cartilage [11–14]. Konttinen *et al.* [15] analysed the expression of 16 MMPs at the mRNA level in trauma and RA, and they found some (e.g. collagenase-3 and the membrane-type matrix metalloproteinase [MT-MMP] MT2-MMP) exclusively present in the rheumatoid tissue.

The precise targets of MMP action in joint tissues are not always clear. In particular, there has been extensive debate concerning their role in the degradation of cartilage proteoglycans relative to that of the related family of a disintegrin, a metalloproteinase and thrombospondin 'aggrecanase' (ADAM-TS) [16,17]. Kozaci *et al.* [18] used a model system of collagen degradation to conclude that stromelysin-1, collagenase-2 and collagenase-3 are unlikely to contribute to proteoglycan degradation, but that collagenases and gelatinase have major roles in type II collagen breakdown. MT1-MMP is expressed by rheumatoid synovial fibroblasts and is regulated by tumour necrosis factor alpha [19]. The identity of the collagenase responsible for cartilage collagen loss is also still a subject of detailed study. There is evidence that specific MMP-13 inhibitors can block interleukin-1-induced collagen loss, and an enhanced cleavage of type II collagen in osteoarthritic cartilage seems to be correlated with MMP-13 activity [20].

The MMP family

The MMP family consists of 25 zinc-dependent and calcium-dependent proteinases in mammalian systems (Table 1), and MMPs are now thought to be the major proteolytic enzymes that facilitate tissue remodelling in both physiological and pathological situations [21–23]. The MMPs do indeed have the combined ability to degrade the major components of the ECM [24].

MMPs can be classified into at least five main groups, according to their substrate specificity, primary structure and cellular localisation; namely, the collagenases, gelatinases, stromelysins, matrilysins and MT-MMPs [25]. There are some MMPs, however, such as macrophage elastase (MMP-12), stromelysin-3 (MMP-11), MMP-19, enamelysin (MMP-20), CA-MMP (MMP-23) and epilysin (MMP-28), that apparently do not fall into any of these categories. In addition, some enzymes, such as MT1-MMP (MMP-14), which displays collagenolytic activity and is membrane associated, may be classified into more than one group.

The collagenases (collagenase-1 [MMP-1], collagenase-2 [MMP-8] and collagenase-3 [MMP-13]) are able to cleave native triple-helical fibrillar collagens (i.e. type I, type II and type III) at a single bond, generating characteristic one-quarter and three-quarter fragments.

Two gelatinases (gelatinase A [MMP-2] and gelatinase B [MMP-9]) have been identified. Gelatinase A is expressed

Table 1

Matrix metalloproteinases (MMPs) and their substrates

MMP	Enzyme	M_r latent	M_r active	Known substrates
MMP-1	Interstitial collagenase (collagenase-1)	55,000	45,000	Collagens I, II, III, VII, VIII and X, gelatin, aggrecan, versican, proteoglycan link protein, casein, α_1-proteinase inhibitor, α_2-M, pregnancy zone protein, ovostatin, nidogen, MBP, proTNF, L-selectin, proMMP-2, proMMP-9
MMP-2	Gelatinase A	72,000	66,000	Collagens I, IV, V, VII, X, XI and XIV, gelatin, elastin, fibronectin, aggrecan, versican, proteoglycan link protein, MBP, proTNF, α_1-proteinase inhibitor, proMMP-9, proMMP-13
MMP-3	Stromelysin-1	57,000	45,000	Collagens III, IV, IX and X, gelatin, aggrecan, versican, perlecan, nidogen, proteoglycan link protein, fibronectin, laminin, elastin, casein, fibrinogen, antithrombin-III, α_2M, ovostatin, α_1-proteinase inhibitor, MBP, proTNF, proMMP-1, proMMP-7, proMMP-8, proMMP-9, proMMP-13
MMP-7	Matrilysin-1 (PUMP-1)	28,000	19,000	Collagens IV and X, gelatin, aggrecan, proteoglycan link protein, fibronectin, laminin, entactin, elastin, casein, transferrin, MBP, α_1-proteinase inhibitor, proTNF, proMMP-1, proMMP-2, proMMP-9
MMP-8	Neutrophil collagenase (collagenase-2)	75,000	58,000	Collagens I, II, III, V, VII, VIII and X, gelatin, aggrecan, α_1-proteinase inhibitor, α_2-antiplasmin, fibronectin
MMP-9	Gelatinase B	92,000	86,000	Collagens IV, V, VII, X and XIV, gelatin, elastin, aggrecan, versican, proteoglycan link protein, fibronectin, nidogen, α_1-proteinase inhibitor, MBP, proTNF
MMP-10	Stromelysin-2	57,000	44,000	Collagens III, IV and V, gelatin, casein, aggrecan, elastin, proteoglycan link protein, fibronectin, proMMP-1, proMMP-8
MMP-11	Stromelysin-3	51,000	44,000	α_1-proteinase inhibitor
MMP-12	Macrophage metalloelastase	54,000	45,000/ 22,000	Collagen IV, gelatin, elastin, α_1-proteinase inhibitor, fibronectin, vitronectin, laminin, proTNF, MBP
MMP-13	Collagenase-3	60,000	48,000	Collagens I, II, III and IV, gelatin, plasminogen activator inhibitor 2, aggrecan, perlecan, tenascin
MMP-14	MT1-MMP	66,000	56,000	Collagens I, II and III, gelatin, casein, elastin, fibronectin, laminin B chain, vitronectin, aggrecan, dermatan sulfate proteoglycan, MMP-2, MMP-13, proTNF
MMP-15	MT2-MMP	72,000	60,000	proMMP-2, gelatin, fibronectin, tenascin, nidogen, laminin
MMP-16	MT3-MMP	64,000	52,000	proMMP-2
MMP-17	MT4-MMP	57,000	53,000	
MMP-18	Xenopus collagenase	55,000	42,000	
MMP-19		54,000	45,000	Collagen IV, gelatin, laminin, nidogen, tenascin, fibronectin, aggrecan, COMP
MMP-20	Enamelysin	54,000	22,000	Amelogenin
MMP-21	XMMP (xenopus)	70,000	53,000	
MMP-22 (MMP-27)	CMMP (chicken)	52,000	43,000	Gelatin, casein
MMP-23	CA-MMP	?	?	
MMP-24	MT5-MMP	63,000	45,000	proMMP-2, proMMP-9, gelatin
MMP-25	MT6-MMP, leukolysin		56,000	Collagen IV, gelatin, fibronectin, fibrin
MMP-26	Matrilysin-2, endometase	28,000		Collagen IV, fibronectin, fibrinogen, gelatin, α_1-proteinase inhibitor, proMMP-9
MMP-28	Epilysin	59,000 (55,000)		Casein

α_2-M, α_2-macroglobulin; COMP, cartilage oligomeric matrix protein; MBP, myelin basic protein; M_r, relative molecular mass; TNF, tumour necrosis factor.

by a broad spectrum of mesenchymal cells, whereas gelatinase B is associated with macrophages and peripheral blood mononuclear cells, as well as activated connective tissue cells and tumours. The gelatinases have a broad substrate specificity and may contribute, together with collagenases, to the degradation of fibrillar collagens, basement membrane components and stromal ECM molecules (e.g. fibronectin).

Stromelysins (stromelysin-1 [MMP-3] and stromelysin-2 [MMP-10]) have one of the broadest substrate spectra of the MMPs and can degrade most ECM components, such as gelatin, fibronectin, laminin and aggrecan, but not triple-helical collagens. They are expressed by synovial fibroblasts from a rheumatoid joint but not by normal synovial cells. Stromelysin-3 (MMP-11), however, has weak proteolytic activity and is activated intracellularly by a furin-like convertase. Both these properties distinguish it from the other two members of the stromelysin group.

Although matrilysins (matrilysin-1 [MMP-7] and matrilysin-2 [MMP-26]) lack the hinge region and the COOH-terminal, hemopexin-like domain common to almost all other members of the MMP subfamily, they are potent proteinases. Matrilysin-1 is expressed by a range of benign and malignant tumours, whereas matrilysin-2 was only recently cloned and detected in uterus, placenta and endometrial tumours.

The group of six cell-associated MT-MMPs (MT1-MMP [MMP-14], MT2-MMP [MMP-15], MT3-MMP [MMP-16], MT4-MMP [MMP-17], MT5-MMP [MMP-24] and MT6-MMP [MMP-25]) seems to be activated intracellularly by a furin-type proprotein convertase. With the exception of MT4-MMP and MT6-MMP, which are membrane bound via a glycosylphosphatidyl-inositol molecule and not via a transmembrane domain, these enzymes also contain a COOH-terminal cytoplasmic tail.

MT1-MMP was shown to be a major activator of proMMP-2 on the cell surface. This activation is thought to be facilitated via a ternary complex of MT1-MMP, TIMP-2 and proMMP-2, enabling cells (e.g. tumour cells) to invade stromal tissue or to cross the basement membrane of blood vessels during metastasis. With the exception of MT6-MMP, which is predominantly expressed in leukocytes, the other MT-MMPs are found in many cell types, although they have not as yet been rigorously studied in relation to arthritic tissues.

Structure and function of MMP domains

MMPs are multidomain proteins consisting of a signal peptide, a propeptide, and the catalytic and COOH-terminal domains, as shown in Figure 1. MT-MMPs and gelatinases have additional features such as a COOH-terminal transmembrane region followed by a short cyto-

Figure 1

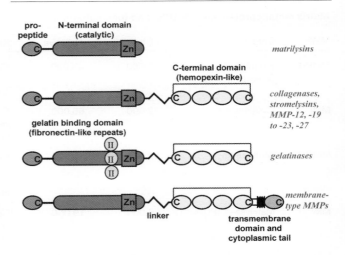

Basic domain structures of the matrix metalloproteinases (MMPs). MMPs consist of: a propeptide (grey), which maintains the enzymes in a latent state; a catalytic domain (blue) with the active site and the catalytic zinc (Zn) (red); and, with the exception of the matrilysins, a COOH-terminal domain (C) (yellow) with homology to the serum protein hemopexin. The latter two domains are connected by a linker peptide. Gelatinases have an insert of three fibronectin type II repeats (turquoise) in the catalytic domain, which is involved in substrate recognition. Membrane-type MMPs contain a transmembrane domain (black) and a cytoplasmic tail (green) at the COOH terminus, which anchors these enzymes in the cell membrane. See Colour figure section.

tail, and three fibronectin type II repeats in the catalytic domain, respectively.

All MMPs are translated with a NH_2-terminal hydrophobic sequence of 18–30 residues that is responsible for trafficking of the enzyme through the endoplasmic reticulum and the Golgi apparatus, and for its subsequent secretion into the extracellular space. The signal peptide is cleaved off during the secretion process. Interestingly, the signal peptide in CA-MMP (MMP-23) contains a transmembrane motif that anchors the enzyme to the membrane. Activation and secretion is achieved by cleavage in a proprotein convertase recognition sequence located between the propeptide and the catalytic domain.

The propeptide domain, N-terminal to the catalytic domain, consists of about 80 residues arranged in three α-helices, and it is responsible for enzyme latency. This domain contains the sequence motif PRCGVPD (also called the 'cysteine switch' motif), which is highly conserved among MMPs. In the latent enzyme, the propeptide domain is located directly opposite the active site cleft and coordinates the catalytic zinc ion with the thiol of the cysteine residue, thus preventing binding of a water molecule required for peptide hydrolysis [26]. Apart from the direct coordination of the zinc ion, several β-structure-like interchain hydrogen bonds are formed between the propeptide and the catalytic site, similar to the bonds established with substrates and inhibitors. It should be noted, however, that the binding orientation of the propeptide is the opposite to that of the substrate

All MMPs (except the MT-MMPs, stromelysin-3 and epilysin, which are activated intracellularly by a furin-type proprotein convertase) probably become activated in a stepwise manner outside the cell by proteolytic cleavage. Activating proteases, like MMPs, serine or cysteine pro-teinases, attack the so-called 'bait region', an exposed and flexible stretch of around 30–40 residues, which probably results in destabilisation of the cysteine switch–zinc inter-actions [26]. These molecular rearrangements promote the full activation of the enzyme by exposing the final cleavage site between propeptide and catalytic domain, generally around residues 80–90, to proteolytic cleavage. The activation of proMMPs (e.g. by other proteinases and MMPs) will be discussed in more detail later.

The MMP catalytic domain consists of approximately 160–170 residues and contains the active centre with the catalytic zinc ion, responsible for substrate hydrolysis and inhibitor interactions. As already described, three con-served histidine residues in the HExxHxxGxxH motif, located 50–55 residues from the COOH-terminal end of the domain, ligate the catalytic zinc ion. X-ray analysis of various MMP catalytic domains, some of which complexed with an inhibitor (i.e. collagenase-1, stromelysin-1, matrilysin-1, collagenase-2 and MT1-MMP), revealed high structural similarity among enzymes.

Essentially, the MMP catalytic domain is made up of a twisted β-sheet covering two long α-helices (helix A and helix B), and of a separate helix at the COOH-terminal end of the domain. The sheet itself consists of four parallel β-strands (strand I, strand II, strand III and strand V) and one antiparallel β-strand (strand IV) (Fig. 2). In addition to the catalytic zinc, a second zinc ion (the so-called 'structural zinc') and one to three calcium ions (depending on the MMP) are also bound in this domain and seem necessary for its function. Two of the three histidine residues coordi-nating the active site zinc are located within helix B, whereas the third histidine is located in the loop between helices B and C and lies opposite the other two histidine residues (Fig. 2).

The typical MMP active site cleft, carved into the surface of the ellipsoidal domain, is relatively flat on the left-hand side (nonprimed) and contains the catalytic zinc in its centre, but is deep on the right-hand side (primed) [27]. Studies using peptide substrates revealed that a substrate is fixed to its cognate MMP through seven intermain-chain hydrogen bonds and that the scissile peptide bond car-bonyl group is directed towards the catalytic zinc ion to be

Figure 2

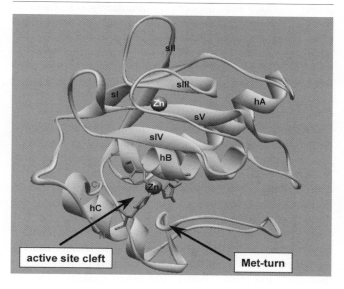

Structure of the catalytic domain of the matrix metalloproteinase MMP-3. The ribbon diagram was created using WebLab Viewer software based on a crystal structure analysis by Gomis-Rüth *et al.* [61]. Strands (sI–sV) and helices (hA–hC) are labelled in black; the catalytic zinc (centre), coordinated by three histidine residues (pink), and the structural zinc (Zn) (top) are labelled in black and white, respectively; and the NH$_2$ terminus (N) and COOH terminus (C) are labelled in red. The active site cleft and the characteristic methionine (Met) turn are indicated with arrows. See Colour figure section.

strongly polarised. For the mechanism of substrate hydrol-ysis by MMPs, it was proposed that the glutamic acid residue within the HExxHxxGxxH motif then polarises a water molecule for a nucleophilic attack on the carbonyl carbon atom of the substrate scissile amino bond.

The sequence requirements for a certain substrate to be cleaved depend on the depth and structure of the catalytic site of the MMP. For example, dominant hydrophobic inter-actions are made through P1′ and P3 residue side chains of the substrate and the respective pockets in the MMP. P1, P2, P3, etc. and P1′, P2′, P3′, etc. indicate peptide substrate residues in the NH$_2$-terminal and COOH-termi-nal directions from the scissile bond, respectively, whereas S1, S2, S3, etc. and S1′, S2′, S3′, etc. indicate the opposing subsites of the MMP [27].

In general, proline and leucine residues at the P3 and P2 positions of the substrate, respectively, are the preferred amino acids for MMPs. A large residue in the P1′ position of the substrate is also preferential for binding to the MMP active site. This residue interacts with the so-called 'speci-ficity pocket' (S1′ pocket), a deep cavity within the MMP active site. The S1′ pocket is a varied structural feature in the active site of MMPs, and it has a major influence on substrate and inhibitor specificity. Stromelysin-1 and MT1-

MMP both have very deep hydrophobic S1′ pockets and prefer residues with aliphatic or aromatic side chains in the P1′ position of the substrate. In fact, synthetic peptides containing unusual amino acids with extremely long side chains in the P1′ position were hydrolysed by MT1-MMP and stromelysin-1 with higher efficiency than peptides containing natural amino acids in the same position.

Collagenases

Studies on the catalytic domains of the collagenases have shown that they contribute to the specificity for the cleavage of triple-helical collagen. We investigated exon 5 of collagenase-1 in this respect by exchanging it with the exon 5 of the noncollagenolytic proteinase MMP-3. Exon 5 harbours major features of the active site including the three histidine ligands of the functional zinc, the S1′ binding site and components of the other substrate binding sites, S2′, S3′ and S1–S3. The overall exon 5 sequence shows a high degree of similarity between collagenase-1 and stromelysin-1. The major variations include the greater hydrophilicity of collagenase-1 and its slightly smaller size. Hence the exchange of exon 5 causes no predictable major structural changes.

The exon 5 mutant of collagenase-1 did demonstrate a change in peptide substrate and small inhibitor specificity as well as binding to N-TIMP-1, the three active N-terminal loops becoming more stromelysin-1-like. The exon 5 mutant also lost most of its ability to cleave type I collagen as well as a reduction in gelatin turnover, indicating that the active site cleft is itself a determinant of specific collagenolytic capacity [28].

A unique feature of the catalytic domain of gelatinases A and B is the presence of three fibronectin type II repeats just upstream of the zinc binding motif, contributing around 20 kDa to the size of the enzyme. These repeats are located between strand V and helix B of the MMP catalytic domain, consist of two double-stranded antiparallel β-sheets and two large irregular loops each, and are important for binding of the substrate in the active site. It was demonstrated that recombinantly expressed repeats bind to denatured type I collagen, denatured type IV and type V collagens, elastin and native type I collagen. While deletion of the three repeats in MMP-2 resulted in decreased gelatinolytic activity and abrogated binding to collagen, TIMP binding was not affected.

Between the catalytic domain and the COOH-terminal hemopexin-like domain lies a variable stretch of 2–72 amino acids, which is termed the 'linker' or 'hinge region'. This region is very extended in the case of collagenases, being rich in proline residues and possibly being responsible for activity versus fibrillar collagens. A hypothetical mechanistic contribution of these linker peptides has been postulated, whereby the proline-rich peptides adopt a helical conformation that might 'unwind' the helix. We analysed the hinge region of collagenase-2 by alanine mutagenesis and found that this region had a pronounced effect on the stability and collagenolytic activity of the enzyme. Notably, some proline residues (shown underlined) were modified to alanine in the sequence Gly-Leu-Ser-Ser-Asn-Pro-Ile-Gln-Pro-Thr-Gly-Pro-Ser-Thr-Pro-Lys-Pro, to show that they were critical to the collagenolytic mechanism [29].

The MMP COOH-terminal domain has strong sequence similarity with the serum protein hemopexin and consists of approximately 200 amino acids. It has the shape of an ellipsoidal disk, as demonstrated by X-ray analysis of the crystal structures of this domain in porcine collagenase-1, human gelatinase A and human collagenase-3. The domain consists of four β-sheets (blades I–IV) with very similar structure, each consisting of four antiparallel β-strands, which are arranged almost symmetrically around a central core. The overall appearance is that of a four-bladed propeller, whereby the innermost strands of all four blades are arranged almost parallel to each other, building a central channel that contains Ca^{2+} and Cl^- ions. The stability of this structure is ensured by a disulfide bond between blades I and IV, which is conserved in all MMPs.

The role of the C-terminal hemopexin-like domain varies widely according to the MMP, one of the most notable being the ability to interact with fibrillar collagens. The hemopexin-like domain of stromelysin-1 was shown to bind to type I and type II collagen, although neither can be cleaved by stromelysin-1. In contrast, all collagenolytic enzymes appear to require the hemopexin-like domain for hydrolysis of triple-helical collagens. In our laboratory, we have prepared C-terminal domain deletion mutants of collagenases, gelatinase A and MT1-MMP to show that, in each case, the domain is absolutely required for 'specific collagenolysis' (i.e. cleavage of type I collagen helix 3/4 from the N-terminus) to occur [3–8].

Mutants of the collagenases comprised of the prodomain and catalytic domain are peptidolytic on removal of the propeptide, but cannot cleave native fibrillar collagen. Cleavage of other collagens (e.g. type IV collagen) by collagenase-3 and other matrix macromolecules does not seem to require the C-terminal domain. Furthermore, 'exchange' of C-terminal domains between MMPs (e.g. N-terminal collagenase-1–C-terminal MMP3, N-terminal collagenase-3–C-terminal MMP-19) generates proteinases that either do not exhibit specific collagen cleaving potential or, in the case of collagenase-3, gelatinase A and gelatinase A-stromelysin-1, exhibit much reduced activity [28,30,31] (Knäuper *et al.*, unpublished data).

Gelatinase A is a remarkable 'collagenase', although it acts very slowly on native collagens relative to denatured forms.

We found that deletion of the collagen–gelatin binding type II fibronectin-like domain caused a loss of the ability of MMP-2 to cleave gelatin efficiently or to bind to collagen or gelatin [32,33]. However, cleavage of native collagen still absolutely required the presence of the C-terminal domain rather than the fibronectin-like domain. Indeed, the mechanism of MMP-2 cleavage of collagen proceeds in two phases: the first resembling that of the interstitial collagenases, and the second being gelatinolysis [31].

The COOH-terminal domain is thus necessary for activity of the collagenases versus fibrillar collagens, but it does not appear to be important for substrate specificity of most other MMPs. McQuibban et al. recently reported a physiological substrate of gelatinase A, monocyte chemoattractant protein-3, however, which was discovered using the gelatinase A hemopexin-like domain as bait in the yeast two-hybrid system [34].

We have constructed and expressed recombinant forms of gelatinase B in which the C-terminal domain has been deleted to compare the activation, catalytic and TIMP binding properties with the full-length enzyme. In vitro, the truncated MMP-9 and wild-type MMP-9 behaved identically when activated by organomercurial or stromelysin-1. When we assessed activation in a cell-based system using either plasminogen or stromelysin-1, both forms of MMP-9 activated at similar rates. Furthermore, the active form of C-truncated gelatinase B showed similar kinetics to wild-type gelatinase B for the turnover of peptide substrates and gelatin. Indeed, the only differences in the behaviour of truncated MMP-9 and full-length MMP-9 was found to be in the rate of binding to TIMP-1.

Full-length TIMP-1 inhibited gelatinase B in a biphasic manner, with a rapid first phase yielding 50–70% inhibition, apparently dependent on the particular enzyme preparation, followed by a slow phase. In comparison, the C-truncated gelatinase B binding to TIMP-1 was difficult to analyse as the data were suggestive of an isomerisation of the enzyme–inhibitor complex [35]. It was apparent that binding of TIMP-1 was severely abrogated by the lack of the C-terminal domain of gelatinase B, reducing the value of the association constant by one to three orders of magnitude [35]. In comparison, association of both forms of gelatinase B with N-TIMP-1 in which the three C-terminal loops have been deleted gave binding constant values similar to those of the slow phase of wild-type TIMP-1–gelatinase B binding. TIMP-2, however, does not show any discrimination in its binding to different forms of gelatinase B. No biological explanation for the 'special' association between TIMP-1 and gelatinase B has been established.

Studies on the domains of gelatinase A have been quite extensive. The effect of deletion of the fibronectin type II-like domain was, to some extent, discussed earlier under collagenases. Apart from a role in the binding of the enzyme to collagen and the turnover of gelatin, this domain does not appear to be required for the turnover of peptide substrates or for the binding of low molecular weight active site inhibitors or TIMPs [32].

The effect of deletion of the C-terminal domain of progelatinase A and the loss of ability to cleave native collagen was also discussed earlier. It has also been shown that the C-domain of gelatinase A is essential for its binding and activation at the surface of many cell types. It has been established that this involves the ability of the C-domain of gelatinase A to interact quite tightly with the inhibitor TIMP-2 as a complex with the membrane-associated MT1-MMP [36–38]. Kinetic studies of the domain interactions between TIMP-2 and gelatinase A show very fast association rates between the full-length proteins that are markedly abrogated by truncation of the TIMP-2 to the N-terminal three loops or of the gelatinase A to remove the C-terminal domain. TIMP-2 binding to the C-domain of gelatinase A is very tight and can occur in the absence of catalytic domain interactions in progelatinase A. The binding has two identifiable components: a charged interaction (salt sensitive) involving the C-terminal tail of the C-terminal three loops of TIMP-2, and a hydrophobic interaction between the remainder of the TIMP-2 and the C-domain of gelatinase A [39].

Our analyses of domain motif function in the membrane-associated MT1-MMP have shown that the C-terminal domain is required for collagenolysis, as already described [40]. Kinetic studies with the TIMPs, however, have shown that the C-domain plays a negligible role in TIMP interactions. TIMP-1 has very little ability to inhibit MT1-MMP for reasons that are not yet entirely clear. However, TIMP-2, TIMP-3 and TIMP-4 are effective inhibitors, either as full-length forms or as the N-terminal three loops, against full-length or C-truncated MT1-MMP. Hence, the complexes of TIMPs with MT1-MMP are all theoretically able to bind the C-domain of MMP2 simultaneously since the necessary binding sites should remain available.

One difference between the MT-MMPs and other MMP family members is the insertion of eight amino acids between strands βII and βIII in the catalytic domain (163-PYAYIREG-170 in MT1-MMP). To investigate the role of this region of MT1-MMP in its function, we have made a number of mutations and deletions in this region. The motif appeared to have no role in the cleavage of peptide substrates or extracellular proteins such as fibrinogen or in the binding of TIMP-2. However, the motif is involved in interactions with progelatinase A, facilitating both the solution-phase MT1-MMP activation mechanism as well as that at the cell surface [41].

The collagenase-3 C-terminal domain deletion abrogates fibrillar collagen cleavage as already discussed, but has no effect on its ability to interact with peptide substrates or inhibitors. Association with TIMP-1, TIMP-2 or TIMP-3 is marginally decreased, suggesting that C-domain interactions are not of great significance [42]. This is of interest in the light of the observation that the activation of collagenase-3 mediated by cell-associated MT1-MMP requires the presence of the C-domain of collagenase-3 [42]. The mechanism underlying this observation remains to be elucidated.

Interactions of the MMPs with their specific natural inhibitors, the TIMPs, predominantly involve the enzyme catalytic domains and the N-terminal three disulfide-bonded loops of the TIMPs. Motifs within these two interacting domains determine a degree of specificity between individual MMPs and TIMPs but these are not well characterised. The C-domain interactions of certain MMPs with the three C-terminal disulfide-bonded loops of the TIMPs, however, do seem to play a major role in the acceleration of association rates in ways that may be biologically relevant.

We have focused our studies on the interactions of TIMPs with MT1-MMP (see earlier) because they are involved in the mechanism for MT1-MMP activation of progelatinase A, apparently bridging the two proteinases to form a trimolecular complex. We found that one specific interaction between TIMP-2 and MT1-MMP could be demonstrated between the hairpin turn of the A and B β strands of TIMP-2 and MT1-MMP. Detailed site-directed mutagenesis of the AB loop showed the residue Tyr36 is almost wholly responsible for the binding of this region to MT1-MMP [43].

We also recently extended our observations to compare TIMP-2 with TIMP4. TIMP-2 and TIMP-4 have a number of similar characteristics with respect to sequence and kinetics of MMP-2 and MT1-MMP interaction, but the latter does not support MT1-MMP activation of progelatinase A. A series of TIMP-4 mutants were produced, including chimeric proteins with TIMP-2 and forms of the C-terminal charged tail that contained sequences from TIMP-2. In biochemical and cell-based studies, we found that TIMP-4 chimeras containing the C-domain of TIMP-2, and even TIMP-4 C-tail mutants containing elements of the TIMP-2 C-tail sequence (Arg186-Pro195), were able to support the formation of gelatinase A–MT1-MMP trimolecular complexes and to support gelatinase A activation (Knäuper *et al.*, unpublished data).

In conclusion, MMPs have a domain structure to facilitate their interaction with activators, substrates and inhibitors. Specific binding to cell membrane or ECM components may also be determined by these domains. These are of importance to focus proteolytic activities at specific peri-cellular sites. For each MMP, a detailed analysis of the relationship between the function of its domains and their specific structure will give valuable new data to aid the design of future novel and specific antiproteinase molecules as potential therapeutics. The mutagenesis and kinetic studies that we have performed have indicated the extent of the task and, with the advent of all the relevant crystal structures, further directed studies may proceed.

MMP cleavage of ECM components

The MMP family contains the only vertebrate proteinases that can specifically degrade triple-helical collagens type I, type II and type III, as described earlier. Cleavage characteristically and specifically occurs at a single locus in all three collagen chains, at a point approximately three-quarters from the N-terminus of the molecule. At physiological temperature, the cleaved triple helix then unwinds, becoming susceptible to attack from other, less specific, proteinases.

The precise MMPs responsible for cartilage collagen cleavage in the arthritides is still open for debate. There are obvious differences in the turnover of collagen between OA and RA with respect to the location of early changes. This may suggest that a different MMP is predominantly responsible for collagen cleavage and that the involvement of different metalloproteinases is temporally distinct in each disease. Changes within the subchondral bone appear to precede cartilage changes in deep layers of cartilage, with subsequent fibrillation of the articular surface in OA. In contrast, early changes in RA appear in the surface layers with the majority of cartilage collagen destruction occurring at the cartilage–pannus junction, although changes within the cartilage matrix may precede and allow penetration by synovial cells.

Collagenase-1 and collagenase-3 are both made by chondrocytes (as are collagenase-2, gelatinase A and MT1-MMP), while collagenase-1 is also produced by the synovial fibroblasts. Hence, some workers consider collagenase-1 may be the foremost collagenase in RA, where the synovium proliferates to form a pannus that can invade cartilage, while collagenase-3 may predominate in OA where the chondrocyte drives the cartilage destruction [13,20,44]. Collagenase-2, previously thought to be restricted to neutrophils, has recently been described in chondrocytes [11] and in synovial cells [45], but a role in cartilage collagen destruction is still unproven [15]. MT1-MMP and gelatinase A (along with all the collagenases) have also been localised to the invading rheumatoid pannus, suggesting a possible role for either (or both) enzymes in disease [46].

MMPs and therapeutic strategies

MMP activity is controlled at several levels, of which gene expression is arguably the most important and is modulated by a variety of growth factors and cytokines [47]. A number of individual polymorphisms of MMP genes have recently been described with some disease associations [48], and associations with arthritic diseases may emerge in future research. After secretion, the activation described earlier (i.e. the proteolytic removal of the propeptide from the latent enzyme) represents one critical step in controlling MMP activity in the ECM. Once activated, regulation in the ECM is effected by natural inhibitors, such as the TIMPs and α_2-macroglobulin [49]. The balance between MMP levels and TIMP levels is thought to be of great importance in determining levels of proteolysis.

Potential strategies for the modulation of MMPs include the development of effectors at the level of gene induction (cytokine inhibitors, receptor antagonists, signal transduction), production (transcription, secretion), zymogen activation (inhibit activating enzyme or prevent conversion of proactive to active enzyme) or enzyme activity (production of TIMPs or inhibition by small molecules). The potential of signal transduction inhibitors for the treatment of arthritis was recently discussed [50] and future directions in the treatment of OA at the level of MMPs has been summarised by Malemud and Goldberg [51].

The direct inhibition by synthetic low molecular weight entities that bind to the zinc and other features of the catalytic site of the enzyme has been most vigorously pursued [17,52]. Early developments led to inhibitors of relatively poor specificity. However, the availability of crystal structures for a number of MMPs has allowed the design and production of inhibitors with increased specificity.

The issue of which MMP (or which other metalloproteinase, such as ADAM-TS4/5 with aggrecanase activity) to inhibit still remains. Van Meurs *et al.* found that active MMPs, particularly stromelysin-1, played a pivotal role in cartilage destruction in both the immune-mediated complex model of arthritis and in antigen-induced arthritis models. Absence of stromelysin-1 did not affect aggrecan depletion in arthritis but did prevent the appearance of collagen cleavage products and cartilage erosions [53,54], suggesting a role for stromelysin-1 in the activation of procollagenases. Elliot and Cawston [55] and Clark *et al.* [22] discuss the issue of whether it is preferable to inhibit the degradation of the proteoglycan or the collagen component of cartilage as a therapeutic strategy for arthritis, but the question of the precise target enzymes remains. There is some support for the concept that the use of a broad-spectrum MMP inhibitor that also inhibits the ADAM proteinases (e.g. TACE, ADAM 17) would be most appropriate in arthritis therapy [55,56].

MMP inhibitors have frequently exhibited toxicity in clinical trials, however, with the development of musculo-skeletal problems such as arthralgia, myalgia and tendinitis. These were predominantly in the upper limbs and were reversible. Interestingly, it has been shown that MT1-MMP-deficient mice not only develop dwarfism and osteopaenia, but also arthritic symptoms and soft tissue fibrosis, demonstrating the important function of this MMP in normal tissue remodelling and suggesting that it would be advantageous to selectively inhibit MMPs active within disease contexts [57].

There are currently no synthetic MMP inhibitors in clinical trials for arthritis due to the failure of early studies, for reasons such as those already outlined. A tetracycline derivative, doxycycline, in subantimicrobial doses (Periostat; CollaGenex Pharmaceuticals Inc., Newtown, PA, USA) is currently the only MMP inhibitor approved by the US Food and Drug Administration and is used as an adjunct therapy in adult periodontitis. The use of tetracyclines for the treatment of arthritic diseases is limited, although doxycycline has been shown to improve some disease parameters as well as reducing the levels of collagenase activity in some patients with RA [58,59].

Concluding remarks

There are now 25 known MMPs, as detailed in this review, but many have not been substantially characterised in relation to arthritic diseases. It will be important for such studies to be carried out in relation to specific disease states. Although it is likely that the MMPs identified are major players, others could have subtle but critical activities in relation to the tissue cells and their interaction with their environment. A proteomics approach [60] should prove useful, if these techniques become sensitive enough, to document the range of proteinases expressed, followed by more detailed studies using quantitative RT-PCR in relation to well-documented disease status. Specific abrogation of individual MMPs in model systems may then give clues vital to the focusing of the design of antiMMP agents as potential therapies.

Glossary of terms

ADAM-TS = a disintegrin, a metalloproteinase and thrombospondin 'aggrecanase'; ECM = extracellular matrix; MMP = matrix metalloproteinase; MT-MMP = membrane-type matrix metalloproteinase; TIMP = tissue inhibitor of metalloproteinases.

References

1. Dayer JM, Krane SM, Russell RG, Robinson DR: **Production of collagenase and prostaglandins by isolated adherent rheumatoid synovial cells.** *Proc Natl Acad Sci USA* 1976, **73:** 945-949. [archival research]
2. Sirum KL, Brinckerhoff CE: **Cloning of the genes for human stromelysin and stromelysin 2: differential expression in rheumatoid synovial fibroblasts.** *Biochemistry* 1989, **28:**8691-8698. [archival research]
3. Woolley DE, Evanson JM: **Collagenase and its natural inhibitors in relation to the rheumatoid joint.** *Connect Tissue Res* 1977, **5:**31-35. [archival research]
4. Hembry RM, Bagga MR, Reynolds JJ, Hamblen DL: **Immunolocalisation studies on six matrix metalloproteinases and their inhibitors, TIMP-1 and TIMP-2, in synovia from patients**

with osteo- and rheumatoid arthritis. *Ann Rheum Dis* 1995, **54**:25-32. [general reference]

5. McCachren SS: **Expression of metalloproteinases and metalloproteinase inhibitor in human arthritic synovium.** *Arthritis Rheum* 1991, **34**:1085-1092. [archival research]

6. Walakovits LA, Moore VL, Bhardwaj N, Gallick GS, Lark MW: **Detection of stromelysin and collagenase in synovial fluid from patients with rheumatoid arthritis and posttraumatic knee injury.** *Arthritis Rheum* 1992, **35**:35-42. [archival research]

7. Lohmander LS, Hoerrner LA, Lark MW: **Metalloproteinases, tissue inhibitor, and proteoglycan fragments in knee synovial fluid in human osteoarthritis.** *Arthritis Rheum* 1993, **36**:181-189. [archival research]

8. Ishiguro N, Ito T, Oguchi T, Kojima T, Iwata H, Ionescu M, Poole AR: **Relationships of matrix metalloproteinases and their inhibitors to cartilage proteoglycan and collagen turnover and inflammation as revealed by analyses of synovial fluids from patients with rheumatoid arthritis.** *Arthritis Rheum* 2001, **44**: 2503-2511. [general reference]

9. Wolfe GC, MacNaul KL, Buechel FF, McDonnell J, Hoerrner LA, Lark MW, Moore VL, Hutchinson NI: **Differential in vivo expression of collagenase messenger RNA in synovium and cartilage.** *Arthritis Rheum* 1993, **36**:1540-1547. [general reference]

10. Mohtai M, Smith RL, Schurman DJ, Tsuji Y, Torti FM, Hutchinson NI, Stetler-Stevenson WG, Goldberg GI: **Expression of 92-kD type IV collagenase/gelatinase (gelatinase B) in osteoarthritic cartilage and its induction in normal human articular cartilage by interleukin 1.** *J Clin Invest* 1993, **92**:179-185. [general reference]

11. Cole AA, Chubinskaya S, Schumacher B, Huch K, CS-Szabo G, Yao J, Mikecz K, Hasty KA, Kuettner KE: **Chondrocyte matrix metalloproteinase-8 − Human articular chondrocytes express neutrophil collagenase.** *J Biol Chem* 1996, **271**:11023-11026. [archival research]

12. Moldovan F, Pelletier JP, Hambor J, Cloutier JM, Martel-Pelletier J: **Collagenase-3 (matrix metalloprotease 13) is preferentially localized in the deep layer of human arthritic cartilage in situ − In vitro mimicking effect by transforming growth factor?** *Arthritis Rheum* 1997, **40**:1653-1661. [general reference]

13. Tetlow LC, Woolley DE: **Comparative immunolocalization studies of collagenase 1 and collagenase 3 production in the rheumatoid lesion, and by human chondrocytes and synoviocytes in vitro.** *Br J Rheumatol* 1998, **37**:64-70. [general reference]

14. Tetlow LC, Adlam DJ, Woolley DE: **Matrix metalloproteinase and proinflammatory cytokine production by chondrocytes of human osteoarthritic cartilage: associations with degenerative changes.** *Arthritis Rheum* 2001, **44**:585-594. [general reference]

15. Konttinen YT, Ainola M, Valleala H, Ma J, Ida H, Mandelin J, Kinne RW, Santavirta S, Sorsa T, Lopez-Otin C, Takagi M: **Analysis of 16 different matrix metalloproteinases (MMP-1 to MMP-20) in the synovial membrane: different profiles in trauma and rheumatoid arthritis.** *Ann Rheum Dis* 1999, **58**:691-697. [general reference]

16. Fosang AJ, Last K, Knauper V, Neame PJ, Murphy G, Hardingham TE, Tschesche H, Hamilton JA: **Fibroblast and neutrophil collagenases cleave at two sites in the cartilage aggrecan interglobular domain.** *Biochem J* 1993, **295**:273-276. [general reference]

17. Bottomley KM, Johnson WH, Walter DS: **Matrix metalloproteinase inhibitors in arthritis.** *J Enzyme Inhib* 1998, **13**:79-101. [general reference]

18. Kozaci LD, Brown CJ, Adcocks C, Galloway A, Hollander AP, Buttle DJ: **Stromelysin 1, neutrophil collagenase, and collagenase 3 do not play major roles in a model of chondrocyte mediated cartilage breakdown.** *J Clin Pathol Mol Pathol* 1998, **51**:282-286. [general reference]

19. Migita K, Eguchi K, Kawabe Y, Ichinose Y, Tsukada T, Aoyagi T, Nakamura H, Nagataki S: **TNF-alpha-mediated expression of membrane-type matrix metalloproteinase in rheumatoid synovial fibroblasts.** *Immunology* 1996, **89**:553-557. [general reference]

20. Billinghurst RC, Dahlberg L, Ionescu M, Reiner A, Bourne R, Rorabeck C, Mitchell P, Hambor J, Diekmann O, Tschesche H, Chen J, Van Wart H, Poole AR: **Enhanced cleavage of type II collagen by collagenases in osteoarthritic articular cartilage.** *J Clin Invest* 1997, **99**:1534-1545. [general reference]

21. Nagase H, Woessner JF: **Matrix metalloproteinases.** *J Biol Chem* 1999, **274**:21491-21494. [key review]

22. Clark IM, Rowan AD, Cawston TE: **Matrix metalloproteinase inhibitors in the treatment of arthritis.** *Curr Opin Anti-Inflamm Immunomodulat Invest Drugs* 2000, **2**:16-25. [general reference]

23. Vu TH, Werb Z: **Matrix metalloproteinases: effectors of development and normal physiology.** *Genes Dev* 2000, **14**:2123-2133. [key review]

24. Birkedal-Hansen H: **Proteolytic remodeling of extracellular matrix.** *COCB* 1995, **7**:728-735. [key review]

25. MEROPS database [http://www.Merops.ac.uk/Merops/index.htm].

26. Nagase H: **Activation mechanisms of matrix metalloproteinases.** *Biol Chem* 1997, **378**:151-160. [general reference]

27. Bode W, Huber R: **Structural basis of the endoproteinase-protein inhibitor interaction.** *Biochim Biophys Acta* 2000, **1477**: 241-252. [key review]

28. Knauper V, Patterson ML, Gomis-Ruth FX, Smith B, Lyons A, Docherty AJ, Murphy G: **The role of exon 5 in fibroblast collagenase (MMP-1) substrate specificity and inhibitor selectivity.** *Eur J Biochem* 2001, **268**:1888-1896. [general reference]

29. Knäuper V, Docherty AJP, Smith B, Tschesche H, Murphy G: **Analysis of the contribution of the hinge region of human neutrophil collagenase (HNC, MMP-8) to stability and collagenolytic activity by alanine scanning mutagenesis.** *FEBS Lett* 1997, **405**:60-64. [general reference]

30. Murphy G, Allan JA, Willenbrock F, Cockett MI, O'Connell JP, Docherty AJP: **The role of the C-terminal domain in collagenase and stromelysin specificity.** *J Biol Chem* 1992, **267**:9612-9618. [general reference]

31. Patterson ML, Atkinson SJ, Knauper V, Murphy G: **Specific collagenolysis by gelatinase A, MMP-2, is determined by the hemopexin domain and not the fibronectin-like domain.** *FEBS Lett* 2001, **503**:158-162. [general reference]

32. Murphy G, Nguyen Q, Cockett MI, Atkinson SJ, Allan JA, Knight CG, Willenbrock F, Docherty AJP: **Assessment of the role of the fibronectin-like domain of gelatinase A by analysis of a deletion mutant.** *J Biol Chem* 1994, **269**:6632-6636. [general reference]

33. Allan JA, Docherty AJP, Barker PJ, Huskisson NS, Reynolds JJ, Murphy G: **Binding of gelatinases A and B to type-I collagen and other matrix components.** *Biochem J* 1995, **309**:299-306. [general reference]

34. McQuibban GA, Gong JH, Tam EM, McCulloch CA, Clark-Lewis I, Overall CM: **Inflammation dampened by gelatinase A cleavage of monocyte chemoattractant protein-3.** *Science* 2000, **289**: 1202-1206. [general reference]

35. O'Connell JP, Willenbrock F, Docherty AJP, Eaton D, Murphy G: **Analysis of the role of the COOH-terminal domain in the activation, proteolytic activity, and tissue inhibitor of metalloproteinase interactions of gelatinase B.** *J Biol Chem* 1994, **269**: 14967-14973. [general reference]

36. Atkinson SJ, Crabbe T, Cowell S, Ward RV, Butler MJ, Sato H, Seiki M, Reynolds JJ, Murphy G: **Intermolecular autolytic cleavage can contribute to the activation of progelatinase A by cell membranes.** *J Biol Chem* 1995, **270**:30479-30485. [general reference]

37. Will H, Atkinson SJ, Butler GS, Smith B, Murphy G: **The soluble catalytic domain of membrane type 1 matrix metalloproteinase cleaves the propeptide of progelatinase A and initiates autoproteolytic activation − Regulation by TIMP-2 and TIMP-3.** *J Biol Chem* 1996, **271**:17119-17123. [general reference]

38. Butler GS, Butler MJ, Atkinson SJ, Will H, Tamura T, Van Westrum SS, Crabbe T, Clements J, d'Ortho M-P, Murphy G: **The TIMP2 membrane type 1 metalloproteinase 'receptor' regulates the concentration and efficient activation of progelatinase A.** *J Biol Chem* 1998, **273**:871-880. [general reference]

39. Willenbrock F, Crabbe T, Slocombe PM, Sutton CW, Docherty AJP, Cockett MI, O'Shea M, Brocklehurst K, Phillips IR, Murphy G: **The activity of the tissue inhibitors of metalloproteinases is regulated by C-terminal domain interactions: a kinetic analysis of the inhibition of gelatinase A.** *Biochemistry* 1993, **32**: 4330-4337. [general reference]

40. d'Ortho M-P, Will H, Atkinson S, Butler GS, Messent A, Gavrilovic J, Smith B, Timpl R, Zardi L, Murphy G: **Membrane-type matrix metalloproteinases 1 and 2 exhibit broad-spectrum proteolytic capacities comparable to many matrix metalloproteinases.** *Eur J Biochem* 1997, **250**:751-757. [general reference]

41. English WR, Holtz B, Vogt G, Knauper V, Murphy G: **Characterization of the role of the 'MT-loop': an eight-amino acid insertion specific to progelatinase A (MMP2) activating**

membrane-type matrix metalloproteinases. *J Biol Chem* 2001, **276**:42018-42026. [general reference]

42. Knäuper V, Murphy G: **Membrane-type matrix metallopro-teinases and cell surface-associated activation cascades for matrix metalloproteinases.** In *Matrix Metalloproteinases*. Edited by Parks WC, Mecham RP. San Diego, CA: Academic Press; 1998:199-218. [general reference]

43. Williamson RA, Hutton M, Vogt G, Rapti M, Knauper V, Carr MD, Murphy G: **Tyrosine 36 plays a critical role in the interaction of the AB loop of tissue inhibitor of metalloproteinases-2 with matrix metalloproteinase-14.** *J Biol Chem* 2001, **276**:32966-32970. [general reference]

44. Lindy O, Konttinen YT, Sorsa T, Ding YL, Santavirta S, Ceponis A, López-Otín C: **Matrix metalloproteinase 13 (collagenase 3) in human rheumatoid synovium.** *Arthritis Rheum* 1997, **40**:1391-1399. [general reference]

45. Hanemaaijer R, Sorsa T, Konttinen YT, Ding Y, Sutinen M, Visser H, van Hinsbergh VW, Helaakoski T, Kainulainen T, Ronka H, Tschesche H, Salo T: **Matrix metalloproteinase-8 is expressed in rheumatoid synovial fibroblasts and endothelial cells. Regulation by tumor necrosis factor-alpha and doxycycline.** *J Biol Chem* 1997, **272**:31504-31509. [general reference]

46. Konttinen YT, Ceponis A, Takagi M, Ainola M, Sorsa T, Sutinen ME, Salo T, Ma J, Santavirta S, Seiki M: **New collagenolytic enzymes cascade identified at the pannus-hard tissue junction in rheumatoid arthritis: Destruction from above.** *Matrix Biol* 1998, **17**:585-601. [general reference]

47. Borden P, Heller RA: **Transcriptional control of matrix metalloproteinases and the tissue inhibitors of matrix metalloproteinases.** *Crit Rev Eukaryot Gene Expr* 1997, **7**:159-178. [general reference]

48. Ye S, Henney AM: **Detecting polymorphisms in MMP genes.** *Methods Mol Biol* 2001, **151**:367-375. [key review]

49. Nagase H, Brew K: **Engineering of tissue inhibitor of metalloproteinases mutants as potential therapeutics.** *Arthritis Res* 2002, **4(suppl 3)**:S51-S61. [general reference]

50. Vincenti MP, Brinckerhoff CE: **Early response genes induced in chondrocytes stimulated with the inflammatory cytokine interleukin-1beta.** *Arthritis Res* 2001, **3**:381-388. [general reference]

51. Malemud CJ, Goldberg VM: **Future directions for research and treatment of osteoarthritis.** *Front Biosci* 1999, **4**:D762-D771. [general reference]

52. Skotnicki JS, Zask A, Nelson FC, Albright JD, Levin JI: **Design and synthetic considerations of matrix metalloproteinase inhibitors.** *Ann NY Acad Sci* 1999, **878**:61-72. [key review]

53. van Meurs J, van Lent P, Stoop R, Holthuysen A, Singer I, Bayne E, Mudgett J, Poole R, Billinghurst C, van der Kraan P, Buma P, van den Berg W: **Cleavage of aggrecan at the ASN³⁴¹-PHE³⁴² site coincides with the initiation of collagen damage in murine antigen-induced arthritis. A pivotal role for stromelysin 1 in matrix metalloproteinase activity.** *Arthritis Rheum* 1999, **42**:2074-2084. [general reference]

54. van Meurs J, van Lent P, Holthuysen A, Lambrou D, Bayne E, Singer I, van den Berg W: **Active matrix metalloproteinases are present in cartilage during immune complex-mediated arthritis: a pivotal role for Stromelysin-1 in cartilage destruction.** *J Immunol* 1999, **163**:5633-5639. [general reference]

55. Elliott S, Cawston T: **The clinical potential of matrix metalloproteinase inhibitors in the rheumatic disorders.** *Drugs Aging* 2001, **18**:87-99. [key review]

56. Conway JG, Andrews RC, Beaudet B, Bickett DM, Boncek V, Brodie TA, Clark RL, Crumrine C, Leenitzer MA, McDougald DL, Han B, Hedeen K, Lin P, Milla M, Moss M, Pink H, Rabinowitz MH, Tippin T, Scates P, Selph J, Stimpson SA, Warner J, Becherer JD: **Inhibition of tumor necrosis factor-α (TNF-α) production and arthritis in the rat by GW3333, a dual inhibitor of TNF-α-converting enzyme and matrix metalloproteinases.** *J Pharm Exp Ther* 2001, **298**:900-908. [general reference]

57. Holmbeck K, Bianco P, Caterina J, Yamada S, Kromer M, Kuznetsov SA, Mankani M, Robey PG, Poole AR, Pidoux I, Ward JM, Birkedal-Hansen H: **MT1-MMP-deficient mice develop dwarfism, osteopenia, arthritis and connective tissue disease due to inadequate collagen turnover.** *PubMed Cell* 1999, **1**:81-92. [general reference]

58. Nordstrom D, Lindy O, Lauhio A, Sorsa T, Santavirta S, Konttinen YT: **Anti-collagenolytic mechanism of action of doxycycline treatment in rheumatoid arthritis.** *Rheumatol Int* 1998, **17**:175-180. [general reference]

59. O'Dell JR: **Is there a role for antibiotics in the treatment of patients with rheumatoid arthritis?** *Drugs* 1999, **57**:279-282. [general reference]

60. Kumar S, Connor JR, Dodds RA, Halsey W, Van Horn M, Mao J, Sathe G, Mui P, Agarwal P, Badger AM, Lee JC, Gowen M, Lark MW: **Identification and initial characterisation of 5000 expressed sequence tags (ESTs) each from adult normal and osteoarthritic cartilage cDNA libraries.** *Ostoarthritis Cartilage* 2001, **9**:641-653. [general reference]

61. Gomis-Rüth FX, Maskos K, Betz M, Bergner A, Huber R, Suzuki K, Yoshida N, Nagase H, Brew K, Bourenko GP, Bartunik H, Bode W: **Mechanism of inhibition of the human matrix metalloproteinase stromelysin-1 by TIMP-1.** *Nature* 1997, **389**:77-81. [general reference]

Supplement Review
Engineering of tissue inhibitor of metalloproteinases mutants as potential therapeutics

Hideaki Nagase* and Keith Brew†

*The Kennedy Institute of Rheumatology Division, Faculty of Medicine, Imperial College of Science, Technology and Medicine, London, UK
†Department of Biomedical Sciences, Florida Atlantic University, Boca Raton, Florida, USA

Correspondence: Hideaki Nagase, The Kennedy Institute of Rheumatology Division, Faculty of Medicine, Imperial College of Science, Technology and Medicine, 1 Aspenlea Road, London W6 8LH, UK. Tel: +44 20 8383 4488; fax: +44 20 8383 4994; e-mail: h.nagase@ic.ac.uk
http://www.med.ic.ac.uk/divisions/template_divisions_general

Received: 2 April 2002
Accepted: 4 April 2002
Published: 9 May 2002

Arthritis Res 2002, **4 (suppl 3)**:S51-S61

This article may contain supplementary data which can only be found online at http://arthritis-research.com/content/4/S3/S051

Chapter summary

Matrix metalloproteinases (MMPs) play a central role in many biological processes such as development, morphogenesis and wound healing, but their unbalanced activities are implicated in numerous disease processes such as arthritis, cancer metastasis, atherosclerosis, nephritis and fibrosis. One of the key mechanisms to control MMP activities is inhibition by endogenous inhibitors called tissue inhibitors of metalloproteinases (TIMPs). This review highlights the structures and inhibition mechanism of TIMPs, the biological activities of TIMPs, the unique properties of TIMP-3, and the altered specificity towards MMPs achieved by mutagenesis. A potential therapeutic use of TIMP variants is discussed.

Keywords: aggrecanase, collagenase, extracellular matrix, matrix metalloproteinases, proteinase inhibitor

Introduction

The extracellular matrix (ECM) holds cells and tissues together, forms organized lattices for cell migration and interaction, and creates correct cellular environments. Timely degradation of the ECM is therefore crucial for controlling cellular behaviour that is required during the development, morphogenesis, and tissue remodelling that are associated with cell differentiation, migration, growth and apoptosis. The major enzymes that are involved in these processes are the members of the MMP family, also called matrixins. Recent studies have also indicated that members of the family called a disintegrin and metalloproteinase (ADAM) also participate.

The activities of these metalloproteinases must therefore be precisely controlled under normal physiological conditions. The disruption of this control results in many diseases, such as arthritis, cancer, atherosclerosis, nephritis,

encephalomyelitis, fibrosis, etc., as a consequence of aberrant turnover of the ECM. While the regulation of the activities of ADAM metalloproteinases are less well understood at the present time, the activities of MMPs are controlled by endogenous inhibitors called TIMPs that are synthesized in a variety of tissues and by a plasma protein α_2-macroglobulin and related molecules. α_2-Macroglobulin, a protein of 725,000 Da, inhibits MMPs and most endopeptidases by entrapment of the enzymes, but its action is thought to be primarily in the fluid phase.

In the tissue, TIMPs are considered to be key inhibitors of MMPs. They form 1:1 enzyme–inhibitor complexes. Four TIMPs are currently identified in humans; they are homologous proteins of 21–29 kDa consisting of two domains, an N-terminal inhibitory domain and a C-terminal domain. The C-terminal domain mediates specific interactions with

---

A glossary of specialist terms used in this chapter appears at the end of the text section. A list of common abbreviations used in this issue appears just before the indexes.

some MMP zymogens. In particular, the binding of TIMP-2 to progelatinase A (proMMP-2) through their C-terminal domains is critical in proMMP-2 activation on the cell surface by membrane-bound membrane type 1 matrix metalloproteinase (MT1-MMP).

TIMP gene expression is regulated by growth factors and cytokines but their levels of modulation are less than those of MMPs. Therefore, elevated levels of MMPs over those of TIMPs are observed in diseases associated with enhanced proteolysis of the ECM. In addition to the inhibitory actions on MMPs, TIMPs have a number of other biological functions that are not attributed to MMP inhibition.

In general, TIMPs inhibit only the members of the MMP family, but recent studies indicate that TIMP-3 is an exception, since it also inhibits the members of the ADAM family, including tumour-necrosis-factor(TNF)-α-converting enzyme (TACE/ADAM-17) and aggrecanase (ADAM with thrombospondin type I domain [ADAMTS]-4 and ADAMTS-5). This suggests a broader importance for TIMPs, particularly TIMP-3 in regulating extracellular metalloproteinases. Mutagenesis of TIMPs at specific sites has been shown to modulate their specificity for MMPs. This suggests that the expression of TIMP variants directed to specific metalloproteinases in a targeted tissue may be a potential therapeutic.

Background: TIMPs and arthritis

Articular cartilage consists of a relatively small number of cells and an abundant ECM. The major components of the ECM are collagen fibrils and aggregating proteoglycan aggrecan. Collagen fibrils, mainly type II collagen together with minor types IX and XI, form a meshwork that provides the tensile strength of the tissue. Aggrecan forms a large aggregated complex interacting with hyaluronan via link proteins and fills the interstitium of the collagen meshwork. Aggrecan provides a hydrated gel that gives cartilage its ability to withstand compression.

In normal cartilage, the turnover and synthesis of ECM macromolecules is at equilibrium, but in rheumatoid arthritis (RA) and osteoarthritis (OA) the loss of ECM components exceeds new synthesis. The primary cause of this imbalance is elevated activity of the proteinase that degrades aggrecan and collagen. Aggrecan loss initially occurs most markedly just beneath the joint surface, which is followed by mechanical failure of the tissue and collagen degradation [1,2].

MMPs are a family of extracellular zinc metalloendopeptidases that function in the turnover of components of the ECM [3,4]. They are produced by many types of cells, but their synthesis is regulated by many factors such as inflammatory cytokines, growth factors, cellular transformation and physical stimuli [3,4].

Certain members of the MMP family have been considered to be the major enzymes that participate in the degradation of aggrecan and collagen in cartilage. Collagenases (MMP-1, MMP-8 and MMP-13), gelatinase A (MMP-2) and gelatinase B (MMP-9), stromelysin 1 (MMP-3), matrilysin 1 (MMP-7) and membrane-type MT1-MMP (MMP-14) are found in cartilage, and most are elevated in the synovium and in the cartilage from patients with RA and OA [5,6].

All of these MMPs cleave the aggrecan core protein at various sites, but the critical site is the Asn341–Phe342 bond located in the interglobular domain located between the two N-terminal globular domains G1 and G2, as this cleavage can release aggrecan molecules from the cartilage [7,8]. The N-terminal fragments with the C-terminal sequence Val-Asp-Ile-Pro-Glu-Asn341 are found in both OA and RA cartilage as well as in normal cartilage [9]. On the contrary, Sandy et al. [10] found that the core protein was cleaved at the Glu373–Ala374 bond, but not at the Asn341–Phe342 bond, when bovine cartilage in culture was stimulated by IL-1. This activity was called 'aggrecanase'. The products resulting from this cleavage accumulate in the synovial fluids of patients with OA or inflammatory joints [11,12].

Two enzymes responsible for this cleavage have been purified and cloned. They are referred to as aggrecanase 1 and aggrecanase 2 (also ADAMTS-4 and ADAMTS-5, members of the ADAM protein family, respectively) [13,14]. Later, it was also found that ADAMTS-1 has aggrecanase activity [15]. The degradation of type II collagen occurs slower than aggrecan degradations in arthritis. This is all due to the action of MMPs, and potential collagenolytic enzymes are MMP-1, MMP-2, MMP-8, MMP-13 and MMP-14.

MMP activities in the tissue are regulated by endogenous inhibitor TIMPs [16]. Four TIMPs (TIMP-1, TIMP-2, TIMP-3, TIMP-4) are found in humans. They are homologous with each other and consist of two domains, an N-terminal inhibitory domain of about 125 amino acids and a C-terminal domain of about 65 amino acids. Each domain is stabilized by three conserved disulfide bonds. While the N-terminal domains of TIMPs (N-TIMPs) are primarily responsible for the inhibition of MMPs [17], the C-terminal domains can also influence their binding affinity. The balance between the metalloproteinases and their endogenous inhibitors is critical for the appropriate maintenance of tissues.

Early work by Dean et al. [18] showed that both MMP levels and TIMP levels were elevated in OA cartilage compared with unaffected cartilage, but that the total amount of MMP was slightly higher than that of TIMP, whereas this balance was reverse in the unaffected cartilage. This subtle difference in the ratio of MMPs and TIMPs is considered to be a cause of the gradual degradation of the cartilage matrix.

TIMP-1, TIMP-2 and TIMP-3 are present in the joint tissue. Some elevated levels of TIMP-1 were reported in synovial fluids [19] and in serum [20,21] of RA patients, but not in the serum of OA patients [22]. However, the changes of TIMP-1 levels are not very large compared with the overexpression of MMPs. Overexpression of TIMP-1 using systemic adenovirus-based gene delivery reduced destruction of the joints of TNF-α transgenic mice [23]. On the contrary, the overexpression of TIMP-1 did not prevent osteochondral injury in the mouse model of collagen-induced arthritis [24]. Since there are differences in specificity among TIMPs, further investigation is clearly needed to elucidate the biological and pathological significance of TIMPs.

Selectivity of TIMPs

Important features of the interaction of TIMPs with MMPs are their high binding affinities and differences in specificity despite their high levels of sequence similarity. TIMP-1 inhibits most MMPs with K_i levels of 0.1–2.8 nM [25]. TIMP-1 has a higher affinity for full-length MMP-1 [26] as compared with MMP-1 that lacks the C-terminal hemopexin domain (see the MMP domain structure composition in the chapter by Murphy et al., this issue). The removal of the hemopexin domain from MMPs often results in an approximately 5-fold to 20-fold increase of the K_i value, indicating that the hemopexin domain assists the interaction of TIMP-1 with MMP. Interestingly, Olson et al. [27] reported that the C-terminal hemopexin-domain-deleted MMP-2 does not bind to TIMP-1. However, N-TIMP-1 is an effective inhibitor of full-length MMP-2 with a K_i value comparable with that of MMP-1. Both the hemopexin and the catalytic domains of MMP-2 are therefore necessary for binding to TIMP-1, or the catalytic domain of MMP-2 may have a significantly different structure from that of the corresponding domain in the full-length enzyme. TIMP-1, however, has little inhibitory activity for MT1-MMP [28,29].

TIMP-2, TIMP-3 and TIMP-4 inhibit all MMPs so far tested. TIMP-2 binds to MMP-2 most tightly. Studies by Hutton et al. [30] indicated that binding was via a two-step mechanism, with a K_i value of 1 μM for the initial step and an association rate for the final step of 33 s^{-1}. The overall dissociation constant was estimated to be 0.6 fM, essentially irreversible. This tight interaction is largely due to the C-terminal domain of TIMP-2 and the C-terminal hemopexin domain of MMP-2 [31]. Removal of the hemopexin domain increases the dissociation constant to 33 pM. TIMP-3 exhibits a relatively low affinity for MMP-3 with $K_i = 67$ nM, but the affinities towards MMP-1 and MMP-2 are 1.2 and 4.3 nM, respectively [32]. TIMP-4 has similar inhibition constants to TIMP-2 for MMP-2 and MT1-MMP [29].

In addition to the inhibitory activity of TIMPs, some TIMPs bind to the zymogen forms of gelatinases. For example, proMMP-2 binds to TIMP-2, TIMP-3 or TIMP-4 through the C-terminal domain of each molecule [33–35], and proMMP-9 (progelatinase B) binds to TIMP-1 and TIMP-3 through C-terminal domain interaction [35,36]. These complexes are potential inhibitors of MMPs. To activate the proMMP-9 of the proMMP-9–TIMP-1 complex by MMP-3, TIMP-1 must be saturated by MMP-3 or other MMPs [37]. Alternatively, TIMP-1 needs to be inactivated by proteolysis [38]. These mechanisms provide precise regulation of MMP activation and the activities of activated MMPs.

Importance of TIMP-2 for the activation of proMMP-2 by MT1-MMP

MT1-MMP was cloned and identified as an activator of proMMP-2 by Sato et al. [39]. This finding is important since proMMP-2 is not readily activated by other tissue proteinases. The activation of proMMP-2 by MT1-MMP, however, requires TIMP-2 [40,41]. In the current model, proMMP-2 secreted from the cell is recruited to the cell surface through the interaction of its C-terminal hemopexin domain and the C-terminal domain of TIMP-2 that is bound to MT1-MMP on the cell surface. The interaction of TIMP-2 and MT1-MMP is via the N-terminal domain of TIMP-2, and therefore the MT1-MMP is inhibited. To activate the cell surface-bound proMMP-2, another molecule of MT1-MMP, free of TIMP-2, needs to be present close to proMMP-2.

The association of two or more molecules of MT1-MMP was recently shown to be through interactions of their hemopexin domains [42]. Disruption of this hemopexin domain association by the overexpression of the MT1-MMP hemopexin domain together with a transmembrane sequence and a cytoplasmic tail prevented proMMP-2 activation. An excess of TIMP-2 also inhibits proMMP-2 activation as it inhibits all MT1-MMP. Activation of MMP-2 and MT1-MMP activity are implicated in tumour cell invasion and neovascularization of endothelial cells [43,44]. This system is therefore likely to be involved in angiogenic processes in rheumatoid synovium.

Itoh et al. [45] have reported that there are two binding modes of TIMP-2 on the cell surface of concanavalin-A-treated fibroblasts: about 50% of TIMP-2 binding is blocked by a peptidyl-hydroxamate inhibitor of MMPs, whereas the other 50% is not blocked by the inhibitor. The former interaction is through MT1-MMP as it is inhibited by a synthetic MMP inhibitor. TIMP-2 bound to the membrane in a hydroxamate inhibitor-insensitive manner specifically inhibits MMP-2 activated on the cell surface but does not inhibit other MMPs, and this inhibitory process is triggered by interaction of the C-terminal domains of the two molecules. This further emphasizes the intricacy of the roles of TIMP-2 in proMMP-2 activation and inhibition.

Unique properties of TIMP-3

Among the four TIMPs, TIMP-3 has a number of unique properties. TIMP-3 was originally found as a 21-kDa protein secreted from chick embryonic fibroblasts transformed with Rous sarcoma virus, but it was strongly bound to the ECM [46]. The protein was later shown to have MMP inhibitory activity [47]. The ECM binding property is due to the interaction of the N-terminal domain of TIMP-3 and the polyanionic components [48]. As well as inhibiting MMPs, TIMP-3 also prevents the shedding of TNF-α receptor [49], L-selectin [50], IL-6 receptor [51] and syndican-1 and syndican-4 [52] from the cell surface.

The enzymes responsible for these activities are yet to be identified, but they are thought to be membrane-bound metalloproteinases belonging to the ADAM family. ADAMs are multidomain proteins consisting of a N-terminal propeptide domain, a metalloproteinase domain, a disintegrin-like domain, an epidermal growth factor-like domain, a transmembrane domain and a cytoplasmic domain. The primary structures of the metalloproteinase domains of ADAMs and MMPs have little sequence similarity except around the catalytic zinc binding motif HEXXHXXGXXH [53]. Indeed, evidence for the unique ability of TIMP-3 to inhibit a member of the ADAM metalloproteinases was first reported for TACE (ADAM-17) [54], and subsequently for ADAMD-10 [55] and ADAM-12 [56]. The apparent K_i value reported against TACE is 182 pM.

Using the N-terminal domain of TIMP-3 expressed in *Escherichia coli*, Kashiwagi et al. [32] have shown that it inhibits two aggrecanases (ADAMTS-4 and ADAMTS-5), a subclass of the ADAM proteinases. The K_i values for ADAMTS-4 and ADAMTS-5 were estimated to be less than 0.5 and 0.1 nM, respectively, whereas the K_i values for MMP-1, MMP-2 and MMP-3 were 1.2, 4.3 and 66.7 nM, respectively. These data suggest that the primary target enzymes of TIMP-3 in cartilage are aggrecanases. TIMP-3 mRNA is expressed in cartilage and skeletal tissue during development of mouse embryo [57], in normal bovine and human articular chondrocytes, and in synoviocytes [58]. The expression of TIMP-3 in chondrocytes in culture is upregulated by transforming growth factor β [59] and by oncostatin M [60]. An antiarthritic agent, calcium pentosan polysulfate, increases the synthesis of TIMP-3 without altering its mRNA levels, and this effect is enhanced in the presence of IL-1 [61]. Elevated TIMP-3 production may be beneficial for the protection of cartilage from degradation not only by preventing the action of aggrecanases and MMPs in cartilage, but also by blocking the release of TNF-α by TACE from synovium.

Another important feature of TIMP-3 is that a point mutation in the C-terminal domain (S156C, G166C, G167C, Y168C or S181C) [62], a splice mutation [63] or a premature termination codon at Glu179 [64] is linked to Sorsby's fundus dystrophy, an autosomal-dominant inherited manuclar disorder that causes irreversible loss of vision with onset in the third or fourth decade of life. Choroidal neovascularization is a feature of this disease that closely resembles the events seen in age-related macular degeneration. Qi et al. [65] reported that the S156C mutant expressed in human retinal pigment epithelial cell lines exhibited reduced MMP inhibitory activity and that the conditioned medium had angiogenic activity, suggesting that increased MMP activity may participate in neovascularization in Sousby's fundus dystrophy.

Yeow et al. [66] also reported that S156C mutant protein slightly reduced MMP inhibitory activity, but this reduction is not considered significant. Their study showed that mutations (S156C and S181C) produced multiple higher-molecular-weight complexes due to aberrant protein–protein interactions, and increased cell adhesiveness to ECM, suggesting possible effects on normal function and turnover of Bruch's membrane.

TIMPs are multifunctional proteins

TIMPs have a number of biological activities other than inhibiting MMPs, some of which are not attributed to inhibition of MMPs. When TIMP-1 was first cloned [67], it was found to be identical to a factor that has erythroid potentiating activity [68].

TIMP-1 also has cell growth-promoting activity on human keratinocytes and other cell types [69,70]. Similar cell growth-promoting activity is seen with TIMP-2 [71,72]. On the contrary, the overexpression of TIMP-1, TIMP-2 and TIMP-3 reduces tumour cell growth (see [73] for review). This may be partially due to the inhibition of MMPs.

TIMP-2, but not TIMP-1, inhibits fibroblast-growth-factor-2-induced human endothelial cell growth [74]. TIMP-2 has metanephritic mesenclynal growth activity and promotes morphogenesis of the ureteric bed by inhibiting its branching and by altering the deposition of basement membrane [75]. The former activity is not due to MMP inhibitory activity, whereas the latter activity is mimicked by a synthetic MMP inhibitor.

The overexpression of TIMP-3 causes apoptotic cell death of a number of cancer cell lines and vascular smooth muscle cells [49,76–78]. Smith et al. [49] suggest that the induction of apoptosis is due to the stabilization of TNF-α receptors, perhaps by inhibiting receptor shedding. Studies by Bond et al. [79] also suggest that the inhibitory activity of TIMP-3 is required for induction of apoptosis. In contrast, TIMP-1 and TIMP-2 suppress the apoptosis of B cells [80] and BB16F10 mouse melanoma cells [81], respectively. Antiapoptotic activity of TIMP-1 is independent of MMP inhibition [80].

Inhibition mechanisms of MMPs by TIMPs

The NMR solution structure of the N-terminal domain of TIMP-2 (N-TIMP-2) revealed a five-stranded β-barrel with a Greek key topology and two α-helices, a structural form known as an OB fold [82]. This category of structure is found in a group of oligonucleotide-binding and oligosaccharide-binding proteins such as staphylococcal nuclease, bacterial entrotoxins and some tRNA synthases [83]. This structure did not, however, identify the MMP interaction site in TIMP or clarify its mechanism of inhibition.

The inhibitory site of TIMP-1 was first proposed from a combination of differential proteinase susceptibility studies [84] and site-directed mutagenesis studies [85]. The former studies were based on the observation that human neutrophil elastase inactivated TIMP-1 by cleaving the inhibitor into 10 and 20 kDa fragments. This cleavage by the elastase was, however, prevented when TIMP-1 formed a complex with MMP-3. The full TIMP-1 activity was recovered from the elastase-treated TIMP-1–MMP-3 complex after dissociation of the complex [84].

Sequence analysis of the TIMP-1 fragments indicated that elastase cleaved the Val69–Cys70 bond of the free TIMP-1, suggesting that the MMP interaction site is located near this region. Based on this information and chemical modification studies, a series of mutagenesis studies were carried out with N-TIMP-1. The mutation of Thr2 to alanine resulted in a more than 100-fold decrease in affinity for MMP-3 and in about a 1000-fold decrease for MMP-1 [85]. Mutation of either Cys1 or Cys70, which are disulfide-bonded in native TIMP-1, decreased the affinity for MMP-3 by more than three orders of magnitude. These studies suggest that residues around the disulfide bond between Cys1 and Cys70, which are conserved among TIMPs, are critical for the interaction with MMPs. The NMR structure of N-TIMP-2 indicated that this region forms an exposed ridge structure on the inhibitor molecule [82].

The mechanism by which TIMP inhibits MMPs was revealed by the crystal structure of the complex of human TIMP-1 and the catalytic domain of MMP-3 [MMP-3(ΔC)] [86], and of the complex of the bovine TIMP-2 with the catalytic domain of MT1-MMP [87], both determined by Bode and colleagues. The structure of the TIMP-1–MMP-3(ΔC) complex shows that TIMP-1 is a 'wedge-shaped' molecule, and its edge corresponding to the aforementioned exposed ridge structure inserts into the catalytic site and substrate binding groove of MMP-3 (Fig. 1).

A schematic display of the secondary structure of TIMP-1 is shown in Fig. 2. Most (75%) of the protein–protein contacts in TIMP-1 are from a contiguous region composed of the N-terminal stretch of Cys1 to Val4 and residues Met66 to Val69 linked by the Cys1–Cys70 disulfide bond. The key feature of this interaction is the binding of residues

Figure 1

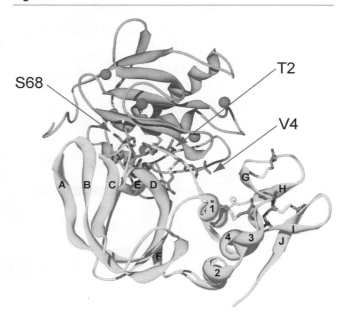

A ribbon diagram of tissue inhibitor of metalloproteinases 1 (TIMP-1) bound to the catalytic domain of matrix metalloproteinase 3 [MMP-3 (ΔC)]. TIMP-1 is shown in green and MMP-3 (ΔC) is shown in light brown. Cystines, Thr2, Val4 and Ser68 in TIMP-1 are indicated: N, blue; O, red; C, grey; and disulfide bonds, yellow. Strands and helices in TIMP-1 are labelled A–J and 1–4, respectively. The catalytic and structural zinc ions are shown in purple, and calcium ions are shown in orange. The image was prepared from the Brookhaven Protein Data Bank entry (1UEA) using the Swiss PDB viewer [91]. See Colour figure section.

1–4 of TIMP-1 to the active site of the enzyme in an analogous fashion to the P1-P1'-P2'-P3' residues of a peptide substrate (the P1 and P1' residues become the new C-terminus and the new N-terminus, respectively, after hydrolysis), but cleavage does not take place. Residues Ser68 and Val69 fit into the substrate binding sites S2 and S3 in an arrangement that is nearly inverted from that of a substrate. A key feature of this interaction is the bidentate coordination of the catalytic Zn^{2+} of the enzyme by the α-amino and carbonyl groups of the N-terminal cysteine of TIMP-1 and the projection of the side chain of Thr2 into the S1' specificity pocket of MMP-3 (Fig. 3a). This mode of interaction is similar to that of a synthetic hydroxamate inhibitor of MMPs (Fig. 3b). The HO group of Thr2 interacts with Glu202 of MMP-3 and displaces a water molecule from the active site that is essential for hydrolysis of a peptide bond.

On binding to TIMP-1, a large conformational change occurs in the N-terminal region of MMP-3. This change involves the disruption of the salt bridge between the α-amino group of the N-terminal Phe83 and the carboxylate side chain of Asp237, and thus results in a movement of 15 Å by the N-terminal region and in an interaction with

Figure 2

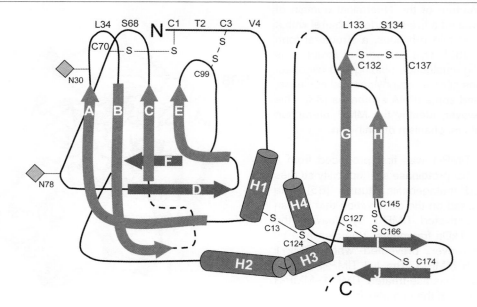

A schematic display of the secondary structure of tissue inhibitor of metalloproteinases 1 (TIMP-1). The crystal structure of TIMP-1 was determined as a complex with the catalytic domain of MMP-3 [86]. Strands (A–J) and helices (H1–H4) are shown. Two glycosylation sites are indicated by diamonds.

Met66 of TIMP-1. Other MMP interaction sites are the A–B loop, the E–F loop, and residues Leu133 and Ser134 of the C-terminal domain (see Fig. 2). The structure of the TIMP-2–MT1-MMP complex shows a similar inhibitor–enzyme interaction to that of the TIMP-1–MMP-3 complex.

Generation of selective TIMP variants

The interaction of residues 2 of TIMP-1 and TIMP-2 with the S1′ site of an MMP appears to be a conserved feature of the TIMP–MMP interaction. Because of the dominant role of the P1′ residue of a substrate in MMP specificity and because of the differences in size of the S1′ specificity pockets of different MMPs, TIMP variants with chemically different side chains at position 2 may be more selective for different MMPs.

Meng *et al.* [88] investigated this possibility by substituting position 2 in N-TIMP with 14 different amino acids and measuring the K_i values of variants against MMP-1, MMP-2 and MMP-3. Table 1 shows that residue 2 has a major role in TIMP–MMP recognition. The absence of a side chain (glycine mutant) reduced the affinity for MMPs by three to five orders of magnitude, reflecting a loss of 33–55% of the free energy of interaction. Thus, although Thr2 is only a small part of the TIMP side of the interaction interface, it has a major role in the stability of the protein–protein interaction, and therefore represents a 'hot spot' for complex formation.

One striking feature of residue 2 in N-TIMP-1 is that mutation at this site significantly alters the affinity for different

Figure 3

(a)

(b)

A schematic representation of **(a)** the N-terminal region of tissue inhibitor of metalloproteinases 1 (TIMP-1) and **(b)** a peptidyl-hydroxamate inhibitor. The scheme of TIMP-1 is based on the crystal structure of the TIMP-1–MMP-3(ΔC) complex [86].

Table 1

K_i values of the N-terminal domain of tissue inhibitor of metalloproteinases 1 (N-TIMP-1) and its variants

Variant	MMP-1	MMP-2	MMP-3
N-TIMP-1	3.0	1.1	1.9
Thr2 to serine	25	2.1	0.5
Thr2 to glycine	18×10^3	103×10^3	1.4×10^3
Thr2 to alanine	2090	307	126
Thr2 to leucine	93	1.0	3.2
Thr2 to isoleucine	262	5.6	20
Thr2 to valine	1.6	4.5	3.0
Thr2 to methionine	11	0.7	0.7
Thr2 to phenylalanine	42	17	13
Thr2 to asparagine	1970	16	44
Thr2 to glutamine	870	12	29
Thr2 to aspartic acid	8130	1250	1110
Thr2 to glutamic acid	5730	433	468
Thr2 to lysine	1670	31	70
Thr2 to arginine	5010	12	28
Thr2 to leucine Val4 to serine Ser38 to alanine	>2000	6.8	196

MMP, matrix metalloproteinase.

Table 2

Relative sequence specificities of matrixins influenced by the P1′ position

	Relative rate of hydrolysis		
P4-P3-P2-P1 ~ P1′-P2′-P3′-P4′	MMP-1	MMP-2	MMP-3
Gly-Pro-Gln-Gly ~ **Ile**-Ala-Gly-Gln	100	100	100
Gly-Pro-Gln-Gly ~ **Leu**-Ala-Gly-Gln	130	88	110
Gly-Pro-Gln-Gly ~ **Val**-Ala-Gly-Gln	9.1	30	53
Gly-Pro-Gln-Gly ~ **Ser**-Ala-Gly-Gln	5.9	15	45
Gly-Pro-Gln-Gly ~ **Phe**-Ala-Gly-Gln	20	55	140
Gly-Pro-Gln-Gly ~ **Met**-Ala-Gly-Gln	110	230	60
Gly-Pro-Gln-Gly ~ **Gln**-Ala-Gly-Gln	28	34	38
Gly-Pro-Gln-Gly ~ **Glu**-Ala-Gly-Gln	<0.5	<0.5	<0.002
Gly-Pro-Gln-Gly ~ **Arg**-Ala-Gly-Gln	<0.5	<0.5	<4.9

MMP, matrix metalloproteinase.

(Table 1). Further experiments are necessary, but the unique structures around the reactive site of TIMPs provide new leads for designing selective MMP inhibitors.

Future prospects

The balance between MMPs and TIMPs is critical for the appropriate maintenance of tissues, and its disruption perturbs tissue homeostasis. A number of MMPs and ADAMTSs play major roles in cartilage matrix breakdown in arthritis. Several potent, orally available MMP inhibitors have been developed by a number of pharmaceutical companies and some were clinically tested for the treatment of arthritis or cancer, but none were found to be efficacious [90]. The reasons for this failure are not clear. It may be due to inhibition of nontargeted metalloproteinases or the inhibitor concentration may not have reached an effective level in the target tissue. In addition, there are general concerns about the safety of synthetic MMP inhibitors. For example, when the broad-spectrum MMP inhibitor Marimastat (British Biotech Pharmaceuticals, Oxford, UK) was used in cancer trials, it caused musculoskeletal problems manifested by tendonitis, joint pain, stiffness and reduced mobility. This may be due to nonselective inhibition of metalloproteinases that are biologically important.

Alternative approaches to preventing accelerated matrix breakdown may be to deliver natural inhibitors or natural inhibitor-derived selective inhibitors to the target tissue using gene transfer technologies.

Concluding remarks

The elucidation of the mode of interaction of TIMPs with MMPs and their inhibition mechanisms has introduced a new opportunity to engineer TIMP so that the variants selectively inhibit MMPs. In combination with gene transfer

MMPs. It is notable, however, that a comparison of the effects of a particular amino acid in the P1′ position of a peptide substrate on k_{cat}/K_m [89] (Table 2) with its effects as residue 2 of TIMP on MMP binding ($1/K_i$) show a poor correlation [88] (Fig. 3). This indicates that there is a large difference between recognition of the P1′ residue of a substrate and residue 2 of TIMP for MMPs. This discrepancy is probably due to a greater loss of conformational entropy associated with peptide substrate–MMP interactions compared with TIMP–MMP interactions. The orientation of residue 2 of TIMP-1 may also be influenced by the rigid structure around the two disulfide bonds in this region. Several mutants show potentially useful changes in specificity (e.g. the Arg2 mutant, which discriminates strongly against MMP-1).

Because the interaction between TIMP and MMP involves multiple sites, more specific mutants with multiple substitutions can be designed. Val4 and Ser68 were chosen because they are part of the core contact region with the MMP (Fig. 4). Substitutions for Val4 and Ser68 have significant effects on specificity (Wei et al., unpublished observations). The properties of the multisite mutants exhibit further enhancement in selectivity. The triple mutant T2L/V45/S68A exhibits high selectivity for MMP-2

Figure 4

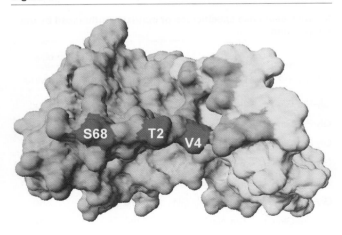

The surface structure of tissue inhibitor of metalloproteinases 1 (TIMP-1). The N-terminal domain and the C-terminal domain are shown in light red and green, respectively. The region within 4 Å contact with the matrix metalloproteinase (MMP) catalytic domain is shown in blue. Mutation sites coloured red modulate the selectivity of N-TIMP-1 against different MMPs. The image was prepared from the Brookhaven Protein Data Bank entry (1UEA) using the Swiss PDB viewer [91]. See Colour figure section.

technologies, it is hopefully possible to deliver a selective TIMP variant to the target tissue. Mutagenesis studies conducted in our laboratories indicate that the rigid nature of the reactive site of TIMP provides a unique mode of interaction with MMPs that is significantly different from those of peptidomimetic synthetic inhibitors. The use of this type of interaction may allow us to design new types of inhibitors. This requires a thorough understanding of the interaction between the target enzyme and the inhibitor. Further investigations of the mode of interaction of TIMP-3 with aggrecanases and TACE are particularly important for the future development of selective inhibitors against these enzymes as potential therapeutics to prevent cartilage matrix breakdown.

Glossary of terms

ADAM = a disintegrin and a metalloproteinase; ADAMTS = ADAM with thrombospondin type I domain; ECM = extracellular matrix; MMP = matrix metalloproteinase; MMP-3 (ΔC) = catalytic domain of MMP-3; MT1-MMP = membrane-type 1 matrix metalloproteinase; N-TIMP = N-terminal domain of tissue inhibitor of metalloproteinases; proMMP = zymogen form of MMP; TACE = tumour-necrosis-factor-alpha-converting enzyme; TIMP = tissue inhibitor of metalloproteinases.

Acknowledgements

The authors thank Dr Rob Visse and Dr Eric Huet for preparation of the illustrations. This work was supported by NIH grant AR40994 and the Wellcome Trust Grant 057508.

References

1. Poole AR, Mort JS, Roughley PJ: **Methods for evaluating mechanisms of cartilage breakdown.** In *Joint Cartilage Degradation: Basic and Clinical Aspects.* Edited by Woessner JF Jr, Howell DS. New York: Marcel Dekker; 1993:225-260. [general reference]
2. Caterson B, Flannery CR, Hughes GE, Little CB: **Mechanisms involved in cartilage proteoglycan catabolism.** *Matrix Biol* 2000, **19**:333-344. [key review]
3. Nagase H, Woessner JF: **Matrix metalloproteinases.** *J Biol Chem* 1999, **274**:21491-21494. [key review]
4. Sternlicht MD, Werb Z: **How matrix metalloproteinases regulate cell behavior.** *Annu Rev Cell Dev Biol* 2001, **17**:463-516. [key review]
5. Konttinen YT, Ainola M, Valleala H, Ma J, Ida H, Mandelin J, Kinne RW, Santavirta S, Sorsa T, López-Otín C, Takagi M: **Analysis of 16 different matrix metalloproteinases (MMP-1 to MMP-20) in the synovial membrane: different profiles in trauma and rheumatoid arthritis.** *Ann Rheum Dis* 1999, **58**:691-697. [general reference]
6. Yoshihara Y, Nakamura H, Obata K, Yamada H, Hayakawa T, Fujikawa K, Okada Y: **Matrix metalloproteinases and tissue inhibitors of metalloproteinases in synovial fluids from patients with rheumatoid arthritis or osteoarthritis.** *Ann Rheum Dis* 2000, **59**:455-461. [general reference]
7. Fosang AJ, Neame PJ, Hardingham TE, Murphy G, Hamilton JA: **Cleavage of cartilage proteoglycan between G1 and G2 domains by stromelysins.** *J Biol Chem* 1991, **266**:15579-15582. [general reference]
8. Fosang AJ, Neame PJ, Last K, Hardingham TE, Murphy G, Hamilton JA: **The interglobular domain of cartilage aggrecan is cleaved by PUMP, gelatinases, and cathepsin B.** *J Biol Chem* 1992, **267**:19470-19474. [general reference]
9. Lark MW, Bayne EK, Flanagan J, Harper CF, Hoerrner LA, Hutchinson NI, Singer II, Donatelli SA, Weidner JR, Williams HR Munford RA, Lohmander LS: **Aggrecan degradation in human cartilage — evidence for both matrix metalloproteinase and aggrecanase activity in normal, osteoarthritic, and rheumatoid joints.** *J Clin Invest* 1997, **100**:93-106. [archival research]
10. Sandy JD, Neame PJ, Boynton RE, Flannery CR: **Catabolism of aggrecan in cartilage explants. Identification of a major cleavage site within the interglobular domain.** *J Biol Chem* 1991, **266**:8683-8685. [archival research]
11. Sandy JD, Flannery CR, Neame PJ, Lohmander LS: **The structure of aggrecan fragments in human synovial fluid. Evidence for the involvement in osteoarthritis of a novel proteinase which cleaves the Glu 373–Ala 374 bond of the interglobular domain.** *J Clin Invest* 1992, **89**:1512-1516. [general reference]
12. Lohmander LS, Hoerrner LA, Lark MW: **Metalloproteinases, tissue inhibitor, and proteoglycan fragments in knee synovial fluid in human osteoarthritis.** *Arthritis Rheum* 1993, **36**:181-189. [general reference]
13. Tortorella MD, Burn TC, Pratta MA, Abbaszade I, Hollis JM, Liu R, Rosenfeld SA, Copeland RA, Decicco CP, Wynn R, Rockwell A, Yang F, Duke JL, Solomon K, George H, Bruckner R, Nagase H, Itoh Y, Ellis DM, Ross H, Wiswall BH, Murphy K, Hillman MC, Hollis GF, Newton RC, Magolda RL, Trzaskos JM, Arner EC: **Purification and cloning of aggrecanase-1: A member of the ADAMTS family of proteins.** *Science* 1999, **284**:1664-1666. [archival research]
14. Abbaszade I, Liu RQ, Yang F, Rosenfeld SA, Ross OH, Link JR, Ellis DM, Tortorella MD, Pratta MA, Hollis JM, Wynn R, Dike JL, George HJ, Hillman MC, Murphy K, Wiswall BH, Copeland RA, Decicco CP, Bruckner R, Nagase H, Itoh Y, Newton RC, Magolda RL, Trazskos JM, Hollis GF, Arner EC, Burn TC: **Cloning and characterization of ADAMTS11, an aggrecanase from the ADAMTS family.** *J Biol Chem* 1999, **274**:23443-23450. [general reference]
15. Kuno K, Okada Y, Kawashima H, Nakamura H, Miyasaka M, Ohno H, Matsushima K: **ADAMTS-1 cleaves a cartilage proteoglycan, aggrecan.** *FEBS Lett* 2000, **478**:241-245. [general reference]
16. Brew K, Dinakarpandian D, Nagase H: **Tissue inhibitors of metalloproteinases: evolution, structure and function.** *Biochim Biophys Acta Protein Struct Mol Enzymol* 2000, **1477**:267-283.[key review]
17. Murphy G, Houbrechts A, Cockett MI, Williamson RA, O'Shea M, Docherty AJP: **The N-terminal domain of tissue inhibitor of metalloproteinases retains metalloproteinase inhibitory activ-**

ity [published erratum appears in *Biochemistry* 1991, **30**: 10362]. *Biochemistry* 1991, **30**:8097-8102. [archival research]

18. Dean DD, Martel-Pelletier J, Pelletier J-P, Howell DS, Woessner JF Jr: **Evidence for metalloproteinase and metalloproteinase inhibitor imbalance in human osteoarthritic cartilage.** *J Clin Invest* 1989, **84**:678-685. [archival research]

19. Kageyama Y, Miyamoto S, Ozeki T, Hiyohsi M, Suzuki M, Nagano A: **Levels of rheumatoid factor isotypes, metalloproteinase-3 and tissue inhibitor of metalloproteinase-1 in synovial fluid from various arthritides.** *Clin Rheumatol* 2000, **19**:14-20. [general reference]

20. Yoshihara Y, Obata K, Fujimoto N, Yamashita K, Hayakawa T, Shinmei M: **Increased levels of stromelysin-1 and tissue inhibitor of metalloproteinases-1 in sera from patients with rheumatoid arthritis.** *Arthritis Rheum* 1995, **38**:969-975. [general reference]

21. Manicourt DH, Fujimoto N, Obata K, Thonar EJ-MA: **Levels of circulating collagenase, stromelysin-1, and tissue inhibitor of matrix metalloproteinases 1 in patients with rheumatoid arthritis. Relationship to serum levels of antigenic keratan sulfate and systemic parameters of inflammation.** *Arthritis Rheum* 1995, **38**:1031-1039. [general reference]

22. Manicourt D-H, Fujimoto, N, Obata K, Thonar EJ-MA: **Serum levels of collagenase, stromelysin-1 and TIMP-1.** *Arthritis Rheum* 1994, **37**:1774-1783. [general reference]

23. Schett G, Hayer S, Tohidast-Akrad M, Schmid BJ, Lang S, Türk B, Kainberger F, Haralambous S, Kollias G, Newby AC, Xu Q, Steiner G, Smolen J: **Adenovirus-based overexpression of tissue inhibitor of metalloproteinases 1 reduces tissue damange in the joints of tumor necrosis factor α transgenic mice.** *Arthritis Rheum* 2001, **44**:2888-2898. [general reference]

24. Apparailly F, Noël D, Millet V, Baker AH, Lisignoli G, Jacquet C, Kaiser MJ, Sany J, Jorgensen C: **Paradoxical effects of tissue inhibitor of metalloproteinases 1 gene transer in collagen-induced arthritis.** *Arthritis Rheum* 2001, **44**:1444-1454. [general reference]

25. Murphy G, Willenbrock F: **Tissue inhibitors of matrix metallo-endopeptidases.** *Methods Enzymol* 1995, **248**:496-510. [general reference]

26. Taylor KB, Windsor LJ, Caterina NCM, Bodden MK, Engler JA. **The mechanism of inhibition of collagenase by TIMP-1:** *J Biol Chem* 1996, **271**:23938-23945. [general reference]

27. Olson MW, Gervasi DC, Mobashery S, Fridman R: **Kinetic analysis of the binding of human matrix metalloproteinase-2 and -9 to tissue inhibitor of metalloproteinase (TIMP-1 and TIMP-2).** *J Biol Chem* 1997, **272**:29975-29983. [general reference]

28. Will H, Atkinson SJ, Butler GS, Smith B, Murphy G: **The soluble catalytic domain of membrane type 1 matrix metalloproteinase cleaves the propeptide of progelatinase A and initiates auto-proteolytic activation. Regulation by TIMP-2 and TIMP-3.** *J Biol Chem* 1996, **271**:17119-17123. [general reference]

29. Bigg HF, Morrison CJ, Butler GS, Bogoyevitch MA, Wang ZP, Soloway PD, Overall CM: **Tissue inhibitor of metalloproteinases-4 inhibits but does not support the activation of gelatinase A via efficient inhibition of membrane type I-matrix metalloproteinase.** *Cancer Res* 2001, **61**:3610-3618. [general reference]

30. Hutton M, Willenbrock F, Brocklehurst K, Murphy G: **Kinetic analysis of the mechanism of interaction of full-length TIMP-2 and gelatinase A — evidence for the existence of a low-affinity intermediate.** *Biochemistry* 1998, **37**:10094-10098. [general reference]

31. Willenbrock F, Crabbe T, Slocombe PM, Sutton CW, Docherty AJP, Cockett MI, O'Shea M, Brocklehurst K, Phillips IR, Murphy G: **The activity of the tissue inhibitors of metalloproteinases is regulated by C-terminal domain interactions: a kinetic analysis of the inhibition of gelatinase A.** *Biochemistry* 1993, **32**:4330-4337. [general reference]

32. Kashiwagi M, Tortorella M, Nagase H, Brew K: **TIMP-3 is a potent inhibitor of aggrecanase 1 (ADAM-TS4) and aggrecanase 2 (ADAM-TS5).** *J Biol Chem* 2001, **276**:12501-12504. [general reference]

33. Overall CM, King AE, Sam DK, Ong AD, Lau TTY, Wallon UM, DeClerck YA, Atherstone J: **Identification of the tissue inhibitor of metalloproteinases-2 (TIMP-2) binding site on the hemopexin carboxyl domain of human gelatinase a by site-directed mutagenesis — The hierarchical role in binding TIMP-2 of the unique cationic clusters of hemopexin modules III and IV.** *J Biol Chem* 1999, **274**:4421-4429. [general reference]

34. Bigg HF, Shi YE, Liu YLE, Steffensen B, Overall CM: **Specific, high affinity binding of tissue inhibitor of metalloproteinases-4 (TIMP4) to the COOH-terminal hemopexin-like domain of human gelatinase A — TIMP-4 binds progelatinase A and the COOH-terminal domain in a similar manner to TIMP-2.** *J Biol Chem* 1997, **272**:15496-15500. [general reference]

35. Butler GS, Apte SS, Willenbrock F, Murphy G: **Human tissue inhibitor of metalloproteinases 3 interacts with both the N- and C-terminal domains of gelatinases A and B — Regulation by polyanions.** *J Biol Chem* 1999, **274**:10846-10851. [general reference]

36. Goldberg GI, Strongin A, Collier IE, Genrich LT, Marmer BL: **Interaction of 92-kDa type IV collagenase with the tissue inhibitor of metalloproteinases prevents dimerization, complex formation with interstitial collagenase, and activation of the proenzyme with stromelysin.** *J Biol Chem* 1992, **267**: 4583-4591. [general reference]

37. Ogata Y, Itoh Y, Nagase H: **Steps involved in activation of the pro-matrix metalloproteinase 9 (progelatinase B)-tissue inhibitor of metalloproteinases-1 complex by 4-amino-phenylmercuric acetate and proteinases.** *J Biol Chem* 1995, **270**:18506-18511. [general reference]

38. Itoh Y, Nagase H: **Preferential inactivation of tissue inhibitor of metalloproteinases-1 that is bound to the precursor of matrix metalloproteinase 9 (progelatinase B) by human neutrophil elastase.** *J Biol Chem* 1995, **270**:16518-16521. [general reference]

39. Sato H, Takino T, Okada Y, Cao J, Shinagawa A, Yamamoto E, Seiki M: **A matrix metalloproteinase expressed on the surface of invasive tumour cells.** *Nature (Lond)* 1994, **370**:61-65. [archival research]

40. Strongin AY, Collier I, Bannikov G, Marmer BL, Grant GA, Goldberg GI: **Mechanism of cell surface activation of 72-kDa type IV collagenase. Isolation of the activated form of the membrane metalloprotease.** *J Biol Chem* 1995, **270**:5331-5338. [general reference]

41. Butler GS, Butler MJ, Atkinson SJ, Will H, Tamura T, van Westrum SS: **The TIMP2 membrane type 1 metalloproteinase 'receptor' regulates the concentration and efficient activation of progelatinase A — a kinetic study.** *J Biol Chem* 1998, **273**:871-880. [general reference]

42. Itoh Y, Takamura A, Ito N, Maru Y, Sato H, Suenaga N, Aoki T, Seiki M: **Homophilic complex formation of MT1-MMP facilitates proMMP-2 activation on the cell surface and promotes tumor cell invasion.** *EMBO J* 2001, **20**:4782-4793. [general reference]

43. Seiki M: **Membrane-type matrix metalloproteinases.** *APMIS* 1999, **107**:137-143. [general reference]

44. Hiraoka N, Allen E, Apel IJ, Gyetko MR, Weiss SJ: **Matrix metalloproteinases regulate neovascularization by acting as pericellular fibrinolysins.** *Cell* 1998, **95**:365-377. [archival research]

45. Itoh Y, Ito A, Iwata K, Tanzawa K, Mori Y, Nagase H: **Plasma membrane-bound tissue inhibitor of metalloproteinases (TIMP)-2 specifically inhibits matrix metalloproteinase 2 (gelatinase A) activated on the cell surface.** *J Biol Chem* 1998, **273**:24360-24367. [general reference]

46. Blenis J, Hawkes SP: **Transformation-sensitive protein associated with the cell substratum of chicken embryo fibroblasts.** *Proc Natl Acad Sci USA* 1983, **80**:770-774. [general reference]

47. Pavloff N, Staskus PW, Kishnani NS, Hawkes SP: **A new inhibitor of metalloproteinases from chicken: ChIMP-3. A third member of the TIMP family.** *J Biol Chem* 1992, **267**:17321-17326. [archival research]

48. Yu WH, Yu SSC, Meng Q, Brew K, Woessner JF: **TIMP-3 binds to sulfated glycosaminoglycans of the extracellular matrix.** *J Biol Chem* 2000, **275**:31226-31232. [general reference]

49. Smith MR, Kung HF, Durum SK, Colburn NH, Sun Y: **TIMP-3 induces cell death by stabilizing TNF-alpha receptors on the surface of human colon carcinoma cells.** *Cytokine* 1997, **9**: 770-780. [general reference]

50. Borland G, Murphy G, Ager A: **Tissue inhibitor of metalloproteinases-3 inhibits shedding of L-selectin from leukocytes.** *J Biol Chem* 1999, **274**:2810-2815. [general reference]

51. Hargreaves PG, Wang FF, Antcliff J, Murphy G, Lawry J, Russell RGG. Croucher PI: **Human myeloma cells shed the interleukin-6**

receptor – inhibition by tissue inhibitor of metalloproteinase-3 and a hydroxamate-based metalloproteinase inhibitor. *Br J Haematol* 1998, **101**:694-702. [general reference]

52. Fitzgerald ML, Wang Z, Park PW, Murphy G, Bernfield M: Shedding of syndecan-1 and -4 ectodomains is regulated by multiple signaling pathways and mediated by a TIMP-3-sensitive metalloproteinase. *J Cell Biol* 2000, **148**:811-824. [general reference]
53. Black RA, White JM: ADAMS – focus on the protease domain. *Curr Opin Cell Biol* 1998, **10**:654-659. [key review]
54. Amour A, Slocombe PM, Webster A, Butler M, Knight CG, Smith BJ, Stephens PE, Shelley C, Hutton M, Knäuper V, Docherty AJP, Murphy G: TNF-Alpha converting enzyme (TACE) is inhibited by TIMP-3. *FEBS Lett* 1998, **435**:39-44. [general reference]
55. Amour A, Knight CG, Webster A, Slocombe PM, Stephens PE, Knäuper V, Docherty AJP, Murphy G: The in vitro activity of ADAM-10 is inhibited by TIMP-1 and TIMP-3. *FEBS Lett* 2000, **473**:275-279. [general reference]
56. Loechel F, Fox JW, Murphy G, Albrechtsen R, Wewer UM: ADAM 12-S cleaves IGFBP-3 and IGFBP-5 and is inhibited by TIMP-3. *Biochem Biophys Res Commun* 2000, **278**:511-515. [general reference]
57. Apte SS, Hayashi K, Seldin MF, Mattei MG, Hayashi M, Olsen BR: Gene encoding a novel murine tissue inhibitor of metalloproteinases (TIMP), TIMP-3, is expressed in developing mouse epithelia, cartilage, and muscle, and is located on mouse chromosome 10. *Dev Dyn* 1994, **200**:177-197. [general reference]
58. Su S, Grover J, Roughley PJ, DiBattista JA, Martel-Pelletier J, Pelletier JP, Zafarullah M: Expression of the tissue inhibitor of metalloproteinases (TIMP) gene family in normal and osteoarthritic joints. *Rheumatol Int* 1999, **18**:183-191. [general reference]
59. Su SM, DiBattista JA, Sun Y, Li WQ, Zafarullah M: Up-regulation of tissue inhibitor of metalloproteinases-3 gene expression by TGF-β in articular chondrocytes is mediated by serine/threonine and tyrosine kinases. *J Cell Biochem* 1998, **70**:517-527. [general reference]
60. Li WQ, Zafarullah M: Oncostatin M up-regulates tissue inhibitor of metalloproteinases-3 gene expression in articular chondrocytes via de novo transcription, protein synthesis, and tyrosine kinase- and mitogen-activated protein kinase-dependent mechanisms. *J Immunol* 1998, **161**:5000-5007. [general reference]
61. Takizawa M, Ohuchi E, Yamanaka H, Nakamura H, Ikeda E, Ghosh P, Okada Y: Production of tissue inhibitor of metalloproteinases 3 is selectively enhanced by calcium pentosan polysulfate in human rheumatoid synovial fibroblasts. *Arthritis Rheum* 2000, **43**:812-820. [general reference]
62. Felbor U, Suvanto EA, Forsius HR, Eriksson AW, Weber BH: Autosomal recessive Sorsby fundus dystrophy revisited: molecular evidence for dominant inheritance. *Am J Hum Genet* 1997, **60**:57-62. [general reference]
63. Tabata Y, Isashiki Y, Kamimura K, Nakao K, Ohba N: A novel splice site mutation in the tissue inhibitor of the metalloproteinases-3 gene in Sorsby's fundus dystrophy with unusual clinical features. *Hum Genet* 1998, **103**:179-182. [general reference]
64. Langton KP, McKie N, Curtis A, Goodship JA, Bond PM, Barker MD, Clarke M: A novel tissue inhibitor of metalloproteinases-3 mutation reveals a common molecular phenotype in Sorsby's fundus dystrophy. *J Biol Chem* 2000, **275**:27027-27031. [general reference]
65. Qi JH, Ebrahem Q, Yeow K, Edwards DR, Fox PL, Anand-Apte B: Expression of Sorsby's fundus dystrophy mutations in human retinal pigment epithelial cells reduces matrix metalloproteinase inhibition and may promote angiogenesis: *J Biol Chem* in press. [general reference]
66. Yeow KM, Kishnani NS, Hutton M, Hawkes SP, Murphy G, Edwards DR: Sorsby's fundus dystrophy tissue inhibitor of metalloproteinases-3 (TIMP-3) mutants have unimpaired matrix metalloproteinase inhibitory activities, but affect cell adhesion to the extracellular matrix. *Matrix Biol* 2002, **21**:75-88. [general reference]
67. Docherty AJP, Lyons A, Smith BJ, Wright EM, Stephens PE, Harris TJR, Murphy G, Raynolds JJ: Sequence of human tissue inhibitor of metalloproteinases and its identity to erythroid-potentiating activity. *Nature (Lond)* 1985, **318**:66-69. [archival research]

68. Gasson JC, Golde DW, Kaufman SE, Westbrook CA, Hewick RM, Kaufman RJ, Wong GG, Temple PA, Leary AC, Brown EL, Orr EC, Clark SC: Molecular characterization and expression of the gene encoding human erythroid-potentiating activity. *Nature (Lond)* 1985, **315**:768-771. [general reference]
69. Bertaux B, Hornebeck W, Eisen AZ, Dubertret L: Growth stimulation of human keratinocytes by tissue inhibitor of metalloproteinases. *J Invest Dermatol* 1991, **97**:679-685. [general reference]
70. Hayakawa T, Yamashita K, Tanzawa K, Uchijima E, Iwata K: Growth-promoting activity of tissue inhibitor of metalloproteinases-1 (TIMP-1) for a wide range of cells. A possible new growth factor in serum. *FEBS Lett* 1992, **298**:29-32. [archival research]
71. Stetler-Stevenson WG, Bersch N, Golde DW: Tissue inhibitor of metalloproteinase-2 (TIMP-2) has erythroid-potentiating activity. *FEBS Lett* 1992, **296**:231-234. [general reference]
72. Hayakawa T, Yamashita K, Ohuchi E, Shinagawa A: Cell growth-promoting activity of tissue inhibitor of metalloproteinases-2 (TIMP-2). *J Cell Sci* 1994, **107**:2373-2379. [general reference]
73. Gomez DE, Alonso DF, Yoshiji H, Thorgeirsson UP: Tissue inhibitors of metalloproteinases – structure, regulation and biological functions [review]. *Eur J Cell Biol* 1997, **74**:111-122. [key review]
74. Murphy AN, Unsworth EJ, Stetler-Stevenson WG: Tissue inhibitor of metalloproteinases-2 inhibits bFGF-induced human microvascular endothelial cell proliferation. *J Cell Physiol* 1993, **157**:351-358. [general reference]
75. Barasch J, Yang J, Qiao JZ, Tempst P, Erdjument-Bromage H, Leung W, Oliver JA: Tissue inhibitor of metalloproteinase-2 stimulates mesenchymal growth and regulates epithelial branching during morphogenesis of the rat metanephros. *J Clin Invest* 1999, **103**:1299-1307. [archival research]
76. Bian J, Wang Y, Smith MR, Kim H, Jacobs C, Jackman J, Kung HF, Colburn NH, Sun Y: Suppression of in vivo tumor growth and induction of suspension cell death by tissue inhibitor of metalloproteinases (TIMP)-3. *Carcinogenesis* 1996, **17**:1805-1811. [general reference]
77. Ahonen M, Baker AH, Kähäri VM: Adenovirus-mediated gene delivery of tissue inhibitor of metalloproteinases-3 inhibits invasion and induces apoptosis in melanoma cells: *Cancer Res* 1998, **58**:2310-2315. [general reference]
78. Baker AH, Zaltsman AB, George SJ, Newby AC: Divergent effects of tissue inhibitor of metalloproteinase-1, -2, or -3 overexpression on rat vascular smooth muscle cell invasion, proliferation, and death in vitro – TIMP-3 promotes apoptosis. *J Clin Invest* 1998, **101**:1478-1487. [general reference]
79. Bond P, Murphy G, Bennett MR, Amour A, Knäuper V, Newby AC, Baker AH: Localization of the death domain of tissue inhibitor of metalloproteinase-3 to the N terminus – metalloproteinase inhibition is associated with proapoptotic activity. *J Biol Chem* 2000, **275**:41358-41363. [general reference]
80. Guedez L, Stetler-Stevenson WG, Wolff L, Wang J, Fukushima P, Mansoor A, Stetler-Stevenson M: In vitro suppression of programmed cell death of B cells by tissue inhibitor of metalloproteinases-1. *J Clin Invest* 1998, **102**:2002-2010. [archival research]
81. Valente P, Fasina G, Melchiori A, Masiello L, Cilli M, Vacca A, Onisto M, Santi L, Stetler-Stevenson WG: TIMP-2 over-expression reduces invasion and angiogenesis and protects B16F10 melanoma cells from apoptosis. *Int J Cancer* 1998, **75**:246-253. [general reference]
82. Williamson RA, Martorell G, Carr MD, Murphy G, Docherty AJP, Freedman RB, Carr MD: Solution structure of the active domain of tissue inhibitor of metalloproteinases-2. A new member of the OB fold protein family. *Biochemistry* 1994, **33**:11745-11759. [archival research]
83. Murzin AG: OB (oligonucleotide/oligosaccharide binding)-fold: common structural and functional solution for non-homologous sequences. *EMBO J* 1993, **12**:861-867. [general reference]
84. Nagase H, Suzuki K, Cawston TE, Brew K. Involvement of a region near valine-69 of tissue inhibitor of metalloproteinases (TIMP)-1 in the interaction with matrix metalloproteinase 3 (stromelysin 1). *Biochem J* 1997, **325**:163-167. [general reference]
85. Huang W, Meng Q, Suzuki K, Nagase H, Brew K: Mutational study of the amino-terminal domain of human tissue inhibitor

of metalloproteinases I (TIMP-1) locates an inhibitory region for matrix metalloproteinases. *J Biol Chem* 1997, **272**:22086-22091. [general reference]

86. Gomis-Rüth FX, Maskos K, Betz M, Bergner A, Huber R, Suzuki K, Yoshida N, Nagase H, Brew K, Bourenkov BP, Bartunik H, Bode W: **Mechanism of inhibition of the human matrix metalloproteinase stromelysin-1 by TIMP-1.** *Nature (Lond)* 1997, **389**:77-81. [archival research]

87. Fernandez-Catalan C, Bode W, Huber R, Turk D, Calvete JJ, Lichte A, Tschesche H, Maskos K: **Crystal structure of the complex formed by the membrane type 1-matrix metalloproteinase with the tissue inhibitor of metalloproteinases-2, the soluble progelatinase a receptor.** *EMBO J* 1998, **17**:5238-5248. [general reference]

88. Meng Q, Malinovskii V, Huang W, Hu YJ, Chung L, Nagase H, Bode W, Maskos K, Brew K: **Residue 2 of TIMP-1 is a major determinant of affinity and specificity for matrix metalloproteinases but effects of substitutions do not correlate with those of the corresponding P1′ residue of substrate.** *J Biol Chem* 1999, **274**:10184-10189. [general reference]

89. Nagase H, Fields GB: **Human matrix metalloproteinase specificity studies using collagen sequence-based synthetic peptides.** *Biopolymers* 1996, **40**:399-416. [key review]

90. Zucker S, Cao J, Chen WT: **Critical appraisal of the use of matrix metalloproteinase inhibitors in cancer treatment.** *Oncogene* 2000, **19**:6642-6650. [key review]

91. Guex N, Peitsch MC: **SWISS-MODEL and the Swiss-Pdb Viewer: an environment for comparative protein modeling.** *Electrophoresis* 1997, **18**:2714-2723. [general reference]

Supplement Review

Tissue engineering: chondrocytes and cartilage

Tim Hardingham, Simon Tew and Alan Murdoch

UK Centre for Tissue Engineering, School of Biological Sciences, University of Manchester, UK.

Correspondence: Tim Hardingham, UK Centre for Tissue Engineering, School of Biological Sciences, University of Manchester, Manchester, UK.
Tel: +44 (0)161 275 5511; fax: +44 (0)161 275 5752; e-mail: tim.hardingham@ukcte.org

Received: 1 March 2002
Revisions requested: 12 March 2002
Revisions received: 12 March 2002
Accepted: 12 March 2002
Published: 9 May 2002

Arthritis Res 2002, **4 (suppl 3)**:S63-S68

This article may contain supplementary data which can only be found online at http://arthritis-research.com/content/4/S3/S063

Chapter summary

Tissue engineering offers new strategies for developing treatments for the repair and regeneration of damaged and diseased tissues. These treatments, using living cells, will exploit new developments in understanding the principles in cell biology that control and direct cell function. Arthritic diseases that affect so many people and have a major impact on the quality of life provide an important target for tissue engineering. Initial approaches are in cartilage repair; in our own programme we are elucidating the signals required by chondrocytes to promote new matrix assembly. These principles will extend to other tissues of the musculoskeletal system, including the repair of bone, ligament and tendon.

Keywords: extracellular matrix, joint disease, osteoarthritis, regenerative medicine

Introduction

Tissue engineering is a new development and in this review we set out some of the principles that underlie it. The potential applications of tissue engineering in medicine are diverse, and as a basis for new treatments for musculoskeletal diseases it is likely to have a major impact in rheumatology and orthopaedics. The progress in research in tissue engineering has been rapid, but it is acknowledged that more basic research is necessary to develop its full potential. This requires the formation and close collaboration of interdisciplinary research teams. One of the focus areas of tissue engineering in our research programme is in cartilage replacement and we summarise some of the strategies being pursued in this area in the newly formed UK Centre for Tissue Engineering in the Universities of Manchester and Liverpool [1].

The principles of tissue engineering

Tissue engineering has emerged through a combination of many developments in biology, material science, engineering, manufacturing and medicine. The strategies developed in tissue engineering involve a range of approaches, the key element of which is the use of biologically based mechanisms to achieve the repair and healing of damaged and diseased tissues. This application distinguishes it from the use of medical devices, and the delivery of an assembled 'tissue equivalent' distinguishes it from a pharmaceutical product. Tissue engineering addresses the problem caused by many injuries and disease processes that result in physically damaged tissues and organs in our bodies which, if left unattended, repair imperfectly or not at all. It is the intervention with an engineered tissue that presents the prospect of achieving successful repair where it would not otherwise occur.

Tissue engineering is part of new wave of developments in biomedicine in which our scientific understanding of how living cells function will enable us to gain control and direct their activity to promote the repair of damaged and diseased tissues. The potential for medical intervention with a tissue engineering solution is seen nowhere better than with the chronic, persistent leg ulcer, which, in a

---

A glossary of specialist terms used in this chapter appears at the end of the text section. A list of common abbreviations used in this issue appears just before the indexes.

patient with diabetes, provides a constant source of discomfort and incapacity. The patient does not lack the inherent capacity to heal a skin wound, but healing is failing to occur naturally at the site of the ulcer. What are lacking are the biological signals, chemical messengers and physical cues that initiate the events of cell migration, blood vessel formation and tissue assembly for normal wound healing. If we can provide these biological signals in a 'tissue engineered' package, we can kick-start a repair process that can be completed by the patient's own tissues.

How can this be achieved? What forms the tissue engineered package? The precise form will vary with the medical application for which it is designed. There are, however, two typical elements: one or more type(s) of living cell with particular tissue functions; and a material support that forms a structure for both culturing the cells in the laboratory and the surgical delivery of the tissue equivalent to the patient. This support might be in the form of a lamella or tubular structure, or in a more complex three-dimensional structure, depending on the clinical application. The 'package' therefore contains several important, and quite different, material components and its assembly involves a manufacturing process that extends from the culture of living cells to the fabrication techniques for 3-dimensional structures, involving engineering and bioreactor design. It also has to be carried out in a regulatory framework that will ensure the monitoring and documenting of all stages of the process. Tissue engineering thus requires the coordination of a range of different disciplines and its development depends on bringing together broadly based research teams to form interdisciplinary collaborations, such as within our research programme at UK Centre for Tissue Engineering, Universities of Manchester and Liverpool [1]. Input is required from cell biologists, molecular biologists, biomaterial scientists, bioengineers and healthcare physicians.

Post genomic research and stem cells
A key to new developments in tissue engineering lies in the current progress in research on living cells. Sequencing the human genome is close to completion and it is one of the inevitable benefits of the post genomic age that a more complete knowledge of the biological signals and cues that trigger natural repair processes will be discovered. It is this knowledge that will be exploited in tissue engineering applications. So, the strategies behind current developments in tissue engineering depend heavily on living cells and tissues, and on our abilities to control their function. The theme that is particularly emphasised in our programmes is that, in many clinical applications, the planned long-term solution will engage the patient's own cells and tissues in the process to complete a biological repair. This is where it differs from the established use of medical devices that have been very successful in some

applications, such as joint replacements, but in which the damaged tissues are replaced with inert nonbiological materials. The applications of tissue engineering will be more diverse than has been possible with the nonbiological devices. These will range from small blood vessel replacement, repair of bone, tendon, ligament and cartilage, healing of skin wounds, nerve regeneration and the repair of problems causing incontinence, to a range of applications in reconstructive surgery. It may also extend to cellular based therapies for degenerative problems in muscle, heart and brain.

To help fuel these aspirations, there are remarkable new developments in stem cell research, which show that we all contain sources of cells that retain the capacity to form the different tissues in our bodies [2]. In addition to embryonic stem cells, which in early embryonic development have all the potential to divide and form all the tissues of the body, it is now recognized that, even as adults, we all contain some cells that retain the ability to form different tissues. It has long been known that these cells can be found in bone marrow (stromal stem cells) but, more recently, evidence has suggested that they can be found in other sites in the body and can even, for example, be harvested from the fat removed at liposuction! There is great interest in these sources of cells for tissue engineering applications, although much research is needed before their full potential (and limitations) will be known.

Research on the biomaterials associated with tissue engineering was initiated ahead of the developments in cell biology. There is currently much research and innovation in the development of new biomaterials. These extend from well-tried polylactates and polyglycolates to novel ceramics, caprolactones and hydrogels. Techniques are being developed for their formation into scaffolds, felts and weaves. Matrix printing devices are being explored for the fabrication of three-dimensional structures with microarchitecture that might mimic complex living organs, such as liver or kidney tissues. Different applications require different material properties to cope both with the required tensile and compressive forces and with elastic deformation and compliance. There is also much innovation occurring in polymer chemistry, but each new polymer or biomaterial requires extensive evaluation to assess how it interacts with living tissue, how long it survives in the body, what wear-products it produces and how it degrades. The ability to generate new chemistry currently far outpaces the speed at which their biological advantages and disadvantages can be thoroughly assessed.

There is also considerable interest in the use of natural biopolymers for tissue engineering applications, such as the long chain polysaccharide hyaluronan and its chemically derivatised forms, and various preparations of natural and recombinant proteins, including collagens and even silk. Many of these materials provide the opportunity for chemically linking biological signaling molecules such as peptides or small proteins, to provide sources of the signaling molecules that will trigger cell responses to help the healing process. For example, these 'smart' materials could be used to provide signals to encourage blood vessel development. When an engineered tissue is placed in the body, it requires the development of a blood supply from the patient for it to become integrated with surrounding tissues; this is essential for the completion of the healing process. The principle exceptions are cartilage, intervertebral disc and cornea, which are largely avascular tissues.

Strategies for articular cartilage repair

Articular cartilage provides its own particular challenges for tissue engineering. Its structure appears simple and it only contains one cell type; however it is has a complex highly organised extracellular matrix (ECM). Articular cartilage is frequently damaged as a result of trauma and degenerative joint diseases that may be driven by changes in biomechanics, cytokines, growth factors and cellular responses [3–6]. Cartilage has no blood vessels, it is not innervated and normal mechanisms of tissue repair, involving the recruitment of cells to the site of damage, do not occur. The challenge for cartilage tissue engineering is to produce cartilage tissue with suitable structure and properties *ex vivo*, which can be implanted into joints to provide a natural repair that with time will become integrated with the patient's tissues.

The physical properties of articular cartilage depend on the structure and organization of the macromolecules in the ECM. They can largely be understood in terms of the contribution made by fibrillar and nonfibrillar components [5]. The structure of collagen gives it impressive tensile properties, which are utilized in a special way in the predominant type II collagen, found in cartilage, to produce a tissue that is not only strong in tension but also resistant to compression. This is achieved by filling the interfibrillar matrix with a very high content of proteoglycan, primarily aggrecan [7,8], which draws water into the tissue as it creates a large osmotic swelling pressure. The osmotic pressure caused by the negatively charged groups on aggrecan create a large difference in the concentration of ions inside the cartilage compared with outside. Water is drawn into the tissue as a result of this osmotic imbalance and, because aggrecan is assembled into large supramolecular aggregates [9], it is too large and immobile to redistribute itself. The water thus swells and expands the aggrecan-rich matrix. This places the collagen network under tension and an equilibrium is achieved when tension in the collagen network balances the swelling pressure. This confers the tissue with compressive resilience and, as aggrecan offers great resistance to any fluid flow, the tissue behaves as a stiff elastic polymer to sudden impact loading, but shows some slow inelastic deformation with

sustained loads. The articular cartilage thus forms a tough but compliant load-bearing surface and these characteristics depend on the integrity of the collagen network and on the retention within it of a high concentration of aggrecan. Part of the challenge of tissue engineering cartilage is thus to provide the essential cells and signals that will establish a cartilage ECM and recapitulate this molecular organisation that forms the basis for the essential mechanical properties of the tissue.

Our tissue engineering approaches to cartilage repair are focussing on developing efficient methods to form cartilage with chondrocytes in culture. This approach depends on the availability of suitably differentiated chondrocytes to produce and maintain the specialised ECM of the tissue. These cells may be obtained through culturing primary autologous/heterologous chondrocytes [10], mesenchymal stem cells [11] and embryonic stem cells [12]. An important factor is the production of chondrocytes in sufficient numbers to form tissue constructs of an appropriate size. In the case of autologous chondrocytes, the expansion of the cell population can be carried out in monolayer culture conditions, although during this process chondrocytes become fibroblastic and lose their characteristic pattern of matrix protein expression [13]. Our initial studies are focussing on human articular chondrocytes, their expansion in monolayer culture under differing conditions and their subsequent potential to re-express a full matrix-producing phenotype.

Gene expression in chondrocytes passaged in monolayer culture

Human articular cartilage was obtained with informed consent from knee replacement operations. The cartilage from regions of the joints with intact tissue were dissected from the underlying bone, chopped finely and digested, first in trypsin for one hour, and subsequently overnight, in 0.08% bacterial collagenase in medium containing 10% foetal bovine serum. Both digestions were at 37°C with constant agitation. Washed, filtered cells were cultured as monolayers in DMEM, containing penicillin/streptomycin and 10% foetal bovine serum. The cells were split at a 1:2 ratio at confluence.

RNA was isolated from chondrocytes at various passages, to build up an initial profile of the changes in gene expression during cell expansion. The level of mRNA expression of a number of ECM markers (including chondrocyte-specific ECM genes [collagen II and aggrecan] and a fibroblast ECM gene [collagen I]) was assessed using RT-PCR. In addition, the expression of transcription factors important to chondrogenesis (SOX9, L-SOX5 and SOX6 [13,14]), of developmentally regulated cartilage genes associated with the further differentiation and hypertrophy of chondrocytes (matrilin-1, indian hedgehog and collagen X) and of other genes (such as the recently cloned xylosyl-

Figure 1

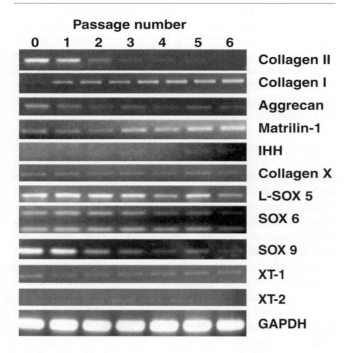

The changes in expression of genes in human articular cartilage chondrocytes with increasing passage in culture, detected using RT-PCR. Passage 0 refers to cells that are freshly isolated from the tissue and have not been cultured. GAPDH, glyceraldehyde phosphate dehydrogenase; IHH, indian hedgehog; XT, xylosyltransferase.

Figure 2

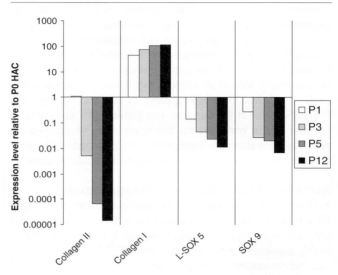

Real time RT-PCR analysis of RNA from human articular cartilage chondrocytes at different passage in culture. The values shown are expression levels of the indicated genes relative to the expression level found in passage (P) 0 cells that are freshly isolated from the tissue.

transferase isoforms [15]) was examined. Probes for these different genes have been designed and tested in the development of specific and sensitive methods to follow changes in gene expression. The changes in expression of these genes in chondrocytes with increasing passage in culture are shown in Fig. 1.

Expression of chondrocyte-specific genes, such as collagen II and aggrecan, decreased with time in culture, whilst collagen I expression increased, as previously reported [16]. Developmentally regulated gene transcripts characteristic of chondrocyte hypertrophy were not expected to be found in significant quantities in mature articular cartilage. Only very low expression of collagen X and indian hedgehog was detected at any stage of monolayer culture. Matrilin-1, however, was detected and its expression tended to increase with culture time. Matrilin-1 is expressed in other nonarticular cartilages and the significance of the expression in articular chondrocytes is currently unknown. Xylosyltransferase expression was examined as a possible indicator of the glycosaminoglycan synthesis of the cells. Two human isoforms have been cloned, but the expression level of both was low and remained the same throughout the culture period.

These initial studies have been extended by using real time, quantitative RT-PCR for the analysis of gene expression levels. This has major advantages over normal RT-PCR as it provides an accurate quantitative assay of gene expression. Polymerase chain reactions have been conducted using an Applied Biosystems 7700 and the amplified product was detected using the fluorescent DNA binding dye SYBR Green. This technique has enabled us to gain accurate data representing changing expression levels between cultured chondrocytes and those freshly isolated from the tissue. Results (Fig. 2) show that the upregulation of collagen I is rapid following the isolation of chondrocytes and their transfer into monolayer culture, and it precedes the downregulation of collagen II. Downregulation of the transcription factors SOX9 and L-SOX5 also precedes changes in collagen II expression. It is also clear that these changes in gene expression are largely complete by passage 5, with little difference between this stage and further culture up to passage 12.

Rates of chondrocyte proliferation

The effects of selected growth factors have also been investigated on the chondrocytes cultured in 10% serum. Published studies, screening an extensive number of growth factors and media supplements [16], have reported that human chondrocytes proliferate most rapidly in medium supplemented with 10% foetal calf serum, platelet-derived growth factor-BB, fibroblast growth factor-2 (FGF-2) and transforming growth factor β-1. When medium containing these supplements was added to human articular cartilage cells at passage 4, they began

Figure 3

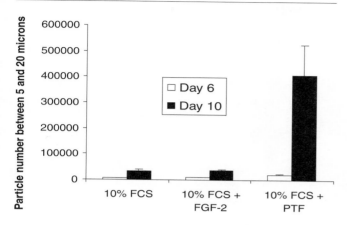

Proliferation of passage 1 human articular cartilage cells grown on tissue culture plastic (24-well plate) in different culture media. FCS, foetal calf serum; FGF-2, fibroblast growth factor-2; PTF, medium containing 10% serum, 5 ng/ml FGF-2, 10 ng/ml platelet-derived growth factor-BB and 1ng/ml transforming growth factor β-1.

to divide far more rapidly than parallel cultures in just 10% serum. The same was evident in these cells cultured in the supplemented medium from the beginning of the first passage. Cells seeded in 24-well plates at 2000 cells/well were counted in medium containing 10% serum, 10% serum + 5 ng/ml FGF-2 or 10% serum, 5 ng/ml fibroblast growth factor-2 (FGF-2), 10 ng/ml platelet derived growth factor-BB and 1ng/ml transforming growth factor β-1 ('PTF media') after 6 and 10 days in culture (Fig. 3). At 6 days, the number of cells in PTF-treated wells was twice that of those in either the control or FGF-2-treated wells, whilst by ten days the difference was ten-fold. This growth factor combination was extremely effective in achieving a rapid expansion of human chondrocytes in culture.

Re-expression of chondrogenic phenotype

A further aim of this project is to quantify the extent to which chondrocytes can re-express a chondrocyte phenotype once placed in a three-dimensional culture environment. The SOX transcription factors, particularly SOX9, appear to be sensitive indicators of the differentiation state of the cell and the expression levels of these genes, as well as those of collagen I, II and aggrecan, will be compared with those of freshly isolated cells. It will be important to determine if the rapid expansion of cell numbers in monolayer culture is detrimental or beneficial to their chondrogenic potential. We have developed sensitive methods of assessing the matrix assembly around chondrocytes, based on determining by confocal fluorescence recovery after photobleaching (confocal-FRAP) the translational diffusion of fluorescent tracer molecules of defined size [17–21]. This will be used to optimize conditions for matrix assembly and develop neocartilage constructs that can form the basis for a tissue engineered product.

Future prospects

Research in tissue engineering is expanding fast worldwide [22], and new UK [23], European [24], Japanese [25] and International [26] societies have begun to provide a forum for worldwide developments. Current advances in cell biology arising in post genomic research will have a major impact on tissue engineering programmes. This will be complemented by the development of novel biomaterials and fabrication methods that will aid the design and effective delivery of tissue engineering treatments to the patient. It is likely that tissue engineering products will become commonplace within 20 years, but it is important to perform a full cost/benefit analysis for such treatments if they are to be funded and fully exploited within the tough constraints of healthcare budgets, such as those in the UK.

Concluding remarks

The application of tissue engineering provides new possibilities for therapeutic intervention and will extend what can be done for individuals with many chronic conditions such as arthritis. A greater focus on strong basic research is now helping to convert some of the past hype in tissue engineering into practical applications.

Glossary of terms

Confocal-FRAP = a technique using the analysis of fluorescent recovery after photobleaching with a confocal microscope to measure self-diffusion and tracer diffusion in polymer networks, such as those found in tissue extracellular matrix; ECM = extracellular matrix; PTF medium = medium containing 10% serum, 5ng/ml FGF-2, 10ng/ml platelet-derived growth factor-BB and 1ng/ml transforming growth factor β-1; SOX genes = (from 'Sry-type high-mobility-group-box') a family of genes that encode for transcription factors important during tissue development; these genes all contain a Sry-type high-mobility-group box, which is a protein motif involved in DNA binding; SOX9, L-SOX5 and SOX6 are expressed in chondrocytes.

Acknowledgements

We acknowledge the support of the Wellcome Trust and the Research Council Award (BBSRC, MRC, EPSRC) for Tissue Engineering: Cellular and Molecular Approaches, to University of Manchester and University of Liverpool.

References

1. **UK Centre for Tissue Engineering in the Universities of Manchester and Liverpool** [http://www.ukcte.org] [website]
2. **National Institutes of Health (USA) website.** [http://www.nih.gov/news/stemcell/primer.htm] [website]
3. Venn G, Billingham MEJ, Hardingham TE: **The increased proteoglycan synthesis in cartilage in experimental canine osteoarthritis does not reflect a permanent change in chondrocyte phenotype.** *Arthritis Rheum* 1995, **38**:525-531. [archival reference]
4. Hazell PK, Dent C, Fairclough JA, Bayliss MT, Hardingham TE: **Changes in glycosaminoglycan epitope levels in knee joint fluid following injury.** *Arthritis Rheum* 1995, **38**:953-959. [archival reference]

5. Hardingham TE: **Articular cartilage**. In *Oxford Textbook of Rheumatology*. Edited by Maddison PJ, Isenberg DA, Woo P, Glass DN. Oxford, New York, Tokyo: Oxford Medical Publications; 1998:405-420. [key review]

6. Goodstone NJ, Hardingham TE: **Tumour necrosis factor alpha is a more potent inducer of nitric oxide synthase than interleukin-1 beta in porcine articular chondrocytes**. *Rheumatology*, in press. [general reference]

7. Hardingham TE, Fosang AJ: **The structure of aggrecan and its turnover in cartilage**. *J Rheumatol* 1995, **22 (Suppl 43)**:86-90. [key review]

8. Fosang AJ, Hardingham TE: **Matrix proteoglycans**. In *Extracellular Matrix Vol 2*. Edited by Comper WD. The Netherlands: Harwood Academic Publishers; 1996:200-229. [key review]

9. Hardingham TE: **Cartilage: aggrecan-hyaluronan-link protein aggregates**. In *Science of Hyaluronan Today*. Edited by Hascall VC, Yanagishita M. Glycoforum Web Site 1998: [http://www.glycoforum.gr.jp] [key review]

10. Brittberg M, Lindahl A, Nilsson A, Ohlsson C, Isaksson O, Peterson L: **Treatment of deep cartilage defects in the knee with autologous chondrocyte transplantation**. *N Engl J Med* 1994, **331**:879-895. [archival reference]

11. Pittenger MF, Mackay AM, Beck SC, Jaiswal RK, Douglas R, Mosca JD, Moorman MA, Simonetti DW, Craig S and Marshak DR: **Multilineage potential of adult human mesenchymal stem cells**. *Science* 1999, **284**:143-147. [archival reference]

12. Thomson JA, Itskovitz-Eldor J, Shapiro SS, Waknitz MA, Swiergiel JJ, Marshall VS, Jones JM: **Embryonic stem cell lines derived from human blastocysts**. *Science* 1998, **282**:1145-1147. [archival reference]

13. Kolettas E, Muir HI, Barrett JC, Hardingham TE: **Chondrocyte phenotype and cell survival are regulated by culture conditions and by specific cytokines through the expression of Sox-9 transcription factor**. *Rheumatology* 2001, **40**:1146-1156. [general reference]

14. Lefebvre V, Li P, de Crombrugghe B: **A new long form of Sox5 (L-Sox5), Sox6 and Sox9 are coexpressed in chondrogenesis and cooperatively activate the type II collagen gene**. *EMBO J* 1998, **17**:2336-2346. [general reference]

15. Gotting C, Kuhn J, Zahn R, Brinkmann T, Kleesiek K: **Molecular cloning and expression of human UDP-D-xylose: proteoglycan core protein β-D-xylosyltransferase and its first isoform XT-II**. *J Mol Biol* 2000, **304**:517-528. [general reference]

16. Jakob M, Démarteau O, Schaefer D, Hintermann B, Dick W, Heberer M, Martin I: **Specific growth factors during the expansion and redifferentiation of adult human articular chondrocytes enhance chondrogenesis and cartilaginous tissue formation *in vitro***. *J Cell Biochem* 2000, **81**:368-377. [general reference]

17. Gribbon P, Hardingham TE: **Macromolecular diffusion of biological polymers measured by confocal fluorescence recovery after photobleaching**. *Biophysical J* 1998, **75**:1032-1039. [key review]

18. Gribbon P, Heng BC, Hardingham TE: **The molecular basis of the solution properties of hyaluronan investigated by confocal-FRAP**. *Biophysical J* 1999, **77**:2210-2216. [general reference]

19. Hardingham TE, Gribbon P: **Confocal-FRAP analysis of ECM molecular interactions**. In *Extracellular Matrix Protocols*. Edited by Streuli C, Grant ME. Totowa, NJ: Humana Press; 2000:83-93. [general reference]

20. Gribbon P, Hardingham TE: **Novel confocal-FRAP techniques for analysis of carbohydrate-protein interactions within the extracellular matrix**. In *Methods in Molecular Biology, Proteoglycan Protocols*. Edited by Lozzo RV. Totowa, NJ: Humana Press; 2001:487-494. [general reference]

21. Gribbon P, Heng BC, Hardingham TE: **The analysis of intermolecular interactions in concentrated hyaluronan solutions suggest no evidence for chain-chain association**. *Biochem J* 2000, **350**:329-335. [general reference]

22. **Tissue Engineering Pages** [http://www.tissue-engineering.net] [website]

23. **Tissue and Cell Engineering Society (UK)** [http://www.tces.org] [website]

24. **European Tissue Engineering Society** [http://www.etes.tissue-engineering.net] [website]

25. **Japanese Tissue Engineering Society** [http://www.med.nagoya-u.ac.jp/oral/jste/index.e.html] [website]

26. **Tissue Engineering Society International** [http://www.ptei.org/tes] [website]

Supplement Review

Insights into integrin–ligand binding and activation from the first crystal structure

Martin J Humphries

Wellcome Trust Centre for Cell-Matrix Research, School of Biological Sciences, University of Manchester, Manchester, UK

Correspondence: Martin J Humphries, Wellcome Trust Centre for Cell-Matrix Research, School of Biological Sciences, University of Manchester, 2.205 Stopford Building, Oxford Road, Manchester M13 9PT, UK. Tel: +44 161 275 5649; fax: +44 161 275 1505; e-mail: martin.humphries@man.ac.uk; departmental website: http://www.sbs.man.ac.uk; personal website: http://www.sbs.man.ac.uk/staff/user.asp?id=406&item=contact_details

Received: 27 February 2002
Revisions requested: 27 February 2002
Revisions received: 28 February 2002
Accepted: 3 March 2002
Published: 9 May 2002

Arthritis Res 2002, **4 (suppl 3)**:S69-S78

This article may contain supplementary data which can only be found online at http://arthritis-research.com/content/4/S3/S069

© 2002 BioMed Central Ltd
(Print ISSN 1465-9905; Online ISSN 1465-9913)

Chapter summary

Integrin receptors transduce bidirectional signals between extracellular adhesion molecules and intracellular cytoskeletal and signalling molecules. The structural basis of integrin signalling is unknown, but the recent publication of the first crystal structure of the extracellular domain of integrin αVβ3 has provided a number of insights. In this review, previous structure–function analyses of integrins that have employed biochemical and molecular biological approaches are placed in the context of the crystal structure, and novel routes to the development of integrin antagonists are discussed.

Keywords: adhesion, cations, extracellular matrix, integrin, structure

Introduction

The integrins are a family of αβ heterodimeric receptors that mediate dynamic linkages between extracellular adhesion molecules and the intracellular actin cytoskeleton. Integrins are expressed by all multicellular animals. In mammals, 18 α-subunit genes and eight β-subunit genes encode polypeptides that combine to form 24 different receptors. Both integrin subunits are noncovalently associated, type I transmembrane proteins with large extracellular domains and short cytoplasmic domains of 700–1100 and 30–50 residues, respectively.

Thousands of studies have investigated the molecular, cellular and organismal basis of integrin function. Gene deletion has demonstrated essential roles for almost all integrins, with the defects suggesting widespread contributions to the maintenance of tissue integrity and the promotion of cellular migration. Integrin–ligand interactions are now considered to provide physical support for cells to maintain cohesion, to permit the generation of traction forces to enable movement, and to organise signalling complexes to modulate differentiation and cell fate.

Animal model studies have also shown integrins to contribute to the progression of many common diseases, and have implicated them as potential therapeutic targets. The use of anti-integrin mAbs and ligand mimetic peptides has validated this suggestion for inflammatory, neoplastic, traumatic and infectious conditions. There is thus intense interest in determining the molecular basis of integrin function to identify approaches for regulating integrin function in disease. The recent publication of an integrin crystal structure promises to aid this process, most obviously by defining the ligand-binding pocket but also by suggesting mechanisms of receptor activation. These topics form the basis of this review.

A glossary of specialist terms used in this chapter appears at the end of the text section. A list of common abbreviations used in this issue appears just before the indexes.

An integrin crystal structure

The first three-dimensional structure of the extracellular domain of an integrin was published in October 2001, a decade and a half after the family was first defined [1]. The team responsible for this landmark study was led by Amin Arnaout (Massachusetts General Hospital, Boston, MA, USA), and comprised crystallographers at the Massachusetts General Hospital and the Argonne National Laboratory, IL, USA, and protein chemists at Merck KGaA in Darmstadt, Germany. The integrin selected for the work was αVβ3, a promiscuous receptor that binds vitronectin, fibronectin, von Willebrand factor and other extracellular matrix ligands. Both subunits of the heterodimer were expressed as full-length, soluble, glycosylated constructs in insect cells, and were crystallised in the presence of Ca^{2+}.

The overall shape of the crystallised conformer (resolved to 3.1 Å) is that of a large 'head' on two 'legs', with the N-termini of both subunits forming the head and the C-termini forming the legs (Fig. 1). Similar images of integrins had been obtained previously from rotary-shadowed and negatively stained specimens analysed by electron microscopy [2,3], and it had been correctly predicted that the legs would be the sites of subunit insertion into the plasma membrane. Furthermore, rotary-shadowed images of the platelet integrin αIIbβ3 bound to its major ligand fibrinogen revealed a highly specific interaction of the head of the integrin with the distal end of the fibrinogen hexamer, suggesting that the head contains the ligand-binding domain [4]. One major difference between the results from these two different structure-determination approaches, however, is the degree of extension of the legs. Both legs are bent in the crystal structure, whereas most electron microscopy images possess straightened legs. The relevance of these differences for receptor activation is discussed later.

In the crystal structure, the head of the integrin contains a seven-bladed β-propeller structure from the α-subunit (comprising seven ~60-amino-acid N-terminal repeats) and a von Willebrand factor A-domain from the β-subunit (termed the βA-domain; Fig. 1). The presence of these two folds had been predicted previously [5,6]. The βA-domain is anchored to the upper face of the β-propeller, with an arginine residue in a 3_{10} helical segment of the βA-domain (between βD and α5) linked to a hydrophobic 'cage' in the central shaft of the β-propeller. The remainder of the head composes an immunoglobulin module into which the βA-domain is inserted.

The α-subunit leg of the integrin contains three large β-sandwich domains. Between the so-called 'thigh' domain and the first of two 'calf' domains is a highly flexible 'knee' (or 'genu'), which is the site of the bend in the crystal structure. The more C-terminal domain of the calf domains contains a site that is cleaved post-translationally to yield

Figure 1

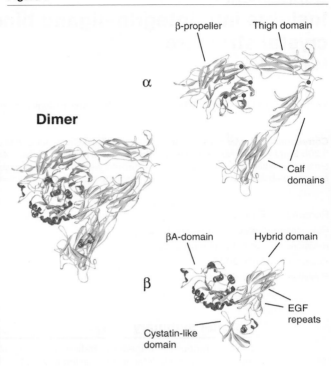

Crystal structure of integrin αVβ3 showing the dimer and individual subunits [1]. The domains that make up each integrin subunit are shown. Secondary structure elements are shown as red α-helices or cyan β-strands/ribbons. Blue circles represent the six cation-binding sites. The plexin–semaphorin–integrin domain and two of the four epidermal growth factor (EGF) repeats in the β-subunit are not visible in the structure. See Colour figure section.

an N-terminal heavy chain and a C-terminal light chain, although the atomic detail is not visible in the structure.

The β-subunit leg contains a plexin–semaphorin–integrin (PSI) domain, four epidermal growth factor-like repeats and a novel cystatin-like fold. The 50-residue PSI domain was also not visible in the structure, but it has been predicted to possess α-helical character [7]. The β-subunit knee region, formed from the conjunction of the hybrid domain, two epidermal growth factor repeats, and the PSI domain, is also bent.

It has previously been shown that truncated αIIb constructs that ended before N-terminal repeats 5, 6 or 7 all associated with their partner subunit β3 [8], and that limited proteolysis of αIIbβ3 bound to a ligand affinity matrix produced a 55/85 kDa heterodimer containing the N-termini of both subunits that reacted with dimer-specific antibodies [9]. The suggestion from these studies that the head region of the integrin contains the major sites of intersubunit association and dimerisation was therefore confirmed by the crystal structure.

Similarly, the spatial relationship between different sub-domains of integrin subunits had been partially determined by protein chemistry. For example, cyanogen bromide cleavage of αIIbβ3, followed by amino acid and N-terminal sequence analysis of the isolated fragments, permitted localisation of all S–S bonds, including a long-range bond joining the N-terminus to the region just after the hybrid domain (C5–C435) [10,11]. Although this bond is not visible in the crystal structure, it is clear that the PSI domain is positioned close enough to the junction between the hybrid domain and the first epidermal growth factor repeat to form the link. The close association of the N-terminal regions of both integrin subunits explains their mutual dependence for folding as assessed using confor-mation-dependent mAbs as probes [12,13]. mAbs that recognise only the α-subunit β-propeller or the βA-domain recognise heterodimeric integrin, while mAbs that are directed against the αA-domain or the legs of either subunit react with their respective monomer.

Integrins actually fall into two subfamilies based on the presence or absence of a 200-amino-acid module in the α-subunit. This module, which is present in nine α-sub-units, shares sequence homology with a von Willebrand factor A-domain, and is inserted between the second and third N-terminal repeats. Although αV lacks an A-domain, the crystal structure does suggest a potential location for the inserted αA-domain, at the side and the top of the β-propeller (see Fig. 3 later).

Prior to the αVβ3 structure, the only region of an integrin for which tertiary structure information was available was the αA-domain, as these domains fold independently and can be expressed in recombinant form. Crystal structures from four α-subunits (α1, α2, αL and αM) have been solved, the first being the αM A-domain [14]. The protein was found to adopt a classical αβ Rossmann fold in which the core of the module was made up of five parallel β-strands and one antiparallel β-strand, decorated peripher-ally by a series of seven α-helices (Fig. 2). A Mg²⁺ ion was located at one end of the module, where it was coordi-nated in an octahedral geometry by residues from three different loops and from a glutamate side chain from another A-domain molecule adjacent in the crystal lattice. This latter interaction was suggested to mimic a ligand–receptor complex [14]. Further crystal forms of the αM and αL A-domains were then reported in which water completed the metal coordination sphere and there was no equivalent of the glutamate ligand [15]. This raised doubts about the relevance of the cation-dependent differ-ence in the A-domain conformation, as discussed later.

The remainder of this review addresses two key questions posed by the integrin structure: how do ligands bind to the two subfamilies of integrin receptors, and how is receptor activation achieved in both types of integrin?

Figure 2

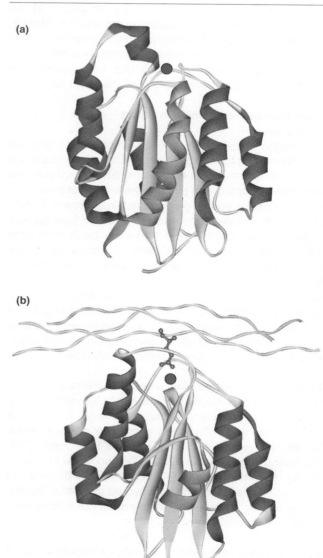

(a)

(b)

Comparison of the crystal structure of the α2 A-domain either **(a)** free or **(b)** complexed with a collagenous peptide [41,47]. Secondary structure elements are shown as red α-helices or cyan β-strands/ribbons. Spheres represent the divalent cation coordinated by the metal ion-dependent adhesion site (MIDAS) motif. The α7 helix is shown in pink. Note the difference in position of α7 in the two structures and the fact that the construct used in (b) contained a truncated α7 helix. The collagen glutamate residue that coordinates the MIDAS cation is shown in green. The MIDAS cation is shown as a blue circle. See Colour figure section.

Ligand-binding sites

The definition of the ligand-binding pocket of an integrin is important because it will generate insights into the relative contributions of different regions of receptor and ligand to the specific binding event. In addition, it will inform the process of drug design by identifying the receptor residues that participate in contacts with ligand. Ultimately, the solution of the tertiary structure of an integrin–ligand complex is needed to provide this information but, in the current absence of such structures, data from a number of experimental approaches have suggested the sites within integrins that bind ligand. This information can now be mapped onto the αVβ3 structure.

Non-αA-domain-containing integrins

Integrin chimeras
Inter-integrin chimeras have been employed to pinpoint sites determining ligand specificity. Subtle differences in the ligand-binding specificity of the related α5- and αV-subunits were recently exploited to pinpoint the regions of the α-subunits responsible, using a gain-of-function approach. The α5 subunit preferentially recognises the so-called 'synergy' site in type III repeat 9 of its ligand fibronectin, binds strongly to RGD peptides containing a C-terminal tryptophan residue (e.g. RGDGW), and binds specifically to the peptide RRETAWA. The high sequence identity (~50%) between α5 and αV permitted the construction of chimeras bearing hybrid native structures. It was reported that repeats 2 and 3 of α5, when introduced into αV, were sufficient to endow αV with the epitopes of all function-blocking anti-α5 mAbs and with the ligand-binding specificity of α5 [16].

The exchange of putative loops between the two subunits, based on the β-propeller prediction that turned out to be correct, led to the identification of a single residue, α5 W157, which was sufficient to convert αV into a receptor that strongly recognised RGDGW and RRETAWA [17]. This finding suggests that W157 (located in the loop connecting repeats 2 and 3) is close to the RGD-binding site on β1. Additional studies that measured the loss of ligand-binding activity in chimeras, while not as convincing, produced similar conclusions.

Similar analyses of the integrin β-subunit have highlighted the importance of the βA-domain. For example, replacement of β1 C187TSEQNC with β3 CYDMKTTC converted the ligand specificity of αVβ1 to be more similar to αVβ3 (i.e. increased binding of fibrinogen, von Willebrand factor and vitronectin) [18]. This sequence is located in a large disulfide-bonded loop between βB and βC adjacent to the cation-binding site in the βA-domain (Fig. 3).

Cross-linking
The discovery that many integrin ligands employ short, acidic peptide motifs (such as RGD and LDV) as key receptor-binding sequences [19] led to the use of chemical cross-linking as a means of pinpointing ligand-binding sites. In the earliest studies, RGD was found to cross-link primarily to the β3 A-domain residues 109–171 or residues 61–203 [20,21], and subsequently a 1:1 stoichiometric β3 (residues 119–131)–RGD complex was detected by mass spectroscopy [22].

Figure 3

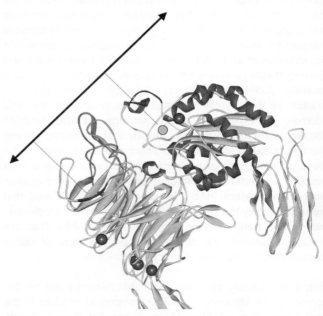

Enlarged view of the potential ligand-binding pocket of integrin αVβ3. The loops on the top of the α-subunit β-propeller implicated in ligand binding are coloured: purple, the 4–1 loop connecting repeats 1–2; orange, the 4–1 loop connecting repeats 2–3; pink, the 4–1 loop connecting repeats 3–4; green, the 2–3 loop in repeat 2; yellow, the 2–3 loop in repeat 3. The potential site for binding the fibronectin synergy sequence in α5β1, the β-strand 4 in repeat 3, is coloured blue (left side of β-propeller). The CYDMKTTC peptide sequence determining ligand specificity in β3 is coloured blue (top of βA-domain). Cations in the αVβ3 crystal structure are shown as blue spheres. The potential site of the metal ion-dependent adhesion site (MIDAS) cation is shown as a green circle. The site of insertion of an αA-domain would be in the orange loop of the β-propeller. The solid double arrow shows the possible orientation of ligand relative to the integrin, with dashed lines indicating speculative contacts with the MIDAS cation and β-strand 4 in repeat 3. See Colour figure section.

Synthetic peptides mimicking putative ligand-binding sites in integrins have been synthesised and tested for their ability to bind ligand directly and to inhibit ligand binding to native integrin. The most definitive study identified two overlapping peptides encompassing residues 204–229 of the β3 A-domain that blocked the binding of fibrinogen to purified αIIbβ3 [23]. The minimal active peptide was subsequently determined to be RNRDA in the α2–α3 loop [24].

Cross-linking has been performed with more potent peptidic ligands, the higher affinity of which might be expected to improve specificity. An LDV-based small molecule inhibitor of α4β1 (BIO-1494) that contained a single reactive amino group was cross-linked to purified or cell-expressed α4β1 [25]. The site of cross-linking was localised by CNBr peptide mapping to β1 (residues 130–146), a region that contains the putative metal binding site in the βA-domain. Similarly, tagged photoreactive cyclic RGD-containing ligands for αIIbβ3 cross-linked specifically to β3 in a cation-dependent manner [26]. Enzymatic and chemical digestions of the radiolabelled conjugate identified β3 (residues 99–118) as the RGD contact site. The similarity between the data generated for LDV and RGD ligands supports the notion of a common ligand-binding pocket for both motifs.

Mutagenesis and mAb epitope mapping
A key assumption underlying the use of epitope mapping to identify ligand-binding sites was that function-blocking mAbs act as competitive inhibitors. This now appears not to be the case, with many anti-integrin mAbs having been shown to function via allosteric mechanisms. The first indication of allosteric inhibition by an anti-integrin mAb came from studies of the binding of a fibronectin fragment and GRGDS peptide to α5β1 [27]. Ligand binding caused a dramatic attenuation of the mAb 13 epitope, and the antibody preferentially recognised the unoccupied conformation of the integrin. This suggested that the antibody inhibits ligand binding either by stabilising the unoccupied state of the receptor or by preventing a conformational change necessary for ligand occupancy. Similar results have subsequently been obtained for many other anti-integrin mAbs.

If anti-functional mAbs recognise integrin sites whose structures are perturbed as a consequence of ligand engagement, then specific sites within the ligand must be responsible for triggering the conformational changes. Using a series of recombinant fragments of fibronectin containing mutations in either the RGD or synergy active sites, the topology of ligand engagement to α5β1 was determined [28]. RGD preferentially perturbed anti-β1 mAb recognition of the integrin, while fragments mutated in the synergy site were unable to block binding of an anti-α5 mAb (P1D6) that mapped to L212 of β1 (β-strand 4 of repeat 3; Fig. 3). Further analysis of the links between ligand binding and mAb binding, in conjunction with the αVβ3 crystal structure, should allow the ligand to be positioned relative to the integrin.

Following the identification of regions within the α-subunit β-propeller and the β-subunit A-domain as putative regions for ligand binding, site-directed mutagenesis has been employed as a method to pinpoint residues contacting the ligand (see [29] for a review). In the α-subunit β-propeller, ligand binding is perturbed by mutations in loops that are predicted to lie on the 'top' of the domain, on the opposite face to the EF-hand-like sequences. In particular, the intra-repeat 2–3 loop of repeat 3 and the inter-repeat 4–1 loops joining repeats 1–2, 2–3 and 3–4 contain the key residues in all integrins tested to date (Fig. 3).

Similar results have come from mAb epitope mapping, where again the 4–1 loops joining repeats 1–2, 2–3 and

3–4 tend to contain key residues. In the integrin β-sub-units, virtually all inhibitory mAbs map to the βA-domain, and mutation of cation-coordinating residues in the βA-domain abolishes ligand binding in all integrins tested.

Alteration of residues within the α3–α4 loop and α4 helix (which are located on the same face as the divalent cation) also appear to be important for several integrins. In a recent study mapping fibrinogen binding sites in αIIbβ3, most of the critical residues were located at the edge of the upper face of the propeller, and several critical residues are located on the side of the propeller domain, in a region corresponding to the anti-α5 mAb P1D6 epitope [30].

Taken together, these data support a model in which the RGD or LDV ligand motif interacts with the cation-binding site in the βA-domain and additional contacts are made with the side of the α-subunit β-propeller (Fig. 3). The critical requirement for a carboxyl group in RGD or LDV has led to the suggestion that it participates in a direct coordination with the integrin-bound cation. Clearly, a ligand–integrin co-crystal is needed to determine the validity of this prediction.

αA-domain-containing integrins
In contrast to the aforementioned situation with non-αA-domain-containing integrins, the major ligand-binding site within those integrins that contain an αA-domain is clearly found within the 200-amino-acid polypeptide module that is inserted within the α-subunit β-propeller. A variety of evidence supports this conclusion, including the mapping of antifunctional mAbs to the αA-domain, the ability of the isolated domain to bind ligand, the inhibitory effects of mutations within the αA-domain on ligand binding, and, most recently, the resolution of the tertiary structure of an αA-domain–ligand complex.

Recombinant αA-domains
In solid-phase assays, the αM A-domain was found to bind to its ligands iC3b, intercellular adhesion molecule (ICAM)-1, ICAM-2, and fibrinogen in a divalent cation-dependent manner [31,32]. The αL A-domain similarly bound directly to purified recombinant ICAM-1 and also inhibited αLβ2-dependent T-cell adhesion to ICAM-1 [33]. The A-domains from α1 and α2 were found to bind to a variety of collagen isotypes, including types I and IV, and laminin in a cation-dependent manner [34–36]. Finally, the αD A-domain has been shown to contain a binding site for vascular cell adhesion molecule-1 [37].

αA-domain mutagenesis and chimeras
Inter-integrin chimeras have proven useful to map ligand-binding sites within αA-domains. Since mouse αLβ2 does not bind human ICAM-1, interspecies chimeras were constructed to identify the ligand-binding regions [38].

Replacement of two noncontiguous regions in the A-domain (residues 119–153 and 218–248) abolished binding. Key residues were found to be M140, E146, T243, and S245, which are located around the cation-binding site. In complementary studies, data from a large number of site-directed mutagenesis experiments, the results of which are summarised in [29], have suggested residues that are critical for interaction of αA-domains with ligands. In addition to cation-coordinating residues, which are essential for the function of all αA-domains, sites within the α3–α4 and βD–α5 loops are frequently implicated. Both loops are located on the top, cation-binding face of the αA-domain.

mAb epitope mapping
Recombinant A-domains of α1, α2, αL, αM, αX and αD have now been shown to contain the epitopes for antifunctional anti-α-subunit mAbs, and interspecies and inter-integrin chimeras have been used to localise antifunctional mAb epitopes to αA-domains. For example, three distinct epitopes within residues 126–150 of the αL A-domain, which is a region close to the cation-binding site, were identified using human–mouse point chimeras [39]. Also, the epitope of anti-α1 mAb AJH10 was localised to the loop between the α3 and α4 helices, which again contributes one of the metal coordination sites of the A-domain [40].

Integrin–ligand co-crystal
Many of these predictions were confirmed in an important study where the crystal structure of a complex between the α2 A-domain and a triple-helical collagen peptide containing a critical GFOGER motif was determined [41]. Three loops on the upper surface of the α2 A-domain that coordinate the cation were found to engage the collagen, with a glutamate residue from the collagen completing the coordination sphere of the metal, and an arginine residue from the same strand of the collagen helix bridging to D219 in the α3–α4 loop on top of the A-domain (Fig. 2). Two phenylalanine residues, one in the same collagen strand as the arginine residue and one in the trailing strand, made further contacts. Hydrogen bonds between the collagen main chain and N154, Y157 (βA–α1 loop) and H258 (βD–α5 loop) of the A-domain were seen.

The use of the glutamate residue for cation coordination suggests that the same mechanism may be employed by other integrin ligands to bind to αA-domains, and it also gives a snapshot of how aspartate-containing ligands may bind to βA-domains in those integrins that lack an αA-domain.

Integrin activation
For the interaction of integrins with their ligands to be meaningful for cellular function, the binding event must be able to trigger signal transduction. In part this will be accomplished by ligands inducing conformational changes in integrins that create effector binding sites and/or exposure of sites to

modifying enzymes. Following the solution of the αVβ3 crystal structure, it is possible to place information that has accumulated from a plethora of studies on integrin activation into a structural context. The long-term aims of this work are to elucidate the structural link between ligand binding and signalling, and to develop strategies for interfering therapeutically in the activation process.

Conformational changes mediating activation
Gross conformational changes in integrins have been detected by a variety of techniques. For almost all of these studies, αIIbβ3 has served as a prototype. For example, treatment of αIIbβ3 with ligand peptides increased its hydrolysis by thrombin and decreased its sedimentation coefficient [42], and platelet activation caused a change in the spatial separation or orientation of the extracellular domains of the two subunits as measured by fluorescence resonance energy transfer [43].

Much work has been carried out on activation-dependent binding of mAbs to integrins, some of which have been called ligand-induced binding sites (LIBS) [44]. Binding of cyclic mimics of different ligand peptides to αIIbβ3 in intact platelets was recently found to trigger distinct conformational alterations in the receptor, as indicated by the differential exposure of LIBS epitopes [45]. This suggests that different ligands may initiate different functional consequences within the receptor. The changes reported by mAbs can be triggered not only from the extracellular side of the integrin in response to ligand binding, but also from the cytoplasmic side of the plasma membrane, suggesting that conformational regulation is an important feature of bidirectional signalling by integrins [46].

Mechanisms of conformational change causing activation
Activation via the αA-domain
As already described, the first crystal structures of the αA-domain, solved for Mg^{2+}-occupied and Mn^{2+}-occupied forms of the αM domain, revealed different structures [14,15]. A comparative analysis revealed a change in metal coordination, a large (10 Å) shift of the C-terminal α7 helix, and the solvent exposure of F302. It was suggested that the movement of the α7 helix in the context of the intact integrin might induce further conformational changes outside of the αA-domain.

Comparison of the tertiary structure of the α2 A-domain–collagen peptide complex with the unoccupied α2 A-domain structure [41,47] revealed similar changes that provide insight into the process of receptor activation (Fig. 2). The central β-sheet did not change appreciably in the two structures, but there were significant changes in cation coordination and helix organisation. A 2.6 Å movement of the cation resulted in the formation of a direct bond with T221 (this residue coordinated via a water molecule in the unoccupied structure), a loss of coordination to D254, and a new coordination to E256. This reorganisation of the upper surface of the A-domain reoriented the side chains of Y157 and H258 such that they were able to fit into grooves in the collagen helix. The shifts in the positions of cation-coordinating loops triggered a rearrangement of the α7 and C helices, the former moving away and down by 10 Å and the latter unwinding. As a consequence of these movements, Y285 in the C helix moved 17 Å and hydrogen bonded with the repositioned α7 helix.

The relevance of the large movement of the α7 helix in both the αM and α2 structures as a consequence of ligand engagement is as yet unclear, but since this sequence is at the C-terminus of the αA-domain, and is therefore connected to the remainder of the subunit, it is tempting to speculate that the conformational change will be propagated through the receptor to initiate signalling. A key question is how the α7 helix contacts the remainder of the integrin, and in particular whether it interacts with the βA-domain to alter its conformation (i.e. whether a ligand-binding event in the αA-domain can have a similar effect to direct ligand binding at the βA-domain).

Activation in non-αA-domain-containing integrins
In contrast to the situation with αA-domain-containing integrins, little is currently known about the intramolecular activation of non-αA-domain-containing integrins. If the ligand-responsive subset of activating mAbs recognises sites that occur naturally in integrins, the location of their epitopes will inform an understanding of the process of receptor activation.

A large number of studies have thus pinpointed activating mAb epitopes by mutagenesis and the use of interspecies integrin chimeras, and these can now be placed in the context of the crystal structure. The overwhelming majority of activating mAbs recognise the β-subunit and, interestingly, while their epitopes are distributed throughout the polypeptide, suggesting large-scale alteration in the conformation of the whole integrin during activation, a number of specific regions appear to be recognised. These regions include the extreme N-terminus of the β-subunit in the PSI domain [48], the βA-domain [49], the hybrid domain [50], and the epidermal growth factor repeats [51,52]. The α1 and α2 helices of the βA-domain, in particular, contain the epitopes for a large number of mAbs, some of which were function blocking and others of which were stimulatory for ligand binding [49]. As these elements are linked to the cation-binding site in the βA-domain, it is conceivable that ligand binding triggers an alteration in their positioning, and that this change is then propagated to the rest of the integrin.

Integrins are relatively large receptors, and a major challenge is to understand how proximal conformational changes in the ligand-binding pocket are passed to the rest of the integrin, and ultimately to the cytoplasmic domains. As there is currently little direct information to inform these issues, any theories will be highly speculative. There is evidence, based on competitive ELISA experiments, that the domains of the α5-subunit and the β1-subunit recognised by mAb JBS5/16 (anti-α5) and mAb 13/12G10 (anti-β1) are spatially close, and that the distance between these two domains increased when α5β1 was occupied by divalent cations [53]. This suggested that divalent cations induced a conformational relaxation in the integrin that resulted in exposure of ligand-binding sites, and that these sites were located near to the interface between the α-subunit and the β-subunit.

The structural homology between the integrin head and heterotrimeric G-proteins would also be consistent with a conformational repositioning of these regions of the receptor [1]. The bending of the legs in the αVβ3 crystal structure, whether a true indication of the native structure of the integrin or a crystallisation artifact, suggests that there are sites in both subunits that exhibit extreme flexibility. While this suggests that the head of the integrin may pivot around the α-subunit thigh–calf junction and the β-subunit hybrid–epidermal growth factor–PSI linkage, it also raises questions about how shape changes induced by ligand binding are able to pass two flexible joints. By constraining the relative position of the membrane-proximal domains of integrin αLβ2 with coiled-coil extensions, it was found that the integrin could be inactivated by bringing its legs close together (with an acid–base coiled coil) and could be activated by keeping them apart (with a base–base extension) [54]. Similarly, proteolytic cleavage of a constrained integrin had the same activating effect [55]. This suggests that a gross repositioning of the legs and cytoplasmic domains underlies integrin activation.

Role of cation-binding sites
The binding of ligands to integrins is universally divalent cation dependent, and occupancy by different cations results in different levels of ligand binding. It is therefore important to consider the location, specificity and functional role of cation-binding sites. Integrin-ligand binding is usually stimulated by Mg^{2+} and Mn^{2+}, and inhibited by Ca^{2+}, as shown first for α5β1 [56]. In the αVβ3 crystal structure, six Ca^{2+}-binding sites are seen (Fig. 1). Four of these lie in β–loop–β structures on the lower face of the β-propeller, and another site is the knee region of the α-subunit. The top face of the βA-domain contains a potential cation-binding site, known as the metal-ion dependent adhesion site (MIDAS), although this is unoccupied in the crystal structure. A novel site is seen adjacent to the MIDAS, however, which the authors termed 'adjacent to MIDAS' (ADMIDAS).

The functional role of the different cation binding sites is discussed later. Apart from their occupancy in the crystal structure, the most convincing evidence that the EF-hand-like sequences in the β-propeller bind calcium derives from the fact that the epitope for Ca^{2+}-dependent mAb CBRM1/20 has been localised to the EF-hand-like sequence in repeat 5 of αM [57].

Crystal structures of αA-domains have proven the presence of a cation-binding site in this module. A characteristic 'DXSXS' motif (D140GSGS in αM) located at the junction of the βA strand and the loop between βA and α1 was found to contribute three of these coordination sites: D140 via a water molecule, and S142 and S144 directly. Two sequentially distant residues, T209 at the C-terminal end of the α3–α4 loop and D242 at the start of the βD–α5 loop, also coordinated, the former directly and the latter via water. Given the sequence and functional homology between the A-domains in both subunits, a similar motif is also highly likely to be found in βA-domains. However, the fact that the crystals were grown in calcium may explain the lack of occupancy.

Until further crystal forms are obtained, it is not clear where Mn^{2+} and Mg^{2+} bind within integrins. However, there is much biochemical evidence to suggest sites. Using the interaction between α5β1 and fibronectin as a model system, a comprehensive analysis of the effects of Mn^{2+}, Mg^{2+}, and Ca^{2+} on ligand binding was carried out [58]. Each cation had distinct effects on ligand-binding capacity: Mn^{2+} promoted high levels of ligand binding, Mg^{2+} promoted low levels of binding, and Ca^{2+} failed to support binding. Ca^{2+} strongly inhibited Mn^{2+}-supported ligand binding, but this inhibition was noncompetitive, suggesting that Ca^{2+} recognises different cation-binding sites to Mn^{2+}. In contrast, Ca^{2+} acted as a direct competitive inhibitor of Mg^{2+}-supported ligand binding, implying that Ca^{2+} can displace Mg^{2+} from the integrin. However, low concentrations of Ca^{2+} greatly increased the apparent affinity of Mg^{2+} for its binding site, suggesting the existence of a distinct high-affinity Ca^{2+}-binding site.

In summary, evidence is accumulating to suggest that non-αA-domain-containing integrins generally contain a cation-binding site that is required for ligand binding and that interacts with Mg^{2+}, Mn^{2+} (to promote binding) or Ca^{2+} (in which case binding does not occur). In addition, occupancy of a separate calcium-binding site, or class of sites, can enhance ligand binding in an allosteric, synergistic manner. The location of the different sites is not yet defined, although it is likely that the Mg^{2+}/Mn^{2+}/Ca^{2+}-binding site is the MIDAS site in the βA-domain. The role of the ADMIDAS site is currently unclear, although it may be an inhibitory Ca^{2+}-binding site [59].

An interesting feature of some LIBS mAbs is that their epitopes are also regulated by divalent cations (for example [53,60]). Since cations also regulate ligand binding, and in some cases the pattern of effects by different cations is the same for mAb and ligand binding [53], it appears that some activating mAbs recognise sites that are regulated by natural modulators of integrin function. One possibility is that cation-responsive activating mAbs recognise naturally occurring conformers of integrins.

Cation effects on integrin conformation have been reported to vary between dimers. Mn^{2+} or ligand induced 9EG7 or 15/7 binding strongly on α4β1, moderately on α5β1, weakly on α2β1, and undetectably on α3β1 and α6β1 [61]. Ca^{2+} uniquely supported constitutive expression of the 9EG7 epitope on α4β1. Thus, not all LIBS mAbs will be faithful reporters of occupancy.

Finally, the different properties of activating antibodies imply that care should be taken in using them as probes of integrin function. It is probable that different mAbs will stabilise different integrin conformers and, if so, the consequences for signalling may also differ.

Concluding remarks

Now that the feasibility of generating a crystal structure of an integrin is proven, many other structural questions can be asked. Key targets for future crystallography studies include different integrin conformers representing different activation states, ligand-occupied integrins, and integrins containing an αA-domain.

Although, as already described, the general location of the ligand-binding pocket of an integrin can now be predicted, the atomic detail will require an integrin–ligand co-crystal. Once this is achieved, the process of drug development based on ligand mimetics will be aided. Interestingly, the allosteric inhibition of ligand binding by antifunctional anti-integrin mAbs implies that it may be feasible to synthesise small molecule inhibitors that function in the same way. Such inhibitors may not possess the agonistic properties of ligand mimetics, and may therefore not suffer from mechanism-related side effects.

As yet, the generation of allosteric integrin inhibitors is in its infancy, although a recent report of the tertiary structure of the αL A-domain in complex with lovastatin has provided an insight into such a mode of action. Statins are drugs used clinically for lowering cholesterol levels, but they are also reported to inhibit the interaction of αLβ2 with ICAM-1 [62,63]. Using nuclear magnetic resonance spectroscopy and X-ray crystallography, the inhibitor was shown to bind to the αL A-domain in a crevice between the central β-sheet and the C-terminal α7 helix. This finding suggests that the inhibitor may function by preventing movement of α7 relative to the rest of the domain and preventing subsequent intramolecular conformational changes [64]. It is possible that a similar approach may be used to develop allosteric inhibitors of the βA-domain, and that this may spawn a new generation of anti-adhesive drugs.

Glossary of terms

ADMIDAS = adjacent to metal ion-dependent adhesion site; LIBS = ligand-induced binding site; MIDAS = metal ion-dependent adhesion site; PSI = plexin–semaphorin–integrin.

Acknowledgements

The work discussed within this review was supported by grants from the Wellcome Trust.

References

1. Xiong JP, Stehle T, Diefenbach B, Zhang R, Dunker R, Scott DL, Joachimiak A, Goodman SL, Arnaout MA: **Crystal structure of the extracellular segment of integrin αVβ3.** *Science* 2001, **294:** 339-345. [general reference]
2. Carrell NA, Fitzgerald LA, Steiner B, Erickson HP, Phillips DR: **Structure of human platelet membrane glycoproteins IIb and IIIa as determined by electron microscopy.** *J Biol Chem* 1985, **260:**1743-1749. [general reference]
3. Nermut MV, Green NM, Eason P, Yamada SS, Yamada KM: **Electron microscopy and structural model of human fibronectin receptor.** *EMBO J* 1988, **7:**4093-4099. [general reference]
4. Weisel JW, Nagaswami C, Vilaire G, Bennett JS: **Examination of the platelet membrane glycoprotein IIb–IIIa complex and its interaction with fibrinogen and other ligands by electron microscopy.** *J Biol Chem* 1992, **267:**16637-16643. [general reference]
5. Springer TA: **Folding of the N-terminal, ligand-binding region of integrin α-subunits into a β-propeller domain.** *Proc Natl Acad Sci USA* 1997, **94:**65-72. [general reference]
6. Tuckwell DS, Humphries MJ: **A structure prediction for the ligand-binding region of the integrin β subunit: evidence for the presence of a von Willebrand factor A domain.** *FEBS Lett* 1997, **400:**297-303. [general reference]
7. Bork P, Doerks T, Springer TA, Snel B: **Domains in plexins: links to integrins and transcription factors.** *Trends Biochem Sci* 1999, **24:**261-263. [general reference]
8. Wilcox DA, Paddock CM, Lyman S, Gill JC, Newman PJ: **Glanzmann thrombasthenia resulting from a single amino acid substitution between the second and third calcium-binding domains of GPIIb: role of the GPIIb amino terminus in integrin subunit association.** *J Clin Invest* 1995, **95:**1553-1560. [general reference]
9. Lam SCT: **Isolation and characterization of a chymotryptic fragment of platelet glycoprotein IIb–IIIa retaining Arg-Gly-Asp binding activity.** *J Biol Chem* 1992, **267:**5649-5655. [general reference]
10. Calvete JJ, Henschen A, Gonzalez-Rodriguez J: **Complete localization of the intrachain disulfide bonds and the N-glycosylation points in the α-subunit of human platelet glycoprotein IIb.** *Biochem J* 1989, **261:**561-568. [general reference]
11. Calvete JJ, Henschen A, Gonzalez-Rodriguez J: **Assignment of disulfide bonds in human platelet GPIIIa. A disulfide pattern for the β-subunits of the integrin family.** *Biochem J* 1991, **274:** 63-71. [general reference]
12. Huang C, Springer TA: **Folding of the β-propeller domain of the integrin αL subunit is independent of the I domain and dependent on the β2 subunit.** *Proc Natl Acad Sci USA* 1997, **94:** 3162-3167. [general reference]
13. Huang C, Lu C, Springer TA: **Folding of the conserved domain but not of flanking regions in the integrin β2 subunit requires association with the α subunit.** *Proc Natl Acad Sci USA* 1997, **94:**3156-3161. [general reference]
14. Lee JO, Rieu P, Arnaout MA, Liddington R: **Crystal structure of the A domain from the α subunit of integrin CR3 (CD11b/CD18).** *Cell* 1995, **80:**631-638. [general reference]
15. Lee JO, Bankston LA, Arnaout MA, Liddington RC: **Two conformations of the integrin A-domain (I-domain): a pathway for activation?** *Structure* 1995, **3:**1333-1340. [key review]

16. Mould P, Askari JA, Humphries MJ: **Molecular basis of ligand recognition by integrin α5β1: Specificity of ligand binding is determined by amino acid sequences in the second and third NH2-terminal repeats of the α subunit.** *J Biol Chem* 2000, **275:** 20324-20336. [general reference]
17. Humphries JD, Askari JA, Zhang XP, Takada Y, Humphries MJ, Mould P: **Molecular basis of ligand recognition by integrin α5β1: Specificity of Arg-Gly-Asp binding is determined by Trp157 of the α subunit.** *J Biol Chem* 2000, **275:**20337-20345. [general reference]
18. Takagi J, Kamata T, Meredith J, Puzon-McLaughlin W, Takada Y: **Changing ligand specificities of αVβ1 and αVβ3 integrins by swapping a short diverse sequence of the β subunit.** *J Biol Chem* 1997, **272:**19794-19800. [general reference]
19. Humphries MJ: **The molecular basis and specificity of integrin–ligand interactions.** *J Cell Sci* 1990, **97:**585-592. [key review]
20. D'Souza SE, Ginsberg MH, Burke TA, Lam SCT, Plow EF: **Localization of an Arg-Gly-Asp recognition site within an integrin adhesion receptor.** *Science* 1988, **242:**91-93. [general reference]
21. Smith JW, Cheresh DA: **The Arg-Gly-Asp binding domain of the vitronectin receptor. Photoaffinity cross-linking implicates amino acid residues 61-203 of the β subunit.** *J Biol Chem* 1988, **263:**18726-18731. [general reference]
22. D'Souza SE, Haas TA, Piotrowicz RS, Byers-Ward V, McGrath DE, Soule HR, Cierniewski C, Plow EF, Smith JW: **Ligand and cation binding are dual functions of a discrete segment of the integrin β3 subunit: cation displacement is involved in ligand binding.** *Cell* 1994, **79:**659-667. [general reference]
23. Charo IF, Nannizzi L, Phillips DR, Hsu MA, Scarborough RM: **Inhibition of fibrinogen binding to GP IIb–IIIa by a GP IIIa peptide.** *J Biol Chem* 1991, **266:**1415-1421. [general reference]
24. Steiner B, Trzeciak A, Pfenninger G, Kouns WC: **Peptides derived from a sequence within β3 integrin bind to platelet αIIbβ3 (GPIIb–IIIa) and inhibit ligand binding.** *J Biol Chem* 1993, **268:**6870-6873. [general reference]
25. Chen LL, Lobb RR, Cuervo JH, Lin K, Adams SP, Pepinsky RB: **Identification of ligand binding sites on integrin α4β1 through chemical crosslinking.** *Biochemistry* 1998, **37:**8743-8753. [general reference]
26. Bitan G, Scheibler L, Greenberg Z, Rosenblatt M, Chorev M: **Mapping the integrin αVβ3–ligand interface by photoaffinity cross-linking.** *Biochemistry* 1999, **38:**3414-3420. [general reference]
27. Mould AP, Akiyama SK, Humphries MJ: **The inhibitory anti-β1 integrin monoclonal antibody 13 recognizes an epitope that is attenuated by ligand occupancy. Evidence for allosteric inhibition of integrin function.** *J Biol Chem* 1996, **271:**20365-20374. [general reference]
28. Mould AP, Askari JA, Aota S, Yamada KM, Irie A, Takada Y, Mardon HJ, Humphries MJ: **Defining the topology of integrin α5β1–fibronectin interactions using inhibitory anti-α5 and anti-β1 monoclonal antibodies. Evidence that the synergy sequence of fibronectin is recognized by the amino-terminal repeats of the α5 subunit.** *J Biol Chem* 1997, **272:**17283-17292. [general reference]
29. Humphries MJ: **Integrin structure.** *Biochem Soc Trans* 2000, **28:** 311-339. [key review]
30. Kamata T, Tieu KK, Springer TA, Takada Y: **Amino acid residues in the αIIb subunit that are critical for ligand binding to integrin αIIbβ3 are clustered in the beta-propeller model.** *J Biol Chem* 2001, **276:**44275-44283. [general reference]
31. Ueda T, Rieu P, Brayer J, Arnaout MA: **Identification of the complement iC3b binding site in the β2 integrin CR3 (CD11b/CD18).** *Proc Natl Acad Sci USA* 1994, **91:**10680-10684. [general reference]
32. Zhou L, Lee DHS, Plescia J, Lau CY, Altieri DC: **Differential ligand binding specificities of recombinant CD11b/CD18 integrin I-domain.** *J Biol Chem* 1994, **269:**17075-17079. [general reference]
33. Randi AM, Hogg N: **I Domain of β2 integrin lymphocyte function-associated antigen-1 contains a binding site for ligand intercellular adhesion molecule-1.** *J Biol Chem* 1994, **269:** 12395-12398. [general reference]
34. Tuckwell D, Calderwood DA, Green LJ: **Humphries MJ. Integrin α2 I-domain is a binding site for collagens.** *J Cell Sci* 1995, **108:**1629-1637. [general reference]

35. Calderwood DA, Tuckwell DS, Eble J, Kuhn K, Humphries MJ: The integrin α1 A-domain is a ligand binding site for collagens and laminin. *J Biol Chem* 1997, **272**:12311-12317. [general reference]

36. Kamata T, Takada Y: Direct binding of collagen to the I domain of integrin α2β1 (VLA-2, CD49b/CD29) in a divalent cation-independent manner. *J Biol Chem* 1994, **269**:26006-26010. [general reference]

37. Van der Vieren M, Crowe DT, Hoekstra D, Vazeux R, Hoffman PA, Grayson MH, Bochner BS, Gallatin WM, Staunton DE: The leukocyte integrin αDβ2 binds VCAM-1: evidence for a binding interface between I domain and VCAM-1. *J Immunol* 1999, **163**:1984-1990. [general reference]

38. Huang C, Springer TA: A binding interface on the I domain of lymphocyte function-associated antigen-1 (LFA-1) required for specific interaction with intercellular adhesion molecule 1 (ICAM-1). *J Biol Chem* 1995, **270**:19008-19016. [general reference]

39. Champe M, McIntyre BW, Berman PW: Monoclonal antibodies that block the activity of leukocyte function-associated antigen 1 recognize three discrete epitopes in the inserted domain of CD11a. *J Biol Chem* 1995, **270**:1388-1394. [general reference]

40. Gotwals PJ, Chi-Rosso G, Ryan ST, Sizing I, Zafari M, Benjamin C, Singh J, Venyaminov SY, Pepinsky RB, Koteliansky V: Divalent cations stabilize the α1β1 integrin I domain. *Biochemistry* 1999, **38**:8280-8288. [general reference]

41. Emsley J, Knight CG, Farndale RW, Barnes MJ, Liddington RC: Structural basis of collagen recognition by integrin α2β1. *Cell* 2000, **101**:47-56. [general reference]

42. Parise LV, Helgerson SL, Steiner B, Nannizzi L, Phillips DR: Synthetic peptides derived from fibrinogen and fibronectin change the conformation of purified platelet glycoprotein IIb–IIIa. *J Biol Chem* 1987, **262**:12597-12602. [general reference]

43. Sims PJ, Ginsberg MH, Plow EF, Shattil SJ: Effect of platelet activation on the conformation of the plasma membrane glycoprotein IIb–IIIa complex. *J Biol Chem* 1991, **266**:7345-7352. [general reference]

44. Ginsberg MH, Frelinger AL, Lam SCT, Forsyth J, McMillan R, Plow EF, Shattil SJ: Analysis of platelet aggregation disorders based on flow cytometric analysis of membrane glycoprotein IIb–IIIa with conformation-specific monoclonal antibodies. *Blood* 1990, **76**:2017-2023. [general reference]

45. Cierniewski CS, Byzova T, Papierak M, Haas TA, Niewiarowska J, Zhang L, Cieslak M, Plow EF: Peptide ligands can bind to distinct sites in integrin αIIbβ3 and elicit different functional responses. *J Biol Chem* 1999, **274**:16923-16932. [general reference]

46. Mastrangelo AM, Homan SM, Humphries MJ, LaFlamme SE: Amino acid motifs required for isolated β cytoplasmic domains to regulate 'in trans' β1 integrin conformation and function in cell attachment. *J Cell Sci* 1999, **112**:217-229. [general reference]

47. Emsley J, King SL, Bergelson JM, Liddington RC: Crystal structure of the I domain from integrin α2β1. *J Biol Chem* 1997, **272**:28512-28517. [general reference]

48. Honda S, Tomiyama Y, Pelletier AJ, Annis D, Honda Y, Orchekowski R, Ruggeri Z, Kunicki TJ: Topography of ligand-induced binding sites, including a novel cation-sensitive epitope (AP5) at the amino terminus, of the human integrin β3 subunit. *J Biol Chem* 1995, **270**:11947-11954. [general reference]

49. Takada Y, Puzon W: Identification of a regulatory region of integrin β1 subunit using activating and inhibiting antibodies. *J Biol Chem* 1993, **268**:17597-17601. [general reference]

50. Puzon-McLaughlin W, Yednock TA, Takada Y: Regulation of conformation and ligand binding function of integrin α5β1 by the β1 cytoplasmic domain. *J Biol Chem* 1996, **271**:16580-16585. [general reference]

51. Bazzoni G, Shih DT, Buck CA, Hemler ME: Monoclonal antibody 9EG7 defines a novel β1 integrin epitope induced by soluble ligand and manganese, but inhibited by calcium. *J Biol Chem* 1995, **270**:25570-25577. [general reference]

52. Wilkins JA, Li A, Ni H, Stupack DG, Shen C: Control of β1 integrin function. Localization of stimulatory epitopes. *J Biol Chem* 1996, **271**:3046-3051. [general reference]

53. Mould AP, Garratt AN, Puzon-McLaughlin W, Takada Y, Humphries MJ: Regulation of integrin function: evidence that bivalent-cation-induced conformational changes lead to the unmasking of ligand-binding sites within integrin α5β1. *Biochem J* 1998, **331**:821-828. [general reference]

54. Lu C, Takagi J, Springer TA: Association of the membrane-proximal regions of the α and β subunit cytoplasmic domains constrains an integrin in the inactive state. *J Biol Chem* 2001, **276**:14642-14648. [general reference]

55. Takagi J, Erickson HP, Springer TA: C-terminal opening mimics 'inside-out' activation of integrin α5β1. *Nat Struct Biol* 2001, **8**: 412-416. [general reference]

56. Gailit J, Ruoslahti E: Regulation of the fibronectin receptor affinity by divalent cations. *J Biol Chem* 1988, **263**:12927-12932. [general reference]

57. Oxvig C, Springer TA: Experimental support for a β-propeller domain in integrin α-subunits and a calcium binding site on its lower surface. *Proc Natl Acad Sci USA* 1998, **95**:4870-4875. [general reference]

58. Mould AP, Akiyama SK, Humphries MJ: Regulation of integrin α5β1–fibronectin interactions by divalent cations. Evidence for distinct classes of binding sites for Mn^{2+}, Mg^{2+}, and Ca^{2+}. *J Biol Chem* 1995, **270**:26270-26277. [general reference]

59. Cierniewska-Cieslak A, Cierniewski CS, Blecka K, Papierak M, Michalec L, Zhang L, Haas TA, Plow EF: Identification and characterization of two cation binding sites in the integrin β3 subunit. *J Biol Chem* 2002, epub ahead of print. [general reference]

60. Dransfield I, Hogg N: Regulated expression of magnesium binding epitope on leukocyte integrin α subunits. *EMBO J* 1989, **8**:3759-3765. [general reference]

61. Bazzoni G, Ma L, Blue ML, Hemler ME: Divalent cations and ligands induce conformational changes that are highly divergent among β1 integrins. *J Biol Chem* 1998, **273**:6670-6678. [general reference]

62. Kallen J, Welzenbach K, Ramage P, Geyl D, Kriwacki R, Legge G, Cottens S, Weitz-Schmidt G, Hommel U: Structural basis for LFA-1 inhibition upon lovastatin binding to the CD11a I-domain. *J Mol Biol* 1999, **292**:1-9. [general reference]

63. Weitz-Schmidt G, Welzenbach K, Brinkmann V, Kamata T, Kallen J, Bruns C, Cottens S, Takada Y, Hommel U: Statins selectively inhibit leukocyte function antigen-1 by binding to a novel regulatory integrin site. *Nat Med* 2001, **7**:687-692. [general reference]

64. McDowall A, Leitinger B, Stanley P, Bates PA, Randi AM, Hogg N: The I domain of integrin leukocyte function-associated antigen-1 is involved in a conformational change leading to high affinity binding to ligand intercellular adhesion molecule 1 (ICAM-1). *J Biol Chem* 1998, **273**:27396-27403. [general reference]

Vascular biology

Supplement Review
Angiogenesis in rheumatoid arthritis
Ewa M Paleolog

Kennedy Institute of Rheumatology Division, Faculty of Medicine, Imperial College of Science, Technology and Medicine, London, UK

Correspondence: Dr Ewa Paleolog, Kennedy Institute of Rheumatology Division, Faculty of Medicine, Imperial College of Science Technology and Medicine, Arthritis Research Campaign Building, 1 Aspenlea Road, Hammersmith, London W6 8LH, UK. Tel: +44 (0)20 8383 4481; fax: +44 (0)20 8383 4499; email: e.paleolog@ic.ac.uk

Received: 20 November 2001
Revisions requested: 21 January 2002
Revisions received: 8 February 2002
Accepted: 9 February 2002
Published: 9 May 2002

Arthritis Res 2002, 4 (suppl 3):S81-S90

This article may contain supplementary data which can only be found online at http://arthritis-research.com/content/4/S3/S081

© 2002 BioMed Central Ltd
(Print ISSN 1465-9905; Online ISSN 1465-9913)

Chapter summary

The expansion of the synovial lining of joints in rheumatoid arthritis (RA) and the subsequent invasion by the pannus of underlying cartilage and bone necessitate an increase in the vascular supply to the synovium, to cope with the increased requirement for oxygen and nutrients. The formation of new blood vessels – termed 'angiogenesis' – is now recognised as a key event in the formation and maintenance of the pannus in RA. This pannus is highly vascularised, suggesting that targeting blood vessels in RA may be an effective future therapeutic strategy. Disruption of the formation of new blood vessels would not only prevent delivery of nutrients to the inflammatory site, but could also lead to vessel regression and possibly reversal of disease. Although many proangiogenic factors are expressed in the synovium in RA, the potent proangiogenic cytokine vascular endothelial growth factor (VEGF) has been shown to a have a central involvement in the angiogenic process in RA. The additional activity of VEGF as a vascular permeability factor may also increase oedema and hence joint swelling in RA. Several studies have shown that targeting angiogenesis in animal models of arthritis ameliorates disease. Our own study showed that inhibition of VEGF activity in murine collagen-induced arthritis, using a soluble VEGF receptor, reduced disease severity, paw swelling, and joint destruction. Although no clinical trials of anti-angiogenic therapy in RA have been reported to date, the blockade of angiogenesis – and especially of VEGF – appears to be a promising avenue for the future treatment of RA.

Keywords: angiogenesis, therapy, VEGF

Introduction

Inflammatory joint diseases such as rheumatoid arthritis (RA) are not only a major cause of disability, but are also frequently associated with increased morbidity and mortality. For example, patients with RA have been found to have a higher prevalence of angina pectoris and stroke than non-patients. Research into the mechanisms underlying musculoskeletal disorders and into the development of newer and more effective therapeutic drugs is thus highly desirable.

RA is a chronic and destructive disease, which typically affects the peripheral joints but may affect any synovial joint in the body. The synovium in RA becomes inflamed and increases greatly in mass, because of hyperplasia of the lining cells. The volume of synovial fluid increases, resulting in joint swelling and pain. Blood-derived cells, including T cells, B cells, macrophages, and plasma cells, infiltrate the sublining of the synovium. Although RA shares these histological features (namely, infiltration and hyperplasia) with other inflammatory arthritides, a particularly characteristic feature of RA is the predilection for the synovium to become locally invasive at the synovial interface with cartilage and bone. This invasive and destructive front (termed 'pannus') causes the erosions observed in

---

A glossary of specialist terms used in this chapter appears at the end of the text section. A list of common abbreviations used in this issue appears just before the indexes.

Figure 1

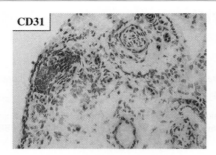
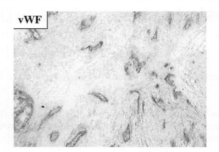

Expression of CD31 and von Willebrand factor in RA synovium. Frozen or paraffin-embedded sections were stained using antibodies against human CD31 or von Willebrand factor (vWf). Samples were then incubated with biotinylated anti-mouse or anti-goat immunoglobulin, followed by streptavidin–horseradish peroxidase. Immune complexes were detected using 3,3′-diaminobenzidine. See Colour figure section.

RA. Progressive destruction of the articular cartilage, sub-chondral bone, and periarticular soft tissues eventually combine to produce the deformities characteristic of long-standing RA. These deformities result in functional deterioration and profound disability in the long term.

An attribute of RA that has long been recognised but has only recently risen to prominence, because of an increased understanding of the underlying mechanisms, is the role of the vasculature in these invasive and destructive processes. There are abundant blood vessels in RA synovium (Fig. 1) and, given the features of RA outlined above – infiltration by blood-derived cells, hyperplasia, oedema, invasiveness – it is perhaps obvious that these vessels are likely to be involved in the development of RA. Indeed, the endothelial cells lining the blood vessels appear to be an active target for the action of cytokines and mitogens, permeability factors, and matrix-degrading enzymes, and the cells' response to these factors both maintains and promotes RA. In particular, the formation of new blood vessels – 'angiogenesis' – has been suggested to be of importance in the pathogenesis of RA, in that the expansion of synovial tissue necessitates a compensatory increase in the number and density of synovial blood vessels. The arthritic synovium is in fact a very hypoxic environment, which is a potent signal for the generation of new blood vessels.

It is now generally accepted that angiogenesis is central to maintaining and promoting RA. It is also possible that a potential method of attenuating development of the pannus is to interfere with its blood supply. This possibility is supported by several recent studies in animal models of arthritis which have suggested that blocking angiogenesis during the course of RA might actually be of therapeutic benefit.

This chapter focuses on the regulation of angiogenesis in RA, on the application of angiogenesis inhibitors in animal models of arthritis, and on the potential for development of new vascular-targeted therapies for treatment of RA.

Historical background

A review in 1982 suggested that in RA, "microcirculatory compromise, concomitant with an increase in metabolic needs of synovial tissue, may initiate tissue injury via anoxia and acidosis, resulting in hydrolytic enzyme release, increased vascular permeability and acceleration of inflammatory processes" [1]. Since that paper by Rothschild and Masi, the number of publications on the PubMed database at the National Library of Medicine citing 'angiogenesis' (or 'angiogenic') and 'arthritis' has risen exponentially, from just 5 in the years 1980–1984, to 130 in 1995–1999. In 2000 and 2001 alone, there were 99 such references (at the time of writing, November 2001).

Changes in the density of blood vessels in the synovium and alterations in endothelial proliferative responses in RA have been shown in a range of studies. For example, the number of synovial blood vessels has been found to correlate with hyperplasia of synovial cells, infiltration of mononuclear cells, and indices of joint tenderness [2]. A morphometric study has suggested that capillaries are distributed more deeply in RA synovium than in normal tissue, although the blood-volume fraction was greater in normal knees than in RA [3]. Another group noted that although perivascular mononuclear-cell infiltration and increased thickness of the synovial lining layer were observed in tissue from both inflamed and noninflamed joints of RA patients, vascular proliferation was seen only in tissues from inflamed joints [4]. Endothelial cells lining blood vessels within RA synovium have been shown to express cell-cycle-associated antigens such as PCNA and Ki67, and integrin $\alpha v \beta 3$, which is associated with vascular proliferation [5,6]. Indices of endothelial proliferation and cell death were shown to be higher in synovia from patients with RA than in controls or individuals with osteoarthritis (OA) [6].

The above observations suggest that in RA synovium, there is active endothelial proliferation. This is not surprising, since a consequence of the synovial hyperplasia associated with RA is an increase in the distance between the proliferating cells and the nearest blood vessels. This situation results in local hypoxia and hypoperfusion. Interestingly, it was first reported more than three decades ago that oxygen tension is low in synovial fluid samples taken from knee joints of people with RA. Lund-Olesen reported that synovial fluid PO_2 was 27 mmHg in patients with RA, versus 43 mmHg in patients with OA and 63 mmHg in controls [7]. The augmented proliferation of the synovial cells imposes an additional demand on the vasculature, further promoting the hypoxic state. Although an increase in local blood flow has been reported, this is unlikely to be sufficient to compensate for the increased requirement for oxygen and nutrients. The increase in synovial fluid volume is also likely to compound the hypoxic state in RA, by reducing synovial capillary flow. Resting intra-articular pressure in chronically inflamed joints has been found to be higher than in normal joints, and this effect would be compounded during movement of joints, inducing acute ischemia in the synovial environment [8].

Such a combination of increased metabolic demand and hypoxia is a potent signal for angiogenesis (Fig. 2). Under normal circumstances, the adult vasculature is mostly quiescent, and angiogenesis does not take place except during wound healing and the female reproductive cycle. Disregulated angiogenesis contributes to the pathology of a number of disease states, during which tissue proliferation outstrips the supply of nutrients and oxygen. These include tumour formation, and indeed parallels have been drawn between tumours and the arthritic synovium, with its attendant features of hyperplasia, oedema, angiogenesis, and invasiveness. In one of the earliest reports concerning angiogenesis and arthritis, Brown and colleagues reported that synovial fluids from patients with RA contained a low-molecular-weight angiogenesis factor apparently identical with that derived from tumours [9]. Subsequently, it was shown that synovial fluids from patients with either RA or OA induced morphological changes in endothelial cells in culture, including the formation of tubular networks morphologically resembling capillaries [10].

Angiogenesis thus contributes to the development and maintenance of RA. Identification of the angiogenic factors has progressed over the intervening years (reviewed [11–14]), and some of the better-characterised proangiogenic stimuli in RA are reviewed in the next section.

Expression of proangiogenic factors in arthritis

A range of growth factors, cytokines, and chemokines are capable of influencing angiogenesis in RA synovium. Many of these substances are thought to act indirectly, by upregulating the expression of more potent and specific angiogenic stimuli (Table 1).

Figure 2

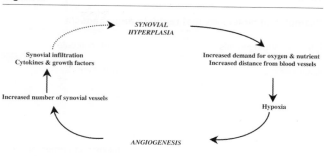

Why does angiogenesis occur in RA? A consequence of the synovial hyperplasia associated with RA is an increase in the distance between the proliferating cells and the nearest blood vessels. This results in hypoxia and hypoperfusion. The augmented proliferation of the synovial cells imposes an additional demand on the vasculature, further promoting hypoxia. This drives angiogenesis, and hence infiltration and hyperplasia.

Several growth factors, which are capable of promoting angiogenesis, are in fact broad-range mitogens. Typical examples are the fibroblast growth factors (FGFs), namely FGF-1 (acidic FGF) and FGF-2 (basic FGF). These polypeptide mitogens elicit a variety of responses depending on the target cell type, including proliferation, migration, and differentiation. Both FGF-1 and FGF-2 are expressed in RA: in macrophages, lining cells, and endothelial cells. Similarly, platelet-derived growth factor (PDGF), which is also a potent mitogen for many cell types, including fibroblasts and smooth muscle cells, is expressed in RA synovium. The heparin-binding cytokine hepatocyte growth factor (HGF; scatter factor) has been reported to be expressed in RA. Hepatocyte growth factor promotes directed and random migration of many epithelial cell types and of vascular endothelial cells, and has been found at significant levels in RA synovial fluids (reviewed [15,16])

In contrast, vascular endothelial growth factor (VEGF) is a relatively endothelial-cell-specific angiogenic factor. The ever-increasing VEGF family is now known to contain at least six related cytokines, although the original member, VEGF, remains the most extensively studied. Alternative mRNA splicing of a single gene yields distinct isoforms of VEGF, with differing properties (Fig. 3). Expression of VEGF is elevated in a range of angiogenesis-associated disease states, such as malignancies, retinal neovascularisation, and psoriasis. VEGF exerts its effects through tyrosine kinase receptors Flt-1 (fms-like tyrosine kinase receptor; also known as VEGF-R1) and Flk-1/KDR (fetal liver kinase receptor/kinase-insert-domain-containing receptor; also known as VEGF-R2) [17,18]. Additional receptors appear to act as co-receptors. For example, neuropilin-1 acts as a co-receptor for VEGF-R2, enhancing the binding and biological activity of the VEGF-165

Table 1

Examples of molecules that regulate angiogenesis

Effect on angiogenesis	Type of molecule	Molecule
Angiogenic stimuli	Growth factors	FGF-1* and FGF-2*, HGF* Placental growth factor* Platelet-derived endothelial-cell growth factor* PDGF-BB* TGF-α, TGF-β* VEGF*
	Cytokines and other mediators	Angiogenin* Ang-1* Granulocyte-colony-stimulating factor* IL-8* Midkine, Pleiotrophin TNFα*
Angiogenesis inhibitors	Cryptic proteins	Angiostatin (plasminogen fragment) Endostatin (collagen XVIII fragment) Fibronectin fragment Kringle 5 (plasminogen fragment) Prolactin 16-kDa fragment Vasostatin (calreticulin fragment)
	Cytokines and other mediators	Cartilage-derived inhibitor Interferon-inducible protein (IP-10) IL-12 Metalloproteinase inhibitors (TIMPs) Plasminogen activator inhibitor Platelet factor-4 Thrombospondin-1

*Expressed in RA. Ang, angiopoietin; FGF, fibroblast growth factor; HGF, hepatocyte growth factor; PDGF, platelet-derived growth factor; TGF, transforming growth factor; VEGF, vascular endothelial growth factor.

Figure 3

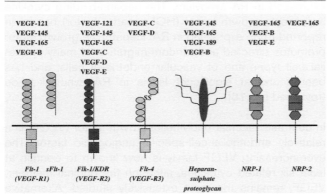

The VEGF family. The binding of VEGF ligands and their splice variants to cell-surface receptors. See Colour figure section.

isoform. A key feature of VEGF is the upregulation of this growth factor by hypoxia [19]. Several distinct molecular mechanisms are thought to be involved in hypoxia-induced upregulation of VEGF expression, including transcriptional control, through transcription factors such as hypoxia-inducible factor-1 (HIF-1), and post-transcriptional stabilisation of VEGF mRNA [20].

The dual activities of VEGF as an endothelial-cell mitogen and a modulator of changes in vascular permeability are of relevance in the pathogenesis of RA. VEGF levels are markedly higher in the serum and synovial fluids of patients with RA than in either patients with OA or normal controls [21–25]. Serum VEGF concentrations in RA patients correlate with levels of C-reactive protein, a marker of inflammation and disease activity [23]. Expression of VEGF mRNA by cells of the lining layer in RA has been reported, and immunohistochemical analyses of synovial biopsies in RA revealed expression of VEGF by synovial lining layers and endothelial cells lining small blood vessels within the pannus [21,26,27]. Synovial fluid neutrophils express VEGF at higher levels than are found in fluids from patients with OA [28]. Moreover, microvascular endothelial cells in the vicinity of VEGF-positive cells express mRNA for VEGF receptors [26,29].

Perhaps the most relevant property of VEGF in the context of angiogenesis and RA is the upregulation of this growth factor by hypoxia. The hypoxic state in the RA joint suggests that the formation of new blood vessels in the pannus may be driven by hypoxia-induced expression of VEGF. Expression of hypoxia-inducible factor-1α by macrophages in RA synovium, predominantly close to the intimal layer but also in the subintimal area, has been described [30]. We have reported that dissociated cells of the synovial membrane in RA respond to hypoxia by upregulating VEGF production. Cells of the synovial membrane in RA were isolated by enzymatic digestion, and after overnight adherence were placed in either normoxic (mean PO_2 140 mmHg) or hypoxic (mean PO_2 60 mmHg) conditions. After 24 hours in hypoxia, release of VEGF was selectively upregulated, whereas production of IL-1β and IL-8 was unaffected. These observations suggest that a component of the formation of new blood vessels observed in RA may result from hypoxia-driven induction of VEGF [23]. To investigate the relation between tissue oxygen levels and synovial VEGF production in inflammatory arthritis in humans, we examined patients undergoing knee arthroscopy. Synovial PO_2 levels were significantly lower in patients with active RA than in patients without RA, and release of VEGF from synovial cells prepared from tissue biopsies was likewise greater for patients with RA. It would appear, therefore, that reduced intra-articular PO_2 is likely to be a stimulus for local VEGF production [31].

We have also recently shown that VEGF is important in the development of joint destruction in RA. We observed a significant correlation between serum VEGF at presentation with early RA and the magnitude of radiological deterioration within the first year, calculated using radiographs of hands and feet, taken at initial presentation and at follow-up after 1 year. Radiographs were scored according to the van der Heijde modification of Sharp's method. Patients with radiological deterioration less than the median rate (change after 1 year = 1.5) had lower circulating VEGF concentrations (358 pg/ml) than those with greater than the median rate of radiological deterioration (change after 1 year = 7.5; serum VEGF = 638 pg/ml; $P < 0.001$) [32]. These results suggest that high serum VEGF levels at an early stage of disease are associated with the increased subsequent damage to joints observed by radiography.

More recent studies have addressed the role in arthritis of another important family of molecules involved in angiogenesis, namely the angiopoietins. These molecules, together with their cell-surface receptors Tie-1 and Tie-2, play a key role in development of the vasculature and have been implicated in the control of vessel stabilisation and regression. The patterns of expression of the best-characterised molecules, angiopoietin (Ang)-1 and Ang-2, during embryonic development and during pathological angiogenesis suggest that Ang-1 may act to stabilise new vessels formed in response to VEGF. In contrast, Ang-2 may destabilise blood vessels, which would lead to new vessel sprouts in the presence of VEGF or to regression of vessels in the absence of VEGF. Expression of Tie-1 and Tie-2 in RA synovium has been reported [33]. Detectable levels of mRNA for Ang-1 and its receptors have been shown in specimens of synovial tissue from patients with juvenile RA, in which expression was signifi-

cantly higher than in tissues from patients with OA or other noninflammatory controls [34]. These observations are perhaps surprising, given that administration of Ang-1 was shown to protect adult mouse vasculature from leaking, countering the permeability activity of VEGF [35].

The levels of an angiogenesis inhibitor, endostatin, were recently reported for patients with RA. VEGF levels in the serum and joint fluid from patients with RA were higher than in patients without RA, whereas endostatin levels were comparable between the groups [36]. My co-workers and I have found that serum levels of the soluble form of the VEGF Flt-1 receptor are raised in RA, as well as in self-limiting arthritis [32]. An inverse relation between the cytokine and its soluble receptor might be predicted. However, raised levels of sFlt-1 observed in RA are presumably insufficient to inhibit VEGF activity. These observations suggest that there may be an imbalance in RA favouring proangiogenic stimuli, whereas inhibitors of angiogenesis such as endostatin are not elevated, or, as in the case of the soluble VEGF Flt-1 receptor, are not increased enough to block the effects of stimuli such as VEGF.

In summary, the invasive pannus in RA is highly vascularised, and numerous growth factors are expressed, which might promote the formation of new blood vessels. Subsequent sections examine the signalling mechanisms involved in the induction of VEGF expression in the context of RA, and the development of new therapies targeting blood vessels in RA.

Angiogenesis blockade in animal models of arthritis

Angiogenesis is clearly a feature of arthritis, with VEGF playing a particularly central role in this process. It seems likely that suppression of the formation of blood vessels should retard the progression of arthritis. There is certainly considerable literature describing the ability of broadly acting angiogenesis inhibitors to modulate disease in animal models. Taxol, TNP-470, and thalidomide – compounds that exert nonspecific anti-angiogenic, as well as other, effects – have all been shown to inhibit pannus formation and neovascularisation [37–39]. For example, in a rat model of arthritis, in which disease is induced by injection of heterologous collagen, leading to synovitis, joint erosion, and associated neovascularisation, TNP-470 was found to suppress established disease. In parallel, there was a marked inhibition of pannus formation and of neovascularisation [37]. TNP-470 has recently been shown to delay onset of arthritis and greatly reduce bone and cartilage destruction if given very early in a transgenic mouse model of arthritis [40].

A hypothesis could also be made that inhibition of VEGF activity should be an effective therapy in RA. We have addressed this hypothesis using the model of collagen-induced arthritis in genetically susceptible mice. To study the association between VEGF and disease severity in murine arthritis, we measured release of this angiogenic cytokine by enzymatically dissociated murine synovial cells. Synovial cells isolated from the knee joints of naive or sham-immunised mice, or from mice immunised with collagen but without arthritis, released little or no detectable VEGF. Onset of arthritis was associated with expression of VEGF, and the levels of VEGF secreted by synovial cells isolated from joints of mice with severe arthritis were significantly higher than from mice with mild disease [41]. We additionally showed that a soluble form of the Flt-1 VEGF receptor (sFlt) significantly reduced disease severity and joint destruction in murine collagen-induced arthritis. Mice treated with a soluble form of this receptor after the onset of arthritis exhibited significantly lower clinical scores and paw swelling than untreated or control-treated animals. These sFlt-treated animals also showed significantly reduced joint inflammation and less destruction of bone and cartilage, as assessed by histology [41].

Later studies, using anti-VEGF polyclonal antibodies, showed the effectiveness of VEGF blockade in collagen-induced arthritis [42,43]. It therefore appears that VEGF plays a unique role in mediating angiogenesis in RA. Our results using sFlt, and more recent, unpublished data using adenovirus-mediated transfer of VEGF antagonists, suggest that blockade of VEGF activity might be of therapeutic benefit in RA.

Anti-TNF-α antibody in RA: effects on angiogenesis

The findings of elevated expression of angiogenic factors in RA suggest that reducing synovial vascularity may be a desirable component of anti-RA therapies. Certain disease-modifying antirheumatic drugs (DMARDs) have been shown to inhibit angiogenesis in experimental systems. These include drugs such as methotrexate (MTX) [44], sulphasalazine, and penicillamine. Combinations of such drugs also affect production of VEGF by synovial cells *in vitro*. For example, bucillamine and gold sodium thiomalate inhibited VEGF production, as did a combination of bucillamine, gold sodium thiomalate, and MTX with dexamethasone [45].

Further insights into the importance of reduced angiogenesis in RA were gained from clinical trials of anti-tumour necrosis factor(TNF)-α antibody infliximab − a chimeric mouse Fv, human IgG1, κ antibody of high affinity. From the earliest trials in 1992, infliximab has shown remarkable therapeutic efficacy, reducing both clinical and laboratory indices of disease activity (reviewed [46,47]). The effects of TNF-α on the angiogenic process are both stimulatory and inhibitory, depending on the system. For example, exposure of endothelial cells to TNF-α has been reported to induce release of VEGF and FGF-2 [48]. Production by

synovial-joint cells of angiogenic cytokines such as VEGF is at least in part induced by TNF-α, as was demonstrated in a study showing reduced synovial-cell VEGF release in the presence of anti-TNF-α antibody: my colleagues and I reported that in the presence of anti-TNF-α antibody, spontaneous release of VEGF by RA synovial-membrane cells was decreased. An even greater reduction was observed in the presence of a combination of IL-1-receptor antagonist and anti-TNF-α antibody (inhibition 45%, $P < 0.05$, versus release from untreated cells) [23]. We therefore postulated that part of the benefit of anti-TNF-α antibody in RA was gained through a reduction in synovial vascularity.

To examine this hypothesis, we measured serum VEGF levels in patients with RA who were treated with anti-TNF-α antibody, and observed significant reductions in circulating concentrations of this angiogenic cytokine. In patients receiving 10 mg infliximab per kilogram of body weight, a reduction in serum VEGF levels of more than 40% was achieved, and even 4 weeks after the treatment with the anti-TNF-α serum, VEGF concentrations were significantly below pre-infusion values. Treatment of RA patients with a combination of multiple infusions of infliximab and MTX resulted in a more prolonged decrease in serum VEGF levels than in patients who received infliximab without MTX. We found that infusion of 10 mg infliximab per kilogram of body weight without MTX reduced the levels of circulating VEGF, although these returned to pre-infusion concentrations after the final infusion. In contrast, in patients who received infliximab as well as MTX, this reduction was maintained up to the end of the trial period [23]. These observations suggest that TNF-α regulates production of VEGF *in vivo*, and that part of the beneficial effect of anti-TNF-α in RA may be a down-modulation in the formation of blood vessels.

In a more recent study, the effects of infliximab on synovial angiogenesis, vascularity, and VEGF expression were investigated [49]. Patients with active RA received a single dose, 10 mg per kilogram of body weight, of anti-TNF-α antibody. Synovial biopsies were taken during arthroscopic examination of the knee joint 1 day before and 2 weeks after treatment, and synovial vascularity was assessed by immunohistochemistry followed by quantitative image analysis. Anti-TNF-α therapy was found to reduce synovial vascularity as assessed by immunostaining for the presence of CD31 and von Willebrand factor. Additionally, a significant reduction in the number of αvβ3-integrin-positive vessels was found. The reduced expression of CD31, von Willebrand factor, and αvβ3 integrin after TNF-α blockade is in agreement with the concept that the balance of new vessel growth and regression is altered such that a net loss of microvessels occurs. Since the endothelial surface plays a key role in mediating cell traffic and delivery of nutrients, such alterations in vascular density may also contribute to therapeutic efficacy. My co-

Table 2

Examples of angiogenesis inhibitors in clinical trials

Action of drug	Drug	Examples of clinical trials	Mode of action
Direct inhibition of endothelial cells	Thalidomide	Phase III non-small-cell lung cancer	Inhibits endothelial cells directly
	Endostatin	Phase I solid tumour	Inhibits endothelial cells
Inhibition of the binding of angiogenic stimuli	Humanised monoclonal anti-human VEGF (bevacizumab)	Phase II metastatic renal cell cancer; phase III with chemotherapy in untreated metastatic colorectal cancer	Monoclonal antibody to VEGF
Inhibition of events downstream of angiogenic stimuli	SU6668	Phase I against advanced tumours	Blocks VEGF, FGF, PDGF receptor signalling
	SU5416	Phase I recurrent head and neck; phase II prostate cancer	Blocks VEGF receptor signalling
Inhibition of matrix breakdown	Marimastat	Phase III small-cell lung cancers	Synthetic MMP inhibitor
	BMS-275291	Phase II/III metastatic non-small-cell lung	Synthetic MMP inhibitor
Inhibition of endothelial–integrin interactions	EMD121974	Phase I in patients with HIV-related Kaposi's sarcoma	Small molecule blocker of integrin on endothelium

FGF, fibroblast growth factor; MMP, matrix metalloproteinase; PDGF, platelet-derived growth factor; VEGF, vascular endothelial growth factor.

workers and I are currently in the process of using power colour Doppler to examine the effects of anti-TNF-α antibody treatment on synovial vascularity.

Angiogenesis: a realistic target for new therapies in RA?

Therapeutic agents and strategies are being devised to either interrupt or inhibit one or more of the pathogenic steps involved in angiogenesis, and blockade of neovascularisation has been effective in many tumour models. Clearly, angiogenesis can be targeted at several different stages, including inhibition of production of stimuli such as VEGF, binding of proangiogenic factors (using antibodies or soluble receptors), interruption of downstream signalling, blockade of matrix degradation, or even the use of anti-angiogenic stimuli such as endostatin. Many of these approaches have been used with varying degrees of success for human cancers (Table 2; for an updated list of angiogenesis inhibitors in clinical trials see [50]).

In terms of inhibiting the action of VEGF, phase I and phase 1b clinical trial data for pharmacological, safety, and pharmacokinetic studies have been reported for anti-VEGF antibody in patients with solid tumours [51]. Another approach is to use inhibitors of receptor tyrosine kinases, such as SU5416 and SU6668, designed by SUGEN, a company of the Pharmacia Corporation based in South San Francisco. SU5416 has been shown to potently inhibit VEGF-dependent tyrosine phosphorylation, ATP-dependent Flk-1 autophosphorylation, and the proliferation of human endothelial cells. Phase I clinical trials in AIDS-related Kaposi's sarcoma and various solid tumours

showed SU5416 to be well tolerated. Most recently, a phase II/III research study of SU5416 in metastatic colorectal cancer completed enrolment [52]. SU6668 is less selective for Flk-1, inhibiting also signalling downstream of the PDGF and the FGF-1 receptors. Currently, SU6668 is in phase I trials for the treatment of advanced solid tumours. None of these compounds is as yet in clinical trials for RA, although our own unpublished data collected using a synthetic inhibitor with relatively greater inhibitory activity for the Flk-1/KDR VEGF receptor showed a significant reduction in clinical score and paw swelling, without any apparent side effects.

The use of anti-angiogenic molecules is less common. In a phase I trial of endostatin at the University of Texas M D Anderson Cancer Center, 25 study patients tolerated the drug well, with few toxic side effects, and two patients showed evidence of some tumour shrinkage [53]. My coworkers and I have recently begun a study in mouse collagen-induced arthritis of K1–5 (protease-activated kringles 1–5), which is related to the potent angiogenesis inhibitor angiostatin. Like several other endogenous anti-angiogenic molecules, angiostatin is a cryptic fragment of a larger molecule lacking in anti-angiogenic activity and is generated as a result of proteolytic cleavage of plasminogen. Angiostatin comprises the first four triple-loop disulfide-linked structures of plasminogen, termed kringle (K) domains. Urokinase-activated plasmin can also convert plasminogen into a molecule containing the intact K1–4 and most of the K5 domains, termed K1–5. This angiogenesis inhibitor K1–5 inhibited the proliferation of endothelial cells more effectively than angiostatin, and suppressed tumour growth and neovascularisation [54]. The effectiveness of treatment with K1–5 treatment in the mouse tumour model prompted us to examine the effects of this inhibitor in the murine model of CIA, and preliminary data are encouraging.

It is not unreasonable to suggest that targeting the newly formed vasculature of the RA pannus, in combination with other therapies such as anti-TNF-α, may lead to a more persistent reduction in pannus volume and hence modify disease progression, but confirmation of this hypothesis requires appropriate clinical trials. Although anti-TNF-α antibody has been shown to reduce serum levels of VEGF by up to 40% in patients with RA, circulating VEGF levels nonetheless remained significantly higher than in healthy individuals [23]. For example, median concentrations of serum VEGF in nonarthritic individuals were equivalent to 160 pg/ml, versus 503 pg/ml in patients with active RA. In patients who received a single infusion of 10 mg/kg infliximab, the maximal change in serum VEGF concentrations was achieved at week 3 (decrease 42%), but the median VEGF concentration was still nearly double that observed in individuals without RA (319 pg/ml). Moreover, not all patients respond to TNF-α blockade. Targeting the inflammatory and vascular components of RA, by combining TNF-α inhibition with angiogenesis blockade, could therefore increase benefit to patients with RA, without augmenting the infection risk.

Concluding remarks
Angiogenesis is, clearly, an important process in the development and perpetuation of RA. Clinical trials in cancer patients of VEGF antibody and small-molecule inhibitors of receptor tyrosine kinases, including those for VEGF, are well under way. It may well be that in the not too distant future, clinical trials of VEGF-targeted therapies may also commence for RA, either alone or in combination with established therapies such as anti-TNF-α antibody.

Naturally, there are undoubted potential drawbacks of anti-angiogenic therapy, such as reduced fertility, impaired healing of fractures, or maybe reduced formation of collateral vessels after an episode of ischaemia. Since patients with RA develop cardiovascular problems at an earlier age than their nonarthritic peers, anti-VEGF therapy might not, therefore, be desirable, in spite of the proven role for VEGF in RA and data showing promising effects of VEGF blockade in animal models. On the other hand, recombinant human VEGF increased the rate and degree of formation of atherosclerotic plaques in the thoracic aorta in a model in cholesterol-fed rabbits, and plasma levels are elevated in atherosclerotic patients [52,53]. It is thus difficult to predict what the results of angiogenesis inhibition in RA might be, and probably only carefully designed clinical trials will answer this question. In theory, at least, anti-angiogenic treatment should not potentially increase the

risk of infection, and a combination of anti-VEGF and infliximab in RA may be beneficial without augmenting potential adverse effects.

Glossary of terms
Ang = angiopoietin; FGF-1 = fibroblast growth factor-1 (acidic FGF); FGF-2 = fibroblast growth factor-2 (basic FGF); Flk-1/KDR = fetal liver kinase receptor/kinase-insert-domain-containing receptor (VEGF-R2); Flt-1 = fms-like tyrosine kinase receptor (VEGF-R1); HGF = hepatocyte growth factor; HIF-1 = hypoxia-inducible factor-1; K = kringle; sFlt-1 = soluble VEGF Flt-1 receptor; Tie = tyrosine kinase with immunoglobulin and epidermal growth factor homology domains.

Acknowledgements
The contributions of Dr Sundeept Ballara, Dr Jadwiga Miotla, Dr Claudia Monaco, Dr Peter Taylor, and Ms Sylvia Young and the support of Professor Marc Feldmann and Professor Ravinder N Maini are gratefully acknowledged. The Kennedy Institute of Rheumatology is a Division of the Faculty of Medicine, Imperial College of Science, Technology and Medicine, and receives a Core Grant from the Arthritis Research Campaign of Great Britain.

References
1. Rothschild BM, Masi AT: **Pathogenesis of rheumatoid arthritis: a vascular hypothesis**. *Semin Arthritis Rheum* 1982, **12**:11-31. [archival research]
2. Rooney M, Condell D, Quinlan W, Daly L, Whelan A, Feighery C, Bresnihan B: **Analysis of the histologic variation of synovitis in rheumatoid arthritis**. *Arthritis Rheum* 1988, **31**:956-963. [archival research]
3. Stevens CR, Blake DR, Merry P, Revell PA, Levick JR: **A comparative study by morphometry of the microvasculature in normal and rheumatoid synovium**. *Arthritis Rheum* 1991, **34**: 1508-1513. [general reference]
4. FitzGerald O, Soden M, Yanni G, Robinson R, Bresnihan B: **Morphometric analysis of blood vessels in synovial membranes obtained from clinically affected and unaffected knee joints of patients with rheumatoid arthritis**. *Ann Rheum Dis* 1991, **50**: 792-796. [general reference]
5. Ceponis A, Konttinen YT, Imai S, Tamulaitiene M, Li TF, Xu JW, Hietanen J, Santavirta S, Fassbender HG: **Synovial lining, endothelial and inflammatory mononuclear cell proliferation in synovial membranes in psoriatic and reactive arthritis: a comparative quantitative morphometric study**. *Br J Rheumatol* 1998, **37**:170-178. [general reference]
6. Walsh DA, Wade M, Mapp PI, Blake DR: **Focally regulated endothelial proliferation and cell death in human synovium**. *Am J Pathol* 1998, **152**:691-702. [general reference]
7. Lund-Olesen K: **Oxygen tension in synovial fluids**. *Arthritis Rheum* 1970, **13**:769-776. [archival research]
8. Jawed S, Gaffney K, Blake DR: **Intra-articular pressure profile of the knee joint in a spectrum of inflammatory arthropathies**. *Ann Rheum Dis* 1997, **56**:686-689. [general reference]
9. Brown RA, Weiss JB, Tomlinson IW, Phillips P, Kumar S: **Angiogenic factor from synovial fluid resembling that from tumours**. *Lancet* 1980, **1 (8170)**:682-685. [archival research]
10. Semble EL, Turner RA, McCrickard EL: **Rheumatoid arthritis and osteoarthritis synovial fluid effects on primary human endothelial cell cultures**. *J Rheumatol* 1985, **12**:237-241. [archival research]
11. Paleolog EM, Fava RA: **Angiogenesis in rheumatoid arthritis: implications for future therapeutic strategies**. *Springer Semin Immunopathol* 1998, **20**:73-94. [key review]
12. Paleolog EM, Miotla JM: **Angiogenesis in arthritis: role in disease pathogenesis and as a potential therapeutic target**. *Angiogenesis* 1998, **2**:295-307. [key review]
13. Ballara SC, Miotla JM, Paleolog EM: **New vessels, new approaches: angiogenesis as a therapeutic target in muscu-**

loskeletal disorders. *Int J Exp Pathol* 1999, **80**:235-250. [key review]

14. Paleolog EM, Miotla JM: **Rheumatoid arthritis: a target for anti-angiogenic therapy?** In *The New Angiotherapy*. Edited by Fan TP, Kohn EC. Totowa, NJ, USA: Humana Press Inc; 2001:129-149. [key review]

15. Koch AE: **The role of angiogenesis in rheumatoid arthritis: recent developments.** *Ann Rheum Dis* 2000, **59 Suppl 1**:I65-71. [key review]

16. Walsh DA, Pearson CI: **Angiogenesis in the pathogenesis of inflammatory joint and lung diseases.** *Arthritis Res* 2001, **3**: 147-153. [key review]

17. Neufeld G, Cohen T, Gengrinovitch S, Poltorak Z: **Vascular endothelial growth factor (VEGF) and its receptors.** *FASEB J* 1999, **13**:9-22. [key review]

18. Ferrara N: **Role of vascular endothelial growth factor in regulation of physiological angiogenesis.** *Am J Physiol Cell Physiol* 2001, **280**:C1358-1366.

19. Shweiki D, Itin A, Soffer D, Keshet E: **Vascular endothelial growth factor induced by hypoxia may mediate hypoxia-initiated angiogenesis.** *Nature* 1992, **359**:843-845. [general reference]

20. Levy NS, Chung S, Furneaux H, Levy AP: **Hypoxic stabilization of vascular endothelial growth factor mRNA by the RNA-binding protein HuR.** *J Biol Chem* 1998, **273**:6417-6423. [general reference]

21. Koch AE, Harlow LA, Haines GK, Amento EP, Unemori EN, Wong WL, Pope RM, Ferrara N: **Vascular endothelial growth factor. A cytokine modulating endothelial function in rheumatoid arthritis.** *J Immunol* 1994, **152**:4149-4156. [general reference]

22. Harada M, Mitsuyama K, Yoshida H, Sakisaka S, Taniguchi E, Kawaguchi T, Ariyoshi M, Saiki T, Sakamoto M, Nagata K, Sata M, Matsuo K, Tanikawa K: **Vascular endothelial growth factor in patients with rheumatoid arthritis.** *Scand J Rheumatol* 1998, **27**:377-380. [general reference]

23. Paleolog EM, Young S, Stark AC, McCloskey RV, Feldmann M, Maini RN: **Modulation of angiogenic vascular endothelial growth factor (VEGF) by TNFα and IL-1 in rheumatoid arthritis.** *Arthritis Rheum* 1998, **41**:1258-1265. [general reference]

24. Nagashima M, Yoshino S, Ishiwata T, Asano G: **Role of vascular endothelial growth factor in angiogenesis of rheumatoid arthritis.** *J Rheumatol* 1995, **22**:1624-1630. [general reference]

25. Lee SS, Joo YS, Kim WU, Min DJ, Min JK, Park SH, Cho CS, Kim HY: **Vascular endothelial growth factor levels in the serum and synovial fluid of patients with rheumatoid arthritis.** *Clin Exp Rheumatol* 2001, **19**:321-324. [general reference]

26. Fava RA, Olsen NJ, Spencer-Green G, Yeo KT, Yeo TK, Berse B, Jackman RW, Senger DR, Dvorak HF, Brown LF: **Vascular permeability factor/endothelial growth factor (VPF/VEGF): accumulation and expression in human synovial fluids and rheumatoid synovial tissue.** *J Exp Med* 1994, **180**:341-346. [general reference]

27. Pufe T, Petersen W, Tillmann B, Mentlein R: **Splice variants VEGF121 and VEGF165 of the angiogenic peptide vascular endothelial cell growth factor are expressed in the synovial tissue of patients with rheumatoid arthritis.** *J Rheumatol* 2001, **28**:1482-1485. [general reference]

28. Kasama T, Kobayashi K, Yajima N, Shiozawa F, Yoda Y, Takeuchi HT, Mori Y, Negishi M, Ide H, Adachi M: **Expression of vascular endothelial growth factor by synovial fluid neutrophils in rheumatoid arthritis (RA).** *Clin Exp Immunol* 2000, **121**:533-538. [general reference]

29. Ikeda M, Hosoda Y, Hirose S, Okada Y, Ikeda E: **Expression of vascular endothelial growth factor isoforms and their receptors Flt-1, KDR, and neuropilin-1 in synovial tissues of rheumatoid arthritis.** *J Pathol* 2000, **191**:426-433. [general reference]

30. Hollander AP, Corke KP, Freemont AJ, Lewis CE: **Expression of hypoxia-inducible factor 1alpha by macrophages in the rheumatoid synovium: implications for targeting of therapeutic genes to the inflamed joint.** *Arthritis Rheum* 2001, **44**:1540-1544. [general reference]

31. Taylor P, Miotla JM, Etherington P, Winlove P, Young Y, Paleolog E, Maini RN: **VEGF release is associated with hypoxia in inflammatory arthritis [abstract].** *Arthritis Rheum* 2000, **43 Suppl 9**:S296. [general reference]

32. Ballara SC, Taylor PC, Reusch P, Marmé D, Feldmann M, Maini RN, Paleolog EM: **Raised serum vascular endothelial growth factor levels are associated with destructive change in inflammatory arthritis.** *Arthritis Rheum* 2001, **44**:2055-2064. [general reference]

33. Uchida T, Nakashima M, Hirota Y, Miyazaki Y, Tsukazaki T, Shindo H: **Immunohistochemical localisation of protein tyrosine kinase receptors Tie-1 and Tie-2 in synovial tissue of rheumatoid arthritis: correlation with angiogenesis and synovial proliferation.** *Ann Rheum Dis* 2000, **59**:607-614. [general reference]

34. Scola MP, Imagawa T, Boivin GP, Giannini EH, Glass DN, Hirsch R, Grom AA: **Expression of angiogenic factors in juvenile rheumatoid arthritis: correlation with revascularization of human synovium engrafted into SCID mice.** *Arthritis Rheum* 2001, **44**:794-801. [general reference]

35. Thurston G, Rudge JS, Ioffe E, Zhou H, Ross L, Croll SD, Glazer N, Holash J, McDonald DM, Yancopoulos GD: **Angiopoietin-1 protects the adult vasculature against plasma leakage.** *Nat Med* 2000, **6**:460-463. [general reference]

36. Nagashima M, Asano G, Yoshino S: **Imbalance in production between vascular endothelial growth factor and endostatin in patients with rheumatoid arthritis.** *J Rheumatol* 2000, **27**:2339-2342. [general reference]

37. Oliver SJ, Cheng TP, Banquerigo ML, Brahn E: **Suppression of collagen-induced arthritis by an angiogenesis inhibitor, AGM-1470, in combination with cyclosporin: reduction of vascular endothelial growth factor (VEGF).** *Cell Immunol* 1995, **166**: 196-206. [general reference]

38. Arsenault AL, Lhotak S, Hunter WL, Banquerigo ML, Brahn E: **Taxol involution of collagen-induced arthritis: ultrastructural correlation with the inhibition of synovitis and neovascularization.** *Clin Immunol Immunopathol* 1998, **86**:280-289. [general reference]

39. Oliver SJ, Cheng TP, Banquerigo ML, Brahn E: **The effect of thalidomide and 2 analogs on collagen induced arthritis.** *J Rheumatol* 1998, **25**:964-969. [general reference]

40. de Bandt M, Grossin M, Weber AJ, Chopin M, Elbim C, Pla M, Gougerot-Pocidalo MA, Gaudry M: **Suppression of arthritis and protection from bone destruction by treatment with TNP-470/AGM-1470 in a transgenic mouse model of rheumatoid arthritis.** *Arthritis Rheum* 2000, **43**:2056-2063. [general reference]

41. Miotla J, Maciewicz R, Kendrew J, Feldmann M, Paleolog E: **Treatment with soluble VEGF receptor reduces disease severity in murine collagen-induced arthritis.** *Lab Invest* 2000, **80**:1195-1205. [general reference]

42. Lu J, Kasama T, Kobayashi K, Yoda Y, Shiozawa F, Hanyuda M, Negishi M, Ide H, Adachi M: **Vascular endothelial growth factor expression and regulation of murine collagen-induced arthritis.** *J Immunol* 2000, **164**:5922-5927. [general reference]

43. Sone H, Kawakami Y, Sakauchi M, Nakamura Y, Takahashi A, Shimano H, Okuda Y, Segawa T, Suzuki H, Yamada N: **Neutralization of vascular endothelial growth factor prevents collagen-induced arthritis and ameliorates established disease in mice.** *Biochem Biophys Res Commun* 2001, **281**:562-568. [general reference]

44. Hirata S, Matsubara T, Saura R, Tateishi H, Hirohata K: **Inhibition of *in vitro* vascular endothelial cell proliferation and *in vivo* neovascularization by low dose methotrexate.** *Arthritis Rheum* 1989, **32**:1065-1073. [general reference]

45. Nagashima M, Wauke K, Hirano D, Ishigami S, Aono H, Takai M, Sasano M, Yoshino S: **Effects of combinations of anti-rheumatic drugs on the production of vascular endothelial growth factor and basic fibroblast growth factor in cultured synoviocytes and patients with rheumatoid arthritis.** *Rheumatology (Oxford)* 2000, **39**:1255-1262. [general reference]

46. Maini RN, Taylor PC, Paleolog E, Charles P, Ballara S, Brennan FM, Feldmann M: **Anti-tumour necrosis factor specific antibody (infliximab) treatment provides insights into the pathophysiology of rheumatoid arthritis.** *Ann Rheum Dis* 1999, **58 Suppl 1**: I56-60. [key review]

47. Feldmann M, Maini RN: **Anti-TNF alpha therapy of rheumatoid arthritis: what have we learned?** *Annu Rev Immunol* 2001, **19**: 163-196. [key review]

48. Yoshida S, Ono M, Shono T, Izumi H, Ishibashi T, Suzuki H, Kuwano M: **Involvement of interleukin-8, vascular endothelial**

growth factor, and basic fibroblast growth factor in tumor necrosis factor alpha-dependent angiogenesis. *Mol Cell Biol* 1997, **17**:4015-4023. [general reference]

49. Taylor P, Patel S, Paleolog E, McCloskey RV, Feldmann M, Maini RN: **Reduced synovial vascularity following TNFα blockade in rheumatoid arthritis [abstract].** *Arthritis Rheum* 1998, **41 Suppl 9**:S295. [general reference]

50. The Angiogenesis Foundation: [http://www.cancer.gov/clinical_trials/doc.aspx?viewid=B0959CBB-3004-4160-A679-6DD204BEE68C]. [online database]

51. Margolin K, Gordon MS, Hol mgren E, Gaudreault J, Novotny W, Fyfe G, Adelman D, Stalter S, Breed J: **Phase Ib trial of intravenous recombinant humanized monoclonal antibody to vascular endothelial growth factor in combination with chemotherapy in patients with advanced cancer: pharmacologic and long-term safety data.** *J Clin Oncol* 2001, **19**:851-856. [general reference]

52. National Cancer Institute: [http://www.sugen.com/webpage_templates/sec.php3?page_name=trials] [relevant website]

53. SUGEN Inc.: [http://www.mdanderson.org/Featured_Sites/Endostatin/] [relevant website]

54. Cao R, Wu HL, Veitonmaki N, Linden P, Farnebo J, Shi GY, Cao Y: **Suppression of angiogenesis and tumor growth by the inhibitor K1-5 generated by plasmin-mediated proteolysis.** *Proc Natl Acad Sci U S A* 1999, **96**:5728-5733. [general reference]

55. Blann AD, Belgore FM, Constans J, Conri C, Lip GY: **Plasma vascular endothelial growth factor and its receptor Flt-1 in patients with hyperlipidemia and atherosclerosis and the effects of fluvastatin or fenofibrate.** *Am J Cardiol* 2001, **87**:1160-1163. [general reference]

56. Celletti FL, Hilfiker PR, Ghafouri P, Dake MD: **Effect of human recombinant vascular endothelial growth factor165 on progression of atherosclerotic plaque.** *J Am Coll Cardiol* 2001, **37**:2126-2130. [general reference]

Supplement Review

Interactions between leukocytes and endothelial cells in gout: lessons from a self-limiting inflammatory response

Dorian O Haskard and R Clive Landis

BHF Cardiovascular Medicine Unit, Faculty of Medicine, Imperial College, Hammersmith Hospital, London, UK

Correspondence: Professor Dorian Haskard, BHF Cardiovascular Medicine Unit, Imperial College School of Medicine, Hammersmith Hospital, Du Cane Road, London W12 ONN, UK. Tel: + 44 (0)20 8383 3064; fax: +44 (0)20 8383 1640; e-mail: d.haskard@ic.ac.uk; http://www.med.ic.ac.uk/divisions/35/index.htm

Received: 15 December 2001
Revisions requested: 21 January 2002
Revisions received: 31 January 2002
Accepted: 1 February 2002
Published: 9 May 2002

Arthritis Res 2002, **4 (suppl 3)**:S91-S97

This article may contain supplementary data which can only be found online at http://arthritis-research.com/content/4/S3/S091

© 2002 BioMed Central Ltd
(Print ISSN 1465-9905; Online ISSN 1465-9913)

Chapter summary

Interactions with endothelium are necessary for leukocytes to pass from the blood into extravascular tissues, and such interactions are facilitated in inflammation by the coordinated expression of endothelial adhesion molecules and chemoattractants. Although the general mechanisms and intracellular pathways of endothelial activation are now fairly well characterised *in vitro*, relatively little detailed information exists on how endothelial activation changes during the course of inflammatory responses and how such change influences the amount of leukocyte recruitment and the types of leukocytes recruited. Having developed a radiolabelled-antibody-uptake technique for quantifying the expression of endothelial adhesion molecules in relation to leukocyte trafficking, we have analysed the acute, self-limiting inflammatory response to injection of monosodium urate (MSU) crystals. Our studies have supported the view that endothelial activation is closely paralleled by leukocyte recruitment at the onset of the response and have highlighted separate vascular and extravascular stages of downregulation. More recent studies addressing the extravascular contribution to downregulation point to an important role for monocyte–macrophage differentiation in limiting further endothelial activation as a consequence of phagocytosis of MSU crystals.

Keywords: endothelium, gout, leukocyte trafficking, macrophage, monocyte

Introduction

This article discusses how the experimental study of gout provides a relatively simple, inflammatory-disease model with which to explore the relation between endothelial-cell activation, leukocyte trafficking, and perivascular activation of leukocytes. We have highlighted important recent advances in the *in vivo* study of endothelial-cell activation that have enabled the link between endothelial-cell activation and leukocyte trafficking to be investigated in detail in an animal model of acute gout. We also discuss recent evidence suggesting a protective role for macrophages in the resolution phase of inflammation.

Historical background

Gout appears to be a simple disease from an aetiological viewpoint, caused by the intra-articular deposition of monosodium urate monohydrate (MSU) crystals in individuals with elevated serum concentrations of uric acid. After the description of the clinical features of gout by Hippocrates in the fourth century BC, landmarks in understanding of the aetiology of gout were the detection of crystals in synovial fluid by Anton van Leeuwenhoek in the seventeenth century, the identification of the main ingredient of gout-associated stones and tophi as uric acid by Scheele and Wollaston, respectively, in the eighteenth

---

A glossary of specialist terms used in this chapter appears at the end of the text section. A list of common abbreviations used in this issue appears just before the indexes.

century, and the association of gout with hyperuricaemia by Garrod in the nineteenth century. However, in the twentieth century the Framlingham study showed that hyperuricaemia does not necessarily lead to clinical gout [1]. Thus, the cumulative incidence of acute gouty arthritis over a 12-year period in hyperuricaemic men (serum uric acid concentrations greater than 8 mg/dl [0.48 mmol/l]) was only 36%. This relatively weak link between hyperuricaemia and gout may be explained at least in part by differences between individuals in the capacity to nucleate and grow MSU crystals. However, we know that other factors besides the presence of crystals are involved in triggering an acute attack of gout, since the presence of crystals can be readily detected in the synovial-fluid samples collected from asymptomatic joints [2]. A possible clue to the role of leukocytes in determining the inflammatory balance in hyperuricemia has come with the observation that the cellular infiltrate in acute gout is predominantly neutrophilic, whereas in asymptomatic gout the leukocytic infiltrate is almost exclusively mononuclear [3,4].

Regulation of expression of endothelial-cell adhesion molecules

Adhesion of leukocytes to vascular endothelium is a prerequisite for their emigration into the tissues in inflammation. The general mechanisms that allow leukocytes to adhere to vascular endothelial cells and migrate into tissues are now quite well understood: they involve sequential capture from free flow via selectins, activation of G-protein-coupled receptors, and subsequent integrin-mediated arrest on the endothelial-cell surface [5–7]. Critical to these interactions is the activation of endothelial cells, which leads to upregulated expression of selectins, chemokines, and integrin ligands on the endothelial-cell surface [8,9].

Activation of endothelial cells occurs in response to changes in the tissue microenvironment and may be classified according to requirement for *de novo* protein synthesis. Stimulation of endothelial cells with agonists such as histamine, C5a, or thrombin leads to the rapid translocation of Weibel–Palade bodies to the luminal surface, with incorporation of presynthesised P-selectin into the plasma membrane and release of IL-8 and von Willebrand factor [10–12]. This process, which is analogous to mast-cell degranulation, provides a rapid but transient mechanism for initiating leukocyte–endothelial-cell interactions within seconds of tissue perturbation. In contrast, a more delayed and sustained response occurs through the stimulation of a programme of gene transcription and *de novo* protein synthesis of adhesion molecules and chemokines that include E-selectin, intercellular adhesion molecule-1 (ICAM-1), vascular cell adhesion molecule-1 (VCAM-1), IL-8, and MCP-1. The agonists that have been best characterised as inducing this transcriptional response are the cytokines IL-1α/β and tumour necrosis factor (TNF)-α [8] Recently, evidence has been provided that IL-1 may

increase the IL-8 content of Weibel–Palade bodies, providing a means by which endothelial cells can mount an augmented immediate response upon subsequent rechallenge [11,12].

Studying endothelial activation *in vivo*

Injection of IL-1 or TNF-α into the skin *in vivo* stimulates a subacute inflammatory response associated with marked leukocyte emigration, which can be quantified by measuring the uptake of intravenously injected radiolabelled leukocytes [13,14]. In order to relate the uptake of leukocytes to endothelial activation, we developed a technique in the pig for quantifying expression of adhesion molecules by measuring the uptake of radiolabelled antibodies, using a differentially radiolabelled nonspecific antibody as an internal control [15]. This allowed us to demonstrate a close relation between the onset of neutrophil recruitment and the expression of E-selectin, both in response to injection of cytokines such as IL-1 or TNF-α and during delayed-hypersensitivity responses [16–18]. A similar approach has since been adopted for measuring endothelial activation and adhesion-molecule expression in models of inflammation in rats [19] and mice [20–24].

Gout as a model for studying endothelial activation and leukocyte trafficking

Developments in understanding of the general mechanisms of leukocyte trafficking now allow us to start dissecting in detail the relation between endothelial activation and leukocyte trafficking in inflammatory rheumatic diseases. Because the aetiology is known, acute gout presents a relatively accessible, self-limiting inflammatory condition upon which to model mechanisms that may underlie other relapsing–remitting diseases. We have particularly addressed the questions of how leukocytes are recruited into the tissues during the amplification phase of the acute attack, and then how the attack spontaneously resolves.

Leukocyte trafficking and endothelial activation during experimental inflammation induced by monosodium urate crystals

Injection of MSU crystals into human skin leads to an erythematous reaction that is maximal at 24 hours and then spontaneously subsides [25]. The response is very similar in pig skin, providing a good model for studying how endothelial activation and leukocyte recruitment relate to the time course of MSU-crystal-induced inflammation. We analysed endothelial activation and leukocyte trafficking by measuring the uptake of differentially radiolabelled anti-E-selectin, neutrophils, and/or mononuclear cells at various times after intracutaneous injection of MSU crystals [26].

Leukocyte recruitment commenced between 1 and 2 hours after injection of MSU crystals, in close parallel with the onset of E-selectin expression (Fig. 1). Unexpectedly, the phase of E-selectin expression and leukocyte

Figure 1

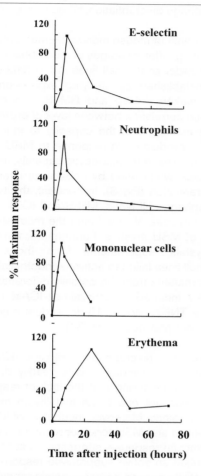

Kinetics of endothelial E-selectin expression, entry of neutrophils and mononuclear cells into the tissues, and erythema in pig skin after injection of monosodium urate (MSU) crystals. Note that E-selectin expression and leukocyte trafficking have returned to near baseline before maximal erythema is seen at 24 hours, indicating a vascular downregulation of the inflammatory response. Erythema subsides spontaneously after 24 hours, in spite of the continued presence of MSU crystals in the tissues, suggesting extravascular downregulating mechanisms (modified from [26], with kind permission from the British Journal of Rheumatology).

recruitment was quite brief, and both had returned to baseline by the peak of erythema at 24 hours. After 24 hours, erythema resolved in spite of the continued presence of MSU crystals in the skin. When the relations between endothelial activation and leukocyte trafficking and the kinetics of the inflammatory response are considered, three conclusions can be drawn. Firstly, initial endothelial activation and leukocyte recruitment were closely connected. Secondly, the transient nature of endothelial E-selectin expression and leukocyte recruitment appeared to limit the entry of leukocytes into the tissues to a relatively early stage of the response. Finally, assuming erythema is a reflection of postmigratory leuko-

cyte activation, mechanisms must exist that reduce the responsiveness of leukocytes to MSU crystals and thereby terminate further endothelial stimulation.

The role of the monocyte in endothelial activation during the onset of acute gout

MSU crystals are able to activate a number of acute inflammatory pathways, which may induce and/or amplify an acute attack of gout. These include the alternative pathway of complement and the kallikrein system, and stimulation of mast-cell degranulation with rapid release of vasoactive mediators and TNF-α [27]. We have focused particularly on the monocyte, because of its potential for the sustained release of endothelial activating factors. Monocytes are known to respond to the phagocytosis of MSU crystals by activating expression of a number of proinflammatory genes, including those encoding interleukin (IL)-1 [28], IL-6 [29], IL-8 [30], TNF-α [31], and Cox-2 [32]. In the case of IL-8, gene transcription follows signalling via tyrosine phosphorylation of extracellularly regulated kinase (ERK)1/ERK2, p38 MAPK (mitogen-activated protein kinase), and JNK (c-Jun N-terminal kinase) [30]. Promoter analysis has demonstrated that transcriptional activation of the IL-8 gene by MSU crystals involves binding of activator protein-1 and the NF-κB complex c-Rel/RelA to the IL-8 promoter [33].

In order to determine which monocyte-derived factors are responsible for activation of expression of endothelial-cell adhesion molecule, we established an *in vitro* model in which MSU-crystal-stimulated monocyte supernatants were transferred to endothelial-cell cultures in the presence of neutralising antibodies to candidate cytokines [34]. These experiments showed that the capacity of MSU-stimulated monocytes to induce expression of the adhesion molecules E-selectin, ICAM-1, and VCAM-1 was entirely attributable to release of TNF-α and IL-1β. Furthermore, when the time course of production of these two cytokines was studied in more detail, IL-1β secretion was found to precede that of TNF-α.

Cytokine-mediated activation of endothelium *in vivo* can be demonstrated by imaging the uptake of intravenously injected anti-E-selectin monoclonal antibody, as shown in rheumatoid arthritis (RA) [35] and inflammatory bowel disease [36]. Using a pig model of MSU-crystal-induced arthritis [37], we found that E-selectin expression and neutrophil recruitment were inhibited approximately 50% in the presence of neutralizing antibodies to TNF-α, a finding consistent with the data found *in vitro* [34] (Fig. 2).

Possible role of the macrophage in downregulating the tissue response

A number of mechanisms have been proposed to account for the spontaneous resolution of acute gout. These include coating of crystals with protective proteins

Figure 2

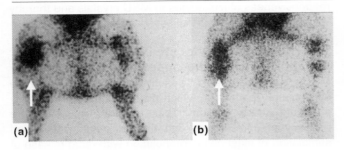

(a)   (b)

Imaging E-selectin expression in MSU crystal-induced arthritis in the pig. Scintigraphic images of anti-E-selectin monoclonal antibody (mAb) uptake in untreated and anti-TNF-α-treated pigs. Scintigraphic images of the hind limbs and abdomen of an untreated **(a)** and an anti-TNF-α-treated animal **(b)** were taken 24 hours after the intra-articular injection of MSU crystals into the right knee and saline solution into the left knee. There is marked uptake of anti-E-selectin mAb into the inflamed joint of the untreated animal, particularly in the region of the joint space (a, arrow). In contrast, anti-E-selectin mAb uptake in the injected knee of an anti-TNF-α treated animal demonstrates a pattern of uptake that is both less intense and less focal (reproduced from [34], with kind permission from Wiley-Liss, Inc., a subsidiary of John Wiley & Sons, Inc.).

[38,39], and anti-inflammatory effects of the hypothalmic–pituitary axis [40,41]. Also, inflammation will decline upon neutrophil apoptosis in the tissues, although neutrophil apoptosis may be delayed by uptake of MSU crystals [42].

Apoptotic neutrophils are rapidly and efficiently phagocytosed by tissue macrophages and possibly also by other resident cells [43]. This is thought to protect tissues from damage due to autolysis and spillage of the apoptotic neutrophil contents, and no doubt reduces the duration and extent of neutrophil-mediated inflammation. Importantly, clearance of apoptotic neutrophils by macrophages occurs without the elaboration of proinflammatory cytokines. Instead, macrophages that have taken up apoptotic neutrophils may generate factors with anti-inflammatory properties, including transforming growth factor-β, platelet-activating factor, and prostaglandin E$_2$ [44]. Evidence for the uptake of apoptotic neutrophils by macrophages in gout exists in the form of the Reiter cell, which can be found in synovial fluid during an acute gout attack [45,46].

It has been known since the 1970s that MSU crystals can be found in asymptomatic joints of hyperuricaemic individuals. When synovial fluid leukocytes associated with crystals were examined, it was observed that >99.5% of internalised crystals were contained within mononuclear cells but almost never within neutrophils [3,4]. This observation raised the possibility that whereas monocytes elicit a proinflammatory response upon uptake of MSU crystals, macrophages might clear crystals without the induction of proinflammatory activity, in a manner analogous to the clearance of apoptotic neutrophils. We therefore addressed directly the possibility that the inflammatory

response to MSU may be influenced by the state of monocyte-to-macrophage differentiation.

We studied a panel of mouse monocyte–macrophage cell lines, representing different stages of macrophage maturation [47]. The order of the cell lines in the differentiation line-up was established by studying expression of the macrophage markers F4/80 and BM 8. The cell lines revealed a close correlation between level of expression of these surface markers and the capacity to ingest MSU crystals. TNF-α production in response to MSU crystals, however, was not linked to phagocytic capacity, in that the most TNF-α was synthesised by cells at an intermediate stage of differentiation (Fig. 3). In contrast, the two most mature macrophage cell types, MH-S and IC21, failed to secrete TNF-α in spite of their being the most efficient at phagocytosis of MSU crystals. Furthermore, after uptake of MSU crystals, supernatants from these mature macrophage cell lines failed to activate endothelial cells. In contrast, supernatants from the partially differentiated cell line RAW264.7 induced endothelial-cell ICAM-1 expression through a TNF-α- and IL-1β-dependent mechanism, in accord with our previous study [34].

Stimulation of the macrophage cell line IC21 with lipopolysaccharide or zymosan led to readily detectable TNF-α production, signifying that the lack of response to MSU crystals was not due to an inability to make proinflammatory cytokines. Moreover, incubation of IC21 cells with both zymosan and MSU together resulted in suppression of the zymosan response, suggesting that MSU crystals may stimulate an active suppressive response. Since suppressor activity passed across a semipermeable filter, this appears to involve the release of as-yet-uncharacterised soluble factors.

We have recently extended these experiments to human monocytes and to macrophages differentiated *in vitro* and obtained very similar results (unpublished observations). Whereas freshly isolated monocytes responded to MSU crystals by releasing IL-1β, TNF-α ,and IL-6, differentiated macrophages from the same individual internalised crystals but failed to generate these cytokines or any other factor capable of activating endothelial-cell adhesion molecule expression [48]. Again, human macrophages were as responsive as monocytes in terms of TNF-α release following zymosan stimulation. Ongoing work is establishing in more detail the profile of proinflammatory and anti-inflammatory genes activated in monocytes and macrophages after uptake of MSU crystals and characterising the receptors and signalling mechanisms involved.

Monocytes and macrophages as partners in the orchestration of acute gout

On the basis of this recent work, we propose a model of gout in which the critical determinant of an acute attack is

Figure 3

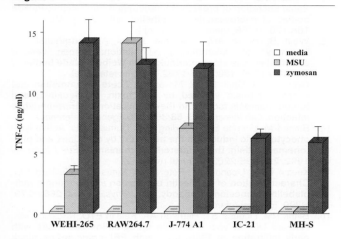

Secretion of TNF-α by macrophage cell lines in response to MSU crystals or zymosan. TNF-α as measured by ELISA in culture supernatants collected from five phagocytically competent macrophage cell lines cultured for 16 hours in the presence of media alone, MSU crystals (0.5 mg/ml), or unopsonized zymosan particles (400 µg/ml). Note that the mature macrophage cell lines IC-21 and MH-S secreted TNF-α in response to zymosan but not to MSU crystals. All these cell lines efficiently phagocytosed MSU crystals. Values are means ± SD of triplicates. (Reproduced from [47], with kind permission from Wiley-Liss, Inc., a subsidiary of John Wiley & Sons, Inc.).

Figure 4

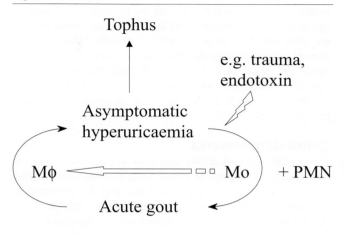

Model of the differential roles of monocytes and macrophages in the inflammatory response to MSU crystals. The model proposes that monocytes play a central role in stimulating an acute attack of gout, whereas differentiated macrophages may play an anti-inflammatory role in terminating an acute attack and in preserving the asymptomatic state (modified from [48], with kind permission from Current Science Ltd). Mo, monocyte; Mφ, macrophage; PMN, polymorphonuclear leukocyte.

not just the presence of free MSU crystals, but also the availability in the extravascular tissues of recently recruited blood monocytes (Fig. 4). In individuals with hyperuricaemia, the asymptomatic state may be maintained by the silent removal by tissue macrophages of small quantities of crystals as and when they precipitate. However, fresh monocyte recruitment may occur in response to any of the well-established precipitants of acute gout (e.g. trauma, infection), perhaps ensuing from initial endothelial activation by mast-cell degranulation and release of TNF-α. Uptake of crystals by monocytes leads to the elaboration of IL-1β and TNF-α, which in turn activates endothelium and amplifies the inflammatory response through the recruitment of neutrophils and further monocytes. Our observations in pig skin suggest that the positive feedback loop is terminated initially at the level of vascular endothelium, by mechanisms shutting off further leukocyte entry into the tissues. Subsequently, the downregulation of postmigratory tissue leukocyte activation and the further elaboration of endothelial activating factors may be achieved by the noninflammatory removal of free crystals by macrophages that have differentiated from recruited monocytes, possibly involving the release of anti-inflammatory mediators. However, the macrophage may not be a completely innocent partner, as it remains possible that the resolution mechanisms induced by MSU crystals could include factors involved in tissue repair (such as proteases and growth factors) that may contribute to the destructive changes associated with tophi.

Acute versus chronic rheumatic diseases
The relation between endothelial activation and monocyte–macrophage differentiation identified in gout provides a platform on which to base an understanding of the kinetics of inflammation in rheumatic diseases that are not self-limiting. In immune-mediated conditions such as RA, a number of influences may limit the downregulating activities of endothelium and macrophages. First, in RA synovium, postcapillary venules come to resemble high endothelial venules found in peripheral lymphoid organs [49]. These high endothelial venules have plump, cuboidal/columnar endothelial cells and are adapted to support sustained rather than self-limited leukocyte recruitment [50,51]. This and other morphological changes characteristic of lymphoid neogenesis are most probably under the control of the B lymphocyte chemo-attractant (BLC/CXCL13) [52,53].

A second important difference in RA is the presence of immune complexes and/or complement, which may subvert the noninflammatory properties of differentiated macrophages by promoting phagocytosis through different receptors. Thus, opsonic serum has been shown to reverse the noninflammatory program of apoptotic neutrophil removal by macrophages, instead rendering the process proinflammatory [54]. Immune complexes in RA may directly trigger the release of proinflammatory cytokines, such as TNF-α, by binding to the immunoglobulin receptor, Fc gamma receptor IIIA [55].

A third difference between the self-limiting inflammatory response in gout and RA is that the prevailing chemokine/cytokine milieu of rheumatoid synovium may favour precursor differentiation to a dendritic cell rather than a tissue macrophage phenotype. Rheumatoid synovium is rich in cytokines, such as IL-4 and IL-15 [56], that skew monocyte differentiation towards dendritic cells [57], but is poor in cytokines, such as M-CSF, that promote the macrophagic end-point [58].

Concluding remarks

The model outlined above can now act as a template for addressing the triangular interactions between monocytes, macrophages, and endothelial cells, and for determining the influence that monocyte–macrophage differentiation has on the control of other inflammatory responses caused by potentially harmful particles. It is clear from the variety of rheumatological syndromes associated with different crystals that the biological effects of crystal deposition vary with the species of crystal involved. This in turn is due to differential cellular responses [31–33], perhaps related to distinct utilisation of cell-surface receptors. The detailed analysis of the various receptor and signalling pathways involved in cellular responses to different crystals may provide important insights that will help us understand the mechanisms underlying the heterogeneity of crystal-related rheumatic diseases.

Glossary of terms

MSU = monosodium urate

References

1. Hall AP, Barry PE, Dawber TR, McNamara PM: **Epidemiology of gout and hyperuricemia. A long-term population study.** *Am J Med* 1967, **42**:27-37. [archival reference]
2. Weinberger A, Schumacher HR, Agudelo CA: **Urate crystals in asymptomatic metatarsophalangeal joints.** *Ann Intern Med* 1979, **91**:56-57. [archival reference]
3. Louthrenoo W, Sieck M, Clayburne G, Rothfuss S, Schumacher HRJ: **Supravital staining of cells in noninflammatory synovial fluids: analysis of the effect of crystals on cell populations.** *J Rheumatol* 1991, **18**:409-413. [archival reference]
4. Pascual E, Jovani V: **A quantitative study of the phagocytosis of urate crystals in the synovial fluid of asymptomatic joints of patients with gout.** *Br J Rheumatol* 1995, **34**:724-726. [archival reference]
5. Springer TA: **Traffic signals on endothelium for lymphocyte recirculation and leukocyte emigration.** *Annu Rev Physiol* 1995, **57**:827-872. [key review]
6. Frenette PS, Wagner DD: **Adhesion Molecules – Part I.** *N Engl J Med* 1996, **334**:1526-1529. [key review]
7. Frenette PS, Wagner DD: **Adhesion molecules—Part II: Blood vessels and blood cells.** *N Engl J Med* 1996, **335**:43-45. [key review]
8. Pober JS, Cotran RS: **Cytokines and endothelial cell biology.** *Physiol Rev* 1990, **70**:427-451. [key review]
9. Cines DB, Pollak ES, Buck CA, Loscalzo J, Zimmerman GA, McEver RP, Pober JS, Wick TM, Konkle BA, Schwartz BS, Barnathan ES, McCrae KR, Hug BA, Schmidt AM, Stern DM: **Endothelial cells in physiology and in the pathophysiology of vascular disorders.** *Blood* 1998, **91**:3527-3561. [key review]
10. Wagner DD: **The Weibel-Palade body: the storage granule for von Willebrand factor and P-selectin.** *Thromb Haemost* 1993, **70**:105-110. [key review]
11. Utgaard JO, Jahnsen FL, Bakka A, Brandtzaeg P, Haraldsen G: **Rapid secretion of prestored interleukin 8 from Weibel-Palade bodies of microvascular endothelial cells.** *J Exp Med* 1998; **188**:1751-1756. [general reference]]
12. Wolff B, Burns AR, Middleton J, Rot A: **Endothelial cell "memory" of inflammatory stimulation: human venular endothelial cells store interleukin 8 in Weibel-Palade bodies.** *J Exp Med* 1998, **188**:1757-1762. [general reference]
13. Cybulsky MI, Chan MKW, Movat HZ: **Acute inflammation and microthrombosis induced by endotoxin, interleukin-1, and tumour necrosis factor and their implication in Gram-negative infection.** *Lab Invest* 1988, **58**:365-378. [general reference]
14. Binns RM, Licence ST, Wooding FBP, Duffus WPH: **Active lymphocyte traffic induced in the periphery by cytokines and phytohemagglutinin: three different mechanisms?** *Eur J Immunol* 1992, **22**:2195-2203. [general reference]
15. Keelan ETM, Licence ST, Peters AM, Binns RM, Haskard DO: **Characterization of E-selectin expression in vivo using a radiolabelled monoclonal antibody.** *Am J Physiol* 1994, **266**:H279-H290. [general reference]
16. Binns RM, Licence ST, Harrison AA, Keelan ETD, Robinson MK, Haskard DO: **In vivo E-selectin upregulation correlates with early infiltration of PMN, later with PBL-entry: mAbs block both.** *Am J Physiol* 1996, **270**:H183-H193. [general reference]
17. Binns RM, Whyte A, Licence ST, Harrison AA, Tsang Y, Haskard DO, Robinson MK: **The role of E-selectin in lymphocyte and polymorphonuclear cell recruitment into cutaneous delayed hypersensitivity reactions in sensitized pigs.** *J Immunol* 1996, **157**:4094-4099. [general reference]
18. Harrison AA, Stocker CJ, Chapman PT, Tsang YT, Huehns TY, Gundel RH, Peters AM, Davies KA, George AJ, Robinson MK, Haskard DO: **Expression of VCAM-1 by vascular endothelial cells in immune- and non-immune inflammatory reactions in the skin.** *J Immunol* 1997, **159**:4546-4554. [general reference]
19. Panes J, Perry MA, Anderson DC, Manning A, Leone B, Cepinskas G, Rosenbloom CL, Miyasaka M, Kvietys PR, Granger DN: **Regional differences in constitutive and induced ICAM-1 expression in vivo.** *Am J Physiol* 1995, **269**:H1955-1964. [general reference]
20. Henninger DD, Panes J, Eppihimer M, Russell J, Gerritsen M, Anderson DC, Granger DN: **Cytokine-induced VCAM-1 and ICAM-1 expression in different organs in the mouse.** *J Immunol* 1997; **158**:1825-1832. [general reference]
21. Hickey MJ, Kanwar S, McCafferty DM, Granger DN, Eppihimer MJ, Kubes P: **Varying roles of E-selectin and P-selectin in different microvascular beds in response to antigen.** *J Immunol* 1999, **162**:1137-1143. [general reference]
22. Harari O, McHale J, Marshall D, Ahmed S, Brown D, Askenase PW, Haskard DO: **Endothelial cell E- and P-selectin up-regulation in murine contact sensitivity is prolonged by distinct mechanisms occurring in sequence.** *J Immunol* 1999, **163**:6860-6866. [general reference]
23. McHale JF, Harari OA, Marshall D, Haskard DO: **TNF-α and IL-1 sequentially induce endothelial ICAM-1 and VCAM-1 expression in MRL/lpr lupus-prone mice.** *J Immunol* 1999, **163**:3993-4000. [general reference]
24. Harari O, Marshall D, McHale J, Ahmed S, Haskard DO: **Limited endothelial E- and P-selectin expression in MRL/lpr lupus-prone mice.** *Rheumatology* 2001, **40**: 889-895. [general reference]
25. Dieppe PA, Doherty M, Papadimitriou GM: **Inflammatory responses to intradermal crystals in healthy volunteers and patients with rheumatic diseases.** *Rheumatol Int* 1982, **2**:55-58. [general reference]
26. Chapman PT, Jamar F, Harrison AA, Schofield JB, Peters AM, Binns RM, Haskard DO: **Characterization of E-selectin expression, leukocyte traffic and clinical sequelae in urate crystal-induced inflammation: an insight into gout.** *Brit J Rheumatol* 1996, **35**:323-334. [general reference]
27. Terkeltaub R: **Pathogenesis of inflammatory manifestations caused by crystals.** In: *Gout, Hyperuricaemia, and Other Crystal-associated Arthropathies.* Edited by Smyth CJ, Holers VM. New York: Marcel Dekker, 1999: 1-14. [key review]
28. Di Giovine FS, Malawista SE, Nuki G, Duff GW: **Interleukin 1 (IL 1) as a mediator of crystal arthritis: stimulation of T cell and synovial fibroblast mitogenesis by urate crystal-induced IL-1.** *J Immunol* 1987,**38**:3213-3218. [general reference]

29. Guerne PA, Terkeltaub R, Zuraw B, Lotz M: **Inflammatory microcrystals stimulate interleukin-6 production and secretion by human monocytes and synoviocytes.** *Arthritis Rheum* 1989, **32**:1443-1452. [general reference]

30. Terkeltaub R, Zachariae C, Santoro D, Martin J, Peveri P, Matsushima K: **Monocyte-derived neutrophil chemotactic factor/interleukin-8 is a potential mediator of crystal-induced inflammation.** *Arthritis Rheum* 1991, **34**:894-903. [general reference]

31. Di Giovine FS, Malawista SE, Thornton E, Duff GW: **Urate crystals stimulate production of tumor necrosis factor alpha from human blood monocytes and synovial cells. Cytokine mRNA and protein kinetics, and cellular distribution.** *J Clin Invest* 1991, **87**:1375-1381. [general reference]

32. Pouliot M, James MJ, McColl SR, Naccache PH, Cleland LG:**Monosodium urate microcrystals induce cyclooxygenase-2 in human monocytes.** *Blood* 1998, **91**:1769-1776. [general reference]

33. Liu R, O'Connell M, Johnson K, Pritzker K, Mackman N, Terkeltaub R: **Extracellular signal-regulated kinase 1/extracellular signal-regulated kinase 2 mitogen-activated protein kinase signaling and activation of activator protein 1 and nuclear factor kappaB transcription factors play central roles in interleukin-8 expression stimulated by monosodium urate monohydrate and calcium pyrophosphate crystals in monocytic cells.** *Arthritis Rheum* 2000, **43**:1145-1155. [general reference]

34. Chapman PT, Yarwood H, Harrison AA, Stocker CJ, Jamar F, Gundel RH, Peters AM, Haskard DO: **Endothelial activation in monosodium urate monohydrate crystal-induced inflammation: in vitro and in vivo studies on the roles of tumor necrosis factor-alpha and interleukin-1.** *Arthritis Rheum* 1997, **40**: 955-965. [general reference]

35. Chapman PT, Jamar F, Keelan ETM, Peters AM, Haskard DO: **Use of a radiolabeled monoclonal antibody against E-selectin for imaging endothelial activation in rheumatoid arthritis.** *Arthritis Rheum* 1996, **39**:1371-1375. [general reference]

36. Bhatti M, Chapman P, Peters AM, Haskard DO, Hodgson H:**Visualizing E-selectin in the detection and evaluation of inflammatory bowel disease.** *Gut* 1998, **43**:40-47. [general reference]

37. Chapman PT, Jamar F, Harrison AA, Binns RM, Peters AM, Haskard DO: **Non-invasive imaging of E-selectin expression by activated endothelium in urate crystal-induced arthritis.** *Arthritis Rheum* 1994, **37**:1752-1756. [general reference]

38. Terkeltaub R, Martin J, Curtiss LK, Ginsberg MH: **Apolipoprotein B mediates the capacity of low density lipoprotein to suppress neutrophil stimulation by particulates.** *J Biol Chem* 1986, **261**:15662-15667. [general reference]

39. Terkeltaub RA, Dyer CA, Martin J, Curtiss LK: **Apolipoprotein (apo) E inhibits the capacity of monosodium urate crystals to stimulate neutrophils. Characterization of intraarticular apo E and demonstration of apo E binding to urate crystals in vivo.** *J Clin Invest* 1991, **87**:20-26. [general reference]

40. Ortiz-Bravo E, Sieck MS, Schumacher HRJ: **Changes in the proteins coating monosodium urate crystals during active and subsiding inflammation. Immunogold studies of synovial fluid from patients with gout and of fluid obtained using the rat subcutaneous air pouch model.** *Arthritis Rheum* 1993, **36**: 1274-1285. [general reference]

41. Getting SJ, Gibbs L, Clark AJ, Flower RJ, Perretti M: **POMC gene-derived peptides activate melanocortin type 3 receptor on murine macrophages, suppress cytokine release, and inhibit neutrophil migration in acute experimental inflammation.** *J Immunol* 1999, **162**:7446-7453. [general reference]

42. Akahoshi T, Nagaoka T, Namai R, Sekiyama N, Kondo H: **Prevention of neutrophil apoptosis by monosodium urate crystals.** *Rheumatol Int* 1997, **16**: :231-235. [general reference]

43. Haslett C, Savill JS, Whyte MK, Stern M, Dransfield I, Meagher LC: **Granulocyte apoptosis and the control of inflammation.** *Philos Trans R Soc Lond B Biol Sci* 1994, **345**:327-333. [key review]

44. Fadok VA, Bratton DL, Konowal A, Freed PW, Westcott JY, Henson PM: **Macrophages that have ingested apoptotic cells in vitro inhibit proinflammatory cytokine production through autocrine/paracrine mechanisms involving TGF-beta, PGE2, and PAF.** *J Clin Invest* 1998, **101**:890-898. [general reference]

45. Savill JS, Wyllie AH, Henson JE, Walport MJ, Henson PM, Haslett C: **Macrophage phagocytosis of aging neutrophils in inflam-mation: programmed cell death in the neutrophil leads to its recognition by macrophages.** *J Clin Invest* 1989, **83**:865-875. [general reference]

46. Selvi E, Manganelli S, De Stefano R, Frati E, Marcolongo R: **CD36 and CD14 immunoreactivity of Reiter cells in inflammatory synovial fluids.** *Ann Rheum Dis* 2000, **59**:399-400. [general reference]

47. Yagnik DR, Hillyer P, Marshall D, Krausz T, Haskard DO, Landis RC: **Non-inflammatory phagocytosis of monosodium urate monohydrate crystals by macrophages: implications for the control of joint inflammation in gout.** *Arthritis Rheum* 2000; **43**: 1779-1789. [general reference]

48. Landis RC, Yagnik DR, Emons V, Mason J, Haskard DO: **Safe disposal of inflammatory monosodium urtae monohydrate crystals by differentiated macrophages.** *Arthritis Rheum* 2001, **44**:S162. [general reference]

49. Iguchi T, Ziff M: **Electron microscopic study of rheumatoid synovial vasculature. Intimate relationship between tall endothelium and lymphoid aggregation.** *J Clin Invest* 1986, **77**: 355-361. [general reference]

50. Freemont AJ: **Molecules controlling lymphocyte-endothelial interactions in lymph nodes are produced in vessels of inflamed synovium.** *Ann Rheum Dis* 1987, **46**:924-928. [general reference]

51. Michie SA, Streeter PR, Bolt PA, Butcher EC, Picker LJ: **The human peripheral lymph node vascular addressin: an inducible endothelial antigen involved in lymphocyte homing.** *Am J Pathol* 1993, **143**:1688-1698. [general reference]

52. Luther SA, Lopez T, Bai W, Hanahan D, Cyster JG: **BLC expression in pancreatic islets causes B cell recruitment and lymphotoxin-dependent lymphoid neogenesis.** *Immunity* 2000, **12**:471-481. [general reference]

53. Shi K, Hayashida K, Kaneko M, Hashimoto J, Tomita T, Lipsky PE, Yoshikawa H, Ochi T: **Lymphoid chemokine B cell attracting chemokine-1 (CXCL13) is expressed in germinal center of ectopic lymphoid follicles within the synovium of chronic arthritis patients.** *J Immunol* 2001, **166**:650-655. [general reference]

54. Meagher LC, Savill JS, Baker A, Fuller RW, Haslett C: **Phagocytosis of apoptotic neutrophils does not induce macrophage release of thromboxane B2.** *J Leukoc Biol* 1992, **52**:269-273. [general reference]

55. Abrahams VM, Cambridge G, Lydyard PM, Edwards JC: **Induction of tumor necrosis factor alpha production by adhered human monocytes: a key role for Fcgamma receptor type IIIa in rheumatoid arthritis.** *Arthritis Rheum* 2000, **43**:608-616. [general reference]

56. McInnes IB, Al-Mughales J, Field M, Leung BP, Huang F-P, Dixon R, Sturrock RD, Wilkinson PC, Liew FY: **The role of interleukin-15 in T-cell migration and activation in rheumatoid arthritis.** *Nat Med* 1996, **2**:175-182. [general reference]

57. Mohamadzadeh M, Berard F, Essert G, Chalouni C, Pulendran B, Davoust J, Bridges G, Palucka AK, Banchereau J: **Interleukin 15 skews monocyte differentiation into dendritic cells with features of Langerhans cells.** *J Exp Med* 2001, **194**:1013-1020.

58. Becker S, Warren MK, Haskill S: **Colony-stimulating factor-induced monocyte survival and differentiation into macrophages in serum-free cultures.** *J Immunol* 1987, **139**: 3703-3709. [general reference].

Supplement Review
VEGF and imaging of vessels in rheumatoid arthritis
Peter C Taylor

The Kennedy Institute Division, Imperial College School of Medicine, London, UK

Correspondence: Peter C Taylor MA, PhD, FRCP, Senior Lecturer and Honorary Consultant Rheumatologist, The Kennedy Institute Division, Imperial College School of Medicine 1 Aspenlea Road London W6 8LH, UK. Tel: 020 8383 4494; fax: 020 8748 3293; email: peter.c.taylor@ic.ac.uk; department website: www.kennedy.ac.uk

Received: 7 December 2001
Accepted: 25 January 2002
Published: 9 May 2002

Arthritis Res 2002, **4 (suppl 3)**:S99-S107

This article may contain supplementary data which can only be found online at http://arthritis-research.com/content/4/S3/S099

Chapter summary

Angiogenesis is a prominent feature of rheumatoid synovitis. Formation of new blood vessels permits a supply of nutrients and oxygen to the augmented inflammatory cell mass and so contributes to perpetuation of joint disease. Vascular endothelial growth factor (VEGF) is a potent endothelial cell-specific growth factor that is upregulated by proinflammatory cytokines and by hypoxia. Serum VEGF concentrations are elevated in rheumatoid arthritis (RA) and correlate with disease activity. Furthermore, serum VEGF measured at first presentation in RA is highly significantly correlated with radiographic progression of disease over the subsequent year. Power Doppler ultrasonography is a sensitive method for demonstrating the presence of blood flow in small vessels and there is a very close relation between the presence or absence of vascular flow signal on power Doppler imaging and the rate of early synovial enhancement on dynamic gadolinium-enhanced magnetic resonance imaging (MRI) of joints with RA. Images obtained by both dynamic enhanced MRI and power Doppler ultrasonography correlate with vascularity of synovial tissue as assessed histologically. In early RA, there is a striking association between joint erosions assessed on high-resolution ultrasonography and vascular signal in power Doppler mode. Collectively, these findings implicate vascular pannus in the erosive phase of disease and strongly suggest that proangiogenic molecules such as VEGF are targets for novel therapies in RA. Animal model data supports this concept. It seems likely that serological and imaging measures of vascularity in RA will become useful tools in the assessment of disease activity and response to therapy.

Keywords: angiogenesis, magnetic resonance imaging, power Doppler ultrasonography, rheumatoid arthritis, VEGF

Introduction

Rheumatoid arthritis (RA) is a common human disease, with a prevalence of about 1%. The clinical presentation is heterogeneous, with a wide spectrum of age of onset, degree of joint involvement, and severity. Up to 90% of patients with aggressive synovitis have radiologic evidence of bone erosion within 2 years of diagnosis, despite treatment [1]. However, at the onset of symptoms, it is difficult to predict which patients will follow a more severe disease course. It is now highly desirable to identify such patients at an early stage in their disease evolution, because of the advent of biologic agents that have the potential not only to significantly improve symptoms and signs of disease in a high proportion of patients [2], but also to arrest structural damage to joints [3]. At present, the economic burden of these new therapies is such that rationing of some sort is inevitable and it is therefore equally desirable to determine whether those patients receiving biologic therapies are responding adequately at an early stage of their treatment.

A glossary of specialist terms used in this chapter appears at the end of the text section. A list of common abbreviations used in this issue appears just before the indexes.

In health, angiogenesis – or growth of new blood vessels from pre-existing vasculature – occurs during growth and the female reproductive cycle. It is also a feature of tissue repair after injury and contributes to the pathogenesis of a number of disease states, including cancer, chronic gingivitis, diabetic retinopathy, and RA. Angiogenesis occurs as a coordinated process comprising proliferation and migration of endothelial cells, followed by the formation of capillary tubes, deposition of basement membrane, and proliferation and migration of pericytes and smooth muscle cells. Anastomoses are created and flow of blood is established. Vascular reorganisation follows, in a process requiring the regression of redundant vessels by apoptosis of endothelial cells [4]. In order to match function of the microvascular bed to local metabolic demand, the developing vessels begin to express vasoactive peptides and their receptors [5].

Angiogenesis in the synovial membrane of patients with RA is considered by many investigators to be an important early step in pathogenesis of RA and in the perpetuation of disease [5,6]. This chapter focuses on recent research findings arising from serologic and imaging measures of vascularity in RA. I discuss the role of vascular endothelial growth factor (VEGF), a marker of angiogenesis, in the pathophysiology of RA, and emerging evidence that serum VEGF concentrations correlate with disease activity and fall when synovitis is successfully suppressed by therapy. I will also discuss the potential of angiogenic markers, such as VEGF, to predict disease outcome. I review developments in imaging technologies that permit assessment of synovial vascularity and discuss their potential application in the evaluation of RA disease activity, prediction of disease progression, and monitoring of response to therapy. I examine the implications of these findings for our understanding of disease pathogenesis and consider the potential of VEGF and angiogenesis as a target for therapy.

Historical background: the role of VEGF in RA

Angiogenesis, regulated by a complex set of inducers and inhibitors, arises when hypoxic, diseased, or injured tissues secrete proangiogenic molecules. Many endothelial growth factors have been demonstrated in RA synovium [6–8] and tenosynovium [9]. Of these, VEGF is the most endothelial-cell-specific factor characterised to date [10–12]. It also induces vascular permeability [13]. In RA synovium, VEGF expression is upregulated in macrophages and fibroblasts [14,15] and we have demonstrated protein expression in synovial endothelial cells by immunohistochemistry [16] (Fig. 1). Co-culture of activated monocytes or neutrophils from RA synovial fluids with unstimulated, semiconfluent RA fibroblast-like synoviocytes results in synergistic increases in the expression and secretion of bioactive VEGF [17]. Furthermore, this induction of VEGF is significantly inhibited by anti-integrin antibodies, a finding implying that VEGF expression in RA

Figure 1

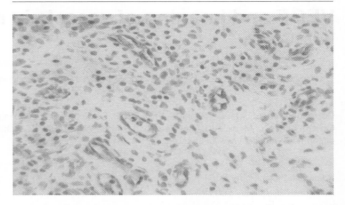

Staining of rheumatoid synovium for vascular endothelial growth factor, showing expression of the factor in endothelial cells. See Colour figure section.

synovitis is regulated not only by proinflammatory cytokines, but also by the physical interaction of activated leukocytes and fibroblast-like synoviocytes [17].

VEGF exists as several isoforms, generated by alternative splicing of VEGF mRNA. RT-PCR analysis shows the VEGF(121) isoform to be expressed constitutively in RA synovial tissues, whereas the VEGF(165) isoform is expressed in less than half the tissues examined [18,19]. Microvascular density is significantly higher in RA synovial tissues expressing VEGF(165) [18]. The proportion of microvessels expressing CD31 that are activated, as assessed by a monoclonal antibody recognising the VEGF/KDR receptor complex, is significantly greater in RA than in osteoarthritis or normal synovial tissue [20]. VEGF receptor Flt-1 (VEGFR-1) protein is expressed on microvessels in close proximity to VEGF protein [19] and there is a close correlation between expression of isoform VEGF(165) and that of its receptors KDR (VEGFR-2) and neuropilin [18].

In the case of inflammatory tissue, several interdependent processes promote angiogenesis. Shear stress on the endothelial wall as a result of increased blood flow may enhance angiogenesis, as may extravasated plasma proteins such as fibrinogen products. Similarly, inflammatory cells – including macrophages, lymphocytes, mast cells, and fibroblasts – and their proangiogenic soluble products promote angiogenesis. Many cytokines promoting inflammation, such as tumour necrosis factor (TNF)-α, IL-1, and IL-8 also have proangiogenic activity. Hypoxia, which is often a feature of inflammation, is a potent inducer of VEGF. Furthermore, hypoxic culture conditions greatly augment the rate of VEGF secretion from cultured synovial fibroblasts stimulated by IL-1 and transforming growth factor (TGF)-β [21]. Direct measurements confirm that the RA joint is a hypoxic environment [22]. Contributory factors include the high metabolic demands of inflamed synovial tissue and the rapid rate of synovial proliferation, such that cells become more distant from the closest blood vessels, compounding the hypoxic state [23]. Tissue hypoxia in the rheumatoid joint results in increased VEGF mRNA stability [24] and enhances VEGF gene transcription through the binding of hypoxia-inducible transcription factors such as HIF-1 and HIF-2. Both of these factors are degraded within minutes of exposure to an oxygen tension >3–5% but are stabilised under conditions of hypoxia (<3% oxygen), then translocated to the nucleus, where they bind to hypoxia-responsive elements on hypoxia-inducible genes to upregulate their expression [25]. Thus, it is possible that the hypoxic environment in the rheumatoid joint, compounded by the high metabolic demands of synovial inflammation, promotes transcriptional changes permissive to perpetuation of synovitis.

Measuring VEGF in RA: relation to disease activity and response to therapy

VEGF is detectable in serum, synovial tissue, and fluids of patients with RA [14,15,26–30]. Human neutrophils secrete VEGF [31], and Kasama et al. report that concentrations of neutrophil-associated VEGF in RA synovial fluids correlate well with free VEGF in joint effusions and with the patient's disease activity [32]. Other investigators find no correlation between VEGF concentrations in serum and synovial fluids from the same RA patients [33]. Synovial fluid VEGF concentrations correlate with matrix metalloproteinase (MMP)-9 concentrations in the fluid in early inflammatory arthritis [34].

The source of VEGF in the serum is unclear. In vitro, human peripheral blood mononuclear cells have been shown to release VEGF in response to cytokines expressed in RA synovium, such as TNF-α [29]. Release of VEGF from platelets has also been reported [35]. Serum VEGF might therefore be derived from platelets, synovial-fluid neutrophils, inflamed synovial tissue, or other sources.

A number of groups have reported that VEGF concentrations are higher in the serum of RA patients than in healthy controls or patients with osteoarthritis [27,33,35–37]. Furthermore, serum VEGF concentrations correlate with individual and composite measures of RA disease activity, including acute phase markers and counts of swollen and tender joints [33,36,37]. In a study of patients attending my early clinics for inflammatory arthritis and established RA, serum VEGF concentrations were higher in patients with early RA than in patients with long-standing, treated RA [36]. This observation may represent a response to therapy, a view supported by studies in which serum VEGF concentrations have been measured before and after commencement of therapy [27,35,36]. In our series, a total of 27 early RA patients responsive to DMARD

(disease-modifying antirheumatic drug) therapy exhibited a significant reduction in serum VEGF concentrations, in contrast to patients unresponsive to DMARD treatment, who showed no such significant change [36]. Treatment of RA patients with anti-TNF-α therapy results in marked reduction, but not normalisation, of serum VEGF concentrations [38]. The correlation of this reduction with changes in clinical and laboratory measures of disease activity suggests that the diminished vascular permeability consequent upon reduced VEGF concentrations contributes to the rapid decrease in counts of swollen joints observed after TNF blockade.

The significant reductions in serum VEGF concentrations following response to therapy in RA suggest that angiogenesis is an important process in perpetuating synovitis and raises the possibility that persistence of joint inflammation indicates an imbalance between inducers and inhibitors of angiogenesis. This concept is supported by the observation that concentrations of endostatin, an angiogenesis inhibitor, are not elevated in serum and synovial fluid samples from patients in whom serum VEGF is elevated [35]. Another naturally occurring inhibitor of angiogenesis is soluble Flt-1, a VEGF antagonist. Soluble Flt-1 (sFlt-1) is an alternatively spliced form of Flt-1, one of the tyrosine kinase receptors that mediate the action of VEGF [12,39,40]. We found that sFlt-1 is higher in groups with both early and long-standing RA than in controls, and that elevated sFlt-1 concentrations correlate with VEGF concentrations in serum of the same RA patients [36]. The raised concentrations of sFlt-1 observed in RA are presumably insufficient to inhibit VEGF activity. This finding is analogous to reports in RA of elevated concentrations of other proinflammatory cytokines and their naturally occurring inhibitors.

Can angiogenic markers predict disease outcome?

My colleagues and I have recently reported that serum VEGF concentrations at presentation with early RA correlate highly significantly with development of radiographic damage over the subsequent year [36] as assessed in radiographs of the hands and feet by the van der Heijde modification of Sharp's method [41] (Fig. 2). We have also observed that RA patients with persistent disease activity despite conventional therapy have relatively high serum VEGF concentrations at first presentation. If confirmed in larger series, these observations would support the case for early introduction of a more aggressive therapeutic regime in patients with highly elevated serum VEGF concentrations early in their disease course. It might also be speculated that, in the future, serial serum measurements of angiogenic markers may help to determine whether vascular pannus, with its potential to cause cartilage and bone destruction, is adequately suppressed at any given stage of disease evolution.

Figure 2

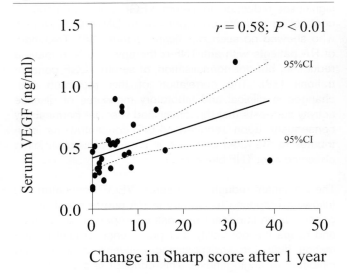

Relation between serum VEGF concentrations, measured at first presentation in a cohort of patients with early RA, and joint damage over the following year, expressed as change in the van der Heijde modification of the Sharp score. Original data reported in [36]. VEGF, vascular endothelial growth factor.

Techniques for imaging synovial vasculature in RA

Blood flows at high velocity in large vessels and can be readily detected by conventional colour Doppler sonography, which encodes the mean Doppler frequency shift. However, at the microvascular level, which is of interest with respect to rheumatoid synovitis, blood flow is at lower velocities that are less readily detectable by conventional colour Doppler sonography. Power Doppler sonography, on the other hand, encodes the amplitude of the power spectral density of the Doppler signal and is a sensitive method for demonstrating the presence of blood flow in small vessels. Several recent studies have demonstrated that power Doppler ultrasound is capable of detecting inflammatory hyperaemia in RA synovitis [42–46]. Furthermore, the signal intensity on power Doppler imaging of synovitis in rheumatoid knee joints correlates well with the histologic assessment of synovial membrane microvascular density in tissue taken at arthroplasty from the previously imaged site [45]. Quantitative assessment of vascularised synovium in metacarpophalangeal joints of patients with RA, as demonstrated by power Doppler, has been reported to correlate with ESR [47]. However, in this cohort of RA patients in the established phase of disease (mean 7.6 years), there was no preponderance of blood flow near joint erosions. In contrast, in a cohort of 39 patients with early RA (disease duration <3 years), we have observed a striking association between the presence of bone erosion in metacarpophalangeal joints and

Figure 3

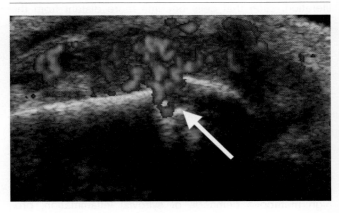

Combined high-resolution ultrasound and power Doppler imaging of a metacarpophalangeal joint in RA, seen in longitudinal section. The red colouring represents vascular signal and the arrow indicates a vascularised erosion. See Colour figure section.

increased intra-articular blood flow at the site of bone damage [48] (Fig. 3). This finding is consistent with the hypothesis that vascularity is associated with the active phase of erosive disease. Laser Doppler imaging of metacarpophalangeal joints in RA has also been reported to correlate with pain scores and synovitis detected on grey-scale high-resolution ultrasound [49]. As disease in many patients with RA continues to progress in spite of suppression of clinically evident synovitis, these noninvasive tools will enhance our ability to detect active vascularised synovium and may also therefore influence the use of DMARD and biologic therapies in such patients.

We have investigated the capability of power Doppler and high-resolution ultrasound imaging to discriminate between patients receiving infliximab or placebo infusions added to pre-existing methotrexate treatment over the first 18 weeks of therapy in a clinical trial [50]. Median reduction in synovial thickness as assessed by high-resolution ultrasound was 50% in the infliximab group, versus an increase of 1.2% in the placebo group ($P = 0.014$). Similarly, median color Doppler area diminished by 98.4% in the infliximab group, versus a reduction of only 30.7% in the placebo group, a statistically significant difference ($P = 0.017$). The total number of vascularised erosions decreased by a median of 1.0 in the infliximab group, whereas there was no change from baseline in the placebo group ($P = 0.001$). In this study, ultrasonographic measures of joint vascularity were better able to discriminate between patients receiving infliximab and those receiving placebo infusions than were changes in DAS28, a composite measure of disease activity.

It has recently been shown that there is a very close relation between the presence or absence of vascular flow signal on power Doppler imaging and the rate of early synovial enhancement on dynamic gadolinium-enhanced magnetic resonance imaging (MRI) of RA metacarpophalangeal joints [51]. The ability to distinguish between RA joint effusion and synovial proliferation using MRI has been greatly improved by the introduction of paramagnetic contrast agents. The early, post-gadolinium synovial membrane enhancement in RA joints, determined by dynamic MRI, is considered to reflect synovial perfusion and permeability [52–54]. Histopathologic analyses of synovial tissue samples obtained from arthrotomy or arthroscopic or blind biopsies from knee joints after dynamic MRI imaging indicate that vascular density and blood-vessel fractional area correlate significantly with the early enhancement rate of synovial membrane [54,55]. Dynamic MRI with a gadolinium-based blood-pool agent has been employed as a technique for measurement of abnormal capillary permeability in synovial tissue of arthritic knees in rabbits [56]. MRI-derived microvascular characteristics comprising plasma volume, fractional leak rate, and permeability-surface area product correlated positively with histologic findings.

A novel approach to detecting angiogenesis *in vivo* using MRI has been described in a tumour model in rabbits. This technique, using a paramagnetic contrast agent targeted to endothelial $\alpha V\beta 3$, an integrin expressed on new blood vessels, by linkage to a monoclonal antibody, successfully provided enhanced and detailed images of rabbit carcinomas and, furthermore, disclosed angiogenic 'hot spots' not visible by standard MRI [57].

Another approach to imaging RA synovial vasculature, which has the disadvantage, relative to the previously described methodologies, that it exposes patients to ionising radiation, is the use of radiolabelled peptides that bind endothelium. For example, a radiolabelled F(ab)2 (antigen-binding fragment) of a monoclonal antibody that recognises an epitope of E-selectin has been successfully used to image RA synovium [58] and a radiolabelled E-selectin binding peptide has been used to image activated synovial endothelium in rat adjuvant arthritis [59]. This is a particularly attractive endothelial adhesion molecule to target, because it is not constitutively expressed but instead is synthesised *de novo* in response to proinflammatory cytokines and expressed on the luminal surface of the endothelium, where it is readily accessible to circulating radioligands [60]. Furthermore, the monoclonal antibody is internalised as a result of receptor recycling, with very little shedding into the general circulation. Nonetheless, positive images of activated endothelium obtained with specific proteins and peptides will inevitably include a component due to nonspecific uptake [61]. Neovascular antigens in inflammatory tissue are other potentially useful targets. Although neovascularisation may be nonspecifically imaged with technetium-labelled isonitriles [62], targeting

epitopes associated with αV integrins, which are specific to new blood vessels [63,64], is a more attractive goal.

Relevance to the understanding of pathogenesis

An inflamed synovium is central to the pathophysiology of RA. Histologically, RA synovitis is characterised by a mononuclear cell infiltrate and luxuriant vasculature [65]. Furthermore, the disease activity in a given joint is correlated with the synovial vascularisation [66,67]. Angiogenesis can be evident on microscopic examination of synovial biopsies from the earliest stages of disease evolution [68] and is observed as a fine network of vessels over the rheumatoid synovium at arthroscopic inspection of RA joints. Angiogenesis is integral to the development of inflammatory pannus, and without it, leukocyte ingress could not occur. Furthermore, formation of new blood vessels permits a supply of nutrients and oxygen to the augmented inflammatory cell mass and so contributes to the perpetuation of synovitis. Studies in experimental models of arthritis suggest that destruction of bone and cartilage may be more closely linked to angiogenesis than to pannus swelling [69,70]. In patients with early RA, my colleagues and I have observed a striking association between the presence of bone erosion on high-resolution ultrasound imaging of metacarpophalangeal joints and increased intra-articular blood flow in power Doppler mode imaging at the site of bone damage [48] These findings implicate vascular pannus in joint destruction in early RA and strongly support the contention that angiogenesis is a potential target for therapy in this disease.

VEGF and angiogenesis as a target for therapy

It is interesting to note that many of the anti-rheumatic drugs used in clinical practice have an effect on the vasculature. Anti-rheumatic drugs including gold, bucillamine, methotrexate, and corticosteroids inhibit production of VEGF by cultured synoviocytes [35]. Methotrexate, at concentrations equivalent to those attained in the serum of RA patients treated with this drug, inhibits basal and stimulated endothelial proliferation *in vitro* [71]. Thiol-containing and gold compounds may modulate neovascularisation indirectly by inhibiting production of monocyte/macrophage-derived angiogenic factors [72,73]. Cyclosporin A is known to inhibit activity of transcription factors of the nuclear factor of activated T-cells family. In addition, cyclosporin A has recently been shown to inhibit migration of primary endothelial cells and angiogenesis induced by VEGF, a novel mechanism that may account for some of the therapeutic activity of this drug in RA [74]. The effect appears to be mediated through inhibition of cyclooxygenase-2, the transcription of which is activated by VEGF in primary endothelial cells. Diminished vascular permeability consequent upon a reduction in VEGF is thought to be a factor contributing to the rapid reduction of joint swelling observed after anti-TNFα therapy [38]. We have shown that TNF blockade is also accompanied by reduced synovial angiogenesis as assessed by immunohistologic analysis of microvascular density and expression of $\alpha V \beta 3$ integrin in synovial biopsy tissue taken before and 4 weeks after a single 10-mg/kg infliximab infusion [16].

Given the evidence discussed so far, there are strong grounds on which to suggest that targeting the newly formed vasculature of the RA pannus might modify disease progression. Identification of new molecular targets for immunotherapeutic intervention in RA ideally requires evidence of synovial tissue expression of the molecule at relevant sites, *in vitro* evaluation of its biologic function, and preclinical studies demonstrating clinical efficacy in experimental models [75]. I have already discussed the first two of these three requirements in considering angiogenesis, and molecules that promote it such as VEGF, as targets for therapy in RA. However, the third requirement, demonstration of clinical efficacy in experimental models, would perhaps represent the most convincing evidence in support of anti-angiogenic strategies in the treatment of human disease.

In collagen-induced arthritis in rats, administration of the anti-angiogenic agent AGM-1470 attenuates the clinical severity of established disease, with reduction in serum concentrations of VEGF [76] and histologic evidence of marked inhibition of pannus formation and neovascularisation [77,78]. In murine collagen-induced arthritis, expression of biologically active VEGF was along a time course that paralleled the expression of VEGFR-1 and VEGFR-2 [79]. Furthermore, in this model, concentrations of VEGF expression correlated with clinical severity of disease and degree of neovascularisation. Administration of anti-VEGF antiserum before the onset of disease significantly delayed the development and severity of arthritis, whereas administration after disease onset had no effect on the progression or ultimate severity of the disease [79]. In another study employing the murine collagen-induced arthritis model, saline, normal rabbit immunoglobulin, or rabbit polyclonal anti-human VEGF(121) antibodies were administered to mice either before or after the onset of clinical disease [80]. Treatment with anti-VEGF antibodies before disease onset significantly delayed the development of arthritis and attenuated the severity of disease expression, although the frequency of the occurrence of disease did not differ from that in either control group. In this study, improvement in clinical and histological parameters of arthritis was observed even when anti-VEGF was administered after the onset of disease. Another approach to VEGF blockade in murine collagen-induced arthritis has been to administer exogenous sFlt-1 linked to polyethylene glycol (sFlt-PEG) to increase its *in vivo* half-life. In this model, daily intraperitoneal administration of this treatment from the first day of clinical arthritis was reported to ameliorate the severity of clinical disease expression and of

bone and cartilage destruction on histopathological assessment [81].

Other anti-angiogenic agents successfully used in preclinical animal studies include the fungal derivative TNP-470 and specific antagonists of $\alpha V \beta 3$. In a transgenic rodent model of inflammatory arthritis, administration of TNP-470 attenuated development of arthritis and alleviated clinical signs if administered at the early stages of clinical disease. Clinical improvement was associated with reduced cartilage and bone destruction [82]. There are preclinical *in vivo* data showing that selective targeting of new blood vessels may result in modification of disease. Intra-articular injections of specific antagonists of $\alpha V \beta 3$ resulted in reduced synovial vascularity in rabbits after induction of arthritis with joint injections of a combination of ovalbumin and basic fibroblast growth factor. Diminished synovial vascularity was associated with a significant decrease in all arthritic parameters, including joint swelling and synovitis. Of note, the beneficial effects of angiogenesis inhibition were apparent in the established phase of disease [70]. Similarly, symptoms of adjuvant-induced arthritis in rats are significantly reduced by prophylactic or therapeutic administration of an orally active $\alpha V \beta 3$ antagonist, with significant improvements in joint integrity seen on MRI [83].

What does the future hold in angiogenesis modulation and imaging of vasculature?

Given the central role played by angiogenesis and VEGF in arthritic disease, it might be predicted that suppression of angiogenesis and/or VEGF activity will be an effective treatment strategy in RA. However, it is possible that such an approach will be limited by toxicities related to inhibition of physiological processes involving VEGF-mediated angiogenesis. Examples include wound healing, the female reproductive cycle, and maintenance of cardiovascular health. Data arising from ongoing clinical trials of anti-angiogenic agents in the treatment of cancers should give valuable insight as to whether these theoretical concerns are well founded or not.

Studies evaluating new imaging technologies suggest that clinical joint examination and plain radiography are relatively insensitive [84] and may thus be insufficient measures for use in future clinical trials designed to assess reduction in symptoms and signs of rheumatoid disease as well as retardation of structural damage to joints. In a double-blind study in early RA in which patients received either infliximab or placebo infusions added to pre-existing, stable methotrexate therapy, my colleagues and I have recently shown that measurement of changes in serum VEGF concentration and ultrasonographic assessments of changes in synovial vascularity are able to discriminate between patients receiving either infliximab or placebo infusions [50]. We have also reported that the serum VEGF concentration at first presentation in early RA significantly correlates with radiological progression over the following year [36]. These findings predict that imaging technologies capable of evaluating synovial vascularity will have a practical value in determining prognosis and in assessment of response to therapy. Of the technologies discussed in this chapter, ultrasonographic imaging methods have the advantage that they are noninvasive, involve no ionising radiation, and are both more widely available and more economical than MRI. Furthermore, rheumatologists can be trained to undertake ultrasonographic imaging, thus obviating the delay incurred in referral to a radiologist.

Concluding remarks

VEGF concentrations are elevated in the serum of patients with RA and correlate with individual and composite measures of the disease activity. Sensitive, noninvasive methods for visualising synovial vascularisation in RA, such as power Doppler sonography, are emerging as clinically important tools in the assessment of disease activity and hold promise as novel means of evaluating the response of patients to therapy. As arresting structural damage to joints becomes a realistic goal in the management of RA, vascular imaging and serologic markers may be more sensitive than disease activity scores in determining at an early stage of treatment which patients are responding satisfactorily.

Glossary of terms

Flt-1 = fms-like tyrosine kinase receptor-1, or VEGF receptor-1 (VEGFR-1); KDR = kinase-insert-domain-containing receptor, or VEGF receptor-2 (VEGFR-2); sFlt-1 = soluble Flt-1; VEGFR = vascular endothelial growth factor receptor.

References

1. Sharp JT, Wolfe F, Mitchell DM, Bloch DA: **The progression of erosion and joint space narrowing scores in rheumatoid arthritis during the first twenty-five years of disease.** *Arthritis Rheum* 1991, **34**:660-668. [archival research]
2. Maini RN, Taylor PC: **Anti-cytokine therapy in rheumatoid arthritis.** *Ann Rev Med* 2000, **51**:207-229. [key review]
3. Taylor PC: **Anti-TNF therapies.** *Curr Opin Rheumatol* 2001, **13**:164-169. [key review]
4. Desmouliere A, Redard M, Darby I, Gabbiani G: **Apoptosis mediates the decrease in cellularity during the transition between granuloma tissue and scar.** *Am J Pathol* 1995, **146**:56-66. [archival research]
5. Walsh DA: **Angiogenesis and arthritis.** *Rheumatology (Oxford)* 1999, **38**:103-112. [key review]
6. Koch A: **Angiogenesis: implications for rheumatoid arthritis.** *Arthritis Rheum* 1998, **41**:951-962. [key review]
7. Paleolog EM, Fava RA: **Angiogenesis in rheumatoid arthritis: implications for future therapeutic strategies.** *Springer Semin Immunopathol* 1998, **20**:73-94. [key review]
8. Paleolog EM, Miotla JM: **Angiogenesis in arthritis: role in disease pathogenesis and as a potential therapeutic target.** *Angiogenesis* 1998, **2**:295-307. [key review]
9. Jain A, Nanchahal J, Troeberg L, Green P, Brennan F: **Production of cytokines, vascular endothelial growth factor, matrix metalloproteinases, and tissue inhibitor of metalloproteinases 1 by tenosynovium demonstrates its potential for tendon destruction in rheumatoid arthritis.** *Arthritis Rheum* 2001, **44**:1754-1760. [general reference]
10. Brown LF, Detmar M, Claffey K, Nagy JA, Feng D, Dvorak AM, Dvorak HF: **Vascular permeability factor/vascular endothelial growth factor: a multifunctional angiogenic cytokine.** *EXS* 1997, **79**:233-269. [key review]
11. Achen MG, Stacker SA: **The vascular endothelial growth factor family; proteins which guide the development of the vasculature.** *Int J Exp Pathol* 1998, **79**:255-265. [general reference]
12. Neufeld G, Cohen T, Gengrinovitch S, Poltorak Z: **Vascular endothelial growth factor (VEGF) and its receptors.** *FASEB J* 1999, **13**:9-22. [general reference]
13. Ferrara N: **The role of vascular endothelial growth factor in pathological angiogenesis.** *Breast Cancer Res Treat* 1995, **36**:127-137. [archival research]
14. Fava RA, Olsen NJ, Spencer-Green G, Yeo KT, Yeo TK, Berse B, Jackman RW, Senger DR, Dvorak HF, Brown LF: **Vascular permeability factor/endothelial growth factor (VPF/VEGF): accumulation and expression in human synovial fluids and rheumatoid synovial tissue.** *J Exp Med* 1994, **180**:341-346. [archival research]
15. Koch AE, Harlow LA, Haines GK, Amento EP, Unemori EN, Wong WL, Pope RM, Ferrara N: **Vascular endothelial growth factor. A cytokine modulating endothelial function in rheumatoid arthritis.** *J Immunol* 1994, **152**:4149-4156. [archival research]
16. Taylor PC, Patel S, Paleolog E, McCloskey RV, Feldmann M, Maini RN: **Reduced synovial vascularity following TNFα blockade in rheumatoid arthritis [abstract].** *Arthritis Rheum* 1998, **41(suppl)**:S295. [general reference]
17. Kasama T, Shiozawa F, Kobayashi K, Yajima N, Hanyuda M, Takeuchi HT, Mori Y, Negishi M, Ide H, Adachi M: **Vascular endothelial growth factor expression by activated synovial leukocytes in rheumatoid arthritis: critical involvement of the interaction with synovial fibroblasts.** *Arthritis Rheum* 2001, **44**:2512-2524. [general reference]
18. Ikeda M, Hosoda Y, Hirose S, Okada Y, Ikeda E: **Expression of vascular endothelial growth factor isoforms and their receptors Flt-1, KDR, and neuropilin-1 in synovial tissues of rheumatoid arthritis.** *J Pathol* 2000, **191**:426-433. [general reference]
19. Pufe T, Petersen W, Tillmann B, Mentlein R: **Splice variants VEGF121 and VEGF165 of the angiogenic peptide vascular endothelial cell growth factor are expressed in the synovial tissue of patients with rheumatoid arthritis.** *J Rheumatol* 2001, **28**:1482-1485. [general reference]
20. Giatromanolaki A, Sivridis E, Athanassou N, Zois E, Thorpe PE, Brekken RA, Gatter KC, Harris AL, Koukourakis IM, Koukourakis MI: **The angiogenic pathway "vascular endothelial growth factor/flk-1(KDR)-receptor" in rheumatoid arthritis and osteoarthritis.** *J Pathol* 2001, **194**:101-108. [general reference]
21. Berse B, Hunt JA, Diegel RJ, Morganelli P, Yeo K, Brown F, Fava RA: **Hypoxia augments cytokine (transforming growth factor-beta (TGF-beta) and IL-1-induced vascular endothelial growth factor secretion by human synovial fibroblasts.** *Clin Exp Immunol* 1999, **115**:176-182. [general reference]
22. Taylor PC, Miotla JM, Etherington P, Winlove P, Young S, Paleolog E, Maini RN: **VEGF release is associated with hypoxia in inflammatory arthritis [abstract].** *Rheumatology (Oxford)* 2000, **40(suppl)**:S7. [general reference]
23. Stevens CR, Blake DR, Merry P, Revell PA, Levick JR: **A comparative study by morphometry of the microvasculature in normal and rheumatoid synovium.** *Arthritis Rheum* 1991, **34**:1508-1513. [general reference]
24. Richard DE, Berra E, Pouyssegur J: **Angiogenesis: how a tumor adapts to hypoxia.** *Biochem Biophys Res Commun* 1999, **266**:718-722. [general reference]
25. Wiesener MS, Turley H, Allen WE, Willam C, Eckardt KU, Talks KL, Wood SM, Gatter KC, Harris AL, Pugh CW, Ratcliffe PJ, Maxwell PH: **Induction of endothelial PAS domain protein-1 by hypoxia: characterisation and comparison with hypoxia-inducible factor-1 alpha.** *Blood* 1998, **92**:2260-2268. [general reference]
26. Jackson JR, Minton JA, Ho ML, Wei N, Winkler JD: **Expression of vascular endothelial growth factor in synovial fibroblasts is induced by hypoxia and and interleukin 1beta.** *J Rheumatol* 1997, **24**:1253-1259. [general reference]
27. Harada M, Mitsuyama K, Yoshida H, Sakisaka S, Taniguchi E, Kawaguchi T, Ariyoshi M, Saiki T, Sakamoto M, Nagata K, Sata M, Matsuo K, Tanikawa K: **Vascular endothelial growth factor in**

patients with rheumatoid arthritis. *Scand J Rheumatol* 1998, **27**:377-380. [general reference]

28. Kikuchi K, Kubo M, Kadono T, Yazawa N, Ihn H, Tamaki K: **Serum concentrations of vascular endothelial growth factor in collagen diseases.** *Br J Dermatol* 1998, **139**:1049-1051. [general reference]

29. Bottomley MJ, Webb NJ, Watson CJ, Holt PJ, Freemont AJ, Brenchley PE: **Peripheral blood mononuclear cells from patients with rheumatoid arthritis spontaneously secrete vascular endothelial growth factor (VEGF): specific up-regulation by tumour necrosis factor-alpha (TNF-alpha) in synovial fluid.** *Clin Exp Immunol* 1999, **117**:171-176. [general reference]

30. Nagashima M, Yoshino S, Ishiwata T, Asano G: Role of vascular endothelial growth factor in angiogenesis of rheumatoid arthritis. *J Rheumatol* 1995, **22**:1624-1630. [general reference]

31. Taichman N, Young S, Cruchley A, Taylor PC, Paleolog E: **Human neutrophils secrete vascular endothelial growth factor.** *J Leukocyte Biol* 1997, **62**:397-400. [general reference]

32. Kasama T, Kobayashi K, Yajima N, Shiozawa F, Yoda Y, Takeuchi HT, Mori Y, Negishi M, Ide H, Adachi M: **Expression of vascular endothelial growth factor by synovial fluid neutrophils in rheumatoid arthritis (RA).** *Clin Exp Immunol* 2000, **121**:533-538. [general reference]

33. Lee SS, Joo YS, Kim WU, Min DJ, Min JK, Park SH, Cho CS, Kim HY: **Vascular endothelial growth factor levels in the serum and synovial fluid of patients with rheumatoid arthritis.** *Clin Exp Rheumatol* 2001, **19**:321-324. [general reference]

34. Fraser A, Fearon U, Reece R, Emery P, Veale DJ: **Matrix metalloproteinase 9, apoptosis, and vascular morphology in early arthritis.** *Arthritis Rheum* 2001, **44**:2024-2028. [general reference]

35. Nagashima M, Wauke K, Hirano D, Ishigami S, Aono H, Takai M, Sasano M, Yoshino S: **Effects of combinations of anti-rheumatic drugs on the production of vascular endothelial growth factor and basic fibroblast growth factor in cultured synoviocytes and patients with rheumatoid arthritis.** *Rheumatology (Oxford)* 2000, **39**:1255-1262. [general reference]

36. Ballara S, Taylor PC, Reusch P Marme D, Maini RN, Paleolog E: **Serum vascular endothelial growth factor (VEGF) and soluble VEGF receptor in inflammatory arthritis.** *Arthritis Rheum* 2001, **44**:2055-2064. [general reference]

37. Sone H, Sakauchi M, Takahashi A, Suzuki H, Inoue N, Iida K, Shimano H, Toyoshima H, Kawakami Y, Okuda Y, Matsuo K, Yamada N: **Elevated levels of vascular endothelial growth factor in the sera of patients with rheumatoid arthritis correlation with disease activity.** *Life Sci* 2001, **69**:1861-1869. [general reference]

38. Paleolog EM, Young S, Stark AC, McCloskey RV, Feldmann M, Maini RN: **Modulation of angiogenic vascular endothelial growth factor (VEGF) by TNFα and IL-1 in rheumatoid arthritis.** *Arthritis Rheum* 1998, **41**:1258-1265. [general reference]

39. Kendall RL, Wang G, Thomas KA: **Identification of a natural soluble form of the vascular endothelial growth factor receptor, FLT-1, and its heterodimerization with KDR.** *Biochem Biophys Res Commun* 1996, **226**:324-328. [archival research]

40. Hornig C, Weich HA: **Soluble VEGF receptors. Recombinant and naturally occurring forms involved in the regulation of angiogenesis.** *Angiogenesis* 1999, **3**:33-39. [general reference]

41. van der Heijde D: **How to read radiographs according to the Sharp/van der Heijde method.** *J Rheumatol* 2000, **27**:261-263. [general reference]

42. Newman JS, Laing TJ, McCarthy CJ, Adler RS: **Power Doppler sonography of synovitis: assessment of therapeutic response – preliminary observations.** *Radiology* 1996, **198**:582-584. [archival research]

43. Hau M, Schultz H, Tony HP, Keberle M, Jahns R, Haerten R, Jenett M: **Evaluation of pannus and vascularization of the metacarpophalangeal and proximal interphalangeal joints in rheumatoid arthritis by high-resolution ultrasound (multidimensional linear array).** *Arthritis Rheum* 1999, **42**:2303-2308. [general reference]

44. Schmidt WA, Volker L, Zacher J, Schlafke M, Ruhnke M, Gromnica-Ihle E: **Colour Doppler ultrasonography to detect pannus in knee joint synovitis.** *Clin Exp Rheum* 2000, **18**:439-444. [general reference]

45. Walther M, Harms H, Krenn V, Radke S, Faehndrich TP, Gohlke F: **Correlation of power Doppler sonography with vascularity of**

the synovial tissue of the knee joint in patients with osteoarthritis and rheumatoid arthritis. *Arthritis Rheum* 2001, **44**:331-338. [general reference]

46. Giovagnorio F, Martinoli C, Coari G: **Power Doppler sonography in knee arthritis—a pilot study.** *Rheumatol Int* 2001, **20**:101-104. [general reference]

47. Qvistgaard E, Rogind H, Torp-Pedersen S, Terslev L, Danneskiold-Samsoe B, Bliddal H: **Quantitative ultrasonography in rheumatoid arthritis: evaluation of inflammation by Doppler technique.** *Ann Rheum Dis* 2001, **60**:690-693. [general reference]

48. Steuer A, Blomley M. Cosgrove D, Maini RN, Taylor PC: **Combined power colour doppler and greyscale ultrasound demonstrate an association between vascularity and erosion in rheumatoid arthritis [abstract].** *Arthritis Rheum* 2000, **43 (suppl)**:S292. [general reference]

49. Ferrel WR, Balint PV, Egan CG, Lockhart JC, Sturrock RD: **Metacarpophalangeal joints in rheumatoid arthritis: laser Doppler imaging – initial experience.** *Radiology* 2001, **220**:257-262. [general reference]

50. Taylor PC, Steuer A, Charles P, Gruber J, Cosgrove D, Blomley M, Wagner C, Marsters P, DeWoody K, Maini RN. **Early RA patients on infliximab therapy show significant changes in sonographic measures of joint vascularity and serum VEGF by 18 weeks [abstract].** *Arthritis Rheum* 2001, **44(suppl)**:S152 [general reference]

51. Szkudlarek M, Court-Payen M, Strandberg C, Klarlund M, Klausen T, Ostergaard M: **Power Doppler ultrasononography for assessment of synovitis in the metacarpophalangeal joints of patients with rheumatoid arthritis; a comparison with dynamic magnetic resonance imaging.** *Arthritis Rheum* 2001, **44**:2018-2023. [general reference]

52. Konig H, Sieper J, Wolf KJ: **Rheumatoid arthritis: evaluation of hypervascular and fibrous pannus with dynamic MR imaging enhanced with Gd-DTPA.** *Radiology* 1990, **176**:473-477. [archival research]

53. Gaffney K, Cookson J, Blake D, Coumbe A, Blades S: **Quantification of rheumatoid synovitis by magnetic resonance imaging.** *Arthritis Rheum* 1995, **38**:1610-1617. [archival research]

54. Gaffney K, Cookson J, Blades S, Coumbe A, Blake D: **Quantitative assessment of the rheumatoid synovial microvascular bed by gadolinium-DTPA enhanced magnetic resonance imaging.** *Ann Rheum Dis* 1998, **57**:152-157. [general reference]

55. Ostergaard M, Stoltenberg M, Lovgreen-Nielsen P, Volck B, Sonne-Holm S, Lorenzen I: **Quantification of synovitis by MRI: correlation between dynamic and static gadolinium-enhanced magnetic resonance imaging and microscopic and macroscopic signs of synovial inflammation.** *Magn Reson Imaging* 1998, **16**:743-754. [general reference]

56. van Dijke CF, Peterfy CG, Brasch RC, Lang P, Roberts TP, Shames D, Kneeland JB, Lu Y, Mann JS, Kapila SD, Genant HK: **MR imaging of the arthritic rabbit knee joint using albumin-(Gd-DTPA)30 with correlation to histopathology.** *Magn Reson Imaging* 1999, **17**:237-245. [general reference]

57. Sipkins DA, Cheresh DA, Kazemi MR, Nevin LM, Bednarski MD, Li KC: **Detection of tumor angiogenesis in vivo by alphaVbeta3-targeted magnetic resonance imaging.** *Nat Med* 1998, **4**:623-626. [general reference]

58. Chapman PT, Jamar F, Keelan ETM, Peters AM, Haskard DO: **Use of a radiolabeled monoclonal antibody against E-selectin for imaging of endothelial activation in rheumatoid arthritis.** *Arthritis Rheum* 1996, **39**:1371-1375. [archival research]

59. Zinn KR, Chaudhuri TR, Smyth CA, Wu Q, Liu HG, Fleck M, Mountz JD, Mountz JM: **Specific targeting of activated endothelium in rat adjuvant arthritis with a 99mTc-radiolabeled E-selectin-binding peptide.** *Arthritis Rheum* 1999, **42**:641-649. [general reference]

60. Keelan ET, Licence ST, Peters AM, Binns RM, Haskard DO: **Characterization of E-selectin expression in vivo with use of a radiolabeled monoclonal antibody.** *Am J Physiol* 1994, **266**:H278-290. [archival research]

61. Jamar F, Chapman PT, Manicourt DH, Glass DM, Haskard DO, Peters AM: **A comparison between 111In-anti-E-selectin mAb and 99Tcm-labelled human non-specific immunoglobulin in radionuclide imaging of rheumatoid arthritis.** *Br J Radiol* 1997, **70**:473-481. [general reference]

62. Scopinaro F, Schillaci O, Scarpini M, Mingazzini PL, Di Macio L, Banci M, Danieli R, Zerilli M, Limiti MR, Centi Colella A: **Tech-**

netium-99m sestamibi: an indicator of breast cancer invasiveness. *Eur J Nucl Med* 1994, **21**:984-987. [archival research]

63. Brooks PC, Montgomery AMP, Rosenfeld M, Reisfeld RA, Hu T, Klier G, Cheresh DA: **Integrin αVβ3 antagonists promote tumor regression by inducing apoptosis of angiogenic blood vessels.** *Cell* 1994, **79**:1157-1164. [archival research]

64. Friedlander M, Brooks PC, Shaffer RW, Kincaid CM, Varner JA, Cheresh DA: **Definition of two angiogenic pathways by distinct αV integrins.** *Science* 1995, **270**:1500-1502. [archival research]

65. FitzGerald O, Bresnihan B: **Synovial membrane cellularity and vascularity.** *Ann Rheum Dis* 1995, **54**:511-515. [archival research]

66. Lindblad S, Hedfors E: **Intraarticular variation in synovitis. Local macroscopic and microscopic signs of inflammatory activity are significantly correlated.** *Arthritis Rheum* 1985, **28**:977-986. [archival research]

67. Ostergaard M, Hansen M, Stoltenberg M, Gideon P, Klarland M, Jensen KE, Lorenzen I: **Magnetic resonance imaging-determined synovial membrane volume as a marker of disease activity and a predictor of progressive joint destruction in the wrists of patients with rheumatoid arthritis.** *Arthritis Rheum* 1999, **42**:918-929. [general reference]

68. Hirohata S, Sakakibara J: **Angioneogenesis as a possible elusive trigger factor in rheumatoid arthritis [letter].** *Lancet* 1999, **353**:1331. [general reference]

69. Firestein GS: **Starving the synovium: angiogenesis and inflammation in rheumatoid arthritis.** *J Clin Invest* 1999, **103**:3-4. [key review]

70. Storgard CM, Stupack DG, Jonczyk A, Goodman SL, Fox RI, Cheresh D: **Decreased angiogenesis and arthritic disease in rabbits treated with alphavbeta3 antagonist.** *J Clin Invest* 1999, **103**:47-54. [general reference]

71. Hirata S, Matsubara T, Saura R, Tateishi H, Hirohata K: **Inhibition of *in vitro* vascular endothelial cell proliferation and *in vivo* neovascularization by low-dose methotrexate.** *Arthritis Rheum* 1989, **32**:1065-1073. [archival research]

72. Koch AE, Cho M, Burrows J, Leibovich SJ, Polverini PJ: **Inhibition of production of macrophage-derived angiogenic activity by the anti-rheumatic agents gold sodium thiomalate and auranofin.** *Biochem Biophys Res Commun* 1988, **154**:205-212. [archival research]

73. Koch AE, Burrows JC, Polverini PJ, Cho M, Leibovich SJ: **Thiol-containing compounds inhibit the production of monocyte/macrophage-derived angiogenic activity.** *Agents Actions* 1991, **34**:350-357. [archival research]

74. Hernandez GL, Volpert OV, Iniguez MA, Lorenzo E, Martinez-Martinez S, Grau R, Fresno M, Redondo JM: **Selective inhibition of vascular endothelial growth factor-mediated angiogenesis by cyclosporin A: roles of the nuclear factor of activated T cells and cyclooxygenase 2.** *J Exp Med* 2001, **193**:607-620. [general reference]

75. Taylor PC, Williams RO, Maini RN: **Immunotherapy for rheumatoid arthritis.** *Curr Opin Immunol* 2001, **13**:611-616. [key review]

76. Oliver SJ, Cheng TP, Banquerigo ML, Brahn E: **Suppression of collagen-induced arthritis by an angiogenesis inhibitor, AGM-1470, in combination with cyclosporin: reduction of vascular endothelial growth factor (VEGF).** *Cell Immunol* 1995, **166**:196-206. [archival research]

77. Peacock DJ, Banquerigo ML, Brahn E: **Angiogenesis inhibition suppresses collagen arthritis.** *J Exp Med* 1992, **175**:1135-1138. [archival research]

78. Oliver SJ, Banquerigo ML, Brahn E: **Suppression of collagen-induced arthritis using an angiogenesis inhibitor, AGM-1470, and a microtubule stabilizer, taxol.** *Cell Immunol* 1994, **157**:291-299. [archival research]

79. Lu J, Kasama T, Kobayashi K, Yoda Y, Shiozawa F, Hanyuda M, Negishi M, Ide H, Adachi M: **Vascular endothelial growth factor expression and regulation of murine collagen-induced arthritis.** *J Immunol* 2000, **164**:5922-5927. [general reference]

80. Sone H, Kawakami Y, Sakauchi M, Nakamura Y, Takahashi A, Shimano H, Okuda Y, Segawa T, Suzuki H, Yamada N: **Neutralization of vascular endothelial growth factor prevents collagen-induced arthritis and ameliorates established disease in mice.** *Biochem Biophys Res Commun* 2001, **281**:562-568. [general reference]

81. Miotla JM, Maciewicz R, Kendrew J, Feldmann M, Paleolog E: **Treatment with soluble VEGF receptor reduces disease severity in murine collagen-induced arthritis.** *Lab Invest* 2000, **80**:1195-1205. [general reference]

82. de Bandt M, Grossin M, Weber AJ, Chopin M, Elbim C, Pla M, Gougerot-Pocidalo MA, Gaudry M: **Suppression of arthritis and protection from bone destruction by treatment with TNP-470/AGM-1470 in a transgenic mouse model of rheumatoid arthritis.** *Arthritis Rheum* 2000, **43**:2056-2063. [general reference]

83. Badger AM, Blake S, Kapadia R, Sarkar S, Levin J, Swift BA, Hoffman SJ, Stroup GB, Miller WH, Gowen M, Lark MW: **Disease-modifying activity of SB 273005, an orally active, non-peptide alphavbeta3 (vitronectin receptor) antagonist, in rat adjuvant-induced arthritis.** *Arthritis Rheum* 2001, **44**:128-137. [general reference]

84. Wakefield RJ, Gibbon WW, Conaghan PG, O'Connor P, McGonagle D, Pease C, Green MJ, Veale DJ, Isaacs JD, Emery P: **The value of sonography in the detection of bone erosions in patients with rheumatoid arthritis.** *Arthritis Rheum* 2000, **43**:2762–2770. [general reference]

Supplement Review
Endothelial activation: intracellular signaling pathways
Jordan S Pober

Yale University School of Medicine, Boyer Center for Molecular Medicine, New Haven, CT, USA

Correspondence: Jordan S Pober, MD, PhD, Professor of Pathology, Immunobiology and Dermatology, Yale University School of Medicine, Boyer Center for Molecular Medicine, 295 Congress Avenue, Room 454, New Haven, CT 06510, USA. Tel: +1 203 737 2292; fax: +1 203 737 2293; e-mail: jordan.pober@yale.edu

Received: 14 November 2001
Revisions requested: 28 January 2002
Revisions received: 4 February 2002
Accepted: 4 February 2002
Published: 9 May 2002

Arthritis Res 2002, **4 (suppl 3)**:S109-S116

This article may contain supplementary data which can only be found online at http://arthritis-research.com/content/4/S3/S109

© 2002 BioMed Central Ltd
(Print ISSN 1465-9905; Online ISSN 1465-9913)

Chapter summary

Tumor necrosis factor (TNF) is the prototypic proinflammatory cytokine and endothelial cells are the principal cellular targets of its actions. Here I review the responses of endothelial cells to TNF, with emphasis on the induction of endothelial leukocyte adhesion molecules. I focus on the biochemistry and cell biology of signal transduction in TNF-treated endothelial cells that lead to the expression of adhesion molecules.

Keywords: adhesion molecules, cytokines, inflammation, leukocytes, tumor necrosis factor

Introduction

Inflammation, defined as the local recruitment and activation of leukocytes, is an essential component of the innate immune response to pathogens and damaged cells. Consequently, mouse and human genetic defects in leukocyte recruitment manifest themselves as an increased frequency and susceptibility to infection and/or as a failure to remove degenerating tissues, such as the stump of a neonatal umbilical cord [1]. The innate inflammatory response has only a limited ability to distinguish normal from infected or damaged cells. Consequently, injury to healthy bystander cells at a site of inflammation is common. Moreover, unresolved inflammation can itself become a disease process, a clear example being rheumatoid arthritis. Inhibition of inflammation in such settings has become a primary goal of therapy irrespective of the underlying cause of the disease. For this reason, it is important to understand how inflammation develops and how it is regulated. In this chapter, I describe how tumor necrosis factor (TNF), an important mediator of innate inflammation, acts on vascular endothelial cells (ECs) to promote the inflammatory response.

Historical background

A description of the inflammatory response to injured tissues at the level of light microscopy was first made over 100 years ago [2]. In those pioneering studies, Cohnheim noted that margination of leukocytes along the luminal surface of the postcapillary venule is the prelude to extravasation. Before the 1980s, these events were generally interpreted as a response of circulating leukocytes to chemoattractant substances elaborated within the tissue, either by infectious microbes (e.g. *N*-formyl peptides) or by the innate response (e.g. complement fragment C5a) [3]. Margination was explained by the observation that such substances not only induced chemotaxis but also triggered adhesion to endothelium, although the increase in adhesion was usually quite small (not more than twofold) [4]. This model did not explain why superfusion of chemotactic

---

A glossary of specialist terms used in this chapter appears at the end of the text section. A list of common abbreviations used in this issue appears just before the indexes.

substances does not cause circulating leukocytes to adhere to endothelium until they reach the venules [5].

Endothelial-cell-based model of inflammation

A re-evaluation of this paradigm began in the mid 1980s with the finding that exposure of ECs to cytokines, such as IL-1 or TNF, caused the ECs to bind 20 to 40 times as many leukocytes as untreated ECs, dwarfing the effects of chemotaxins [6]. The change in EC adhesivity arose from the induction of new surface proteins, collectively designated as endothelial leukocyte adhesion molecules (ELAMs), that bind counter-receptor proteins expressed on leukocytes [7]. Cytokine-treated ECs are also a source of chemoattractant cytokines (chemokines) that contribute to adhesion by activating the affinity of leukocyte counter-receptors for ELAMs [7]. These observations, combined with new experimental models such as parallel plate flow chambers and *ex vivo* videomicroscopy, led to the current multistep model of leukocyte recruitment centered on the responses of the vascular ECs lining postcapillary venules rather than on responses of leukocytes [8,9]. In brief, resting ECs are now viewed as noninteractive with leukocytes, so that random encounters with circulating white cells are short-lived, leaving both cells unaltered. Microbes and other inflammatory stimuli induce resident macrophages to release cytokines such as TNF or IL-1, which induce venular ECs to synthesize and express new proteins on their luminal cell surface. Critically, cytokine-treated ECs express several new ELAMS, namely E-selectin and integrin-ligands such as intercellular adhesion molecule-1 (ICAM-1) and vascular cell adhesion molecule-1 (VCAM-1), that can interact with blood leukocytes. (Mouse ECs, but not human ones, also upregulate P-selectin in response to TNF or IL-1.) Cytokine-activated ECs also synthesize, secrete, and display (in association with cell-surface proteoglycans) chemokines on their luminal surface. Circulating leukocytes that bump into cytokine-activated ECs rapidly form low-affinity interactions mediated by binding to E-selectin and/or VCAM-1. Shear force, imparted by flowing blood, causes these interactions to be rapidly broken, only to reform rapidly as the leukocyte is displaced. Multiple iterations of these processes results in rolling of the leukocyte on the EC surface. Rolling, but not free-flowing, leukocytes encounter and respond to the surface-displayed chemokines, causing cell spreading and clustering of surface integrins (such as LFA-1 and VLA-4) at the contact area with the ECs. These leukocyte integrins are the counter-receptors for ICAM-1 and VCAM-1 on ECs, and enhanced interactions by clustered integrins produce firm attachment to the ECs. Bound chemokines also stimulate leukocyte chemokinesis, resulting in crawling on the EC surface. As crawling leukocytes reach the junction between ECs, they extravasate through the junction into the tissue space, resulting in inflammation.

Several refinements of this EC-based model of inflammation are worth noting. One point involves the specialized nature of venular ECs. Although ICAM-1 is upregulated by TNF or IL-1 on essentially all ECs lining the microvasculature, E-selectin and VCAM-1 are normally confined to ECs of the postcapillary venule, the site of leukocyte rolling and margination [10]. However, in certain disease states (e.g. psoriasis), capillaries also may express these molecules, and the pattern of leukocyte extravasation changes to match that of expression of adhesion molecules [11]. In addition, the patterns of adhesion molecule expression (and chemokine expression) are dynamic. For example, expression of E-selectin, associated with neutrophil extravasation, peaks early (at 2–4 hours) after TNF addition, corresponding to the onset of neutrophil recruitment. VCAM-1, which is more closely associated with binding of mononuclear leukocytes, typically peaks at later times (12–24 hours) after TNF addition, corresponding to the onset of T-cell recruitment [12]. Finally, the EC response to TNF can be modified by T-cell-derived cytokines. For example, IFN-γ prolongs the expression of E-selectin [13], whereas IL-4 suppresses the expression of E-selectin while promoting that of VCAM-1 [14]. These alterations in the EC surface produce corresponding changes in the nature of the inflammatory leukocyte populations that are recruited. Specifically, IFN-γ favors recruitment of leukocytes associated with inflammation of the T-helper-1 type (dependent on E-selectin), whereas IL-4 favors inflammation of the T-helper-2 type (independent of E-selectin) [15]. In other words, the spatial, temporal, and qualitative patterns of EC adhesion molecule expression govern the location, evolution, and nature of the inflammatory response.

The biochemistry of TNF signaling in endothelial cells

A central role of TNF in inflammation has been established by observations that many inflammatory reactions are impaired in TNF or TNF-receptor (TNFR) knockout mice [16] and that, in humans, TNF inhibitors (soluble receptors or neutralizing antibodies) are effective anti-inflammatory therapeutics [17]. As I have noted, proinflammatory actions of TNF on ECs generally involve new protein synthesis. In general, these changes are initiated by new gene transcription [7]. Two specific transactivating (transcription) factors, NF-κB and activator protein-1 (AP-1), are essential (although probably not sufficient) for TNF induction of ELAMs [18]. The evidence for this conclusion is that the E-selectin, ICAM-1, and VCAM-1 genes each contain DNA sequences in their 5′ flanking regions that bind various forms of NF-κB and AP-1 in electrophoretic-mobility-shift assays and that mutations of these sequences reduce TNF responses of transfected promoter–reporter genes. In addition, transfection experiments of wild-type and mutant forms of NF-κB and AP-1 subunits into cultured ECs can regulate in the expression of E-selectin, ICAM-1, and VCAM-1.

An active area of research in the 1990s was the elucidation of signaling pathways through which TNF could activate NF-κB and AP-1. Human ECs, like most other cell types, express two different TNFRs, designated TNFR1 (CD120a) and TNFR2 (CD120b) [19]. Signaling is initiated when ligand-occupied receptors recruit the binding of intracellular adaptor proteins to the intracellular portions of the receptor molecules (reviewed in [20,21]). Initially, ligand-occupied TNFR1 binds TNF-receptor-associated death-domain protein (TRADD) through interactions of homologous regions, called 'death domains' (DDs), expressed in both proteins [22]. The original DD was so named because it was found in the death-inducing receptor Fas as well as in an adaptor protein recruited to ligand-occupied Fas, called Fas-associated DD protein (FADD). The three-dimensional structure of the TNFR1 DD has recently been solved by two separate groups of researchers, and two interactive TRADD binding sites have been defined [23,24]. Unoccupied TNFR1 associates with a DD-containing protein, called silencer of DDs (SODD), which is displaced by TRADD upon TNF binding [25]. Receptor-bound TRADD can recruit FADD through DD interactions and thereby mimic the death-activation responses of Fas [26].

TRADD recruitment also initiates the recruitment of two other adaptor proteins that have been linked to activation of NF-κB and for AP-1, namely receptor interacting protein (RIP) and TNF-receptor-associated factor 2 (TRAF2). RIP is a serine/threonine kinase that contains a DD that mediates binding to TRADD [27]. The mechanism of action of RIP is unclear; kinase-inactive RIP can function when overexpressed, but this may involve recruitment of endogenous RIP molecules with an intact kinase activity. Thymocytes from knockout mice lacking RIP cannot activate NF-κB in response to TNF but can still respond to TNF by activating AP-1 [28]. TRAF2 binds to the N-terminal domain of TRADD, i.e. outside the DD [29]. TRAF2 contains an N-terminal RING domain, which is essential for its signaling, a series of zinc fingers, and C-terminal TRAF domains shared with other members of the TRAF family. The TRAF domains mediate both self-association and binding to adaptor proteins (e.g. TRADD). Unlike RIP, TRAF2 has no known enzymatic activities (although RING domains may act as E3 ubiquitin ligases) [30]. Embryonic fibroblasts lacking TRAF2 show a partially impaired ability of TNF to activate NF-κB and show complete loss of TNF-induced activation of AP-1 [31]. (The incomplete effect of TRAF2 deficiency may arise because of redundancy with TRAF5 [32].) TRAF2 may indirectly contribute to NF-κB activation by recruiting and/or stabilizing the interactions of RIP with its downstream targets [33]. Overexpression of either RIP or TRAF2 in wild-type cells can initiate both NF-κB and AP-1 signaling independent of TNF, TNFR1, or TRADD, possibly by driving association of adaptor proteins in a nonphysiological manner.

The physiological downstream targets of RIP or TRAF2 remain uncertain. Both the NF-κB and the AP-1 pathways are activated by members of the mitogen-activated-protein kinase (MAPK) kinase kinase (MAP3K, also known as MEKK) family. Experiments in gene-knockout embryonic fibroblasts implicate MEKK-1 in the AP-1 pathway [34] and MEKK3 in the NF-κB pathway [35] activated by TNF. Several different MEKKs can phosphorylate and activate a cytosolic enzymatic complex called IκB kinase (IKK) [36]. This multiprotein complex contains at least two active kinases (IKK-α and IKK-β), as well as a regulatory protein that lacks kinase activity, called IKK-γ, or NEMO. Studies in gene-knockout animals point to IKK-β as the crucial component that mediates TNF-induced phosphorylation of cytosolic inhibitor of κB (IκB) proteins [37,38] and show that IKK-γ (NEMO) is required for this response [39].

In unstimulated cells, IκB proteins normally sequester dimeric NF-κB complexes in the cytosol, preventing their entry into the nucleus where gene transcription occurs [40]. In response to TNF, IκB proteins are phosphorylated by IKK upon critical serine residues, and, once phosphorylated, are rapidly ubiquitinated and then degraded by the cytosolic proteosome. This process occurs within 15 minutes of treating human umbilical-vein-derived endothelial cells (HUVECs) with TNF. In HUVECs, TNF causes degradation of IκB-α, -β, and -ε [41,42]. Once an IκB protein is degraded, the associated NF-κB is free to move from the cytosol to the nucleus and activate transcription by binding to specific DNA sequences in the enhancers of target genes. In HUVECs, TNF-activated NF-κB is formed of homodimers or heterodimers involving three different members of the Rel family, namely p50 (also called NF-κB1), p65 (also called Rel A), and c-Rel. Homodimers of p50 appear to be constitutively present in the nucleus and are not regulated by IκB degradation. A recent report has suggested that IκB-α and IκB-β associate primarily with p50/p65 or p50/c-Rel heterodimers, whereas IκB-ε associates primarily with p50/c-Rel or c-Rel homodimers [42]. Minor variations in a κB-binding DNA sequence may favor binding of one form of NF-κB over another. In experiments using electrophoretic-mobility-shift assay, the three E-selectin elements preferentially bind p50/p65 heterodimers [43–45]. The VCAM-1 promoter contains two tandem κB-binding sites that also appear to preferentially bind p50/p65 [46,47]. In contrast, the ICAM-1 promoter contains one κB element that may preferentially bind p50/c-Rel heterodimers or c-Rel heterodimers [42,48].

AP-1 activation occurs when an MAP3K, probably MEKK-1, phosphorylates and activates several MAP2Ks (also known as MEKs), which, in turn, phosphorylate and activate several MAPKs (also known as stress-activated protein kinases, or SAPKs) such as c-Jun N-terminal kinase (JNK)-1 and -2 and p38 MAPK [49]. JNK-1 and -2 phosphorylate the transactivating domain of c-Jun, a component of AP-1, and thereby enable AP-1 to activate gene transcription. Normally, c-Jun forms heterodimers with members of the Fos family, such as c-Fos or FosB, but c-Jun also can heterodimerize with activating transcription factor 2 (ATF2) to form a variant form of AP-1. TNF increases the binding of c-Jun/ATF2 to a DNA sequence in the E-selectin promoter [50]. Transfected E-selectin promoter–reporter genes lacking the c-Jun/ATF2-binding site are much less active than wild type [51], and E-selectin transcription does not occur in mice lacking ATF2 [52]. The transcriptional potential of ATF2, like that of c-Jun, can be increased by phosphorylation of its transactivating domain, catalyzed by p38 MAP kinase. However, while overexpression of a c-Jun mutant that cannot be phosphorylated (or of dominant negative JNK isoforms) will inhibit E-selectin transcription, a mutant form of ATF2 that cannot be phosphorylated is not inhibitory [51]. This suggests that c-Jun/ATF2 is necessary for E-selectin transcription but that only the c-Jun subunit needs to be phosphorylated for efficient gene transactivation. Both ICAM-1 and VCAM-1 also contain AP-1 binding sites (commonly called tetrahydrophorbol response elements, or TREs) that bind AP-1 in TNF-treated ECs [53,54]. In this case, AP-1 consists of c-Jun/cFos heterodimers. The significance of the canonical TRE in the VCAM-1 promoter has been questioned because this element is lacking in mice [54]. However, human and mouse VCAM-1 may not be regulated in the same manner, and a role of AP-1 in VCAM-1 transcription has been demonstrated using promoter–reporter genes in human ECs, although the site where AP-1 appears to bind in the model is distinct from the consensus TRE and is instead located between the two κB-binding elements [55].

Although the activation of NF-κB and AP-1 may involve divergent pathways, these factors interact in the nucleus through concomitant binding of gene coactivators, such as histone acetyl transferases like CREB-binding protein (CBP), or p300 [56]. The steric positioning of individual transcription factors bound to DNA, which permits coordinate interactions with coactivators, may depend upon DNA bending, controlled by proteins such as the high-mobility-group protein HMG-Y1 [43–45]. The basic unit of such coordinated complexes has been called an 'enhanceosome'. The three NF-κB binding sites and the AP-1 binding site in the E-selectin promoter appear to fit this definition.

E-selectin transcription and AP-1 activation are both transient in TNF-treated HUVECs [57], but NF-κB activation is not [41]. A decrease in phospho-c-Jun/ATF2, resulting from shutting off of JNK activity, probably accounts for the termination of E-selectin transcription [57]. Once the gene turns off, E-selectin cannot be effectively reinduced by TNF without a rest period of 18–24 hours. During the refractory period, it can be reinduced by IL-1 or CD40 ligand, and reinduction correlates with the reactivation of JNK. Since JNK activation is mediated by TRAF proteins and since TNF, IL-1, and CD40 ligand all use distinct TRAF proteins (although CD40 ligand does recruit TRAF2 and TRAF6 as well as TRAF3 and TRAF5), an attractive explanation for receptor-specific desensitization is that specific TRAFs are somehow selectively inactivated. TRAF proteins contain RING domains that can act as ubiquitin E3 ligases [30], and it is possible that ubiquitination is involved in TRAF inactivation and is responsible for the reduction of JNK and AP-1 activity. This speculation is supported by the observation that TRAF activation by CD30 in T cells is terminated by TRAF ubiquitination and degradation [58].

In some cells, TNF signaling may involve signaling pathways in addition to those described above, including the activation of phosphatidylinositol-3 kinase and protein kinase B (also known as Akt) [59]; activation of neutral or acidic sphingomyelinases to generate ceramide [60]; *de novo* sphingosine-1 phosphate (S-1P) synthesis [61]; and a Ras/Raf/ERK growth-control pathway [62]. My laboratory has shown that the Akt and ceramide pathways do not contribute to adhesion molecule expression in ECs [63,64]. It is possible that the S-1P and Ras pathways do participate in ELAM regulation, but, if so, the biochemical links to ELAM gene transcription are unknown.

The cell biology of TNF signaling in ECs

The biochemical view of TNF signaling described above is well supported by genetic and molecular data. However, my colleagues and I believe that it is an incomplete description, because it does not consider the capacity of cells to regulate interactions of receptors and adaptor proteins through control of their subcellular localization. Much of our recent work has focused upon this aspect of TNF signaling. HUVECs have very little TNFR1 on their surface; the predominant surface receptor is TNFR2 [65,66]. Although TNFR2 can directly bind TRAF2 (as well as TRAF1), it does not activate expression of adhesion molecules in these cells [19] (although it can do so, independently of ligand, when overexpressed) [67]. However, the presence of TNFR2 increases the cells' sensitivity to TNF [19], consistent with the hypothesis of ligand passing from a higher-affinity (TNFR2) to a lower-affinity (TNFR1) receptor [68].

When TNF binds to ECs, much of it is rapidly internalized. Most of the internalized ligand follows a coated-pit/coated-vesicle pathway, winding up in endosomal/lysosomal compartments [65]. TNFR2 shows a similar pattern of internalization, and it is likely that most TNF uptake is mediated via this nonsignaling receptor. Surprisingly, a significant fraction of internalized TNF molecules end up associated with mitochondria [69] and a third TNF-binding protein (of approximately 60 kDa) has been identified in the inner membrane of this organelle [69]. The complete identity of this molecule, the pathway by which TNF is transported to the mitochondria, and the function, if any, of mitochrondial TNF are still unknown.

In cultured HUVECs, as in many other cell types, the majority of TNFR1 molecules are located within the Golgi apparatus, retained there through an undefined interaction involving the DD [65,66]. Until recently, the cellular and subcellular distributions of TNFR1 were known only from studies of cultured cells. Interestingly, in our initial analysis of a human tissue, namely the kidney, my colleagues and I found that TNFR1 was confined mainly to the Golgi apparatus of golmerular and peritubular capillary ECs [70], consistent with findings in studies in vitro (although the absence of TNFR1 in cell types other than ECs was unexpected). The role of the Golgi population of receptors is unknown. Plasma-membrane receptors can be internalized to an ER-like compartment in response to MAPK-mediated phosphorylation [71]. My colleagues at Cambridge University and I have recently found that Golgi receptors can be mobilized to appear on the cell surface by stimulation of cultured ECs with histamine (Jun Wang et al., unpublished observations).

When HUVECs are exposed to noxious stimuli, TNFR1 is shed from the surface [72]. This response is mediated by a protease inhibited by the compound TAPI (TACE protease inhibitor), and thus likely to be identical to TNF-α-converting enzyme (TACE). Shedding of receptors both desensitizes HUVECs to TNF [72] and serves as a source for soluble receptor (sTNFR), a natural inhibitor of TNF function [73]. The Golgi pool of receptors could thus be a reservoir for replacing shed receptors on the surface or could serve as a precursor pool for increasing the number of shed receptors. Our recent observations indicate that the same signals that mobilize receptors from the Golgi apparatus also favor receptor shedding, supporting the latter hypothesis (Jun Wang et al., unpublished observations). The importance of receptor shedding is highlighted by the finding that deficiencies in shedding receptors due to structural mutations in TNFR1 underlie TNFR-associated periodic syndrome (TRAPS), characterized by febrile episodes related to overreaction to TNF [74].

Even though only a minority of TNFR1 molecules are present on the plasma membrane, these molecules are critically important, because they are the only population that interacts with TRADD upon TNF treatment [75]. The cellular compartment(s) in which FADD, RIP, and TRAF2 are recruited to the TNFR1/TRADD complex is unknown. However, my colleagues and I and others have also observed that treatments that reduce membrane trafficking (e.g. endocytosis) also block TNF signaling [76,77], and such observations imply that TNFR1 signaling com-

plexes move from the plasma membrane in order to signal efficiently. My colleagues and I also have found that internalized receptors rapidly dissociate from TRADD, potentially limiting signaling [76].

A recent idea in receptor function is that activated receptors efficiently interact with adaptor proteins (and engage in crosstalk with other receptors) only when the relevant proteins are brought into proximity within cholesterol- and sphingomyelin-rich patches of the plasma membrane called lipid rafts [78,79]. In ECs and certain other cell types, lipid rafts bind cytoskeletal scaffolding proteins called caveolins [80]. Caveolin binding causes the rafts to invaginate, forming specialized organelles known as caveolae. Although caveolae were first identified for their role in initiating transcellular vesicular transport, they are now (additionally) thought to facilitate signaling and permit receptor crosstalk. It is thus noteworthy that in ECs, TRAF2 is normally associated with caveolin-1 [67]. This finding suggests that the TNFR1 signaling complex, through binding of TRAF2, can be recruited via caveolin-1 to caveolae, where interactions with other signaling pathways may occur.

Concluding remarks

TNF-mediated induction of ELAM gene expression in vascular ECs is a central event in inflammation. Over the past 10 years, a reasonably good biochemical model has been developed of how TNF can activate two families of transcription factors, namely NF-κB and AP-1, whose activation is necessary for expression of ELAM genes. Our current focus of investigation is how this biochemical model operates within the living ECs, where various interactive components may either be segregated or brought together in response to ligand binding. The more complete picture of TNF signaling, which is being developed from these studies, may lead to new, more nuanced therapeutic approaches to regulating the inflammatory process.

Glossary of terms

ATF = activating transcription factor; DD = death domain; ELAM = endothelial leukocyte adhesion molecule; FADD = Fas-associated DD protein; HUVEC = human umbilical-vein-derived endothelial cell; IKK = IκB kinase; JNK = c-Jun N-terminal kinase; MAPK = mitogen-activated protein kinase; MEK = MAPK kinase (also called MAP2K); MEKK = MEK kinase (also called MAP3K); RIP = receptor interacting protein; TRADD = TNF-receptor-associated death-domain protein; TRAF = TNF-receptor-associated factor; TRE = tetrahydrophorbol response element.

Acknowledgements

The studies presented from the laboratory have been supported by the NIH (HL36003). I would like to acknowledge members of my laboratory, past and present, who have contributed to this project, including Drs Tucker Collins, David Johnson, Lynne Lapierre, John Doukas, David Briscoe, Mark Slowik, Linda De Luca, Karin Karmann,

Peter Petzelbauer, Wang Min, Lisa Madge, Martin Kluger, Xiao Feng, and Mary Lou Gaeta. Many of the studies described herein were performed in collaboration with Dr John R Bradley and his laboratory group at Cambridge University.

References

1. Etazioni A, Doerschuk CM, Harlan JM: **Of man and mouse: leukocyte and endothelial adhesion molecule deficiencies.** *Blood* 1999, **94**:3281-3288. [key review]
2. Cohnheim J. *Lectures in General Pathology.* Translated by Al McKee from the 2nd German edn. London: New Sydenham Society; 1989. [archival reference]
3. Robbins SL, Angell M, Kumar V (Eds). **Chapter 2: Inflammation and repair.** In *Basic Pathology.* 4th edn. Philadelphia: WB Saunders; 1981:28-61. [archival reference]
4. Tonnesen MG, Smedly LA, Henson PM: **Neutrophil-endothelial cell interactions. Modulation of neutrophil adhesiveness induced by complement fragments C5a and C5a des arg and formyl-methionyl-leucyl-phenylalanine in vitro.** *J Clin Invest* 1984,**74**:1581-1592. [general reference]
5. Bjork J, Hugli TE, Smedegard G: **Microvascular effects of anaphylatoxins C3a and C5a.** *J Immunol* 1985, **134**:1115-1119. [general reference]
6. Bevilacqua MP, Pober JS, Wheeler ME, Cotran RS, Gimbrone MA Jr: **Interleukin-1 acts on cultured human vascular endothelial cells to increase the adhesion of polymorphonuclear leukocytes, monocytes and related leukocyte cell lines.** *J Clin Invest* 1985, **76**:2003-2011. [general reference]
7. Pober JS, Cotran RS: **Cytokines and endothelial cell biology.** *Physiol Rev* 1990, **70**:427-451. [key review]
8. Butcher EC: **Leukocyte-endothelial cell recognition: three (or more) steps to specificity and diversity.** *Cell* 1991, **67**:1033-1036. [key review]
9. Springer TA: **Traffic signals for lymphocyte recirculation and leukocyte emigration: the multistep paradigm.** *Cell* 1994, **76**: 301-314. [key review]
10. Petzelbauer P, Bender J, Wilson J, Pober JS: **Heterogeneity of dermal microvascular endothelial cell antigen expression and cytokine responsiveness in situ and in cell culture.** *J Immunol* 1993, **151**:5062-5072. [general reference]
11. Petzelbauer P, Pober JS, Keh A, Braverman IM: **Inducibility and expression of microvascular endothelial adhesion molecules in lesional, perilesional, and uninvolved skin of psoriatic patients.** *J Invest Dermatol* 1994, **103**:300-305. [general reference]
12. Briscoe DM, Cotran RS, Pober JS: **Effects of tumor necrosis factor, lipopolysaccharide, and IL-4 on the expression of vascular cell adhesion molecule-1 in vivo. Correlation with CD3+ T cell infiltration.** *J Immunol* 1992, **149**:2954-2960. [general reference]
13. Doukas J, Pober JS: **IFN-gamma enhances endothelial activation induced by tumor necrosis factor but not IL-1.** *J Immunol* 1990, **145**:1727-1733. [general reference]
14. Thornhill MH, Wellicome SM, Mahiouz DL, Lanchbury JS, Kyan-Aung U, Haskard DO: **Tumor necrosis factor combines with IL-4 or IFN-gamma to selectively enhance endothelial cell adhesiveness for T cells. The contribution of vascular cell adhesion molecule-1-dependent and -independent binding mechanisms.** *J Immunol* 1991, **146**:592-598. [general reference]
15. Austrup F, Vestweber D, Borges E, Lohning M, Brauer R, Herz U, Renz H, Hallmann R, Scheffold A, Radbruch A, Hamann A: **P- and E-selectin mediate recruitment of T-helper-1 but not T-helper-2 cells into inflamed tissues.** *Nature* 1997, **385**:81-83. [general reference]
16. Douni E, Akassoglou K, Alexopoulou L, Georgopoulos S, Haralambous S, Hill S, Kassiotis G, Kontoyiannis D, Pasparakis M, Plows D, Probert L, Kollias G: **Transgenic and knockout analyses of the role of TNF in immune regulation and disease pathogenesis.** *J Inflamm* 1995, **47**:27-38. [key review]
17. Feldmann M, Maini RN, Bondeson J, Taylor P, Foxwell BM, Brennan FM: **Cytokine blockade in rheumatoid arthritis.** *Adv Exp Med Biol* 2001, **490**:119-127. [key review]
18. Collins T, Read MA, Neish AS, Whitley MZ, Thanos D, Maniatis T: **Transcriptional regulation of endothelial cell adhesion molecules: NF-kappa B and cytokine-inducible enhancers.** *FASEB J* 1995, **9**:899-909. [key review]
19. Slowik MR, De Luca LG, Fiers W, Pober JS: **Tumor necrosis factor activates human endothelial cells through the p55 tumor necrosis factor receptor but the p75 receptor contributes to activation at low tumor necrosis factor concentration.** *Am J Pathol* 1993, **143**:1724-1730. [general reference]
20. Ledgerwood EC, Pober JS, Bradley JR: **Recent advances in the molecular basis of TNF signal transduction.** *Lab Invest* 1999, **79**:1041-1050. [key review]
21. Madge LA, Pober JS: **TNF signaling in vascular endothelial cells.** *Exp Mol Pathol* 2001, **70**:317-325. [key review]
22. Hsu H, Xiong J, Goeddel DV: **The TNF receptor 1-associated protein TRADD signals cell death and NF- kappa B activation.** *Cell* 1995, **81**:495-504. [general reference]
23. Telliez JB, Xu GY, Woronicz JD, Hsu S, Wu JL, Lin L, Sukits SF, Powers R, Lin LL: **Mutational analysis and NMR studies of the death domain of the tumor necrosis factor receptor-1.** *J Mol Biol* 2000, **300**:1323-1333. [general reference]
24. Sukits SF, Lin LL, Hsu S, Malakian K, Powers R, Xu GY: **Solution structure of the tumor necrosis factor receptor-1 death domain.** *J Mol Biol* 2001, **310**:895-906. [general reference]
25. Jiang Y, Woronicz JD, Liu W, Goeddel DV: **Prevention of constitutive TNF receptor 1 signaling by silencer of death domains.** *Science* 1999, **283**:543-546. [general reference]
26. Hsu H, Shu HB, Pan MG, Goeddel DV: **TRADD-TRAF2 and TRADD-FADD interactions define two distinct TNF receptor 1 signal transduction pathways.** *Cell* 1996, **84**:299-308. [general reference]
27. Hsu H, Huang J, Shu HB, Baichwal V, Goeddel DV: **TNF-dependent recruitment of the protein kinase RIP to the TNF receptor-1 signaling complex.** *Immunity* 1996, **4**:387-396. [general reference]
28. Kelliher MA, Grimm S, Ishida Y, Kuo F, Stanger BZ, Leder P: **The death domain kinase RIP mediates the TNF-induced NF-kappaB signal.** *Immunity* 1998, **8**:297-303. [general reference]
29. Park YC, Ye H, Hsia C, Segal D, Rich RL, Liou H-C, Myszka DG, Wu H: **A novel mechanism of TRAF signaling revealed by structural and functional analyses of the TRADD-TRAF2 interaction.** *Cell* 2000, **101**:777-787. [general reference]
30. Lorick KL, Jensen JP, Fang S, Ong AM, Hatakeyama S, Weissman AM: **RING fingers mediate ubiquitin-conjugating enzyme (E2)-dependent ubiquitination.** *Proc Natl Acad Sci U S A* 1999, **96**: 11364-11369. [general reference]
31. Yeh WC, Shahinian A, Speiser D, Kraunus J, Billia F, Wakeham A, de la Pompa JL, Ferrick D, Hum B, Iscove N, Ohashi P, Rothe M, Goeddel DV, Mak TW: **Early lethality, functional NF-kappaB activation, and increased sensitivity to TNF-induced cell death in TRAF2-deficient mice.** *Immunity* 1997, **7**:715-725. [general reference]
32. Tada K, Okazaki T, Sakon S, Kobarai T, Kurosawa K, Yamaoka S, Hashimoto H, Mak TW, Yagita H, Okumura K, Yeh WC, Nakano H: **Critical roles of TRAF2 and TRAF5 in tumor necrosis factor-induced NF-kappa B activation and protection from cell death.** *J Biol Chem* 2001, **276**:36530-36534. [general reference]
33. Devin A, Cook A, Lin Y, Rodriguez Y, Kelliher M, Liu Z: **The distinct roles of TRAF2 and RIP in IKK activation by TNF-R1: TRAF2 recruits IKK to TNF-R1 while RIP mediates IKK activation.** *Immunity* 2000, **12**:419-429. [general reference]
34. Xia Y, Makris C, Su B, Li E, Yang J, Nemerow GR, Karin M: **MEK kinase 1 is critically required for c-Jun N-terminal kinase activation by proinflammatory stimuli and growth factor-induced cell migration.** *Proc Natl Acad Sci U S A* 2000, **97**:5243-5248. [general reference]
35. Yang J, Ling Y, Guo Z, Cheng J, Huang J, Deng L, Liao W, Chen Z, Liu Z-g, Su B: **The essential role of MEKK3 in TNF-induced NF-κB activation.** *Nat Immunol* 2001, **2**:620-624. [general reference]
36. Karin M: **The beginning of the end: IkappaB kinase (IKK) and NF-kappaB activation.** *J Biol Chem* 1999, **274**:27339-27342. [key review]
37. Tanaka M, Fuentes ME, Yamaguchi K, Durnin MH, Dalrymple SA, Hardy KL, Goeddel DV: **Embryonic lethality, liver degeneration, and impaired NF-κB activation in IKK-b-deficient mice.** *Immunity* 1999, **10**:421-429. [general reference]
38. Li ZW, Chu W, Hu Y, Delhase M, Deerinck T, Ellisman M, Johnson R, Karin M: **The IKKbeta subunit of IkappaB kinase (IKK) is essential for nuclear factor kappaB activation and prevention of apoptosis.** *J Exp Med* 1999, **189**:1839-1845. [general reference]

39. Rudolph D, Yeh WC, Wakeham A, Rudolph B, Nallainathan D, Potter J, Elia AJ, Mak TW: **Severe liver degeneration and lack of NF-kappaB activation in NEMO/IKKgamma-deficient mice.** *Genes Dev* 2000, **14**:854-862. [general reference]

40. Baldwin AS Jr: **The NF-kappa B and I kappa B proteins: new discoveries and insights.** *Annu Rev Immunol* 1996, **14**:649-683. [key review]

41. Johnson DR, Douglas I, Jahnke A, Ghosh S, Pober JS: **A sustained reduction in IkappaB-beta may contribute to persistent NF-kappaB activation in human endothelial cells.** *J Biol Chem* 1996, **271**:16317-16322. [general reference]

42. Spiecker M, Darius H, Liao JK: **A functional role of I kappa B-epsilon in endothelial cell activation.** *J Immunol* 2000, **164:** 3316-3322. [general reference]

43. Lewis H, Kaszubska W, DeLamarter JF, Whelan J: **Cooperativity between two NF-kappa B complexes, mediated by high-mobility-group protein I(Y), is essential for cytokine-induced expression of the E-selectin promoter.** *Mol Cell Biol* 1994, **14:** 5701-5709. [general reference]

44. Schindler U, Baichwal VR: **Three NF-kappa B binding sites in the human E-selectin gene required for maximal tumor necrosis factor alpha-induced expression.** *Mol Cell Biol* 1994, **14:** 5820-5831. [general reference]

45. Whitley MZ, Thanos D, Read MA, Maniatis T, Collins T: **A striking similarity in the organization of the E-selectin and beta interferon gene promoters.** *Mol Cell Biol* 1994, **14**:6464-6475. [general reference]

46. Shu HB, Agranoff AB, Nabel EG, Leung K, Duckett CS, Neish AS, Collins T, Nabel GJ: **Differential regulation of vascular cell adhesion molecule 1 gene expression by specific NF-kappa B subunits in endothelial and epithelial cells.** *Mol Cell Biol* 1993, **13**:6283-6289. [general reference]

47. Ahmad M, Marui N, Alexander RW, Medford RM: **Cell type-specific transactivation of the VCAM-1 promoter through an NF-kappa B enhancer motif.** *J Biol Chem* 1995, **270**:8976-8983. [general reference]

48. Parry GC, Mackman N: **A set of inducible genes expressed by activated human monocytic and endothelial cells contain kappa B-like sites that specifically bind c-Rel-p65 heterodimers.** *J Biol Chem* 1994, **269**:20823-20825. [general reference]

49. Baud V, Karin M: **Signal transduction by tumor necrosis factor and its relatives.** *Trends Cell Biol* 2001, **11**:372-377. [key review]

50. De Luca LG, Johnson DR, Whitley MZ, Collins T, Pober JS: **cAMP and tumor necrosis factor competitively regulate transcriptional activation through and nuclear factor binding to the cAMP-responsive element/activating transcription factor element of the endothelial leukocyte adhesion molecule-1 (E-selectin) promoter.** *J Biol Chem* 1994, **269**:19193-19196. [general reference]

51. Min W, Pober JS: **TNF initiates E-selectin transcription in human endothelial cells through parallel TRAF-NF-kappa B and TRAF-RAC/CDC42-JNK-c-Jun/ATF2 pathways.** *J Immunol* 1997, **159**:3508-3518. [general reference]

52. Reimold AM, Grusby MJ, Kosaras B, Fries JW, Mori R, Maniwa S, Clauss IM, Collins T, Sidman RL, Glimcher MJ, Glimcher LH: **Chondrodysplasia and neurological abnormalities in ATF-2-deficient mice.** *Nature* 1996, **379**:262-265. [general reference]

53. Stade BG, Messer G, Riethmuller G, Johnson JP: **Structural characteristics of the 5' region of the human ICAM-1 gene.** *Immunobiology* 1990, **182**:79-87. [general reference]

54. Cybulsky MI, Allan-Motamed M, Collins T: **Structure of the murine VCAM1 gene.** *Genomics* 1993, **18**:387-391. [general reference]

55. Ahmad M, Theofanidis P, Medford RM: **Role of activating protein-1 in the regulation of the vascular cell adhesion molecule-1 gene expression by tumor necrosis factor-α.** *J Biol Chem* 1998, **273**:4616-4621. [general reference]

56. Gerritsen ME, Williams AJ, Neish AS, Moore S, Shi Y, Collins T: **CREB-binding protein/p300 are transcriptional coactivators of p65.** *Proc Natl Acad Sci U S A* 1997, **94**:2927-2932. [general reference]

57. Karmann K, Min W, Fanslow WC, Pober JS: **Activation and homologous desensitization of human endothelial cells by CD40 ligand, tumor necrosis factor, and interleukin 1.** *J Exp Med* 1996, **184**:173-182.

58. Duckett CS and Thompson, CB: **CD30-dependent degradation of TRAF2: implications for negative regulation of TRAF signaling and the control of cell survival.** *Genes Dev* 1997, **11**:2810-2821. [general reference]

59. Ozes ON, Mayo LD, Gustin JA, Pfeffer SR, Pfeffer LM, Donner DB: **NF-kappaB activation by tumour necrosis factor requires the Akt serine-threonine kinase.** *Nature* 1999, **401**:82-85. [general reference]

60. Kolesnick RN, Kronke M: **Regulation of ceramide production and apoptosis.** *Annu Rev Physiol* 1998, **60**:643-665. [key review]

61. Xia P, Gamble JR, Rye KA, Wang L, Hii CS, Cockerill P, Khew-Goodall Y, Bert AG, Barter PJ, Vadas MA: **Tumor necrosis factor-alpha induces adhesion molecule expression through the sphingosine kinase pathway.** *Proc Natl Acad Sci U S A* 1998, **95**:14196-14201. [general reference]

62. Xu XS, Vanderziel C, Bennett CF, Monia BP: **A role for c-Raf kinase and Ha-Ras in cytokine-mediated induction of cell adhesion molecules.** *J Biol Chem* 1998, **273**:33230-33238. [general reference]

63. Madge LA, Pober JS: **A phosphatidylinositol 3-kinase/Akt pathway, activated by tumor necrosis factor or interleukin-1, inhibits apoptosis but does not activate NFkappaB in human endothelial cells.** *J Biol Chem* 2000, **275**:15458-15465. [general reference]

64. Slowik MR, De Luca LG, Min W, Pober JS: **Ceramide is not a signal for tumor necrosis factor-induced gene expression but does cause programmed cell death in human vascular endothelial cells.** *Circ Res* 1996, **79**:736-747. [general reference]

65. Bradley JR, Thiru S, Pober JS: **Disparate localization of 55-kd and 75-kd tumor necrosis factor receptors in human endothelial cells.** *Am J Pathol* 1994, **146**:27-32. [general reference]

66. Gaeta ML, Johnson DR, Kluger MS, Pober JS: **The death domain of tumor necrosis factor receptor 1 is necessary but not sufficient for Golgi retention of the receptor and mediates receptor desensitization.** *Lab Invest* 2000, **80**:1185-1194. [general reference]

67. Feng X, Gaeta ML, Madge LA, Yang JH, Bradley JR, Pober JS: **Caveolin-1 associates with TRAF2 to form a complex that is recruited to tumor necrosis factor receptors.** *J Biol Chem* 2001, **276**:8341-8349. [general reference]

68. Tartaglia LA, Pennica D, Goeddel DV: **Ligand passing: the 75-kDa tumor necrosis factor (TNF) receptor recruits TNF for signaling by the 55-kDa TNF receptor.** *J Biol Chem* 1993, **268**:18542-18548. [general reference]

69. Ledgerwood EC, Prins JB, Bright NA, Johnson DR, Wolfreys K, Pober JS, O'Rahilly S, Bradley JR: **Tumor necrosis factor is delivered to mitochondria where a tumor necrosis factor-binding protein is localized.** *Lab Invest* 1998, **78**:1583-1589. [general reference]

70. Al-Lamki RS, Wang J, Skepper JN, Thiru S, Pober JS, Bradley JR: **Expression of tumor necrosis factor receptors in normal kidney and rejecting renal transplants.** *Lab Invest* 2001, **81**:1503-1515. [general reference]

71. Cottin V, Van Linden A, Riches DW: **Phosphorylation of tumor necrosis factor receptor CD120a (p55) by p42(MAPK/ERK2) induces changes in its subcellular localization.** *J Biol Chem* 1999, **274**:32975-32987. [general reference]

72. Madge LA, Sierra-Honigmann MR, Pober JS: **Apoptosis-inducing agents cause rapid shedding of tumor necrosis factor receptor 1 (TNFR1). A nonpharmacological explanation for inhibition of TNF-mediated activation.** *J Biol Chem* 1999, **274**:13643-13649. [general reference]

73. Wallach D, Engelmann H, Nophar Y, Aderka D, Kemper O, Hornik V, Holtmann H, Brakebusch C: **Soluble and cell surface receptors for tumor necrosis factor.** *Agents Actions Suppl* 1991, **35:** 51-57. [key review]

74. Galon J, Aksentijevich I, McDermott MF, O'Shea JJ, Kastner DL: **TNFRSF1A mutations and autoinflammatory syndromes.** *Curr Opin Immunol* 2000, **12**:479-486. [key review]

75. Jones SJ, Ledgerwood EC, Prins JB, Savidge J, Johnson DR, Pober JS, Bradley JR: **TNF recruits TRADD to the plasma membrane but not the trans-Golgi network, the principal subcellular location of TNF-R1.** *J Immunol* 1999, **162**:1042-1048. [general reference]

76. Bradley JR, Johnson DR, Pober JS: **Four different classes of inhibitors of receptor-mediated endocytosis decrease TNF-induced gene expression in human endothelial cells**. *J Immunol* 1993, **150**:5544-5555. [general reference]

77. Schutze S, Machleidt T, Adam D, Schwandner R, Wiegmann K, Kruse ML, Heinrich M, Wickel M, Kronke M: **Inhibition of receptor internalization by monodansylcadaverine selectively blocks p55 tumor necrosis factor receptor death domain signaling**. *J Biol Chem* 1999, **274**:10203-10212. [general reference]

78. Simons K, Toomre D: **Lipid rafts and signal transduction**. *Nat Rev Mol Cell Biol* 2000, **1**:31-39. [key review]

79. Galbiati F, Razani B, Lisanti MP: **Emerging themes in lipid rafts and caveolae**. *Cell* 2001, **106**:403-411. [key review]

80. Schlegel A, Lisanti MP: **The caveolin triad: caveolae biogenesis, cholesterol trafficking, and signal transduction**. *Cytokine Growth Factor Rev* 2001, **12**:41-51. [key review]

Immunology

Supplement Review
The immunological synapse
Michael L Dustin

Department of Pathology, New York University School of Medicine, Skirball Institute for Biomolecular Medicine, New York, NY, USA

Correspondence: Department of Pathology, New York University School of Medicine, Program in Molecular Pathogenesis, Skirball Institute for Biomolecular Medicine, 540 First Ave, New York, NY 10016, USA. Tel: +1 212 263 3207; fax: +1 212 263 5711; e-mail: dustin@saturn.med.nyu.edu; website: www.saturn.med.nyu.edu/groups/Dustin

Received: 26 November 2001
Accepted: 11 December 2001
Published: 9 May 2002

Arthritis Res 2002, 4 (suppl 3):S119-S125

This article may contain supplementary data which can only be found online at http://arthritis-research.com/content/4/S3/S119

Chapter summary

T-cell activation requires interaction of T-cell antigen receptors with proteins of the major histocompatibility complex (antigen). This interaction takes place in a specialized cell–cell junction referred to as an immunological synapse. The immunological synapse contains at least two functional domains: a central cluster of engaged antigen receptors and a surrounding ring of adhesion molecules. The segregation of the T-cell antigen receptor (TCR) and adhesion molecules is based on size, with the TCR interaction spanning 15 nm and the lymphocyte-function-associated antigen-1 (LFA-1) interaction spanning 30–40 nm between the two cells. Therefore, the synapse is not an empty gap, but a space populated by both adhesion and signaling molecules. This chapter considers four aspects of the immunological synapse: the role of migration and stop signals, the role of the cytoskeleton, the role of self-antigenic complexes, and the role of second signals.

Keywords: activation, adhesion, immunological synapse, inhibition, signaling

Introduction

The immunological synapse (IS) is a specialized cell–cell junction between a thymus-derived lymphocyte (T cell) and an antigen-presenting cell (APC) [1,2]. Initiation of an antigen-specific immune response is based on the interaction between T-cell receptors (TCRs) and major histocompatibility complex proteins that have bound antigenic peptides (MHCps) [3,4]. Because the TCRs and MHCps are attached to the surface of the T cell and the APC, respectively, the initiation of an immune response requires a molecular grasp between the T cell and the APC – a synapse. A current focus of research on the IS is to determine how this supramolecular structure contributes to T-cell sensitivity and to the fidelity of the T-cell response. Four areas in which the concept of the IS is contributing to our understanding of T-cell activation are the coordination of antigen recognition and T-cell migration; the role of

the cytoskeleton in T-cell activation; the mechanism of sensitive antigen recognition by T cells; and the integration of the adaptive and innate immune responses.

Historical background

The formation of the IS has been followed over time in live T cells interacting with planar bilayers [2] and studied at specific time points in fixed cell–cell conjugates [5]. The T cell forms an adhesion zone with the antigen-presenting bilayer; this zone is then surrounded by areas of close contact where TCR can reach the MHCp. If the TCR engagement exceeds a threshold rate and level, the T cell stops migrating and forms a ring of engaged TCRs at the periphery of the nascent IS (Fig. 1a). This pattern takes ~30 seconds to form and corresponds to the peak of TCR-associated tyrosine phosphorylation and Ca^{2+} mobilization. Within a few more seconds, the sites of TCR

A glossary of specialist terms used in this chapter appears at the end of the text section. A list of common abbreviations used in this issue appears just before the indexes.

engagement move from the periphery of the contact area to the center of the contact area to form the mature IS (Fig. 1b). During this time, the disk-like region of LFA-1–ICAM-1 (intercellular adhesion molecule-1) interaction appears to give way to the centrally moving TCR, but the LFA-1–ICAM-1 interactions maintain the contact area and evolve into a ring of ~5 µm outer diameter (Fig. 1c). It is not clear if the same TCRs move from the outside to the center or if new TCRs are continually recruited. The interaction of the TCRs with agonist MHCp complexes has a short half-life (~5 seconds) [6], and it is known that TCRs are degraded after effective engagement [7]. However, at some point in IS formation, the interaction of the TCRs and the major histocompatibility complex protein (MHC)–peptide complexes change so that they no longer dissociate. Thus, while serial engagement may dominate in the nascent IS, parallel engagement of at least 50 TCRs is characteristic of the center of the mature IS. These observations have emphasized the concept that biochemical reactions are highly compartmentalized in the IS, in such a way that the location of receptor and signaling molecules must be considered if we are to to understand the biochemical basis of T-cell activation [8].

Migration and the immunological synapse

T-cell activation requires a sustained signal. The duration of signaling required to initiate proliferation of T cells is at least 2 hours [9–11] but may be much longer to achieve appropriate differentiation of helper T cells [12]. T cells migrate continually between the blood and the secondary lymphoid tissues where they encounter APCs. In the absence of an immune response, the T cell completes this cycle about twice a day [13]. During the initiation of an immune response, the T cells are held in the antigen-exposed lymph nodes or the spleen for 2–3 days and then effector cells are released after the third day [14]. *In vitro* T-cell recognition of agonist MHCp in the context of the adhesion molecule ICAM-1 delivers a stop signal to migrating T cells [15]. This stop signal is the first stage in the formation of an IS [2].

The mechanism of the stop signal is not known, but it appears to involve the polarization of the T-cell toward the source of antigen, as indicated by the position of the microtubule organizing center (MTOC) and the associated Golgi apparatus [16]. The environment of the T-cell–APC interaction regulates the stop signal. One example of this is that APCs with agonist MHCp do not stop T cells in three-dimensional collagen gels *in vitro* [17]. The mechanism of this effect is not known, but it may involve chemokine gradients [18] or interactions with extracellular matrix that prevent T-cell polarization toward the APCs. In lymph nodes, however, T cells are not exposed to collagen fibers, which are sequestered in reticular fibers [19]. Reticular fibers may provide a weakly adhesive reticular scaffold decorated with APCs that define corridors

Figure 1

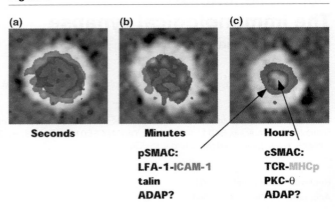

The development of the immunological synapse. Images adapted from [2] based on fluorescence microscope images of T-cell interaction with agonist MHC–peptide complexes (green) and ICAM-1 (red) in a supported planar bilayer with a T cell. The accumulation of fluorescence represents interactions in different time frames. **(a)** Within seconds, the T cell attaches to the substrate using LFA-1/ICAM-1 interactions in the center based on TCR signaling triggered at the periphery of the contact area. **(b)** Over a period of minutes, the engaged TCRs are translocated to the center of the contact area. **(c)** The final pattern, with a central cluster of engaged TCRs surrounded by a ring of engaged LFA-1, is stable for hours. Molecular markers for the cSMAC and pSMAC are indicated. For scale, the pSMAC is ~5 µm across. ADAP, adhesion and degranulation adapter protein; cSMAC, central supramolecular activation cluster; ICAM, intercellular adhesion molecule; LFA, lymphocyte-function-associated antigen; MHCp, major histocompatibility complex protein complexed to a foreign or self-peptide; PKC-θ, a protein kinase C isoform that is activated by DAG but not Ca^{2+}; pSMAC, peripheral supramolecular activation cluster – the ring of LFA-1 and talin on the T cell and ICAM-1 on the antigen-presenting cell in the mature immunological synapse; TCR, T-cell antigen receptor. See Colour figure section.

through which the T cells migrate [19]. Based on the lymph node environment and *in vitro* data, it is most likely that the IS coordinates T-cell migration and the antigen recognition process to allow full activation of T cells by small numbers of APCs that express the appropriate MHCp. When there are only a few APCs with agonist MHCp, it seems more efficient to have the T cell stop upon interaction with agonist MHCp-bearing APCs rather than having the T cells interact transiently with both agonist-MHCp-bearing and -deficient APCs equally, because the former procedure maximizes the interaction with the agonist MHCp and favors activation early in an immune response. This view is supported by *in vivo* data demonstrating clustering of polarized T cells around dendritic cells [20,21].

The cytoskeleton and the immunological synapse

Our expectations about molecular interaction in the IS have been shaped by early molecular definition of the molecules involved in this process [22]. The complex of the LFA-1 with ICAM-1 (~48 nm) is more than three times as large as the complex of the TCRs with MHCp (~15 nm) [23–25]. Therefore, the LFA-1/ICAM-1 and TCR/MHC interactions segregate into different compartments within the contact area [26]. This receptor segregation forms receptor aggregates whose size and organization are determined by the rigidity of the membrane, the kinetics of the interactions, and the degree of differences in molecular size of the participating receptor–ligand pairs [27]. This immediate segregation may be the initial trigger of receptor clustering and signaling in the nascent IS [28]. These events take happen in seconds and set the stage for the formation of the mature synapse.

The formation of the synapse is highly active and depends on an intact actin cytoskeleton. The formation of the central cluster of TCR has a superficial similarity to antibody-mediated capping, in that it requires an intact actino-myosin cytoskeleton. A plausible model based on this similarity has been proposed and initial results support some aspects of the model [29]. However, the IS has many elements that are completely absent in capping of cross-linked antigen receptors. For example, most capping is based on a network of interactions on a membrane surface that lead to cross-linking, whereas receptor aggregation is a cell–cell contact is more likely to result from membrane fluctuations, receptor–ligand size differences, and interaction kinetics. These components have been incorporated in a physical model by Chakraborty and colleagues [27]. The predictions of this model are remarkably concordant with the observations on the formation of the IS. This more physical view is compatible with an active role for the cortical cytoskeleton, because signaling-induced changes in cytoskeletal dynamics in activated T cells will profoundly regulate the Brownian bending movements of the membrane that are required for movement of the receptor interactions. This model could be described as a physical and mathematical elaboration on the kinetic-segregation model [28]. Thus, the early signals from the TCRs that trigger increased actin polymerization may induce the membrane fluctuations that drive the maturation of the IS. Both the capping and the kinetic-segregation models predict that cytoskeletal dynamics are critical for IS formation.

Signaling pathways activated during synapse formation

The TCR activates three major transcription-factor families. In addition to regulation of gene expression, intermediates and side branches of these signaling pathways also appear to be partly responsible for formation of the immuological synapse. The importance of this concept is that these signaling pathways play an important role in creating the physical environment for sustained signaling.

The initial events at the engaged TCR activate a tyrosine kinase cascade that requires the participation of three families of tyrosine kinases: the src family, the syk family, and the tec family. The src family kinase p56[lck] and the syk family kinase ZAP-70 are sufficient for phosphorylation of the immunotyrosine activation motifs (ITAMs) in the cytoplasmic domains of the TCR complex [30]. These phosphorylation events then enable tyrosine phosphorylation of the transmembrane adapter protein called linker of activated T cells (LAT), and phosphoLAT recruits enzymes including phospholipase Cγ (PLCγ), the Grb2/SOS complex, phosphatidylinositol-3-kinase and the GADS/SLP-76/NCK/VAV complex [31], which links LAT to activation of the small G protein Rac and recruitment of PKC-θ. The recruitment of PLCγ leads to cleavage of phospatidyl-inositol-4,5-bisphosphate (PI-4,5-P$_2$) to diacylglycerol (DAG) and inositol-1,4,5-trisphosphate (IP$_3$). IP$_3$ activates Ca^{2+} channels in the endoplasmic reticulum to release Ca^{2+} into the cytoplasm, and depletion of this store opens plasma-membrane capacitative Ca^{2+} channels that enable sustained cytoplasmic Ca^{2+} elevation [32]. Full activation of PLCγ for sustained Ca^{2+} signals requires activation of members of the Tec family protein kinase, Itk, which is recruited to the membrane PI-3,4,5-P$_3$, a product of phosphatidylinositol-3-kinase activation. Sustained Ca^{2+} elevation activates calcineurin, leading to dephosphorylation and nuclear translocation of NFAT (nuclear factor of activated T cells) [33]. The activation of RAS by Grb2/SOS and also by Ras-GRP leads to activation of AP-1 (activation protein 1). Activation of AP-1 is also promoted by the Jun kinase, which is regulated by p21rac downstream of VAV and other guanine nucleotide exchange factors. The third major family of transcription factors activated by the TCR is the PKCθ/IκB/inhibitor of κB kinase pathway leading to phosphorylation and degradation of IκB, the regulatory subunit of the nuclear factor-κB (NF-κB) transcription factor [34]. All three of these pathways also feed back on the synapse through effects on the cytoskeleton and regulation of adhesion. For example, the adhesion and degranulation protein (ADAP) identifies a signaling pathway linking the TCR to LFA-1 regulation [35,36].

The mechanisms that turn off signaling in the synapse are poorly understood. The broad regulatory mechanisms that have been identified are phosphatases and ubiquitin-pathway-mediated degradation [37–39]. It is apparent that activation of tyrosine kinase signaling pathways lead to recruitment of tyrosine phosphatases that may be involved in turning off signals. The most notable is SHP-1, an SH2 domain containing tyrosine phosphatase-1 that is deficient in motheaten mice. The SH2 domains of SHP-1 interact with immunotyrosine-based inhibitory motifs in the cytoplasmic domains of inhibitory receptors such as the killer inhibitory receptors and receptors expressed in T cells such as LAIR [40,41]. When an immunotyrosine-based inhibitory motif is phosphorylated by an active Src family kinase it recruits SHP-1, which can extinguish downstream signaling by ITAM-containing receptors [42]. It has also been shown that SHP-1 can be recruited to partially phosphorylated ITAMs and therefore may play an important role in negative signaling by antagonist MHCp [39].

The second process that appears to downregulate signaling is TCR degradation through a ubiquitin-mediated pathway [43]. Ubiquitin is added to substrates by an enzyme (E1) that is linked to the substrate by an adapter (E3). The adapter for addition of ubiquitin to the TCR complex is not known for certain, but may include members of the cbl family of ring finger domain containing E3s [44]. Cbl-b has also been implicated in regulating phosphatidylinositol-3-kinase (PI-3-K) [45]. TCR degradation takes place both in lysosomes and via the proteosome. How the TCR is delivered to the proteosome is not clear, but some TCR is internalized via clathrin-coated pits. The relatively fast off-rate for TCR-MHCp interaction suggests that it should be easy for TCR to dissociate from MHCp prior to internalization. However, studies in planar bilayers suggest that the kinetics of the TCR–MHCp interaction is substantially slower in the central cluster of the IS than in solution. Photobleaching experiments suggest, in fact, that the interactions become irreversible [2]. These irreversible complexes may require a more radical strategy for their destruction that would involve removal of an entire large membrane fragment from either the T cell or APC to accommodate internalization by one cell or the other. Consistent with this, fragments containing MHCp, CD80, and ICAM-1 are transferred from the APC to the T cell [46,47]. This process results in significant loss of molecules from the APC but does not reduce the cell's viability. It is not clear if the internalized TCR continues to signal before it is degraded or if all signaling takes place at the cell surface. When TCR internalization is suppressed by presenting MHCp on supported planar bilayers, from which the TCR cannot pull the MHC molecules, it is clear that endosomal structures collect near the central cluster [48]. These endosomes contain CD45 and the glycolipid GM1, a marker for glycolipid- and cholesterol-enriched membrane domains known as rafts. T cell–APC contacts lack these synaptic endosomes, perhaps because TCR can extract MHCp from the APC to achieve internalization of 'locked in' TCR-MHCp interactions. Once the TCR–MHCp interactions are internalized, they may meet CD45- and GM1-containing endosomes at other sites inside the cell. The purpose of these endomembrane structures for T-cell activation is not known. TCR downregulation clearly resets the threshold of the T cell for subsequent interactions and thus TCR downregulation can certainly be seen as a desensitizing mechanism [49].

The role of self MHCp in T-cell sensitivity to foreign MHCp

Any single TCR interacts with a degenerate spectrum of MHCp: null MHCps alone do not activate T cells, and agonist MHCp, the model foreign MHCp, induces full T-cell activation. Weak agonists induce a subset of T-cell responses, and antagonists interfere with T-cell responses to agonists. Approximately half of the TCR–MHCp binding energy comes from the TCR contacts with the MHC molecule [50]. Thus, the remaining peptides can be further divided. Some null peptides actively interfere with the TCR interactions and thus allow no interaction of the TCR with MHC, while other null peptides are neutral and allow the TCR to interact with MHC. The kinetics of this latter group of null MHCp are too fast to induce a response in mature T cells [51]. Self-peptides that form MHCp that are agonists, weak agonists or antagonists all induce apoptosis of immature T cells *in vivo* [51]. In contrast, a subset of null MHCps enhances positive selection. Thus, most mature T cells face APCs that are loaded with a mixture of null peptides (self). These mature T cells are triggered by APC bearing a few agonist/weak agonist MHCp mixed with diverse null MHCp. Naïve T cells respond to approximately 300 agonist MHCps on the APC, while memory T cells require only 50 agonist MHCps [52]. A single agonist MHCp is sufficient to trigger cytotoxic T-cell killing [53].

How is the high sensitivity of immune recognition achieved? Can a single agonist MHCp achieve T-cell activation, or do other MHCps promote this process? Wülfing *et al.* tested the hypothesis that some null MHCps contribute to T-cell activation through analysis of proliferation and formation of the IS [54]. They found that an interacting null MHCp contributes to IS formation and T-cell activation triggered by subthreshold amounts of agonist MHCp. It was demonstrated that fluorescently labeled null MHCps were accumulated in the center of the IS and synergized with trace levels of agonist MHCp for T-cell actvation. In contrast, the subset of null MHCp that does not interact with the TCR did not synergize with agonist MHC for T-cell activation and did not cluster in the center of synapses. Thus, agonist MHCps do not have to do it alone: they are substantially helped by this subset of null MHCps. We propose that this functional subset of MHCps be termed co-agonists. These experiments provide proof in principle that very weak TCR–co-agonist MHCp interactions can contribute to T-cell activation by the stronger TCR–agonist MHCp interactions. It will now be important to establish how prominent these synergizing null MHCps are in the self-peptide repertoire. The density of these complexes may vary with the specific APC types and between different TCR and MHC molecules. While contributing to sensitive recognition of MHCp by T cells, it is also possible that these null MHCps may contribute to autoimmune disease.

Integration of adaptive and innate responses

The IS is not limited to adhesion molecules and MHC–peptide complexes. The activation of naïve T cells involves a system of checks and balances that are integrated to make activation decisions. An important aspect of this integration is that T cells test both the MHC–peptide complex and the status of the innate immune response in the APC. In response to evolutionarily conserved microbial products such as lipopolysaccharide, the APC can be become activated. This increases expression of a number of molecules including the MHCp, adhesion molecules, and ligands for costimulatory receptors. Ligands for co-stimulatory receptors include CD80 and B7-DC (also know at PDL2) [55]. CD28 is the receptor for CD80 and by binding CD80 it indirectly transduces an innate immune system signal that can be integrated with the TCR signal. CD28–CD80 interactions are very inefficient due to the low density of CD28 and its low lateral mobility on naïve T cells [56]. Upon immunological synapse formation, CD28–CD80 interactions are facilitated and focused in the central region of the immunological synapse, very close to the site of TCR engagement. However, CD28–CD80 interaction does not help the TCR–MHCp interaction, which sets it apart from adhesion molecules such as LFA-1 and CD2[56]. This suggests a sequential model for T-cell response to TCR and innate signals. The formation of the IS corresponds to the antigen signal. Once this signal is received, the T-cell becomes competent to receive the signal through CD28. While this is an attractive hypothesis, there are a number of results that still must be reconciled. First, Sprent and colleagues have shown that the CD28–CD80 interaction is very effective at mediating the transfer of APC membrane proteins to the T-cell in a process that appears to require adhesion but does not require antigen [47]. This implies an interaction of CD28 and CD80 in the absence of TCR signals. The basis of this interaction is yet to be determined but might involve preclustering of CD80 on the APC membrane, as recently reported by Mellman and colleagues [57]. Such preclustering might partially overcome the low expression and mobility of CD28 on the T cell. It has also been shown that the MHCp and CD80 do not necessarily have to be presented on the same APC, in vivo or in vitro [58]. Thus, IS formation with one APC may facilitate the CD28–CD80 interaction in a contact with a second APC. Additional work will be required to understand the full implications of the low mobility of CD28 in diverse interactions in vivo. It will be important to determine if other secondary signals are dependent on IS formation.

Future prospects

Studies on the IS are still in their early days. The relation between IS formation and migration must be explored in vivo. This is important because it is difficult to simulate the in vivo environment in vitro. T cells and APCs can be labeled in vitro and transferred into recipient mice or endogenously labeled through GFP transgenes or knock-in mutant mice. The likely variables are the local extracellular matrix and chemokine gradients. This may be approached either in organ culture or by true in vivo imaging on live animals with natural perfusion of the lymphoid organs. The

latter will be most important, since afferent lymph is essential to maintain lymph node architecture and interactions. Blood perfusion is also likely to be critical to maintain the viability of cells deep in the lymph node. The depth of imaging needed can be achieved with two-photon excitation. The relationship between IS formation and the cytoskeleton needs to be experimentally tested using very specific genetic, biochemical, and imaging approaches. The entire question of self-MHCp and the prevalence of co-agonist MHCp in this group now takes on great importance. If the proportion of co-agonist MHCp differs between APCs, then these self-peptides could play an important role in autoimmunity as well as in normal responses to pathogens. Finally, the field of co-stimulation is exploding. There are additional recent members of the CD28/B7 family of receptors and ligands and there are also new molecular families that are implicated in providing co-stimulatory signals. The relation of these signals to the IS will need to be addressed through genetic, biochemical, and imaging experiments in the future.

Concluding remarks

In summary, the IS concept provides a number of insights into the process of T-cell activation. First, it provides a stop signal that coordinates antigen recognition and T-cell migration. Second, the essential role of the actin cytoskeleton in T-cell activation is related to the role of actin in IS formation. Third, the sensitivity of T-cell to agonist MHCp is related to the role of weakly interacting, but probably more abundant, self MHCp in promoting IS formation. Finally, the IS provides a framework for orderly integration of the TCR and innate immune signals such as CD28–CD80 interaction.

Glossary of terms

AP-1 = activation protein 1 – a transcription factor composed of Jun and Fos oncogene products; APC = antigen-presenting cell – generally a cell dedicated to the process of generating MHCps from intact antigens and then interacting with T cells to allow possible TCR-MHCp interactions and T-cell activation; cSMAC = central supramolecular activation cluster – the cluster of molecules including TCR and PKC-θ on the T cell and MHC-peptide complexes on the antigen-presenting cell in the mature immunological synapse; Grb2/SOS = a complex that links to phosphorylated LAT and activates guanine nucleotide exchange and activation of RAS; ICAM-1 = intercellular adhesion molecule-1 – type I transmembrane glycoprotein of the immunoglobulin superfamily that interacts with the integrins LFA-1 and Mac-1; IS = immunological synapse – the junction between a T cell and an APC bearing antigenic MHC–peptide complexes; ITAM = immunotyrosine activation motifs; LFA-1 = lymphocyte-function-associated antigen-1 – a member of the integrin family of adhesion molecules that interacts with ICAMs 1, 2, and 3; MHC = major histocompatibility complex protein – class I and class II proteins from this gene locus encode type I transmembrane glycoproteins with peptide-binding grooves to hold foreign or self-peptides; MHCp = major histocompatibility complex protein complexed to a foreign or self-peptide; NFAT = nuclear factor of activated T cells; PKC-θ = a protein kinase C isoform that is activated by DAG but not Ca^{2+}; PLCg = phospholipase Cg; pSMAC = peripheral supramolecular activation cluster – the ring of LFA-1 and talin on the T cell and ICAM-1 on the antigen-presenting cell in the mature immunological synapse; RAS = a small G protein that regulates the mitogen-activated protein kinase pathway; Ras-GRP = a protein that mediates an alternative pathway to activation of Ras that is stimulated by DAG; TCR = T-cell antigen receptor – type I transmembrane protein generated by somatic recombination of gene segments to generate millions of possible MHCp-binding receptors; Two-photon microscopy = a technique based on using mode-locked titanium-sapphire lasers to excite fluorescence of visible light fluorophores with two photons of infrared light. The use of infrared light provides excellent penetration. The two-photon excitation is achieved only at the focal point of the laser beam, so all fluorescence can be collected to generate the image – even highly scattered photons. Effective penetration is of the order of 500 mm; VAV = an oncogene product that acts as a guanine nucleotide exchange factor for Rac and may also contribute to recruitment of PKC-θ.

Acknowledgements

I thank my colleagues at Washington University and Stanford University for contributions to prepublication work described in this chapter. I also thank S Alzabin and E Block for critical reading of this chapter and R Barrett for preparation of the manuscript.

References

1. Paul WE, Seder RA: **Lymphocyte responses and cytokines.** *Cell* 1994, **76**:241-251. [key review]
2. Grakoui A, Bromley SK, Sumen C, Davis MM, Shaw AS, Allen PM, Dustin ML: **The immunological synapse: A molecular machine controlling T cell activation.** *Science* 1999, **285**:221-227. [general reference]
3. Hedrick SM, Nielsen EA, Kavaler J, Cohen DI, Davis MM: **Sequence relationships between putative T-cell receptor polypeptides and immunoglobulins.** *Nature* 1984, **308**:153-158. [general reference]
4. Babbitt BP, Allen PM, Matsueda G, Haber E, Unanue E: **Binding of immunogenic peptides to Ia histocompatibility molecules.** *Nature* 1985, **317**:359-361. [general reference]
5. Monks CR, Freiberg BA, Kupfer H, Sciaky N, Kupfer A: **Three-dimensional segregation of supramolecular activation clusters in T cells.** *Nature* 1998, **395**:82-86. [general reference]
6. Matsui K, Boniface JJ, Steffner P, Reay PA, Davis MM: **Kinetics of T-cell receptor binding to peptide/I-Ek complexes: correlation of the dissociation rate with T cell responsiveness.** *Proc Natl Acad Sci USA* 1994, **91**:12862-12866. [general reference]
7. Valututti S, Müller S, Cella M, Padovan E, Lanzavecchia A: **Serial triggering of many T-cell receptors by a few peptide-MHC complexes.** *Nature* 1995, **375**:148-151. [general reference]
8. Dustin ML, Chan AC: **Signaling takes shape in the immune system.** *Cell* 2000, **103**:283-294. [key review]
9. Iezzi G, Karjalainen K, Lanzavecchia A: **The duration of antigenic stimulation determines the fate of naive and effector T cells.** *Immunity* 1998, **8**:89-95. [general reference]
10. Wong P, Pamer EG: **Cutting edge: antigen-independent CD8 T cell proliferation.** *J Immunol* 2001, **166**:5864-5868. [general reference]
11. Kaech SM, Ahmed R: **Memory CD8+ T cell differentiation: initial antigen encounter triggers a developmental program in naive cells.** *Nat Immunol* 2001, **2**:415-422. [general reference]
12. Lanzavecchia A, Sallusto F: **The instructive role of dendritic cells on T cell responses: lineages, plasticity and kinetics.** *Curr Opin Immunol* 2001, **13**:291-298. [key review]
13. Mackay CR, Marston WL, Dudler L: **Naive and memory T cells show distinct pathways of lymphocyte recirculation.** *J Exp Med* 1990, **171**:810-817. [general reference]
14. Sprent J, Miller JFAP: **Interaction of thymus lymphocytes with histoincompatible cells. II. Recirculating lymphocytes derived from antigen-activated thymus cells.** *Cell Immunol* 1972, **3**:385-404. [general reference]
15. Dustin ML, Bromely SK, Kan Z, Peterson DA, Unanue ER: **Antigen receptor engagement delivers a stop signal to migrating T lymphocytes.** *Proc Natl Acad Sci U S A* 1997, **94**:3909-3913. [general reference]
16. Kupfer A, Singer SJ: **Cell biology of cytotoxic and helper T cell functions. Immunofluorescence microscopic studies of single cells and cell couples.** *Annu Rev Immunol* 1989, **7**:309-337. [key review]
17. Gunzer M, Schafer A, Borgmann S, Grabbe S, Zanker KS, Brocker EB, Kampgen E, Friedl P: **Antigen presentation in extracellular matrix: interactions of T cells with dendritic cells are dynamic, short lived, and sequential.** *Immunity* 2000, **13**:323-332. [general reference]
18. Bromley SK, Peterson DA, Gunn MD, Dustin ML: **Cutting edge: hierarchy of chemokine receptor and tcr signals regulating T cell migration and proliferation.** *J Immunol* 2000, **165**:15-19. [general reference]
19. Kaldjian EP, Gretz JE, Anderson AO, Shi Y, Shaw S: **Spatial and molecular organization of lymph node T cell cortex: a labyrinthine cavity bounded by an epithelium-like monolayer of fibroblastic reticular cells anchored to basement membrane-like extracellular matrix.** *Int Immunol* 2001, **13**:1243-1253. [general reference]
20. Ingulli E, Mondino A, Khoruts A, Jenkins MK: **In vivo detection of dendritic cell antigen presentation to CD4(+) T cells.** *J Exp Med* 1997, **185**:2133-2141. [general reference]
21. Reichert P, Reinhardt RL, Ingulli E, Jenkins MK: **Cutting edge: in vivo identification of TCR redistribution and polarized IL-2 production by naive CD4 T cells.** *J Immunol* 2001, **166**:4278-4281. [general reference]
22. Springer TA: **Adhesion receptors of the immune system.** *Nature* 1990, **346**:425-433. [key review]
23. Garcia KC, Degano M, Stanfield RL, Brunmark A, Jackson MR, Peterson PA, Teyton L, Wilson IA: **An αβ T cell receptor structure at 2.5Å resolution and its orientation in the TCR-MHC complex.** *Science* 1996, **274**:209-219. [general reference]
24. Xiong JP, Stehle T, Diefenbach B, Zhang R, Dunker R, Scott DL, Joachimiak A, Goodman SL, Arnaout MA: **Crystal structure of the extracellular segment of integrin αVβ3.** *Science* 2001, **6**:6. [general reference]
25. Casasnovas JM, Stehle T, Liu JH, Wang JH, Springer TA: **A dimeric crystal structure for the N-terminal two domains of intercellular adhesion molecule-1.** *Proc Natl Acad Sci U S A* 1998, **95**:4134-4139. [general reference]
26. Dustin ML, Olszowy MW, Holdorf AD, Li J, Bromley S, Desai N, Widder P, Rosenberger F, van der Merwe PA, Allen PM, Shaw AS: **A novel adapter protein orchestrates receptor patterning and cytoskeletal polarity in T cell contacts.** *Cell* 1998, **94**:667-677. [general reference]
27. Qi SY, Groves JT, Chakraborty AK: **Synaptic pattern formation during cellular recognition.** *Proc Natl Acad Sci U S A* 2001, **98**:6548-6553. [general reference]
28. van der Merwe PA, Davis SJ, Shaw AS, Dustin ML: **Cytoskeletal polarization and redistribution of cell-surface molecules during T cell antigen recognition.** *Semin Immunol* 2000, **12**:5-21. [key review]
29. Dustin ML, Cooper JA: **The immunological synapse and the actin cytoskeleton: molecular hardware for T cell signaling.** *Nat Immunol* 2000, **1**:23-29. [key review]
30. Weiss A, Littman DR: **Signal transduction by lymphocyte antigen receptors.** *Cell* 1994, **76**:263-274. [key review]

31. Zhang W, Trible RP, Zhu M, Liu SK, McGlade CJ, Samelson LE: **The association of Grb2, Gads and phospholipase C-γ1 with phosphorylated LAT tyrosine residues: the effect of tyrosine mutations on T cell antigen receptor-mediated signaling.** *J Biol Chem* 2000, **275**:23355-23361. [general reference]

32. Lewis RS, Cahalan MD: **Potassium and calcium channels in lymphocytes.** *Annu Rev Immunol* 1995, **13**:623-653. [key review]

33. Avni O, Rao A: **T cell differentiation: a mechanistic view.** *Curr Opin Immunol* 2000, **12**:654-659. [key review]

34. Sun Z, Arendt CW, Ellmeier W, Schaeffer EM, Sunshine MJ, Gandhi L, Annes J, Petrzilka D, Kupfer A, Schwartzberg PL, Littman DR: **PKC-θ is required for TCR-induced NK-κB activation in mature but not immature T lymphocytes.** *Nature* 2000, **404**:402-407. [general reference]

35. Griffiths EK, Krawczyk C, Kong YY, Raab M, Hyduk SJ, Bouchard D, Chan VS, Kozieradzki I, Oliveira-Dos-Santos AJ, Wakeham A, Ohashi PS, Cybulsky MI, Rudd CE, Penninger JM: **Positive regulation of T cell activation and integrin adhesion by the adapter Fyb/Slap.** *Science* 2001, **293**:2260-2263. [general reference]

36. Peterson EJ, Woods ML, Dmowski SA, Derimanov G, Jordan MS, Wu JN, Myung PS, Liu QH, Pribila JT, Freedman BD, Shimizu Y, Koretzky GA: **Coupling of the TCR to integrin activation by Slap-130/Fyb.** *Science* 2001, **293**:2263-2265. [general reference]

37. Dittel BN, Stefanova I, Germain RN, Janeway CA Jr.: **Cross-antagonism of a T cell clone expressing two distinct T cell receptors.** *Immunity* 1999, **11**:289-298. [general reference]

38. Johnson KG, LeRoy FG, Borysiewicz LK, Matthews RJ: **TCR signaling thresholds regulating T cell development and activation are dependent upon SHP-1.** *J Immunol* 1999, **162**:3802-3813. [general reference]

39. Liu H, Rhodes M, Wiest DL, Vignali DA: **On the dynamics of TCR:CD3 complex cell surface expression and downmodulation.** *Immunity* 2000, **13**:665-675. [general reference]

40. Lanier LL: **NK cell receptors.** *Annu Rev Immunol* 1998, **16**:359-393. [key review]

41. Sathish JG, Johnson KG, Fuller KJ, LeRoy FG, Meyaard L, Sims MJ, Matthews RJ: **Constitutive association of SHP-1 with leukocyte-associated Ig-like receptor-1 in human T cells.** *J Immunol* 2001, **166**:1763-1770. [general reference]

42. Binstadt BA, Brumbaugh KM, Dick CJ, Scharenberg AM, Williams BL, Colonna M, Lanier LL, Kinet JP, Abraham RT, Leibson PJ: **Sequential involvement of Lck and SHP-1 with MHC-recognizing receptors on NK cells inhibits FcR-initiated tyrosine kinase activation.** *Immunity* 1996, **5**:629-638. [general reference]

43. Yu H, Kaung G, Kobayashi S, Kopito RR: **Cytosolic degradation of T-cell receptor alpha chains by the proteasome.** *J Biol Chem* 1997, **272**:20800-20804. [general reference]

44. Wang HY, Altman Y, Fang D, Elly C, Dai Y, Shao Y, Liu YC: **Cbl promotes ubiquitination of the T cell receptor zeta through an adaptor function of Zap-70.** *J Biol Chem* 2001, **276**:26004-26011. [general reference]

45. Fang D, Liu YC: **Proteolysis-independent regulation of PI3K by Cbl-b-mediated ubiquitination in T cells.** *Nat Immunol* 2001, **2**:870-875. [general reference]

46. Huang JF, Yang Y, Sepulveda H, Shi W, Hwang I, Peterson PA, Jackson MR, Sprent J, Cai Z: **TCR-mediated internalization of peptide-MHC complexes acquired by T cells.** *Science* 1999, **286**:952-954. [general reference]

47. Hwang I, Huang JF, Kishimoto H, Brunmark A, Peterson PA, Jackson MR, Surh CD, Cai Z, Sprent J: **T cells can use either T cell receptor or CD28 receptors to absorb and internalize cell surface molecules derived from antigen-presenting cells.** *J Exp Med* 2000, **191**:1137-1148. [general reference]

48. Johnson KG, Bromley SK, Dustin ML, Thomas ML: **A supramolecular basis for CD45 regulation during T cell activation.** *Proc Natl Acad Sci U S A* 2000, **97**:10138-10143. [general reference]

49. Valitutti S, Muller S, Dessing M, Lanzavecchia A: **Signal extinction and T cell repolarization in T helper cell-antigen-presenting cell conjugates.** *Eur J Immunol* 1996, **26**:2012-2016. [general reference]

50. Manning TC, Schlueter CJ, Brodnicki TC, Parke EA, Speir JA, Garcia KC, Teyton L, Wilson IA, Kranz DM: **Alanine scanning mutagenesis of an alphabeta T cell receptor: mapping the energy of antigen recognition.** *Immunity* 1998, **8**:413-425. [general reference]

51. Williams CB, Engle DL, Kersh GJ, Michael White J, Allen PM: **A kinetic threshold between negative and positive selection based on the longevity of the T cell receptor-ligand complex.** *J Exp Med* 1999, **189**:1531-1544. [general reference]

52. Peterson DA, DiPaolo RJ, Kanagawa O, Unanue ER: **Negative selection of immature thymocytes by a few peptide-MHC complexes: differential sensitivity of immature and mature T cells.** *J Immunol* 1999, **162**:3117-3120. [general reference]

53. Sykulev Y, Joo M, Vturina I, Tsomides TJ, Eisen HN: **Evidence that a single peptide-MHC complex on a target cell can elicit a cytolytic T cell response.** *Immunity* 1996, **4**:565-571. [general reference]

54. Wülfing C, Sumen C, Sjaastad MD, Wu LC, Dustin ML, Davis MM: **Contribution of costimulation and endogenous MHC ligands to T cell recognition.** *Nat Immunol*, in press. [general reference]

55. Tseng SY, Otsuji M, Gorski K, Huang X, Slansky JE, Pai SI, Shalabi A, Shin T, Pardoll DM, Tsuchiya H: **B7-DC a new dendritic cell molecule with potent costimulatory properties for T cells.** *J Exp Med* 2001, **193**:839-846. [general reference]

56. Bromley SK, Laboni A, Davis SJ, Whitty A, Green JM, Shaw AS, Weiss A, Dustin ML: **The immunological synapse and CD28-CD80 interactions.** *Nat Immunol*, in press. [general reference]

57. Turley SJ, Inaba K, Garrett WS, Ebersold M, Unternaehrer J, Steinman RM, Mellman I: **Transport of peptide-MHC class II complexes in developing dendritic cells.** *Science* 2000, **288**:522-527. [general reference]

58. Mandelbrot DA, Kishimoto K, Auchincloss H Jr, Sharpe AH, Sayegh MH: **Rejection of mouse cardiac allografts by costimulation in trans.** *J Immunol* 2001, **167**:1174-1178. [general reference]

Supplement Review
The instructive role of dendritic cells on T-cell responses
Federica Sallusto and Antonio Lanzavecchia

Institute for Research in Biomedicine, Bellinzona, Switzerland

Correspondence: Antonio Lanzavecchia, Institute for Research in Biomedicine, Via Vincenzo Vela 6, CH-6500 Bellinzona, Switzerland.
Tel: +41 (0)91 8200 310; fax: +41 (0)91 8200 312; e-mail: lanzavecchia@irb.unisi.ch

Received: 27 February 2002
Accepted: 4 March 2002
Published: 9 May 2002

Arthritis Res 2002, **4 (suppl 3)**:S127-S132

This article may contain supplementary data which can only be found online at http://arthritis-research.com/content/4/S3/S127

© 2002 BioMed Central Ltd
(Print ISSN 1465-9905; Online ISSN 1465-9913)

Chapter summary

Immune responses are initiated in the T-cell areas of secondary lymphoid organs where naïve T lymphocytes encounter dendritic cells (DCs) that present antigens taken up in peripheral tissues. DCs represent the interface between the universe of foreign and tissue-specific antigens and T lymphocytes, and they are the key players in the regulation of cell-mediated immunity. We discuss how the nature of the DC maturation stimuli and the density and quality of DCs present in the T-cell areas of secondary lymphoid organs determine the magnitude and class of the T-cell response.

Keywords: dendritic cells, effector and memory T cells, T-cell activation, T-cell tolerance

Introduction

DCs possess specialized features, such as pathogen recognition, antigen capturing and processing machinery, migratory capacity and costimulatory molecules, that allow them to act as the professional antigen presenting cells (APC) [1]. DCs represent the interface between the universe of foreign and tissue-specific antigens and T lymphocytes. They also play a role in all aspects of T-cell responses, from the deletion of self-reactive thymocytes to the generation of effector and memory cells, as well as the induction of peripheral tolerance.

In this review, we shall discuss how DCs provide a qualitative and quantitative framework for T-cell antigen recognition. We shall first summarize the requirements for T-cell activation and differentiation in terms of concentration of peptide–MHC complexes, costimulatory molecules and cytokines. We shall then consider how DCs assemble these components and deliver them, as discrete short-lived packets, to the T-cell areas. Finally, we shall discuss how the nature of the DC maturation stimuli determines the density and quality of antigen-carrying DCs and, consequently, the magnitude and class of T-cell responses.

Activation and differentiation of naïve T lymphocytes

The signals that lead to T-cell activation are generated at the level of the immunological synapse, a specialized area of contact between T cells and APC where adhesion molecules and TCRs segregate into distinct supramolecular complexes [2,3]. At the synapse, the TCRs are sequentially triggered by peptide–MHC complexes, a process that allows the signal to be sustained for as long as the synapse is in place [4,5]. Synapses are stable in the absence of disturbing influences, but they can be disrupted by cell division, by death of APC or by external influences, such as collagen or chemokines. T cells continuously search for antigen and can rapidly shift from one APC to another offering a higher level of stimulation. While the duration of TCR stimulation depends on the duration of the synapse, the intensity of signal that T cells receive is dependent both on the level of peptide–MHC complexes

A glossary of specialist terms used in this chapter appears at the end of the text section. A list of common abbreviations used in this issue appears just before the indexes.

S127

that trigger TCRs and the level of costimulatory molecules that amplify the signalling process [6].

The efficiency of signal transduction varies with the nature of the APC and the T cell's developmental stage [6,7]. In activated, effector and memory T cells, TCR triggering is efficiently coupled to signal transduction pathways so that the cells can respond to low doses of antigens even in the absence of costimulation. In contrast, TCRs are inefficiently coupled in naïve T cells. Engagement of CD28 by B7 molecules expressed by professional APC recruits membrane rafts containing kinases and adapters to the synapse, and amplifies up to 100-fold the signalling process initiated by the TCRs. In the absence of costimulation, naïve T cells can thus be activated only by extremely high (nonphysiologic) doses of antigens and they require a prolonged stimulation, while in the presence of costimulation they can respond to ~100-fold lower doses of antigen and can also respond more rapidly. Depending on the antigen dose and the level of costimulation, naïve T cells require between 6 and >30 hours of TCR stimulation to become committed to cell division, while memory/effector T cells respond within 0.5–2 hours [7].

Once committed to division, T cells proliferate rapidly in response to IL-2, which is produced in an autocrine or paracrine fashion by activated T cells. We have shown that the duration of TCR stimulation together with polarizing cytokines determines the progressive differentiation of CD4$^+$ and CD8$^+$ T cells, leading to the generation of terminally differentiated effector cells as well as intermediates [8,9]. T cells that receive a short TCR stimulation proliferate, but fail to differentiate to effector cells and retain the lymph-node homing capacity characteristic of naïve T cells. In contrast, T cells that receive a prolonged TCR stimulation in the presence of IL-12 or IL-4 differentiate to Th1 or Th2 cells. As part of their differentiation programme, Th1 and Th2 cells lose the lymph-node homing receptors and acquire receptors that control their migration to inflamed nonlymphoid tissues where they can execute effector functions.

T cells interact with DCs in a highly dynamic environment where they have to compete to achieve a level of TCR stimulation sufficient to drive their activation and differentiation processes. We suggest that the progressive process of T-cell differentiation combined with the stochastic stimulation of proliferating T cells by random T cell–DC interactions leads to the generation of both intermediates and terminally differentiated cells within the same responding clone (Fig. 1) (F Sallusto, unpublished data). We consider this intraclonal diversification as a fundamental property of the immune system since, on the one hand, it prevents clonal exhaustion and, on the other, it allows the generation of distinct T-cell subsets that play a role in effector and memory responses [5]. The intraclonal

Figure 1

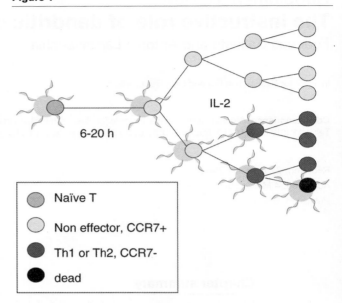

Stochastic stimulation of proliferating T cells leads to intraclonal functional diversification. By establishing immunological synapses with dendritic cells (DCs), naïve T cells (green) achieve stimulation and become committed to proliferate in response to autocrine or paracrine IL-2. T-cell receptor stimulation is sustained by serial encounters with DCs and, in the presence of polarizing cytokines (IL-12 and IL-4, not shown), drives T-cell differentiation to Th1 or Th2 effector cells that have lost CCR7 expression (red). T cells receiving a shorter stimulation do not acquire effector function and do retain lymph-node homing capacity (yellow). An excessive stimulation leads to activation-induced cell death (black). See Colour figure section.

differentiation model is supported by the existence of distinct subsets of memory cells: 'central memory' cells that represent intermediates, and 'effector memory' cells that represent terminally differentiated cells [10].

The DC maturation process
DCs that migrate from tissues to lymph nodes have a life expectancy of only a few days and can therefore be viewed as disposable packets, each carrying a given amount of peptide–MHC complexes, costimulatory molecules and cytokines. These packets are assembled during DC maturation, a process that is initiated by pathogens and/or inflammatory stimuli. The production of homogeneous populations of human immature DCs from human peripheral blood monocytes cultured with granulocyte/macrophage-colony-stimulating factor and IL-4 [11] has been instrumental in identifying the maturation stimuli and in dissecting the DC maturation process (Fig. 2).

DC maturation is triggered and modulated by a variety of receptors for microbial products, cytokines and T cells [12,13]. Human monocyte derived and myeloid DCs express several Toll-like receptors such as TLR2 and TLR4 that trigger maturation in response to bacterial peptidoglycan

Figure 2

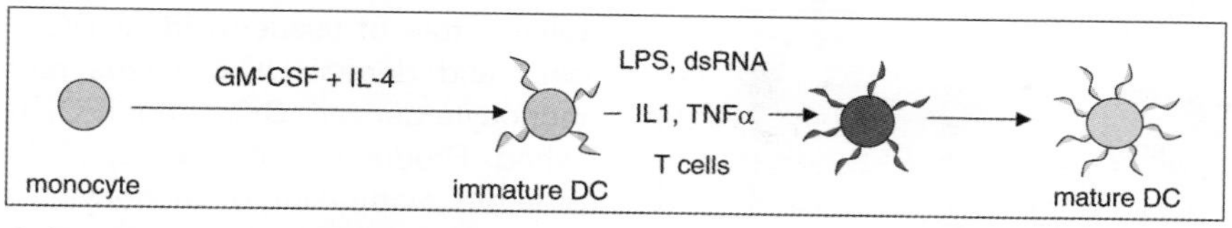

		monocyte	immature DC		mature DC
Antigen capture	macropinocytosis	++		+	-
	Mannose R++		+		-
	FcR	++		+	-
Antigen presentation	Class II synthesis	+		++	-
	Class II halflife	10 h		>>	>100 h
	Class I synthesis	+		++	++
Costimulation	ICAM-1	-		+	+
	B7	-		+	+
Migration	CCR5	+		-	-
	MIP-1β	-		++	-
	CCR7	-		+	+
	ELC, TARC	-		-	+
Cytokines	TNF-α	-		2-6 h	-
	IL-6	-		2-6 h	-
	IL-10	-		8-24 h	-
	IL-12	-		8-16 h	-

The maturation programme studied in monocyte-derived dendritic cells. DC, dendritic cells; ELC, endothelial-like cells; FcR, receptors for crystallizable fragment [of antibody]; GM-CSF, granulocyte/macrophage-colony-stimulating factor; ICAM-1, intracellular adhesion molecule-1; LPS, lipopolysaccharide; MIP, macrophage inflammatory protein; TARC, thymus- and activation-regulated chemokine. See Colour figure section.

and lipopolysaccharide, respectively. Interestingly, these receptors are absent in plasmacytoid DCs (also known as interferon-producing cells [IPC]) that instead express TLR9, which mediates the response to CpG DNA [14,15]. The differential responsiveness of myeloid and plasmacytoid DCs to pathogens underlines a division of labour between human DC subsets. DC maturation can be also triggered by tumour necrosis factor (TNF)-α and IL-1, and can be inhibited by IL-10. Finally, all DC types are exquisitely sensitive to T-cell feedback signals delivered by activated T cells through CD40 ligand (CD40L).

The maturation process coordinately regulates antigen capturing, processing and presentation, expression of costimulatory molecules, cytokine production and lifespan. Immature DCs are extremely efficient in antigen capture since they possess high levels of constitutive macropinocytosis and express endocytic receptors for microbial patterns, such as the mannose receptor [16]. Maturation increases synthesis of MHC class II molecules, while decreasing their degradation, thus favouring the rapid accumulation of long-lived peptide–MHC complexes, which are retained for several days, while class II synthesis is shut off [17]. Presentation on MHC class I molecules is also enhanced by an approximately 10-fold increase in the rate of synthesis, which is sustained in mature DCs [18]. DCs are capable of transporting phagocytosed antigens from the endocytic compartment to the cytosol, leading to their 'cross-presentation' to CD8+

T cells [19,20]. Finally, maturation stimuli upregulate the expression of B7.1 and B7.2, thus enhancing the T-cell stimulatory capacity of DCs. While the upregulation of MHC molecules ensures higher capacity for antigen presentation, upregulation of costimulatory molecules ensures an efficient amplification of signalling in naïve T cells.

Cytokine production by DCs is subject to a tight regulation, which is particularly relevant in the case of IL-12 and IFN-I, the major Th1-polarizing cytokines [21]. IL-12 production is elicited by most pathogens and is boosted by activated T cells through CD40L [22]. In contrast, IL-12 is not induced by other maturation stimuli such as TNF-α, IL-1, and cholera toxin. IL-12 production can be modulated by cytokines and mediators present during induction of maturation: IFN-γ and IL-4 enhance IL-12 production induced by appropriate stimuli, while prostaglandin E_2 and IL-10 exert an inhibitory effect. In addition, one has to consider that IL-12 production is restricted to a narrow temporal window, 8–16 hours after induction of DC maturation [9]. In summary, the Th1-polarizing capacity of DCs is contingent on a number of variables that include the lineage of DCs, the microenvironment in which they are stimulated, the maturation stimuli, and the kinetics of maturation (Fig. 3).

Dynamic changes in DC type and concentration impact on T-cell responses

Because the half-life of mature DCs is short and because cytokine production is transient, the number and type of

Figure 3

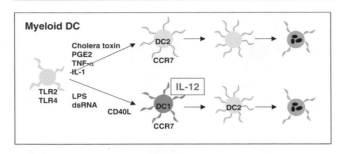

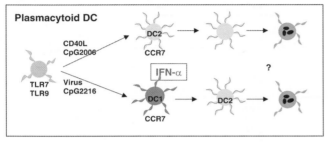

Reactivity, flexibility, kinetics and exhaustion in myeloid and plasmacytoid dendritic cells (DCs). The figure summarizes the properties of immature myeloid and plasmacytoid DCs. Indicated are the most relevant Toll-like receptors (TLR) and chemokine receptors, and the response to various maturation stimuli. DC1 and DC2 refer to the capacity of the cells to induce Th1 and Th2 responses, respectively. CD40L, CD40 ligand; LPS, lipopolysaccharide; PGE2, prostaglandin E_2. See Colour figure section.

DCs present in the T-cell areas will reflect, in highly dynamic fashion, the conditions of the tissues from which the lymph is drained. Under steady-state conditions, only a few tissue-resident DCs 'spontaneously' mature and migrate to the draining lymph nodes, carrying antigens and apoptotic bodies taken up in peripheral tissues [23]. These migrating DCs do not induce effector responses, but rather trigger an abortive T-cell proliferation that leads to immunological tolerance [24,25]. It is possible that spontaneously matured DCs deliver to T cells a qualitatively distinct tolerizing signal. Alternatively, according to the progressive differentiation model, we suggest that the low frequency and short lifespan of these DCs, together with the low level of antigen and B7, may deliver a weak stimulus to T cells, which is not sufficient to sustain proliferation and to promote differentiation.

When pathogens (or adjuvants) are present in peripheral tissues, resident DCs are activated *en masse* and migrate to the draining lymph nodes. At the same time monocytes are recruited from peripheral blood into inflamed tissues, where they rapidly differentiate to DCs that capture antigens and, on maturation, migrate to the draining lymph nodes. This mechanism sustains antigen sampling and presentation for extended periods of time. Maturing DCs

produce large amounts of inflammatory cytokines and chemokines that promote monocyte recruitment [26]. The relative role of tissue-resident DCs, such as Langerhans cells and dermal DCs, versus recruited DCs, such as monocyte-derived DCs and IPC, remains to be established. Production of IFN-I by IPC may be important to promote maturation of monocytes and to protect them from the cytopathic effects of viruses [27,28].

In summary, under inflammatory conditions, the T-cell areas of draining lymph nodes receive large numbers of highly stimulatory DCs for a sustained period of time. The high DC density and the high levels of antigen and B7 molecules deliver a strong and sustained stimulation to specific T cells, leading to their rapid proliferation and differentiation. High levels of IL-2 are produced under these conditions and drive clonal expansion of committed T cells irrespective of whether they continue to receive TCR stimulation. One should also consider that DC–T cell interaction results in a reciprocal stimulation. Activated T cells trigger DCs via CD40L or TNF-related activation-induced cytokine, improving their T-cell stimulatory capacity, boosting IL-12 production, and prolonging their lifespan [29]. It is possible that regulatory T cells may suppress antigen presentation by DCs via production of inhibitory cytokines or by direct contact [30].

There is growing evidence that the capacity of DCs to induce Th1 or Th2 responses is contingent on appropriate stimulation and timing (Fig. 3). As already discussed, myeloid DCs produce IL-12 only in response to some pathogens or CD40L, and within a narrow time window. In addition, IPC produce large amounts of IFN-I, another Th1-polarizing cytokine, in response to viruses but not in response to CD40L; again, only within a narrow time window. In contrast, Th2 responses may be induced by DCs that do not produce Th1-polarizing cytokines, either because they have been conditioned by nonpermissive stimuli or because they have exhausted their IL-12 or IFN-I-producing capacity. In this case, Th2 polarization is driven by IL-4 produced by T cells themselves or derived from exogenous sources, such as natural killer T cells or mast cells. It is worth considering that the dynamics of DC migration to the draining lymph nodes may lead to preferential generation of Th1 cells during the early phases of the immune response, when active DCs enter the T-cell areas in large numbers. This is followed by induction of Th2 and nonpolarized T cells at later time points when the influx of DCs ceases and the DCs surviving in the T-cell area exhaust their IL-12-producing capacity [31].

Competition for DC shaping T-cell responses

The availability of antigen-presenting DCs and of antigen-specific T-cell precursors represents the limiting factors in the immune responses. There is growing evidence that responding T cells compete *in vivo* for access to DCs and that this competition can be relieved by providing more DCs [32]. At the initial phase of a primary response, the low frequency of naïve T cells specific for a given antigen makes competition among responding cells unlikely. However, as the responding cells proliferate, competition for sustained TCR stimulation will increase, particularly among cells of the same clone, which have the same avidity and occupy the same niche. This intraclonal competition contributes to functional diversification: T cells achieving a sustained stimulation differentiate to effector cells, while those receiving a short stimulation remain in an intermediate state giving rise to central memory T cells. In contrast, interclonal competition may take place preferentially in secondary responses due to the larger numbers of antigen-specific cells present, and may therefore explain the selection of high-avidity T cells under these circumstances.

Conclusions

It is becoming increasingly clear that DCs provide the adaptive immune system with the essential function of context discrimination. DCs can integrate multiple stimuli from pathogens, inflammatory cytokines and T cells, and can provide distinct outputs in terms of antigen presentation, costimulation and cytokine production. Like other cells involved in the innate immune response, DCs produce large amounts of inflammatory chemokines that contribute to the recruitment of DC precursors in inflamed tissues, thus sustaining antigen sampling in peripheral tissue and presentation to T cells in lymph nodes. Finally, the T-cell activation and differentiation programme translates antigen concentration, cytokine and costimulatory molecule composition, and DC density into distinct cell fates ranging from tolerance to inflammation, cytotoxicity and memory.

Glossary of terms

APC = antigen presenting cells; CD40L = CD40 ligand; DC = dendritic cell; IPC = interferon-producing cells.

Acknowledgement

A Lanzavecchia is supported by the Helmut Horten Foundation and by the Swiss National Science Foundation (grant no. 31-63885). This work was supported in part by the European Community (contract no. QLK2-CT-201-0105).

References

1. Banchereau J, Steinman RM: **Dendritic cells and the control of immunity.** *Nature* 1998, **392**:245-252. [general reference]
2. Monks CR, Freiberg BA, Kupfer H, Sciaky N Kupfer A: **Three-dimensional segregation of supramolecular activation clusters in T cells.** *Nature* 1998, **395**:82-86. [general reference]
3. Grakoui A, Bromley SK, Sumen C, Davis MM, Shaw AS, Allen PM, Dustin ML: **The immunological synapse: a molecular machine controlling T cell activation.** *Science* 1999, **285**:221-227. [general reference]
4. Lanzavecchia A, Iezzi G, Viola A: **From TCR engagement to T cell activation: a kinetic view of T cell behavior.** *Cell* 1999, **96**: 1-4. [general reference]
5. Lanzavecchia A, Sallusto F: **Antigen decoding by T lymphocytes: from synapses to fate determination.** *Nat Immunol* 2001, **2**:487-492. [general reference]
6. Viola A, Schroeder S, Sakakibara Y, Lanzavecchia A: **T lymphocyte costimulation mediated by reorganization of membrane microdomains.** *Science* 1999, **283**:680-682. [general reference]
7. Iezzi G, Karjalainen K, Lanzavecchia A: **The duration of antigenic stimulation determines the fate of naive and effector T cells.** *Immunity* 1998, **8**:89-95. [general reference]
8. Iezzi G, Scheidegger D, Lanzavecchia A: **Migration and function of antigen-primed nonpolarized T lymphocytes in vivo.** *J Exp Med* 2001, **193**:987-993. [general reference]
9. Langenkamp A, Messi M, Lanzavecchia A, Sallusto F: **Kinetics of dendritic cell activation: impact on priming of TH1, TH2 and nonpolarized T cells.** *Nat Immunol* 2000, **1**:311-316. [general reference]
10. Sallusto F, Lenig D, Forster R, Lipp M, Lanzavecchia A: **Two subsets of memory T lymphocytes with distinct homing potentials and effector functions.** *Nature* 1999, **401**:708-712. [general reference]
11. Sallusto F, Lanzavecchia A: **Efficient presentation of soluble antigen by cultured human dendritic cells is maintained by granulocyte/macrophage colony-stimulating factor plus interleukin 4 and downregulated by tumor necrosis factor alpha.** *J Exp Med* 1994, **179**:1109-1118. [general reference]
12. Reis e Sousa C, Sher A, Kaye P: **The role of dendritic cells in the induction and regulation of immunity to microbial infection.** *Curr Opin Immunol* 1999, **11**:392-399. [general reference]
13. Lanzavecchia A, Sallusto F: **The instructive role of dendritic cells on T cell responses: lineages, plasticity and kinetics.** *Curr Opin Immunol* 2001, **13**:291-298. [general reference]
14. Kadowaki N, Ho S, Antonenko S, Malefyt RW, Kastelein RA, Bazan F, Liu YJ: **Subsets of human dendritic cell precursors express different toll-like receptors and respond to different microbial antigens.** *J Exp Med* 2001, **194**:863-869. [general reference]
15. Jarrossay D, Napolitani G, Colonna M, Sallusto F, Lanzavecchia A: **Specialization and complementarity in microbial molecule recognition by human myeloid and plasmacytoid dendritic cells.** *Eur J Immunol* 2001, **31**:3388-3393. [general reference]
16. Sallusto F, Cella M, Danieli C, Lanzavecchia A: **Dendritic cells use macropinocytosis and the mannose receptor to concentrate macromolecules in the major histocompatibility class II compartment: downregulation by cytokines and bacterial products.** *J Exp Med* 1995, **182**:389-400. [general reference]
17. Cella M, Engering A, Pinet V, Pieters J, Lanzavecchia A: **Inflammatory stimuli induce accumulation of MHC class II complexes on dendritic cells.** *Nature* 1997, **388**:782-787. [general reference]
18. Cella M, Salio M, Sakakibara Y, Langen H, Julkunen I, Lanzavecchia A: **Maturation, activation, and protection of dendritic cells induced by double-stranded RNA.** *J Exp Med* 1999, **189**:821-829. [general reference]
19. Albert ML, Sauter B, Bhardway N: **Dendritic cells acquire antigen from apoptotic cells and induce class I-restricted CTLs.** *Nature* 1998, **392**:86-89. [general reference]
20. Rodriguez A, Regnault A, Kleijmeer M, Ricciardi-Castagnoli P, Amigorena S: **Selective transport of internalized antigens to the cytosol for MHC class I presentation in dendritic cells.** *Nat Cell Biol* 1999, **1**:362-368. [general reference]
21. Kalinsky P, Hilkens C, Wierenga E, Kapsenberg M: **T cell priming by type-1 and type-2 polarized dendritic cells: the concept of a third signal.** *Immunol Today* 1999, **20**:561-567. [general reference]
22. Cella M, Scheidegger D, Palmer Lehmann K, Lane P, Lanzavecchia A, Alber G: **Ligation of CD40 on dendritic cells triggers production of high levels of interleukin-12 and enhances T cell stimulatory capacity: T–T help via APC activation.** *J Exp Med* 1996, **184**:747-752. [general reference]
23. Huang FP, Platt N, Wykes M, Major JR, Powell TJ, Jenkins CD, MacPherson GG: **A discrete subpopulation of dendritic cells transports apoptotic intestinal epithelial cells to T cell areas of mesenteric lymph nodes.** *J Exp Med* 2000, **191**:435-444. [general reference]
24. Kurts C, Kosaka H, Carbone FR, Miller JF, Heath WR: **Class I-restricted cross-presentation of exogenous self-antigens leads to deletion of autoreactive CD8(+) T cells.** *J Exp Med* 1997, **186**:239-245. [general reference]
25. Hernandez J, Aung S, Redmond WL, Sherman LA: **Phenotypic and functional analysis of CD8(+) T cells undergoing peripheral**

deletion in response to cross-presentation of self-antigen. *J Exp Med* 2001, **194**:707-717. [general reference]

26. Sallutso F, Palermo B, Lenig D, Meittinen M, Matikainen S, Julkunen I, Forster R, Burgstahler R, Lipp M, Lanzevecchia A: **Distinct patterns and kinetics of chemokine production regulate dendritic cell function.** *Eur J Immunol* 1999, **29**:1617-1625. [general reference]

27. Siegal FP, Kadowaki N, Shodell M, Fitzgerald-Bocarsly PA, Shah K, Ho S, Antonenko S, Liu YJ: **The nature of the principal type 1 interferon-producing cells in human blood.** *Science* 1999, **284**:1835-1837. [general reference]

28. Cella M, Jarrossay D, Facchetti F, Alebardi O, Nakajima H, Lanzavecchia A, Colonna M: **Plasmacytoid monocytes migrate to inflamed lymph nodes and produce large amounts of type I interferon.** *Nat Med* 1999, **5**:919-923. [general reference]

29. Wong BR, Josien R, Lee SY, Sauter B, Li H, Steinman RM, Choi Y: **TRANCE (tumor necrosis factor [TNF]-related activation-induced cytokine), a new TNF family member predominantly expressed in T cells, is a dendritic cell-specific survival factor.** *J Exp Med* 1997, **186**:2075-2080. [general reference]

30. Vendetti S, Chai JG, Dyson J, Simpson E, Lombardi G, Lechler R: **Anergic T cells inhibit the antigen-presenting function of dendritic cells.** *J Immunol* 2000, **165**:1175-1181. [general reference]

31. Lanzavecchia A, Sallusto F: **Dynamics of T lymphocyte responses: intermediates, effectors and memory cells.** *Science* 2000, **290**:92-97. [general reference]

32. Kedl RM, Rees WA, Hildeman DA, Schaefer B, Mitchell T, Kappler J, Marrack P: **T cells compete for access to antigen-bearing antigen-presenting cells.** *J Exp Med* 2000, **192**:1105-1113. [general reference]

Supplement Review

Humanized mice as a model for rheumatoid arthritis

Rüdiger Eming*, Kevin Visconti*, Frances Hall*†, Chiyoko Sekine*, Kayta Kobayashi*, Qun Chen*, Andrew Cope*‡, Satoshi Kanazawa§, Matija Peterlin§, Antonius Rijnders¶, Annemieke Boots¶, Jan Meijerink¶ and Grete Sønderstrup*

*Department of Microbiology and Immunology, Stanford University School of Medicine, Stanford, California, USA
†Weatherall Institute of Molecular Medicine, Oxford, UK
‡The Kennedy Institute of Rheumatology, Imperial College, London ,UK
§Department of Microbiology and Immunology, University of California, San Francisco, California, USA
¶NV Organon, Oss, The Netherlands

Correspondence: Grete Sønderstrup, Stanford University School of Medicine, Department of Microbiology and Immunology, Sherman Fairchild Building, Room D345, 299 Campus Drive, Stanford, CA 94305-5124, USA. Tel: +1 650 723 5893; fax: +1 650 723 9180; e-mail: gretes@stanford.edu

Received: 18 February 2002
Revisions requested: 18 February 2002
Revisions received: 28 February 2002
Accepted: 4 March 2002
Published: 9 May 2002

Arthritis Res 2002, **4 (suppl 3)**:S133-S140

This article may contain supplementary data which can only be found online at http://arthritis-research.com/content/4/S3/S133

© 2002 BioMed Central Ltd
(Print ISSN 1465-9905; Online ISSN 1465-9913)

Chapter summary

Genetic susceptibility to rheumatoid arthritis (RA), a common autoimmune disease, is associated with certain HLA-DR4 alleles. Treatments are rarely curative and are often tied to major side effects. We describe the development of a humanized mouse model wherein new, less toxic, vaccine-like treatments for RA might be pretested. This model includes four separate transgenes: HLA-DR*0401 and human CD4 molecules, a RA-related human autoantigenic protein (HCgp-39), and a T-cell receptor (TCRαβ) transgene specific for an important HCgp-39 epitope, eliciting strong Th1 responses in the context of HLA-DR*0401.

Keywords: autoimmunity, HCgp-39, HLA-DR4 transgenic mice, rheumatoid arthritis, T-cell receptor transgenic mice

Introduction

RA is a chronic autoimmune disease affecting about 1% of the general population. RA is characterized by symmetrical inflammation of synovial joints and has often been classified with a group of organ-specific autoimmune diseases including multiple sclerosis, type 1 diabetes, and pemphigus vulgaris. RA differs from these diseases in several aspects, however, and RA patients may develop extra-articular disease manifestations such as rheumatoid nodules, rheumatic lung disease, and vasculitis, suggestive of a more generalized autoimmune process.

Genetic predisposition to develop RA is strongly associated with a number of human leukocyte antigen (HLA) class II alleles, which all share a collection of positively charged amino acids at positions 70–72 of the DRB1 chain, called the 'shared epitope' (reviewed by Winchester [1]). HLA class II molecules function by selecting and presenting immunogenic peptide epitopes to the CD4+ T cells of the immune system. HLA class II molecules also have a major role in positive and negative selection in the thymus of the T-cell receptor (TCR) repertoire released to the periphery. It has been suggested that these

A glossary of specialist terms used in this chapter appears at the end of the text section. A list of common abbreviations used in this issue appears just before the indexes.

mechanisms are in part responsible for the HLA-associated disease susceptibility in RA and other organ-specific autoimmune diseases [2].

There are contrasting opinions on how normal immune regulation breaks down in RA. One opinion argues that RA is a disease controlled and perpetuated by antigen-presenting cells (APC), such as dendritic cells, macrophages, and B cells, and also including conventionally nonprofessional APC such as synoviocytes and fibroblasts [3]. The other opinion stresses that CD4+ T cells play an essential role in sustaining chronic autoimmunity in RA [4]. Two relatively recent murine models with spontaneous development of clinical arthritis may provide a reconciliation of these views and a better understanding of the mechanisms behind the development of RA [5,6].

The primary disease phenotype detected in several different tumor necrosis factor (TNF)-α transgenic mice with constitutive expression of human TNF has been an inflammatory arthritis similar to RA [5,7]. This phenotype is essentially preserved when these mice are backcrossed to a severe combined immune deficiency background, which lacks the development of B cells and T cells, indicating that arthritis can develop without the participation of lymphocytes. The importance of TNF-α is further supported by trials in humans, in which antagonizing TNF-α by means of anti-TNF-α monoclonal antibodies or TNF receptor antagonists is very effective in controlling arthritis symptoms, while disease activity usually rebounds if treatment is stopped [8]. It is possible that high local or systemic TNF-α production, for example in connection with infection, may function as a trigger of disease activity in RA. However, TNF-α may also exert its function indirectly through the upregulation of other cytokines [9], and it has been reported that APC populations in the rheumatoid joints have strong expression of IL-1β [10].

Spontaneous RA-like arthritis was also observed in a murine TCR transgenic model, (KRNxNOD) [6]. This TCR was originally chosen because it was specific for bovine ribonuclease in the context of I-A^k. The transgenic TCR$\alpha\beta$-positive cells were completely deleted in I-A^k mice, however, and in attempts to rescue the transgenic CD4+ T cells from deletion these mice were crossed to a number of different inbred mouse strains. Surprisingly, all the TCR transgene-positive animals developed arthritis within the first few weeks of life after the first cross to the nonobese diabetic mouse strain (NOD) [6]. These transgenic T cells were, in the context of the I-Ag^7 allele of the NOD, activated by a cross-reactive self-protein, glucose-6-phosphate isomerase (GPI), which is a ubiquitously expressed murine protein [11]. Transfer of purified GPI-specific autoantibodies from (KRNxNOD) mice could induce arthritis in healthy mice of the inbred balb/c and C57/B6 strains but not in mice of the inbred NOD strain, which is deficient in complement factor C'5 [12], and the (KRNxNOD) mice did not develop arthritis after backcrossing to knockout mice lacking the B-cell compartment [13]. Although GPI-specific autoantibodies seem to be essential for arthritis development in the (KRNxNOD) model, TCR transgenic CD4 T cells hold the real key to development of the disease phenotype, since the production of the GPI-specific autoantibodies is contingent on the help from CD4 T cells.

In a different TCR transgenic model system investigating the influenza hemagglutinin (HA)-specific TCR transgenic model (TS1) crossed with various transgenic lines expressing the HA as 'neo-self-antigens', Cope *et al.* have shown that the TCR $\alpha\beta$-positive T cells could change from a predominantly Th2 phenotype in TS1 single-transgenic mice to a Th1 phenotype after passing positive and negative selection in the thymus of the double-transgenic (TS1xHA) mice [14]. It is well established in several experimental models of inflammatory arthritis that the level of specific (auto)antibodies of IgG2a subtype, which is dependent on Th1 help, in the individual animal is directly correlated to the risk of developing arthritis [15–18]. The IgG subtype of the GPI autoantibodies has not been reported in the (KRNxNOD) arthritis model. It is possible, however, that the T helper cell evolution and the cytokine response pattern elicited by TCR$\alpha\beta$ transgene-positive T cells on the NOD background are the most important part of the (KRNxNOD) mice.

GPI-specific autoantibodies, which have undergone somatic mutation, have been detected in humans with RA [19]. Although it is unknown what role these autoantibodies play in disease, it is possible that components similar to those active in the (KRNxNOD) mouse may also be implicated in the autoimmune process in RA in humans.

In view of the strong genetic association between particular HLA class II alleles and RA, we assume that CD4+ T cells play a significant role in the pathogenesis of this disease. CD4+ T cells might supply some sort of generalized immune activation similar to the two transgenic arthritis models already mentioned [5,6]. It is possible that the activation of dendritic cells and macrophages, together with an upregulation of accessory molecules and homing receptors locally in the joints, perhaps secondary to infection, can lower the threshold for activation of autoreactive Th1 cells. From studies of autoantigen-specific CD4+ T-cell responses in humans, including T-cell proliferation and different cytokine assays, it is known that not only do many patients demonstrate autoreactive T-cell responses *in vitro*, but autoreactive T-cell responses can also be detected in healthy control individuals of appropriate HLA genotype [20–22]. Why do these autoreactive T cells only rarely cause disease, and what are the differences in the immune responses of healthy individuals compared with those of patients with autoimmune diseases?

Special cytokine patterns are often taken as an indication of an activation of a unique T-cell subpopulation. We have hypothesized that the individual CD4+ T-cell epitopes of a given autoantigen in the setting of one particular HLA class II allele in a healthy *in vivo* study subject would activate a distinct CD4+ T-cell population. To test this hypothesis, we have studied cytokine responses in healthy HLA-DR4 transgenic mice after immunization with intact protein antigen, followed by cytokine measurement after *in vitro* re-stimulation with the individual peptide epitopes. Although immunization with antigen in incomplete Freund's adjuvant (IFA) might bias the cytokine responses to a certain degree, comparative studies using other forms of immunization with antigen-pulsed dendritic cells or DNA vaccination should ultimately resolve this problem.

We chose to analyze the CD4 T-cell immune responses to the human cartilage autoantigen, HCgp-39, in the setting of the RA-associated HLA-DR*0401 (DRA*0101/DRB1*0401) HLA class II molecule [23]. To augment the autoreactive T-cell responses of these mice, a TCRαβ transgene was added to the model. The TCR construct was produced from a selected T-cell hybridoma specific for a HCgp-39 peptide epitope, which induced a significant IFN-γ response.

Development of HLA class II transgenic mice

The original HLA class II transgenic mouse model was designed to serve as an *in vivo* animal model in which several aspects of the human CD4+ T-cell immune responses could be studied after immunization with either endogenous or exogenous protein antigen [24]. Transgenic mice with the RA-susceptible DR*0401 allele and the RA nonassociated DRA/DRB1*0402 (DR*0402) allele, which had IDE in place of the QKR sequence of the 'shared epitope', were produced using cDNA matching the entire human coding sequences for the DRA and DRB1 chains expressed under the direction of the I–E alpha promoter [25].

To obtain sufficient selection of CD4+ T cells, it was necessary to introduce a correctly expressed human CD4 transgene and to delete the murine major histocompatibility complex class II genes [24]. This was achieved by crossbreeding with a human-CD4 transgenic line provided by Dr D Littman, and the murine class II-negative Aβ line from Dr D Mathis and Dr C Benoist [26,27]. After these changes, the cell surface expression of the HLA-DR*0401 molecule increased two to three times, and the CD4+ T-cell counts increased accordingly [24]. However, all our HLA class II transgenic mice, which were carefully selected from between six and 15 different transgenic founder lines per HLA specificity, had preserved normal lymphoid architecture and correct tissue-specific expression of the introduced HLA molecules in the thymus, the lymph nodes and the spleen. These mice had normal CD4+ T-cell function

and, similar to HLA-DR4+ humans, they did not develop spontaneous autoimmune diseases [24].

Choice of human autoantigen

The human cartilage protein HCgp-39 was chosen as a model autoantigen because it was a proven target for T-cell autoimmunity in RA patients [23,28]. A significant fraction of RA patients had shown signs of previous T-cell activation specific for a number of the immunogenic peptides from the protein, suggesting that it might be a possible target for future immunotherapy in RA. Our choice of prototype antigen, however, did not imply that HCgp-39 was supposed to have a unique role in the pathogenesis of RA.

Epitope mapping of HCgp-39 protein in HLA-DR*0401 and HLA-DR*0402 transgenic mice

CD4+ T-cell epitope mapping after immunization of DR*0401 and DR*0402 transgenic mice with recombinant HCgp-39 in IFA was performed using the T-cell hybridoma technique, which is described in detail in Cope *et al.* [23]. These experiments, involving 16 HLA-DR*0401 and 12 HLA-DR*0402 transgenic mice of appropriate genotypes, revealed three major immunogenic HCgp-39 epitopes (peptides 100–115, 262–277, and 322–337) in DR*0401 mice and two major epitopes (peptides 22–37, and 298–313) in DR*0402 mice [23]. A number of minor HCgp-39-specific T-cell epitopes were also identified [23]. Investigation of peptide–HLA complex stability for the major immunogenic HCgp-39 epitopes showed that the immunogenicity of DR*0401 and DR*0402 peptide epitopes was strongly related to the kinetic stability in all conditions, from the acidic endosomal compartment in the presence of the peptide editor HLA-DM to the neutral cell surface conditions [29].

HCgp-39-specific cytokine production in HLA-DR*0401 transgenic mice

Early cytokine studies in DR*0401 and DR*0402 transgenic mice had shown that intact HCgp-39 protein elicited strong IFN-γ and TNF-α responses in DR*0401 transgenic mice, while fairly small IFN-γ responses were detected in the DR*0402 transgenic mice [23]. TNF-α responses were not detected in the DR*0402 transgenic mice after *in vivo* immunization with HCgp-39 [23]. The intact HCgp-39 protein, as well as the individual HCgp-39 peptides, induced only small amounts of IL-2 in DR*0401 transgenic mice (Hall F, manuscript in preparation).

Two immunodominant peptide epitopes (peptides 100–115 and 322–337) appeared to be responsible for the majority of the IFN-γ elicited in response to HCgp-39 immunization. The Th2-type cytokine IL-5, however, was predominantly generated by peptide 100–115, while moderate amounts of TNF-α and intermediate levels of IL-10 could be driven by either peptide 100–115 or peptide 322–337 (Hall F, manuscript in preparation). The third major epitope (peptide 262–277) elicited small amounts of each of the five cytokines tested, and the significance of this reactivity pattern is unknown.

The bulk of the TNF-α was produced in response to the two minor peptide epitopes, peptides 256–271 and 334–349 (Hall F, manuscript in preparation). Considering the low frequencies of T cells responding to these two peptide epitopes [23], this response was (on a per-cell basis) approximately 50 times higher than the TNF-α produced in response to peptides 100–115 and 322–337. On a per-cell basis, peptides 256–271 and 334–349 elicited about the same IFN-γ levels as peptide 322–337, but no IL-5 or IL-10 responses were detected after re-stimulation with either of these 'minor' peptides (Hall F, manuscript in preparation).

The two T-cell epitopes 256–271 and 334–349 had been selected for further studies because they had elicited T-cell proliferative responses in the majority of both the HLA-DR4-positive RA patients and the HLA-DR4-positive human control subjects studied [23] (Sønderstrup G, unpublished results, 1998). Peptides 256–271 and 334–349 may therefore activate a unique subset of CD4 T cells. However, it should be emphasized that HCgp-39 functioned as a foreign antigen in the HLA-DR*0401 transgenic mice, while it was a self-protein in humans.

Cytokine responses after immunization with synthetic peptide versus intact protein antigen

Since a major objective was to identify a TCR for production of TCR transgenic mice in which disease might be induced, we chose to focus on peptide epitope 322–337 that exhibited a Th1 cytokine pattern. Figure 1a shows the IFN-γ response of four individual HLA-DR*0401+/human CD4+/murine I-Aβ−/− mice after immunization with recombinant HCgp-39 protein in IFA followed by *in vitro* re-stimulation with medium only (control), intact HCgp-39 protein (20 μg/ml), and the specific peptide 322–337 (10 μg/ml) for 24, 48, and 74 hours. Three of the four mice produced high IFN-γ levels to both protein and peptide, while mouse 1 responded much less (Fig. 1a).

In a similar study of four additional DR*0401 transgenic mice that were immunized with the synthetic peptide 322–337, 100 μg in IFA (Fig. 1b), lymph-node T cells preferentially responded with high levels of IFN-γ to the synthetic peptide itself. The IFN-γ responses to intact HCgp-39 protein were about 10 times lower (Fig. 1b).

These data suggest that the responding CD4+ T-cell population activated *in vivo* following immunization with a synthetic peptide may be different from the T-cell population responding to the same amino acid sequence if processed from the native protein antigen. T-cell clones that recognize the same peptide–HLA complex, which will only respond after *in vitro* re-stimulation with the synthetic peptide but not the intact protein antigen, have been described earlier as type b T cells [23,30]. In a recent study of antigen processing and presentation of the immunodominant HCgp-39 epitopes using HLA-DM-positive and HLA-DM-negative human APC, we have also shown that intact HCgp-39 protein must be processed via the endosomal compartment in the presence of HLA-DM molecules to induce activation of the peptide 322–337-specific T-cell hybridoma clones [31].

TCR transgenic mice specific for peptide 322–337 in the context of HLA-DR*0401

Detailed studies of more than 10 T-cell hybridomas, including antigen titration, N-terminal and C-terminal truncation studies as well as a complete set of alanine-substituted peptides across the wild-type sequence of peptide 322–337, revealed that although all the peptide 322–337-specific T-cell hybridomas recognized the same peptide–HLA complex, they fell into two groups with distinct response patterns (Hall F, manuscript in preparation). Approximately one-half of the T-cell hybridomas were completely unaffected by alanine substitutions outside of the 9mer core epitope. The second group of the peptide 322–337-specific T-cell hybridomas produced less IL-2, and these hybridomas usually required a relatively high antigen concentration. The latter group of T cells was sensitive to both alanine substitutions in the 9mer core region of the peptide that bound in the groove of the HLA-DR*0401 molecule and to substitutions in the N-terminal overhanging amino acids. These residues were presumably TCR contact residues since they only influenced T-cell responsiveness and had no influence on peptide–HLA binding (Hall F, manuscript in preparation).

We consequently chose to produce two separate TCR αβ constructs using a T-cell hybridoma representing each of these two different response patterns. The two TCR α-chain and TCR β-chain constructs were produced using the pTαcass and the pTβcass kindly provided by D Mathis and C Benoist [32]. The first TCR αβ construct, TCR/18B1, which was produced using a T-cell hybridoma from the N-terminal overhang-dependent group, was TCRVα11, Vβ14. Six TCR transgenic founders transmitting at least the TCR β-chain transgene were obtained. The 18B1/TCR β-chain was selected both by I-Aq and DR*0401+ mice. Three of these lines have been tested on the DR*0401 background and they all responded to both the nominal peptide and the HCgp-39 protein.

FACS analyses demonstrated that the transgenic TCRVβ-chain was expressed on more than 95% of CD4+ T cells. Less than 1% of the T cells expressed other TCRV β-chains. However, the transgenic T cells did not show an *in vivo* activated phenotype. The founder lines of TCR/18B1, which are still in an early stage of evaluation, will be tested

Figure 1

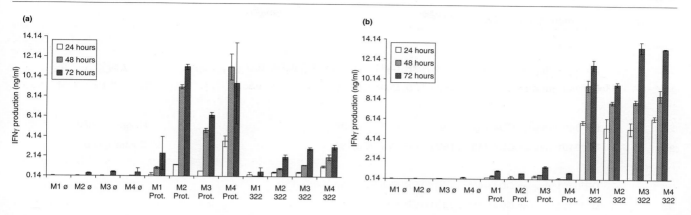

(a) IFN-γ responses following immunization with HCgp-39 protein. The IFN-γ responses of four different DR*0401 transgenic mice immunized with recombinant HCgp-39 in incomplete Freund's adjuvant following *in vitro* re-stimulation with either intact protein or immunodominant peptide epitope 322–337. (b) IFN-γ responses following immunization with peptide 322–337. The contrasting IFN-γ responses elicited by either intact protein antigen or peptide 322–337 after immunization of four similar DR*0401 mice with the synthetic peptide 322–377 itself.

for incorporation of the appropriate TCRVα-chain by means of polymerase chain reaction using specific primers. DR*0401/peptide 322–337 tetramers are under development and will be used to determine the exact levels of expression of the transgenic TCRαβ combination.

The second TCR transgene, 14H2, was TCRVβ6. Unexpectedly, the 14H2/TCR was only selected on an I-Aq-positive background. Several transgenic founder lines expressing and transmitting the TCR transgene were obtained. When these mice were backcrossed to the DR*0401/human CD4/I-Aβ−/− genetic background, however, no Vβ6-positive T cells (0–1%) could be detected in the periphery. Non-TCR transgenic littermates with the full DR*0401+/human CD4+/I-Aβ−/− genotype usually express between 2 and 5% Vβ6-positive T cells. It is currently unclear whether the absence of Vβ6-positive T cells in these mice is due to a lack of positive selection or due to a complete deletion of the T cells expressing the transgenic TCRVβ6 chain by thymic negative selection.

To rescue the 14H2/TCR transgene, founder lines that express transgenic TCRVα and Vβ chains on the I-Aq genetic background will be backcrossed to an HLA-DR*0401+ transgenic line on the NOD genetic background, which is less efficient in negative selection. Inhibition studies have shown that the 14H2 T-cell hybridoma exclusively interacts with the human CD4 molecule (Sønderstrup G, unpublished results, 2001), and separate attempts to rescue thymic selection of the transgenic 14H2/TCR are in progress by crossing the 14H2/TCR transgene onto a DR*0401+/I-Aβ−/−/DBA/1J background without human CD4. Finally, the 14H2/TCR transgene will also be crossed with HLA-DR*0405 transgenic mice on the NOD background. The HLA-DR*0405

allele, which is closely related to the DR*0401 allele, is also associated with susceptibility to RA [2].

HCgp-39 transgenic mice

The human HCgp-39 protein [33] and the murine counterpart, Brp39 [34], show more than 80% sequence homology, but they differ significantly in the areas that are found to be important for T-cell recognition in HLA-DR*0401 transgenic mice [24]. We therefore produced transgenic mice carrying the human HCgp-39 protein expressed under the murine collagen type II promoter (CoII), which directs expression to the synovial joints and the eye [35].

An optimal founder line for the CoII-HCgp-39 mice was identified after intercrossing with DR*0401+/human CD4+/I-Aβ−/− mice by following the HCgp-39 protein content of synovial joint cartilage over three generations. Since the CoII-HCgp-39 transgene functioned as a neo-self-antigen, the DR*0401 transgenic mice were tolerant to HCgp-39. However, they did break tolerance and developed specific antibodies of IgG1, IgG2a, and IgE isotypes after sequential immunization with HCgp-39 in complete Freund's adjuvant followed by immunizations in IFA (Hall F, manuscript in preparation). We expect to find a qualitative difference in the HCgp-39-specific immune responses of DR*0401/CoII-HCgp-39 double-transgenic mice compared with DR*0401 single transgenic mice.

Future prospects: strategies for triggering *in vivo* activation of the TCR αβ? transgenic T cells

FACS analysis using anti-CD25, anti-CD44, and anti-CD69 monoclonal antibodies does not indicate increased levels of activated CD4+ T cells in the DR*0401+, 18B1/TCR double-transgenic mice. One major objective is thus to activate the CD4+ T cells carrying the transgenic

Table 1

Genotypes of experimental animal groups

Group	Genotype	
1A	DR*0401+/human CD4+/Aβ−/−, 18B1/TCR, Coll-HCgp-39, TET-Coll-TNF-α	
1B	DR*0401+/human CD4+/Aβ−/−, 18B1/TCR, Coll-HCgp-39	Control group
2A	DR*0401+/human CD4+/Aβ−/−, 18B1/TCR, Coll-HCgp-39	HCgp-39 in IFA
2B	DR*0401+/human CD4+/Aβ−/−, 18B1/TCR, Coll-HCgp-39	Control group
3A	DR*0401+/human CD4+/Aβ−/−, 18B1/TCR, Coll-HCgp-39, Ii-HCgp-39	
3B	DR*0401+/human CD4+/Aβ−/−, 18B1/TCR, Ii-HCgp-39	
3C	DR*0401+/human CD4+/Aβ−/−, 18B1/TCR	Control group

The table shows the detailed genotypes of the different groups of multitransgenic mice that will be used to explore the influence of joint-specific CD4 T cells in the development of inflammatory arthritis in the humanized *in vivo* mouse model. Coll, collagen type II promoter; HCgp39, human cartilage glycoprotein 39; IFA, incomplete Freund's adjuvant; Ii, invariant chain; TET, tetracycline-inducible TNF-α transgene.

TCRαβ combination of these mice *in vivo*, and this might be achieved by simple immunization with the HCgp-39 protein or the cognate peptide. However, an immunization approach may be hampered by processing problems or by reverse effects of other HCgp-39 T-cell epitopes. Two separate strategies will therefore be pursued in parallel. The first uses transgenic mice carrying a tetracycline-inducible TNF-α transgene expressed under the murine Coll, which theoretically should induce local activation of the APC similar to the TNF-α transgenic mice [5]. Founder mice are currently under selection. A second transgenic approach will target the peptide 322–337 sequence to the endosomal compartment of professional APC. This approach will use a DNA construct that substitutes the oligonucleotide sequence of peptide 322–337 for the CLIP sequence of the murine invariant chain and insert this cDNA into a modification of a murine invariant chain cassette vector developed by D Mathis and C Benoist [36].

Different combinations of these humanized mice will be used to explore whether clinical arthritis can be induced in mice by triggering the APC with local TNF-α release (group 1A), by activating the transgenic TCR with its specific antigen/peptide as a vaccination in CFA (group 2A), or by *in vivo* activation of the TCR transgene by crossing with a transgenic line (group 3B), which expresses the cognate peptide as a transgene under the invariant chain promoter. Mice of the genotypes show in Table 1 will be monitored in groups of 10 mice for development of clinical arthritis up to 30 weeks of age.

Assuming that the control mice (groups 1B, 2B, and 3C) will not develop disease spontaneously, occurrence of arthritis in mice of group 1A will suggest a major role for local APC in the development of arthritis. Arthritis after immunization of group 2A mice will imply a major role for CD4 T cells in arthritis development. Arthritis in group 3A mice, which carry the HCgp-39 epitope as a neo-self-antigen both in the APC (expressed under the invariant chain promoter) and locally in the joints (expressed under the Coll promoter), but not in group 3B mice, which only express the HCgp-39 epitope in the APC, will indicate that joint antigen-specific CD4 T cells may be very important in disease induction. Arthritis in group 3B mice, but not in group 3A mice, will suggest that high local expression of autoantigen plays a key role in keeping self-reactivity in check. Finally, arthritis occurrence in both group 3A and group 3B mice will indicate that generalized immune activation plays a major role in RA.

Concluding remarks

This HLA-DR*0401 transgenic mouse model was designed to provide an *in vivo* animal model that would faithfully replicate certain aspects of an HLA-DR*0401-positive human CD4 T-cell immune system, and therefore these mice were not expected to develop arthritis or other autoimmune disease manifestations spontaneously. The addition of a neo-self-antigen, the human autoantigenic protein HCgp-39, which in humans can be produced by several different cell types in many different tissues during inflammatory conditions, was expected to provide antigen specificity to the autoimmune responses of these humanized mice. As outlined in Table 1, the further addition of the HCgp-39-specific TCR transgene was anticipated to enlarge the autoantigen-specific Th1 response to this human neo-self-antigen. A small population of TCR transgene-positive cells, which may have escaped negative selection in the thymus but later encounter their specific peptide presented in the periphery in the context of HLA-DR*0401 molecules, may then be activated and expanded in the lymph nodes and the spleen. These humanized mice would be expected to reproduce some of the most important features of human RA and provide a model of inducible arthritis, which alone or in connection with cell transfer experiments can be used to develop and pretest vaccine-like immunomodulatory therapies for AR in humans.

Glossary of terms

CollI = collagen type II promoter; DM = HLA-DM, a non-peptide-binding HLA class II molecule, which facilitates exchange of peptides of already formed peptide/HLA class II complexes, mostly in the acidic endosomal compartment of the antigen-presenting cell; GPI = glucose-6-phosphate isomerase; HA = influenza hemagglutinin; HCgp-39 = human cartilage glycoprotein 39; HLA-DR*0401 = DRA, DRB1*0401; HLA-DR*0402 = DRA, DRB1*0402; HLA-DR*0405 = DRA, DRB1*0405; IFA = incomplete Freund's adjuvant; NOD = nonobese diabetic (mouse); TS1 = influenza hemagglutinin-specific TCR transgenic model.

Acknowledgements

RE was supported by Deutche Forschungsgemeinschaft, FH by The Arthritis Research Campaign, UK, AC by the Wellcome Trust, and GS by the National Institutes of Health (AR44647).

Funds for research

Funding possibilities for arthritis research could be applied for at the NIH (National Institute for Arthritis Skin and Musculo-Skeletal Diseases), the Arthritis Foundation (USA), and the Arthritis Research Campaign (ACR) (UK).

References

1. Winchester R: The molecular basis of susceptibility to rheumatoid arthritis. Adv Immunol 1994, 56:389-466. [key review]
2. Todd JA, Acha-Orbea H, Bell JI, Chao N, Fronek Z, Jacob CO, McDermott M, Sinha AA, Timmerman L, Steinman L, McDevitt HO: A molecular basis for MHC class II-associated autoimmunity. Science 1988, 240:1003-1009. [key review]
3. Firestein GS, Zvaifler NJ: How important are T cells in chronic rheumatoid synovitis?: II. T cell-independent mechanisms from beginning to end. Arthritis Rheum 2002, 46:298-308. [review]
4. Panayi GS, Corrigall VM, Pitzalis C: Pathogenesis of rheumatoid arthritis. The role of T cells and other beasts. Rheum Dis Clin North Am 2001, 27:317-334. [review]
5. Keffer J, Probert L, Cazlaris H, Georgopoulos S, Kaslaris E, Kioussis D, Kollias G: Transgenic mice expressing human tumour necrosis factor: a predictive genetic model of arthritis. EMBO J 1991, 10:4025-4031. [general reference]
6. Kouskoff V, Korganow AS, Duchatelle V, Degott C, Benoist C, Mathis D: Organ-specific disease provoked by systemic autoimmunity. Cell 1996, 87:811-822. [general reference]
7. Butler DM, Malfait AM, Mason LJ, Warden PJ, Kollias G, Maini RN, Feldmann M, Brennan FM: DBA/1 mice expressing the human TNF-alpha transgene develop a severe, erosive arthritis: characterization of the cytokine cascade and cellular composition. J Immunol 1997, 159:2867-2876. [general reference]
8. Feldmann M, Bondeson J, Brennan FM, Foxwell BM, Maini RN: The rationale for the current boom in anti-TNFalpha treatment. Is there an effective means to define therapeutic targets for drugs that provide all the benefits of anti-TNFalpha and minimise hazards? Ann Rheum Dis 1999, 58 (Suppl 1): I27-I32. [review]
9. Feldmann M, Brennan F, Paleolog E, Taylor P, Maini RN: Anti-tumor necrosis factor alpha therapy of rheumatoid arthritis. Mechanism of action. Eur Cytokine Network 1997, 8:297-300. [review]
10. Ulfgren AK, Grondal L, Lindblad S, Khademi M, Johnell O, Klareskog L, Andersson U: Interindividual and intra-articular variation of proinflammatory cytokines in patients with rheumatoid arthritis: potential implications for treatment. Ann Rheum Dis 2000, 59:439-447. [general reference]
11. Mangialaio S, Ji H, Korganow AS, Kouskoff V, Benoist C, Mathis D: The arthritogenic T cell receptor and its ligand in a model of spontaneous arthritis. Arthritis Rheum 1999, 42:2517-2523. [general reference]
12. Korganow AS, Ji H, Mangialaio S, Duchatelle V, Pelanda R, Martin T, Degott C, Kikutani H, Rajewsky K, Pasquali JL, Benoist C, Mathis D: From systemic T cell self-reactivity to organ-specific autoimmune disease via immunoglobulins. Immunity 1999, 10:451-461. [general reference]
13. Ji H, Korganow AS, Mangialaio S, Hoglund P, Andre I, Luhder F, Gonzalez A, Poirot L, Benoist C, Mathis D: Different modes of pathogenesis in T-cell-dependent autoimmunity: clues from two TCR transgenic systems. Immunol Rev 1999, 169:139-146. [general reference]
14. Riley MP, Shih FF, Jordan MS, Petrone AL, Cerasoli DM, Scott P, Caton AJ: CD4+ T cells that evade deletion by a self peptide display Th1-biased differentiation. Eur J Immunol 2001, 31: 311-319. [general reference]
15. Cope AP, Fugger LH, Chu W, Sønderstrup-McDevitt G: Collagen induced arthritis in HLA-DR4/human CD4 transgenic mice. In Genetic Diversity of HLA. Functional and Medical Implications. Edited by Charron D. Paris: EDK; 1997:634-637. [general reference]
16. Brand DD, Marion TN, Myers LK, Rosloniec EF, Watson WC, Stuart JM, Kang AH: Autoantibodies to murine type II collagen in collagen-induced arthritis: a comparison of susceptible and nonsusceptible strains. J Immunol 1996, 157:5178-5184. [general reference]
17. Andersson EC, Hansen BE, Jacobsen H, Madsen LS, Andersen CB, Engberg J, Rothbard JB, McDevitt GS, Malmstrom V, Holmdahl R, Svejgaard A, Fugger L: Definition of MHC and T cell receptor contacts in the HLA-DR4 restricted immunodominant epitope in type II collagen and characterization of collagen-induced arthritis in HLA-DR4 and human CD4 transgenic mice. Proc Natl Acad Sci USA 1998, 95:7574-7579. [general reference]
18. Hollo K, Glant TT, Garzo M, Finnegan A, Mikecz K, Buzas E: Complex pattern of Th1 and Th2 activation with a preferential increase of autoreactive Th1 cells in BALB/c mice with proteoglycan (aggrecan)-induced arthritis. Clin Exp Immunol 2000, 120:167-173. [general reference]
19. Schaller M, Burton DR, Ditzel HJ: Autoantibodies to GPI in rheumatoid arthritis: linkage between an animal model and human disease. Nat Immunol 2001, 2:746-753. [general reference]
20. Sønderstrup G, Durinovic-Bélló I: Human T cell responses to islet cell antigens. In Molecular Pathology of Insulin-Dependent Diabetes Mellitus. Current Directions in Autoimmunity, vol. 4. Edited by von Herrath MG. Basle: Karger AG; 2001:239-251. [review]
21. Zhang J, Markovic-Plese S, Lacet B, Raus J, Weiner HL, Hafler DA: Increased frequency of interleukin 2-responsive T cells specific for myelin basic protein and proteolipid protein in peripheral blood and cerebrospinal fluid of patients with multiple sclerosis. J Exp Med 1994, 179:973-984. [general reference]
22. Budinger L, Borradori L, Yee C, Eming R, Ferencik S, Grosse-Wilde H, Merk HF, Yancey K, Hertl M: Identification and characterization of autoreactive T cell responses to bullous pemphigoid antigen 2 in patients and healthy controls. J Clin Invest 1998, 102:2082-2109. [general reference]
23. Cope AP, Patel SD, Hall F, Congia M, Hubers HA, Verheijden GF, Boots AM, Menon R, Trucco M, Rijnders AW, Sonderstrup G: T cell responses to a human cartilage autoantigen in the context of rheumatoid arthritis-associated and nonassociated HLA-DR4 alleles. Arthritis Rheum 1999, 42:1497-1507. [general reference]
24. Sønderstrup G, Cope AP, Patel S, Congia M, Hain N, Hall FC, Parry SL, Fugger LH, Michie S, McDevitt HO: HLA class II transgenic mice: models of the human CD4+ T-cell immune response. Immunol Rev 1999, 172:335-343. [key review]
25. Fugger LP, Michie SA, Rulifson I, Lock CB, Sønderstrup-McDevitt G: Expression of HLA-DR4 and human CD4 transgenes in

mice determines the variable region β-chain T-cell repertoire and mediates an HLA-DR restricted immune response. *Proc Natl Acad Sci USA* 1994, **91**:6151-6155. [general reference]

26. Killeen N, Sawada S, Littman DR: **Regulated expression of human CD4 rescues helper T cell development in mice lacking expression of endogenous CD4.** *EMBO J* 1993, **12:** 1547-1553. [general reference]

27. Cosgrove D, Gray D, Dierich A, Kaufman J, Lemeur M, Benoist C, Mathis D: **Mice lacking MHC class II molecules.** *Cell* 1991, **66:** 1051-1066. [general reference]

28. Verheijden GF, Rijnders AW, Bos E, Coenen-de Roo CJ, van Staveren CJ, Miltenburg AM, Meijerink JH, Elewaut D, de Keyser F, Veys E, Boots AM: **Human cartilage glycoprotein-39 as a candidate autoantigen in rheumatoid arthritis.** *Arthritis Rheum* 1997, **40**:1115-1125. [general reference]

29. Hall FC, Rabinowitz J, Belmares M, Patil N, Busch R, Cope AP, Patel S, McConnel HM, Mellins ED, Sønderstrup G: **Relationship between dissociation kinetics and immunogenicity of HLA-DR4/peptide complexes.** *Eur J Immunol* 2002, **32**:662-670. [general reference]

30. Viner NJ, Nelson CA, Unanue ER: **Identification of a major I-Ek-restricted determinant of hen egg lysozyme: limitations of lymph node proliferation studies in defining immunodominance and crypticity.** *Proc Natl Acad Sci USA* 1995, **92**:2214-2218. [general reference]

31. Patil NS, Hall FC, Drover S, Spurrell DR, Bos E, Cope AP, Sønderstrup G, Mellins ED: **Autoantigenic HCgp39 epitopes are presented by the HLA-DM dependent presentation pathway in human B cells.** *J Immunol* 2001, **166**:33-41. [general reference]

32. Kouskoff V, Signorelli K, Benoist C, Mathis D: **Cassette vectors directing expression of T cell receptor genes in transgenic mice.** *J Immunol Methods* 1995, **180**:273-280. [general reference]

33. Hakala BE, White C, Recklies AD: **Human cartilage gp-39, a major secretory product of articular chondrocytes and synovial cells, is a mammalian member of a chitinase protein family.** *J Biol Chem* 1993, **268**:25803-25810. [general reference]

34. Morrison BW, Leder P: **neu and ras initiate murine mammary tumors that share genetic markers generally absent in c-myc and int-2-initiated tumors.** *Oncogene* 1994, **9**:3417-3426. [general reference]

35. Metsaranta M, Garofalo S, Smith C, Niederreither K, de Crombrugghe B, Vuorio E: **Developmental expression of a type II collagen/beta-galactosidase fusion gene in transgenic mice.** *Dev Dyn* 1995, **204**:202-210. [general reference]

36. van Santen H, Benoist C, Mathis D: **A cassette vector for high-level reporter expression driven by a hybrid invariant chain promoter in transgenic mice.** *J Immunol Methods* 2000, **245:** 133-137. [general reference]

Supplement Review
Multiple roles for tumor necrosis factor-α and lymphotoxin α/β in immunity and autoimmunity

Hugh McDevitt, Sibyl Munson, Rachel Ettinger and Ava Wu

Department of Microbiology and Immunology, and Department of Medicine, Stanford University Medical Center, Stanford, California, USA

Correspondence: Hugh McDevitt, Department of Microbiology and Immunology, and Department of Medicine, Stanford University Medical Center, Stanford, CA 94305, USA. Tel: +1 650 723 5893; fax: +1 650 723 9180; e-mail: hughmcd@stanford.edu

Received: 29 January 2002
Accepted: 3 March 2002
Published: 9 May 2002

Arthritis Res 2002, **4 (suppl 3)**:S141-S152

This article may contain supplementary data which can only be found online at http://arthritis-research.com/content/4/S3/S141

Chapter summary

Tumor necrosis factor (TNF)-α and lymphotoxin (LT) α/β play multiple roles in the development and function of the immune system. This article focuses on three important aspects of the effects of these cytokines on the immune response and on autoimmunity. In several experimental systems (Jurkat T cells, murine T-cell hybridomas), TNF-α appears to cause a downregulation of signaling through the TCR, revealed by changes in calcium flux, activation of p21, p23 and ZAP70, and a decrease in nuclear activation of NF-κB. Previous and present results suggest that TNF-α interferes in some manner with signaling through the TCR, at a locus yet to be delineated. Transgenic expression of LTβR-Fc in nonobese diabetic (NOD) transgenic mice results in prevention of type 1 diabetes in NOD mice as long as the level of expression of the fusion protein (under the control of the cytomegalovirus promoter) remains above a level of 2–3 μg/ml. Once the expression levels of the fusion protein have dropped below this critical level, the diabetic process resumes and the animals become diabetic at 40–50 weeks of age, whereas nontransgenic littermates develop diabetes by 25–30 weeks of age. The paradoxical effects of neonatal TNF-α administration in NOD mice in increasing incidence of and hastening onset of type 1 diabetes, while neonatal anti-TNF administration completely prevents all signs of islet cell autoimmunity, are due partly to the low levels of CD4$^+$CD25$^+$ T cells in NOD mice. These low levels are reduced by a further 50% on neonatal administration of nontoxic levels of TNF-α. In contrast, neonatal administration of anti-TNF-α results in a dramatic increase in the levels of CD4$^+$CD25$^+$ regulatory T cells, to levels beyond those seen in wild-type untreated NOD mice. TNF-α and LTα/β thus have pleomorphic regulatory effects on the development and expression of autoimmunity.

Keywords: autoimmunity, immunity, lymphotoxin α/β, tumor necrosis factor alpha

Introduction and historical background

The cytokines TNF-α and LTα/β and their receptors play key roles in the development of the immune system and in immune regulation, inflammation, and autoimmunity. Manipulation of these cytokines in their receptors has revealed numerous aspects of their function in both health and disease, particularly in autoimmune diseases. Recent basic studies and corresponding clinical trials have revealed a major role for TNF-α in the pathogenesis of rheumatoid arthritis (RA), with a dramatic response in two-thirds of the patients to TNF blockade, either with a monoclonal antibody or with a soluble TNF receptor. Similarly, recent findings have shown that blockade of LTα/β by soluble LTβ receptor can suppress the normal immune response and interfere with the development of autoimmune diabetes in the NOD mouse.

A glossary of specialist terms used in this chapter appears at the end of the text section. A list of common abbreviations used in this issue appears just before the indexes.

Table 1

Diseases in which tumor necrosis factor (TNF) blockade causes exacerbation

Disease	Intervention	Result	Mechanism	References
1. Multiple sclerosis	Anti-TNF, soluble TNFR	Increase in CNS lesions and disease activity	? T-cell activation	[1,2]
2. Experimental allergic encephalomyelitis (EAE)	TNF-α null mutation	Failure of usual regression of T-cell reactivity; prolonged exacerbation of EAE	? T-cell activation	[3]
3a. Murine 'lupus' in (NZB×NZW)F1 mice	TNF administration (adult)	3–4 month delay in disease onset	? Inhibition of T-cell activation	[4]
3b. Murine 'lupus' in (NZB×NZW)F1 mice	Anti-TNF administration (adult)	Earlier disease onset with increased severity	? T-cell activation	[5]
3c. Murine 'lupus' in (NZB×NZW)F1 mice	Heterozygous TNF null mutant	Earlier disease onset with increased severity	? T-cell activation	[6]
3d. Murine 'lupus' in (NZB×NZW)F1 mice	Anti-IL-10 administration (adult)	Delayed onset and decreased severity	Increase in endogenous TNF, leading to decreased T-cell activation	[5]
4a. Type 1 diabetes mellitus in (NOD) mice	TNF i.p. in adult mice	Delayed onset, decreased incidence of diabetes	? Inhibition of T-cell activation	[7]
4b. Type 1 diabetes mellitus in (NOD) mice	Anti-TNF in adult mice	Variable, earlier onset with increased incidence	? T-cell activation	[8]

CNS, central nervous system; i.p., intraperitoneally; NOD, nonobese diabetic; TNFR, TNF receptor.

This review will focus primarily on the effects of TNF and TNF blockade, and of LTα/β and a blockade of this cytokine with soluble LTβ receptor in several autoimmune diseases, both in spontaneous models in the mouse and in patients with autoimmune disease.

Effects of TNF-α and TNF-α blockade on T-cell function in autoimmunity

There is a growing body of evidence that blockade of TNF action in patients and experimental animals increases disease activity and severity in some, but not all, T-cell-dependent autoimmune diseases. Diseases in which blockade of TNF action causes exacerbation or prolongation of pre-existing autoimmune diseases, or the appearance of new signs of autoimmunity, are presented in Table 1.

Diseases such as multiple sclerosis, experimental allergic encephalomyelitis, and type 1 diabetes (T1DM) are all T-cell mediated as well as T-cell dependent. Murine 'lupus' in the (NZB × NZW)F1 strain is antibody mediated, but clearly T-cell dependent for the development of the pathogenic IgG autoantibodies. The findings presented in Table 1 have been confirmed in all cases by at least two separate studies, and in most cases by several studies. Many possible mechanisms for these results have been excluded in one or more of the diseases listed. These excluded mechanisms include alterations in CD4+/CD8+ ratios, alterations in Th1/Th2 ratios, alterations in levels of expression of Fas and Fas ligand, and effects on levels of expression of IL-12, IL-4, etc. [8,9].

Several lines of evidence suggest that TNF levels inversely affect T-cell responsiveness and TCR signal transduction [4,8–14]. These studies have documented a decrease in T-cell proliferation, cytokine production, and calcium flux in normal T cells and TCR transgenic T cells, following chronic exposure to TNF in both *in vitro* and *in vivo* studies. More recently, Cope and coworkers [15] have demonstrated a decrease in phosphorylation of CD3zeta p21, p23, and ZAP 70 in T-cell hybridomas cultured *in vitro* in the presence of nontoxic levels of TNF-α.

In our own laboratory (Munson *et al.*, manuscript in preparation), in collaboration with the laboratory of Dr Arthur Weiss, we have found that chronic 5-day exposure of Jurkat T cells to nontoxic levels of TNF results in a 90% reduction in TCR-mediated nuclear activation of NF-κB (as detected by a reporter construct encoding a NF-κB binding site coupled to the luciferase gene) after TCR stimulation. These results suggest that the immunostimulatory effects of TNF blockade in many autoimmune diseases (Table 1) may be due to release of T cells from endogenous TNF-α-mediated inhibition. If so, this would imply that chronic TNF-α exposure in some manner downregulates signal transduction mediated by the TCR.

Because TNF has such pleotropic effects, and because tumor necrosis factor receptor 1 (55 kb) (TNFR1) and tumor necrosis factor receptor 2 (75 kb) (TNFR2) are so widely expressed, it is possible, and indeed probable, that other not mutually exclusive mechanisms may also contribute to the effects presented in Table 1.

Table 2

Diseases in which tumor necrosis factor (TNF) blockade is therapeutic

Disease	Intervention	Result	Mechanism	Reference
1a. Rheumatoid arthritis	Anti-TNF, soluble TNFR	65% of patients have a dramatic decrease in disease activity	Blockade of TNF-induced inflammatory response (? decreased macrophage activation)	[16]
1b. Rheumatoid arthritis	Anti-TNF, soluble TNFR	Up to 15% of patients develop α-dsDNA antibodies. 0.2% develop mild SLE	? T-cell activation	[16]
1c. Rheumatoid arthritis	Anti-TNF, soluble TNFR	A few patients develop CNS findings suggestive of MS	? T-cell activation	[17]
2. Crohn's disease	Anti-TNF, soluble TNFR	Dramatic decrease in disease activity in up to 80% of patients	? Decreased monocyte/macrophage activation	[18]
3. Psoriasis	Anti-TNF	Dramatic clearing of skin lesions, decrease in associated arthritis	Blockade of TNF-induced inflammation	[19]

CNS, central nervous system; MS, multiple sclerosis; SLE, systemic lupus erythematosus; TNFR, TNF receptor.

Diseases in which TNF blockade is therapeutic

Diseases in which blockade of TNF action has been shown to be therapeutic are presented in Table 2. Three diseases (RA, Crohn's disease, and psoriasis) form an interesting group that contrasts sharply with the diseases in which TNF blockade causes exacerbation (Table 1). RA is thought by many to be a T-cell-mediated disease but, unlike the diseases in which TNF blockade causes exacerbation (Table 1), anti-TNF therapy results in a dramatic decrease in symptoms, and in some cases a near complete remission, although the disease recurs relatively promptly after cessation of anti-TNF therapy.

Much less is known or conjectured about the pathogenesis of Crohn's disease and psoriasis. With respect to Crohn's disease, recent evidence indicates that one of the principal predisposing genetic factors is a series of mutations in the NOD 2 gene, a regulator of NF-κB, a master regulator of genes involved in inflammation [20,21]. These genes are expressed in monocytes and macrophages, and are thought to be a part of the innate immune response. The prominence of macrophage-produced cytokines (IL-1, TNF-α, and IL-6) in RA and the prominence of a gene expressed in monocytes and active in the innate immune system suggest that those diseases in which TNF blockade is therapeutic may primarily be the result of overproduction of TNF and related cytokines by macrophages and monocytes. This is perhaps initially triggered by activated T cells, but the major mediator of inflammation is the macrophage rather than the T cell.

Some of the side effects of anti-TNF therapy in RA (development of anti-dsDNA antibodies, development of overt systemic lupus erythematosus, and central nervous system lesions suggestive of multiple sclerosis [Table 2]) are known manifestations of the diseases presented in Table 1, in which blockade of TNF action leads to exacerbation.

Effects of neonatal administration of TNF and anti-TNF on T1DM in the NOD mouse

Table 3 presents the effects of neonatal administration of nontoxic doses of TNF-α to newborn NOD mice, which results in a striking increase in incidence and a much earlier onset of diabetes. Additionally, administration of anti-TNF in doses beginning at 20 μg/g body weight and rising to 100 μg every other day for the first 21 days after birth results in complete and prolonged (1 year) absence of both diabetes and almost all signs of islet cell autoimmunity [10]. Recent evidence has shown that NOD mice treated in the neonatal period with TNF have a further sharp decrease in their already low levels of CD4+CD25+ regulatory T cells. Conversely, anti-TNF treatment in the neonatal period results in a dramatic *increase* in these CD4+CD25+ regulatory T cells. Preliminary studies suggest that the increase in CD4+CD25+ T cells alone is sufficient to explain the complete prevention of T1DM, since regular transfer of small numbers of these T cells to young NOD mice prevents the development of T1DM.

While this effect on regulatory T cells may be the primary explanation for the effect of neonatal TNF and anti-TNF on T1DM, there is another possibility. It has been postulated [9] that, by decreasing TCR signaling, neonatal TNF exposure results in a decrease in thymic T-cell-negative selection, particularly of autoreactive T cells. Correspondingly, neonatal exposure to anti-TNF, by increasing signaling through the TCR, may result in an increase in thymic T-cell-negative selection of autoreactive T cells, thus preventing diabetes.

The second model of T1DM presented in Table 3 is that induced in C57BL/6 mice by introduction of a transgene encoding the rat insulin promoter coupled to the TNF-α coding sequence. These mice develop early severe insulitis,

Table 3

Effect of neonatal tumor necrosis factor (TNF) and anti-TNF therapy on type 1 diabetes (T1DM) models

Model	Intervention	Result	Mechanism	References
1a. T1DM in NOD mice	TNF, 1–2 µg i.p., q.o.d for 21 days from birth	Increased incidence and earlier onset of diabetes ? Decrease in thymic T-cell-negative selection	? Further decrease in CD4$^+$CD25$^+$ regulatory T cells	[9,10] (A Wu and HO McDevitt, unpublished observations)
1b. T1DM in NOD mice	Anti-TNF, 20–100 µg i.p., q.o.d. for 21 days from birth	Complete, prolonged (1 year) absence of diabetes and islet cell autoimmunity ? Increase in thymic T-cell-negative selection	Dramatic increase in CD4$^+$CD25$^+$ regulatory T cells	[9,10] (A Wu and HO McDevitt, unpublished observations)
2. T1DM in C57BL/6 mice expressing RIP-TNF	TNF overexpressed in β cells	Severe insulitis, but diabetes never occurs (unless transgenic RIP-B7.1 is introduced)	RIP-TNF appears to have induced a Th2 shift in islet-reactive T cells	[11,12]

i.p., intraperitoneally; NOD, nonobese diabetic; q.o.d., every other day; RIP, rat insulin promoter; Th2, T helper cell type 2.

due to the overexpression of TNF in the β-islet cells. Despite this severe continuing insulitis, however, these transgenic animals never develop diabetes, and can be induced to do so only on introduction of a second transgene, rat insulin promoter-B7.1 [11,12].

Analysis of this model indicates that there is an increase in the number of macrophages and dendritic cells attracted to the islets by the local expression of TNF-α. Despite this, the T cells in the islets of these mice appear to be 'tolerant' to islet cell autoantigens, and the T cells have undergone a Th2 shift in the β-islet cell reactive T-cell population. While this model appears to be distinct from that in the wild-type NOD mouse, it is noteworthy that the severe prolonged insulitis in these animals does not result in the development of islet cell destruction, but does result in a form of T-cell tolerance; presumably due to some type of downregulation or alteration in T-cell function, an effect similar to the effects described in Table 1 (part 3a).

Potential mechanisms

Among the potential mechanisms by which blockade of TNF action might increase or activate autoimmunity (Table 1), an inverse effect of TNF levels on signal transduction through the TCR and/or a direct effect of TNF levels on T-cell apoptosis in the periphery mediated by TNFR2 are the most prominent (Table 4).

There are several reasons for the first of these two prominent potential mechanisms. First, it is difficult to envision how TNF blockade could activate macrophage function, antigen presentation or any other of the inflammatory functions of TNF-α. Second, several lines of evidence (see earlier) indicate that *in vitro* or *in vivo* exposure to TNF is capable of decreasing the T-cell response as measured by

T-cell proliferation, cytokine production, and calcium flux. Third, preliminary studies by Cope and coworkers [15] and Munson *et al.* (manuscript in preparation) have shown that chronic exposure to TNF is capable of decreasing the activation of several of the proximal proteins in the TCR signaling pathway, and is also capable of decreasing TCR-mediated activation of NF-κB. The latter effect is important, since signaling by TNF through one arm of the TNF receptor signaling pathway and signaling by the TCR can both result in activation of NF-κB.

The possibility that TNF acts by increasing T-cell programmed death via TNFR2 must also be considered, since both mechanisms could be operative. The functions of TNFR1 are well characterized and include the induction of programmed cell death via the caspase-8 pathway, as well as the activation of a large array of molecules involved in the inflammatory response, primarily through the activation of NF-κB. The functions of TNFR2 are less well characterized.

Studies in R1, R2 or double-receptor-deficient mice have shown that TNFR1 is responsible for a number of host defense and inflammatory responses [22]. TNFR2-deficient mice have dramatically increased serum levels of TNF in response to endotoxin, and they show exacerbated inflammation in several inflammatory models [22]. This suggests that a primary role of TNFR2 is to suppress or regulate TNF-mediated inflammatory responses. The TNFR1 receptor is the high-affinity receptor for soluble TNF [23], but it is expressed at much lower levels on T cells and peritoneal exudate macrophages [22]. This difference in expression levels makes evaluation of the phenotype of receptor-deficient mice complex. Thus, in TNFR2-deficient mice, experimental allergic encephalomyelitis is a much more severe and acute disease [24]. It

Table 4

Mechanisms

Intervention	Potential mechanisms
1. Adult TNF therapy (delays type 1 diabetes, prevents β-cell destruction, and delays glomerulonephritis in B/WF1 mice)	1. A decrease in TCR signal transduction and effector T-cell function mediated through TNFR1 2. An increase in T-cell apoptosis mediated by TNFR2 3. Very little effect has been found on CD4+CD25+ regulatory T cells in adult mice
2. Adult anti-TNF therapy (variably hastens type 1 diabetes, increases B/W F1 nephritis, and increases late EAE)	1. An increase in TCR signal transduction and effector T-cell function through TNFR1 2. A decrease in T-cell apoptosis through TNFR2 3. Very little effect has been found on CD4+CD25+ regulatory T cell numbers by anti-TNF
3. Neonatal TNF therapy (increases diabetes incidence and hastens onset in NOD mice)	1. Further decreases CD4+CD25+ regulatory T cells, possibly via TNFR2-mediated T-cell apoptosis 2. Possible activation of macrophages and dendritic cells, increasing insulitis 3. A decrease in TCR signal transduction via TNFR1, permitting potentially autoreactive T cells to escape negative selection, emigrate to the periphery and cause diabetes
4. Neonatal anti-TNF therapy (completely prevents type 1 diabetes in NOD mice)	1. Dramatically increases CD4+CD25+ regulatory T cells, possibly by blocking TNFR2-mediated T-cell apoptosis 2. Possibly decreases macrophage and dendritic cell activation so that regulatory T cells can function effectively 3. Possibly increases TCR signal transduction so that autoreactive T cells are negatively selected in the thymus and/or in the periphery

EAE, experimental allergic encephalomyelitis; NOD, nonobese diabetic; TCR, T-cell receptor; TNF, tumor necrosis factor; TNFR1, tumor necrosis factor receptor 1 (55 kb); TNFR2, tumor necrosis factor receptor 2 (75 kb).

is not clear whether this is due to the lack of a downregulatory influence of TNFR2 or to the increased levels of TNF that are released in inflammatory responses because of the lack of the R2 receptor [25–31].

The TNF and TCR signaling pathways

With respect to the specific effects of TNF on signal transduction through the TCR, it should be noted that Cope and coworkers have reported that chronic TNF exposure of T-cell hybridomas results in a downregulation of activation of CD3zeta p21 and 23 and ZAP 70 [15]. It is not clear how TNF exposure leads to a decrease in the activation of these proximal TCR signal transduction proteins. However that decreased activation is achieved, it would be expected to lead to a decrease in activation of PLC-γ and PKC, and a corresponding decrease in the activation pathway from CD28 to NF-κB.

As noted earlier, Munson et al. (manuscript in preparation) have shown in Jurkat T cells that chronic exposure to low levels of TNF-α leads to a striking reduction in TCR-induced NF-κB activation after a 5-day period of incubation. TNF exposure may act through both pathways to result in a decrease in NF-κB activation. This would be expected to result in a decrease in T-cell activation and

T-cell response. Conversely, exposure to anti-TNF and blockade of all endogenous TNF should prevent the normal endogenous TNF effects on NF-κB activation. In both these latter observations [15] (Munson et al., manuscript in preparation), the pathways and signaling proteins that are affected by chronic exposure to TNF are unknown, and they are extremely difficult to identify because of the complexity of both signaling pathways.

Actual and potential interactions between cell receptor signaling pathways (receptor cross-talk): interaction between TNF-α and the insulin receptor

Insulin resistance is an important metabolic abnormality often associated with stress, infections, cancer and obesity, and is especially prominent in non-insulin-dependent diabetes. Increased production of TNF-α is frequently observed in the first three of these conditions.

In obesity, it has been observed that adipocytes produce low levels of TNF-α that increase in obesity [32]. In 1994, Spiegelman and associates found that TNF-α inhibits signaling from the insulin receptor [33] and that this was associated with reduced tyrosine kinase activity of the insulin receptor [34]. Subsequently, Spiegelman's group showed that this reduced signaling through the insulin receptor was due to the induction of serine phosphorylation of insulin receptor substrate-1 (IRS-1). Serine phosphorylation converts IRS-1 into an inhibitor of insulin receptor tyrosine kinase activity [35]. (In 1997, Hotamisligil and coworkers also demonstrated that TNF contributes to obesity by increasing the release of leptin from adipocytes [36].)

The effects of TNF on signaling through the insulin receptor were verified earlier this year when White and coworkers [37] showed that TNF-α, insulin, and insulin growth factor-1 all act to serine phosphorylate IRS-1 on serine 307. Serine 307 phosphorylation of IRS-1 by TNF-α requires the action of MEK (also activated in the TNF signaling pathway), while serine 307 phosphorylation by insulin and insulin growth factor-1 requires association of JNK-1 with IRS-1, and the activation of the phosphatidylinositol 3-kinases.

This is an excellent example of receptor cross-talk. Insulin, insulin growth factor-1 and TNF-α all stimulate inhibitory phosphorylation of serine 307 on IRS-1 but do so through the use of different kinase pathways, all intersecting at IRS-1 and serine 307. A similar type of interaction may explain many other receptor cross-talk phenomena, possibly including the effect of TNF on downregulation of signaling through the TCR.

Interactions between TNF and IL-10
As noted by Ishida *et al.* [5], chronic administration of anti-IL-10 to adult (3–4 months old) (NZB × NZW)F1 female mice (which would be expected to remove the inhibitory effects of IL-10 and to lead to an exacerbation of disease) paradoxically results in a delay in the onset of glomerulonephritis. This paradoxical result is almost entirely due to the failure of IL-10 to downregulate TNF-α production by macrophages and T cells, since simultaneous administration of anti-TNF with anti-IL-10 results in no effect on disease in this model. Thus, endogenous TNF, unopposed by IL-10, exerts the same delaying and preventive effect that is seen with administration of TNF in these mice [4,5]. (Anti-TNF administration alone caused a much earlier onset of fatal nephritis in these mice [5].)

It is clear from the observations already cited [4,5] that TNF-α, IFN-γ, and other inflammatory cytokines have an intimate reciprocal relationship with IL-10 [38]. This is another example of receptor cross-talk, in this case 'cross-inhibition'. When this inhibition is released, macrophages are then capable of increasing their production of inflammatory cytokines such as TNF.

Interactions between TNF and the TCR
Developing evidence [9,15] (Munson *et al.*, manuscript in preparation) has shown that chronic TNF exposure downregulates components of both the TNF and the TCR signaling pathways. This evidence indicates that TNF has an effect both at the level of NF-κB expression, a very distal part of activation through both the TNF and TCR, and at the very proximal locus of activation of the CD3 components of the TCR.

Effect of TNF-α on Jurkat TCR activation
Jurkat T cells were cultured in the presence or absence of human recombinant TNF (10 ng/ml) for 1–6 days. Cells were then transfected with various transcription factor binding site–luciferase reporter constructs, incubated overnight, and washed and stimulated with phorbol 12-myristate 13-acetate and ionomycin or with anti-CD3 alone or in combination with anti-CD28, in the absence of TNF. Cells were cotransfected with a plasmid encoding a truncated CD25 molecule that could be used for normalizing the transfection efficiency by staining for anti-CD25 and performing FACS analysis.

TNF treatment for 3–5 days resulted in an 86% decrease in NF-κB-binding to a class I NF-κB binding site–luciferase reporter construct following stimulation with phorbol 12-myristate 13-acetate and ionomycin, and resulted in an 83% decrease following stimulation with anti-CD3 + anti-CD28 after normalization for transfection efficiency. Likewise, TNF treatment resulted in similar decreases in AP-1 binding to an AP-1 luciferase reporter, as well as decreases in luciferase production from a dual NF–AT–AP-1 composite reporter. Phosphoblots revealed very little difference in phosphorylation.

The findings cited in previous sections indicate that exposure to TNF-α affects both proximal and distal parts of the TCR signal transduction pathways. To obtain a survey of changes in expression (either up or down) in components of both the TNF and TCR signaling pathways, experiments currently underway will utilize gene expression profiling as the first step in assessing the effect of chronic TNF-α exposure on TCR signal transduction. These experiments will utilize the 'lymphochip' originally used by Alizadeh *et al.* [39] to analyze gene expression in large B-cell lymphoma and, more recently, in Jurkat T cells under a variety of stimulation conditions. These experiments are currently in progress and should permit a more comprehensive assessment of changes in gene expression in both of these receptor signaling pathways. An understanding of precisely how TNF exposure indirectly regulates TCR signal transduction may lead to the development of methods for compensating for the effects of TNF blockade in those autoimmune diseases where this is an appropriate therapeutic measure.

The role of LTα/β and LTβ receptor in autoimmunity
Administration of the soluble extracellular domain of LTα/β coupled to the Fc fragment of IgG as a fusion protein (LTβR-Fc) to NOD mice, either by injection [40] or by

transgenic expression transcribed from the cytomegalovirus (CMV) promoter [41], prevents T1DM in NOD mice. The mechanisms of this prevention and the possible undesirable side effects of these interventions are currently unknown. There are three principal, nonexclusive mechanisms for the effects of LTβ receptor blockade.

The first mechanism is prevention of MAdCAM-1 expression, causing defective T-cell, B-cell, and dendritic-cell homing and localization to peripheral lymphoid organs. Second is the interruption of the positive feedback circuit between LTαβ/LTβ receptor, B lymphocyte chemoattractant (BLC) and BLR-1 (and SLC and ELC), resulting in improper localization of T cells, B cells, and dendritic cells within the spleen and the lymph nodes, thus causing altered or defective T cell, B cell, and antigen-presenting cell (APC) interactions [40,41]. Finally, since soluble LTβ receptor binds both LTα/β and LIGHT (whose cognate receptor is the herpes virus entry mediator [HVEM]), the immunoregulatory effects of the soluble LTβR-Fc may be mediated by blockade of the interaction between LIGHT, LTα/β, and the LTβ receptor.

There is abundant evidence (reviewed in [42–44]) describing the critical role of LTα/β and the LTβ receptor in the development of the immune system. This ligand–receptor pair, as well several other ligand–receptor pairs within the TNF-α superfamily, and a number of transcription factors, chemokines and chemokine receptors have all been shown to be required for proper lymph-node genesis [42–50]. Many of these gene products operate at the very earliest stages of lymph-node formation, as well as at later stages in this process. These effects are beyond the scope of the present discussion, which will focus on the effects of the lack of the LTβ receptor on immune system function, primarily in autoimmunity.

Inhibition of LTαβ signaling through the LTβ receptor in adult mice, by the use of a blocking monoclonal antibody against LTβ receptor or a soluble LTβR-Fc fusion protein, induces marked changes in mice receiving this treatment [40,41,51–54]. In the spleen, discreet B-cell follicles are markedly reduced or absent, follicular dendritic cell (FDC) clusters are lacking, and the marginal zone shows radical changes, with absence of staining with MOMA-1 (a marker for marginal metallophilic macrophages) and reduced staining for ER-TR9 on marginal zone macrophages. In addition, the normal staining for MAdCAM-1 in the marginal zone is absent in treated mice. The normal boundary between the B-cell and T-cell zones in the white pulp of the spleen is disrupted, and the population of ER-TR7+ reticular fibroblasts normally seen around the outside of the white pulp in the marginal zone is absent. Furthermore, germinal centers did not form in these mice following immunization with sheep red blood cells [55].

A single injection of LTβR-Fc was sufficient to eliminate MAdCAM-1 expression 1 week later [40]. Some of the other changes noted earlier required several injections of the fusion protein. Several injections of the LTβR-Fc fusion protein resulted in a progressive decrease in the level of sheep red blood cell-specific IgG1, IgG2a, and IgM responses [40].

Similar changes in splenic architecture, B-cell and T-cell zone abnormalities, and absence of staining for MAdCAM-1 were also seen in BALB/c mice expressing a transgenic LTβR-Fc fusion protein under the control of the CMV promoter [55]. In this transgenic model, the CMV promoter does not become activated until days 2–3 after birth, by which time the development and population of lymph nodes has occurred [55].

The LTβ receptor has two ligands, LTα/β and LIGHT, another member of the TNF superfamily. The binding of LIGHT to a second receptor, the HVEM, functions as a costimulatory ligand–receptor pair that can promote T-cell proliferation and IFNγ production. Until very recently there were no reagents that could effectively block LIGHT activity in vivo. However, a very recent publication [56] has utilized a soluble HVEM-Fc receptor molecule to block the action of LIGHT in vivo. These studies showed that the HVEM-Fc was capable of downregulating the T-cell response to stimulation with concanavalin A and anti-CD3. Furthermore, multiple injections of HVEM-Fc in 5-week-old to 6-week-old NOD mice (100 µg per injection) was capable of decreasing the development of T1DM in the NOD recipients from 80% at 25 weeks to 25%. It is thus clear that at least part of the effects of the soluble LTβR-Fc are due to blockade of the interaction of LIGHT with HVEM.

The preliminary results presented in this recent study [56] did not demonstrate the extensive morphological changes in the spleen and lymph nodes that are seen with the soluble LTβR-Fc. Clearly, further studies need to be carried out, but it appears that the effects of LTβR-Fc on the morphology in the spleen and lymph nodes, the absence of the marginal zone, and of staining with MOMA-1 and MadCAM-1 antibodies indicate that the effects of blockade through the LTβ receptor may involve LTα/β, LIGHT, and MadCAM-1. The initial results indicate that LTβR-Fc is more effective in preventing diabetes than is HVEM-Fc.

Several studies over the past 4 years [13–15] (Munson *et al.*, manuscript in preparation) have revealed that LTαβ/LTβ receptor are critical for the development of natural killer cells, dendritic APCs, and FDCs. Membrane lymphotoxin is required for dendritic cells to infiltrate the lymph nodes, while mature FDC networks require LTβ receptor expression by stromal cells, and LTαβ and TNF expression by B cells. FDC development is dependent on TNF signaling and on LTβ receptor signaling by B cells (Munson *et al.*, manuscript in preparation).

Mebius *et al.* [57] showed that, during fetal lymph node development, the lymph node post-capillary high endothelial venules express MAdCAM-1. This permits the early lymphoid precursor cells that are $\alpha_4\beta_7^+$, CD45+, CD4+ and CD3− to enter the lymph-node anlage. These cells also express surface LTβ and the chemokine receptor BLR-1 (CXCR5), and are capable of becoming natural killer cells, dendritic APCs, and follicular cells [58–60]. More recently, the mediators by which LTαβ/LTβ receptor signaling attracts B cells, dendritic APCs, and FDC to the developing lymph node follicle have been delineated [61–63]. The picture that emerges from these studies can be briefly summarized as follows.

Membrane-bound LTβ (produced by CD45+, CD4+, CD3− lymphoid precursors; see earlier) [57,61–63] binds to LTβ receptor on stromal cells, leading to the release of BLC (CCL13). By binding to its receptor on B cells (BLR-1, CXCR5), BCL attracts B cells to the area in the lymph nodes and the spleen where production of BLC is maximal. BLC binding to its receptor leads to B-cell activation and increased expression of LTαβ, which then leads to a further increase in expression of BLC, thus establishing a positive feedback loop. By inducing upregulation of membrane-bound LTαβ, BLC promotes further FDC development. At the same time, by binding to its receptor, LTαβ also stimulates induction of SLC (6 C-kine), a weak B-cell chemoattractant and a strong T-cell chemoattractant. SLC expression is induced in the region immediately adjacent to the B-cell region, creating a T-cell-rich region in the patterns seen in normal lymph nodes and spleen.

LTαβ binding to LTβ receptor also drives the expression of PNAd, MAdCAM-1 and V-CAM on the post-capillary high endothelial venules in the developing lymphoid tissue. SLC expression by endothelial cells and stromal cells, driven by LTαβ/LTβ receptor, also results in the expression of ELC by stromal cells. ELC is a strong T-cell chemoattractant, and the combined action of SLC and ELC, both binding to CCR7 on T cells, results in the well-defined segregation of T-cell and B-cell zones in normal lymphoid tissue. SLC and ELC also bind to CCR7 on dendritic cell precursors, thus attracting these cells to the developing lymphoid architecture.

Chemokines, triggered by the binding of LTαβ to LTβ receptor (and also by TNF-α binding to its receptors), thus establish the normal microarchitecture of the lymph node and the spleen.

From the presented results, it is clear that LTβ receptor blockade by a LTβR-Fc fusion protein will have multiple effects. These include a decrease in B-cell production of LTαβ and BLC, a decrease in expression of PNAd, MAdCAM-1, and VCAM-1, and a decrease in SLC, and to a lesser extent, ELC production by stromal cells in the T-cell zone. These effects explain many of the manifestations seen in LTβ receptor-deficient and LTβ-deficient mice, and in mice expressing a LTβR-Fc fusion protein: the loss of the marginal zone in the spleen; the partial mixing and disruption of normal T-cell/B-cell zone separation in the splenic white pulp and lymph nodes; the decrease in MAdCAM-1 expression; the decrease or absence of primary follicles and FDC clusters; and the diminution in T-cell–B-cell–APC interactions, resulting in isotype-switching defects in specific antibody responses [40,41].

The effect of LTβR-Fc on development of T1DM in the NOD mouse

Injection of relatively large doses of LTβR-Fc in NOD mice at 12 weeks of age, when insulitis is already well established in untreated littermates, results in nearly complete reversal of insulitis, and in failure to develop diabetes up to 30 weeks of age [40]. Expression of LTβR-Fc, under the control of the CMV promoter, prevents diabetes in NOD mice during the period in which expression of the fusion protein is greater than 2 μg/ml serum [41]. When expression of the transgene fusion protein drops below this critical level, however, the mice begin to develop diabetes, at approximately 40–50 weeks of age, with an incidence of 40% at the end of 1 year.

Both of these findings show that blockade of the LTαβ/LTβ receptor ligand–receptor system is capable of downregulating the diabetic process and of preventing the development of T1DM. Furthermore, the second study [41] shows that once the level of transgenic fusion protein has fallen below a critical level, the immune system is perfectly capable of reinstituting the diabetic process, leading to overt clinical diabetes.

It should be noted that in NOD LTβR-Fc mice, there was very little diminution in insulitis; the size of lymphocytic infiltrates in the islets and the frequency of insulitis were indistinguishable between transgene-positive and transgene-negative littermates. This result suggests that the ability of lymphocytes to migrate to areas of inflammation is not impaired under this type of treatment, but that the ability to generate a sufficient diabetogenic T-cell response that would result in islet cell destruction is impaired, possibly because of interference with normal T cell–B cell and T cell–APC interactions.

Two major mechanisms for the effects of LTβR-Fc can thus be envisioned to explain the observed effects. First, it is possible that interference with LTαβ binding to its receptor may decrease the expression of adhesins and integrins sufficiently to prevent insulitis and diabetes.

Earlier studies from this laboratory [64] have shown that administration of a monoclonal antibody to the α_4 integrin in young NOD mice is capable of preventing the development of diabetes in these animals. Thus, interference with $\alpha_4\beta_7$ and $\alpha_4\beta_1$ binding to their respective receptors can prevent the development of diabetes. However, the finding that insulitis persists in mice expressing a LTβR-Fc fusion protein would indicate that these lymphocytes are capable of entering inflamed areas.

The second possible mechanism for diabetes prevention may involve the effect of LT$\alpha\beta$/LTβ receptor blockade in interfering with normal separation between T-cell and B-cell zones, normal dendritic cell localization, and faulty interactions of T cells with both B cells and APCs [65]. In the latter case (i.e. in LTβR-Fc transgenic mice), where the degree of interference with this ligand–receptor system is presumably less than that induced by injection of very high doses of the fusion protein, it may be possible to prevent the development of diabetes with doses of the fusion protein that do not seriously interfere with the development of the normal immune response to environmental antigens.

LTα/β or LTβ null mutations, leading to LTβ deficiency, prevent autoimmunity not only in NOD mice [40,41], but also in experimental allergic encephalomyelitis and experimental murine colitis models [66,67]. Near-complete LT$\alpha\beta$ blockade (as in [40]) may cause increased susceptibility to infection. Conversely, lesser degrees of blockade (as in [41]) (indicated by the persistence of insulitis) may result in prevention of diabetogenesis for shorter periods, requiring repeated administration, albeit with less severe immune suppressive side effects.

Effect of transgenic expression of a soluble LTβ receptor on diabetes in NOD mice

F9 LTβR-Fc transgenic mice were followed for the development of diabetes by expanding the population to 40–50 female mice, along with nontransgenic littermates. This experiment was carried out in two different founder lines: one expressing high (0.8–30 µg/ml) levels of the transgene protein (line 1610), and one expressing lower (0.38–1.1 µg/ml) levels of the transgene protein (line 201). The 201 line developed diabetes at almost the same rate as nontransgenic littermates (albeit slightly delayed). However, female mice in the 1610 line did not develop diabetes by 30 weeks of age, with the exception of one animal in a group of 26 females. Examination of these animals by histology and immunohistochemistry showed that the 1610 line at 6 and 12 weeks demonstrated similar anatomical abnormalities in the spleen, the lymph node, and Peyer's patches as had been noted in the original LTβR-Fc transgenic mice described earlier.

In the 1610 NOD line (unlike results in BALB/c mice), LTβR-Fc protein expression began at relatively high levels on embryonic day 16.5, reaching 2–30 µg transgene protein/ml serum by neonatal day 7. Over the next 10–12 weeks, however, the fusion protein concentrations fell to an average of 3 µg/ml at 10 weeks of age, and to less than 2 µg/ml at 20 weeks of age [41]. This is an unusual result, since transcription from the CMV promoter normally is expected to occur in many tissues throughout life. In the LTβR-Fc BALB/c mice, levels of LTβR-Fc remain constant up to 40–50 weeks of age.

Beginning at 35–40 weeks of age, female NOD 1610 mice unexpectedly began to develop diabetes, such that almost 50% of them developed diabetes by 65 weeks. Thus, once the LTβR-Fc protein levels fell to 1–2 µg/ml or lower, the diabetic process was capable of resuming. This resumption led to the development of T1DM, albeit 15–30 weeks after the nontransgenic littermate females.

Histologic analysis of these mice at 12 and 17–19 weeks of age showed that they had almost the same degree of insulitis as seen in control littermates (unlike the results described by Fu and coworkers [40]). The anatomical abnormalities in the spleen, which were seen in 4-week-old to 12-week-old mice, were greatly reduced by 30 weeks of age, with the exception of the redevelopment of the marginal zone. At 20 and 30 weeks, the structure of the marginal zone and the expression of MAdCAM-1 and MOMA-1 were still absent.

Soluble LTβR-Fc fusion protein therefore prevents T1DM in NOD mice, while levels remain above a critical threshold. Of great interest, following the decay of fusion-protein expression, the diabetic process spontaneously restarts and leads to development of overt diabetes in 50% of mice, with a 30-week delay (roughly the time period during which higher levels of the fusion protein were expressed) [41].

The results of this study are significant because they indicate that relatively low levels of a LTβR-Fc fusion protein are capable of inducing LTβ receptor blockade and of preventing the diabetic process in genetically susceptible NOD mice. Furthermore, it is clear from this study that no permanent inhibition of the immune response is induced by expression of the soluble LTβ receptor. This, of course, raises the possibility that the LTβR-Fc fusion protein, given at carefully determined times and doses, might permit prevention of the development of T1DM without significant degrees of suppression of the immune response to foreign antigens.

Effect of TNF-α and its blockade on the development of CD4+CD25+ regulatory T cells in the NOD mouse
Introduction
CD4+CD25+ T cells are derived from the thymus and have gained recent attention as mediators of peripheral tolerance

[68–70], as well as potentially having a role in the protection of a transplanted organ from immunological attack [70]. These cells are found in many mouse strains, including the NOD mouse, and in humans. CD4+CD25+ T cells act essentially as suppressor T cells in the periphery. These cells are anergic and do not respond to stimulation with anti-CD3, they are capable of suppressing the antigen-specific activation of CD4+CD25− T cells, they require cell–cell contact for this suppression to be effective, and they may function through the expression of CTLA-4 molecules on these T cells interacting with B7 (on either APCs or on the target T-cell population) [68].

The NOD mouse is a well-defined animal model used to study T1DM. Our laboratory has previously demonstrated that neonatal administration of TNF (first 3 weeks of life) accelerates the onset of and increases the incidence of T1DM in the NOD mouse, while neonatal administration of anti-TNF completely abrogates all manifestations of T1DM for up to 1 year [71]. Neonatal TNF administration also further decreases the number and function of CD4+CD25+ regulatory T cells. Neonatal administration of anti-TNF, in contrast, increases the number of CD4+CD25+ T cells and does not alter the ability of these cells to suppress disease in a transfer system. These data suggest that the numbers and function of this regulatory population may be regulated in either a positive or negative manner by their cytokine (specifically, TNF) milieu.

Initial results
Ourselves and other workers [72] have shown that the NOD mouse is numerically deficient in the CD4+CD25+ T-cell population, suggesting a compromised ability to maintain a state of nonresponsiveness to self-antigens. Direct supplementation of the neonatal NOD mouse with three injections of 2×10^5 CD4+CD25+ T cells can significantly delay the onset of T1DM in this mouse model. Continued weekly administration of similar small numbers of CD4+CD25+ T cells results in failure to develop diabetes for as long as this treatment is continued. These data highlight the potential therapeutic value and the potency of these cells, and are compatible with the concept that the anti-TNF-induced increase in CD4+CD25+ T cells is the basis for the failure of anti-TNF-treated mice to develop diabetes.

Future studies
There is abundant evidence that the thymus of the NOD mouse displays significant anatomical abnormalities that are thought to be related to the T1DM disease process. The precise relationship is unknown. The NOD thymus exhibits giant perivascular spaces with abnormal retention of thymocytes and with premature signs of age-associated breakdown of the thymic epithelium [73–75]. To the extent that the NOD thymic architecture could influence the selection and ultimate trafficking of CD4+CD25+ T cells, it becomes important to understand the development of CD4+CD25+ T cells in the thymus. There is little to no information available in this area of study. There is no data available regarding the development of CD4+CD25+ T cells, and how TNF and/or anti-TNF may affect their development. These studies are currently under way.

Concluding remarks
The studies presented in this review, as well as a number of studies from the literature, make it clear that TNF-α and its receptors (TNFR1 and TNFR2), LTβ receptor and its LTα/β and LIGHT ligands, and the interaction of LIGHT with HVEM are all important regulators of the development and maintenance of structural integrity and function of the T cells in their interactions with other T cells, B cells and APCs in the development of the normal immune response and in the development of autoimmunity. Further understanding of the molecular basis for the downregulation of the immune response produced by pharmacological doses of TNF-α may lead to the development of new therapies to prevent the excessive stimulation of the immune system seen in TNF blockade, as occurs in RA.

Furthermore, a detailed understanding of the effects of soluble LTβ receptor and soluble HVEM receptor on the function of T cells, and the interaction of T cells with other T cells and with APCs in the white pulp of the spleen and the developing follicles in the lymph nodes, may lead to relatively nontoxic methods for downregulating the autoimmune response in diseases such as T1DM, where individuals at risk in the prediabetic stage can be identified and subjected to this kind of blocking therapy.

Glossary of terms
BLC = B lymphocyte chemoattractant; CMV = cytomegalovirus; FDC = follicular dendritic cell; HVEM = herpes virus entry mediator; IRS-1 = insulin receptor substrate-1; LTα/β = lymphotoxin α/β (α2β1, αα1β2); LTβR-Fc = the extra cellular domain of LTα/β coupled to the Fc fragment of IgG as a fusion protein; NOD = nonobese diabetic; T1DM = type 1 diabetes, juvenile onset, insulin-dependent diabetes mellitus, due to insulin deficiency; TNFR1 = tumor necrosis factor receptor 1 (55 kb); TNFR2 = tumor necrosis factor receptor 2 (75 kb).

References
1. van Oosten BW, Barkhof F, Truyen L, Boringa JB, Bertelsmann FW, von Blomberg BM, Woody JN, Hartung HP, Polman CH: **Increased MRI activity and immune activation in two multiple sclerosis patients treated with the monoclonal anti-tumor necrosis factor antibody cA2.** *Neurology* 1996, **47**:1531-1534. [general reference]
2. The Lenercept Multiple Sclerosis Study Group and The University of British Columbia MS/MRI Analysis Group: **TNF neutralization in MS: results of a randomized, placebo-controlled multicenter study.** *Neurology* 1999, **53**:457-465. [general reference]
3. Kassiotis G, Kollias G: **Uncoupling the proinflammatory from the immunosuppressive properties of tumor necrosis factor (TNF) at the p55 TNF receptor level: implications for pathogenesis and therapy of autoimmune demyelination.** *J Exp Med* 2001, **193**:427-434. [general reference]

4. Jacob CO, McDevitt HO: **Tumour necrosis factor-alpha in murine autoimmune 'lupus' nephritis.** *Nature* 1988, **331**:356-358. [general reference]

5. Ishida H, Muchamuel T, Sakaguchi S, Andrade S, Menon S, Howard M: **Continuous administration of anti-interleukin 10 antibodies delays onset of autoimmunity in NZB/W F1 mice.** *J Exp Med* 1994, **179**:305-310. [general reference]

6. Kontoyiannis D, Kollias G: **Accelerated autoimmunity and lupus nephritis in NZB mice with an engineered heterozygous deficiency in tumor necrosis factor.** *Eur J Immunol* 2000, **30**:2038-2047. [general reference]

7. Jacob CO, Aiso S, Michie SA, McDevitt HO, Acha-Orbea H: **Prevention of diabetes in nonobese diabetic mice by tumor necrosis factor (TNF): similarities between TNF-alpha and interleukin 1.** *Proc Natl Acad Sci USA* 1990, **87**:968-972. [general reference]

8. Cope A, Ettinger R, McDevitt HO: **The role of TNFα and related cytokines in the development and function of the autoreactive T-cell repertoire.** *Res Immunol* 1997, **148**:307-313. [key review]

9. Cope AP, Liblau RS, Yang XD, Congia M, Laudanna C, Schreiber RD, Probert L, Kollias G, McDevitt HO: **Chronic tumor necrosis factor alters T cell responses by attenuating T cell receptor signaling.** *J Exp Med* 1997, **185**:1573-1584. [general reference]

10. Yang XD, Tisch R, Singer SM, Cao ZA, Liblau RS, Schreiber RD, McDevitt HO: **Effect of tumor necrosis factor alpha on insulin-dependent diabetes mellitus in NOD mice. I. The early development of autoimmunity and the diabetogenic process.** *J Exp Med* 1994, **180**:995-1004. [general reference]

11. Picarella DE, Kratz A, Li CB, Ruddle NH, Flavell RA: **Transgenic tumor necrosis factor (TNF)-alpha production in pancreatic islets leads to insulitis, not diabetes. Distinct patterns of inflammation in TNF-alpha and TNF-beta transgenic mice.** *J Immunol* 1993, **150**:4136-4150. [general reference]

12. McSorley SJ, Soldera S, Malherbe L, Carnaud C, Locksley RM, Flavell RA, Glaichenhaus N: **Immunological tolerance to a pancreatic antigen as a result of local expression of TNFalpha by islet beta cells.** *Immunity* 1997, **7**:401-409. [general reference]

13. Quattrocchi E, Walmsley M, Browne K, Williams RO, Marinova-Mutafchieva L, Buurman W, Butler DM, Feldmann M: **Paradoxical effects of adenovirus-mediated blockade of TNF activity in murine collagen-induced arthritis.** *J Immunol* 1999, **163**:1000-1009. [general reference]

14. Gordon C, Ranges GE, Greenspan JS, Wofsy D: **Chronic therapy with recombinant tumor necrosis factor-alpha in autoimmune NZB/NZW F1 mice.** *Clin Immunol Immunopathol* 1989, **52**:421-434. [general reference]

15. Isomaki P, Panesar M, Annenkov A, Clark JM, Foxwell BM, Chernajovsky Y, Cope AP: **Prolonged exposure of T Cells to TNF down-regulates TCRzeta and expression of the TCR/CD3 complex at the cell surface.** *J Immunol* 2001, **166**:5495-5507. [general reference]

16. Feldmann M, Maini RN: **Anti-TNF alpha therapy of rheumatoid arthritis: what have we learned?** *Annu Rev Immunol* 2001, **19**:163-196. [key review]

17. Mohan N, Edwards ET, Cupps TR, Oliverio PJ, Siegel JN: **Demyelination diagnosed during etanercept (TNF receptor fusion protein) therapy [abstract].** *Arthritis Rheum* 2000, **43**:S228. [general reference]

18. Sandborn WJ, Hanauer SB: **Antitumor necrosis factor therapy for inflammatory bowel disease: a review of agents, pharmacology, clinical results, and safety.** *Inflamm Bowel Dis* 1999, **5**:119-133. [general reference]

19. Chaudhari U, Romano P, Mulcahy LD, Dooley LT, Baker DG, Gottlieb AB: **Efficacy and safety of infliximab monotherapy for plaque-type psoriasis: a randomised trial.** *Lancet* 2001, **357**:1842-1847. [general reference]

20. Hugot JP, Chamaillard M, Zouali H, Lesage S, Cezard JP, Belaiche J, Almer S, Tysk C, O'Morain CA, Gassull M, Binder V, Finkel Y, Cortot A, Modigliani R, Laurent-Puig P, Gower-Rousseau C, Macry J, Colombel JF, Sahbatou M, Thomas G: **Association of NOD2 leucine-rich repeat variants with susceptibility to Crohn's disease.** *Nature* 2001, **411**:599-603. [general reference]

21. Ogura Y, Bonen DK, Inohara N, Nicolae DL, Chen FF, Ramos R, Britton H, Moran T, Karaliuskas R, Duerr RH, Achkar JP, Brant SR, Bayless TM, Kirschner BS, Hanauer SB, Nunez G, Cho JH: **A frameshift mutation in NOD2 associated with susceptibility to Crohn's disease.** *Nature* 2001, **411**:603-606. [general reference]

22. Peschon JJ, Torrance DS, Stocking KL, Glaccum MB, Otten C, Willis CR, Charrier K, Morrissey PJ, Ware CB, Mohler KM: **TNF receptor-deficient mice reveal divergent roles for p55 and p75 in several models of inflammation.** *J Immunol* 1998, **160**:943-952. [general reference]

23. Grell M, Wajant H, Zimmermann G, Scheurich P: **The type 1 receptor (CD120a) is the high-affinity receptor for soluble tumor necrosis factor.** *Proc Natl Acad Sci USA* 1998, **95**:570-575. [general reference]

24. Eugster HP, Frei K, Bachmann R, Bluethmann H, Lassmann H, Fontana A: **Severity of symptoms and demyelination in MOG-induced EAE depends on TNFR1.** *Eur J Immunol* 1999, **29**:626-632. [general reference]

25. Tartaglia LA, Goeddel DV, Reynolds C, Figari IS, Weber RF, Fendly BM, Palladino MA Jr: **Stimulation of human T-cell proliferation by specific activation of the 75-kDa tumor necrosis factor receptor.** *J Immunol* 1993, **151**:4637-4641. [general reference]

26. Zheng L, Fisher G, Miller RE, Peschon J, Lynch DH, Lenardo MJ: **Induction of apoptosis in mature T cells by tumour necrosis factor.** *Nature* 1995, **377**:348-351. [general reference]

27. Wang B, Kondo S, Shivji GM, Fujisawa H, Mak TW, Sauder DN: **Tumour necrosis factor receptor II (p75) signalling is required for the migration of Langerhans' cells.** *Immunology* 1996, **88**:284-288. [general reference]

28. Sheehan KC, Pinckard JK, Arthur CD, Dehner LP, Goeddel DV, Schreiber RD: **Monoclonal antibodies specific for murine p55 and p75 tumor necrosis factor receptors: identification of a novel in vivo role for p75.** *J Exp Med* 1995, **181**:607-617. [general reference]

29. Riminton DS, Sedgwick JD: **Novel concepts of tumor necrosis factor action in autoimmune pathology. Biologic and gene therapy of autoimmune disease.** In *Current Directions in Autoimmunity.* Edited by Theofilopoulos AN. Basel: Karger; 2000. [key review]

30. Wallach D, Varfolomeev EE, Malinin NL, Goltsev YV, Kovalenko AV, Boldin MP: **Tumor necrosis factor receptor and Fas signaling mechanisms.** *Annu Rev Immunol* 1999, **17**:331-367. [key review]

31. Cantrell D: **T cell antigen receptor signal transduction pathways.** *Annu Rev Immunol* 1996, **14**:259-274. [key review]

32. Hotamisligil GS, Arner P, Caro JF, Atkinson RL, Spiegelman BM: **Increased adipose tissue expression of tumor necrosis factor-alpha in human obesity and insulin resistance.** *J Clin Invest* 1995, **95**:2409-2415. [general reference]

33. Hotamisligil GS, Murray DL, Choy LN, Spiegelman BM: **Tumor necrosis factor alpha inhibits signaling from the insulin receptor.** *Proc Natl Acad Sci USA* 1994, **91**:4854-4858. [general reference]

34. Hotamisligil GS, Budavari A, Murray D, Spiegelman BM: **Reduced tyrosine kinase activity of the insulin receptor in obesity-diabetes. Central role of tumor necrosis factor-alpha.** *J Clin Invest* 1994, **94**:1543-1549. [general reference]

35. Hotamisligil GS, Peraldi P, Budavari A, Ellis R, White MF, Spiegelman BM: **IRS-1-mediated inhibition of insulin receptor tyrosine kinase activity in TNF-alpha- and obesity-induced insulin resistance.** *Science.* 1996, **271**:665-668. [general reference]

36. Kirchgessner TG, Uysal KT, Wiesbrock SM, Marino MW, Hotamisligil GS: **Tumor necrosis factor-alpha contributes to obesity-related hyperleptinemia by regulating leptin release from adipocytes.** *J Clin Invest* 1997, **100**:2777-2782. [general reference]

37. Rui L, Aguirre V, Kim LK, Shulman GI, Lee A, Corbould A, Dunaif A, White MF: **Insulin/IGF-1 and TNF-alpha stimulate phosphorylation of IRS-1 at inhibitory Ser307 via distinct pathways.** *J Clin Invest* 2001, **107**:181-189. [general reference]

38. Moore KW, de Waal Malefyt R, Coffman RL, O'Garra A: **Interleukin-10 and the interleukin-10 receptor.** *Annu Rev Immunol* 2001, **19**:683-765. [key review]

39. Alizadeh AA, Eisen MB, Davis RE, Ma C, Lossos IS, Rosenwald A, Boldrick JC, Sabet H, Tran T, Yu X, Powell JI, Yang L, Marti GE, Moore T, Hudson J Jr, Lu L, Lewis DB, Tibshirani R, Sherlock G, Chan WC, Greiner TC, Weisenburger DD, Armitage JO, Warnke R, Levy R, Wilson W, Grever MR, Byrd JC, Botstein D, Brown PO, Staudt LM: **Distinct types of diffuse large B-cell lymphoma identified by gene expression profiling.** *Nature* 2000, **403**:503-511. [general reference]

40. Wu Q, Salomon B, Chen M, Wang Y, Hoffman LM, Bluestone JA, Fu YX: **Reversal of spontaneous autoimmune insulitis in nonobese diabetic mice by soluble lymphotoxin receptor.** *J Exp Med* 2001, **193**:1327-1332. [general reference]

41. Ettinger R, Munson SH, Chao CC, Vadeboncoeur M, Toma J, McDevitt HO: **A critical role for lymphotoxin-beta receptor in the development of diabetes in nonobese diabetic mice.** *J Exp Med* 2001, **193**:1333-1340. [general reference]

42. Ware CF, VanArsdale TL, Crowe PD, Browning JL: **The ligands and receptors of the lymphotoxin system.** *Curr Top Microbiol Immunol* 1995, **198**:175-218. [key review]

43. Rennert PD, Browning JL, Mebius R, Mackay F, Hochman PS: **Surface lymphotoxin alpha/beta complex is required for the development of peripheral lymphoid organs.** *J Exp Med* 1996, **184**:1999-2006. [general reference]

44. Fu YX, Chaplin DD: **Development and maturation of secondary lymphoid tissues.** *Annu Rev Immunol* 1999, **17**:399-433. [key review]

45. Kim D, Mebius RE, MacMicking JD, Jung S, Cupedo T, Castellanos Y, Rho J, Wong BR, Josien R, Kim N, Rennert PD, Choi Y: **Regulation of peripheral lymph node genesis by the tumor necrosis factor family member TRANCE.** *J Exp Med* 2000, **192**:1467-1478. [general reference]

46. Wigle JT, Oliver G: **Prox1 function is required for the development of the murine lymphatic system.** *Cell* 1999, **98**:769-778. [general reference]

47. Naito A, Azuma S, Tanaka S, Miyazaki T, Takaki S, Takatsu K, Nakao K, Nakamura K, Katsuki M, Yamamoto T, Inoue J: **Severe osteopetrosis, defective interleukin-1 signalling and lymph node organogenesis in TRAF6-deficient mice.** *Genes Cells* 1999, **4**:353-362. [general reference]

48. Shinkura R, Kitada K, Matsuda F, Tashiro K, Ikuta K, Suzuki M, Kogishi K, Serikawa T, Honjo T: **Alymphoplasia is caused by a point mutation in the mouse gene encoding Nf-kappa b-inducing kinase.** *Nat Genet* 1999, **22**:74-77. [general reference]

49. Burkly L, Hession C, Ogata L, Reilly C, Marconi LA, Olson D, Tizard R, Cate R, Lo D: **Expression of relB is required for the development of thymic medulla and dendritic cells.** *Nature* 1995, **373**:531-536. [general reference]

50. Weih F, Carrasco D, Durham SK, Barton DS, Rizzo CA, Ryseck RP, Lira SA, Bravo R: **Multiorgan inflammation and hematopoietic abnormalities in mice with a targeted disruption of RelB, a member of the NF-kappa B/Rel family.** *Cell* 1995, **80**:331-340. [general reference]

51. Cao X, Shores EW, Hu-Li J, Anver MR, Kelsall BL, Russell SM, Drago J, Noguchi M, Grinberg A, Bloom ET: **Defective lymphoid development in mice lacking expression of the common cytokine receptor gamma chain.** *Immunity* 1995, **2**:223-238. [general reference]

52. Forster R, Mattis AE, Kremmer E, Wolf E, Brem G, Lipp M: **A putative chemokine receptor, BLR1, directs B cell migration to defined lymphoid organs and specific anatomic compartments of the spleen.** *Cell* 1996, **87**:1037-1047. [general reference]

53. Mackay F, Majeau GR, Lawton P, Hochman PS, Browning JL: **Lymphotoxin but not tumor necrosis factor functions to maintain splenic architecture and humoral responsiveness in adult mice.** *Eur J Immunol* 1997, **27**:2033-2042. [general reference]

54. Sun Z, Unutmaz D, Zou YR, Sunshine MJ, Pierani A, Brenner-Morton S, Mebius RE, Littman DR: **Requirement for RORgamma in thymocyte survival and lymphoid organ development.** *Science* 2000, **288**:2369-2373. [general reference]

55. Ettinger R, Browning JL, Michie SA, van Ewijk W, McDevitt HO: **Disrupted splenic architecture, but normal lymph node development in mice expressing a soluble lymphotoxin-beta receptor-IgG1 fusion protein.** *Proc Natl Acad Sci USA* 1996, **93**:13102-13107. [general reference]

56. Wang J, Lo JC, Foster A, Yu P, Chen HM, Wang Y, Tamada K, Chen L, Fu YX: **The regulation of T cell homeostasis and autoimmunity by T cell-derived LIGHT.** *J Clin Invest* 2001, **108**:1771-1780. [general reference]

57. Mebius RE, Rennert P, Weissman IL: **Developing lymph nodes collect CD4+CD3− LTbeta+ cells that can differentiate to APC, NK cells, and follicular cells but not T or B cells.** *Immunity* 1997, **7**:493-504. [general reference]

58. Wu Q, Wang Y, Wang J, Hedgeman EO, Browning JL, Fu YX: **The requirement of membrane lymphotoxin for the presence**

of dendritic cells in lymphoid tissues. *J Exp Med* 1999, **190**:629-638. [general reference]

59. Endres R, Alimzhanov MB, Plitz T, Futterer A, Kosco-Vilbois MH, Nedospasov SA, Rajewsky K, Pfeffer K: **Mature follicular dendritic cell networks depend on expression of lymphotoxin beta receptor by radioresistant stromal cells and of lymphotoxin beta and tumor necrosis factor by B cells.** *J Exp Med* 1999, **189**:159-168. [general reference]

60. Gonzalez M, Mackay F, Browning JL, Kosco-Vilbois MH, Noelle RJ: **The sequential role of lymphotoxin and B cells in the development of splenic follicles.** *J Exp Med* 1998, **187**:997-1007. [general reference]

61. Ngo VN, Korner H, Gunn MD, Schmidt KN, Riminton DS, Cooper MD, Browning JL, Sedgwick JD, Cyster JG: **Lymphotoxin alpha/beta and tumor necrosis factor are required for stromal cell expression of homing chemokines in B and T cell areas of the spleen.** *J Exp Med* 1999, **189**:403-412. [general reference]

62. Luther SA, Lopez T, Bai W, Hanahan D, Cyster JG: **BLC expression in pancreatic islets causes B cell recruitment and lymphotoxin-dependent lymphoid neogenesis.** *Immunity* 2000, **12**:471-481. [general reference]

63. Ansel KM, Ngo VN, Hyman PL, Luther SA, Forster R, Sedgwick JD, Browning JL, Lipp M, Cyster JG: **A chemokine-driven positive feedback loop organizes lymphoid follicles.** *Nature* 2000, **406**:309-314. [general reference]

64. Michie SA, Sytwu HK, McDevitt JO, Yang XD: **The roles of alpha 4-integrins in the development of insulin-dependent diabetes mellitus.** *Curr Top Microbiol Immunol* 1998, **231**:65-83. [key review]

65. Cyster JG: **Chemokines and cell migration in secondary lymphoid organs.** *Science* 1999, **286**:2098-2102.

66. Suen WE, Bergman CM, Hjelmstrom P, Ruddle NH: **A critical role for lymphotoxin in experimental allergic encephalomyelitis.** *J Exp Med* 1997, **186**:1233-1240. [general reference]

67. Mackay F, Browning JL, Lawton P, Shah SA, Comiskey M, Bhan AK, Mizoguchi E, Terhorst C, Simpson SJ: **Both the lymphotoxin and tumor necrosis factor pathways are involved in experimental murine models of colitis.** *Gastroenterology* 1998, **115**:1464-1475. [general reference]

68. Sakaguchi S: **Regulatory T cells: controllers of immunologic self-tolerance.** *Cell* 2000, **101**:455-458. [general reference]

69. Shevach E: **Certified professionals: CD4+CD25+ suppressor T cells.** *J Exp Med* 2001, **193**:F41-F45. [general reference]

70. Wu DY, Goldschneider I: **Tolerance to cyclosporin A-induced autologous graft-versus-host disease is mediated by a CD4+CD25+ subset of recent thymic emigrants.** *J Immunol* 2001, **166**:7158-7164. [general reference]

71. Yang XD, Tisch R, Singer AM, Cao ZA, Liblau RS, Schreiber RD, McDevitt HO: **Effect of tumor necrosis factor alpha on insulin dependent diabetes mellitus in NOD mice. I. The early development of autoimmunity and the diabetogenic process.** *J Exp Med* 1994, **185**:1573-1584. [general reference]

72. Salomon B, Lenschow DJ, Rhee L, Ashourian N, Singh B, Sharpe A, Bluestone JA: **B7/CD28 costimulation is essential for the homeostasis of CD4+CD25+ immunoregulatory T cells that control autoimmune diabetes.** *Immunity* 2000, **12**:431-440. [general reference]

73. Savino W, Carnaud C, Luan JJ, Bach JF, Dardenne M: **Characterization of the extracellular matrix-containing perivascular spaces in the NOD mouse thymus.** *Diabetes* 1993, **42**:134-140. [general reference]

74. O'Reilly LA, Healy D, Simpson E, Chandler P, Lund T, Ritter MA, Cooke A: **Studies on the thymus of non-obese diabetic (NOD) mouse: effect of transgene expression.** *Immunology* 1994, **82**:275-286. [general reference]

75. Nabarra B, Andrianarison I: **Thymic reticulum of autoimmune mice. 3. Ultrastructural study of NOD (non obese diabetic) mouse thymus.** *Int J Exp Pathol* 1991, **72**:275-287. [general reference]

Supplement Review

HLA-B27: natural function and pathogenic role in spondyloarthritis

Andrew McMichael* and Paul Bowness*†

*MRC Human Immunology Group, Weatherall Institute of Molecular Medicine, John Radcliffe Hospital, Oxford, UK
†Nuffield Orthopaedic Centre, Oxford, UK

Correspondence: Paul Bowness, MRC Human Immunology Group, Weatherall Institute of Molecular Medicine, John Radcliffe Hospital, Oxford OX3 9DS, UK. Tel: +44 (0)1865 222 334; fax: +44 (0)1865 222 502; e-mail: pbpwness@molbiol.ox.ac.uk; department website: http://users.imm.ox.ac.uk/groups/mrc-hiu

Received: 22 February 2002
Accepted: 25 February 2002
Published: 9 May 2002

Arthritis Res 2002, **4 (suppl 3)**:S153-S158

This article may contain supplementary data which can only be found online at http://arthritis-research.com/content/4/S3/S153

© 2002 BioMed Central Ltd
(Print ISSN 1465-9905; Online ISSN 1465-9913)

Chapter summary

The human leukocyte antigen HLA-B27 is strongly associated with development of a group of inflammatory arthritides collectively known as the spondyloarthritides. We have set out to define the natural immunological function of HLA-B27, and then to apply this knowledge to understand its pathogenic role. Human leukocyte antigen class 1 molecules bind antigenic peptides for cell surface presentation to cytotoxic T lymphocytes. HLA-B27 binds and presents peptides from influenza, HIV, Epstein–Barr virus, and other viruses. This leads to vigorous and specific cytotoxic T lymphocyte responses, which play an important role in the body's immune response to these viruses. HLA-B27 thus carries out its natural function highly effectively. Although many theories have been proposed to explain the role of HLA-B27 in the pathogenesis of spondyloarthropathy, we favour those postulating that the pathogenic role of HLA-B27 stems from its natural function. For example, the 'arthritogenic' peptide hypothesis suggests that disease results from the ability of HLA-B27 to bind a unique peptide or a set of antigenic peptides. Additionally, a number of lines of evidence from our laboratory and other laboratories have suggested that HLA-B27 has unusual cell biology. We have recently demonstrated that HLA-B27 is capable of forming disulfide-bonded homodimers. These homodimers are expressed on the cell surface and are ligands for a number of natural killer and related immunoreceptors, expressed on a variety of cell types including natural killer cells, T lymphocytes and B lymphocytes, and members of the monocyte/macrophage lineage. We are currently investigating the possibility that such interactions could be involved in disease pathogenesis.

Keywords: cytotoxic C cell, HLA-B27, peptide, spondyloarthritis

Introduction

This chapter will first describe the natural function of HLA-B27, before presenting possible mechanisms by which HLA-B27 might be involved in disease pathogenesis. We will review the data available from HLA-B27 transgenic animals, from structural studies and from biochemical analysis of HLA-B27 function. A concluding section will identify key lines of current and future research.

Historical background

Possession of the human leukocyte antigen (HLA) class 1 allele HLA-B27 is strongly associated with development of the spondyloarthritides, a group of related diseases including ankylosing spondylitis and reactive arthritis (see Table 1). Ankylosing spondylitis is a common inflammatory rheumatic disease, affecting up to 0.5% of the population. The association of HLA-B27 with ankylosing spondylitis

---

A glossary of specialist terms used in this chapter appears at the end of the text section. A list of common abbreviations used in this issue appears just before the indexes.

Table 1

HLA-B27-associated spondyloarthritides

Disease	HLA-B27 frequency (%) (approximate)
Ankylosing spondylitis	96
Undifferentiated spondyloarthropathy	70
Reactive arthritis	30–70
Colitis-associated spondyloarthritis	33–75
Psoriatic spondyloarthritis	40–50
Juvenile enthesitis-related arthritis	70
Iritis	50
Cardiac conduction defects with aortic incompetence	Up to 88

was first described in 1973 [1], and is among the strongest described for a HLA locus. A recent study found that 94% of ankylosing spondylitis patients are HLA-B27-positive, compared with 9.4% of controls, giving an odds ratio of 161 with a 95% confidence interval of 113–230 [2]. HLA-B27 is also less significantly associated with reactive arthritis [3] and with the spondyloarthritis associated with psoriasis and inflammatory bowel disease [4]. These conditions share clinical features including arthritis of the spine and large joints, and involvement of the skin, eye, genital mucosa and heart.

While the pathogenic role of HLA-B27 in the spondyloarthropathies is unknown, numerous theories have been proposed. These theories are reviewed in [5], and many are applicable to the HLA associations with other autoimmune diseases (reviewed in [6]). Some theories suggest that the pathogenic role of HLA-B27 is independent of its immune function; for example, suggesting that HLA-B27 acts as a receptor for a disease-causing microorganism or is even merely a genetic marker for the true gene responsible. We favour theories suggesting that the pathogenic role of HLA-B27 stems from its immunological role. The 'arthritogenic' peptide theory (see later) proposes that HLA acts to present antigens to T cells. Alternatively, it is possible that HLA-B27 itself acts as a source of antigen, providing peptides that can be presented by other HLA molecules.

The finding that the natural role of HLA molecules is peptide binding and presentation to T cells [7,8] led to the suggestion that the spondyloarthropathies result from the ability of HLA-B27 to bind a unique set of peptides [9]. This 'arthritogenic' peptide hypothesis proposes that disease results from an HLA-B27-restricted cytotoxic T-cell response to a peptide or peptides found only in joint and other affected tissues. Such a peptide could be bound and presented by all disease-associated HLA-B27 subtypes

(see later), but not by other class I molecules. Pathogenic T cells might be primed in the joint or at other sites such as the genital or gut mucosa. A modification of this original hypothesis could entail a breakdown of self-tolerance by initial HLA-B27-restricted presentation of a peptide or peptides derived from one of the triggering pathogens.

If the disease association of HLA-B27 is indeed a consequence of its physiological role in peptide presentation, HLA-B27-restricted cytotoxic T lymphocytes (CTL), specific for self-epitopes or bacterial epitopes, should be demonstrable in the involved joints of patients with spondyloarthropathies. Although Yersinia-specific and Salmonella-specific clones have been isolated from two patients with reactive arthritis [10], many groups have found predominant CD4 T-cell responses to triggering bacteria within the joint.

Although an arthritogenic peptide model of disease causation is supported by the epidemiological and functional studies of HLA-B27 subtypes (see later), evidence from patients and from transgenic models (see later) suggests that other factors and mechanisms need to be considered.

Animal models of HLA-B27-associated disease

Rats and mice carrying HLA-B27 as a transgene provide strong evidence that HLA-B27 is directly involved in disease pathogenesis. These animals can develop illnesses similar to the spondyloarthropathies. Rats carrying a high copy number of HLA-B*2705 transgenes develop an illness characterized by peripheral and axial arthritis, gut inflammation, and genital and skin lesions [11]. Interestingly, rats kept in germ-free conditions do not develop the inflammatory intestinal or peripheral joint disease [12]. It appears that this disease can be transferred by foetal liver cells alone, suggesting that antigen presentation by HLA-B27 in peripheral tissues such as joints is not essential for development of disease [13].

Mice transgenic for HLA-B27 do not normally develop disease. However, spontaneous inflammatory arthritis develops in mice transgenic for HLA-B27 but lacking murine beta-2-microglobulin (β2m), following transfer from germ-free to conventional conditions [14]. In the absence β2m, these animals express very low levels of class 1 molecules. Although normally conformed HLA-B27 is not expressed in these mice, HLA-B27 heavy chains (not associated with β2m) can be detected on the cell surface of concanavalin A-treated peripheral blood leukocytes using the monoclonal antibody HC10 [15].

HLA-B27 structure and function

Much is now known of the molecular structure, peptide-binding specificity and cell biology of HLA-B27. Solution of the crystal structure of HLA-B27, crystallized with a mixture of self-peptides [16], showed that short peptides are bound in an extended conformation within a peptide binding groove. A common arginine residue was found at the second position of all bound peptides. The long side chain of this arginine was accommodated in the 'B' or '45' pocket, comprising in HLA-B27 a unique combination of residues: 45E, 67C, 34V, 26G and 24T. Amino acid analysis of self-peptides eluted from HLA-B27 has confirmed the presence of this arginine residue at the second position [17,18]. Arginine at the second position of the bound peptide is thus an anchor residue for HLA-B27.

There are also preferences for particular amino acids at other positions, with these preferences differing between different HLA-B27 subtypes. HLA-B*2705 thus appears to bind peptides with C terminal amino acids that are either aromatic, hydrophobic or positively charged, whereas HLA-B*2702 can probably only accommodate aromatic or hydrophobic residues at this position [18]. Finally, measurement of the ability of different peptides to bind to HLA-B27 has confirmed the importance of the P2 arginine (for example [19,20]), and also confirmed that different subtypes probably bind different but overlapping subsets of peptides [21,22].

Molecular epidemiological studies have confirmed the association of HLA-B*2702, HLA-B*2704, and HLA-B*2705 with spondyloarthritis first described by Breur-Vriesendorp et al. [23,24]. However, molecular epidemiological studies of other subtypes have produced somewhat conflicting results. Thus, although HLA-B*2703 and HLA-B*2706 have been reported as not associated with disease [24,25], spondyloarthropathy patients bearing these subtypes have subsequently been described [26]. This is an important area of research as these subtypes differ principally in their peptide-binding specificities, and these findings, if confirmed, would support arthritogenic peptide models of pathogenesis.

The role of HLA-B27 in immune responses to viral infection
We have shown that individuals infected with influenza A or HIV make vigorous CTL responses to specific viral peptide epitopes that are presented by HLA-B27 [27,28]. Evidence that HLA-B27-restricted CTL play a major role in HIV infection has recently come from long-term studies of the viral sequence. For certain patients, viral 'escape' mutants that no longer bind to HLA-B27 accumulate after a number of years. These patients, but not those retaining the original viral sequence, progressed to develop AIDS [29].

Using the response to influenza nucleoprotein residues 383–391 as a model, we previously defined the rules for peptide binding to HLA-B27, and identified the key residues for subsequent recognition by the T-cell receptor for antigen (TCR) of cytotoxic T cells [19]. Both healthy and spondyloarthritis patients made good HLA-B27-

restricted CTL responses, showing that there is nothing abnormal about the natural function of HLA-B27 in patients with spondyloarthropathy. These findings have also allowed us to predict which residues of a potential arthritogenic peptide could be flexible or conserved if molecular mimicry plays a role in disease pathogenesis.

Finally, we have also shown that the TCR of CTL recognizing the HLA-B27/influenza nucleoprotein peptide combination use a highly conserved repertoire of TCRs [30]. This has lead to studies of the TCR repertoire in patients with spondyloarthropathy, which found evidence of expanded T-cell populations [31], of which some bear identical or almost identical TCRBV chain sequences. One interpretation of these findings is that these oligoclonal expansions are driven by a self-antigen within the joint, presumably presented by HLA-B27 (May et al., unpublished data).

New developments and future prospects in the study of peptide presentation by HLA-B27
The generation of fluorogenic multimeric major histocompatibility complexes (usually tetramers) has recently proven invaluable for phenotypic analysis of viral responses ex vivo [32]. This technique is now also being applied to the study of autoimmune disease, and has recently been reviewed in Arthritis Research [33]. We have made fluorescent HLA-B27/β2m/peptide tetramers for use in studying T-cell recognition of defined complexes, such as with the influenza peptide [34].

Recent advances in genomics and bioinformatics promise to revolutionize our investigation of autoimmune and infectious diseases. For example, 'search' programs have been developed that can identify potential HLA-B27-binding epitopes as well as those likely to be generated by the proteosome. These methods have now been exploited to hunt for potential arthritogenic peptides within the genome of Chlamydia trachomatis, one of the organisms known to trigger reactive arthritis. Peptides have been identified and immune responses detected in both HLA-B27 transgenic mice and in patients with reactive arthritis (following C. trachomatis infection) using both enzyme-linked immunospot (ELISPOT) assays and tetrameric HLA-B27/β2m/peptide complexes [35].

HLA-B27 cell biology and disease
Another distinct, but not necessarily exclusive, possibility is that unique features of the biochemistry or cell biology of HLA-B27 predispose to disease development. A number of lines of evidence suggest that HLA-B27 may not behave like most other class 1 molecules.

An early observation that cell surface HLA-B27 molecules were peptide-receptive lead to the suggestion that disease might result from presentation to T cells of extra-

Figure 1

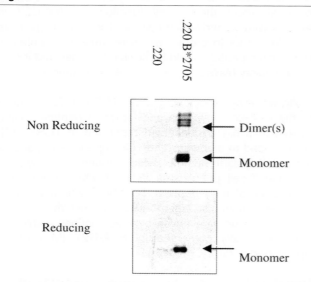

Disulfide-bonded HLA-B27 heavy chain homodimers are present in HLA-B*2705 transfected LBL721.220 cells. HC-10 western blot shown under non-reducing (upper panel) and reducing (lower panel) conditions. The left-hand lane shows untransfected 721.220 cells.

cellular peptides not normally accessible to the class 1 processing pathway [36]. Unusually long peptides have been isolated bound to HLA-B27 [37]. We have recently shown that HLA-B27 heavy chains can form homodimers *in vitro* that are dependent on disulfide bonding through their cysteine 67 residues [38]. These homodimers do not contain β2m but are capable of peptide binding, and adopt a different conformation to 'standard' β2m-associated HLA-B27 complexes; for example, reacting with the monoclonal antibody HC10. These 'HC-B27' homodimers can be detected at the cell surface of HLA-B27-transfected cell lines, and are more abundantly expressed when

the cell's antigen-presenting function is impaired (Bird *et al.*, unpublished observations).

Figure 1 shows an example of HLA-B27 heavy chain homodimer expression in the cell line LBL721.220. A key role for the unpaired cysteine at position 67 of the HLA-B27 alpha 1 helix is suggested by site-directed mutagenesis (Bird *et al.*, unpublished observations). Figure 2 shows a molecular model of a HLA-B27 homodimer. A disulfide bond is shown between position 67 of the two HLA-B27 heavy chains. It is not yet known whether HC-B27 homodimer expression is specific for, or indeed correlates with, spondyloarthropathy, or whether HLA-B27-negative patients with spondyloarthritis express homodimers of other HLA alleles. Interestingly, we have recently observed HLA-B27 homodimer expression at the cell surface of HLA-B27+/β2m knockout mice.

These and other findings have lead to two novel hypotheses for disease causation. Colbert and colleagues have proposed that homodimer formation is a symptom of HLA-B27 'misfolding' within the endoplasmic reticulum, and that accumulation of misfolded protein results in a potentially proinflammatory intracellular stress response [39]. Alternatively, we have suggested that HLA-B27 heavy chain homodimers may be expressed at the cell surface, where they may act as a proinflammatory target or receptor for humoral or cell-mediated autoimmune responses.

We have recently shown that tetrameric complexes of HLA-B27 heavy chain homodimers bind to certain natural killer (NK) and related receptors, expressed on lymphocytes, NK cells and cells of the monocyte/macrophage lineage. (Kollnberger *et al.*, unpublished data). The functional outcome of the interaction of HLA-B27 with NK receptors and other immunoreceptors is as yet unclear. Although many killer immunoglobulin-like receptors have inhibitory effects, there is accumulating evidence that

Figure 2

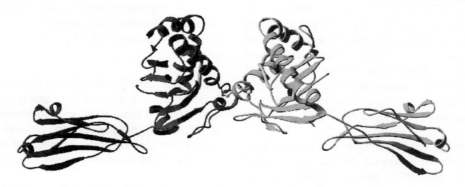

Hypothetical molecular model of the HLA-B27 heavy chain homodimer structure. The alpha 1, 2, and 3 domains of two HLA-B27 molecules are shown in ribbon form, bound peptide shown. Orientation: cell surface at bottom of picture. See Colour figure section.

Figure 3

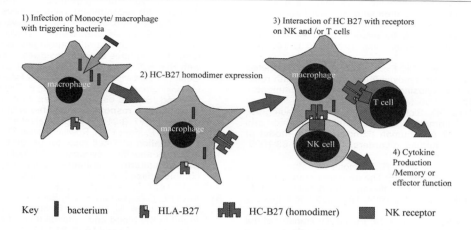

1) Infection of Monocyte/ macrophage with triggering bacteria

2) HC-B27 homodimer expression

3) Interaction of HC B27 with receptors on NK and /or T cells

4) Cytokine Production /Memory or effector function

Key   bacterium   HLA-B27   HC-B27 (homodimer)   NK receptor

Hypothetical model for the role of HLA-B27 homodimers in the pathogenesis of spondyloarthritis. NK, natural killer. See Colour figure section.

expression of certain receptors is associated with prolonged survival of memory T cells [40].

One possible model of disease causation is presented in Figure 3. We first show infection of HLA-B27-expressing cells by an organism capable of triggering spondyloarthropathy. This infection results in interference of the cellular antigen-presenting function and consequent expression of aberrant HLA-B27 homodimers [2]. Notably, other stresses at other sites (e.g. mucosae) could have similar effects. Cell-surface B27 homodimers engage NK or related immunoreceptors expressed on lymphocytes or other cells within the joint, resulting in local cytokine production or enhanced cellular activity [4], and hence perpetuating joint inflammation. Since both CD8 and CD4 T cells can express NK receptors, such a hypothesis could explain the involvement of either cells in disease pathogenesis (expanded populations of both CD4 and CD8 T cells are found in reactive arthritis [31]).

An alternative explanation for the involvement of CD4 T cells in spondyloarthropathy has been suggested by recent evidence from Gaston's group showing that HLA-B27 can itself be recognized by CD4 T cells. Different patterns of reactivity have been identified, and it has been suggested that empty or homodimeric forms are being recognized [41]. This is an exciting area for future study.

Concluding remarks
Work from our group and other groups has shown that HLA-B27 appears to excel at its natural function of binding and presenting viral peptide epitopes to cytotoxic T cells. We have suggested that HLA-B27 may, however, act as a 'double-edged sword'. Thus, certain features of its peptide binding ability or cell biology (perhaps those favouring excellent antiviral responses) might also lead to

autoimmunity. The recent demonstration that HLA-B27 can interact with a number of different immunoreceptors on different cell types has opened up promising new avenues of research into clarifying its role in the pathogenesis of spondyloarthropathy.

Glossary of terms
β2m = beta-2-microglobulin; HC10 = a monoclonal antibody with specificity for HLA class I heavy chains; HC-B27 = β2m-unassociated HLA-B27 heavy chain homodimer.

Acknowledgement
This work was funded by the Medical Research Council and Arthritis Research Campaign.

References
1. Brewerton DA, Caffrey M, Hart FD, James DCO, Nichols A, Sturrock RD: **Ankylosing spondylitis and HL-A27.** *Lancet* 1973, i:904-907. [archival research]
2. Brown MA, Pile KD, Kennedy LG, Calin A, Darke C, Bell J, Wordsworth BP, Cornelis F: **HLA class I associations of ankylosing spondylitis in the white population in the United Kingdom.** *Ann Rheum Dis* 1996, **55**:268-270. [general reference]
3. Brewerton DA, Caffrey M, Hart FD, James DCO, Nichols A, Sturrock RD: **Reiters disease and HL-A27.** *Lancet* 1974, ii:996-998. [archival research]
4. Orchard TR, Thiyagaraja S, Welsh KI, Wordsworth BP, Hill Gaston JS, Jewell DP: **Clinical phenotype is related to HLA genotype in the peripheral arthropathies of inflammatory bowel disease.** *Gastroenterology* 2000, **118**:274-278. [general reference]
5. Allen RL, Bowness P, McMichael A: **The role of HLA-B27 in spondyloarthritis.** *Immunogenetics* 1999, **50**:220-227. [key review]
6. Hall F, Bowness P: **HLA and disease: from molecular function to disease association.** In: *HLA and MHC: Genes, Molecules and Function.* Edited by Browning M, McMichael AJ. Oxford: Bios Scientific; 1996:353-381. [key review]
7. Townsend A, Rothbard J, Gotch F, Bahadur B, Wraith D, McMichael A: **The epitopes of influenza nucleoprotein recognized by cytotoxic T lymphocytes can be defined with short synthetic peptides.** *Cell* 1986, **44**:959-968. [archival research]

8. Gotch F, Rothbard J, Howland K, Townsend A, McMichael A: **Cytotoxic T lymphocytes recognise a fragment of influenza virus matrix protein in association with HLA-A2.** *Nature* 1987, **326**:881-882. [archival research]

9. Benjamin R, Parham P: **Guilt by association: HLA B27 and ankylosing spondylitis.** *Immunol Today* 1990, **11**:137-142. [key review]

10. Hermann E, Yu DT, Meyer zBK, Fleischer B: **HLA-B27-restricted CD8 T cells derived from synovial fluids of patients with reactive arthritis and ankylosing spondylitis [see comments].** *Lancet* 1993, **342**:646-650. [archival research]

11. Hammer RE, Maika SD, Richardson JA, Tang J-P, Taurog JD: **Spontaneous inflammatory disease in transgenic rats expressing HLA-B27 and human β2m: an animal model of HLA-B27-associated human disorders.** *Cell* 1990, **63**:1099-1112. [archival research]

12. Taurog JD, Richardson JA, Croft JT, Simmons WA, Zhou M, Fernandez SJL, Balish E, Hammer RE: **The germfree state prevents development of gut and joint inflammatory disease in HLA-B27 transgenic rats.** *J Exp Med* 1994, **180**:2359-2364. [general reference]

13. Breban M, Hammer RE, Ricardson JA, Taurog JD: **Transfer of the inflammatory disease of HLA-B27 transgenic rats by bone marrow engraftment.** *J Exp Med* 1993, **178**:1607-1616. [general reference]

14. Khare SD, Luthra HS, David CS: **Spontaneous inflammatory arthritis in HLA-B27 transgenic mice lacking beta 2-microglobulin: a model of human spondyloarthropathies.** *J Exp Med* 1995, **182**:1153-1158. [general reference]

15. Khare SD, Hansen J, Luthra HS, David CS: **HLA-B27 heavy chains contribute to spontaneous inflammatory disease in B27/human beta2-microglobulin (beta2m) double transgenic mice with disrupted mouse beta2m.** *J Clin Invest* 1996, **98**:2746-2755. [general reference]

16. Madden DR, Gorga JC, Strominger JL, Wiley DC: **The structure of HLA B27 reveals nonamer self-peptides bound in an extended conformation.** *Nature* 1991, **353**:321-325. [archival research]

17. Jardetzky TS, Lane WS, Robinson RA, Madden DR, Wiley DC: **Identification of self peptides bound to purified HLA-B27.** *Nature* 1991, **353**:326-329. [archival research]

18. Rotzschke O, Falk F, Stevanovic S, Gnau V, Jung G, Rammensee H-G: **Dominant aromatic/aliphatic C-terminal anchor in HLA-B*2702 and B*2705 peptide motifs.** *Immunogenetics* 1994, **39**:74-77. [general reference]

19. Bowness P, Allen RL, McMichael AJ: **Identification of T cell receptor recognition residues for a viral peptide presented by HLA B27.** *Eur J Immunol* 1994, **24**:2357-2363. [general reference]

20. Colbert RA, Rowland-Jones SL, McMichael AJ, Frelinger JA: **Allele-specific B pocket transplant in class 1 major histocompatibility complex protein changes requirement for anchor residue at P2 of peptide.** *Proc Natl Acad Sci USA* 1993, **90**:6879-6883. [general reference]

21. Tanigaki N, Fruci D, Vigneti E, Starace G, Rovero P, Londei M, Butler RH, Tosi R: **The peptide binding specificity of HLA-B27 subtypes.** *Immunogenetics* 1994, **40**:192-198. [general reference]

22. Colbert RA, Rowland-Jones SL, McMichael AJ, Frelinger JA: **Differences in peptide presentation between B27 subtypes: the importance of the P1 side chain in maintaining high affinity peptide binding to B*2703.** *Immunity* 1994, **1**:121-130. [general reference]

23. Breur-Vriesendorp S, Dekker-Says A, Ivanyi P: **Distribution of HLA-B27 subtypes in patients with ankylosing spondylitis: the disease is associated with a common determinant of the various B27 molecules.** *Ann Rheum Dis* 1987, **46**:353-356. [archival research]

24. Hill AVS, Allsopp CEM, Kwiatowski D, Anstey NM, Greenwood BM, McMichael AJ: **HLA class I typing by PCR: HLA-B27 and an African subtype.** *Lancet* 1991, **337**:640-642. [general reference]

25. Lopez-Larrea C, Sujirachato K, Mehr N, Chiewsilp P, Isarangkura D, Kanga U, Dominguez O, Coto E, Pena M, Setien F, Gonzalez-Roces S: **HLA-B27 subtypes in Asian patients with ankylosing spondylitis. Evidence for new associations.** *Tissue Antigens* 1995, **45**:169-176. [general reference]

26. Khan MA: **HLA-B27 polymorphism and association with disease [editorial] [see comments].** *J Rheumatol* 2000, **27**:1110-1114. [key review]

27. Nixon DF, Townsend ARM, Elvin JG, Rizza CR, Gallwey J, McMichael AJ: **HIV-1 gag-specific cytotoxic T lymphocytes defined with recombinant vaccinia virus and synthetic peptides.** *Nature* 1988, **336**:484-487. [archival research]

28. Huet S, Nixon DF, Rothbard J, Townsend ARM, Ellis SA, McMichael AJ: **Structural homologies between two HLA B27 restricted peptides suggest residues important for interaction with HLA B27.** *Int Immunol* 1990, **2**:311-316. [general reference]

29. Goulder PJ, Phillips RE, Colbert RA, McAdam S, Ogg G, Nowak MA, Giangrande P, Luzzi G, Morgan B, Edwards A, McMichael AJ, Rowland JS: **Late escape from an immunodominant cytotoxic T-lymphocyte response associated with progression to AIDS.** *Nat Med* 1997, **3**:212-217. [general reference]

30. Bowness P, Moss PAH, Rowland-Jones SL, Bell JI, McMichael AJ: **Conservation of T-cell receptor usage by HLA B27-restricted influenza-specific cytotoxic T-lymphocytes suggests a general pattern for antigen-specific major histocompatibility complex class-i-restricted responses.** *Eur J Immunol* 1993, **23**:1417-1421. [general reference]

31. Allen RL, Gillespie GM, Hall F, Edmonds S, Hall MA, Wordsworth BP, McMichael AJ, Bowness P: **Multiple T cell expansions are found in the blood and synovial fluid of patients with reactive arthritis.** *J Rheumatol* 1997, **24**:1750-1757. [general reference]

32. Altman JD, Moss P, Goulder P, Barouch DH, McHeyzer WM, Bell JI, McMichael AJ, Davis MM: **Phenotypic analysis of antigen-specific T lymphocytes.** *Science* 1996, **274**:94-96. [general reference]

33. Sun MY, Bowness P: **MHC class I multimers.** *Arthritis Res* 2001, **3**:265-269. [key review]

34. Bowness P, Allen RL, Barclay DN, Jones EY, McMichael AJ: **Importance of a conserved TCR J alpha-encoded tyrosine for T cell recognition of an HLA B27/peptide complex.** *Eur J Immunol* 1998, **28**:2704-2713. [general reference]

35. Kuon W, Holzhutter HG, Appel H, Grolms M, Kollnberger S, Traeder A, Henklein P, Weiss E, Thiel A, Lauster R, Bowness P, Radbruch A, Kloetzel PM, Sieper J: **Identification of HLA-B27-restricted peptides from the Chlamydia trachomatis proteome with possible relevance to HLA-B27-associated diseases.** *J Immunol* 2001, **167**:4738-4746. [general reference]

36. Benjamin RJ, Madrigal J, Parham P: **Peptide binding to empty HLA-B27 molecules of viable human cells.** *Nature* 1991, **351**:74-77. [general reference]

37. Urban RG, Chicz RM, Lane WS, Strominger JL, Rehm A, Kenter MJH, Uytdehaag FGCM, Ploegh H, Uchanska ZB, Ziegler A: **A subset of HLA-B27 molecules contains peptides much longer than nonamers.** *Proc Natl Acad Sci USA* 1994, **91**:1534-1538. [general reference]

38. Allen RL, O'Callaghan CA, McMichael AJ, Bowness P: **Cutting edge: HLA-B27 can form a novel beta 2-microglobulin-free heavy chain homodimer structure.** *J Immunol* 1999, **162**:5045-5048. [general reference]

39. Mear JP, Schreiber KL, Munz C, Zhu X, Stevanovic S, Rammensee HG, Rowland-Jones SL, Colbert RA: **Misfolding of HLA-B27 as a result of its B pocket suggests a novel mechanism for its role in susceptibility to spondyloarthropathies.** *J Immunol* 1999, **163**:6665-6670. [general reference]

40. Young NT, Uhrberg M, Phillips JH, Lanier LL, Parham P: **Differential expression of leukocyte receptor complex-encoded Ig-like receptors correlates with the transition from effector to memory CTL.** *J Immunol* 2001, **166**:3933-3941. [general reference]

41. Boyle LH, Goodall JC, Opat SS, Gaston JS: **The recognition of HLA-B27 by human CD4(+) T lymphocytes.** *J Immunol* 2001, **167**:2619-2624. [general reference]

Cytokines

Supplement Review

The contrasting roles of IL-2 and IL-15 in the life and death of lymphocytes: implications for the immunotherapy of rheumatological diseases

Thomas Waldmann

Metabolism Branch, National Cancer Institute, National Institutes of Health, Bethesda, MD, USA

Correspondence: Thomas Waldmann, Metabolism Branch, National Cancer Institute, NIH, Bethesda, MD 20892, USA.
Tel: +1 301 496 6656; fax: +1 301 496 9956; e-mail: tawald@helix.nih.gov

Received: 19 December 2001
Accepted: 10 February 2002
Published: 9 May 2002

Arthritis Res 2002, **4 (suppl 3)**:S161-S167

This article may contain supplementary data which can only be found online at http://arthritis-research.com/content/4/S3/S161

Chapter summary

Interleukin-15 (IL-15) is a 14–15-kDa member of the 4α helix bundle family of cytokines that stimulate T and NK (natural killer) cells. IL-15 and IL-2 utilize heterotrimeric receptors that include the cytokine-specific private receptors IL-2Rα and IL-15Rα, as well as two receptor elements that they share, IL-2Rβ and γc. Although IL-2 and IL-15 share two receptor subunits and many functions, at times they provide contrasting contributions to T-cell-mediated immune responses. IL-2, through its pivotal role in activation-induced cell death (AICD), is involved in peripheral tolerance through the elimination of self-reactive T cells. In contrast, IL-15 in general manifests anti-apoptotic actions and inhibits IL-2-mediated AICD. IL-15 stimulates the persistence of memory phenotype CD8+ T cells, whereas IL-2 inhibits their expression. Abnormalities of IL-15 expression have been described in patients with rheumatoid arthritis or inflammatory bowel disease and in diseases associated with the retrovirus HTLV-I (human T-cell lymphotropic virus I). Humanized monoclonal antibodies that recognize IL-2Rα, the private receptor for IL-2, are being employed to inhibit allograft rejection and to treat T-cell leukemia/lymphoma. New approaches directed toward inhibiting the actions of the inflammatory cytokine, IL-15, are proposed for an array of autoimmune disorders including rheumatoid arthritis as well as diseases associated with the retrovirus HTLV-I.

Keywords: interleukin-2, interleukin-15, rheumatoid arthritis

Introduction

Intracellular communications involved in immune responses are often mediated by cytokines that show a high degree of redundancy and pleiotropy, controlling a wide range of functions in various cell types. Disordered expression of cytokines has been shown to play a role in autoimmune diseases such as rheumatoid arthritis (RA). In particular, abnormalities of TNF-α and such downstream mediators of proinflamatory activity as IL-1, IL-6, granulocyte/macrophage-colony-stimulating factor (GM-CSF),

and inflammatory chemokines have been demonstrated in RA [1]. Recently, disorders involving interleukin (IL)-15 have been demonstrated in this autoimmune disease as well [2–10]. IL-2 and IL-15 utilize heterotrimeric receptors that include cytokine-specific private receptors IL-2Rα and IL-15Rα respectively, as well as two receptor elements, IL-2Rβ and γc, that they share [11–14]. We and others have shown that although IL-2 and IL-15 share two receptors and therefore share many functions, they also provide distinct and at times contrasting contributions to the life and

A glossary of specialist terms used in this chapter appears at the end of the text section. A list of common abbreviations used in this issue appears just before the indexes.

death of lymphocytes [15–19]. IL-2, through its pivotal role in activation-induced cell death (AICD), is involved in peripheral tolerance through the elimination of self-reactive T cells [20]. In contrast, IL-15 in general manifests anti-apoptotic actions and inhibits AICD and stimulates the persistence of memory phenotype CD8+ T cells [17,18]. Abnormalities of IL-15 expression have been reported in inflammatory, autoimmune, and neoplastic diseases [2–10,21–24]. In particular, abnormally high levels of IL-15 transcription and translation are observed in human T-cell lymphotropic virus I (HTLV-I)-associated diseases such as the neurological disorder tropical spastic para-paresis/HTLV-I associated myelopathy (TSP/HAM) [23,24]. Furthermore, abnormalities of IL-15 expression have been noted in patients with autoimmune diseases such as RA and inflammatory bowel disease [2–10, 21–24]. Therapeutic agents are being developed to target the receptor and signaling elements shared by IL-2 and IL-15 to provide effective treatment for such autoimmune disorders as well as the leukemia/lymphomas that are associated with the retrovirus HTLV-I [9,10,19].

Historical background

Two separate groups simultaneously reported the recognition of the novel cytokine now known as IL-15, which was recognized as novel on the basis of the ability of culture supernatants from two cell lines, CV-1/EBNA and the HTLV-I-associated HuT-102, to stimulate proliferation of the cytokine-dependent murine T cell CTLL-2 in the absence of IL-2 [12,13]. During studies to define patho-genic mechanisms that underlie the IL-2-independent pro-liferation of HTLV-I-associated adult T-cell leukemia cells, our group found that the ATL (adult T-cell leukemia) cell line HuT-102 secretes a 14–15-kDa lymphokine, which we provisionally designated IL-T, that stimulates T-cell pro-liferation and induces activation of large, granular lympho-cytes [12,25]. In addition, we showed that IL-T-mediated stimulation requires the expression of the IL-2Rβ subunit [12]. Grabstein and co-workers simultaneously reported a cytokine they designated IL-15, which was isolated from the supernatant of the simian kidney epithelial-cell line CV-1/EBNA [13]. IL-15 shared many characteristics with IL-T, including an apparent molecular mass of 14–15 kDa, as well as a signaling pathway in T and natural killer (NK) cells that utilized the IL-2Rβ and γc subunits of the IL-2 receptor. By use of an appropriate anti-cytokine antibody, IL-T and IL-15 were shown to be identical [19].

IL-2/IL-15 cytokine family

Cytokines exhibit a high degree of redundancy and pleiotropy, which is explained in part by the sharing of common receptor subunits among members of the cytokine receptor family. Each cytokine has its own private receptor, but may also share public receptor subunits with other cytokines. This is the case in the IL-2 receptor system. The IL-2R is made up of at least three distinct membrane components: the 55-kDa alpha chain (IL-2Rα); the 70–75-kDa β chain (IL-2Rβ); and the 64-kDa common γ chain (γc) chain, which is shared with other members of this system, including IL-4, IL-7, IL-9, IL-15, and IL-21. IL-2 and IL-15 also share the IL-2Rβ subunit [11–14].

The regulation of IL-15 expression

IL-2 and IL-15 exhibit major differences in the levels of control of their synthesis and secretion and in their sites of synthesis [19,26,27]. IL-2 is produced by activated T cells and its expression is regulated predominantly at the levels of mRNA transcription and message stabilization. In contrast, there is widespread constitutive expression of IL-15 mRNA in a variety of tissues, including placenta, skeletal muscle, kidney, lung, heart, fibroblasts, and activated monocytes [13,19].

The regulation of IL-15 expression is multifaceted. Modest control occurs at the level of transcription, whereas a dominant control occurs post-transcriptionally, at the levels of translation and intercellular trafficking [19,26,28]. Although IL-15 mRNA is widely expressed constitutively, it has been difficult to demonstrate IL-15 within the cells or the supernatants of cells that express such IL-15 mRNA. Multiple controlling elements impede the translation of IL-15 mRNA, including a long 5′ UTR containing IL-13 upstream AUGs, an unusually long (48-amino-acid) IL-15 signal peptide, and an inhibitory element in the C terminus of the IL-15 mature coding sequence or protein [19,26,27]. These multiple negative regulatory features controlling IL-15 expression may be required, in light of the potency of IL-15 as an inflammatory cytokine that stimulates the expression of TNF-α, IL-1β, and inflammatory chemokines, which if indiscriminately expressed could lead to inflammatory autoimmune diseases. In terms of a more positive role for IL-15, by maintaining a pool of trans-lationally inactive mRNA, cells may respond rapidly to an intracellular infection by transforming the IL-15 mRNA into a form that can be translated effectively, yielding secreted IL-15 that may activate T and NK cells that could then aid in the host response to the invading pathogen.

The shared and contrasting roles of IL-2 and IL-15 in the life and death of lymphocytes

Functions mediated by IL-2 and IL-15 may be evaluated with regard to the fundamental goals of the immune system, which may be considered to include the generation of a rapid innate and adapative response to invading pathogens; the maintenance of a specific memory response to these pathogens; and the elimination of host-reactive T cells, to yield tolerance to self.

As might be anticipated from their sharing of the IL-2Rβ and γc subunits in T and NK cells, IL-15 and IL-2 share a number of biological activities, including stimulation of the proliferation of activated CD4+CD8+ as well as γδ subsets of T cells [19,29–31]. IL-2 and IL-15 also facilitate the induction of cytolytic effector cells, including CTL and LAK cells [19,29–31]. In addition, both IL-2 and IL-15 act as chemoattractants for T cells. The two cytokines stimulate the proliferation of NK cells and can synergize with IL-12 to facilitate their synthesis of IFN-γ and TNF-α [31]. Both cytokines induce the proliferation and immunoglobulin synthesis by human B cells stimulated with anti-IgM or CD40 ligand [32].

A major advance emerging from work in our laboratory and those of others is that although IL-2 and IL-15 share two receptor subunits and some functions, they also provide distinct and at times contrasting contributions to the life and death of lymphocytes [15–19]. Although IL-2 is an important growth and survival factor, it also plays a critical role in Fas-mediated activation-induced cell death (AICD) of CD4 T cells [20]. Receptor-mediated stimulation of CD4 T cells by antigen at high concentration (or by CD3 plus CD28) induces the expression of IL-2 and the IL-2 receptor, which in turn interact to yield T-cell activation and T-cell cycling. Antigen stimulation of the cycling T cells at this stage through the T-cell antigen receptor increases the transcription and surface expression of the death-effector molecule Fas ligand (FasL). The interaction of FasL with Fas then leads to death of the self-reactive T cells [20]. My colleagues and I showed that IL-15, in contrast, acts to extend the survival of lymphocytes, both by acting as a growth factor and by inhibiting IL-2-mediated AICD of CD4 T cells [17]. In ex vivo studies, CD4+ T cells from IL-15 transgenic mice that we developed did not manifest IL-2-mediated AICD.

In addition to their distinct actions on AICD, IL-2 and IL-15 play opposing roles in the homeostasis of CD8+ memory phenotype T cells [17]. Zhang and Ku and their co-workers [15,16] reported that the division and survival of CD8+ T cells of memory phenotype is stimulated by IL-15. We in turn showed that our transgenic mice had abnormally elevated numbers of CD8+ memory phenotype T cells. Furthermore, we defined a role for IL-15 and its receptor in the HTLV-I-associated neurological disease tropical spastic paraparesis (TSP/HAM) [33]. The number of circulating MHC class I restricted antigen (amino acids 11–19 of the HTLV-I-encoded tax protein) specific memory CD8+ cells that have been suggested to be involved in the pathogenesis of TSP was shown by tetramer technology to be markedly increased in the circulation of patients with HTLV-I. My colleagues and I studied the persistence of such CD8-antigen-specific T cells ex vivo in the presence of antibodies to the IL-2 or IL-15 cytokines or to their receptors and showed that the ex vivo addition to IL-15 or to IL-2Rβ of antibodies that inhibit IL-15 action to such mononuclear cells ex vivo led to the rapid reduction (within six days) in the number of such antigen-specific memory and effector cytotoxic CD8+

cells, whereas antibodies to IL-2 or to its private IL-2Rα receptor did not have this effect [33]. In this system, IL-15 both increased the proliferation of the CD8 cells and reduced their death by apoptosis.

These conclusions concerning the distinct functional roles manifested by IL-2 and IL-15, derived from ex vivo studies, are supported by the analysis of knockout mice with disrupted cytokine and cytokine-receptor genes as well as from the study of transgenic mice. IL-2$^{-/-}$ and IL-2Rα null mice developed massive enlargement of peripheral lymphoid organs and polyclonal T- and B-cell expansion, as well as autoimmune diseases, including hemolytic anemia and inflammatory bowel disease, that are related to the impaired AICD [34,35]. In contrast to this phenotype, mice genetically deficient in IL-15 (IL-15$^{-/-}$) or its receptor (IL-15Rα) did not manifest lymphoid enlargement, high immunoglobulin levels, or autoimmune disease. Rather, they displayed a marked reduction in the number of thymic and peripheral NK cells, NK T cells, and intestinal intraepithelial lymphocytes (IELs). Furthermore, they manifested a marked reduction in memory phenotype CD8+ T cells [36,37].

Taken together, these studies support the view that in their special adaptive immune functions, IL-2 and IL-15 favor opposing actions that tend to emphasize one or the other of the two competing major goals of the immune response. IL-2, through its contribution to AICD for CD4 cells and its interference with the persistence of CD8+ memory phenotype T cells, favors the elimination of selected lymphocytes that are directed toward self-antigens and thus IL-2 plays a critical role in the maintenance of peripheral self-tolerance. In contrast, IL-15 through its inhibition of IL-2-mediated AICD and its positive role in the maintenance of CD8+ memory phenotype cells, favors the maintenance and survival of CD4 and CD8 T cells. The persistence of memory phenotype CD8+ T cells mediated by IL-15 is of value in maintaining a specific immune response to foreign pathogens. However, IL-15 expression carries with it the risk to the organism of the survival of self-reactive T cells that could lead to the development of autoimmune diseases.

Aberrant IL-15 expression in retroviral diseases
Increased IL-15 expression has been observed in retroviral diseases and neoplasia [23,24]. HTLV-I-infected T cells of patients with the neurological disorder TSP/HAM express the HTLV-I-encoded transactivator p40^{tax}. The expression of tax leads to the induction of IL-15 and IL-15Rα, and to the expression of IL-2 and IL-2Rα. The induction of IL-15 and IL-15R expression involves NF-κB and IRF-1 or interferon regulatory factor (IRF)-4 [23,24,38]. The ex vivo proliferation of HTLV-I-infected T cells in TSP/HAM can be partially inhibited by an antibody to IL-15 or to IL-2 and can be virtually abrogated by the simultaneous administration of antibodies to both cytokines or to both cytokine receptors,

suggesting that these two cytokines mediate autocrine/paracrine stimulatory systems as a consequence of HTLV-I infection. IL-15 also appears to play a role in the expression of antigen-specific MHC I restricted memory phenotype CD8+ cells that participate in the pathogenesis of TSP/HAM. In patients with TSP/HAM, tetramer technology showed that 3% to over 20% of their CD8 cells were MHC class I restricted, antigen-specific cells (directed to amino acids 11–19 of the tax protein transactivator) [33]. The number of such cells that persisted for six days in *ex vivo* cultures of patient peripheral blood mononuclear cells was decreased in the presence of antibodies to IL-15 or to its receptor. This observation is in accord with the view, presented above, that IL-15 plays a major role in the generation and persistence of antigen-specific CD8+ memory and effector cells. An increased production of IL-15 by HTLV-I-associated T cells is also observed in ATL, an aggressive leukemia of mature CD4 cells that is associated with HTLV-I [23]. Taken as a whole, the evidence supports the view that the retrovirus-induced IL-15 and its private receptor play meaningful roles in the pathogenesis and persistence of both autoimmune and leukemic disorders associated with HTLV-I infection.

Abnormalities of IL-15 expression in inflammatory autoimmune diseases including RA

Feldmann and co-workers proposed that TNF-α is at the apex of a cytokine cascade that includes IL-1β, IL-6, GM-CSF, and a series of inflammatory chemokines, including Mip1α, Mip1β, and IL-8, that are intimately involved in the development and progression of RA [1]. McInnes and co-workers have reported abnormalities of IL-15 in this disease and have suggested that IL-15 may precede TNF-α in the cytokine cascade [2,3,8]. In particular, IL-15-activated T cells can induce TNF synthesis by macrophages in RA via a mechanism dependent on cell contact [3]. Those workers reported the presence of high concentrations of IL-15 in RA synovial fluid and showed that IL-15 is expressed by cells of the synovial membrane lining. Nevertheless, the presence of rheumatoid factor in the fluids may yield specious high estimates for IL-15 assessed by an ELISA. Harada and co-workers showed that freshly isolated cells from synovial tissues strongly expressed mRNA for IL-15 and in comparison with cells from osteoarthritis tissues could spontaneously release large amounts of IL-15 in culture [4]. The IL-15 could stimulate the proliferation of synovial-tissue T cells from RA patients. Klimiuk and co-workers also showed high levels of IL-15 as well as TNF-α in the serum of patients with RA [7]. Synovial fluids in RA contain chemotactic and T-cell-stimulatory activities attributable in part to IL-15. Oppenheimer-Marks and co-workers showed that IL-15 is produced by endothelial cells in rheumatoid tissues and that this cytokine markedly increases transendothelial migration of both CD4 and CD8 cells [6]. Furthermore,

they showed that IL-15 leads to the accumulation of T cells in RA synovial tissues engrafted into mice with severe combined immune deficiency (SCID) *in vivo*. In a parallel murine model, the intra-articular injection of IL-15 induced a local tissue inflammatory infiltrate consisting predominately of T lymphocytes. These data suggest that IL-15 can recruit and activate T cells into the synovial membrane, possibly contributing to the pathogenesis of RA. Ziolkowska and co-workers also suggested that IL-15 plays an important role in the pathogenesis of RA, in part by inducing IL-17 in the joints of RA patients: this cytokine is known to stimulate synoviocytes to release several mediators of inflammation, including IL-6, IL-8, GM-CSF, and prostaglandin E_2 [39]. Finally, as noted below, the injection of inhibitors of IL-15 action suppressed the development of collagen-induced arthritis [9,10]. In summary, these reports suggest a role for IL-15 in the development of inflammatory RA and imply that antagonists to IL-15 action may have therapeutic potential in this disease.

Therapy directed toward IL-15 and IL-15 receptor subunits

The majority of therapeutic trials directed toward the IL-2/IL-2R or IL-15/IL-15R systems have focused on the alpha subunit of the IL-2 receptor. Such efforts directed toward IL-2Rα have met with considerable success in the treatment of leukemia and select autoimmune disorders and in the prevention of allograft rejection [40]. However, efforts targeting IL-2Rα have limitations. In particular, antibodies to IL-2Rα do not inhibit the actions of IL-15, a cytokine that does not bind to this subunit. They also do not act on resting NK or NK T cells that express IL-2Rβ and γc but not IL-2Rα. Additional limitations are suggested by our discussion above of the role of IL-2R in the elimination of memory T cells and in AICD, where antibody-mediated inhibition of AICD may prevent the generation of peripheral tolerance to host antigens targeted in autoimmunity and to the transplatation antigens expressed on the allografts. In addition, the role of IL-2 in the termination of memory cells directed toward self-antigens is not desirable. Finally, blockade of IL-2/IL-2R interaction could prevent the development and persistence of CD4+CD25+ (IL-2Rα+) negative regulatory cells that normally would inhibit the development and maintenance of autoimmune diseases [41]. Due to these limitations in therapy directed toward IL-2Rα, therapy directed toward IL-15 receptor is being developed for use in organ tranplantation protocols and for application to the treatment of autoimmune disorders, as well as for diseases caused by the retrovirus HTLV-I. The administration of an IL-15 inhibitor, the soluble high-infinity IL-15R receptor chain linked to the immunoglobulin Fc element, prevented the development of murine collagen-induced arthritis and inhibited allograft rejection [9]. Furthermore, an IL-15 receptor antagonist produced by mutation of a glutamine residue within the C-terminus of IL-15 to aspartic acid competitively inhibited IL-15-triggered cellular proliferation [10]. The administration of this IL-15 mutant markedly attenutated antigen-specific delayed hypersensitivity responses in mice and enhanced the acceptance of pancreatic islet cell allografts [10].

Our own therapeutic approaches directed toward IL-15 have focused on the IL-2Rβ receptor subunit shared by IL-2 and IL-15 [42]. A humanized version of Mikβ1, an antibody directed toward IL-2Rβ that is used by both IL-2 and IL-15 and that inhibits IL-15 action on T and NK cells, prolonged cardiac allograft survival in cynomolgus monkeys [42]. In our initial clinical trial, we are evaluating the antibody Mikβ1 in the therapy of patients with T-cell-type large granular lymphocytic leukemia associated with hematocytopenia. The monoclonal large granular lymphocytes involved in this disease respond to IL-15 and express IL-2Rβ and γc but not IL-2Rα [43]. In addition, this monoclonal antibody will soon be evaluated in the treatment of autoimmune diseases where abnormalities of IL-15 have been demonstrated, including RA, multiple sclerosis, and TSP/HAM.

Future prospects

Abnormalities of IL-15 expression caused by HTLV-I tax-mediated transactivation of IL-15 have been demonstrated in the abnormal T cells in HTLV-I-associated ATL and in TSP/HAM. Abnormalities of IL-15 expression may also be involved in the pathogenesis of inflammatory autoimmune disorders such as RA and inflammatory bowel disease. Although these observations are interesting, they are not sufficient to warrant the conclusion that a disorder of IL-15 expression is a meaningful element in the pathogenesis of these disorders. However, the clinical application of new therapeutic agents that target IL-15 or the receptor used by IL-15 may aid in determining if there is a role played by IL-15 in such autoimmune disorders as TSP/HAM and RA. In particular, IL-15R-directed therapeutic studies of TSP/HAM would involve tetramer technology to define the effect of therapy on the number of circulating antigen-specific (tax aa 11–19) CD8+ cells. Similarly, IL-15/IL-15R-directed therapy of RA should be monitored for its impact on serum concentrations of TNF-α and on the activity of the disease.

Additional efforts are directed toward developing an inhibitor of Janus kinase 3 (JAK3) as an agent for controlled immunosuppression in transplantation protocols and in the treatment of RA. Expression of JAK3 is limited largely to lymphocytes and hematopoietic cells. Furthermore, JAK3 is activated by the cytokines that use γc, including IL-15, IL-2, IL-4, IL-7, IL-9, and IL-21, but is not essential for signaling by other cytokines. JAK3 is defective in an autosomal form of severe combined immunodeficiency disease (SCID) in humans, in which immunodeficiency but no disorders of other systems are found [44,45]. Furthermore, mice made JAK3-deficient by homologous recombination manifest an absence of NK cells and abnormalities of T and B cells but do not have

disorders in nonimmunological systems [46]. Finally, JAK3 is constitutively activated in some cell lines in IL-2-independent HTLV-I-associated adult T-cell leukemia [47,48]. Taken together, these observations suggest that drugs that inhibit JAK3 action may be of value as antileukemia agents and in the therapy of autoimmune diseases, associated with abnormal production of IL-15.

In conclusion, our emerging understanding of the IL-15/IL-15R system, including the definition of the actions that this cytokine manifests — both those that are shared with IL-2 and those that are distinct — is opening new possibilities for the development of more rational immune interventions directed toward IL-15 and IL-15 receptors that may be of value in the treatment of cancer, the prevention of allograft rejection, the therapy of diseases associated with the retrovirus HTLV-I, and the treatment of autoimmune diseases such as RA.

Glossary of terms

AICD = activation-induced cell death: a multi-step process involved in peripheral tolerance, initiated by stimulation of T-cell receptors (TCRs)/CD3 and inducing the expression and interaction of the induced IL-2 and IL-2 receptors (IL-2Rs). When the cell cycling induced by this interaction is followed by restimulation of TCR/CD3, these events lead to the induction of the cell-death-effector Fas ligand, which interacts with the Fas receptor, culminating in the death of the self-reactive T cell; ATL = adult T-cell leukemia: an aggressive malignancy of mature lymphocytes expressing CD3, CD4, and CD25 (IL-2Rα), caused by the retroviruses HTLV-I; FasL = Fas ligand; HTLV-I = human T-cell lymphotropic virus I: a retrovirus, found predominantly in Japan, the Caribbean Islands, and sub-Saharan Africa, which induces the expression of IL-2, IL-15, and their private receptors and which is the etiological agent of a number of human diseases including inflammatory arthritis, myositis, adult T-cell leukemia, and the neurological disorder tropical spastic paraparesis/HTLV-I-associated myelopathy (TSP/HAM); IL-15Rα = cytokine-specific private receptor for IL-15; IL-2Rα = cytokine-specific private receptor for IL-2; tax = transactivator (protein); TSP/HAM = tropical spastic paraparesis/HTLV-I-associated myelopathy: a demyelinating neurological disease caused by the retrovirus HTLV-I and associated with progressive weakness and bowel and bladder dysfunction.

References

1. Feldmann M, Brennan FM, Maini RN: **Role of cytokines in rheumatoid arthritis.** *Annu Rev Immunol* 1996, 14:397-440. [key review]
2. McInnes IB, al-Mughales J, Field M, Leung BP, Huang FP, Dixon R, Sturrock RD, Wilkinson PC, Liew FY: **The role of interleukin-15 in T-cell migration and activation in rheumatoid arthritis.** *Nat Med* 1996, 2:175-182. [key review]
3. McInnes IB, Leung BP, Sturrock RD, Field M, Liew FY: **Interleukin-15 mediates T cell-dependent regulation of tumor necrosis factor-alpha production in rheumatoid arthritis.** *Nat Med* 1997, 3:189-195. [general reference]

4. Harada S, Yamamura M, Okamoto H, Morita Y, Kawahima M, Aita T, Makino Y: **Production of interleukin-7 and interleukin-15 by fibroblast-like synoviocytes from patients with rheumatoid arthritis.** *Arthritis Rheum* 1999, 42:1508-1516. [general reference]

5. Kirmar I, Vaener B, Nielsen OH: **Interleukin-15 and its role in chronic inflammatory diseases.** *Inflamm Res* 1998, 47:285-289. [key review]

6. Oppenheimer-Marks N, Brezinschek RI, Mohamadzadeh M, Vita R, Lipsky PE: **Interleukin 15 is produced by endothelial cells and increases the transendothelial migration of T cells in vitro and in the SCID mouse-human rheumatoid arthritis model in vivo.** *J Clin Invest* 1998, 101:1261-1272. [general reference]

7. Klimiuk PA, Sierakowski S, Latosiewicz R, Cylioik B, Skowronski J, Chwiecko J: **Serum cytokines in different histological variants of rheumatoid arthritis.** *J Rheumatol* 2001, 28:1211-1217. [general reference]

8. McInnes IB, Liew FY: **Interleukin 15: A proinflamatory role in rheumatoid arthritis synovitis.** *Immunol Today* 1998, 19:75-79. [key review]

9. Ruchatz H, Leung BP, Wei XQ, McInnes IB, and Liew FY: **Soluble IL-15 receptor alpha-chain administration prevents murine collagen-induced arthritis: a role for IL-15 in development of antigen-induced immunotherapy.** *J Immunol* 1998, 160:5654-5660. [general reference]

10. KimYS, Maslinski W, Zheng XX, Stevens AC, Li XC, Tesch GH, Kelley VR, Strom TB: **Targeting the IL-15 receptor with an antagonist IL-15 mutant/Fc γ2a protein blocks delayed-type hypersensitivity.** *J Immunol* 1998, 160:5742-5748. [general reference]

11. Waldmann TA: **The interleukin-2 receptor.** *J Biol Chem* 1991, 266:2681-2684. [key review]

12. Bamford RN, Grant AJ, Burton JD, Peters C, Kurys G, Goldman CK, Brennan J, Roessler E, Waldmann TA: **The interleukin (IL) 2 receptor β chain is shared by IL-2 and a cytokine, provisionally designated IL-T, that stimulates T-cell proliferation and the induction of lymphokine-activated killer cells.** *Proc Natl Acad Sci U S A* 1994, 91:4940-4944. [archival research]

13. Grabstein KH, Eisenman J, Shanebeck K, Rauch C, Srinivasan S, Fung V, Beers C, Richardson J, Schoenborn MA, Ahdieh M, Johnson L, Alderson MR, Watson JD, Anderson DM, Giri JG: **Cloning of a T cell growth factor that interacts with the beta chain of the interleukin-2 receptor.** *Science* 1994, 264: 965-968. [archival research]

14. Giri JG, Kumaki S, Ahdieh M, Friend DJ, Loomis A, Shanebeck K, DuBose R, Cosman D, Park LS, Anderson DM: **Identification and cloning of a novel IL-15 binding protein that is structurally related to the alpha chain of the IL-2 receptor.** *EMBO J* 1995, 14:3654-3663. [archival research]

15. Zhang X, Sun S, Hwang I, Tough DF, Sprent J: **Potent and selective stimulation or memory-phenotype CD8+ T cells in vivo by IL-15.** *Immunity* 1998, 8:591-599. [general reference]

16. Ku CC, Murakami M, Sakamoto A, Kappler J, Marrack P: **Control of homeostasis of CD8+ memory T cells by opposing cytokines.** *Science* 2000, 288: 675-678. [general reference]

17. Marks-Konczalik J, Dubois S, Losi JM Sabzevari, H Yamada, N Feigenbaum L, Waldmann TA, Tagaya Y: **IL-2-induced activation-induced cell death is inhibited in IL-15 transgenic mice.** *Proc Natl Acad Sci U S A* 2000, 97: 11445-11450. [general reference]

18. Waldmann TA, Dubois S, Tagaya Y: **Contrasting roles of IL-2 and IL-15 in the life and death of lymphocytes: implications for immunotherapy.** *Immunity* 2001, 14:105-110. [key review]

19. Waldmann T, Tagaya Y: **The multifaceted regulation of interleukin-15 expression and the role of this cytokine in NK cell differentiation and host response to intracellular pathogens.** *Ann Rev Immunol* 1999, 17:19-49. [key review]

20. Lenardo MJ: **Fas and the art of lymphocyte maintenance.** *J Exp Med* 1996, 183: 721-724. [key review]

21. Kirman I, Nielsen OH: **Increased numbers of interleukin-15 expressing cells in active ulcerative colitis.** *Am J Gastroenterol* 1996, 91:1789-1794. [general reference]

22. Kivisakk P, Matusevicius D, He B, Soderstrom M, Fredrikson S, Link H: **IL-15 mRNA expression is up-regulated in blood and cerebrospinal fluid mononuclear cells in multiple sclerosis (MS).** *Clin Exp Immunol* 1998, 111:193-197. [general reference]

23. Azimi N, Brown K, Bamford RN, Tagaya Y, Siebenlist U, Waldmann TA: **Human T cell lymphotropic virus type I Tax protein trans-activates interleukin 15 gene transcription through an NF-kappaB site.** *Proc Natl Acad Sci U S A* 1998, 95:2452-2457. [general reference]

24. Azimi N, Jacobson S, Leist T, Waldmann TA: **Involvement of IL-15 in the pathogenesis of human T lymphotropic virus type I-associated myelopathy/tropical spastic paraparesis: implications for therapy with a monoclonal antibody directed to the IL-2/15Rβ receptor.** *J Immunol* 1999 163: 4064-4072. [general reference]

25. Burton JD, Bamford RN, Peters C, Grant AJ, Kurys G, Goldman CK, Brennan J, Roessler E, Waldmann TA: **A lymphokine, provisionally designated interleukin T and produced by a human adult T-cell leukemia line, stimulates T-cell proliferation and the induction of lymphokine-activated killer cells.** *Proc Natl Acad Sci U S A* 1994, 91:4935-4939. [archival record]

26. Bamford RN, DeFilippis AP, Azimi N, Kurys G, Waldmann TA: **The 5′ untranslated region, signal peptide, and the coding sequence of the carboxyl terminus of IL-15 participate in its multifaceted translational control.** *J Immunol* 1998, 160: 4418-4426. [general reference]

27. Onu A, Pohl T, Krause H, Bulfone-Paus S: **Regulation of IL-15 secretion via the leader peptide of two IL-15 isoforms.** *J Immunol* 1997, 158:255-262. [general reference]

28. Kurys G, Tagaya Y, Bamford R, Hanover JA, Waldmann TA: **The long signal peptide isoform and its alternative processing direct the intracellular trafficking of IL-15.** *J Biol Chem* 2000, 275:30653-30659. [general reference]

29. Kennedy MK, Park LS: **Characterization of interleukin-15 (IL-15) and the IL-15 receptor complex.** *J Clin Immunol* 1996, 16: 134-143. [key review]

30. Inagaki-Ohara K, Nishimura H, Mitani A, Yoshikai Y: **Interleukin-15 preferentially promotes the growth of intestinal intraepithelial lymphocytes bearing gamma delta T cell receptor in mice.** *Eur J Immunol* 1997, 27:2885-2891. [general reference]

31. Carson WE, Ross ME, Baiocchi RA, Marien MJ, Boiani N, Grabstein K, Caligiuri MA: **Endogenous production of interleukin 15 by activated human monocytes is critical for optimal production of interferon-gamma by natural killer cells in vitro.** *J Clin Invest* 1995, 96:2578-2582. [general reference]

32. Armitage RJ, Macduff BM, Eisenman J, Paxton R, Grabstein KH: **IL-15 has stimulatory activitity for the induction of B cell proliferation and differentiation.** *J Immunol* 1995, 154:483-490. [archival research]

33. Azimi N, Nagai M, Jacobson S, Waldmann T: **Interleukin 15 is an essential factor for the persistence of the Tax-specific CD8 cells in HAM/TSP patients.** *Proc Natl Acad Sci U S A*, in press. [general reference]

34. Sadlack B, Kuhn R, Schorle H, Rajewsky K, Muller W, Horak I: **Development and proliferation of lymphocytes in mice deficient for both interleukins-2 and-4.** *Eur J Immunol* 1994, 24: 281-284. [general research]

35. Willerford DM, Chen J, Ferry JA, Davidson L, Ma A, Alt FW: **Interleukin-2 receptor α chain regulates the size and content of the peripheral lymphoid compartment.** *Immunity* 1995, 3:521-530. [general research]

36. Lodolce JP, Boone DL, Chai S, Swain RE, Dassopoulis T, Trettin S, Ma A: **IL-15 receptor maintains lymphoid hemeostatsis by supporting lymphocyte homing and proliferation.** *Immunity* 1998, 9: 668-676. [general reference]

37. Kennedy MK, Glaccum M, Brown SN, Butz EA, Viney JL, Embers M, Matsuki N, Charrier K, Sedger L, Willis CR, Brasel K, Morrissey PJ, Stocking K, Schuh JC, Joyce S, Peschon JJ: **Reversible defects in natural killer and memory CD8 T cell lineages in interleukin 15-deficient mice.** *J Exp Med* 2000, 191: 771-780. [general reference]

38. Mariner JM, Lantz V, Waldmann TA, Azimi N. **Human T cell lymphotropic virus type I Tax protein activates interleukin 15 receptor alpha gene expression through the action of NF-κB.** *J Immunol* 2001, 166:2 602-2609. [general reference]

39. Ziolkowska M, Koc A, Luszczkiewicz G, Ksiezopolska-Pietrzak K, Klimczak E, Chawalinska-Sadowska H, Maslinski W: **High levels of IL-17 in rheumatoid arthritis patients; IL-15 triggers in vitro IL-17 production via cydosporin A-sensitive mechanism.** *J Immunol* 2000, 164:2832-2838. [general reference]

40. Waldmann TA, White JD, Goldman CK, Top L, Grant A, Bamford R, Roessler E, Horak ID, Zaknoen S, Kasten-Sportes C, England R, Horak E, Mishra B, Dipre M, Hale P, Fleisher TA, Junghans RP,

Jaffe ES, Nelson DL: **The interleukin receptor: a target for monoclonal antibody treatment of human T-cell lymphotrophic virus I-induced adult T-cell leukemia.** *Blood* 1993, **82**:1701-1712. [key review]

41. Shevach EM: **Certified professionals: CD4+ CD25+ suppressor T cells.** *J Exp Med* 2001, **193**:F41-F45. [key review]

42. Tinubu SA, Hakimi J, Kondas JA, Bailon P, Familletti PC, Spence C, Crittenden MD, Parenteau GL, Dirbas FM, Tsudo M, Bacher JD, Kasten-Sportès C, Martinucci JL, Goldman CK, Clark RE, Waldmann TA: **A humanized antibody directed to the interleukin-2 receptor β chain prolongs primate cardiac allograft survival.** *J Immunol* 1994, **153**:4330-4338. [general reference]

43. Tsudo M, Goldman CK, Bongiovanni KF, ChanWC, Winton EF, Yagita M, Grimm EA, Waldmann TA: **The p75 peptide is the receptor for interleukin 2 expressed on large granular lymphocytes and is responsible for the interleukin 2 activation of these cells.** *Proc Natl Acad Sci U S A* 1987, **84**:5394-5398. [archival research]

44. Russsell SM, Tayebi N, Nakajima H, Riedy MC, Roberts JL, Aman MJ, Migone TS, Noguchi M, Markert ML, Buckley RH, O'Shea JJ, Leonard WJ: **Mutation of Jak3 in a patient with SCID: essential role of Jak3 in lymphoid development.** *Science* 1995, **270**:797-800. [general reference]

45. Macchi P, Villa A, Gillani S, Sacco MG, Frattini A, Porta F, Ugazio AG, Johnston JA, Candotti F, O'Shea JJ, Vezzoni P, Notarangelo LD: **Mutations of Jak3 gene in patients with autosomal severe combined immune deficiency (SCID).** *Nature* 1995, **377**:65-68. [general reference]

46. Nosaka T, van Deursen JM, Tripp RA, Thierfelder WE, Witthuhn BA, McMickle AP, Doherty PC, Grosveld GC, Ihle JN: **Defective lymphoid development in mice lacking Jak3.** *Science* 1995, **270**:800-802. [general reference]

47. Migone TS, Lin JX, Cereseto A, Mulloy JC, O'Shea JJ, Franchini G, Leonard WJ: **Constitutively activated Jak-STAT pathway in T cells transformed with HTLV-1.** *Science* 1995, **269**:79-81. [general reference]

48. Xu X, Kang SH, Heidenreich O, Okerholm M, O'Shea JJ, Nerenberg MI: **Constitutive activation of different Jak tyrosine kinases in human T cell leukemia virus type I (HTLV-1) tax protein or virus-transformed cells.** *J Clin Invest* 1995, **96**:1548-1555. [general reference]

Supplement Review
The role of human T-lymphocyte–monocyte contact in inflammation and tissue destruction
Danielle Burger and Jean-Michel Dayer

Division of Immunology and Allergy, Clinical Immunology Unit, University Hospital, Geneva, Switzerland

Correspondence: Dr D Burger, Clinical Immunology Unit, University Hospital, 24 rue Micheli-du-Crest, CH-1211 Geneva 14, Switzerland.
Tel: +41 22 372 9376; fax: +41 22 372 9369; e-mail: danielle.burger@hcuge.ch

Received: 28 February 2002
Revisions requested: 1 March 2002
Revisions received: 4 March 2002
Accepted: 7 March 2002
Published: 9 May 2002

Arthritis Res 2002, **4 (suppl 3)**:S169-S176

This article may contain supplementary data which can only be found online at http://arthritis-research.com/content/4/S3/S169

© 2002 BioMed Central Ltd
(Print ISSN 1465-9905; Online ISSN 1465-9913)

Chapter summary

Contact-mediated signaling of monocytes by human stimulated T lymphocytes (T_L) is a potent proinflammatory mechanism that triggers massive upregulation of the proinflammatory cytokines IL-1 and tumor necrosis factor-α. These two cytokines play an important part in chronic destructive diseases, including rheumatoid arthritis. To date this cell–cell contact appears to be a major endogenous mechanism to display such an activity in monocyte-macrophages. Since T_L and monocyte-macrophages play a pivotal part in the pathogenesis of chronic inflammatory diseases, we investigated the possible ligands and counter-ligands involved in this cell–cell interaction. We also characterized an inhibitory molecule interfering in this process, apolipoprotein A-I. This review aims to summarize the state of the art and importance of contact-mediated monocyte activation by stimulated T_L in cytokine production in rheumatoid arthritis and mechanisms that might control it.

Keywords: cytokines, inflammation, monocytes, rheumatoid arthritis, T lymphocytes

Introduction

Inflammation is usually the consequence of tissue damage and its purpose is to direct plasma factors and immune cells to the lesion site to eradicate infection and repair damaged tissue. In pathological conditions such as chronic inflammation, infiltration of immune cells into the target tissue precedes tissue damage; the lesion occurs after infiltration of immune cells. Based on observations in animal models it is usually thought that the first cells to infiltrate the tissue are T lymphocytes (T_L), suggesting a pathogenic role for the latter cells. However, the mechanisms underlying the extravasation of T cells into the joint are still elusive [1]. T cell cytokines such as IL-4, IL-10, IL-13, and transforming growth factor (TGF)-β have predominantly anti-inflammatory effects and, in the human

system, IFN-γ alone displays weak activation capacity in terms of IL-1β and tumor necrosis factor (TNF)-α induction, suggesting that soluble factors produced by T cells are not pathological mediators. Therefore, T cells might exert a pathological effect through direct cellular contact with monocyte-macrophages (Mϕ). Studies carried out during the past ten years in our laboratory proved the premise that IL-1β and TNF-α are markedly increased in this interaction [2–8]. This was further confirmed by others [9–12]. This review aims to assess the importance of contact-mediated monocyte activation by stimulated T_L resulting in cytokine production, and its relevance to chronic inflammatory conditions as exemplified by rheumatoid arthritis (RA). Possible modulations and controls of this mechanism are discussed.

A glossary of specialist terms used in this chapter appears at the end of the text section. A list of common abbreviations used in this issue appears just before the indexes.

Historical background

The history of contact-mediated activation of Mφ by stimulated T_L (reviewed in (13)) began in the mid-eighties when it was observed that the expression of membrane-associated IL-1 (IL-1α) in mouse Mφ was mediated by both soluble factors and direct contact with T cells. The importance of cellular contact was confirmed by experiments showing that IL-1 was induced upon T cell-Mφ contact with both Th1 and Th2 cells in the absence of lymphokine release. We also observed that direct contact with stimulated T cells was a potent stimulus of Mφ activation. Although observations have shown that the induction of murine Mφ effector functions mediated by T_L in living cell co-cultures involved signals delivered by cell–cell contact together with IFN-γ, fixed, stimulated T cells induced TNF production in Mφ in the absence of IFNγ. Furthermore, when isolated plasma membranes from different stimulated T-cell clones were used, both stimulated Th1 and Th2 cells were able to activate Mφ, establishing that direct contact with stimulated T cells was a potent mechanism inducing Mφ effector functions.

Triggering of cytokine production in chronic inflammation

Based on histology, function, animal models and clinical studies, Mφ appear to play a key role in chronic inflammation by producing large amounts of IL-1 and TNF-α under various stimuli. In chronic inflammation, infiltration of T_L into the target tissue precedes tissue damage suggesting that their effect is pathogenic. Angiogenesis and proliferation of resident cells accompany this infiltration. However, Mφ are rapidly found in the lesion and interactions occur between T_L and Mφ. These interactions lead to IL-1 and TNF-α production, a process that is potentiated by many other factors including IFN-γ, IL-15, and IL-18; T cell cytokines such as IL-4, IL-10, IL-13, and TGF-β are inhibitory (Fig. 1). Our previous seminal studies and further works by others strongly argue that direct cellular contact with stimulated T cells is a major pathway for the production of IL-1 and TNF-α in Mφ [13]. Indeed, contact-mediated activation of Mφ by stimulated T_L is as potent as optimal doses of lipopolysaccharide (LPS) or phorbol myristate acetate in inducing IL-1β and TNF-α production in monocytes and cells of the monocytic lineage, such as THP-1 cells [13]. We therefore postulate that this mechanism is highly relevant to the pathogenesis and maintenance of chronic inflammation in diseases such as RA.

Relevance of contact-mediated activation of Mφ to chronic inflammatory diseases

T lymphocytes are likely to play a pivotal role in the pathogenesis of RA [1]. In RA, T_L displaying a mature helper phenotype (i.e. CD3+ CD4+ CD45RO+) are the main infiltrating cells in the pannus, at percentages ranging from 16% of total cells in 'transitional areas' to 75% in 'lymphocyte-rich areas' [14,15]. The latter are to be found in perivascular

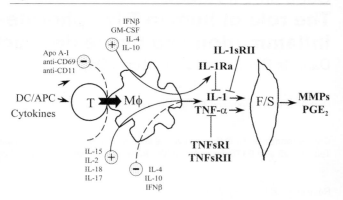

Figure 1

Scheme of the activation cascade from T lymphocytes (T_L) to monocyte-macrophages (Mφ) and fibroblasts/synoviocytes (F/S). Activated T_L trigger Mφ to produce proinflammatory cytokines that in turn induce the production of matrix-destructive metalloproteinases (MMPs) and prostaglandin E_2 (PGE_2), the latter products being involved in cartilage destruction and bone resorption. These processes are controlled by proinflammatory factors (IL-15, IL-2, IL-18, IL-17) and anti-inflammatory factors (IL-4, IL-10, granulocyte/macrophage colony stimulating factor [GM-CSF], IFN-β). Furthermore, naturally occurring inhibitors (IL-1sRII, IL-1Ra, tumor necrosis factor [TNF]sRI, TNFsRII) inhibit the activity of IL-1 and TNF-α, the production of which is blocked by apolipoprotein (apo) A-I and decreased by exogenous antibodies to CD69 and β2-integrins (CD11b>CD11c>CD11a). APC, antigen presenting cells; DC, dendritic cells.

regions, around 'high endothelial venule'-like vessels, where T_L extravasation occurs forming germinal center-like structures [16]. Although they are the most abundant infiltrating cells in the pannus, the importance of T_L in RA pathogenesis has been mainly proven in animal models [1]. Indeed, T cells from RA patients that were transferred to SCID mice induced arthritis [17]. Although evidence suggests that T_L play a pathogenic part in chronic inflammatory diseases, the mechanism by which they exert their pathogenicity has not been clearly elucidated [1], thus contact-mediated induction of proinflammatory cytokines in Mφ might represent one of these mechanisms.

T cell signaling of Mφ by direct cell–cell contact

The activation of effector cells mediated by stimulated T_L has been abundantly substantiated in the T-B lymphocyte model for the induction of cell proliferation and antibody secretion, which require both direct cell–cell contact and soluble signals. Indeed, B cells can be activated in the absence of antigen by direct contact with activated T cells. A considerable amount of signaling crosstalk was observed in T and B cells, that triggered various synchronized signals resulting in the activation of effector functions in both cell types, as recently exemplified in RA [18]. Similarly, ample data exist regarding the crosstalk between dendritic cells and T_L. However, much less is known about the crosstalk between T_L and Mφ, other than antigen presentation.

Table 1

Depending on T-cell stimulus, various products are induced in monocytes upon cell–cell contact

Stimulus	Type of T cell	Type of monocyte	Products	References
PHA/PMA	PB T_L, HUT-78 cells, Jurkat cells, synovial and PB T cell clones: CD4+; CD8+; Th1; and Th2	PB monocytes, THP-1 cells	TNF-α, IL-1β, IL-6, IL-8, IL-1α, IL-1Ra, TNFsRs, MMP-1 MMP-9, TIMP-1	[2–6,8,62]
PdBu/ionomycine	PB T_L	PB monocytes	TNF-α, IL-10	[19]
anti-CD3	PB T_L, synovial T cells	PB monocytes, THP-1 cells	TNF-α, IL-10, IL-1β; MMP-1	[4,12,19,22,62]
anti-CD3 and anti-CD28 or specific Ag	Th1 cell clones	THP-1 cells	IL-1β, low IL-1Ra	[7]
anti-CD3 and anti-CD28 or specific Ag	Th2 cell clones	THP-1 cells	IL-1Ra, low IL-1β	[7]
Cytokines*	PB T_L, synovial T cells, Th1 and Th2 cell clones	PB monocytes	TNF-α, IL-1β	[9–12,20,63]
Anti-CD3	PB T_L	PMA/IFN-γ-treated U937 cell	TNF-α, IL-10, IL-12 and IL-4	[64]

*IL-2 or IL-15 alone or in combination with IL-6 and TNF-α. Ag, antigen; MMP, matrix metalloproteinase; PB, peripheral blood; PHA, phytohemagglutinin; PMA, phorbol myristate acetate; Th, T helper cell; TIMP, tissue inhibitor of matrix metalloproteinases; TL, T lymphocyte; TNF, tumor necrosis factor; TNFsRs, TNF soluble receptors. Modified and published with permission from *European Cytokine Network* [13].

Most T cell types, including T cell clones, freshly isolated T_L, and T cell lines (such as HUT-78 cells) induce IL-1 and TNF-α in Mϕ [2,3,5,13]. Various stimuli other than phytohemagglutinin/phorbol myristate acetate induce T_L to activate monocytes by direct cellular contact: cross-linking of CD3 by immobilized anti-CD3 mAb with or without cross-linking of the co-stimulatory molecule CD28 [7,12,19]; antigen recognition on antigen-specific T cell clones [7]; and cytokines [9,10,20]. Furthermore, depending on T cell type and T cell stimulus, direct cell–cell contact with stimulated T_L can induce different patterns of products in Mϕ (Table 1). This suggests that multiple ligands and counter-ligands are involved in the contact-mediated activation of Mϕ, which are differentially induced in T cells depending on the stimulus. Recent studies by Brennan *et al.* [12] have led to the concept that, based on their effect on Mϕ, T_L can be classified as cytokine-activated T_L (T_{ck}) (which are likely to be present in RA synovium [12]) or T-cell-receptor-activated T_L. In some cases, an imbalance in production of proinflammatory versus anti-inflammatory cytokines has been observed, where Th1 cell clones preferentially induce IL-1β rather than IL-1Ra production, and cytokine-stimulated T_L induce TNF-α production but not that of IL-10 [7,9]. Besides, we demonstrated that upon contact with stimulated T cells, the balance between IL-1β and IL-1Ra production in monocytes is ruled by Ser/Thr phosphatase(s) [8] and that contact-activated THP-1 cells express membrane-associated protease(s), neutralizing TNF-α activity both by degrading the latter cytokine and by cleaving its receptors at the cell surface [6]. Thus triggering these intra- and extra-cellular processes by direct contact with stimulated T_L may regulate the proinflammatory cytokines and their inhibitors. The balance of their production in monocytes dictates, in part, the outcome of the inflammatory process, as depicted in Figure 1.

Cell surface molecules involved in contact-mediated monocyte activation

A critical issue arising from these observations is the identity of the molecules on the T cell surface that are involved in contact-mediated signaling of Mϕ activation, as well as their counter-ligands. It has been postulated that T cell membrane-associated TNF-α was involved in Mϕ activation. However, fixed, stimulated Th2 cells from a T cell line that did not express membrane-associated TNF induced both TNF and IL-1 production in Mϕ [21] demonstrating that TNF-α might play a part, but not a primary one. We have shown that neither soluble TNF-α receptors nor IL-1Ra block T cell signaling of the monocytic cell line THP-1. Besides, neutralizing antibodies to TNF-α, IL-1, IL-2, IFN-γ, and granulocyte/macrophage colony stimulating factor all failed to affect monocyte activation by membranes from stimulated T cells [2–4]. Similarly, although lymphotoxin (LT)-α receptor is expressed in Mϕ, it is not likely that membrane-associated LT is involved in Mϕ signaling upon contact with stimulated T cells, since Th2 cells do not express LT at either protein or mRNA levels. It must be emphasized that the contact between T_L and Mϕ could involve different ligands and counter-ligands in the murine and the human systems.

In addition to membrane-associated cytokines, other surface molecules have been assessed for their ability to activate Mϕ upon contact with stimulated T cells (e.g. lymphocyte function-associated antigen [LFA]-1/intercellular adhesion molcule-1, CD2/LFA 3, CD40/CD40L, and lymphocyte activation antigen-3. Thus CD40/CD40L interaction was shown to be involved in the contact activation of both human and mouse Mφ by T_L stimulated for 6 hours [22]. However, when stimulated for 24 hours, T_L isolated from both CD40L knockout and wild type mice triggered Mφ activation, although to a lesser extent [23]. In our system, where human T_L were stimulated for 48 hours and expressed a high capacity to induce cytokines in Mφ, we never observed any inhibition of contact-induced cytokine production, by blocking antibodies to either CD40L or soluble CD40. Furthermore, HUT-78 cells, which efficiently induce cytokine production in Mφ, do not express CD40L mRNA in resting or activated condition [24]. Finally, THP-1 cells that respond to contact-mediated activation by membranes of stimulated T cells do not express CD40. Another study of ours shows that in cocultures of living cells stimulated with IL-15, Th1- but not Th2-clones induce IL-1β production in monocytes [20]. In the latter system, blockade of the CD40–CD40L interaction results in inhibition of IL-1β production while IL-1Ra induction is unaffected. This differential effect indicates the selective relevance of CD40–CD40L engagement upon monocyte activation by Th1 clones. However, the levels of CD40L expression did not differ in Th1 and Th2 cell clones, implying that additional, unidentified molecule(s) preferentially expressed by Th1 cells are involved in their capacity to induce IL-1β. Therefore, CD40–CD40L might be a cofactor in contact-mediated activation of Mφ by stimulated T_L. Lymphocyte activation gene (LAG)-3 might also be one of the latter factors since it is able to synergize with low amounts of CD40L in inducing TNF-α and IL-12 on monocyte-derived dendritic cells [11]. In our system LAG-3 did not induce the production of IL-1β and TNF-α (unpublished results). Others have found that soluble CD23 induces cytokine production on monocytes [25]. In monocytes, the counter-ligands of CD23 are CD11b/CD18 and CD11c/CD18 rather than CD21. LFA-1 (CD11a/CD18) and CD69 also contribute to the activation of human monocytic cells by stimulated T cells [2,26]. This was substantiated by a study showing that IL-15 induced synovial T cells from RA patients to activate the production of TNF-α by Mφ. This effect was inhibited by antibodies to CD69, LFA-1 and intracellular adhesion molecule-1 [10].

Together these studies suggest that some known surface molecules are indeed involved in T cell signaling of Mφ. However, inhibitors (e.g. antibodies) of these molecules fail to abolish monocyte activation altogether, suggesting that the factor(s) required for T cell signaling of human monocytes by direct contact remain(s) to be identified.

Intracellular pathways involved in cytokine production by monocyte-macrophages upon contact with stimulated T lymphocytes

Depending on the type of stimulus, different intracellular pathways are used in Mφ for the production of the same cytokine. Some stimuli (i.e. microbial products) can induce the production of TNF-α, IL-1β, and IL-1Ra in human Mφ. In other cases, IL-1Ra might be induced in the absence of IL-1 induction, but from what is known at present, all stimuli eliciting IL-1β production also trigger IL-1Ra production, at least in Mφ. The tight control of proinflammatory cytokine production is indeed a prerequisite to avoid a cascade of events that could lead to uncontrolled inflammation. It is also well known that the production of both IL-1β and TNF-α is tightly regulated at several levels, including the dissociation between transcription and translation [27]. For example, stimuli such as C5a, hypoxia, blood clotting, or surface contact are not sufficient to provide a signal for translation, despite a vigorous signal for transcription [28]. Consequently, some stimuli might provide signals for complete cytokine gene transcription but no translational signaling. IL-1β and TNF-α translation can be blocked by pyridinyl-imidazol compounds that bind and inactivate the mitogen-activated protein kinase p38 [28].

Lipopolysaccharide has been the most frequently used stimulus for *in vitro* studies aimed at identifying transduction pathways underlying cytokine production in Mφ. Components of the transduction pathways that are induced by toll-like receptor 4 [29,30] and lead to the translocation of nuclear factor (NF)-κB, AP-1, protein kinase C [31], and p44/42 (extracellular signal-regulated kinase) [32] are all likely to be also involved in cytokine gene induction by other stimuli. Other components of transcription pathways leading to cytokine synthesis have been identified after signaling by engagement of cell surface molecules. The engagement of CD45 leading to TNF-α production in monocytes adopts a unique signaling pathway (phosphoinositol-3 kinase [PI3-K]) and pathways shared with LPS (NF-κB and p38 kinase). Furthermore, different products induced by the same stimulus can depend on different signaling pathways (e.g. PI3-K pathway selectively controls IL-1Ra, and not IL-1β, in 'septic' leukocytes [33]).

Upon T-cell-contact-mediated activation of Mφ, different pathways are involved in the induction of IL-10 or TNF-α [34,35]. Interestingly, PI3-K is mainly involved in IL-10 induction whereas NF-κB is involved in TNF-α production, suggesting that PI3-K is preferentially involved in pathways controlling the production of anti-inflammatory factors. T cells activated by a different stimulus also induce these two pathways [12]. Indeed, T cells that had been activated for eight days using a cocktail of cytokines and designated T_{ck} induced TNF-α production in resting monocytes in a cell-contact-dependent manner [12]. The same results were obtained with RA synovial T cells, suggesting that T_{ck} resemble RA synovial joint T cells in terms of contact-mediated cytokine induction in monocytes. In this system, TNF-α production was abrogated by blockade of the transcription factor NF-κB but enhanced by PI3-kinase inhibitors. Production of TNF-α, induced in monocytes by peripheral blood T cells that were stimulated by crosslinked anti-CD3, was not affected by NF-κB and was inhibited in the presence of PI3-kinase inhibitors. The premise that T_{ck} behave similarly to RA T cells further confirms the importance of T cells in inducing TNF-α in chronic inflammatory rheumatoid tissue. We recently demonstrated that PI3-kinase might represent a checkpoint signaling molecule favoring IL-1Ra synthesis over that of IL-1β [36]. Furthermore, upon contact with stimulated T cells, the balance between IL-1β and IL-1Ra production in monocytes was also regulated by Ser/Thr phosphatase(s) [8].

Modulation of contact-mediated activation of monocyte-macrophages

Since the contact-mediated activation of Mφ is a major pathway toward cytokine production, the modulation of this mechanism (i.e. the blockade of IL-1 and TNF-α production at the triggering level of contact-mediated activation) would be of therapeutic interest. We established that therapeutic agents used in RA and multiple sclerosis (i.e. leflunomide [37] and IFN-β [38,39], respectively) affect the contact-mediated activation of monocytes. Leflunomide inhibits the ability of stimulated T_L to trigger IL-1β production in monocytes, resulting in an enhancement of the IL-1Ra/IL-1β molar ratio [40]. Similar results were obtained with IFN-β. Indeed, upon contact-mediated activation of monocytes, IFN-β not only inhibited IL-1β and TNF-α but it also stimulated IL-1Ra [41,42], due to the fact that IFN-β interfered with the activation of both T_L and monocytes. However, surface molecules of T_L that we found to be involved in contact-signaling of monocytes (i.e. TNF-α, CD25, CD69, CD18, CD11a, CD11b, CD11c, CD40L, and LAG-3) were not modulated by IFN-β or leflunomide, suggesting that other surface activators on T_L are involved in the contact-mediated activation of monocytes by stimulated T_L. While CD40–CD40 ligand engagement is required, it may not be sufficient for human Th1 cell induction of IL-2- or IL-15-driven, contact-dependent IL-1β production by Mφ [20]. These effects are similar to those observed in patients *in vivo*, suggesting the occurrence of contact-mediated activation of monocytes *in vivo*.

Identification of a specific inhibitor of T-cell contact-mediated activation of monocyte-macrophages

The inhibition of T cell signaling of monocytes might be important because it would maintain a low level of monocyte activation within the blood stream. We recently identified apolipoprotein (apo) A-I as being a specific inhibitor of contact-mediated activation of monocytes [43]. These results were further confirmed by using recombinant apo A-I [42]. Apo A-I is a 'negative acute-phase protein' and the main protein of high-density lipoproteins (HDL). Variations of apo A-I concentration were observed in several inflammatory diseases [44]. In RA, the levels of circulating apo A-I and HDL-cholesterol in untreated patients were lower than in normal controls [45–47]. In contrast, apo A-I was enhanced in synovial fluid of RA patients [48], although its concentrations remained 10-fold lower in synovial fluid than in plasma. The elevation of apo A-I levels in synovial fluid of RA patients was accompanied by an enhancement in cholesterol, suggesting an infiltration of HDL particles in the inflamed joint. This putative regulatory mechanism might, however, be overcome by serum amyloid A (SAA), a positive acute-phase protein, which is not only produced in the liver but also in the RA synovium [49]. Indeed SAA can displace apo A-I from HDL, and HDL-associated SAA displays proinflammatory activity [50]. Recently, it was shown that the inflammatory condition in juvenile RA was associated with hypo-high density lipoproteinemia and a significant decrease in apo A-I concentration in patient plasma [51]. Furthermore, in collaboration with B Bresnihan (Dublin, Ireland), we observed that apo A-I was present in the perivascular region of RA synovium but not in normal tissue (manuscript in preparation). In systemic lupus erythematosus, apo A-I plasma concentrations are diminished. This decrease is associated with the presence of anti-apo A-I antibodies in 32% of patients [52]. In patients with multiple sclerosis undergoing IFN-β therapy, levels of apo A-I proved to be lower in a subgroup of patients experiencing relapses and/or progression [53]. Furthermore, increasing evidence strongly supports the contention that inflammatory responses are an integral part of atherosclerosis [54]. Indeed, Mφ and T_L are present at all stages of lesion development, and the earliest lesion (fatty streak) consists predominantly of Mφ and T_L. In addition, transfer of CD4+ T cells aggravates atherosclerosis in immunodeficient apo E knockout mice [55]. Therefore, T_L-signaling of monocytes may occur in atherosclerosis. Gene transfer of apo A-I reduced atherosclerosis in several mouse models [56]. This phenomenon has been attributed to the function of HDL-associated apo A-I in lipid metabolism and transport. However, the premise that apo A-I inhibit contact-mediated activation of Mφ by T_L suggests that HDL has protective functions at several levels in atherosclerosis, including cytokine production by Mφ. Furthermore, the incidence of atherosclerotic heart disease is higher in patients with systemic lupus erythematosus and RA [57], in agreement with the inverse correlation of the concentration of HDL with the incidence of atherosclerosis.

With the exception of atherosclerosis, which had not been considered a chronic inflammatory disease until recently, and despite the scarcity of studies having dealt with the levels of HDL in 'classical' chronic inflammatory diseases, it seems that chronic inflammation is associated with low levels of HDL-associated apo A-I. We thus hypothesize that in these diseases, a vicious circle sets in, which is responsible for the maintenance of inflammation (Fig. 2).

Figure 2

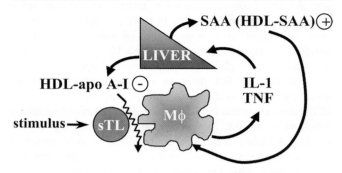

Scheme of the relationship between chronic inflammation, acute-phase proteins and homeostasis of cytokines. The liver produces both apolipoprotein (apo) A-I and serum amyloid A (SAA). IL-1β and TNF-α differentially regulate the production of acute-phase proteins by increasing the production of SAA (a proinflammatory factor) and decreasing that of apo A-I (an anti-inflammatory factor). The decreased level of apo A-I results in a better activation of monocyte-macrophages (Mφ) by direct contact with stimulated T lymphocytes (sTL), enhancing the production of IL-1 and TNF. The increased levels of SAA result in the substitution of apo A-I by SAA on high-density lipoprotein (HDL), and SAA–HDL further stimulates the production of cytokines by Mφ.

The identification of HDL-associated apo A-I ligand(s) on stimulated T cells might lead to the elucidation of the mechanisms and molecules involved in T cell signaling of monocytes. HDL-associated apo A-I has been shown to bind specifically to a number of cell-surface molecules, including HDL binding protein [58], scavenger receptor B1, HDL binding protein-2, cubilin [59], ATP-binding cassette A1 transporter [60], and a 95 kDa protein at the surface of human fetal hepatocytes [61]. All these proteins display a high molecular weight (≥80 kDa) and to date have not been identified (not searched) on T cells. In conclusion, the identification of apo A-I as an important regulator of T_L–Mφ interaction sheds new light on the role of HDL-associated apo A-I in innate and acquired immune response, and could be extended to other diseases.

Dissociation of IL-1β and IL-1Ra production in monocytes in contact with stimulated T lymphocytes due to the presence of HDL-associated apo A-I

Although HDL inhibited the production of TNF-α and IL-1β in both peripheral blood monocytes and THP-1 cells, this did not apply to IL-1Ra. Indeed, in peripheral blood mononuclear cells that were stimulated by either phytohemagglutinin or an antigen (tetanus toxoid), IL-1Ra production was not significantly inhibited, contrasting with the obvious inhibition of IL-1β and TNF-α production (Fig. 3). Furthermore, this indicates that apo A-I was able to inhibit contact-mediated Mφ activation when T_L were stimulated by either nonspecific stimuli or antigens.

Figure 3

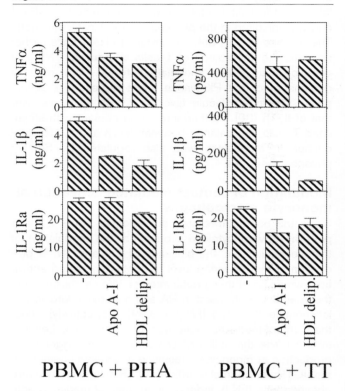

Apolipoprotein (apo) A-I does not significantly inhibit IL-1Ra production in peripheral blood mononuclear cells (PBMC) stimulated by either phytohemagglutinin (PHA) or tetanus toxoid (TT).
Conditions: 0.4 × 10⁶ cells/well/200 μl; 5 μg/ml polymyxin; 1 μg/ml PHA; 10 μg/ml TT; 48 hour incubation for PHA, 72 hours for TT.

Concluding remarks

To date, direct cell–cell contact with stimulated T_L is the main pathway triggering activation of Mφ in the absence of infectious agents. The potency of this mechanism suggests that it is a major pathway by which T_L exert their pathogenic effect in chronic inflammatory diseases of autoimmune etiology. Many more investigations are needed to identify the surface molecules (ligands and counter-ligands) involved in this process. However, the control of contact-mediated signaling of monocytes by apo A-I might represent the first step toward developing novel agents that interfere with the inflammatory response induced by cell–cell contact, which leads to tissue destruction in chronic inflammatory diseases.

Glossary of terms

apo = apolipoprotein; HDL = high-density lipoprotein; LAG = lymphocyte activation gene; LFA = lymphocyte-function-associated antigen; LT = lymphotoxin; PI3-K = phosiphinositol-3 kinase; PMA = phorbol myristate acetate; SAA = serum amyloid A; T_{ck} = cytokine-activated T lymphocyte; T_L = T lymphocytes.

Acknowledgments

The authors gratefully acknowledge Mrs Roswitha Rehm for skilful reading of the manuscript. Unpublished results reported here were part of projects supported by grant #31-50930-97 from the Swiss National Science Foundation as well as grants from the Swiss Society for Multiple Sclerosis, and the Hans Wilsdorf Foundation.

References

1. Firestein GS, Zvaifler NJ: **How important are T cells in chronic rheumatoid synovitis?: II. T cell-independent mechanisms from beginning to end.** *Arthritis Rheum* 2002, **46**:298-308. [key review]
2. Vey E, Zhang JH, Dayer J-M: **IFN-gamma and 1,25(OH)2D3 induce on THP-1 cells distinct patterns of cell surface antigen expression, cytokine production, and responsiveness to contact with activated T cells.** *J Immunol* 1992, **149**:2040-2046. [archival reference]
3. Isler P, Vey E, Zhang JH, Dayer JM: **Cell surface glycoproteins expressed on activated human T-cells induce production of interleukin-1 beta by monocytic cells: a possible role of CD69.** *Eur Cytokine Netw* 1993, **4**:15-23. [archival reference]
4. Lacraz S, Isler P, Vey E, Welgus HG, Dayer JM: **Direct contact between T lymphocytes and monocytes is a major pathway for induction of metalloproteinase expression.** *J Biol Chem* 1994, **269**:22027-22033. [archival reference]
5. Li JM, Isler P, Dayer JM, Burger D: **Contact-dependent stimulation of monocytic cells and neutrophils by stimulated human T-cell clones.** *Immunology* 1995, **84**:571-576. [archival reference]
6. Vey E, Burger D, Dayer JM: **Expression and cleavage of tumor necrosis factor-alpha and tumor necrosis factor receptors by human monocytic cell lines upon direct contact with stimulated T cells.** *Eur J Immunol* 1996, **26**:2404-2409. [archival reference]
7. Chizzolini C, Chicheportiche R, Burger D, Dayer JM: **Human Th1 cells preferentially induce interleukin (IL)-1 beta while Th2 cells induce IL-1 receptor antagonist production upon cell/cell contact with monocytes.** *Eur J Immunol* 1997, **27**:171-177. [general reference]
8. Vey E, Dayer JM, Burger D: **Direct contact with stimulated T cells induces the expression of IL-1 beta and IL-1 receptor antagonist in human monocytes. Involvement of serine/threonine phosphatases in differential regulation.** *Cytokine* 1997, **9**:480-487. [general reference]
9. Sebbag M, Parry SL, Brennan FM, Feldmann M: **Cytokine stimulation of T lymphocytes regulates their capacity to induce monocyte production of tumor necrosis factor-alpha, but not interleukin-10: Possible relevance to pathophysiology of rheumatoid arthritis.** *Eur J Immunol* 1997, **27**:624-632. [general reference]
10. McInnes IB, Leung BP, Sturrock RD, Field M, Liew FY: **Interleukin-15 mediates T cell-dependent regulation of tumor necrosis factor-alpha production in rheumatoid arthritis.** *Nat Med* 1997, **3**:189-195. [general reference]
11. Avice MN, Sarfati M, Triebel F, Delespesse G, Demeure CE: **Lymphocyte activation gene-3, a MHC class II ligand expressed on activated T cells, stimulates TNF-alpha and IL-alpha production by monocytes and dendritic cells.** *J Immunol* 1999, **162**:2748-2753. [general reference]
12. Brennan FM, Hayes AL, Ciesielski CJ, Green P, Foxwell BM, Feldmann M: **Evidence that rheumatoid arthritis synovial T cells are similar to cytokine-activated T cells: involvement of phosphatidylinositol 3-kinase and nuclear factor kappaB pathways in tumor necrosis factor alpha production in rheumatoid arthritis.** *Arthritis Rheum* 2002, **46**:31-41. [general reference]
13. Burger D: **Cell contact-mediated signaling of monocytes by stimulated T cells: a major pathway for cytokine induction.** *Eur Cytokine Netw* 2000, **11**:346-353. [key review]
14. Tak PP, Smeets TJM, Daha MR, Kluin PM, Meijers KAE, Brand R, Meinders AE, Breedveld FC: **Analysis of the synovial cell infiltrate in early rheumatoid synovial tissue in relation to local disease activity.** *Arthritis Rheum* 1997, **40**:217-225. [general reference]
15. Smeets TJ, Kraan MC, Galjaard S, Youssef PP, Smith MD, Tak PP: **Analysis of the cell infiltrate and expression of matrix metalloproteinases and granzyme B in paired synovial biopsy specimens from the cartilage-pannus junction in patients with RA.** *Ann Rheum Dis* 2001, **60**:561-565. [general reference]
16. Tak PP, Bresnihan B: **The pathogenesis and prevention of joint damage in rheumatoid arthritis: advances from synovial biopsy and tissue analysis.** *Arthritis Rheum* 2000, **43**:2619-2633. [key review]
17. Mima T, Saeki Y, Ohshima S, Nishimoto N, Matsushita M, Shimizu M, Kobayashi Y, Nomura T, Kishimoto T: **Transfer of rheumatoid arthritis into severe combined immunodeficient mice. The pathogenetic implications of T cell populations oligoclonally expanding in the rheumatoid joints.** *J Clin Invest* 1995, **96**:1746-1758. [archival reference]
18. Takemura S, Klimiuk PA, Braun A, Goronzy JJ, Weyand CM: **T cell activation in rheumatoid synovium is B cell dependent.** *J Immunol* 2001, **167**:4710-4718. [general reference]
19. Parry SL, Sebbag M, Feldmann M, Brennan FM: **Contact with T cells modulates monocyte IL-10 production. Role of T cell membrane TNF-alpha.** *J Immunol* 1997, **158**:3673-3681. [general reference]
20. Ribbens C, Dayer JM, Chizzolini C: **CD40-CD40 ligand (CD154) engagement is required but may not be sufficient for human T helper 1 cell induction of interleukin-2- or interleukin-15-driven, contact-dependent, interleukin-1beta production by monocytes.** *Immunology* 2000, **99**:279-286. [general reference]
21. Suttles J, Miller RW, Tao X, Stout RD: **T cells which do not express membrane tumor necrosis factor-alpha activate macrophage effector function by cell contact- dependent signaling of macrophage tumor necrosis factor-alpha production.** *Eur J Immunol* 1994, **24**:1736-1742. [archival reference]
22. Wagner DH, Stout RD, Suttles J: **Role of the CD40-CD40 ligand interaction in CD4(+) T cell contact-dependent activation of monocyte interleukin-1 synthesis.** *Eur J Immunol* 1994, **24**:3148-3154. [archival reference]
23. Stout RD, Suttles J, Xu J, Grewal IS, Flavell RA: **Impaired T cell-mediated macrophage activation in CD40 ligand-deficient mice.** *J Immunol* 1996, **156**:8-11. [archival reference]
24. Gauchat J-F, Aubry J-P, Mazzei G, Life P, Jomotte T, Elson G, Bonnefoy J-Y: **Human CD40-ligand: molecular cloning, cellular distribution and regulation of expression by factors controlling IgE production.** *FEBS Lett* 1993, **315**:259-266. [archival reference]
25. Hermann P, Armant M, Brown E, Rubio M, Ishihara H, Ulrich D, Caspary RG, Lindberg FP, Armitage R, Maliszewski C, Delespesse G, Sarfati M: **The vitronectin receptor and its associated CD47 molecule mediates proinflammatory cytokine synthesis in human monocytes by interaction with soluble CD23.** *J Cell Biol* 1999, **144**:767-775. [general reference]
26. Manié S, Kubar J, Limouse M, Ferrua B, Ticchioni M, Breittmayer JP, Peyron JF, Schaffar L, Rossi B: **CD3-stimulated Jurkat T-cells mediate IL-1β production in monocytic THP-1 cells: role of LFA-1 molecule and participation of CD69 T-cell antigen.** *Eur Cytokine Netw* 1993, **4**:7-13. [archival reference]
27. Schindler R, Gelfand JA, Dinarello CA: **Recombinant C5a stimulates transcription rather than translation of interleukin-1 (IL-1) and tumor necrosis factor: translational signal provided by lipopolysaccharide or IL-1 itself.** *Blood* 1990, **76**:1631-1638. [archival reference]
28. Dinarello CA: **IL-1beta.** In *Cytokine Reference.* Edited by Oppenheim JJ, Feldmann M. New York, London: Academic Press; 2000:351-374. [key review]
29. Aderem A, Ulevitch RJ: **Toll-like receptors in the induction of the innate immune response.** *Nature* 2000, **406**:782-787. [key review]
30. Beutler B: **Toll-like receptors: how they work and what they do.** *Curr Opin Hematol* 2002, **9**:2-10. [key review]
31. Shapira L, Takashiba S, Champagne C, Amar S, Van Dyke TE: **Involvement of protein kinase C and protein tyrosine kinase in lipopolysaccharide-induced TNF-alpha and IL-1 beta production by human monocytes.** *J Immunol* 1994, **153**:1818-1824. [archival reference]
32. Liu MK, Herrera Velit P, Brownsey RW, Reiner NE: **CD14-dependent activation of protein kinase C and mitogen-activated protein kinases (p42 and p44) in human monocytes treated with bacterial lipopolysaccharide.** *J Immunol* 1994, **153**:2642-2652. [archival reference]
33. Learn CA, Boger MS, Li L, McCall CE: **The phosphatidylinositol 3-kinase pathway selectively controls sIL-1RA not interleukin-1beta production in the septic leukocytes.** *J Biol Chem* 2001, **276**:20234-20239. [general reference]

34. Foey AD, Green P, Foxwell B, Feldmann M, Brennan F: **Cytokine-stimulated T cells induce macrophage IL-10 production dependent on phosphatidylinositol 3-kinase and p70S6K: implications for rheumatoid arthritis.** *Arthritis Res* 2002, **4**:64-70. [general reference]

35. Foxwell B, Browne K, Bondeson J, Clarke C, de Martin R, Brennan F, Feldmann M: **Efficient adenoviral infection with IkappaB alpha reveals that macrophage tumor necrosis factor alpha production in rheumatoid arthritis is NF-kappaB dependent.** *Proc Natl Acad Sci USA* 1998, **95**:8211-8215. [general reference]

36. Hyka N, Kaufmann MT, Chicheportiche R, Dayer JM, Burger D: **Interferon-beta induces interleukin-1 receptor antagonist production in human monocytes through PI3-kinase-STAT1 signaling pathway [abstract].** *Autoimmunity Rev* 2002, **1**:64. [general reference]

37. Tugwell P, Wells G, Strand V, Maetzel A, Bombardier C, Crawford B, Dorrier C, Thompson A for the Leflunomide Rheumatoid Arthritis Investigators Group: **Clinical improvement as reflected in measures of function and health-related quality of life following treatment with leflunomide compared with methotrexate in patients with rheumatoid arthritis: sensitivity and relative efficiency to detect a treatment effect in a twelve-month, placebo-controlled trial.** *Arthritis Rheum* 2000, **43**:506-514. [general reference]

38. Smeets TJ, Dayer JM, Kraan MC, Versendaal J, Chicheportiche R, Breedveld FC, Tak PP: **The effects of interferon-beta treatment of synovial inflammation and expression of metalloproteinases in patients with rheumatoid arthritis.** *Arthritis Rheum* 2000, **43**:270-274. [general reference]

39. Arnason BG: **Treatment of multiple sclerosis with interferon beta.** *Biomed Pharmacother* 1999, **53**:344-350. [key review]

40. Déage V, Burger D, Dayer JM: **Exposure of T lymphocytes to leflunomide but not to dexamethasone favors the production by monocytic cells of interleukin-1 receptor antagonist and the tissue-inhibitor of metalloproteinases-1 over that of interleukin-1beta and metalloproteinases.** *Eur Cytokine Netw* 1998, **9**:663-668. [general reference]

41. Coclet-Ninin J, Dayer JM, Burger D: **Interferon-beta not only inhibits interleukin-1 beta and tumor necrosis factor-alpha but stimulates interleukin-1 receptor antagonist production in human peripheral blood mononuclear cells.** *Eur Cytokine Netw* 1997, **8**:345-349. [general reference]

42. Franceschini G: **Apolipoprotein function in health and disease: insights from natural mutations.** *Eur J Clin Invest* 1996, **26**:733-746. [archival review]

43. Hyka N, Dayer JM, Modoux C, Kohno T, Edwards CK, III, Roux-Lombard P, Burger D: **Apolipoprotein A-I inhibits the production of interleukin-1beta and tumor necrosis factor-alpha by blocking contact-mediated activation of monocytes by T lymphocytes.** *Blood* 2001, **97**:2381-2389. [general reference]

44. Burger D, Dayer JM: **High-density lipoprotein-associated apolipoprotein A-I: the missing link between infection and chronic inflammation?** *Autoimmunity Rev* 2002, **1**:111-117. [key review]

45. Park YB, Lee SK, Lee WK, Suh CH, Lee CW, Lee CH, Song CH, Lee J: **Lipid profiles in untreated patients with rheumatoid arthritis.** *J Rheumatol* 1999, **26**:1701-1704. [general reference]

46. Doherty NS, Littman BH, Reilly K, Swindell AC, Buss JM, Anderson NL: **Analysis of changes in acute-phase plasma proteins in an acute inflammatory response and in rheumatoid arthritis using two-dimensional gel electrophoresis.** *Electrophoresis* 1998, **19**:355-363. [general reference]

47. Lakatos J, Harsagyi A: **Serum total, HDL, LDL cholesterol, and triglyceride levels in patients with rheumatoid arthritis.** *Clin Biochem* 1988, **21**:93-96. [general reference]

48. Ananth L, Prete PE, Kashyap ML: **Apolipoproteins A-I and B and cholesterol in synovial fluid of patients with rheumatoid arthritis.** *Metabolism* 1993, **42**:803-806. [archival reference]

49. O'Hara R, Murphy EP, Whitehead AS, Fitzgerald O, Bresnihan B: **Acute-phase serum amyloid A production by rheumatoid arthritis synovial tissue.** *Arthritis Res* 2000, **2**:142-144. [general reference]

50. Patel H, Fellowes R, Coade S, Woo P: **Human serum amyloid A has cytokine-like properties.** *Scand J Immunol* 1998, **48**:410-418. [general reference]

51. Tselepis AD, Elisaf M, Besis S, Karabina SA, Chapman MJ, Siamopoulou A: **Association of the inflammatory state in active juvenile rheumatoid arthritis with hypo-high-density lipoproteinemia and reduced lipoprotein-associated platelet-activating factor acetylhydrolase activity.** *Arthritis Rheum* 1999, **42**:373-383. [general reference]

52. Dinu AR, Merrill JT, Shen C, Antonov IV, Myones BL, Lahita RG: **Frequency of antibodies to the cholesterol transport protein apolipoprotein A1 in patients with SLE.** *Lupus* 1998, **7**:355-360. [general reference]

53. Sena A, Pedrosa R, Ferret-Sena V, Almeida R, Andrade ML, Morais MG, Couderc R: **Interferon beta-1a therapy changes lipoprotein metabolism in patients with multiple sclerosis.** *Clin Chem Lab Med* 2000, **38**:209-213. [general reference]

54. Ross R: **Atherosclerosis – an inflammatory disease.** *N Engl J Med* 1999, **340**:115-126. [general reference]

55. Zhou X, Nicoletti A, Elhage R, Hansson GK: **Transfer of CD4(+) T cells aggravates atherosclerosis in immunodeficient apolipoprotein E knockout mice.** *Circulation* 2000, **102**:2919-2922. [general reference]

56. Tangirala RK, Tsukamoto K, Chun SH, Usher D, Pure E, Rader DJ: **Regression of atherosclerosis induced by liver-directed gene transfer of apolipoprotein A-I in mice.** *Circulation* 1999, **100**:1816-1822. [general reference]

57. Manzi S, Wasko MC: **Inflammation-mediated rheumatic diseases and atherosclerosis.** *Ann Rheum Dis* 2000, **59**:321-325. [general reference]

58. Fidge NH: **High-density lipoprotein receptors, binding proteins, and ligands.** *J Lipid Res* 1999, **40**:187-201. [key review]

59. Kozyraki R, Fyfe J, Kristiansen M, Gerdes C, Jacobsen C, Cui S, Christensen EI, Aminoff M, de la Chapelle A, Krahe R, Verroust PJ, Moestrup SK: **The intrinsic factor-vitamin B12 receptor, cubilin, is a high-affinity apolipoprotein A-I receptor facilitating endocytosis of high-density lipoprotein.** *Nat Med* 1999, **5**:656-661. [general reference]

60. Chambenoit O, Hamon Y, Marguet D, Rigneault H, Rosseneu M, Chimini G: **Specific docking of apolipoprotein A-I at the cell surface requires a functional ABCA1 transporter.** *J Biol Chem* 2001, **276**:9955-9960. [general reference]

61. Bocharov AV, Vishnyakova TG, Baranova IN, Patterson AP, Eggerman TL: **Characterization of a 95 kDa high affinity human high density lipoprotein-binding protein.** *Biochemistry* 2001, **40**:4407-4416. [general reference]

62. Miltenburg AMM, Lacraz S, Welgus HG, Dayer JM: **Immobilized anti-CD3 antibody activates T cell clones to induce the production of interstitial collagenase, but not tissue inhibitor of metalloproteinases, in monocytic THP-1 cells and dermal fibroblasts.** *J Immunol* 1995, **154**:2655-2667. [archival reference]

63. Avice MN, Demeure CE, Delespesse G, Rubio M, Armant M, Sarfati M: **IL-15 promotes IL-12 production by human monocytes via T cell-dependent contact and may contribute to IL-12-mediated IFN-gamma secretion by CD4+ T cells in the absence of TCR ligation.** *J Immunol* 1998, **161**:3408-3415. [general reference]

64. Chabot S, Charlet D, Wilson TL, Yong VW: **Cytokine production consequent to T cell--microglia interaction: the PMA/IFN gamma-treated U937 cells display similarities to human microglia.** *J Neurosci Methods* 2001, **105**:111-120. [general reference]

Supplement Review

Cytokine regulation in RA synovial tissue: role of T cell/macrophage contact-dependent interactions

Fionula Mary Brennan and Andrew David Foey

Kennedy Institute of Rheumatology Division, Faculty of Medicine, Imperial College of Science, Technology and Medicine, London, UK

Correspondence: Fionula Mary Brennan, Imperial College of Science, Technology and Medicine, Kennedy Institute of Rheumatology Division, Faculty of Medicine, 1 Aspenlea Road, London, W6 8LH, UK. Tel: +44 (0)20 8383 4451; fax: +44 (0)20 8563 0399; e-mail: f.brennan@ic.ac.uk

Received: 9 January 2002
Accepted: 5 March 2002
Published: 9 May 2002

Arthritis Res 2002, **4 (suppl 3)**:S177-S182

This article may contain supplementary data which can only be found online at http://arthritis-research.com/content/4/S3/S177

Chapter summary

Several groups have documented the expression of cytokines in rheumatoid arthritis synovial tissue over the past 15 years or so. These studies have indicated that most cytokines examined are expressed at the mRNA levels at least, and many other cytokines are found in abundance as proteins. Our attention has recently focused on the mechanisms that induce and regulate tumour necrosis factor and IL-10. Other workers and ourselves have found that cell–cell contact is an important signal for the induction of cytokines, and our work has demonstrated that tumour necrosis factor and IL-10 production in rheumatoid arthritis synovial joint cells cultures is dependent on T cell/macrophage interaction. In this chapter, we review recent advances in this area and also highlight areas where new therapeutic intervention opportunities arise.

Keywords: cognate, differentiation, macrophage, signalling, T cells

Historical background

It is now well accepted that the spontaneous production of proinflammatory cytokines (in particular, tumour necrosis factor [TNF] and IL-1) produced locally in the inflamed synovial joint contribute directly/indirectly to the pathogenesis of rheumatoid arthritis (RA) [1]. These observations have arisen from *ex vivo* studies on human synovial cultures, immunohistochemical and mRNA analysis of synovium, and *in vivo* studies in animal models of arthritis.

These investigations led to the development of several TNF and IL-1 inhibitors, two of which are currently licensed Remicade (chimeric anti-TNF antibody) and Enbrel (TNF-receptor fusion protein). While such therapies targeting TNF in chronic inflammatory disease are very successful [2], it is also apparent that long-term blockade of a cytokine such as TNF, which is important in

innate and acquired immunity, may lead to an increase in latent and/or opportunistic infections. This is now apparent, with a small but significant increase in unusual infections, as well as the re-emergence of latent tuberculosis, particularly in Central and Eastern Europe [3].

There is thus a need to understand what mechanisms lead to the production of proinflammatory cytokines in RA synovial tissue, and further to determine how this is linked to homeostatic regulation. It has been observed that while the production of proinflammatory cytokines and enzymes is increased in RA, this is offset to some degree by the action of the endogenous anti-inflammatory cytokines and cytokine inhibitors. Of particular importance in this respect is IL-10, an important regulator of TNF-α and IL-1β spontaneously produced by macrophages in the rheumatoid joint [4,5]. Thus, if endogenous IL-10 is blocked in RA synovial

---

A glossary of specialist terms used in this chapter appears at the end of the text section. A list of common abbreviations used in this issue appears just before the indexes.

cell cultures, the spontaneous production of both TNF and IL-1 increases significantly [4]. There is therefore an important need to develop therapies that block proinflammatory pathways but leave unaffected those pathways that regulate immunoregulatory cytokines such as IL-10.

Cognate-dependent interactions

Histological studies of synovium in RA have indicated that this tissue is very cellular, and that several different cell types including macrophages and T cells are in close proximity [6]. This may suggest that contact signals between macrophages and T cells could be of importance *in vivo* in modulating macrophage function. We have found that TNF-α production in RA synovium is T-cell dependent, as removal of CD3-positive T cells from RA synovial mononuclear cells resulted in significant reduced macrophage TNF-α production [7]. Furthermore, this signal was abrogated if physical contact between the two cell types was blocked.

Direct-contact-mediated interactions have been studied by several groups using transformed T-cell lines and monocytic lines, and have been found to play a role in inducing the synthesis of several cytokines including IL-1β, TNF-α, IL-10 and metalloproteinases [8–12]. We have studied T cell/monocyte cognate interactions using cells isolated from the peripheral blood of normal donors. Importantly, we observed that the manner in which T cells were activated influenced the profile of cytokines induced in the monocytes. Thus, if blood T cells were activated with cross-linked anti-CD3, this induced the production of TNF-α and IL-10 in monocytes [12]. However, if the T cells were stimulated with a cocktail of cytokines (TNF-α, IL-2 and IL-6) for 8 days (bystander activation), TNF-α production followed but IL-10 production did not [11]. These observations suggested to us that cytokine-stimulated T cells (Tck) may be the actual T cells in RA synovial tissue that induce macrophage TNF-α production, because they induce an unbalanced, proinflammatory cytokine response from monocytes and they could be part of a vicious cycle (Fig. 1). Indeed, in addition to the mechanism of T-cell activation determining the cytokine profile produced by monocytic cells, the corresponding T-cell phenotype would also appear to be important, as one study [13] suggested a differential regulation of monocyte-derived cytokine production by Th1-like and Th2-like cells. This study describes CD4$^+$ Th1 clones inducing high levels of IL-1β production by THP-1 monocytes, whereas Th2 clones induced higher levels of IL-1ra. This implies that Th1 cells are proinflammatory whereas Th2 cells are anti-inflammatory.

The hypothesis that RA T cells mimic the action of Tck cells is attractive since T cells found in RA synovium have unusual characteristics. The T cells are relatively small and noncycling, but have features of activation, with over one-

Figure 1

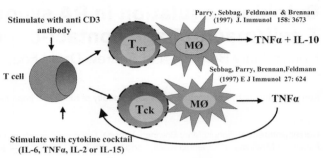

Bystander activation - "vicious cycle"

Cytokine disequilibrium induced by cytokine-stimulated T cells (Tck). Mϕ, monocytes; T$_{tcr}$, T-cell-receptor-dependent stimulated T cells.

half expressing HLA class II, VLA antigens, CD25 and CD69 [14,15]. T-cell receptor analysis has not revealed a consistent pattern, and responses to putative autoantigens have not been easy to reproduce (reviewed in [16]). Based on these features and the low capacity of T cells to produce T-cell-derived cytokines, it has been proposed that T cells in the joint may not be involved in the later stages of the disease [17]. We have, however, proposed that they are involved in disease pathology through the activation of macrophages to induce TNF. The environment of the RA synovium is favourable to Tck cells, as it is rich in cytokines. Unutmaz *et al.* described bystander-activated T cells generated from normal peripheral blood mononuclear cells (PBMC) with IL-2, IL-6 and TNF-α [18]. We found that IL-15 could, by itself, mimic the IL-6/TNF-α/IL-2 cocktail used to activate Tck [11]. IL-15 is of particular interest as it is found in RA synovium [19] and can activate peripheral blood T cells to induce TNF-α synthesis in U937 cells or in adherent RA synovial cells in a contact-dependent manner [20,21]

Other cognate cell-to-cell interactions occur in the synovial joint, which contribute to the disease pathology observed in RA. These interactions include endothelial cell/T cell and fibroblast/T cell interactions. During the early stages of inflammation there is a large cellular infiltration from the peripheral circulation to the synovial joint, where interactions between T cells and vascular endothelium drive further extravasation and infiltration by the expression of cell adhesion molecules, chemokines and cytokines [22–25]. In addition, the earliest infiltrating cells, neutrophils, can be activated by contact-mediated interaction with T cells, as determined by the ability of these neutrophils to be primed for respiratory burst by formyl-methionine leucine phenylalanine peptide [26].

As the pathology of RA progresses to chronic inflammation and pannus forms at the cartilage–pannus junction, the interactions between T cells and fibroblasts/ macrophages predominate. The interaction between stimulated T cells and dermal fibroblasts or synoviocytes has recently been shown to induce MMP-1 (collagenase) and TIMP-1, with an imbalance in favour of the proinflammatory MMP-1 [27], also inhibiting the synthesis of type I and type III collagen by fibroblast cells [28].

Studies undertaken thus far have documented the potent stimulatory activity of T cells on monocyte cytokine production during the pathology of RA. The abundance of T cells and monocytes in the peripheral circulation, which have the potential to physically interact with each other, however, does not seem to induce cytokine production. This led to the hypothesis and subsequent characterisation of an inhibitory factor, apolipoprotein A-1, preventing monocyte activation in the plasma/serum [29]. The presence of apolipoprotein A-1 and subsequent inhibition of T-cell-mediated macrophage activation may suggest this molecule to have a useful anti-inflammatory therapeutic effect in chronic inflammatory diseases such as RA.

Cell surface molecules

As contact-dependent signals have been demonstrated to be of importance, much attention has focused on the probable candidate molecules on the surface of cells mediating these functions. Specific surface interaction molecules that have been reported to mediate induction of monocyte cytokine synthesis include CD69, LFA-1 [8,30], CD44 [31], CD45 [32], CD40 [33], membrane TNF [12], and signalling lymphocytic activation molecule [34]. Our studies further demonstrated that T cells activated through the T-cell receptor complex induced monocyte IL-10 synthesis, which was partially dependent on endogenous TNF-α and IL-1, and that T-cell membrane TNF-α was an important contact-mediated signal [12,35]. However, IL-10 synthesis still occurred when TNF-α and IL-1 were neutralised, suggesting that there are other TNF/IL-1-independent signals required for IL-10 synthesis.

While TNF clearly plays a role in IL-10 production, there are other signals independent of TNF and IL-1 that may be involved. Of particular interest are members of the TNF/TNF-receptor family, which include CD40, CD27, CD30, OX-40 and LTβ. The ligands of these TNF-receptor molecules have been described as upregulated on T-cell activation. In addition, CD40L, 4-1BB, CD27L and CD30 have been described to be released as soluble molecules after activation [36–39]. The interaction between CD40L and CD40 has been suggested to be important for inducing both IL-1 and IL-12 synthesis following T-cell interaction with monocytes [33,40] and, more recently, to mediate IL-10 production by human microglial cells on interaction with anti-CD3-stimulated T cells [41]. In addition, we have recently shown that CD40L/CD40 interaction mediates cognate induction of macrophage IL-10

Figure 2

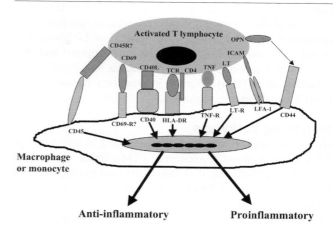

Potential ligand/counter ligand interactions involved in cytokine production by macrophages. HLA-DR, human leukocyte antigen – class II, subtype DR; ICAM, intracellular adhesion molecule; LT, lymphotoxin; MMP, matrix metalloproteinase; OPN, osteoprotegrin; RNI, reactive nitrogen intermediates; TCR, T-cell receptor; TNF, tumour necrosis factor.

[42]. The potential involvement of these ligand/counter ligand pairs on cells interacting in synovial membrane tissue is represented in Figure 2.

Differentiation status

In addition to the stimulus encountered by the T cells, our data has indicated the importance of the differentiation state of the monocyte in determining cytokine profiles in response to activated T cells. We observed that CD40 signalling augmented lipopolysaccharide (LPS)-induced IL-10 production by monocytes, but also observed that CD40 ligation induced IL-10 production by differentiated monocytes (macrophages) in the absence of LPS. Indeed, the priming mechanism of the macrophage determined the cytokine profile: macrophage-colony-stimulating factor preprogrammed macrophages to produce both IL-10 and TNF-α on stimulation by CD40L or Tck, whereas IFN-γ priming resulted predominantly in TNF-α [42].

IFN-γ-primed macrophages, however, can produce an endogenous IL-10 activity that is not secreted into the supernatant on cell contact with either Tck or CD40L transfectants, as neutralisation of endogenous IL-10 resulted in a marked increase in TNF-α production. This observation may agree with the report of membrane-associated IL-10 [43] and may highlight differences in the ability of these two types of macrophage-like cells to process cytokines.

Macrophage-colony-stimulating factor can usually be readily detected in the RA joint, while IFN-γ is scarce (reviewed in [44]). This may indicate why both TNF-α and

IL-10 are found in synovial membrane cell cultures. This preprogramming of macrophages would appear to be irrespective of the triggering stimulus because macrophages stimulated by either Tck, CD40 ligation or LPS result in similar cytokine profiles. It would thus appear that the route of differentiation of the monocyte is critical in the induction of IL-10 in cognate interactions between activated T cells and macrophages.

Signalling pathways

TNF-α synthesis in monocytes in response to some stimuli (LPS) but not others (zymosan or CD45 ligation) is NF-κB dependent [32,45,46]. It is thus of interest to observe that Tck-induced, but not T-cell-receptor-dependent stimulated T cell (Ttcr)-induced, TNF-α production in monocytes is NF-κB dependent. Furthermore, whereas phosphatidylinositol 3-kinase (PI3K) inhibitors blocked Ttcr induction of TNF-α, they paradoxically augmented TNF-α in monocytes stimulated by Tck cells. Importantly, we then found that RA T cells behaved like Tck cells, in that the induction of TNF-α in resting peripheral blood monocytes was NF-κB dependent but superinduced if PI3K was blocked. An identical result was observed if NF-κB or PI3K was blocked in the RA synovial cell cultures.

IL-10 production in monocytes/macrophages is equally complex. In response to LPS, IL-10 production is dependent on endogenous IL-1 and TNF-α. Furthermore, there is selective mitogen-activated protein kinase (MAPK) utilisation where IL-10 production was dependent on p38 MAPK, and TNF-α production was dependent on both p38 MAPK and p42/44 MAPK [47]. The involvement of p38 MAPK activity in IL-10 production subsequently led to the characterisation of the downstream effector, hsp27, as an anti-inflammatory mediator [48].

Little is known, however, regarding the involvement of the PI3K pathway in macrophage production of IL-10. PI3K and its downstream substrate p70S6K mediate IL-10-induced proliferative responses but not anti-inflammatory effects [49]. A recent study from our laboratory has described Tck-induced macrophage IL-10 production to be dependent on PI3K and p70S6K, whereas TNF-α production is negatively regulated by PI3K and is p70S6K dependent [50]. This suggests that IL-10 and TNF-α share a common component, p70S6K, but differentially utilise PI3K activity. These results are reproduced in the spontaneous cytokine production by RA synovial mononuclear cells (RA-SMCs) and by cocultures of RA synovial T cells with macrophages (RA-T/macrophage cocultures), further suggesting the relevance of this Tck/macrophage cognate coculture system as a model for cytokine production occurring in the inflamed synovium of the rheumatoid joint.

Although many other studies have implicated other signalling cascades in the induction of IL-10 production, not much work exists on the signalling required in macrophages stimulated by cognate interactions with fixed activated T cells. PKC and cAMP signalling have been implicated in IL-10 and TNF-α production and are currently under investigation in our group. Preliminary results would suggest that both these cascades differentially regulate IL-10 and TNF-α.

Studies undertaken by other groups have reported the involvement of the cAMP/PKA pathway in the induction of IL-10 production by human PBMC. The membrane-permeable dibutyryl cAMP was capable of elevating IL-10 mRNA and of augmenting LPS-induced IL-10 production, but on its own was incapable of producing IL-10 protein [51]. This work also demonstrated a role for PKC in the induction of IL-10 by LPS using the PKC inhibitors, calphostin C and H-7. This result contradicts our data but may reflect that this study used PBMC, a heterogeneous population, as compared with purified monocyte-derived macrophages.

In addition, the selective inhibition of phosphodiesterase type IV by rolipram was found to augment LPS-induced IL-10 production by murine peritoneal macrophages. The mechanism of this was thought to be as a consequence of LPS inducing the anti-inflammatory mediator, prostaglandin E_2, which in turn upregulates intracellular cAMP via stimulation of adenylate cyclase activity [52].

Concluding remarks

The cognate activation of macrophages by T cells has focused almost exclusively on the membrane interactions mediating the macrophage effector function, such as nitric oxide release, phagocytosis, B-cell help and, more recently, the cytokine profiles induced. The control of T-cell-induced IL-10 and TNF-α production by monocyte-derived macrophages is complex and is regulated at many levels. These levels include priming of the monocyte/macrophage, T-cell stimulation, and hence specific ligand/receptor interaction, and the resulting signal cascades and crosstalk between them. The continued study of these contact-mediated interactions, the signal transduction distal to the receptor and how they compare between the induction of IL-10 and TNF-α may discover potential therapeutic targets selectively affecting proinflammatory TNF-α production without affecting anti-inflammatory IL-10 production. Such targets will prove to be of great benefit in the treatment of such chronic inflammatory diseases as RA.

Glossary of terms

MAPK = mitogen-activated protein kinase; PI3K = phosphatidylinositol 3-kinase; Tck = cytokine-stimulated T cells; Ttcr = T-cell-receptor-dependent stimulated T cells.

Acknowledgements

Andy Foey is funded by a Wellcome Trust project grant. Prof Fionula Brennan and The Kennedy Institute are supported by a core grant from the Arthritis and Rheumatism Campaign.

References

1. Feldmann M, Brennan FM, Maini RN: **Role of cytokines in rheumatoid arthritis.** *Annu Rev Immunol* 1996, **14**:397-440. [key review]
2. Feldmann M, Maini RN: **Anti-TNF alpha therapy or rheumatoid arthritis: what have we learned?** *Annu Rev Immunol* 2001, **19**: 163-196. [key review]
3. Keane J, Gershon S, Wise RP, Mirabile-Levens E, Kasznica J, Schwieterman WD, Siegel JN, Braun MM: **Tuberculosis associated with infliximab, a tumor necrosis factor alpha-neutralizing agent.** *N Engl J Med* 2001, **345**:1098-1104. [general reference]
4. Katsikis PD, Chu CQ, Brennan FM, Maini RN, Feldmann M: **Immunoregulatory role of interleukin 10 in rheumatoid arthritis.** *J Exp Med* 1994, **179**:1517-1527. [general reference]
5. Chomarat P, Vannier E, Dechanet J, Rissoan MC, Banchereau J, Dinarello CA, Miossec P: **Balance of IL-1 receptor antagonist/IL-1 beta in rheumatoid synovium and its regulation by IL-4 and IL-10.** *J Immunol* 1995, **154**:1432-1439. [general reference]
6. Duke O, Panayi GS, Janossy G, Poulter LW: **An immunohistological analysis of lymphocyte subpopulations and their microenvironment in the synovial membranes of patients with rheumatoid arthritis using monoclonal antibodies.** *Clin Exp Immunol* 1982, **49**:22-30. [archival research]
7. Brennan FM, Hayes AL, Ciesielski CJ, Green P, Foxwell BMJ, Feldmann M: **Evidence that rheumatoid arthritis synovial T cells are similar to cytokine-activated T cells: involvement of phosphatidylinositol 3-kinase and nuclear factor κB pathways in tumour necrosis factor α production in rheumatoid arthritis.** *Arthritis Rheum* 2002, **46**:31-41. [general reference]
8. Isler P, Vey E, Zhang JH, Dayer JM: **Cell surface glycoproteins expressed on activated human T cells induce production of interleukin-1 beta by monocytic cells: a possible role of CD69.** *Eur Cytokine Network* 1993, **4**:15-23. [general reference]
9. Lacraz S, Isler P, Vey E, Welgus HG, Dayer JM: **Direct contact between T lymphocytes and monocytes is a major pathway for induction of metalloproteinase expression.** *J Biol Chem* 1994, **269**:22027-22033. [archival research]
10. Suttles J, Miller RW, Tao X, Stout RD: **T cells which do not express membrane tumour necrosis factor-alpha activate macrophage effector function by cell contact-dependent signalling of macrophage tumour necrosis factor-alpha production.** *Eur J Immunol* 1994, **24**:1736-1742. [general reference]
11. Sebbag M, Parry SL, Brennan FM, Feldmann M: **Cytokine stimulation of T lymphocytes regulates their capacity to induce monocyte production of tumor necrosis factor-alpha, but not interleukin-10: possible relevance to pathophysiology of rheumatoid arthritis.** *Eur J Immunol* 1997, **27**:624-632. [archival research]
12. Parry SL, Sebbag M, Feldmann M, Brennan FM: **Contact with T cells modulates monocyte IL-10 production: role of T cell membrane TNF-alpha.** *J Immunol* 1997, **158**:3673-3681. [archival research]
13. Chizzolini C, Chicheportiche R, Burger D, Dayer JM: **Human Th1 cells preferentially induce interleukin (IL)-1beta while Th2 cells induce IL-1 receptor antagonist production upon cell/cell contact with monocytes.** *Eur J Immunol* 1997, **27**:171-177. [general reference]
14. Salmon M, Gaston JS: **The role of T-lymphocytes in rheumatoid arthritis.** *Br Med Bull* 1995, **51**:332-345. [key review]
15. Nanki T, Lipsky PE: **Cytokine, activation marker, and chemokine receptor expression by individual CD4+ memory T cells in rheumatoid arthritis.** *Arth Res* 2000, **2**:415-423. [general reference]
16. Goronzy JJ, Zettl A, Weyand CM: **T cell receptor repertoire in rheumatoid arthritis.** *Int Rev Immunol* 1998, **17**:339-363. [general reference]
17. Firestein GS, Zvaifler NJ: **How important are T cells in chronic rheumatoid synovitis?** *Arthritis Rheum* 1990, **33**:768-773. [key review]
18. Unutmaz D, Pileri P, Abrignani S: **Antigen-independent activation of naive and memory resting T cells by a cytokine combination.** *J Exp Med* 1994, **180**:1159-1164. [archival research]
19. McInnes IB, al-Mughales J, Field M, Leung BP, Huang FP, Dixon R, Sturrock RD, Wilkinson PC, Liew FY: **The role of interleukin-15 in T-cell migration and activation in rheumatoid arthritis.** *Nat Med* 1996, **2**:175-182. [general reference]
20. McInnes IB, Leung BP, Sturrock RD, Field M, Liew FY: **Interleukin-15 mediates T cell-dependent regulation of tumor necrosis factor-alpha production in rheumatoid arthritis.** *Nat Med* 1997, **3**:189-195. [general reference]
21. McInnes IB, Liew FY: **Interleukin 15: a proinflammatory role in rheumatoid arthritis synovitis.** *Immunol Today* 1998, **19**:75-79. [key review]
22. Lou J, Dayer J-M, Grau GE, Burger D: **Direct cell/cell contact with stimulated T lymphocytes induces the expression of cell adhesion molecules and cytokines by human brain microvascular endothelial cells.** *Eur J Immunol* 1996, **26**:3107-3113. [general reference]
23. Lou J, Ythier A, Burger D, Zheng L, Juillard P, Lucas R, Dayer J-M, Grau GE: **Modulation of soluble and membrane-bound TNF-induced phenotypic and functional changes of human brain microvascular endothelial cells by recombinant TNF binding protein I.** *J Neuroimmunol* 1997, **77**:107-115. [general reference]
24. Yarwood H, Mason JC, Mahiouz D, Sugars K, Haskard DO: **Resting and activated T cells induce expression of E-selectin and VCAM-1 by vascular endothelial cells through a contact-dependent but CD40 ligand-independent mechanism.** *J Leukoc Biol* 2000, **68**:233-242. [general reference]
25. Monaco C, Andreakos E, Young S, Feldmann M, Paleolog E: **T cell-mediated signalling to vascular endothelium: Induction of cytokines, chemokines and tissue factor.** *J Leukoc Biol* 2002, in press. [general reference]
26. Li JM, Isler P, Dayer J-M, Burger D: **Contact-dependent stimulation of monocytic cells and neutrophils by stimulated human T-cell clones.** *Immunology* 1995, **84**:571-576. [general reference]
27. Burger D, Rezzonico R, Li JM, Modoux C, Pierce RA, Welgus HG, Dayer JM: **Imbalance between interstitial collagenase and tissue inhibitor of metalloproteinases 1 in synoviocytes and fibroblasts upon direct contact with stimulated T lymphocytes: involvement of membrane-associated cytokines.** *Arthritis Rheum* 1998, **41**:1748-1759. [archival research]
28. Rezzonico R, Burger D, Dayer JM: **Direct contact between T lymphocytes and human dermal fibroblasts or synoviocytes down-regulates types I and III collagen production via cell-associated cytokines.** *J Biol Chem* 1998, **273**:18720-18728. [general reference]
29. Hyka N, Dayer J-M, Modoux C, Kohno T, Edwards CK, Roux-Lombard P, Burger D: **Apolipoprotein A-I inhibits the production of interleukin-1β and tumour necrosis factor-α by blocking contact-mediated activation of monocytes by T lymphocytes.** *Blood* 2001, **97**:2381-2389. [archival research]
30. Manie S, Kubar J, Limouse M, Ferrua B, Ticchioni M, Breittmayer J-P, Peyron J-F, Schaffar L, Rossi B: **CD3-stimulated Jurkat T cells mediate IL-1β production in monocytic THP-1 cells. Role of LFA-1 molecule and participation of CD69 T cell antigen.** *Eur Cytokine Network* 1993, **4**:7-13. [general reference]
31. Zembala M, Siedlar M, Ruggiero I, Wieckiewicz J, Mytar B, Mattei M, Colizzi V: **The MHC class-II and CD44 molecules are involved in the induction of tumour necrosis factor (TNF) gene expression by human monocytes stimulated with tumour cells.** *Int J Cancer* 1994, **56**:269-274. [general reference]
32. Hayes AL, Smith C, Foxwell BM, Brennan FM: **CD45-induced tumor necrosis factor alpha production in monocytes is phosphatidylinositol 3-kinase-dependent and nuclear factor-kappaB-independent.** *J Biol Chem* 1999, **274**:33455-33461. [archival research]
33. Wagner DH Jr, Stout RD, Suttles J: **Role of the CD40–CD40 ligand interaction in CD4+ T cell contact-dependent activation of monocyte interleukin-1 synthesis.** *Eur J Immunol* 1994, **24**: 3148-3154. [general reference]
34. Isomaki P, Aversa G, Cocks BG, Luukkainen R, Saario R, Toivanen P, de Vries JE, Punnonen J: **Increased expression of signaling lymphocytic activation molecule in patients with rheumatoid arthritis and its role in the regulation of cytokine production in rheumatoid synovium.** *J Immunol* 1997, **159**: 2986-2993. [general reference]
35. Wanidworanun C, Strober W: **Predominant role of tumor necrosis factor-alpha in human monocyte IL-10 synthesis.** *J Immunol* 1993, **151**:6853-6861. [general reference]
36. Graf D, Muller S, Korthauer U, van Kooten C, Weise C, Kroczek RA: **A soluble form of TRAP (CD40 ligand) is rapidly released after T cell activation.** *Eur J Immunol* 1995, **25**:1749-1754. [general reference]

37. Michel J, Langstein J, Hofstadter F, Schwarz H: **A soluble form of CD137 (ILA/4-1BB), a member of the TNF receptor family, is released by activated lymphocytes and is detectable in sera of patients with rheumatoid arthritis.** *Eur J Immunol* 1998, **28**: 290-295. [general reference]

38. Pizzolo G, Vinante F, Chilosi M, Dallenbach F, Josimovic-Alasevic O, Diamantstein T, Stein H: **Serum levels of soluble CD30 molecule (Ki-1 antigen) in Hodgkin's disease: relationship with disease activity and clinical stage.** *Br J Haematol* 1990, **75**: 282-284. [general reference]

39. Cheng J, Zhou T, Liu C, Shapiro JP, Brauer MJ, Kiefer MC, Barr PJ, Mountz JD: **Protection from Fas-mediated apoptosis by a soluble form of the Fas molecule.** *Science* 1994, **263**:1759-1762. [general reference]

40. Shu U, Kiniwa M, Wu CY, Maliszewski C, Vezzio N, Hakimi J, Gately M, Delespesse G: **Activated T cells induce interleukin-12 production by monocytes via CD40–CD40 ligand interaction.** *Eur J Immunol* 1995, **25**:1125-1128. [general reference]

41. Chabot S, Williams G, Hamilton M, Sutherland G, Yong VW: **Mechanisms of IL-10 production in human microglia–T cell interaction.** *J Immunol* 1999, **162**:6819-6828. [general reference]

42. Foey AD, Feldmann M, Brennan FM: **Route of monocyte differentiation determines their cytokine production profile: CD40 ligation induces interleukin 10 expression.** *Cytokine* 2000, **12**: 1496-1505. [general reference]

43. Fleming SD, Campbell PA: **Macrophages have cell surface IL-10 that regulates macrophage bactericidal activity.** *J Immunol* 1996, **156**:1143-1150. [general reference]

44. Brennan FM, Maini RN, Feldmann M: **Cytokine expression in chronic inflammatory disease.** *Br Med Bull* 1995, **51**:368-384. [key review]

45. Foxwell BMJ, Browne K, Bondeson J, Clarke C, de Martin R, Brennan FM, Feldmann M: **Efficient adenoviral infection with IκBα reveals that TNFα production in rheumatoid arthritis is NF-κB dependent.** *Proc Natl Acad Sci USA* 1998, **95**:8211-8215. [general reference]

46. Bondeson J, Foxwell BMJ, Brennan FM, Feldmann M: **Defining therapeutic targets by using adenovirus: blocking NF-kB inhibits both inflammatory and destructive mechanisms in rheumatoid synovium but spares anti-inflammatory mediators.** *Proc Natl Acad Sci USA* 1999, **96**:5668-5673. [general reference]

47. Foey AD, Parry SL, Williams LM, Feldmann M, Foxwell BM, Brennan FM: **Regulation of monocyte IL-10 synthesis by endogenous IL-1 and TNF-alpha: role of the p38 and p42/44 mitogen-activated protein kinases.** *J Immunol* 1998, **160**:920-928. [archival research]

48. De AK, Kodys KM, Yeh BS, Miller-Graziano C: **Exaggerated human monocyte IL-10 concomitant to minimal TNF-alpha induction by heat-shock protein 27 (Hsp27) suggests Hsp27 is primarily an antiinflammatory stimulus.** *J Immunol* 2000, **165**:3951-3958. [general reference]

49. Crawley JB, Williams LM, Mander T, Brennan FM, Foxwell BM: **Interleukin-10 stimulation of phosphatidylinositol 3-kinase and p70 S6 kinase is required for the proliferative but not the antiinflammatory effects of the cytokine.** *J Biol Chem* 1996, **271**:16357-16362. [general reference]

50. Foey AD, Green P, Foxwell BMJ, Feldmann M, Brennan F: **Cytokine stimulated T cells induce IL-10 production dependent on phosphatidylinositol 3-kinase and p70S6K: implications for rheumatoid arthritis.** *Arthritis Res* 2002, **4**:64-70. [archival research]

51. Meisel C, Vogt K, Platzer C, Randow F, Liebenthal C, Volk HD: **Differential regulation of monocytic tumor necrosis factor-alpha and interleukin-10 expression.** *Eur J Immunol* 1996, **26**: 1580-1586. [general reference]

52. Kambayashi T, Jacob CO, Zhou D, Mazurek N, Fong M, Strassmann G: **Cyclic nucleotide phosphodiesterase type IV participates in the regulation of IL-10 and in the subsequent inhibition of TNF-alpha and IL-6 release by endotoxin-stimulated macrophages.** *J Immunol* 1995, **155**:4909-4916. [general reference]

Supplement Review

Chemokine receptors on dendritic cells promote autoimmune reactions

Joost J Oppenheim*, De Yang*, Arya Biragyn†, OM Zack Howard* and Paul Plotz‡

*Laboratory of Molecular Immunoregulation, Center for Cancer Research, National Cancer Institute, Frederick, MD, USA
†Experimental Transplantation and Immunology Branch, Center for Cancer Research, National Cancer Institute, Frederick, MD, USA
‡Intramural Research Program, National Institute of Arthritis and Musculoskeletal and Skin Diseases, National Institutes of Health, Bethesda, MD, USA

Correspondence: Joost J Oppenheim, Laboratory of Molecular Immunoregulation, Building 560, Room 21-89A, National Cancer Institute, Frederick, MD 21702-1201, USA. Tel: +1 301 846 1551; fax: +1 301 846 7042; e-mail: Oppenhei@ncifcrf.gov

Received: 14 January 2002
Revisions requested: 16 January 2002
Revisions received: 19 January 2002
Accepted: 10 February 2002
Published: 9 May 2002

Arthritis Res 2002, 4 (suppl 3):S183-S188

This article may contain supplementary data which can only be found online at http://arthritis-research.com/content/4/S3/S183

© 2002 BioMed Central Ltd
(Print ISSN 1465-9905; Online ISSN 1465-9913)

Chapter summary

This paper presents a brief review of several lines of evidence suggesting that chemokine receptors on dendritic cells play an important role in breaking tolerance to self and in inducing autoimmunity. First, we have shown that an idiotypic self-antigen obtained from malignant murine lymphomas, when covalently linked to selected chemokines or defensins that interact with receptors on immature dendritic cells (iDCs), has the capacity to break tolerance to self and induce humoral or cell-mediated anti-tumor responses. Since unlinked antigens mixed with the same chemokines or defensins or antigens fused with a mutant ligand deficient in receptor-binding capacity were not immunogenic, we propose that delivery of an antigen coupled to a ligand for receptors on iDCs promotes the processing and subsequent presentation of the antigen, resulting in immunoadjuvant effects. In a second study, we observed that two of five aminoacyl tRNA synthetases (aaRSs) – which act as autoantigens to which some patients with myositis have autoantibodies – were chemotactic for activated monocytes, T cells, and iDCs. These aaRSs interacted with either CC chemokine receptor (CCR)5 or CCR3, as was shown by desensitization with chemokines and the response of cell lines transfected with the chemokine receptor. Presumably, these autoantigens therefore have the capacity to attract inflammatory cells, including iDCs, to infiltrate affected muscle cells. These observations suggest the hypothesis that antigens delivered to receptors on iDCs are potent immunogens capable of breaking self-tolerance to tumor antigens to induce autoimmune diseases.

Keywords: aminoacyl + RNA synthetase, autoimmune myositis, chemokine receptors, dendritic cells, idiotypic lymphoma antigen

Introduction: characteristics of dendritic cells

It is now well established that dendritic cells (DCs) are pivotal antigen-presenting cells with the unique capacity to initiate primary as well as secondary immune responses. 'Immature' dendritic cells (iDCs) can be generated in vitro from CD34+ hematopoietic stem cells or from CD14+ monocytes by incubation with granulocyte/monocyte-colony-stimulating factor plus tumor necrosis factor-α or IL-4 for 7 days. In the course of this differentiation process, the DC precursors lose the CD34 and CD14 markers and express a number of novel phenotypic markers and cell-surface receptors [1–4]. After an additional 2 days of CD40 ligation or incubation with proinflammatory agents such as bacterial lipopolysaccharide or cytokines such as tumor necrosis factor-α, the iDCs become mature DCs (mDCs), with

---

A glossary of specialist terms used in this chapter appears at the end of the text section. A list of common abbreviations used in this issue appears just before the indexes.

Figure 1

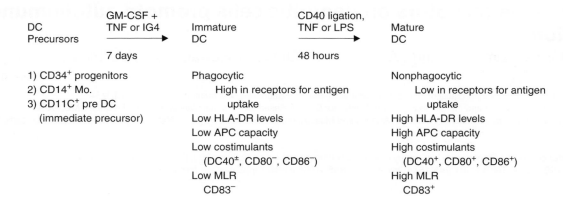

In vitro stages of differentiation and maturation of dendritic cells. The phenotypic and functional characteristics of immature and mature dendritic cells are compared. APC, antigen-presenting cell; DC, dendritic cell; GM-CSF, granulocyte/macrophage-colony-stimulating factor; HLA-DR, histocompatibility leukocyte antigen; LPS, lipopolysaccharide; MLR, mixed leukocyte reaction; TNF, tumor necrosis factor.

consistent changes in their phenotypic markers as shown in Fig. 1.

The differences in the functional capabilities of iDCs and mDCs are relevant to understanding their respective roles in adaptive immunity and autoimmunity [2]. The iDCs can phagocytose particulate and larger soluble antigens and can enzymatically process them to generate small peptide fragments that can be presented to T cells on cell-surface MHC (major histocompatibility complex) antigens. However, the expression of MHC class II and costimulatory proteins by iDCs is low and hence these cells have little or no capacity to present antigens until they differentiate into mDCs. The mDCs lose their capacity to phagocytose particles and process antigens, but are induced by proinflammatory stimulants to express high levels of MHC class II alloantigens on their surface, along with processed antigenic peptides and costimulatory surface markers such as CD40, CD80, and CD86 (see Fig. 1). Thus, by expressing costimulatory molecules, mDCs can induce a second signal in T cells that, together with the first signal generated by TCR in response to the MHC-peptide complex, results in an immune rather than a tolerogenic/anergic response.

The changes in receptor expression from DC precursors to iDCs and to mDCs enables DCs as they mature to respond to a new set of ligands with consequent changes in the trafficking pattern of DCs [3]. For example, as precursors of DC become iDCs they become responsive to a wide range of proinflammatory stimuli and migrate towards sites of infections and injuries [2–5]. The iDCs express many receptors for proinflammatory cytokines as well as chemoattractant factors which equip iDCs with the capacity to respond to many exogenous and endogenous danger signals [4]. Chemoattractant receptors enable iDCs to migrate towards inflammatory sites where

chemoattractants are being produced. Once they are there, they phagocytize and process self-antigens from cellular debris and foreign antigens from invading microorganisms. The interaction of chemoattractants with their receptors initiates a signal-transduction cascade that, in addition to activating cell migration, activates a number of genes, resulting in the production and secretion of a variety of mediators and effector molecules including cytokines such as IL-1, IL-2, IL-4, IL-12, IL-15, and TGF-β (transforming growth factor-β) chemokines ([6,7] and unpublished observations).

Expression of chemokine receptors by dendritic cells

The presence of 'danger' signals such as inflammatory mediators and components of infectious organisms at the peripheral inflammatory site serve to induce the maturation of iDCs [4]. As DCs mature, they lose many of their receptors, but they gain CCR7 and CXCR5, which enable them to migrate along concentration gradients of constitutively produced chemokines such as SLC/CCL21, ELC/CCL19, and BLC/CXCL13 to the site of origin of these chemokines in lymphoid tissues [5] (Fig. 2). It is in the well-organized lymphoid tissues that mDCs expressing a particular peptide–MHC complex have a better chance of encountering those few T lymphocytes expressing a TCR that can recognize the antigen on the DC, thus initiating an immune response. By directing the trafficking and homing of iDCs and mDCs, respectively, chemokine receptors therefore presumably play a crucial role in the uptake and delivery of antigenic signals and initiation of adaptive immune responses.

Role of defensins in adaptive immunity

A number of disparate nonchemokine ligands have been shown to have the ability to activate chemokine receptors

Figure 2

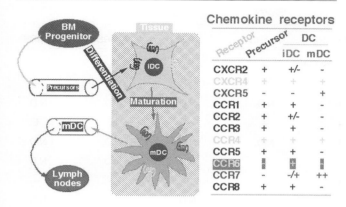

Chemokine receptors			
Receptor	Precursor	DC iDC	mDC
CXCR2	+	+/-	-
CXCR4	+	+	+
CXCR5	-	-	+
CCR1	+	+	-
CCR2	+	+/-	-
CCR3	+	+	-
CCR4	+	+	+
CCR5	+	+	-
CCR6	▪	+	-/+
CCR7	-	-/+	++
CCR8	+	+	-

Changes in chemokine receptor expression in the course of maturation of dendritic cells. The *in vivo* traffic route of dendritic cells as they mature is depicted, along with the changes in the expression of chemokine receptors. BM, bone marrow; CC indicates the presence of adjoining cysteines in sequence; DC, dendritic cell; iDC, immature dendritic cell; mDC, mature dendritic cell. See Colour figure section.

on iDCs and as a consequence to have major effects on adaptive immune responses. One example is the defensins, which interact with chemokine receptors. We have shown that β defensins interact with cells expressing CCR6, the receptor for a chemokine known as LARC/MIP-3α/CCL20, present on iDCs, resting memory CD4 cells, and a subset of B lymphocytes [8]. Defensins at micromolar concentrations have direct microbicidal activities, but at 1/10 to 1/100 micromolar concentrations, the β defensins derived from keratinocytes and mucosal epithelial cella activate and induce chemotactic migration of CCR6+ cells. Although the receptor for α defensins has not been identified, it is inhibitable by pertussis toxin and therefore also is a Gαi-protein-coupled receptor, like the chemokine receptors [9]. The possibility that α defensins interact with chemokine-like receptors on iDCs may account for our previous findings showing that α defensins are remarkably potent adjuvants that enhance both T-helper (Th)$_1$ cell-mediated responses and Th$_2$-type humoral antibody responses in mice to concomitantly administered antigens such as keyhole limpet hemocyanin (KLH) and ovalbumin [10,11].

Role of receptors on dendritic cells in breaking tolerance to 'self-tumor' antigens

The observed adjuvant effects of defensins on soluble antigens led us to examine the ability of β defensins to augment a weaker anti-tumor response. The anti-tumor effect of β defensins and selected chemokines was tested by linking them to an idotypic immunoglobulin antigen (Id) or its unique Fv Fragment (sFv) present on malignant murine lymphomas [12]. These linked fusion constructs were administered either as a naked DNA vaccine intra-

muscularly or as recombinant fusion proteins. The results revealed that Id or sFv by themselves were not immunogenic [12,13]. Furthermore, mixtures of chemokines or murine β defensins (mBD2 and mBD3) and Id had no significant protective effect. Only when the β defensins or chemokines were covalently linked to the tumor antigen was an immunogenic anti-tumor effect achieved [12,13]. The Id–mBD2 fusion product yielded more cellular than humoral immunity, while Id–mBD3 induced predominantly antibody responses to the tumor antigens. Consequently, mBD2, but not mBD3, had a protective effect and induced prolonged tumor survival in 20–50% of mice challenged with tumors. The humoral immune effects of mBD3 fusion products resembled that of MDC/CCL22, which interacts with CCR4 and is known to favor the induction of TH2 responses. Alternatively, mBD2 mimicked the cell-mediated anti-tumor effects of MIP3α/CCL20, which also interacts with CCR6 and MCP3/CCL7, a chemokine that is known to interact with chemokine receptors CCR1, CCR2, and CCR3, which favors Th$_1$-cell-mediated immune responses [14]. These findings suggest that the identity of the chemokine or defensin–receptor interaction on iDCs plays a role in determining whether humoral or cellular immunity is induced [13]. Because only Id antigens fused to chemokines or defensins were effective in inducing an immune response, and because these fused proteins were still functionally active inducers of *in vitro* chemotaxis of iDCs [13], presumably interaction of the fusion product with the chemokine receptor favors antigen uptake and processing and subsequent presentation by antigen-presenting cells. This hypothesis is supported by the inability of control fusion constructs (using mutated or an inactive β pro-defensin moiety) that do not bind or activate the receptors on iDCs to elicit any immune response [13]. Thus, linking of sFv antigen to a functional chemokine or defensin, like a postage stamp, may help deliver the antigen more effectively to the iDCs in part by directing the migration of iDCs to the site of antigen production when used as a DNA vaccine. Since Id antigen actually represents an overexpressed normal clonal B-cell immunoglobulin product, these experiments actually break tolerance and produce an immune response to a self-antigen: in other words, they induce an 'autoimmune' response to the tumor.

Role of receptors on dendritic cells in autoimmune myositis

There have been several recent reports of a second type of nonchemokine ligand, namely tyrosyl tRNA synthetase (TyrRS) being chemotactic for neutrophils by selectively interacting with one of the receptors for IL-8, CXCR-1 [15,16]. This surprising result motivated us to evaluate the chemoattractant activities of other aminoacyl tRNA synthetases (aaRSs) to which some patients with idiopathic inflammatory myopathic (dermatomyositis and polymyositis or related diseases) develop autoantibodies [17].

Table 1

Chemotactic activity of aminoacyl tRNA synthetases

Leukocyte subpopulation	HisRS	MHRS	1–48 HisRS	AsnRS	SerRS	AspRS	LysRS
Neutrophils	–	–	–	–	–	–	–
Monocytes	–	–	–	–	–	–	–
IL-2-activated monocytes	+	–	+	N.D.	N.D.	N.D.	N.D.
Lymphocytes	+	–	+	+	+	±	±
CD8 T cells	±	–	±	N.D.	N.D.	N.D.	N.D.
CD4 T cells	+	–	+	+	N.D.	N.D.	N.D.
iDCs	+	–	+	+	–	+	–
mDCs	–	–	–	–	N.D.	N.D.	N.D.

–, absent response; +, positive response; ±, variable response; N.D., not done. AsnRS, asparaginyl tRNA synthetase; AspRS, aspartyl tRNA synthetase; HisRS, histidyl tRNA synthetase; iDC, immature dendritic cells; LysRS, lysyl tRNA synthetase; mDCs, mature dendritic cells; MHRS, mutated HisRS; SerRS, seryl tRNA synthetase.

Of the five aaRSs tested, two to which patients had autoantibodies were shown to be chemotactic for T lymphocytes, IL-2-activated monocytes, and immature dendritic cells (iDCs). They were not chemotactic for neutrophils, unstimulated monocytes, or mature dendritic cells (mDCs) (Table 1).

We tested histidyl tRNA synthetase (HisRS), the most frequently targeted aaRS in myositis, since 20–30% of patients have autoantibodies to it. We also tested the N-terminal coiled-coil domain of HisRS 1–48 with which autoantibodies react and found it to be a less potent chemotactic stimulant of IL-2-activated monocytes and T cells but not of iDCs. In contrast, a construct lacking the N-terminal domain (HisRS 61–509) was not chemotactic for any leukocyte subset. Furthermore, a mutated variant of HisRS, MHRS, also lacked any chemotactic activity.

Next, we investigated the possibility that HisRS utilized a G-coupled protein receptor by testing its susceptibility to pertussis toxin. Indeed, the chemotactic response of HisRS was inhibited by this toxin. Furthermore, we examined the desensitizing effects of a panel of chemokines to determine whether HisRS acted on a chemokine receptor. Preincubation with either RANTES/CCL5 or MIP-1β/CCL4, which uses CCR5, inhibited the subsequent chemotactic response of T cells to HisRS. Conversely, preincubation with HisRS selectively blocked the chemotactic response to these chemokines. Furthermore, HisRS was an equipotent chemoattractant for HEK293 cells transfected with CCR5, but not for cells transfected with CCR1 or CCR3. These observations thus identified CCR5 as a receptor for HisRS.

Although the incidence of autoantibody formation to asparaginyl tRNA synthetase (AsnRS) is less than 5%, this synthetase was also chemotactic for T cells and iDCs.

We therefore tested AsnRS on a panel of cell lines transfected with chemokine receptors to identify its receptors and established that AsnRS was chemotactic for HEK293 cells transfected with CCR3. In contrast, three additional aaRSs to which no autoantibodies have been detected, namely seryl tRNA synthetase (SerRS), lysyl tRNA synthetase (LysRS), and aspartyl tRNA synthetase (AspRS) were not chemotactic for iDCs. Even though SerRS was chemotactic for lymphocytes expressing CCR3, it had no effect on iDCs. Consequently, the presence of autoantibodies to an aaRS appear to correlate with the capacity of the synthetase to have chemotactic effects on iDCs expressing receptors, suggesting that these antigens may contribute to myositis not only by inducing autoantibodies, but also by attracting inflammatory cells into affected muscle tissue. Indeed, three lines of evidence support this hypothesis. One is that infiltrates of mononuclear cells, including DCs, have been detected in striated muscle of patients with myositis [18]. Another is that CCR5 as well as CCR2 have been detected on cells infiltrating inflamed muscle tissue, and the degenerating and regenerating muscles themselves express low levels of CCR5 in myositis [19–21]. And finally, injection of naked DNA coding for HisRS into mice induces local myositis at the injection site [22].

Role of receptors on dendritic cells in pathogenesis of autoimmune disease

Another group of nonchemokine ligands that are well known to interact with CCR5 and CXCR4 are the envelope proteins gp120 and gp41 of HIV-1 (as reviewed [23]). They initially interact with CD4, and the result is a conformational change that enables the envelope proteins to interact with chemokine receptors as a prerequisite for the entry of HIV-1 into cells. This interaction with chemokine receptors is evident from the inability of monocytotropic HIV-1 to infect subjects homozygous for the

Δ32 CCR5 variant [24,25]. This variant is retained in the cytoplasm and is not expressed on the cell surface. Furthermore, heterozygotes develop AIDS more slowly than homozygotes [26]. It is relevant to our findings that subjects heterozygous for Δ32 CCR5 also have a lower incidence of autoimmune diseases, including rheumatoid arthritis, Crohn's disease, and multiple sclerosis [27–30]. The mechanistic basis for the lower incidence of autoimmunity in such heterozygotes is elucidated to some extent by the phenotypic characteristics of CCR5 knockout mice [31]. Such mice have reduced resistance to several microbial pathogens and are protected from lipopolysaccharide-induced endotoxemia. The finding that cellular immune responses of CCR5-deficient mice are diminished suggests that ligation of CCR5 promotes Th_1 polarization of immune responses [32]. This hypothesis is supported by observations that ligands, such as MIP-1α and RANTES, that utilize CCR5 favor induction of cytokine production by Th_1 cells [32]. These reports suggest that CCR5 ligation may favor the development of Th_1-type autoimmune conditions. Consequently, myositis may be a Th1 condition and this may account for the low incidence of autoantibody formation in these patients.

Our studies have shown that diverse chemoattractants for iDCs also have the capacity to break self-tolerance, resulting in the capacity to reject tumors or promulgate autoimmunity [33]. These findings suggest the hypothesis that antigens with chemotactic effects for receptors expressed by iDCs may be more effectively processed and presented to T cells, thus initiating and promulgating autoimmune responses or tumor immunity. Our observations suggest that the proinflammatory chemokine-like properties of some proteins provide a danger signal that not only amplifies innate inflammatory reactions, but also elicits adaptive immune responses, including the formation of autoantibodies.

Furthermore, the observation that the administration of an idiotypic tumor antigen derived from lymphomas, when linked to chemokines or β defensins as a fusion product, can apparently also break the tolerant or anergic state to that antigen further highlights the immuno-enhancing/adjuvant consequences of antigens interacting with receptors on iDCs. This idea is certainly supported by abundantly documented observations that antigens interacting with receptors on antigen-presenting cells are 10,000-fold more effectively processed by the MHC class II pathway than are pinocytosed antigens [34].

Therapeutic implications

Of course, many questions remain unanswered. For example, it is unclear why only a minority of patients with myositis develop autoantibodies selectively to aaRS. Perhaps myositis is predominantly based on Th_1 cytokine responses, with a lower incidence of autoantibody pro-

duction than is seen in Th_2 autoimmune-based conditions. Since aaRSs are present in all nucleated cell types, the selective targeting of these particular autoantigens to muscle tissues in myositis is another puzzle awaiting solution. Nevertheless, our observations suggest that the autoantigenic aaRS has a causal role in this disease process and identifies several chemokine receptors, namely CCR5 and CCR3, as potential targets for therapeutic intervention in patients with autoimmune myositis.

Concluding remarks

Overall, our results lead to the prediction that ligands that interact with receptors on DC are likely to have immuno-adjuvant effects. This suggests that the relatively small proportion of self-antigens that are thought to be capable of inducing autoimmune conditions are more likely than most self-antigens to have domains that mimic ligands for receptors on iDCs. The observation that some aaRSs fall into that category is provocative, but additional autoantigens need to be examined to support this hypothesis.

Glossary of terms

aaRS = aminoacyl tRNA synthetase; AsnRS = asparaginyl tRNA synthetase; AspRS = aspartyl tRNA synthetase; CC indicates the presence of adjoining cysteines in sequence; CCL = CC chemokine ligand; CCR = CC chemokine receptor; DC = dendritic cell; HisRS = histidyl tRNA synthetase; Id = idiotypic immunoglobulin; iDC = immature dendritic cell; LARC = liver- and activation-regulated chemokine; LysRS = lysyl tRNA synthetase; mBD = murine β defensin; MCP = monocyte chemotactic protein; MDC = macrophage-derived chemokine; mDC = mature dendritic cell; MHRS = mutated HisRS; MIP = macrophage inflammatory protein; RANTES = regulated-upon-activation normal T cell expressed and secreted; SerRS = seryl tRNA synthetase; sFv = lymphoma-specific single-chain immunoglobulin (consisting of linked Vh and V2 domains of lymphoma immunoglobulin).

Acknowledgements

We are grateful for the infinite patience and fortitude of Ms Cheryl Fogle, who retyped this draft on innumerable occasions, and to Dr Ruth Neta for her critical, constructive comments. The contents of this publication do not necessarily reflect the views or policies of the Department of Health and Human Services, nor does mention of trade names, commercial products, or organizations imply endorsement by the US Government. The publisher or recipient acknowledges the right of the US Government to retain a nonexclusive, royalty-free license in and to any copyright covering the article.

References

1. Lanzavecchia A, Sallusto F: **The instructive role of dendritic cells on T cell responses: lineages, plasticity and kinetics.** *Curr Opin Rheumatol* 2001, **13**:291-298. [key review]
2. Banchereau J, Steinman RM: **Dendritic cells and the control of immunity.** *Nature* 1998, **392**:245-251. [key review]
3. Sallusto F, Schaerli P, Loetscher P, Schaniel C, Denig D, Mackay C R, Qin S, Lanzavecchia A: **Rapid and coordinated switch in chemokine receptor expression during dendritic cell maturation.** *Eur J Immunol* 1998, **28**:2760-2769. [general reference]
4. Matzinger P: **An innate sense of danger.** *Semin Immunol* 1998, **10**:399-415. [key review]

5. Sallusto F, Palermo B, Lenig D, Miettinen M, Matikainen S, Julkunen I, Forster R, Burgstahler R, Lipp M, Lanzavecchia A: **Distinct patterns and kinetics of chemokine production regulate dendritic cell function.** *Eur J Immunol* 1999, **29**:1617-1625. [general reference]

6. Granucci F, Vizzardelli C, Pavelka N, Feau S, Persico M, Virzi E, Rescigno M, Moro G, Ricciardi-Castagnoli P: **Inducible IL-2 production by dendritic cells revealed by global gene expression analysis.** *Nat Immunol* 2001, **2**:882-888. [general reference]

7. Vissers JL, Hartgers FC, Lindhout E, Teunissen MB, Fidor CG, Adema G: **Quantitative analysis of chemokine expression by dendritic cell subsets in vitro and in vivo.** *J Leukoc Biol* 2001, **69**:785-793. [general reference]

8. Yang D, Chertov O, Bykovskaia SN, Chen Q, Buffo M J, Shogan J, Anderson M, Schroder JM, Wang JM, Howard OMZ, Oppenheim JJ: **Beta-defensins: linking innate and adaptive immunity through dendritic and T cell CCR6.** *Science* 1999, **286**:525-528. [general reference]

9. Yang D, Chen Q, Chertov O, Oppenheim JJ: **Human neutrophil defensins selectively chemoattract naive T and immature dendritic cells.** *J Leukoc Biol* 2000, **68**:9-14. [general reference]

10. Tani K, Murphy WJ, Chertov O, Salcedo R, Koh CY, Utsunomiya I, Funakoshi S, Asai O, Hermann S, Wang J, Kwak L, Oppenheim JJ: **Defensins act as potent adjuvants that promote cellular and humoral immune response in mice to a lymphoma idiotype and carrier antigens.** *J Int Immunol* 2000, **12**:691-700. [general reference]

11. Lillard JW Jr, Boyaka PN, Chertov O, Oppenheim JJ, McGhee JR: **Mechanisms for induction of acquired host immunity by neutrophil peptide defensins.** *Proc Natl Acad Sci U S A* 1999, **96**:651-656. [general reference]

12. Biragyn A, Tani K, Grimm MC, Weeks SD, Kwak LW: **Genetic fusion of chemokines to a self tumor antigen induces protective, T-cell dependent antitumor immunity.** *Nat Biotechnol* 1999, **17**:253-258. [general reference]

13. Biragyn A, Surehnu M, Yang D, Ruffini PA, Haines BA, Klyushnenkova E, Oppenheim JJ, Kwak LW: **Mediators of innate immunity that target immature, but not mature, dendritic cells induce antitumor immunity when genetically fused with non-immunogenic tumor antigens.** *J Immunol* 2001, **167**:6644-6653. [key review]

14. Sato N, Ahuja SK, Quinones M, Kostecki V, Reddick RL, Melby PC, Kuziel WA, Ahuja SS: **CC chemokine receptor (CCR)2 is required for langerhans cell migration and localization of T helper cell type 1 (Th1)-inducing dendritic cells. Absence of CCR2 shifts the Leishmania major-resistant phenotype to a susceptible state dominated by Th2 cytokines, b cell outgrowth, and sustained neutrophilic inflammation.** *J Exp Med* 2000, **192**:205-218. [general reference]

15. Wakasugi K, Schimmel P: **Two distinct cytokines released from a human aminoacyl-tRNA synthetase.** *Science* 1999, **284**:147-151. [general reference]

16. Wakasugi K, Schimmel P: **Highly differentiated motifs responsible for two cytokine activities of a split human tRNA synthetase.** *J Biol Chem* 1999, **274**:23155-23159. [general reference]

17. Targoff IN: **Update on myositis-specific and myositis-associated autoantibodies.** *Curr Opin Rheumatol* 2000, **12**:475-481. [key review]

18. Nagaraju K, Raben N, Villalba ML, Danning C, Loeffler LA, Lee E, Tresser N, Abati A, Fetsch P, Plotz PH: **Costimulatory markers in muscle of patients with idiopathic inflammatory myopathies and in cultured muscle cells.** *Clin Immunol* 1999, **92**:161-169. [general reference]

19. Adams EM, Kirkley J, Eidelman G, Dohlman J, Plotz PH: **The predominance of beta (CC) chemokine transcripts in idiopathic inflammatory muscle diseases.** *Proc Assoc Am Physicians* 1997, **109**:275-285. [general reference]

20. Confalonieri P, Bernasconi P, Megna P, Galbiati S, Cornelio F, Mantegazza R: **Increased expression of beta-chemokines in muscle of patients with inflammatory myopathies.** *J Neuropathol Exp Neurol* 2000, **59**:164-169. [general reference]

21. De Rossi M, Bernasconi P, Baggi F, de Waal Malefyt R, Mantegazza R: **Cytokines and chemokines are both expressed by human myoblasts: possible relevance for the immune pathogenesis of muscle inflammation.** *Int Immunol* 2000, **12**:1329-1335. [general reference]

22. Blechynden LM, Lawson MA, Tabarias H, Garlepp MJ, Sherman J, Raben N, Lawson CM: **Myositis induced by naked DNA immunization with the gene for histidyl-tRNA synthetase.** *Hum Gene Ther* 1997, **8**:1469-1480. [general reference]

23. Wang JM, Oppenheim JJ: **Interference with the signaling capacity of CC chemokine receptor 5 can compromise its role as an HIV-1 entry coreceptor in primary T lymphocytes.** *J Exp Med* 1999, **190**:591-595. [key review]

24. Liu R, Paxton WA, Choe S, Ceradini D, Martin SR, Horuk R, MacDonald ME, Stuhlmann H, Koup RA, Landau NR: **Homozygous defect in HIV-1 coreceptor accounts for resistance of some multiply-exposed individuals to HIV-1 infection.** *Cell* 1996, **86**:367-377. [general reference]

25. Samson M, Libert F, Doranz BJ, Rucker J, Liesnard C, Farber CM, Saragosti S, Lapoumeroulie C, Cognaux J, Forceille C, Muyldermans G, Collman RG, Doms RW, Vassart G, Parmentier M: **Resistance to HIV-1 infection in Caucasian individuals bearing mutant alleles of the CCR-5 chemokine receptor gene.** *Nature* 1996, **382**:772-725. [general reference]

26. Dean M, Jacobson LP, McFarlane G, Margolick JB, Jenkins FJ, Howard OMZ, Dong HF, Goedert JJ, Buchbinder S, Gomperts E, Vlahov D, Oppenheim JJ, O'Brien SJ, Carrington M: **Reduced risk of AIDS lymphoma in individuals heterozygous for the CCR5-delta32 mutation.** *Cancer Res* 1999, **59**:3561-3564. [general reference]

27. Zang YC, Samanta AK, Halder JB, Hong J, Tejada-Simon MV, Rivera VM, Zhang JZ: **Aberrant T cell migration towards RANTES and MIP-1 alpha in patients with multiple sclerosis. Overexpression of chemokine receptor CCR5.** *Brain* 2000, **123**:1874-1882. [general reference]

28. Garred P, Madsen HO, Peterson J, Marquart H, Hansen TM, Freisleben Sorensen S, Volck B, Svejgaard A, Anderson V: **CC chemokine receptor 5 polymorphism in rheumatoid arthritis.** *J Rheumatol* 1998, **25**:1462-1465. [general reference]

29. Gomez-Reino JJ, Pablos JL, Carreira PE, Santiago B, Serrano L, Vicario JL, Balsa A, Figueroa M, de Juan MD: **Association of rheumatoid arthritis with a functional chemokine receptor, CCR5.** *Arthritis Rheum* 1999, **42**:989-992. [general reference]

30. Herfarth H, Pollok-Kopp B, Goke M, Press A, Oppermann M: **Polymorphism of CC chemokine receptors CCR2 and CCR5 in Crohn's disease.** *Immunol Lett* 2001, **77**:113-117. [general reference]

31. Zhou Y, Kurihara T, Ryseck RP, Yang Y, Ryan C, Loy J, Warr G, Bravo R: **Impaired macrophage function and enhanced T cell-dependent immune response in mice lacking CCR5, the mouse homologue of the major HIV-1 coreceptor.** *J Immunol* 1998, **160**:4018-4025. [general reference]

32. Andres PG, Beck PL, Mizoguchi E, Mizoguchi A, bhan AK, Dawson T, Kuziel WA, Maeda N, MacDermott RP, Podolsky DK, Reinecker HC: **Mice with a selective deletion of the CC chemokine receptors 5 or 2 are protected from dextran sodium sulfate-mediated colitis: lack of CC chemokine receptor 5 expression results in a NK1.1+lymphocyte-associated Th2-type immune response in the intestine.** *J Immunol* 2000, **164**:6303-6312. [general reference]

33. Bender A, Ernst N, Iglesias A, Dornmair K, Wekerle H, Hohlfeld R: **T cell receptor repertoire in polymyositis: clonal expansion of autoaggressive CD8+ T cells.** *J Exp Med* 1995, **181**:1863-1868. [general reference]

34. Watts C: **Capture and processing of exogenous antigens for presentation on MHC molecules.** *Annu Rev Immunol* 1997, **15**:821-850. [key review]

Supplement Review

How are the regulators regulated? The search for mechanisms that impose specificity on induction of cell death and NF-κB activation by members of the TNF/NGF receptor family

David Wallach, Thangavelu U Arumugam, Mark P Boldin, Giuseppina Cantarella*, Koluman A Ganesh, Yuri Goltsev, Tanya M Goncharov, Andrew V Kovalenko, Akhil Rajput, Eugene E Varfolomeev and Si Qing Zhang

Department of Biological Chemistry, Weizmann Institute of Science, Rehovot, Israel
*Institute of Pharmacology, University of Catania, Catania, Italy

Correspondence: Prof David Wallach, Department of Biological Chemistry, Ullman Building, Weizmann Institute of Science, Rehovot 76100, Israel. Tel: +972 8 934 3941; fax: +972 8 934 3165; e-mail: David.Wallach@weizmann.ac.il; departmental website: http://www.weizmann.ac.il/Biological_Chemistry/; personal website: http://www.weizmann.ac.il/Biological_Chemistry/scientist/Wallach/david_wallach.html

Received: 18 December 2001
Accepted: 5 February 2002
Published: 9 May 2002

Arthritis Res 2002, **4 (suppl 3)**:S189-S196

This article may contain supplementary data which can only be found online at http://arthritis-research.com/content/4/S3/S189

© 2002 BioMed Central Ltd
(Print ISSN 1465-9905; Online ISSN 1465-9913)

Chapter summary

Signals emanating from receptors of the tumor necrosis factor/nerve growth factor (TNF/NGF) family control practically all aspects of immune defense and, as such, constitute potential targets for therapeutic intervention through rational drug design. Indeed, arrest of these signals by blocking ligand–receptor interactions enables effective suppression of a variety of activities that are implicated in various pathologies, such as T and B lymphocyte activation and growth, inflammation, fibroblast proliferation, and cell death. To be therapeutically useful, however, inhibition of signaling should be restricted by determinants of specificity, at least to the same degree observed when blocking activation of individual receptors. In spite of their broad range of functions, receptors of the TNF/NGF family are known to activate just a few signaling pathways. Of these, the most extensively studied are the activation of the caspase protease cascade, which leads to cell death, and the activation of NF-κB (nuclear factor-κB) transcription factors through protein phosphorylation cascades. Until recently, most studies of the two pathways have solely focused on the core signaling complexes that are shared by the different receptors: death-inducing complexes containing the cysteine proteases caspase-8 and caspase-10, bound to the adapter protein MORT1/FADD (mediator of receptor-induced toxicity/Fas-associated DD protein), and the NF-κB-activating complex, composed of the protein kinases IKK1 (IκB kinase 1) and IKK2 (IκB kinase 2) and the regulatory subunit NEMO (NF-κB essential modulator; the 'IKK signalosome'). Knowledge has begun to emerge of additional molecules and mechanisms that affect these basic signaling complexes and impose specificity on their function.

Keywords: apoptosis, caspase, NF-κB, signaling, tumor necrosis factor

Introduction

The tumor necrosis factor (TNF) ligand and TNF/nerve growth factor (NGF) receptor families provide a unique point of view of biological regulation. (For a list of alternative names of receptors and ligands, see website [1]. See Fig. 1 for a schematic presentation of the known interactions

---

A glossary of specialist terms used in this chapter appears at the end of the text section. A list of common abbreviations used in this issue appears just before the indexes.

Figure 1

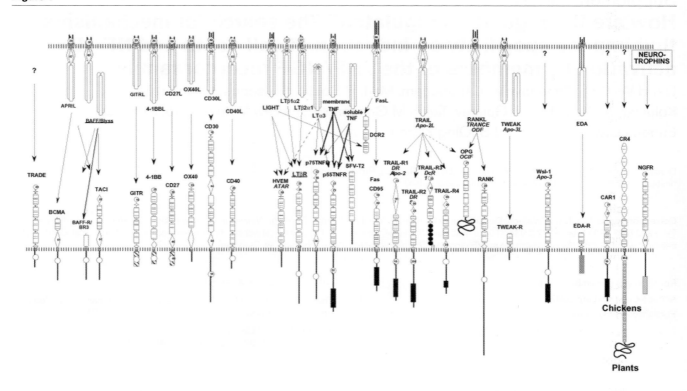

Schematic drawing of the known interactions between members of the TNF ligand family and members of the TNF/NGF receptor families. Death domains are indicated as black boxes (or gray boxes, in the cases of NGF-R and EDAR). EDAR, ectodysplasin-A receptor; NGF, nerve growth factor; NGF-R, receptor for nerve growth factor; TNF, tumor necrosis factor.

between them.) These receptors and ligands are expressed in almost all cells and trigger a wide range of different, in part contrasting, cellular activities [2–5]. They help to regulate practically every aspect of immune defense, as well as certain developmental processes. All of these activities are mediated by a unique set of apparently few signaling proteins, which are shared by the different receptors [6].

Understanding how such a heterogeneous group of functions can be elicited by a limited number of signaling proteins and, just as importantly, how the signaling system 'decides' which of its potential downstream pathways will be activated in a given situation is not solely a matter of academic interest. As demonstrated by the efficacy of anti-TNF therapy in diseases such as rheumatoid arthritis [7], understanding the mechanisms of action of the TNF/NGF receptor family at the molecular level bears immense therapeutic potential. Studies in our laboratory have helped to elucidate two aspects of specificity in the functioning of the signaling pathways: mechanisms that determine whether cell death or a noncytocidal effect is induced, and mechanisms that impose specificity of action on the enzymes that activate the highly pleiotropic nuclear factor-κB (NF-κB) transcription factors.

A cell death pathway that is independent of, yet controlled by, gene activation

Several members of the TNF/NGF receptor family are capable of inducing cell death. Those doing so most effectively, collectively known as 'death receptors,' share an intracellular motif, the so-called 'death domain,' through which their cytotoxic activities are mediated. Much of our current understanding of their mode of toxicity arises out of studies of the earliest-known members of the TNF ligand family, TNF itself and lymphotoxin-α. Almost from the first, it was noted that the ability of these cytokines to kill cells is independent of protein synthesis, but, rather, is strongly potentiated by inhibitors of protein synthesis [8–10].

Once it became evident that this cytotoxicity is receptor mediated [11], it followed that the cytocidal effect is exerted by activation of death-inducing signaling proteins that pre-exist in the living cell. It also followed that there exist in cells protein-synthesis-dependent 'antideath' functions. One could further deduce from these early studies of TNF cytotoxicity that the protein-synthesis-dependent 'antideath' functions are in part activated by TNF itself [12].

Current knowledge of the molecular mechanisms of cell death induction by the death receptors enables delineation of a continuous pathway that begins with the triggering of receptor signaling by ligands and ends with certain specific morphological and functional manifestations of programmed cell death. Acting on the assumption that the apoptotic mechanism activated by the death receptors involves solely cellular components that have pre-existed in the cell before death is triggered, attempts to identify these components have centered on analyses of the protein–protein interactions initiated by the stimulated receptors.

Two-hybrid screens led firstly to the identification of three adapter proteins, MORT1/FADD [13,14], TRADD [15], and RIP [16], all of which contain death domains that bind to the death domains in the receptors. Subsequent two-hybrid screens and analysis of the composition of the signaling complex associated with the death receptor Fas led to the identification of caspase-8 (MACH/FLICE [MORT1-associated CED3 homologue/FADD-like interleukin-1-converting enzyme]), a cysteine protease that is recruited to the receptor complex through its binding to MORT1/FADD and, once activated there, initiates the cell death process [17,18]. A close homologue of caspase-8, caspase-10, is similarly recruited and also serves to initiate the apoptotic process [19–21].

Once activated, caspase-8 and caspase-10 activate other members of the caspase family, the so-called 'executioner caspases' such as caspase-3 and caspase-7, either by direct proteolytic processing of their precursors or indirectly, by triggering the release of cytochrome *c* from the mitochondria: cytochrome *c* activates caspase-9, which in turn processes and activates caspase-3 and caspase-7. The 'executioner' caspases cleave target proteins that play critical roles in specific aspects of the death pathway. Two such examples are the processing of I-CAD/DFF-45 (inhibitor of caspase-activated deoxyribonuclease/45-kDa subunit of DNA fragmentation factor) that leads to DNA degradation [22] and the cleavage products of gelsoline, which participate in the process of membrane blebbing [23].

The straightforward nature of the aforementioned pathway (Fig. 2) highlights the need to clarify its regulation. If all that it takes for the death receptor to trigger cell death is just a short series of molecular interactions leading from receptor activation to the eventual death events, how is it that these same receptors so often elicit effects that are not at all cytotoxic, and may even stimulate cell growth?

Knowledge emerging from the many laboratories that have addressed this question implies that the 'decision' taken by the death receptors either to induce cell death or to exert noncytocidal effects is actually a summing up of multiple 'antideath' mechanisms that act at various mechanistic levels [24]. Some of the mechanisms that prevent the

Figure 2

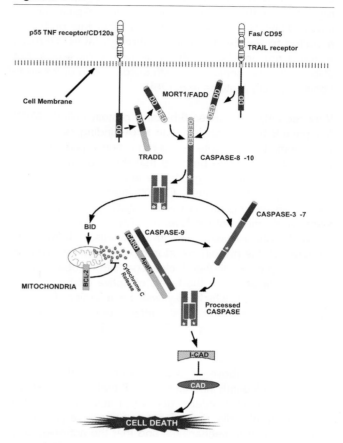

Schematic drawing of the caspase pathway leading to cell death induction by members of the TNF receptor family. DD, death domain; DED, death-effector domain; TNF, tumor necrosis factor. For other abbreviations, see Glossary of terms.

induction of cell death do so by arresting the recruitment of the death-signaling proteins, thus enabling the receptors to trigger other signaling molecules specifically involved in noncytocidal functions.

Quite interestingly, however, protective mechanisms that act by harnessing the same molecules that are dedicated to the induction of cell death to noncytocidal functions also seem to exist. Studies of the impact of targeted disruption of the genes encoding caspase-8 and its adapter protein, MORT1/FADD, revealed that apart from signaling for cell death, these same proteins also participate in the processes triggering development of the heart muscle in mammalian embryos and, at least in the case of MORT1/FADD, triggering lymphocytic growth as well [25–27].

Knowledge of the mechanisms that direct these death molecules to noncytocidal functions is just beginning to emerge. One of the proteins shown to participate in this regulation is the enzymatically inactive caspase homologue cFLIP. Several studies indicate that this protein is recruited to the death receptors through MORT1/FADD, where it not only blocks the activation of caspases, but also, perhaps in conjunction with caspase-8, recruits additional signaling proteins (e.g. [28]).

Very recently, a caspase-8-binding protein called CARY (caspase-8 binding protein with RNA-binding motifs) that also seems to contribute to this regulation was discovered in our laboratory. We propose that this protein acts at a postreceptor level to regulate the activation of caspase-8 in the cytosol. Because CARY itself is cleaved by caspase-8, its impact on the apoptotic process is transient. Modulations of the level of CARY in the cytoplasm, either by its release from the nucleus, where large amounts of this protein are stored, or by phosphorylation of its caspase-8-mediated cleavage site, probably contribute to variations in the levels of active caspase molecules in the cell, which may well be a critical factor in determining whether or not the effects of caspase activity result in cell death (Fig. 3) (Goncharov MT *et al.*, manuscript in preparation).

As mentioned above, it was evident from the earliest studies of cell death induction by TNF that while the death mechanism itself is independent of protein synthesis, the vulnerability of cells to TNF cytotoxicity is regulated by protein synthesis mechanisms and that the activities of at least some of the proteins protecting cells from TNF cytotoxicity are induced by TNF itself. A major advance towards understanding this regulatory process was the identification of the NF-κB transcription factor family as involved in the induction of cellular self-resistance to TNF cytotoxicity. The NF-κB transcription factors are known to be activated by almost all of the members of the TNF/NGF receptor family. Suppressing the activity of these transcription factors greatly sensitizes cells to the cytotoxic effects of TNF and various other agents (reviewed in [29]). Indeed, the genes for several of the proteins known to play a role in regulating the cytotoxic effects of members of the TNF/NGF family are regulated by NF-κB (e.g. [30]).

Specificity in the activation of NF-κB

An additional major challenge to our understanding of the nature of specificity in the signaling mechanisms of the TNF/NGF family of receptors is posed by the way they activate NF-κB. The core mechanism that activates NF-κB was recently elucidated and was found to consist of a macromolecular complex known as the IKK signalosome [31]. This complex is composed of two protein kinases, IKK1 and IKK2. Both kinases phosphorylate IκB (inhibitor of κB), an NF-κB inhibitory molecule, at specific sites, thus targeting it for ubiquitinilation and consequent proteasomal degradation.

Figure 3

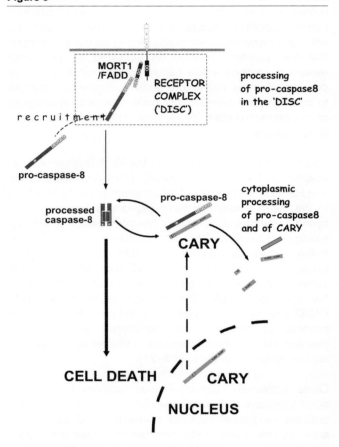

A hypothetical model describing the proposed role of CARY (caspase-8 binding protein with RNA-binding motifs) in controlling postreceptor cleavage of pro-caspase-8. For abbreviations, see Glossary of terms.

Almost all of the receptors of the TNF/NGF family are able to activate NF-κB and involve this activation in a significant part of their gene regulatory effects, influencing a broad spectrum of cellular functions, only some of which concern cell death. Some of the NF-κB-regulated functions contribute to innate immunity and others to adaptive immunity; still others affect certain aspects of embryonic development. In every case, however, NF-κB activation by the receptors was found to be mediated by the same basic NF-κB-activating mechanism, the IKK signalosome.

Knowledge of the ways in which specificity is imposed on this core mechanism is only now beginning to emerge. Studies carried out mainly in the laboratory of David Goeddel have demonstrated involvement of two adapter proteins, TRAF2 and RIP, in the activation of NF-κB by TNF. TRAF2 is a member of a family of adapter proteins that shares among its members a C-terminal protein-binding motif, the TRAF domain [32]. Other members of the TRAF family are also known to participate in NF-κB activation by members of the TNF/NGF receptor family, as well as by some other receptors [33]. RIP is a death-domain-containing adapter protein that is recruited to the p55 TNF receptor by the binding of RIP to TRADD, another death-domain-containing protein, directly associated with this receptor [34,35].

Our own attempts to contribute to the understanding of specificity in NF-κB activation have focused on exploring the identity of the signaling proteins acting downstream of these adapter proteins. By means of two-hybrid screens, we succeeded in identifying several novel proteins that bind to TRAF2 and, when overexpressed, modulate NF-κB activation, suggesting that they participate in the activation of NF-κB or in its regulation. One of the novel TRAF2-binding proteins, a protein kinase that we called NIK (NF-κB-inducing kinase) causes dramatic activation of NF-κB when overexpressed. On the other hand, over-expression of kinase-deficient mutants of this enzyme was found to block the activation of NF-κB by a variety of different inducers [36]. This indiscriminate inhibition implies that NIK is intimately associated with the core mechanism of NF-κB activation. Indeed, subsequent studies revealed that NIK binds directly to IKK1 and phosphorylates it [37].

Although there are still large gaps in our understanding of NIK function, the evidence that is accumulating indicates that this kinase possesses the ability to activate NF-κB in response to specific inducers and for specific purposes. Even though both the p55 TNF receptor and the lympho-toxin-β receptor involve TRAF2 in NF-κB activation, NIK is apparently activated only by the latter [38,39]. Stimulation of the IKK signalosome by TNF leads to the activation of an NF-κB complex comprising the NF-κB subunits p65 (RelA) and p50, and of IκB, through phosphorylation of IκB induced by IKK2 (and consequent degradation of IκB). However, stimulation of the IKK signalosome by NIK also leads to the formation of another NF-κB subspecies, p52, through induced phosphorylation of a p52 precursor, p100 (NF-κB2) by IKK1 (and consequent proteolytic processing of p100) (Fig. 4) [40,41].

It is not yet known which additional inducers other than lymphotoxin-β involve NIK in their effect on NF-κB. However, the phenotypes of mice with a natural point mutation in NIK (the *aly* strain) and of mice with targeted disruption of the NIK gene indicate that NIK specifically mediates the effects of NF-κB-inducing agents that serve to regulate adaptive immunity [39,42].

Among the proteins found in our two-hybrid screens to bind to the other NF-κB activating adapter protein, RIP, we focused on one, which we have initially called RAP2 (the second RIP-associated-protein found in our screens). Unlike NIK, RAP-2 was found to be devoid of any enzymatic function. Nevertheless, it dramatically modulated NF-κB activa-

Figure 4

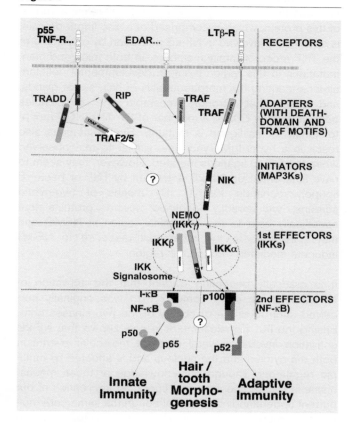

A model depicting the nuclear-factor-κB-activating pathways described in this essay. For abbreviations, see Glossary of terms.

tion. At low expression levels, it somewhat potentiated the activation of NF-κB by a variety of agents, while at higher expression levels, it strongly inhibited such activation.

This same protein was independently identified in several other laboratories, where it has been called NEMO, IKKγ, IKKAP1, and FIP3 [43–46]. Studies coming out of these laboratories revealed that NEMO also binds to the two protein kinases comprising the IKK signalosome, and in fact constitutes an integral part of this macromolecular complex. The coincidental identification of NEMO through its binding to RIP and to the IKKs suggested that this protein may function as a molecular link between the IKK signalosome and specific inducers.

Indeed, in further analysis we found that NEMO is recruited to the TNF receptor complexes along with the other signalosome components [47]. It was later determined that a RIP homologue, RIP2/RICK, also binds to NEMO and recruits the signalosome to a RICK-activating intracellular receptor molecule, Nod1 [48]. Certain viral proteins have also been shown to regulate the signalo-some function by binding to NEMO [46,49].

A more recent development in the study of NEMO function was the interesting finding that the C-terminal region of this protein, which is comprised of a zinc finger domain, is specifically involved in NF-κB activation by only some of the TNF receptor family members. In both mice and man, mutations in this region result in developmental deficiencies concerning the morphogenesis of hair, sweat glands, and teeth that strongly resemble the deficiencies observed when EDAR, a member of the TNF/NGF receptor family, or its ligand is mutated. Such mutations also result in a hyper-IgM syndrome, similar to that observed when the CD40 ligand is mutated. However, they seem to have little effect on NF-κB activation by TNF or bacterial lipopolysaccharide [50,51]. By means of two-hybrid screens, we recently identified several proteins that specifically bind to the C-terminal region in NEMO and may participate in the differential response to NF-κB inducers mediated through this region.

It is gradually becoming evident that the activation of NF-κB is much more complex than was originally perceived soon after the discovery of the two kinases comprising the IKK signalosome. It is now known that NF-κB activation involves several different molecular events in both the cytosol and the nucleus and is affected by multiple regulators. Though our knowledge of these mechanisms is still fragmentary, one important implication of our current understanding is that, although the same core molecular complex, the IKK signalosome, participates in the activation of NF-κB by a variety of different inducers, this core complex displays sufficient complexity of interaction to allow for specificity of regulation.

Concluding remarks

With some regret, we are watching the gradual replacement of the simple and elegant initial models of signaling mechanisms for cell death and NF-κB activation by members of the TNF/NGF receptor family with models of much greater complexity. This loss of elegance is surely worthwhile, as the new, more complex models further our understanding of the ways in which the simple set of signaling molecules known to be activated by members of the TNF/NGF receptor family can coordinate the broad and heterogeneous range of activities controlled by these receptors, without apparent self-contradiction. In essence, we are gradually learning that this simple set of signaling molecules constitutes only the framework within which a much more complex set of molecules interacts, imposing specificity on its action.

There is also an obvious applicative value to this emerging complexity. Understanding the workings of biological regulation at the molecular level provides us with potential tools for medical manipulation of pathological deregulation. It was the search for molecules that provide self-resistance to TNF cytotoxicity that led researchers in our laboratory and several others to the discovery, more than a decade ago, of soluble TNF receptors in body fluids [52–55]. This finding paved the way toward the current use of engineered soluble TNF receptors to block TNF function in diseases, such as rheumatoid arthritis, in which TNF is a causative factor. One can just as well expect that identification of regulatory molecules that impose specificity on the function of TNF/NGF receptors will lead to more refined disease therapies designed to specifically block the deleterious effects of these receptors, without obliterating the beneficial ones.

Glossary of terms

CARY = caspase-8-binding protein with RNA-binding motifs; DFF-45 = 45-kDa subunit of DNA fragmentation factor; FADD = Fas-associated death-domain protein; FIP3 = 14.7-K interacting protein 3; FLICE = FADD-like inteleukin-1-converting enzyme; I-CAD = inhibitor of caspase-activated deoxyribonuclease; IKK = IκB kinase; IKKAP1 = IκB kinase-associated protein 1; MACH = MORT1-associated CED3 homologue; MORT = mediator of receptor-induced toxicity; NEMO = NF-κB essential modulator; NIK = NF-κB-inducing kinase; RAP2 = RIP-associated protein; RICK = RIP-like interacting CLARP kinase; RIP = receptor-interacting protein; TRADD = TNF-receptor-1-associated death-domain protein; TRAF = TNF-receptor-associated factor.

Acknowledgements

DW was supported in part by grants from Inter-Lab Ltd, Nes Ziona, Israel; Ares Trading SA, Switzerland; the European Commission Grant; the Joseph and Bessie Feinberg Foundation; and the German–Israeli Project Cooperation (DIP).

References

1. The Human Genome Organization Gene Nomenclature Committee: http://www.gene.ucl.ac.uk/nomenclature/genefamily/tnftop.html (HGNC Gene Family Nomenclature) [online database].
2. Wallach D, Bigda J, Engelmann H: **The TNF family and related molecules.** In *The Cytokine Network and Immune Functions.* Edited by Thèze J. Oxford: Oxford University Press; 1999:51-84. [key review]
3. Locksley RM, Killeen N, Lenardo MJ: **The TNF and TNF receptor superfamilies: integrating mammalian biology.** *Cell* 2001, **104:** 487-501. [key review]
4. Wallach D: **TNF ligand and TNF/NGF receptor families.** In *Cytokine Reference.* Edited by Oppenheim JJ, Feldmann M. London: Academic Press; 2000:1565-1586. [key review]
5. http://www.apnet.com/cytokinereference/ (Wallach D: **TNF ligand and TNF/NGF receptor families.** In *Cytokine Reference.* Edited by Oppenheim JJ, Feldmann M. London: Academic Press).
6. Wallach D, Varfolomeev EE, Malinin NL, Goltsev YV, Kovalenko AV, Boldin MP: **Tumor necrosis factor receptor and Fas signaling mechanisms.** *Annu Rev Immunol* 1999, **17:**331-367. [key review]
7. Feldmann M, Maini RN: **Anti-TNF alpha therapy of rheumatoid arthritis: what have we learned?** *Annu Rev Immunol* 2001, **19:** 163-196. [key review]
8. Williams TW, Granger GA: **Lymphocyte in vitro cytotoxicity: mechanism of human lymphotoxin-induced target cell destruction.** *Cell Immunol* 1973, 6:171-185. [archival research]
9. Rosenau W, Goldberg ML, Burke GC: **Early biochemical alterations induced by lymphotoxin in target cells.** *J Immunol* 1973, 111:1128-1135. [archival research]
10. Ruff MR, Gifford GE: **Rabbit tumor necrosis factor: mechanism of action.** *Infect Immun* 1981, 31:380-385. [archival research]

11. Engelmann H, Holtmann H, Brakebusch C, Shemer Avni Y, Sarov I, Nophar Y, Hadas E, Leitner O, Wallach D: **Antibodies to a soluble form of a tumor necrosis factor receptor have TNF-like activity.** *J Biol Chem* 1990, 265:14497-14504. [archival research]

12. Wallach D: **Preparations of lymphotoxin induce resistance to their own cytotoxic effect.** *J Immunol* 1984, 132:2464-2469. [archival research]

13. Boldin MP, Varfolomeev EE, Pancer Z, Mett IL, Camonis JH, Wallach D: **A novel protein that interacts with the death domain of Fas/APO1 contains a sequence motif related to the death domain.** *J Biol Chem* 1995, 270:7795-7798. [general reference]

14. Chinnalyan AM, O'Rourke K, Tewari M, Dixit VM: **FADD, a novel death domain-containing protein, interacts with the death domain of Fas and initiates apoptosis.** *Cell* 1995, 81:505-512. [general reference]

15. Hsu H, Xiong J, Goeddel DV: **The TNF receptor 1-associated protein TRADD signals cell death and NF- kappa B activation.** *Cell* 1995, 81:495-504. [general reference]

16. Stanger BZ, Leder P, Lee TH, Kim E, Seed B: **RIP: a novel protein containing a death domain that interacts with Fas/APO-1 (CD95) in yeast and causes cell death.** *Cell* 1995, 81:513-523. [general reference]

17. Boldin MP, Goncharov TM, Goltsev YV, Wallach D: **Involvement of MACH, a novel MORT1/FADD-interacting protease, in Fas/APO1- and TNF receptor-induced cell death.** *Cell* 1996, 85:803-815. [general reference]

18. Muzio M, Chinnaiyan AM, Kischkel FC, O'Rourke K, Shevchenko A, Ni, Scaffidi C, Bretz JD, Zhang M, Gentz R, Mann M, Krammer PH, Peter ME, Dixit VM: **FLICE, a novel FADD-homologous ICE/CED-3-like protease, is recruited to the CD95 (Fas/APO-1) death–inducing signaling complex.** *Cell* 1996, 85:817-827. [general reference]

19. Vincenz C, Dixit VM: **Fas-associated death domain protein interleukin-1beta-converting enzyme 2 (FLICE2), an ICE/Ced-3 homologue, is proximally involved in CD95- and p55-mediated death signaling.** *J Biol Chem* 1997, 272:6578-6583. [general reference]

20. Kischkel FC, Hellbardt S, Behrmann I, Germer M, Pawlita M, Krammer PH, Peter ME: **Cytotoxicity-dependent APO-1 (Fas/CD95)-associated proteins form a death-inducing signaling complex (DISC) with the receptor.** *EMBO J* 1995, 14:5579-5588. [general reference]

21. Wang J, Chun HJ, Wong W, Spencer DM, Lenardo MJ: **Caspase-10 is an initiator caspase in death receptor signaling.** *Proc Natl Acad Sci U S A* 2001, 98:13884-13888. [general reference]

22. Sakahira H, Enari M, Nagata S: **Cleavage of CAD inhibitor in CAD activation and DNA degradation during apoptosis.** *Nature* 1998, 391:96-99. [general reference]

23. Kothakota S, Azuma T, Reinhard C, Klippel A, Tang J, Chu K, McGarry TJ, Kirschner MW, Koths K, Kwiatkowski DJ, Williams LT: **Caspase-3-generated fragment of gelsolin: effector of morphological change in apoptosis.** *Science* 1997, 278:294-28. [general reference]

24. Wallach D, Kovalenko AV, Varfolomeev EE, Boldin MP: **Death-inducing functions of ligands of the tumor necrosis factor family: a Sanhedrin verdict.** *Curr Opin Immunol* 1998, 10:279-288. [key review]

25. Varfolomeev EE, Schuchmann M, Luria V, Chiannilkulchai N, Beckmann JS, Mett IL, Rebrikov D, Brodianski VM, Kemper OC, Kollet O, Lapidot T, Soffer D, Sobe T, Avraham KB, Goncharov T, Holtmann H, Lonai P, Wallach D: **Targeted disruption of the mouse Caspase 8 gene ablates cell death induction by the TNF receptors, Fas/Apo1, and DR3 and is lethal prenatally.** *Immunity* 1998, 9:267-276. [general reference]

26. Yeh W, de la Pompa JL, McCurrach ME, Shu H, Elia AJ, Shahinian A, Ng M, Wakeham A, Khoo W, Mitchell K, El-Deiry WS, Lowe SW, Goeddel DV, Mak TW: **FADD: essential for embryo development and signaling from some, but not all, inducers of apoptosis.** *Science* 1998, 279:1954-1958. [general reference]

27. Zhang J, Cado D, Chen A, Kabra NH, Winoto A: **Fas-mediated apoptosis and activation-induced T-cell proliferation are defective in mice lacking FADD/Mort1.** *Nature* 1998, 392:296-300. [general reference]

28. Kataoka T, Budd RC, Holler N, Thome M, Martinon F, Irmler M, Burns K, Hahne M, Kennedy N, Kovacsovics M, Tschopp J: **The caspase-8 inhibitor FLIP promotes activation of NF-kappaB and Erk signaling pathways.** *Curr Biol* 2000, 10:640-648. [general reference]

29. Wallach D: **Cell death induction by TNF: a matter of self control.** *Trends Biochem Sci* 1997, 22:107-109. [key review]

30. Micheau O, Lens S, Gaide O, Alevizopoulos K, Tschopp J: **NF-kappaB signals induce the expression of c-FLIP.** *Mol Cell Biol* 2001, 21:5299-5305. [general reference]

31. Karin M, Ben-Neriah Y: **Phosphorylation meets ubiquitination: the control of NF-[kappa]B activity.** *Annu Rev Immunol* 2000, 18:621-663. [key review]

32. Rothe M, Wong SC, Henzel WJ, Goeddel DV: **A novel family of putative signal transducers associated with the cytoplasmic domain of the 75 kDa tumor necrosis factor receptor.** *Cell* 1994, 78:681-692. [general reference]

33. Wajant H, Henkler F, Scheurich P: **The TNF-receptor-associated factor family: scaffold molecules for cytokine receptors, kinases and their regulators.** *Cell Signal* 2001, 13:389-400. [key review]

34. Ting AT, Pimentel-Muinos FX, Seed B: **RIP mediates tumor necrosis factor receptor 1 activation of NF-kappaB but not Fas/APO-1-initiated apoptosis.** *EMBO J* 1996, 15:6189-6196. [general reference]

35. Kelliher MA, Grimm S, Ishida Y, Kuo F, Stanger BZ, Leder P: **The death domain kinase RIP mediates the TNF-induced NF-kappaB signal.** *Immunity* 1998, 8:297-303. [general reference]

36. Malinin NL, Boldin MP, Kovalenko AV, Wallach D: **MAP3K-related kinase involved in NF-kappaB induction by TNF, CD95 and IL-1.** *Nature* 1997, 385:540-544. [general reference]

37. Régnier CH, Song HY, Gao X, Goeddel DV, Cao Z, Rothe M: **Identification and characterization of an IkB kinase.** *Cell* 1997, 90:373-383. [general reference]

38. Matsushima A, Kaisho T, Rennert PD, Nakano H, Kurosawa K, Uchida D, Takeda K, Akira S, Matsumoto M: **Essential role of nuclear factor (NF)-kappaB-inducing kinase and inhibitor of kappaB (IkappaB) kinase alpha in NF-kappaB activation through lymphotoxin beta receptor, but not through tumor necrosis factor receptor I.** *J Exp Med* 2001, 193:631-636. [general reference]

39. Yin L, Wu L, Wesche H, Arthur CD, White JM, Goeddel DV, Schreiber R D: **Defective lymphotoxin-beta receptor-induced NF-kappaB transcriptional activity in NIK-deficient mice.** *Science* 2001, 291:2162-2165. [general reference]

40. Xiao G, Harhaj EW, Sun SC: **NF-kappaB-inducing kinase regulates the processing of NF-kappaB2 p100.** *Mol Cell* 2001, 7:401-409. [general reference]

41. Senftleben U, Cao Y, Xiao G, Greten FR, Krahn G, Bonizzi G, Chen Y, Hu Y, Fong A, Sun SC, Karin M: **Activation by IKKalpha of a second, evolutionary conserved, NF-kappa B signaling pathway.** *Science* 2001, 293:1495-1499. [general reference]

42. Shinkura R, Kitada K, Matsuda F, Tashiro K, Ikuta K, Suzuki M, Kogishi K, Serikawa T, Honjo T: **Alymphoplasia is caused by a point mutation in the mouse gene encoding Nf-kappa b-inducing kinase.** *Nat Genet* 1999, 22:74-77. [general reference]

43. Yamaoka S, Courtois G, Bessia C, Whiteside ST, Weil R, Agou F, Kirk HE, Kay RJ, Israel A: **Complementation cloning of NEMO, a component of the IkappaB kinase complex essential for NF-kappaB activation.** *Cell* 1998, 93:1231-1240. [general reference]

44. Rothwarf DM, Zandi E, Natoli G, Karin M: **IKK-gamma is an essential regulatory subunit of the IkappaB kinase complex.** *Nature* 1998, 395:297-300. [general reference]

45. Mercurio F, Murray BW, Shevchenko A, Bennett BL, Young DB, Li JW, Pascual G, Motiwala A, Zhu HI, Mann M, Manning AM: **kappaB kinase (IKK)-associated protein 1, a common component of the heterogeneous IKK complex.** *Mol Cell Biol* 1999, 19:1526-1538. [general reference]

46. Li Y, Kang J, Friedman J, Tarassishin L, Ye J, Kovalenko A, Wallach D, Horwitz MS: **Identification of a cell protein (FIP-3) as a modulator of NF-kappaB activity and as a target of an adenovirus inhibitor of tumor necrosis factor alpha-induced apoptosis.** *Proc Natl Acad Sci U S A* 1999, 96:1042-1047. [general reference]

47. Zhang SQ, Kovalenko A, Cantarella G, Wallach D: **Recruitment of the IKK signalosome to the p55 TNF receptor: RIP and A20 bind to NEMO (IKKgamma) upon receptor stimulation.** *Immunity* 2000, 12:301-311. [general reference]

48. Inohara N, Koseki T, Lin J, del Peso L, Lucas PC, Chen FF, Ogura Y, Nunez G: **An induced proximity model for NF-kappa B activation in the Nod1/RICK and RIP signaling pathways.** *J Biol Chem* 2000, **275**:27823-27831. [general reference]

49. Harhaj EW, Sun SC: **IKKgamma serves as a docking subunit of the IkappaB kinase (IKK) and mediates interaction of IKK with the human T-cell leukemia virus Tax protein.** *J Biol Chem* 1999, **274**:22911-22914. [general reference]

50. Jain A, Ma CA, Liu S, Brown M, Cohen J, Strober W: **Specific missense mutations in NEMO result in hyper-IgM syndrome with hypohydrotic ectodermal dysplasia.** *Nat Immunol* 2001, **2**: 223-228. [general reference]

51. Doffinger R, Smahi A, Bessia C, Geissmann F, Feinberg J, Durandy A, Bodemer C, Kenwrick S, Dupuis-Girod S, Blanche S, Wood P, Rabia SH, Headon DJ, Overbeek PA, Le Deist F, Holland SM, Belani K, Kumararatne DS, Fischer A, Shapiro R, Conley ME, Reimund E, Kalhoff H, Abinun M, Munnich A, Israel A, Courtois G, Casanova JL: **X-linked anhidrotic ectodermal dysplasia with immunodeficiency is caused by impaired NF-kappaB signaling.** *Nat Genet* 2001, **27**:277-285. [general reference]

52. Engelmann H, Aderka D, Rubinstein M, Rotman D, Wallach D: **A tumor necrosis factor-binding protein purified to homogeneity from human urine protects cells from tumor necrosis factor toxicity.** *J Biol Chem* 1989, **264**:11974-11980. [archival research]

53. Olsson I, Lantz M, Nilsson E, Peetre C, Thysell H, Grubb A, Adolf G: **Isolation and characterization of a tumor necrosis binding protein from urine.** *Eur J Haematol* 1989, **42**:270-275. [archival research]

54. Seckinger P, Isaaz S, Dayer JM: **Purification and biologic characterization of a specific tumor necrosis factor a inhibitor.** *J Biol Chem* 1989, **264**:11966-11973. [archival research]

55. Engelmann H, Novick D, Wallach D: **Two tumor necrosis factor binding proteins purified from human urine. Evidence for immunological cross reactivity with cell surface tumor-necrosis-factor receptors.** *J Biol Chem* 1990, **265**:1531-1536. [archival research]

Supplement Review
Studies of T-cell activation in chronic inflammation
Andrew P Cope

The Kennedy Institute of Rheumatology Division, Faculty of Medicine, Imperial College, London, UK

Correspondence: Andrew P Cope, The Kennedy Institute of Rheumatology Division, Faculty of Medicine, Imperial College, Arthritis Research Campaign Building, 1 Aspenlea Road, Hammersmith, London W6 8LH, UK. Tel: +44 (0)20 8383 4444; fax: +44 (0)20 8383 4499; e-mail: andrew.cope@ic.ac.uk

Received: 3 January 2002
Accepted: 21 January 2002
Published: 9 May 2002

Arthritis Res 2002, **4 (suppl 3)**:S197-S211

This article may contain supplementary data which can only be found online at http://arthritis-research.com/content/4/S3/S197

© 2002 BioMed Central Ltd
(Print ISSN 1465-9905; Online ISSN 1465-9913)

Chapter summary

The strong association between specific alleles encoded within the MHC class II region and the development of rheumatoid arthritis (RA) has provided the best evidence to date that CD4+ T cells play a role in the pathogenesis of this chronic inflammatory disease. However, the unusual phenotype of synovial T cells, including their profound proliferative hyporesponsiveness to TCR ligation, has challenged the notion that T-cell effector responses are driven by cognate cartilage antigens in inflamed synovial joints. The hierarchy of T-cell dysfunction from peripheral blood to inflamed joint suggests that these defects are acquired through prolonged exposure to proinflammatory cytokines such as tumour necrosis factor (TNF)-α. Indeed, there are now compelling data to suggest that chronic cytokine activation may contribute substantially to the phenotype and effector function of synovial T cells. Studies reveal that chronic exposure of T cells to TNF uncouples TCR signal transduction pathways by impairing the assembly and stability of the TCR/CD3 complex at the cell surface. Despite this membrane-proximal effect, TNF selectively uncouples downstream signalling pathways, as is shown by the dramatic suppression of calcium signalling responses, while Ras/ERK activation is spared. On the basis of these data, it is proposed that T-cell survival and effector responses are driven by antigen-independent, cytokine-dependent mechanisms, and that therapeutic strategies that seek to restore T-cell homeostasis rather than further depress T-cell function should be explored in the future.

Keywords: inflammation, rheumatoid arthritis, signal transduction, T cells, TNF

Introduction and historical background

Evolving concepts of disease mechanisms for rheumatoid arthritis (RA) have provided a paradigm for understanding the pathogenesis of autoimmune disease. This paradigm proposes that genetic and environmental factors shape a complex series of molecular and cellular interactions leading to a chronic inflammatory response. CD4+ T lymphocytes have featured prominently because the genetic elements most strongly associated with RA susceptibility or severity are encoded within the MHC class II region (discussed in this issue in the chapters by H McDevitt, and G Sønderstrup). Precisely how effector T cells initiate

and promote the inflammatory process in RA, however, remains far from clear. Much effort has focussed on establishing the molecular nature of antigenic reactivity, in the belief that the established chronic phase of the disease is antigen-driven. Animal models of inflammatory arthritis would certainly lend support to this view. However, the results of detailed phenotypic and functional analyses of chronically activated T cells derived from inflamed joints are difficult to reconcile with traditional models of cartilage-antigen-driven inflammatory disease in patients with RA. This chapter aims to explore this theme in more depth, beginning with an outline of the molecular events that

---

A glossary of specialist terms used in this chapter appears at the end of the text section. A list of common abbreviations used in this issue appears just before the indexes.

dictate the differentiation of T helper (Th) cells at the outset of adaptive immune responses in regional lymph nodes. Much of the remainder of the discussion focuses on the different ways in which, in the longer term, the chronic inflammatory process influences maturation, differentiation, and function of effector T cells at sites of inflammation. I conclude by speculating about how our understanding of T-cell activation in chronic inflammation may influence future therapy, and discuss this in the context of the prevailing view that in a susceptible host, chronic inflammatory disease occurs through a failure of regulatory T cells to downregulate the inflammatory process.

Acquisition of transcriptional competence during differentiation of T helper cells

There is now good evidence that there exists a coordinated programme of molecular events initiated at the outset of T-cell differentiation that leads to the generation of CD4+ Th effector cells [1]. This process of differentiation is characterised by a distinctive pattern of cytokine production and is important because its outcome dictates the host response to foreign pathogens such as *Listeria monocytogenes* infection or to parasitic infestation [2]. For cytokine genes, at least three stages are thought to be required for the acquisition of transcriptional competence in T cells: an initiation phase, a commitment phase, and a phase of acute gene transcription (Fig. 1). The existence of these stages has been deduced largely from experiments in which monospecific T cells are stimulated *in vitro* in bulk cultures from naïve precursors [3,4]. During the initiation phase, naïve T cells are engaged through their T-cell receptors (TCRs) by MHC/peptide complexes expressed on the surface of dendritic cells. Only those T cells that form a functional immunological synapse are likely to differentiate [5]. At this point, intracellular signalling pathways emanating from stable clusters of TCR/CD3 complexes are integrated with those from cytokine receptors following engagement by cytokines. For example, IL-12 and IL-18 are important for differentiation of Th1 cells but also play a key role in innate immunity. In polarised Th cells, some cytokines activate families of transcription factors called 'signal transducers and activators of transcription', or STATs, such as STAT4 for IL-12 (Th1), or STAT6 for IL-4 (Th2) [6]. The initial engagement phase may last from hours to days, and in general will result in the production of IL-2 and entry of the cell into the cell cycle. At this stage, cells are incapable of producing Th1 (IFN-γ) or Th2 (IL-4) cytokines, despite optimal stimulation by antigenic peptide and cytokines. Moreover, surprisingly few T cells progress beyond this early stage of maturation.

The commitment phase is characterised at the molecular level by the induction and recruitment of Th-subset-specific transcription factors. Those considered to be lineage-specific include GATA-3 and c-Maf for Th2 cells [7,8], and T-bet and ERM for Th1 cells [9,10]. Once these factors are expressed, differentiation is stabilised and maintained even in the absence of further TCR stimulation (see Fig. 1, middle panel). The third phase, that of acute gene transcription, is determined by secondary contact with antigen and necessitates the recruitment of nuclear factor of activated T cells (NFAT) together with subset-specific transcription factors to the transcriptosome complex (see Fig. 1, right panel). This process is thought to be monoallelic and stochastic, probably because it depends upon chromatin accessibility [1,6]. Thus, specific loci become transcriptionally active through a series of changes to chromatin structure, including chromatin decondensation and remodelling, and recruitment of complexes to the nuclear matrix [11]. Within 48 hours of stimulation, new clusters of DNase-hypersensitive sites can be detected, as demonstrated for the IL-4 gene [12], possibly through the coordinated action of STATS and other transcription factors such as the binding of p300 and of calcium-binding proteinC/EBP (CCAAT/enhancer binding protein) to DNA elements [1,6]. These sites are markers of stable, differentiated T cells. Coincident with these changes in the nucleus are overall increases in histone acetylation, histone phosphorylation, and DNA demethylation [13,14], which occur during the S phase of the cell cycle [15].

Full commitment to a specific lineage is established gradually and in most cases takes place in regional lymph nodes. According to this model, Th cells can be thought of as being in 'antigen mode', since the transcriptional programme required for effector function is absolutely determined by antigen and TCR signalling pathways. It follows from this that the expression and stability of the TCR on the T-cell surface, its avidity for MHC/peptide complexes, the signal strength, and the integrity of protein tyrosine kinases and signalling adaptor molecules would be essential in determining both qualitative and quantitative characteristics of the immune response [16].

T-cell differentiation in chronic inflammation – clues from the rheumatoid joint

While these molecular events go some way towards explaining why some CD4+ T cells differentiate into Th1 cell subsets and produce IFN-γ while others are destined to become Th2 cells producing IL-4, IL-5, and IL-13, much less is known about the events that regulate T-cell effector responses in the context of chronic immunoinflammatory responses. Part of the problem lies in accessibility to T cells at sites of inflammation available for study, the heterogeneity of T-cell subsets recruited to these sites, the unpredictable immunomodulatory effects of drug therapy, and the relapsing and remitting nature of the disease process itself. Notwithstanding these issues, it has been possible to draw some tentative conclusions based on the phenotype of T cells isolated from inflamed tissue such as the RA synovial joint.

Figure 1

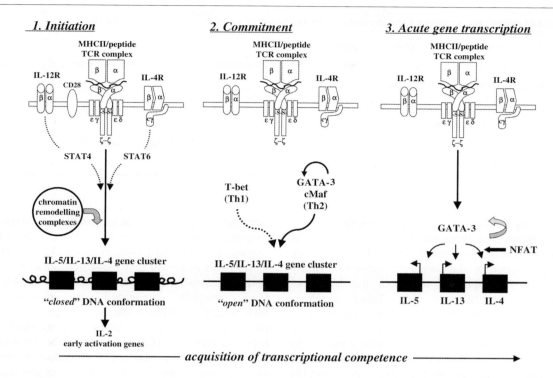

Acquisition of transcriptional competence during differentiation of T helper cells. Th cells become productive effectors of immunoinflammatory responses following a complex series of molecular events dependent upon membrane-proximal TCRs and cytokine receptor signals. Chromatin remodelling is an essential step in the process leading to a switch from the 'closed' to 'open' DNA conformation. This in turn permits accessibility of Th-subset-specific transcription factors and accessory factors to the promoter elements of the Th2 gene cluster, as illustrated here. Ultimately, NFAT is recruited to the transcriptosome, after which cytokine gene transcription proceeds. c-Maf, transcription factor specific for Th2 cells; ERM, transcription factor specific for Th1 cells; GATA-3, transcription factor specific for Th2 cells; NFAT, nuclear factor of activated T cells; STAT, signal transducer and activator of transcription; T-bet, transcription factor specific for Th1 cells; TCR, T-cell receptor; Th, T helper (cell).

What do the available data tell us about T-cell activation and differentiation in established chronic inflammation? The evidence for chronic immune activation is unambiguous (Table 1). This is best illustrated by histological analyses of sections of synovial tissue in which, in subsets of patients with more severe RA, there exist perivascular follicular lymphoid-like structures resembling germinal centres of lymphoid organs [17,18]. Lymphoid aggregates in synovial tissue are rich in T cells, B cells expressing MHC class II, and dendritic cells, and their precise cellular organisation is thought to depend on the local expression of cytokines and chemokines [19]. *Ex vivo*, flow cytometric analysis reveals a memory phenotype for synovial tissue and fluid T cells expressing CD45RO but low levels of CD45RB [20,21], suggestive of past or persistent antigenic stimulation. Their cell surface carries other markers of activation, such as CD69, CD44, and HLA-DR, as well as the chemokine receptors CCR4, CCR5, CXCR3, and CX_3CR1, whose selective expression may facilitate homing to synovial joints [20,22]. Synovial T cells persist in the joint, possibly through an environment that favours cell survival. The expression of stromal cell derived survival

factors such as IFN-α may contribute [23]. The demonstration of both significant and premature telomere shortening would also suggest that these cells undergo progressive self-replication *in situ* [24], and so by the time the inflammatory process is established, subsets of synovial T cells may already be approaching the stage of terminal differentiation or senescence.

While there is a general consensus that in inflamed synovial joints there is enrichment of Th1 T cells [25], the demonstration of significant populations of polarised Th1 subsets has been difficult, even with the advent of intracellular staining techniques [26,27]. Indeed, expression of cytokines cannot be detected easily without stimulation, and even after stimulation with anti-CD3 and anti-CD28, the frequency of cytokine-expressing cells may be very low, necessitating pharmacological stimulants (e.g. phorbol ester and ionophore) to demonstrate the presence of cytokine-producing T cells. Nonetheless, the finding of a paucity of Th2-cytokine-expressing T cells by many laboratories has been more consistent [25,28], and recently there are data to suggest that naïve RA peripheral

Table 1

Characteristics of chronically activated T lymphocytes in the synovium of patients with rheumatoid arthritis

1   T lymphocytes are found in follicular lymphoid aggregates

2   The cell-surface phenotype is suggestive of chronic immune activation, e.g. expression of CD45RO, CD69, and subsets of chemokine receptors

3   T cells are terminally differentiated, with significant telomere loss

4   Synovial T cells are hyporesponsive to TCR ligation

5   Synovial T cells exist in an environment favouring cell survival

6   There is an imbalance of pro- and anti-inflammatory cytokines, with a predominance of macrophage products in inflamed joints

7   There is a bias towards the development of T helper (Th)1 cells

blood T cells may be refractory to Th2 differentiation [29]. According to these data, there exists in vivo an imbalance between proinflammatory cytokines and anti-inflammatory cytokines whereupon a deficiency of anti-inflammatory cytokines might be expected to favour the failure of immunoregulatory mechanisms [30]. Taken together, these experimental observations go some way towards supporting the idea that in inflamed synovial joints, the T cell is in a state of chronic immune activation, if not to say a state of chronic stress or exhaustion, and that the default regulatory mechanisms operating in the nonsusceptible host are absent or insufficient.

Synovial T cells are hyporesponsive to TCR engagement

The low levels of constitutive cytokine expression in synovial T cells is puzzling, given their activated phenotype. More puzzling is the finding that they proliferate very poorly in vitro in response to either mitogen, recall antigens, or CD3 ligation with specific agonistic monoclonal antibodies (Table 1, and [31–33]). Indeed, suppression of proliferative and cytokine responses has led some workers in the field to conclude that terminally differentiated T cells may not contribute to the established inflammatory response [34]. However, this does not seem compatible with the histopathological features of inflamed joints outlined above.

There are several possible reasons for the unusual phenotype of synovial T cells, which may have to do with both spatial and temporal parameters. Firstly, the anatomy and cellular environment of inflamed synovial tissue are different from the architecture and cellular constituents of lymph nodes, with hypoxia and extremes of extracellular pH imposing significant pathophysiological effects (discussed in this issue in chapters by P Taylor and E Paleolog). Secondly, extensive analysis of the inflammatory environment demonstrates that the cytokine milieu in RA synovial tissue is different from that expressed in a lymph node during primary interactions between dendritic cells and precursors of Th cells, with a strong predominance of macrophage products [30]. Accordingly, the expression of

cytokine receptors and the acquisition of chronic cytokine responsiveness is likely to be a distinguishing feature of chronically activated T cells in inflamed joints. Historically, it has been assumed that T-cell activation in the rheumatoid joint would be driven by peptide fragments of cartilage antigens presented by disease-associated MHC-class-II molecules [35,36]. However, this model now has to take into account the fact that synovial T cells are hyporesponsive to TCR engagement. These findings raise the possibility that during the evolution of immune and inflammatory responses, the balance of stimulation shifts from 'antigen mode', in which T cells are engaged through the TCR/CD3 complex during the early phases of Th differentiation, to 'inflammation mode', in which T-cell activation and effector responses are driven by proinflammatory cytokines (Fig. 2).

A model of T-cell activation in chronic inflammation

Almost a decade ago, we began to think about ways to explore how the chronic inflammatory process might influence T-cell autoreactivity and effector responses, in the belief that this might contribute to an understanding of the immunopathogenic processes involved in the chronic phase of RA. Our approach was influenced to a great extent by a series of observations arising from a larger programme of work in the laboratory and by others, which sought to document in depth the broad range of cytokines expressed in rheumatoid joints. The observations of particular importance included the findings that tumour necrosis factor (TNF)-α bioactivity persists in synovial joint cell cultures and in vivo [37–40]; that both high-affinity p55 and p75 tumour-necrosis-factor receptors (TNFRs) are upregulated on synovial joint T cells [41]; that TNFRs are expressed in lymphoid aggregates and colocalise with ligand [42]; and that expression of the naturally occurring TNF inhibitors, the soluble TNFRs, is also increased in synovial fluid but is insufficient to completely neutralise bioactive TNF in vivo [43]. The implication of these findings was that synovial mononuclear-cell infiltrates, including T cells, are chronically exposed to TNF in vivo. We

Figure 2

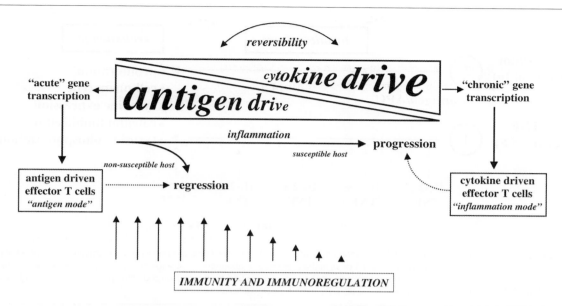

A model for the role of CD4+ T cells in the pathogenesis of chronic inflammation. Antigen drive predominates during the early phase of inflammatory responses ('antigen mode'). In a nonsusceptible host, the immune response resolves through mechanisms such as activation-induced cell death and/or the production of immunoregulatory cytokines. In the susceptible host, additional T cells are recruited to sites of inflammation through bystander activation, or by stimulation with self antigens released from inflamed tissues. As the inflammatory process progresses, chronic cytokine production induces profound nondeletional T-cell hyporesponsiveness. Hyporesponsive T cells function as effector cells and sustain the chronic inflammatory process through predominantly antigen independent mechanisms ('inflammation mode'). It is proposed that by reversing T-cell hyporesponsiveness, antigen-dependent responses that serve to regulate the inflammatory process (e.g. through expression of immunoregulatory cytokines) are restored.

therefore predicted that the environment generated in chronically inflamed joints must be very different from that provided by an acute inflammatory or infectious episode (Table 1), and that chronic exposure to inflammatory cytokines might have effects distinct from those induced after short-term exposure.

We set out to mimic chronic exposure to cytokines by culturing antigen-activated T cells in the presence of TNF. This *in vitro* model was very similar to that used in many laboratories to explore the effects of cytokines such as IFN-γ, IL-4, and IL-12 on T-cell differentiation [3,4], with the exception that recombinant TNF was added repeatedly to T-cell cultures to mimic better the sustained TNF signalling we believed existed in inflamed joints (Fig. 3) [44]. The principal finding that chronic, as opposed to acute, exposure to TNF suppressed T-cell activation was unambiguous, and could not have been predicted from published data at that time, which suggested that TNF was costimulatory and a growth factor for T cells [45]. These results have been confirmed in other laboratories [46–48] and have been supported further through extensive analyses of both human and murine T-cell lines and clones *in vitro,* as well as from experiments *in vivo* undertaken in T-cell receptor transgenic mice treated with recombinant TNF, anti-TNF, or after intercrossing to

human-TNF-globin transgenic mice [49,50]. The findings are summarised in Table 2. Two lines of evidence convinced us that these unexpected findings were potentially important and worthy of further investigation. The first was the observation that peripheral blood T-cell responses from patients with RA were dramatically and rapidly restored after treatment with anti-TNF (infliximab, Remicade™) [44] and that these immunological parameters closely followed clinical improvement [51]. The second line of evidence came from a series of studies undertaken in TCR transgenic mice. These experiments revealed that repeated injections of otherwise healthy transgenic mice with anti-TNF enhanced T-cell responses to cognate peptide antigen, and implied that physiological concentrations of TNF had immunomodulatory properties *in vivo* [49].

The immunomodulatory effects of TNF in the initiation and resolution of autoimmunity

Until the late 1980s, it was assumed that TNF was both proinflammatory and co-stimulatory [30]. How could these initial observations be reconciled with the immunosuppressive effects outlined above? An extensive series of studies in mice deficient for TNF or TNFR have confirmed that TNF has potent immunomodulatory effects *in vivo*, capable of regulating T-cell autoreactivity and autoimmunity when

Figure 3

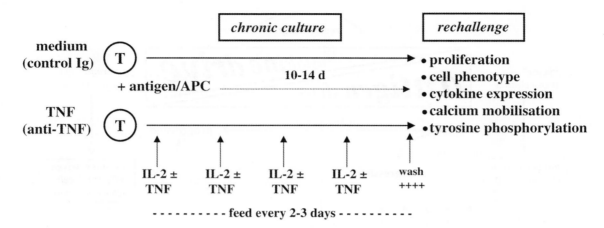

Model for studying the effects of TNF on T-cell differentiation and maturation. T cells are stimulated with cognate antigen in the presence of irradiated antigen-presenting cells for periods of up to 14 days in the presence or absence of recombinant TNF. Cytokines are added to cultures every 2 or 3 days. At the end of the culture period, T cells are washed extensively and then rechallenged with specific antigen or anti-CD3 mAb in the absence of TNF. APC, antigen-presenting cell; T, T cell; TNF, tumour necrosis factor-α.

Table 2

Characteristics of CD4+ T cells chronically exposed to tumour necrosis factor

1	Upregulation of activation antigens such as CD69
2	Induction of nondeletional, proliferative hyporesponsiveness
3	Suppression of cytokine production
4	Uncoupling of TCR signal transduction pathways
5	Repression of CD28 gene transcription

studied in autoimmune-susceptible strains of mice [50]. Indeed, the suppressive effects of chronic TNF were entirely consistent with the studies of Jacob and McDevitt [52], as well as Gordon and colleagues [53], who first demonstrated the disease-protecting effects of chronic TNF therapy in the NZB/W F$_1$ lupus-prone mouse. Similar effects were reported subsequently in murine models of type I diabetes [54,55]. Using a mouse model of multiple sclerosis, Kollias and colleagues demonstrated that while acute TNF exposure is important for T-cell priming to cognate antigen, chronic TNF is required for resolution of T-cell reactivity to myelin antigens [56]. They found that the initiation of T-cell reactivity to myelin basic protein or myelin oligodendrocyte glycoprotein in TNF-deficient mice of the H-2^b strain, which is normally resistant to experimental autoimmune encephalomyelitis, was dramatically impaired, consistent with the idea that TNF was an absolute pre-requisite for T-cell priming by antigen. However, by following the T-cell responses to self-antigens over time, it became apparent that while antigen reactivity peaked and then declined to concentrations no longer detectable in wild-type mice, responses gradually increased and became sustained in TNF-deficient littermates many weeks after immunisation. This sustained and uncontrolled autoreactivity to myelin oligodendrocyte glycoprotein correlated closely with the development of a chronic demyelinating disease in an otherwise disease-resistant strain [56]. These data provide compelling evidence to suggest that while short-term TNF is important for antigen priming, sustained TNF expression is necessary for resolution of T-cell responses (Fig. 4).

How does chronic TNF attenuate T-cell activation?

The potent immunodulatory effects of prolonged TNF exposure *in vitro* and *in vivo* in both mouse and man has prompted us to explore in more depth the molecular and biochemical basis for these findings, in the belief that an understanding of the processes involved might unravel one of nature's immunosuppressive mechanisms. Therefore, we began to study TNF effects on T-cell hybridomas, since these cells could be propagated in the absence of accessory cells. Using this model, we found that the suppression of IL-2 production (to 10% of that in control T cells) was the most profound that we had observed to date. Our first series of experiments revealed that chronic TNF stimulation increased the threshold for T-cell activation through the TCR, such that more peptide/MHC complexes were required for longer periods of time for TNF-treated T cells to commit to IL-2 production [57]. Closer scrutiny of TNF-treated T cells revealed both dose- and time-dependent reductions in expression of the TCR/CD3 complex at the cell surface, as determined by flow cytometry or by cell surface immunoprecipitation experiments. In contrast, levels of expression of CD3ε in

Figure 4

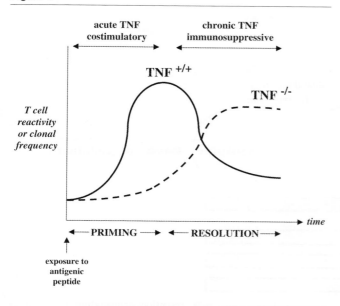

The immunomodulatory effects of TNF during the evolution of the immune response. After TCR ligation, TNF is costimulatory and required for antigen priming. As the immune response proceeds over time, TNF is required to suppress subsequent clonal expansion (TNF$^{+/+}$; unbroken line). In TNF-deficient animals (TNF$^{-/-}$; dotted line), immune responses are delayed, but, once established, they fail to resolve, leading to persistent antigen reactivity. TNF, tumour necrosis factor-α.

whole-cell lysates from the same cells were unimpaired [57]. An understanding of the process of TCR/CD3 complex assembly provided the first clues as to the most likely mechanism for this unexpected observation.

TNF impairs assembly and stability of the TCR/CD3 complex at the cell surface

Current concepts of TCR/CD3 complex assembly have been based largely on detailed molecular analyses in T-cell hybridomas using metabolic labelling and pulse-chase experiments. They describe a process where, for full function, the polymorphic TCR$\alpha\beta$ chains associate with the invariant chains (CD3 γ, δ, and ε and TCRζ) consisting of noncovalently linked $\gamma\varepsilon$ and $\delta\varepsilon$ heterodimers and disulphide-linked ζ–ζ homodimers, which transmit signals inside the cell (Fig. 5). Association of TCRζ dimers with newly synthesized hexameric complexes ($\alpha\beta\gamma\varepsilon\delta\varepsilon$) results in the transport and subsequent expression of the complete TCR/CD3 complex ($\alpha\beta\gamma\varepsilon\delta\varepsilon\zeta_2$) at the cell surface. Studies in T-cell hybridomas have revealed that TCRζ is synthesized at ~10% of the rate of other components [58], and therefore the amount of TCRζ available in a given T cell is thought to regulate TCR/CD3 expression at the cell surface.

Our results predicted that expression of TCRζ may be one target of chronic TNF stimulation. Indeed, following closely

the kinetics of IL-2 downregulation, western blotting analysis of whole-cell lysates revealed that chronic stimulation with TNF suppressed the expression of TCRζ in a dose- and time-dependent fashion, while concentrations of the protein tyrosine kinases ZAP-70, p56Lck, and p59Fyn were not altered [57]. Furthermore, immunoprecipitation of CD3ε-containing complexes revealed normal concentrations of CD3ε, γ and δ, indicating that TNF had selective effects on TCRζ expression. Given that TCRζ might be rate limiting for TCR/CD3 assembly, the data were consistent with a model in which TNF appeared to disrupt the assembly of TCR/CD3 complexes through its effects on TCRζ expression. Profound reduction in concentrations of cell-surface biotinylated TCRζ in TNF-treated T cells strongly supported this notion [57].

A second unexpected experimental observation provided further evidence that persistent TNF signalling in T cells could perturb TCR/CD3 expression at the cell surface. Immunoblotting analysis of unstimulated and TNF-stimulated T cells revealed that the expression of the novel transmembrane adaptor protein TRIM (T-cell-receptor-interacting molecule) was markedly downregulated by TNF treatment [59; Isomäki and Cope, unpublished data]. Closer examination revealed that TRIM expression was reduced by TNF before changes in TCRζ expression could be detected, and that reconstitution of both TRIM and TCRζ expression was required to fully restore TCR responsiveness in TNF-treated cells. The implications of these findings have only recently become apparent, through studies of TRIM expression in human peripheral blood and Jurkat T cells. In collaborative studies with Dr Burkhart Schraven, it was found that the half-life of TCR/CD3 complexes in stable Jurkat clones overexpressing TRIM is increased [60]. This in turn leads to increased cell-surface expression of TCR and enhanced signalling responses as determined by intracellular calcium mobilisation. We can conclude from these experiments that sustained TNF signals in T cells impair TCR/CD3 assembly not only through its effects on TCRζ expression, but also by reducing the half-life of assembled complexes at the cell surface by downregulating the expression of TRIM (see Fig. 5). The kinetics of these changes, as well as the precise interactions between TCRζ and TRIM, are now being studied. Nevertheless, the findings provided a molecular basis for the profound hyporesponsiveness of T cells after TNF stimulation and predicted that downstream TCR signalling pathways might be significantly attenuated as a consequence of these structural constraints.

TNF attenuates membrane-proximal TCR signalling pathways

One of the earliest events detected after TCR ligation is the phosphorylation of tandemly arranged tyrosine residues within immunoreceptor tyrosine-based activation motifs (ITAMs) of TCRζ chain and CD3γ, δ, and ε chains

Figure 5

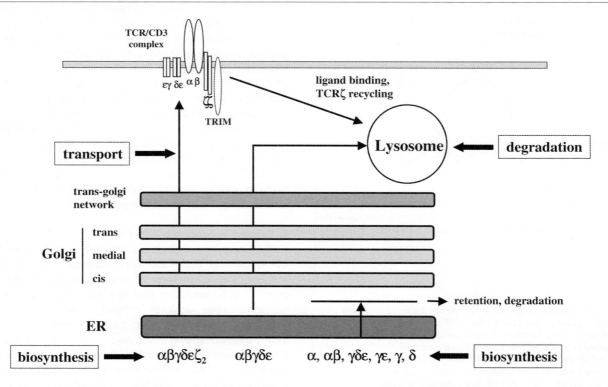

Assembly and degradation of the TCR/CD3 complex. TCRζ and TRIM are required for assembly and stability of the TCR/CD3 complex at the cell surface (see text for further details). ER, endoplasmic reticulum; TCR, T-cell receptor; TRIM, T-cell-receptor-interacting molecule.

by Src family kinases, notably Lck and Fyn [61]. In contrast to CD3 chains, which contain just one ITAM, TCRζ carries three, providing the TCR/CD3 complex with a signal sensor and amplification module [62,63]. In addition, TCRζ plays a role in proofreading extracellular signals, since differences in the quality, intensity, and duration of the antigenic stimulus are translated into specific patterns of TCRζ phosphorylation [64]. Once phosphorylated, TCRζ ITAMs function as docking sites for protein tyrosine kinases of the Syk family, such as ZAP-70 [65]. The phosphorylation of several adaptor proteins by ZAP-70 and Src kinases then serves as a link between membrane-proximal phosphorylation events and the activation of downstream signalling pathways leading to IL-2 production, T-cell proliferation, and effector responses [61].

Given that TCRζ functions as a signal-amplification module as well as a key component of TCR/CD3 complex assembly, we reasoned that reduced expression of TCRζ homodimers by TNF might impair membrane-proximal tyrosine phosphorylation events. A comprehensive analysis of signalling pathways in control and TNF-treated T cells has shown that concentrations of phospho-TCRζ are reduced in TNF-treated T cells after TCR ligation [57]. Furthermore, in spite of normal Lck kinase activity, the recruitment of

ZAP-70 to phospho-TCRζ through its SH2 domains and its subsequent phosphorylation were also impaired. The transmembrane adaptor protein linker for activation of T cells (LAT) is an *in vivo* substrate for ZAP-70 kinase, and plays a key role in linking membrane-proximal events with both calcium and Ras/MAPK (mitogen-activated protein kinase) pathways [66,67]. LAT phosphorylation was substantially reduced in TNF-treated cells, and, as predicted, intracellular calcium mobilisation was also dramatically attenuated [57]. The precise mechanisms for the down-regulation of TCRζ expression by TNF are not clear. However, TCRζ mRNA is reduced in T cells treated with higher concentrations of TNF (2.5 ng/ml). Furthermore, TNF may also reduce TCRζ concentrations indirectly through the generation of reactive oxygen species, since culture of TNF-treated T cells with the glutathione precursor, *N*-acetylcysteine, reverses some but not all of the signalling defects we had documented in TNF-treated T cells, possibly by restoring TCRζ expression [57]. Regardless of the mechanisms, the data were consistent with a model in which proximal signalling was impaired as a direct result of the effects of TNF on TCRζ expression and phosphorylation and suggested a novel mechanism whereby the inflammatory process might suppress T-cell reactivity in RA synovial joints.

Selective uncoupling of downstream signalling by TNF

Since the transmembrane adaptor protein LAT functions as a pivotal bifurcation point for downstream Ras/ERK (extracellular signal-regulated kinase) and calcium signalling pathways [67], the reductions in concentrations of phosphorylated LAT would predict that these downstream pathways should be attenuated in TNF-treated T cells. Several lines of preliminary evidence suggest that this prediction may be too simplistic. We have been struck by the extent to which TCR-induced calcium responses are attenuated in TNF-treated T cells [49,57]. However, very recent experiments have documented additional defects in calcium signalling that arise through mechanisms independent of the effects of TNF on membrane-proximal phosphorylation events and TCR/CD3 expression. For example, while TNF depletes to only a modest extent the thapsigargin-depletable intracellular calcium pool, TNF attenuates to a much greater extent the influx of calcium through store-operated I_{CRAC} (calcium-release-activated calcium current) channels ([68], and Fig. 6). The activation of I_{CRAC} calcium channels and influx of extracellular calcium contributes significantly to the amplitude, duration, and kinetics of the total calcium signal, which in turn is known to profoundly influence gene expression in T cells [69]. We believe that this may provide an additional mechanism through which TNF attenuates gene transcription through calcium/NFAT-dependent pathways, and may go some way to explain the profound proliferative and cytokine hyporesponsiveness following TCR ligation that we have observed after chronic TNF exposure.

We next undertook a systematic analysis of the Ras/ERK pathway in control and TNF-treated T cells, expecting to document similar degrees of attenuation. The results were unexpected. While concentrations of TCR-induced GTP-Ras are only modestly reduced in TNF-treated T cells, phosphorylation of Raf-1, activation of ERK1/2, induction of c-Fos, and TCR-induced expression of CD69 are unambiguously preserved. These results would predict that AP (activator protein)-1 transactivation is likely to be spared in TNF-treated T cells. If this is found to be the case, the data define a novel biochemical basis for acquired suppression of T-cell activation based upon selective attenuation of the calcium but not of the Ras/ERK pathways (Fig. 7). At the biochemical level, this result is of particular interest given the observations that anergic T cells have reciprocal defects, namely, reductions in TCR-induced Ras/ERK activation, while calcium responses are spared [70,71].

Aberrant signal transduction pathways in synovial T cells in rheumatoid arthritis

The effects of chronic TNF described above have provided an experimental framework for exploring the role of inflammatory cytokines in regulating the phenotype of synovial T cells from inflamed joints of patients with RA. Many of the features of T cells chronically exposed to TNF resemble RA synovial T cells (see Tables 1 and 2). Most notable among these are the nondeletional, reversible T-cell hyporesponsiveness [31–33], the upregulation of cell-surface antigens [20], and the repression of CD28 gene expression [72]. These similarities suggest that TNF may play a role in driving this phenotype, and raise the intriguing possibility that there may also be similarities in terms of the aberrations of intracellular signalling pathways that might account for this phenotype.

The pioneering studies of Verweij and colleagues in this field have perhaps most comprehensively and systematically documented proximal TCR signalling in synovial-fluid T cells [73]. The most relevant to this discussion is the downregulation of TCRζ chain expression in synovial-fluid T cells in comparison with peripheral blood, as determined by flow cytometry, immunoblotting, or immunohistochemistry [73,74]. Expression and phosphorylation of p36LAT and its recruitment to the plasma membrane is also reduced in synovial-fluid T cells [75], and both this phenomenon and the loss of TCRζ expression can be reversed at least partially by restoring concentrations of glutathione by culturing T cells ex vivo with N-acetylcysteine [73,75]. This is an important finding, since it indicates that TCR signalling pathways are sensitive to reactive oxygen species and redox potential. More recent data indicate that the generation of such oxygen species is regulated by Ras, which is itself expressed in a constitutively active GTP bound form in synovial T cells, and that increased concentrations of these oxygen species may influence the tertiary structure and conformation of LAT at the plasma membrane [76].

The similarities between synovial T cells and T cells generated in vitro after repeated TNF stimulation extend further to calcium responses, including influx through I_{CRAC} channels, which are also attenuated in peripheral blood and joint T cells from patients [77,78], as well as in Jurkat T cells treated with TNF [79]. Using a completely different approach, Isaacs and colleagues have compared the characteristics of anergic CD4[+] T cells and RA synovial T cells at the mRNA level by differential display RT-PCR [80]. One striking transcriptional event common to both sets of T cells was the downregulation of calmodulin, a gene whose product plays an important role in coupling calcium responses to downstream pathways. Indeed, transcription of calmodulin in RA synovial T cells was less than 1% that in synovial samples from patients with reactive arthritis, who served as the controls in these studies. Expression in synovial T cells was lower than that observed in paired peripheral blood T cells. Interestingly, calmodulin transcripts increased 5- to 10-fold after TNF blockade in vivo in all six patients studied. Thus, the findings of impaired calcium responses on the one hand, and constitutively active Ras on the other, provide compelling evidence of

Figure 6

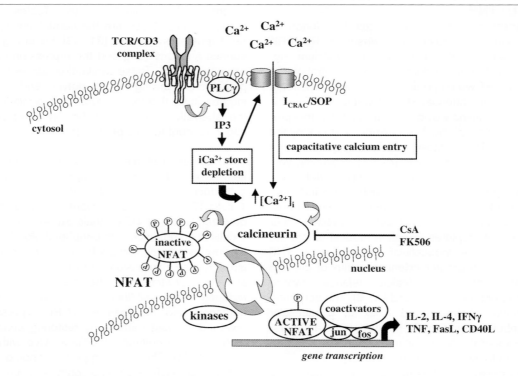

The calcium/calcineurin/NFAT signalling pathway in T cells. After TCR ligation and PLCγ1 activation, newly synthesized IP3 binds to tetrameric IP3 receptor complexes inducing the release of intracellular calcium stores from the sarco-endoplasmic reticulum. Store depletion leads directly to the opening of I_{CRAC} or store-operated channels (SOC) in the plasma membrane through mechanisms that are unclear. This leads ultimately to activation of the serine phosphatase calcineurin, dephosphorylation of NFAT, and translocation of this transcription factor to the nucleus. For many genes, NFAT binds cooperatively to AP-1 complexes for optimal gene transcription. AP, activator protein; CsA, cyclosporin A; iCa^{2+}, intracellular calcium; I_{CRAC}, calcium-release-activated calcium current; IP, inositol phosphate; P, phosphate group; PLCγ, phospholipase Cγ; TCR, T-cell receptor.

selective uncoupling of TCR signalling in chronically active T cells *in vivo*, similar to that observed in TNF-treated T cells (see Fig. 7). Moreover, direct comparisons of peripheral blood and joint T cells have established hierarchical attenuation of signalling pathways from peripheral blood to the joint, with the most profound defects being observed in the joint [73–75], suggesting that these signalling anomalies are not inherited but are likely to be acquired through chronic exposure to the environment in inflamed joints over prolonged periods of time.

Are there any clues suggesting selective activation of downstream signalling pathways leading to specific transcriptional events at the nuclear level? Data up to now are scarce, but there are isolated reports of constitutive NF-κB activation in RA synovial T cells [81]. The finding of constitutive activation of NF-κB in synovial T cells is of particular interest given the recent studies demonstrating the beneficial therapeutic effects of a T-cell selective NF-κB inhibitory compound (SP100030) in collagen-induced arthritis [82]. The same group have documented attenuation of adjuvant arthritis in rats using dominant negative

IKKβ (inhibitor of NF-κB kinase β) delivered by adenoviral vector [83], although when this approach is used, inhibition of NF-κB would not be confined to T cells. In addition, a recent analysis of constitutive MAPK activation in synovial tissue suggests that there may be preferential activation of ERK in lymphoid aggregates in perivascular tissue [84]. It is perhaps premature to draw any firm conclusions about which transcription factors are active in synovial T cells, other than to state that there is evidence for constitutive activation of pathways *in vivo* that exert a potential for promoting the inflammatory process, and perhaps cell survival.

Implications for the pathogenesis of chronic inflammatory disease

The effects of TNF on downstream TCR signalling pathways outlined above, together with the studies of calcium signalling in synovial T cells from patients with RA, predict that transactivation of NFAT should be dramatically reduced in the synovial joint. If this indeed is the case, then it provides a molecular framework for exploring further how the inflammatory process might influence

Figure 7

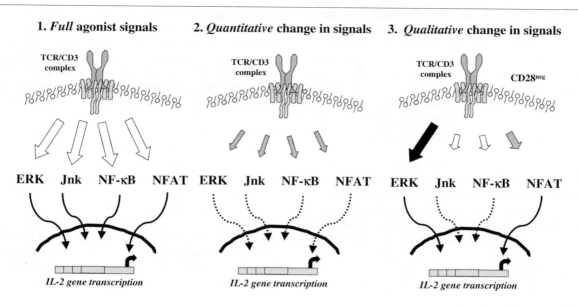

TCR signal transduction pathways. Engagement and stabilisation of TCR/CD3 complexes leads to a membrane-proximal cascade of tyrosine phosphorylation events that ultimately lead to the activation of kinases and transcription factors directly involved in gene transcription. Ligation of TCR and costimulatory receptors leads to activation of multiple pathways, including ERK, JNK, NF-κB, and NFAT (left panel). Impaired assembly and stability of the TCR/CD3 complex would be expected to attenuate all downstream pathways (middle panel). However, chronic TNF stimulation leads to selective uncoupling of TCR signalling, such that TCR-induced calcium/NFAT responses are impaired, while Ras/ERK activation is spared (right panel). The effects of proinflammatory cytokines on the activation of these specific pathways are not included here. ERK, extracellular signal-regulated kinase; Jnk, c-Jun N-terminal kinase; NF, nuclear factor; NFAT, nuclear factor of activated T cells; TCR, T-cell receptor.

immunity and inflammation *in vivo*. For example, NFAT is required for the transcription of many genes involved in the initiation of the immune response, cell growth and differentiation, the induction of immunoregulatory cytokines, host defence, and resolution of the immune response through activation-induced cell death [85]. Accordingly, defects in this pathway would lead not only to depressed immunity and the failure to generate productive Th effector responses, but also to the failure of tolerance by impaired TCR-induced expression of FasL (Fas ligand), attenuation of activation-induced cell death, and the failure to mount significant immunoregulatory responses.

Our own studies of the effects of chronic TNF signalling emphasise the potential for cytokine-dependent, antigen-independent effector mechanisms, driven perhaps through chronic stimulation of the NF-κB pathway. Sustained NF-κB activation would promote trafficking to sites of inflammation, as well as enhance the survival of cells in the inflamed joint, thereby promoting effector responses dependent on cell-to-cell interactions [86,87]. Preliminary phenotyping and genotyping analyses in our laboratory suggest that a number of potential candidates may be upregulated on the cell surface of TNF-treated T cells as a direct consequence of chronic NF-κB activation. These include RANK (receptor activator of nuclear factor κB)

ligand, whose upregulation enhances osteoclastogenesis and bone resorption; β integrins, which promote T-cell trafficking to inflamed joints; and CD69, a surface antigen that has been shown to promote signalling between macrophages and T cells and inflammatory cytokine production [87]. This switch from 'antigen mode' to 'inflammation mode' and the generation of antigen-independent effector responses in T cells (see Fig. 2) suggests that conventional therapeutic approaches for modulating T-cell reactivity may need to be revised.

Future prospects for therapy

It has long been recognised that cellular immunity and, in particular, T-cell activation are restored after treatment with remission-inducing therapy, regardless of the disease-modifying agent. We now know that anti-TNF treatment is no exception [44]. The question of whether inflammatory disease remits as a consequence of the recovery of immune competence or in spite of it has never been addressed in depth. On the basis of the available data, we can only conclude that recovery of T-cell reactivity is compatible with attenuation of the disease process and does not seem to exacerbate the inflammatory process. The possibility that normalisation of function of a subset of specific T cells with anti-inflammatory activity occurs is consistent with this conclusion.

Results from several laboratories, including our own, suggest that therapeutic strategies aimed at restoring T-cell homeostasis should be given serious consideration, and should in addition take into account the effects of the inflammatory process on thymic function [50,80,88,89]. This therapeutic approach is in line with the thesis proposing that susceptibility to autoimmunity arises not through clonal expansion of autoaggressive effector T cells as a primary event, but more through the failure of the adaptive immune system to regulate an inflammatory response [90].

How could recovery of T-cell regulatory activity be achieved in man? A major challenge in the short term will be to define more precisely a phenotype for regulatory T-cell subsets so that their frequency can be studied in peripheral blood and at sites of inflammation. It would be of particular interest to establish whether their TCR signalling responses and regulatory function correlate inversely with disease activity. Such studies might include analyses of the new generation of 'suppressor' T cells such as IL-10-producing, Tr1-like CD4$^+$ cells, CD4$^+$CD25$^+$ regulatory T cells, or IL-16-producing CD8$^+$ T cells [91–94]. If, in the longer term, antigenic specificity can be established, T-cell responsiveness could be restored towards 'normal' (but *not* beyond) by combining peptide therapy with anti-TNF. Precise knowledge of the specific TCR signalling defects could facilitate the monitoring of such therapy, so that any potential for rebound hyper-reactivity of bystander T cells and its deleterious consequences, including systemic autoimmune disease, could be substantially reduced [95,96]. Anti-TNF in combination with nondepleting anti-CD4 or anti-CD3 mAb might have similar beneficial therapeutic effects.

There exists an alternative to the hypothesis that the acquisition of T-cell hyporesponsiveness promotes the inflammatory process. For example, defective T-cell reactivity at sites of inflammation may turn out to be an essential adaptive response for suppressing autoreactivity, as suggested by studies in mice (50,88). In this event, it would be important to understand how the inflammatory process uncouples signalling pathways, since this might facilitate the development of novel immunosuppressive agents. Rather than target pathways that are already suppressed, such as the calcium/calcineurin pathway, these strategies might attenuate those that are dominant and that drive the inflammatory process. According to this model, the Ras/ERK and NF-κB signalling pathways would be good candidates.

Concluding remarks
The molecular events that shape the early phase of Th cell differentiation in regional lymph nodes are quite likely to be distinct from those imposed by the environment of an inflamed joint. It follows from this that the design of strategies for manipulating T-cell effector responses should be governed by the chronicity of the immune response. Until now, therapies that target T cells have been based largely upon the potency of agents in acute immunoinflammatory responses in the laboratory. With a growing knowledge base of the characteristics and phenotype of chronically activated T cells, we can look forward to a new generation of therapeutics targeting selective intracellular pathways involved directly in promoting the chronic inflammatory process. Whether such strategies will necessitate targeted immunoablation or restoration of T-cell homeostasis remains to be seen. However, when considering the available options, it should be borne in mind that protection against foreign pathogens is the primary function of the immune system and that this immunity is provided to the host at the expense of a huge propensity for cross-reactivity to self tissue antigens. My own bias, which is derived in part from the working model illustrated in Fig. 2, would be to focus on methods of reconstituting the immune system of patients with the regulatory networks that keep this cross-reactivity in check and the vast majority of individuals in good health.

Glossary of terms
c-Maf = a transcription factor specific for Th2 cells; ERM = a transcription factor specific for Th1 cells; I$_{CRAC}$ = calcium-release-activated calcium current; ITAM = immunoreceptor tyrosine-based activation motifs; GATA-3 = a transcription factor specific for Th2 cells; T-bet = a transcription factor specific for Th1 cells.

Acknowledgements
I gratefully acknowledge Professors Marc Feldmann, David Wallach, and Hugh McDevitt, in whose laboratories much of this work was undertaken, my mentor Professor Tiny Maini for guidance and support throughout my career, and members of the 'Cope lab', who are continuing with this work. These studies have been funded by The Wellcome Trust and the Arthritis Research Campaign.

References
1. Avni O, Rao A: **T cell differentiation: a mechanistic view.** *Curr Opin Immunol* 2000, **12**:654-659. [key review]
2. Mossman TR, Coffman RL: **TH1 and TH2 cells: different patterns of lymphokine secretion lead to different functional properties.** *Annu Rev Immunol* 1989, **7**:145-173. [key review]
3. Seder RA, Paul WE, Davis MM, Fazekas de St Groth B: **The presence of interleukin 4 during in vitro priming determines the lymphokine-producing potential of CD4+ T cells from T cell receptor transgenic mice.** *J Exp Med* 1992, **176**:1091-1098. [general reference]
4. Hosken NA, Shibuya K, Heath AW, Murphy KM, O'Garra A: **The effect of antigen dose on CD4+ T helper cell phenotype development in a T cell receptor-alpha beta-transgenic model.** *J Exp Med* 1995, **182**:1579-1584. [general reference]
5. Dustin ML, Cooper JA: **The immunological synapse and the actin cytoskeleton: molecular hardware for T cell signaling.** *Nat Immunol* 2000, **1**:23-29. [key review]
6. Murphy KM, Ouyang W, Farrar JD, Yang J, Ranganath S, Asnagli H, Afkarian M, Murphy TL: **Signaling and transcription in T helper development.** *Annu Rev Immunol* 2000, **18**:451-494. [key review]
7. Ouyang W, Ranganath SH, Weindel K, Bhattacharya D, Murphy TL, Sha WC, Murphy KM: **Inhibition of Th1 development mediated by GATA-3 through an IL-4-independent mechanism.** *Immunity* 1998, **9**:745-755. [archival research]
8. Ho IC, Hodge MR, Rooney JW, Glimcher LH: **The proto-oncogene c-maf is responsible for tissue-specific expression of interleukin-4.** *Cell* 1996, **85**:973-983. [archival research]

9. Szabo SJ, Kim ST, Costa GL, Zhang X, Fathman CG, Glimcher LH: **A novel transcription factor, T-bet, directs Th1 lineage commitment.** *Cell* 2000, **100**:655-669. [archival research]

10. Ouyang W, Jacobson NG, Bhattacharya D, Gorham JD, Fenoglio D, Sha WC, Murphy TL, Murphy KM: **The Ets transcription factor ERM is Th1-specific and induced by IL-12 through a Stat4-dependent pathway.** *Proc Natl Acad Sci U S A* 1999, **96**:3888-3893. [general reference]

11. Vignali M, Hassan AH, Neely KE, Workman JL: **ATP-dependent chromatin-remodeling complexes.** *Mol Cell Biol* 2000, **20**: 1899-1910. [key review]

12. Ouyang W, Lohning M, Gao Z, Assenmacher M, Ranganath S, Radbruch A, Murphy KM: **Stat6-independent GATA-3 autoactivation directs IL-4-independent Th2 development and commitment.** *Immunity* 2000, **12**:27-37. [general reference]

13. Blackwood EM, Kadonaga JT: **Going the distance: a current view of enhancer action.** *Science* 1998, **281**:61-63. [general reference]

14. Fitzpatrick DR, Shirley KM, McDonald LE, Bielefeldt-Ohmann H, Kay GF, Kelso A: **Distinct methylation of the interferon gamma (IFN-gamma) and interleukin 3 (IL-3) genes in newly activated primary CD8+ T lymphocytes: regional IFN-gamma promoter demethylation and mRNA expression are heritable in CD44(high)CD8+ T cells.** *J Exp Med* 1998, **188**:103-117. [general reference]

15. Bird JJ, Brown DR, Mullen AC, Moskowitz NH, Mahowald MA, Sider JR, Gajewski TF, Wang CR, Reiner SL: **Helper T cell differentiation is controlled by the cell cycle.** *Immunity* 1998, **9**:229-237. [general reference]

16. Germain RN, Stefanova I: **The dynamics of T cell receptor signaling: complex orchestration and the key roles of tempo and cooperation.** *Annu Rev Immunol* 1999, **17**:467-522. [key review]

17. Young CL, Adamson TC, Vaughan JH, Fox RI: **Immunohistologic characterization of synovial membrane lymphocytes in rheumatoid arthritis.** *Arthritis Rheum* 1984, **27**:32-39. [general reference]

18. Wagner UG, Kurtin PJ, Wahner A, Brackertz M, Berry DJ, Goronzy JJ, Weyand CM: **The role of CD8+ CD40L+ T cells in the formation of germinal centers in rheumatoid synovitis.** *J Immunol* 1998, **161**:6390-6397. [general reference]

19. Takemura S, Braun A, Crowson C, Kurtin PJ, Cofield RH, O'Fallon WM, Goronzy JJ, Weyand CM: **Lymphoid neogenesis in rheumatoid synovitis.** *J Immunol* 2001, **167**:1072-1080. [general reference]

20. Cush JJ, Lipsky PE: **Phenotypic analysis of synovial tissue and peripheral blood lymphocytes isolated from patients with rheumatoid arthritis.** *Arthritis Rheum* 1988, **31**:1230-1238. [general reference]

21. Thomas R, McIlraith M, Davis LS, Lipsky PE: **Rheumatoid synovium is enriched in CD45RBdim mature memory T cells that are potent helpers for B cell differentiation.** *Arthritis Rheum* 1992, **35**:1455-1465. [general reference]

22. Katschke KJ Jr, Rottman JB, Ruth JH, Qin S, Wu L, LaRosa G, Ponath P, Park CC, Pope RM, Koch AE: **Differential expression of chemokine receptors on peripheral blood, synovial fluid, and synovial tissue monocytes/macrophages in rheumatoid arthritis.** *Arthritis Rheum* 2001, **44**:1022-1032. [general reference]

23. Salmon M, Scheel-Toellner D, Huissoon AP, Pilling D, Shamsadeen N, Hyde H, D'Angeac AD, Bacon PA, Emery P, Akbar AN: **Inhibition of T cell apoptosis in the rheumatoid synovium.** *J Clin Invest* 1997, **99**:439-446. [general reference]

24. Koetz K, Bryl E, Spickschen K, O'Fallon WM, Goronzy JJ, Weyand CM: **T cell homeostasis in patients with rheumatoid arthritis.** *Proc Natl Acad Sci U S A* 2000, **97**:9203-9208. [general reference]

25. Simon AK, Seipelt E, Sieper J: **Divergent T-cell cytokine patterns in inflammatory arthritis.** *Proc Natl Acad Sci U S A* 1994, **91**:8562-8566. [general reference]

26. Morita Y, Yamamura M, Kawashima M, Harada S, Tsuji K, Shibuya K, Maruyama K, Makino H: **Flow cytometric single-cell analysis of cytokine production by CD4+ T cells in synovial tissue and peripheral blood from patients with rheumatoid arthritis.** *Arthritis Rheum* 1998, **41**:1669-1676. [general reference]

27. Ronnelid J, Berg L, Rogberg S, Nilsson A, Albertsson K, Klareskog L: **Production of T-cell cytokines at the single-cell level in patients with inflammatory arthritides: enhanced activity in synovial fluid compared to blood.** *Br J Rheumatol* 1998, **37**:7-14. [general reference]

28. Dolhain RJ, van der Heiden AN, ter Haar NT, Breedveld FC, Miltenburg AM: **Shift toward T lymphocytes with a T helper 1 cytokine-secretion profile in the joints of patients with rheumatoid arthritis.** *Arthritis Rheum* 1996, **39**:1961-1969. [general reference]

29. Davis LS, Cush JJ, Schulze-Koops H, Lipsky PE: **Rheumatoid synovial CD4+ T cells exhibit a reduced capacity to differentiate into IL-4-producing T-helper-2 effector cells.** *Arthritis Res* 2001, **3**:54-64. [general reference]

30. Feldmann M, Brennan FM, Maini RN: **Role of cytokines in rheumatoid arthritis.** *Annu Rev Immunol* 1996, **14**:397-440. [key review]

31. Malone DG, Wahl SM, Tsokos M, Cattell H, Decker JL, Wilder RL: **Immune function in severe, active rheumatoid arthritis. A relationship between peripheral blood mononuclear cell proliferation to soluble antigens and synovial tissue immunohistologic characteristics.** *J Clin Invest* 1984, **74**:1173-85. [general reference]

32. Emery P, Panayi GS, Nouri AM: **Interleukin-2 reverses deficient cell-mediated immune responses in rheumatoid arthritis.** *Clin Exp Immunol* 1984, **57**:123-129. [general reference]

33. Emery P, Panayi GS, Welsh KI, Cole BC: **Relationship of HLA-DR4 to defective cellular immunity in rheumatoid arthritis using PPD, and mycoplasma and lectin mitogens.** *J Rheumatol* 1985, **12**:859-864. [general reference]

34. Firestein GS, Xu WD, Townsend K, Broide D, Alvaro-Gracia J, Glasebrook A, Zvaifler NJ: **Cytokines in chronic inflammatory arthritis. I. Failure to detect T cell lymphokines (interleukin 2 and interleukin 3) and presence of macrophage colony-stimulating factor (CSF-1) and a novel mast cell growth factor in rheumatoid synovitis.** *J Exp Med* 1988, **168**:1573-1586. [general reference]

35. Stastny P. **Association of the B-cell alloantigen DRw4 with rheumatoid arthritis.** *N Engl J Med* 1978, **298**: 869-871. [archival research]

36. Panayi GS, Wooley PH, Batchelor JR: **HLA-DRw4 and rheumatoid arthritis.** *Lancet* 1979, **1**:730. [key review]

37. Buchan G, Barrett K, Turner M, Chantry D, Maini RN, Feldmann M: **Interleukin-1 and tumour necrosis factor mRNA expression in rheumatoid arthritis: prolonged production of IL-1α.** *Clin Exp Immunol* 1988, **73**:449-455. [general reference]

38. Saxne T, Palladino MA Jr, Heinegard D, Talal N, Wollheim FA: **Detection of tumor necrosis factor alpha but not tumor necrosis factor beta in rheumatoid arthritis synovial fluid and serum.** *Arthritis Rheum* 1988, **31**:1041-1045. [archival research]

39. Brennan FM, Chantry D, Jackson A, Maini R, Feldmann M: **Inhibitory effect of TNF alpha antibodies on synovial cell interleukin-1 production in rheumatoid arthritis.** *Lancet* 1989, **2**: 244-247. [archival research]

40. Chu CQ, Field M, Feldmann M, Maini RN: **Localization of tumor necrosis factor alpha in synovial tissues and at the cartilage-pannus junction in patients with rheumatoid arthritis.** *Arthritis Rheum* 1991, **34**:1125-1132. [archival research]

41. Brennan FM, Gibbons DL, Mitchell T, Cope AP, Maini RN, Feldmann M: **Enhanced expression of tumor necrosis factor receptor mRNA and protein in mononuclear cells isolated from rheumatoid arthritis synovial joints.** *Eur J Immunol* 1992, **22**: 1907-1912. [archival research]

42. Deleuran BW, Chu CQ, Field M, Brennan FM, Mitchell T, Feldmann M, Maini RN: **Localization of tumor necrosis factor receptors in the synovial tissue and cartilage-pannus junction in patients with rheumatoid arthritis. Implications for local actions of tumor necrosis factor alpha.** *Arthritis Rheum* 1992, **35**:1170-1178. [archival research]

43. Cope AP, Aderka D, Doherty M, Engelmann H, Gibbons D, Jones AC, Brennan FM, Maini RN, Wallach D, Feldmann M: **Increased levels of soluble tumor necrosis factor receptors in the sera and synovial fluid of patients with rheumatic diseases.** *Arthritis Rheum* 1992, **35**:1160-1169. [archival research]

44. Cope AP, Londei M, Chu NR, Cohen SB, Elliott MJ, Brennan FM, Maini RN, Feldmann M: **Chronic exposure to tumor necrosis factor (TNF) in vitro impairs the activation of T cells through the T cell receptor/CD3 complex; reversal in vivo by anti-TNF antibodies in patients with rheumatoid arthritis.** *J Clin Invest* 1994, **94**:749-760. [archival research]

45. Yokota S, Geppert TD, Lipsky PE: **Enhancement of antigen- and mitogen-induced human T lymphocyte proliferation by tumor necrosis factor-alpha.** *J Immunol* 1988, **140**:531-536. [general reference]

46. Lorenz HM, Antoni C, Valerius T, Repp R, Grunke M, Schwerdtner N, Nusslein H, Woody J, Kalden JR, Manger B: **In vivo blockade of TNF-alpha by intravenous infusion of a chimeric monoclonal TNF-alpha antibody in patients with rheumatoid arthritis. Short term cellular and molecular effects.** *J Immunol* 1996, **156**:1646-1653. [general reference]

47. Maurice MM, van der Graaff WL, Leow A, Breedveld FC, van Lier RA, Verweij CL: **Treatment with monoclonal anti-tumor necrosis factor alpha antibody results in an accumulation of Th1 CD4+ T cells in the peripheral blood of patients with rheumatoid arthritis.** *Arthritis Rheum* 1999, **42**:2166-2173. [general reference]

48. Berg L, Lampa J, Rogberg S, van Vollenhoven R, Klareskog L: **Increased peripheral T cell reactivity to microbial antigens and collagen type II in rheumatoid arthritis after treatment with soluble TNFalpha receptors.** *Ann Rheum Dis* 2001, **60**:133-139. [general reference]

49. Cope AP, Liblau RS, Yang XD, Congia M, Laudanna C, Schreiber RD, Probert L, Kollias G, McDevitt HO: **Chronic tumor necrosis factor alters T cell responses by attenuating T cell receptor signaling.** *J Exp Med* 1997, **185**:1573-1584. [general reference]

50. Cope AP. **Regulation of autoimmunity by proinflammatory cytokines.** *Curr Opin Immunol* 1998, **10**:669-676. [key review]

51. Elliott MJ, Maini RN, Feldmann M, Kalden JR, Antoni C, Smolen JS, Leeb B, Breedveld FC, Macfarlane JD, Bijl H, Woody J: **Randomised double-blind comparison of chimeric monoclonal antibody to tumour necrosis factor alpha (cA2) versus placebo in rheumatoid arthritis.** *Lancet* 1994, **344**:1105-1110. [archival research]

52. Jacob CO, McDevitt HO: **Tumour necrosis factor-α in murine autoimmune 'lupus' nephritis.** *Nature* 1988, **331**:356-358. [archival research]

53. Gordon C, Ranges GE, Greenspan JS, Wofsy D: **Chronic therapy with recombinant tumor necrosis factor-alpha in autoimmune NZB/NZW F1 mice.** *Clin Immunol Immunopathol* 1989, **52**:421-434. [general reference]

54. Satoh J, Seino H, Abo T, Tanaka SI, Shintani S, Ohta S, Tamura K, Sawai T, Nobunaga T, Ohteki T, Kumagai K, Toyota T: **Recombinant human tumor necrosis factor α suppresses autoimmune diabetes in non-obese diabetic mice.** *J Clin Invest* 1989, **84**:1345-1348. [general reference]

55. Jacob CO, Aiso S, Michie SA, McDevitt HO, Acha-Orbea H: **Prevention of diabetes in nonobese diabetic mice by tumor necrosis factor (TNF): similarities between TNF-alpha and interleukin 1.** *Proc Natl Acad Sci U S A* 1990, **87**:968-972. [general reference]

56. Kassiotis G, Kollias G: **Uncoupling the proinflammatory from the immunosuppressive properties of tumor necrosis factor (TNF) at the p55 TNF receptor level. Implications for pathogenesis and therapy of autoimmune demyelination.** *J Exp Med* 2001, **193**:427-434. [general reference]

57. Isomäki P, Panesar M, Annenkov A, Clark JM, Foxwell BM, Chernajovsky Y, Cope AP: **Prolonged exposure of T cells to TNF down-regulates TCRzeta and expression of the TCR/CD3 complex at the cell surface.** *J Immunol* 2001, **166**:5495-5507. [general reference]

58. Minami Y, Weissman AM, Samelson LE, Klausner RD: **Building a multichain receptor: synthesis, degradation, and assembly of the T-cell antigen receptor.** *Proc Natl Acad Sci U S A* 1987, **84**:2688-2692. [general reference]

59. Bruyns E, Marie-Cardine A, Kirchgessner H, Sagolla K, Shevchenko A, Mann M, Autschbach F, Bensussan A, Meuer S, Schraven B: **T cell receptor (TCR) interacting molecule (TRIM), a novel disulfide-linked dimer associated with the TCR-CD3-zeta complex, recruits intracellular signaling proteins to the plasma membrane.** *J Exp Med* 1998, **188**:561-575. [general reference]

60. Kirchgessner H, Dietrich J, Scherer J, Isomäki P, Korinek V, Hilgert I, Bruyns E, Leo A, Cope AP, Schraven B: **The transmembrane adaptor protein TRIM regulates T cell receptor (TCR) expression and TCR-mediated signaling via an association with the TCR zeta chain.** *J Exp Med* 2001, **193**:1269-1284. [general reference]

61. Weiss A, Littman DR: **Signal transduction by lymphocyte antigen receptors.** *Cell* 1994, **76**:263-274. [key review]

62. Irving BA, Weiss A: **The cytoplasmic domain of the T cell receptor zeta chain is sufficient to couple to receptor-associated signal transduction pathways.** *Cell* 1991, **64**:891-901. [archival research]

63. Letourneur F, Klausner RD: **Activation of T cells by a tyrosine kinase activation domain in the cytoplasmic tail of CD3 epsilon.** *Science* 1992, **255**:79-82. [archival research]

64. Sloan-Lancaster J, Shaw AS, Rothbard JB, Allen PM: **Partial T cell signaling: altered phospho-zeta and lack of zap70 recruitment in APL-induced T cell anergy.** *Cell* 1994, **79**:913-922. [general reference]

65. Chan AC, Iwashima M, Turck CW, Weiss A: **ZAP-70: a 70 kd protein-tyrosine kinase that associates with the TCR zeta chain.** *Cell* 1992, **71**:649-662. [archival research]

66. Zhang W, Sloan-Lancaster J, Kitchen J, Trible RP, Samelson LE: **LAT: the ZAP-70 tyrosine kinase substrate that links T cell receptor to cellular activation.** *Cell* 1998, **92**:83-92. [archival research]

67. Finco TS, Kadlecek T, Zhang W, Samelson LE, Weiss A: **LAT is required for TCR-mediated activation of PLCgamma1 and the Ras pathways.** *Immunity* 1998, **9**:617-626. [general reference]

68. Clark JM, Isomäki P, Panesar M, Anenkov A, Chernajowsky Y, Cope AP: **Prolonged stimulation by TNF uncouples T-cell receptor (TCR) signalling pathways at multiple levels [abstract].** *Immunol* 2001, 104:OP269. [general reference]

69. Feske S, Giltnane J, Dolmetsch R, Staudt LM, Rao A: **Gene regulation mediated by calcium signals in T lymphocytes.** *Nat Immunol* 2001, **2**:316-324. [general reference]

70. Kang SM, Beverly B, Tran AC, Brorson K, Schwartz RH, Lenardo MJ: **Transactivation by AP-1 is a molecular target of T cell clonal anergy.** *Science* 1992, **257**:1134-1138. [general reference]

71. Schwartz RH. **T cell clonal anergy.** *Curr Opinion Immunol* 1997, **9**:351-357. [key review]

72. Bryl E, Vallejo AN, Weyand CM, Goronzy JJ: **Down-regulation of cd28 expression by TNF-alpha.** *J Immunol* 2001, **167**:3231-3238. [general reference]

73. Maurice MM, Lankester AC, Bezemer AC, Geertsma MF, Tak PP, Breedveld FC, van Lier RA, Verweij CL: **Defective TCR-mediated signaling in synovial T cells in rheumatoid arthritis.** *J Immunol* 1997, **159**:2973-2978. [general reference]

74. Berg L, Ronnelid J, Klareskog L, Bucht A: **Down-regulation of the T cell receptor CD3zeta chain in rheumatoid arthritis (RA) and its influence on T cell responsiveness.** *Clin Exp Immunol* 2000, **120**:174-182. [general reference]

75. Gringhuis SI, Leow A, Papendrecht-Van Der Voort EA, Remans PH, Breedveld FC, Verweij CL: **Displacement of linker for activation of T cells from the plasma membrane due to redox balance alterations results in hyporesponsiveness of synovial fluid T lymphocytes in rheumatoid arthritis.** *J Immunol* 2000, **164**:2170-2179. [general reference]

76. Remans PHJ, van Laar JM, Reedquist KA, Papendrecht EAM, Levarht NEW, Bos JI, Breedveld FC, Verweij CL: **Deregulated Ras and Rap1 signalling in rheumatoid arthritis synovial fluid T lymphocytes leads to persistent reactive oxygen species production and chronic oxidative stress [abstract].** *Arthritis Rheum* 2001, **44**:S2034. [general reference]

77. Allen ME, Young SP, Michell RH, Bacon PA: **Altered T lymphocyte signaling in rheumatoid arthritis.** *Eur J Immunol* 1995, **25**:1547-1554. [general reference]

78. Carruthers DM, Arrol HP, Bacon PA, Young SP: **Dysregulated intracellular Ca2+ stores and Ca2+ signaling in synovial fluid T lymphocytes from patients with chronic inflammatory arthritis.** *Arthritis Rheum* 2000, **43**:1257-1265. [general reference]

79. Church LD, Goodall JE, Rider DA, Bacon PA, Young SP: **TNF-α modulates TCR-induced intracellular calcium signalling in T cells: implications for sphingomyelinase activation [abstract].** *Immunology* 2001, 104:OP165. [general reference]

80. Ali M, Ponchel F, Wilson KE, Francis MJ, Wu X, Verhoef A, Boylston AW, Veale DJ, Emery P, Markham AF, Lamb JR, Isaacs JD: **Rheumatoid arthritis synovial T cells regulate transcription of several genes associated with antigen-induced anergy.** *J Clin Invest* 2001, **107**:519-528. [general reference]

81. Collantes E, Valle Blazquez M, Mazorra V, Macho A, Aranda E, Munoz E: **Nuclear factor-kappa B activity in T cells from**

patients with rheumatic diseases: a preliminary report. *Ann Rheum Dis* 1998, **57**:738-741. [general reference]

82. Gerlag DM, Ransone L, Tak PP, Han Z, Palanki M, Barbosa MS, Boyle D, Manning AM, Firestein GS: **The effect of a T cell-specific NF-kappa B inhibitor on in vitro cytokine production and collagen-induced arthritis.** *J Immunol* 2000, **165**:1652-1658. [general reference]

83. Tak PP, Gerlag DM, Aupperle KR, van de Geest DA, Overbeek M, Bennett BL, Boyle DL, Manning AM, Firestein GS: **Inhibitor of nuclear factor kappaB kinase beta is a key regulator of synovial inflammation.** *Arthritis Rheum* 2001, **44**:1897-1907. [general reference]

84. Schett G, Tohidast-Akrad M, Smolen JS, Schmid BJ, Steiner CW, Bitzan P, Zenz P, Redlich K, Xu Q, Steiner G: **Activation, differential localization, and regulation of the stress-activated protein kinases, extracellular signal-regulated kinase, c-JUN N-terminal kinase, and p38 mitogen-activated protein kinase, in synovial tissue and cells in rheumatoid arthritis.** *Arthritis Rheum* 2000, **43**:2501-2512. [general reference]

85. Rao A, Luo C, Hogan PG: **Transcription factors of the NFAT family: regulation and function.** *Annu Rev Immunol* 1997, **15**: 707-747. [key review]

86. Lacraz S, Isler P, Vey E, Welgus HG, Dayer JM: **Direct contact between T lymphocytes and monocytes is a major pathway for induction of metalloproteinase expression.** *J Biol Chem* 1994, **269**:22027-22033. [general reference]

87. McInnes IB, Leung BP, Sturrock RD, Field M, Liew FY: **Interleukin-15 mediates T cell-dependent regulation of tumor necrosis factor-alpha production in rheumatoid arthritis.** *Nature Med* 1997, **3**:189-195. [general reference]

88. Cope A, Ettinger R, McDevitt H: **The role of TNF alpha and related cytokines in the development and function of the autoreactive T-cell repertoire.** *Res Immunol* 1997, **148**:307-312. [key review]

89. Goronzy JJ, Weyand CM: **Thymic function and peripheral T-cell homeostasis in rheumatoid arthritis.** *Trends Immunol* 2001, **22**:251-255. [key review]

90. Mason D, Powrie F: **Control of immune pathology by regulatory T cells.** *Curr Opin Immunol* 1998, **10**:649-655. [key review]

91. Groux H, O'Garra A, Bigler M, Rouleau M, Antonenko S, de Vries JE, Roncarolo MG: **A CD4+ T-cell subset inhibits antigen-specific T-cell responses and prevents colitis.** *Nature* 1997, **389**: 737-742. [general reference]

92. Stephens LA, Mottet C, Mason D, Powrie F: **Human CD4(+)CD25(+) thymocytes and peripheral T cells have immune suppressive activity in vitro.** *Eur J Immunol* 2001, **31**: 1247-1254. [general reference]

93. Jonuleit H, Schmitt E, Stassen M, Tuettenberg A, Knop J, Enk AH: **Identification and functional characterization of human CD4(+)CD25(+) T cells with regulatory properties isolated from peripheral blood.** *J Exp Med* 2001, **193**:1285-1294. [general reference]

94. Klimiuk PA, Goronzy JJ, Weyand CM: **IL-16 as an anti-inflammatory cytokine in rheumatoid arthritis.** *J Immunol* 1999, **162**: 4293-4299. [general reference]

Signalling

Supplement Review

High-efficiency gene transfer into nontransformed cells: utility for studying gene regulation and analysis of potential therapeutic targets

Nicole J Horwood, Clive Smith, Evangelos Andreakos, Emilia Quattrocchi, Fionula M Brennan, Marc Feldmann and Brian MJ Foxwell

Kennedy Institute of Rheumatology Division, Imperial College Faculty of Medicine, London, UK

Correspondence: Brian MJ Foxwell, Kennedy Institute of Rheumatology Division, Imperial College Faculty of Medicine, Charing Cross Campus, ARC Building, 1 Aspenlea Road, London, UK. Tel: +44 (0)20 8383 4444; fax: +44 (0)20 8563 0399; e-mail: b.foxwell@ic.ac.uk

Received: 22 January
Revisions requested: 23 January 2002
Revisions received: 14 February 2002
Accepted: 3 March 2002
Published: 9 May 2002

Arthritis Res 2002, **4 (suppl 3)**:S215-S225

This article may contain supplementary data which can only be found online at http://arthritis-research.com/content/4/S3/S215

Chapter summary

The elucidation of the signalling pathways involved in inflammatory diseases, such as rheumatoid arthritis, could provide long sought after targets for therapeutic intervention. Gene regulation is complex and varies depending on the cell type, as well as the signal eliciting gene activation. However, cells from certain lineages, such as macrophages, are specialised to degrade exogenous material and consequently do not easily transfect. Methods for high-efficiency gene transfer into primary cells of various lineages and disease states are desirable, as they remove the uncertainties associated with using transformed cell lines. Significant research has been undertaken into the development of nonviral and viral vectors for basic research, and as vehicles for gene therapy. We briefly review the current methods of gene delivery and the difficulties associated with each system. Adenoviruses have been used extensively to examine the role of various cytokines and signal transduction molecules in the pathogenesis of rheumatoid arthritis. This review will focus on the involvement of different signalling molecules in the production of tumour necrosis factor alpha by macrophages and in rheumatoid synovium. While the NF-κB pathway has proven to be a major mediator of tumour necrosis factor alpha production, it is not exclusive and work evaluating the involvement of other pathways is ongoing.

Keywords: adenovirus, gene transfer, macrophage, NF-κB, rheumatoid arthritis

Introduction

The revolution in biological knowledge in the past two decades, with the ability to manipulate, sequence, clone and transfect DNA, has resulted in the sequencing of multiple prokaryotic and eukaryotic genomes, and has spawned a whole new industry, the biotechnology industry – now a major segment of the pharmaceutical industry. This has led to the development of important new drugs, such as cytokines, as well as monoclonal antibodies and receptor Fc fusion proteins.

In this chapter, we will present evidence, using tumour necrosis factor (TNF)-α as our example, that gene regulation is complex and varies depending on the cell type, as

A glossary of specialist terms used in this chapter appears at the end of the text section. A list of common abbreviations used in this issue appears just before the indexes.

well as the signal eliciting gene activation. Analysis of gene regulation is typically performed in transformed cell lines with, for example, footprinting analysis and DNase protection to evaluate which portions of DNA are 'protected' by transcription factors. With genes induced by multiple signals, such as TNF-α, however, it is not clear whether every signal operates in the same way in every cell. Prior literature suggested they did not, since in human T-cell lines (JURKAT), TNF-α synthesis was nuclear factors of activated T cells (NFAT)-dependent and NF-κB-independent, whereas in murine macrophages it was NF-κB dependent [1]. Hence, while a useful indicator, knowledge of the sites in the promoter for transcription factors would not have yielded any definitive data pertaining to a given circumstance.

We will also present evidence that there are new approaches of high-efficiency gene delivery that do permit the elucidation of gene function in physiological and pathological circumstances. The technique we have developed employs replication-deficient adenoviruses, but other efficient delivery systems can also be equally valuable for defining gene function. However, their utility may depend on the particular cell system being investigated.

The problem of gene delivery

Certain molecular techniques, while yielding new information, have limitations. DNA transfer by transfection has low efficiency in easily transfectable transformed cell lines (e.g. HEK 293, COS, CHO), but almost no efficiency in normal 'primary' cells. Low-efficiency DNA transfection need not be a rate-limiting step, as cells stably transfected with DNA can be detected, sorted or cloned. However, there are problems that cannot be overcome. One problem is that transfectable cells from certain lineages such as macrophages, a cell type of major importance in inflammation and chronic rheumatoid diseases, are specialised to degrade exogenous material (such as DNA) and consequently do not transfect. Gene function in one cell type may not be identical to that in another; hence, conclusions made in transfectable cell lineages may not extrapolate to other nontransfectable cells. Furthermore, transformed cell lines have enormous abnormalities in their genomes, with deletions, duplications and alterations in chromosome number.

We therefore explored methods of DNA delivery to nontransformed cells, both normal and cells from pathological sites, that yield effective DNA transfer into >90% of cells. This level of transfer would permit the inhibition of signalling pathways by the inserted DNA. This DNA may encode an endogenous inhibitor (e.g. inhibitor of kappa B alpha [IκBα], which binds NF-κB), a dominant negative (i.e. blocks normal or 'wild type' product), mutation of a kinase or transcription factor, a DNA encoding an antisense mRNA, or even a DNA encoding a single-chain antibody variable region.

Methods of DNA delivery

Current gene delivery systems can be broadly categorised into two main groups: nonviral (plasmid DNA, DNA-coated gold particles, liposomes and polymer DNA complexes), and viral vectors (adenovirus, retrovirus, adeno-associated virus, lenti-virus and herpes virus).

Nonviral vectors

Nonviral vectors attract considerable interest as they lack some of the risks inherent with viral vectors. Nonviral DNA delivery is less toxic, less immunogenic, and easier to prepare. However, DNA delivery is significantly less efficient and gene expression only occurs over a short duration, posing serious limitations and opportunities for the use of these systems for long-term treatment of rheumatic and other diseases. In addition, inflammatory responses following *in vivo* delivery of DNA and lipid–DNA complexes have been reported [2–4]. The exact mechanism is currently unknown, but might be related to the presence of unmethylated CpG motifs in plasmid DNA propagated in bacteria.

Naked or plasmid DNA
DNA can be directly administered to skeletal muscle via an intramuscular injection of 'naked' plasmid DNA. However, gene expression was restricted to cells nearest the route of injection, and less than 1% of the plasmid DNA was incorporated into the cells [5]. Systemic administration has been even less successful. Intravenous injection of naked plasmid DNA showed no gene expression, even in the liver, where the highest uptake was observed [6]. Liu *et al.* have more recently shown that it is possible to achieve systemic administration of naked DNA under hydrostatic pressure by injecting a large volume of DNA solution via the tail vein of mice [7]. Although these experiments demonstrate that it may be possible to deliver naked DNA to cells, this is not a feasible option for exploring gene function.

Gene gun
Particle-mediated ('gene gun') gene transfer has been applied to various cells and tissues. Gold particles coated with plasmid DNA are propelled at the target tissue at pressures of 150–200 psi. The efficiency of this system varies, with skin cells showing the greatest uptake of 10–20% [8]. This system has been used to deliver a nucleic acid-based hepatitis B vaccine to both mice and humans, and is presently in clinical trials [9]. The major limitations are the shallow penetration of particles, associated cell damage, and the inability to deliver the DNA systemically.

Cationic lipids and polymers
Cationic lipids, such as cationic derivatives of cholesterol and diacylglycerol, quarternary ammonium detergents, and lipid derivatives of polyamines condense plasmid DNA to form particles based on the electrostatic interaction and to

protect it from degradation. Mahato *et al.* reported clearance of liposome plasmid DNA from the circulation within 60 min, resulting in extensive accumulation in the lung and liver after intravenous injection in mice [6]. DNA complex properties, such as molecular weight, particle size, and electrical charge, are important considerations for biodistribution of carriers after intravenous injection. The development of carrier systems that escape undesired tissue uptake and exhibit target cell-specificity is therefore required to make this a viable *in vivo* system [10]. Although this method improves the ability of DNA to evade swift degradation, delivery to target cells is still elusive and expression of the transgene is short lived.

Cationic polymers (amino acids) are soluble in water, are biodegradable, are not significantly immunogenic, and have multiple functional groups that can be chemically modified. These cationic polymers are also more effective at condensing DNA than cationic lipids. Among various poly(amino acids) available, poly(glutamic acid) and poly(lysine) have been widely used as carrier backbones.

Viral vectors

Since the evolution and survival of viruses is based on their ability to infect cells and to replicate their genes, it is not surprising that viral vectors have proven to be the most efficient vehicles for DNA delivery to cells both *in vitro* and *in vivo*. Viruses also permit greater duration of transgene expression. This is particularly relevant when attempting to treat chronic conditions, such as rheumatoid arthritis (RA), osteoarthritis, cystic fibrosis, or muscular dystrophy, where enduring transgene expression is desirable. Viral vectors are capable of delivering exogenous cDNA to the synovium, enabling effective levels of intra-articular transgene expression following direct injection to the joint. The expression of certain gene products has proven to be sufficient to inhibit the progression of disease in animals with experimental arthritis, even when the virus is administered after onset of inflammation (see later).

Adeno-associated virus

Adeno-associated virus (AAV) is a single-stranded DNA parvovirus that causes no known pathology in humans. AAV infection involves attachment to a variety of cell surface receptors (heparan sulfate, integrins, and fibroblast growth factor receptor 1) followed by clathrin-dependent or clathrin-independent internalisation [11]. Although the wild-type AAV integrates into a specific locus (AAVS1) on the human chromosome 19, recombinant AAV vectors do not because they lack the rep gene. Consequently, gene expression is transient [12]. Transgenes of up to 5 kb can be accommodated within the 4.68 kb single-stranded DNA virus, and AAV infects a wide variety of dividing and nondividing cells. Recombinant AAV encodes no viral proteins, reducing its immunogenicity and capacity to stimulate an inflammatory response.

Two different groups have recently shown that AAV encoding IL-4 promotes long-term (up to 7 months) protection from articular cartilage destruction and amelioration of disease severity in mice with collagen-induced arthritis (CIA) [13,14]. Additionally, intra-articular injection of AAV encoding soluble TNF receptor I significantly decreased synovial hyperplasia, and cartilage and bone destruction, in TNF-α transgenic mice [15].

Herpes simplex viruses

The herpes simplex virus (HSV) offers several potential benefits that could be useful for treating arthritic conditions. More than one-half of the 152 kb genome of HSV is not required for replication *in vitro*, and large genes or multiple genes can therefore be accommodated by this vector. HSV also develops latency in certain cell types, where the viral genome persists for the life of the host cell without integrating into the genome and without altering host cell metabolism. Although most of the immediate-early genes are inactivated, HSV vectors still express low levels of some viral proteins, resulting in an inflammatory response [16]. Administration of HSV-derived vectors as DNA–liposome complexes improves *in vivo* transduction efficiency by evading the host anti-HSV immunity during systemic administration [15,17]. The delivery of a HSV vector encoding human interleukin-1 receptor antagonist (IL-1Ra) to the joints of rabbits with experimental arthritis has been shown to ameliorate inflammation [18].

Retroviruses

Retroviruses derived from the Moloney murine leukaemia virus have been used extensively in the laboratory and in clinical trials. They are able to incorporate 8–10 kb exogenous DNA, and they contain no native viral coding sequences. Retroviruses integrate their genome into that of the host cell, resulting in sustained transgene expression. This feature of retroviruses also presents a potential hazard beccause insertional mutagenesis could occur following random integration of the provirus into the host genome. This vector is currently used to treat the rare lethal immune disorder, severe combined immunodeficiency-X1, in children [19]. Successful application of these vectors for the study of gene function and gene therapy, however, has often proven difficult because they are unable to transduce quiescent cells [20].

Immortalised embryonic DBA/1 fibroblasts, infected with a retrovirus expressing murine IFN-β *ex vivo* and subsequently implanted intraperitoneally into mice immunised with bovine type II collagen, were able to prevent the onset of arthritis or to ameliorate existing disease [21]. Recent work by Croxford *et al.* has shown that fibroblasts, transduced with retroviral vectors expressing IL-10, could inhibit experimental allergic encephalomyelitis, which is a central nervous system autoimmune disease mediated by the action of CD4+ T cells, macrophages, and proinflammatory cytokines [22].

Figure 1

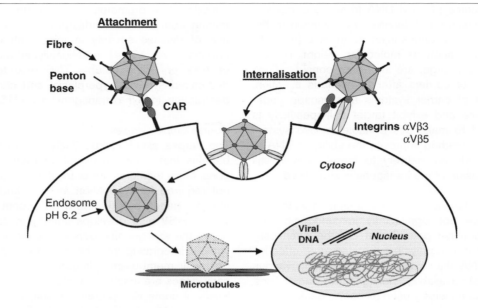

Schematic representation of the adenoviral attachment and internalisation. CAR, Coxsackievirus and adenovirus receptor. See Colour figure section.

Transgene expression, similar to that observed with *ex vivo* administration, has been achieved using direct administration of high-titre retroviruses into the arthritic joint [23,24]. However, high-titre preparations of Moloney murine leukaemia virus-based vectors have been difficult to generate routinely, and this has limited studies involving direct retroviral-mediated gene delivery.

The only clinical trial on gene therapy of RA involving nine patients was performed in the USA using a retroviral vector containing the cDNA for IL-1Ra. Synovial tissue was removed by joint surgery, and cells were expanded and infected *in vitro* before being re-introduced into the joint space. Synovial tissue was removed 1 week later by joint arthroplasty for analysis, showing evidence of IL-1Ra expression at both mRNA and protein levels. This study of local *ex vivo* retroviral gene therapy of RA demonstrated that safe and effective transgene expression could be achieved [25].

Adenoviruses
The remainder of this review will focus on the development and use of adenoviruses *in vitro* and *in vivo*. Replication-deficient adenoviruses are one of the most widely used systems for preclinical experimentation owing to their efficiency and technically straightforward methods for generating high-titre recombinant adenoviruses [26,27]. Adenoviral particles are ~70–100 nm non-enveloped icosahedrons that contain a ~35 kb double-stranded DNA genome and can infect a wide range of cell types.

Adenoviruses are endocytosed by attachment of their fibre protein to the coxsackievirus and adenovirus receptor (CAR) [28]. This process is facilitated by interactions between the penton base protein and integrins on the cell surface. This latter interaction induces release of the fibre protein and initiates internalisation of bound virions into early endosomes via clathrin-coated pits. After internalisation and endosomal escape, adenovirus particles undergo a stepwise disassembly programme and, finally, delivery of viral DNA to the nucleus. This viral DNA exists as extra-chromosomal DNA, resulting in transient gene expression (Fig. 1). The first generation of adenoviruses commonly used for preclinical research are devoid of the E1, E3 regions of the viral genome (Fig. 2). This prevents virus replication while providing the space required to insert your gene of interest. The ability of adenoviruses to infect nearly 100% of cells, quiescent and dividing, makes it an extremely useful vehicle for gene delivery.

Heterogeneity of gene regulation: dependent on cell type and signals
Adenoviruses have been used to analyse macrophages (monocytes differentiated for 2 days with macrophage colony stimulating factor) stimulated to produce TNF-α by a range of signals. Lipopolysaccharide (LPS), UV light, and phorbol 12-myristate 13-acetate (PMA) were shown to be NF-κB dependent, while zymosan and anti-CD45 were NF-κB independent, demonstrating that within a single cell type the stimulus determined the signalling pathway [29]. Again there were differences in T-cell-

Figure 2

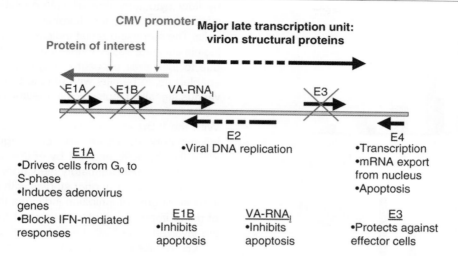

Schematic diagram of the adenoviral genome. In the first generation of adenoviral vectors, the E1A, E1B and E3 regions have been deleted to allow for insertion of your gene of interest. CMV, cytomegalovirus. See Colour figure section.

dependent stimulation of macrophage TNF-α production, with T-cell receptor-activated T cells showing NF-κB-independent TNF-α production whereas bystander cytokine-activated T cells were driving NF-κB-dependent TNF-α [30]. The production of TNF-α in antigen-activated T cells was different from that in macrophages because in cell lines it appeared to be NF-κB independent.

A variety of cytokines and cytokine inhibitors produced by macrophages have been tested for their dependence on NF-κB using the IκBα adenovirus. It appears that NF-κB regulates essentially all proinflammatory cytokines, although not with every stimulus. Second, NF-κB does not regulate anti-inflammatory cytokines, such as IL-10, IL-11 or IL-1Ra, but has moderate effects on shedding of soluble TNF receptor. Third, there were differences within a single study (e.g. LPS) in the degree to which different proinflammatory cytokines were NF-κB dependent. IL-6 was ~80% inhibited, whereas TNF and IL-1 were 60% inhibited and IL-8 was only inhibited by 30–40%. The results varied with different stimuli; for example, with TNF-α stimulation, IL-8 is >60% NF-κB dependent. The reasons for these differences are not known. However, it is possible that other transcription factors are used for IL-1 and IL-8 production in response to LPS [31].

Work by Pope et al. has shown that PMA-treated macrophages, infected with a dominant negative CCAAT/ enhancer binding protein beta (C/EBPβ) adenovirus, produce 60% less TNF-α in response to LPS. Furthermore, dominant negative versions of both C/EBPβ and c-Jun, but not NF-κB p65, suppressed PMA-induced TNF-α secretion, demonstrating that C/EBPβ and c-Jun contribute to TNF-α regulation in normal macrophages [32].

The importance of using the appropriate model for studying gene regulation, and thereby identify potential targets for therapy, has been aptly demonstrated by studies on the NF-κB-inducing kinase (NIK). This enzyme was identified as kinase for IKK1/α, a part of the IκB kinase (IKK) signalosome. Several studies on NIK have shown evidence that NIK acts as a gateway for multiple activators of NF-κB, including the key inflammatory factors, TNF-α, IL-1 and LPS. However, these studies have been exclusively performed in transformed cell lines [33–35]. We confirmed these results in cell lines using an adenovirus encoding a dominant negative version of NIK. However, introduction of the same construct into primary human cells of fibroblast, myeloid or endothelial lineage showed no role for NIK in TNF-α, LPS or IL-1 signalling (Figs 3 and 4) [36]. Rather, the role of NIK was restricted to NF-κB induction by activation of the lymphotoxin beta receptor (LTβR) (Fig. 4) [36]. This supported studies in cells from mice defective in NIK expression or function that showed that NIK function was restricted to LTβR signalling [37]. Together, these data highlight the diversity inherent in signalling pathways and the potent effect that transformation has on cell function.

Use of adenoviruses for analysis of RA and its models
In vitro analysis on synovial tissue
As the pathology of RA is concentrated in the synovium, analysis of this tissue can provide major insights into its pathogenesis. A key question was therefore whether adenoviruses could effectively infect human synovial cells in vitro and, if so, whether all cell types infect equally. It was found that >90% of synovial cells were infected at a multiplicity of virus of 40:1 using a β-galactosidase

Figure 3

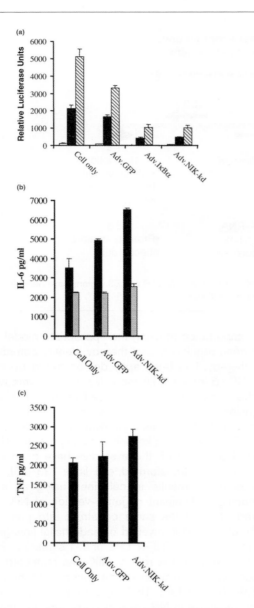

(a) Nuclear factor-kappa B (NF-κB)-dependent gene induction in HeLa 57A cells is NF-κB-inducing kinase (NIK) dependent. HeLa 57A cells were infected with Adv.GFP, Adv.IκBα, or Adv.NIK-kd as indicated (moi 50) and left for 24 hours to allow transgene expression. Cells were stimulated for 4 hours with vehicle (no shading), with 25 ng/ml tumor necrosis factor (TNF)-α (solid shading), or with 10 ng/ml IL-1α (hashed shading). Cell lysates were then prepared and luciferase activities assessed ($n = 3$, ± SEM). **(b, c)** NIK is not required for lipopolysaccharide (LPS)-induced or TNF-α-induced cytokine expression in primary human macrophages. Primary human macrophage colony stimulating factor-differentiated macrophages were infected with Adv.GFP or Adv.NIK-kd as indicated (moi 100) and left for 24 hours to allow transgene expression. Cells were then stimulated for a further 24 hours with vehicle (no shading), with 10 ng/ml LPS (hashed shading), or with 25 ng/ml TNF-α (solid shading). Cell supernatants were collected and secreted IL-6 and TNF-α levels were determined by enzyme-linked immunopsorbent assay ($n = 3$, ± SEM).

reporter virus (Fig. 5) [31]. Furthermore, it was established by flow cytometry that all subpopulations of cells were infected; macrophages, fibroblasts and also >80% of T cells. The surprising result indicated that cells from pathological sites are easier to infect than resting cells, probably due to their prior exposure to cytokines. This observation enabled us, in parallel with others, to evaluate the role of various signalling molecules in rheumatoid synovium.

With the IκBα adenovirus, we showed that multiple pro-inflammatory cytokines are downregulated: TNF-α by 70%, IL-6 by 80%, and IL-1 by ~50% (as shown in Fig. 5). In contrast, anti-inflammatory mediators were not affected. These results parallel prior studies with macrophages. The variable degree of inhibition indicates that, while NF-κB is of major importance, other important transcription factors are involved, especially for IL-1 and IL-8. The blockage of NF-κB resulted in the downregulation of degradative enzymes, with matrix metalloproteinases MMP-1 and MMP-3 markedly reduced. In contrast, the tissue inhibitor of matrix metalloproteinases, TIMP-1, was not downregulated [38]. Taken together, the local effects of NF-κB blockade would be very beneficial for RA. Much work has been carried out to define the inducers of NF-κB and to subsequently generate inhibitors (e.g. inhibitors of IKK2).

Adenoviral-mediated gene delivery of a non-degradable IκBα, or dominant negative versions of C/EBPβ or c-Jun, has been examined to determine the contribution of each transcription factor to IL-6 and IL-8 expression by RA fibroblast-like synoviocytes. Inhibition of NF-κB activation significantly reduced the spontaneous and IL-1β-induced secretion of IL-6 and IL-8. Conversely, inhibition of C/EBPβ and c-Jun/AP-1 had little or no effect on the production of either IL-6 or IL-8 [39].

The p38 mitogen-activated protein kinase (MAPK) is an important regulator of cytokine production, including TNF-α. While drugs blocking p38 MAPK (e.g. SB203570) were effective at blocking LPS-induced TNF-α, they were less effective at blocking spontaneous synovial TNF-α production. Specific p38 MAPK inhibitors, encoded in adenoviral constructs, were constructed to examine their effectiveness in rheumatoid synovial cultures. It was found that up to 80% of spontaneously produced TNF-α was inhibited (Ciesielski *et al.*, manuscript in preparation).

In vivo effects on animal models of arthritis

Adenoviral vectors have been extensively used in preclinical studies on gene therapy of RA using a number of animal models of arthritis. Two main strategies have been employed: systemic delivery, whereby vectors are injected intravenously; and local delivery, whereby genes are transferred to the joint, either via direct injection into the joint (*in vivo*), or by infecting autologous synovial cells *in vitro* and transferring the transformed cells into the joint (*ex vivo*).

Figure 4

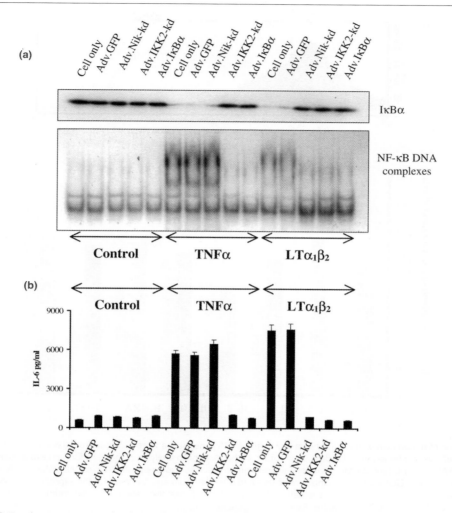

Nuclear factor-kappa B (NF-κB)-inducing kinase (NIK) is dispensable for tumour necrosis factor (TNF) receptor but is essential for lymphotoxin beta-receptor (LTβR)-induced NF-κB activation in primary human skin fibroblasts. Primary human skin fibroblasts were infected with Adv.GFP, Adv.NIK-kd, Adv.IKK2-kd or Adv.IκBα (moi 50) and left for 24 hours to allow transgene expression. **(a)** Cells were stimulated with vehicle (control), with 25 ng/ml TNF-α or with 50 ng/ml LTα1β2 for 30 min prior to the preparation of cytosolic and nuclear extracts. Cytosolic IκBα levels were determined by western blotting (upper panel). Nuclear NF-κB DNA-binding activities were determined by electrophoretic mobility shift assay (EMSA) (lower panel). **(b)** Cells were stimulated with vehicle (control), with 25 ng/ml TNF-α or with 50 ng/ml LTα1β2 for 24 hours, and secreted IL-6 levels were determined by enzyme-linked immunosorbent assay ($n = 3$, ± SEM).

Modulation and suppression of experimental arthritis has been achieved by the systemic gene delivery of a variety of anti-inflammatory and immunosuppressive proteins. Sustained amelioration of murine CIA was demonstrated in our studies. An adenovirus encoding IL-10, when injected intravenously, produced elevated serum levels of murine IL-10 that reduced cell-mediated immune reactivity and IFN-γ production without affecting antibody responses. Interestingly, IL-10 was also able to suppress adenovirus-induced hepatic inflammation, a limitation of the first-generation adenoviral vectors [40].

Systemic delivery of an adenovirus encoding the cytotoxic T lymphocyte antigen CTLA4-Ig, an inhibitor of the CD28/CD80 and CD86 interaction between T cells and antigen-presenting cells, has also been investigated by our group. This treatment was similarly very effective, even if administered after onset of arthritis, being just as effective as protein delivery in optimal concentrations [41]. With the systemic injection of an adenovirus encoding an immunogenic protein, strikingly different results were obtained. The human p55 TNF receptor coupled to a mouse IgG Fc fusion protein gene, inserted into an adenoviral vector and

Figure 5

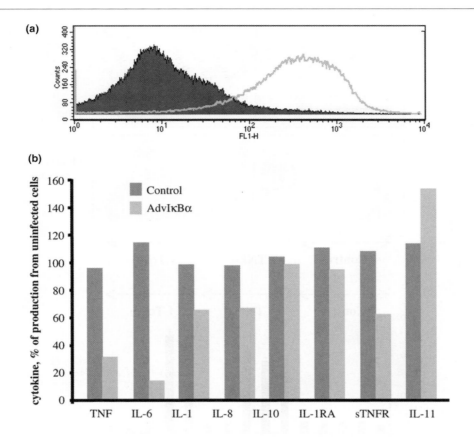

(a) Efficiency of infection of rheumatoid arthritis (RA) joint cell cultures. RA joint tissues were obtained from the synovium from patients with RA undergoing surgery. Cells were infected with Advβgal (moi 40) for 48 hours prior to analysis of the cells for βgal expression by fluorescence activated cell sorting (FACS). (B) Effect of IκBα transgene expression on cytokine expression in RA joint cell cultures. RA joint cells were infected with AdvIκBα or AdvO (moi 40). Culture supernatants were harvested after 48 hours and analysed for the expression of various cytokines by enzyme-linked immunosorbent assay. Data are representative of samples from at least five patients. IL-1RA, interleukin-1 receptor antagonist; TNF, tumour necrosis factor; sTNFR, soluble TNF receptor. See Colour figure section.

injected systemically in arthritic mice, induced elevated serum levels of the fusion protein and ameliorated CIA for up to 7–10 days. Then, a dramatic inflammatory rebound was observed and treated mice appeared sicker than controls. These findings confirm prior reports on the role of host immune reactions elicited more towards the product of gene transduction than to the virus itself.

The group of Robbins and Evans has reported successful treatment of murine CIA with an adenovirus encoding IL-4 [42]. This treatment was also effective in the rat model of adjuvant arthritis after disease onset, and decreased levels of TNF-α, IL-1β, macrophage inflammatory protein-2, and CCL5 (the chemokine ligand for CCR5) were reported [43].

A local intra-articular approach has also been investigated using adenoviral vectors. As mutations in the tumour suppressor protein p53 are observed in synovial cells from some RA patients, overexpression of p53 by adenoviral

gene transfer in synovial cell cultures *in vitro*, and in synovial tissue *in vivo*, has been achieved in a rabbit model of arthritis, and resulted in significant apoptosis. In addition, the intra-articular injection of p53 adenovirus determined a rapid induction of synovial apoptosis in the rabbit knee joint without affecting cartilage metabolism [44].

Makorov *et al.* have shown in a rat model of arthritis that local injection of a retrovirus expressing a mutant, non-degradable IκBα, induces improvements in joint disease [45]. This work is supported by experiments using another member of the NF-κB pathway; inhibitor of NF-κB kinase beta (IKKβ). Intra-articular injection of adenovirus encoding IKKβ-wt into the joints of normal rats caused significant paw swelling and histologic evidence of synovial inflammation. Increased IKK activity was detectable in the IKKβ-wt-injected ankle joints, coincident with enhanced NF-κB DNA binding activity, while a dominant negative version of IKKβ significantly ameliorated disease severity of adjuvant arthritis, and determined a significant decrease in NF-κB DNA expression [46].

The work described here regarding animal models of arthritis has been supplemented by a number of studies using retroviruses that were used to infect cell lines *in vitro* and then injected systemically *in vivo* [47].

Future prospects

The working draft covering 97% of the human genome was completed in June 2000. It is expected that the 'finished' sequence of greater than 99.99% accuracy will be completed within the next year. Analysis of the current sequence shows 38,000 predicted genes and many of these have no known function. Expectations within the pharmaceutical industry have been high that this knowledge will be transformed into therapeutic targets and new drugs. These expectations have so far not been met because crucial roadblocks remain in the elucidation of target genes for drug development. Expectations have been raised about the possibility of performing drug development '*in silico*' using genetic information, but successes from this approach remain to be achieved.

The ability to explore gene function both *in vitro* and *in vivo* is paramount to the elucidation of gene regulation and potential targets for therapeutic intervention. While substantial work has been undertaken to determine the signalling pathways controlling TNF-α production and other inflammatory mediators, the roles of a multitude of cytokines, cytokine receptors, kinases and phosphatases remain to be explored.

Research into developing high-efficiency vectors for transgene delivery is a continually evolving field of research. Current research into developing cationic lipids/polymers for cell-specific delivery via receptor-mediated endocytosis, such as galactose, mannose, lactose, transferrin, epidermal growth factor, asialoglycoprotein and antibodies, may provide valuable advances allowing the targeting of specific cell populations [10]. Combining advances in DNA delivery via directed cationic lipids and polymers, and improved adenoviral or other viral vectors, looks to be a promising approach to evade clearance and to deliver stable gene expression to specific cells [48,49].

Although adenoviruses have proved valuable tools for preclinical research, the first generation of E1, E3 deleted vectors still contains native viral-coding sequences expressed at low levels, resulting in inflammatory responses (Fig. 2) [50]. Furthermore, expression of these viral proteins leads to the clearance of transduced cells, limiting transgene expression [51]. Recently described helper-dependent, or gutless, adenoviral vectors may overcome many of these problems. These adenoviruses do not encode any viral coding sequences and have shown an excellent expression profile in a variety of animal models, as well as reduced toxicity after local or systemic delivery [52]. Expression of the transgene can be detected for many months and the gutted adenoviruses do not elicit an immune response in animals previously immunised against the same adenovirus serotype [53].

Concluding remarks

There has been much progress in the development of methods of gene transfer into normal cells and cells from pathological sites. These techniques can be used to test the function of genes, allegedly known or unknown both *in vivo* and *in vitro*. These approaches can be used to elucidate important pathways, and to help confirm or define therapeutic targets.

Glossary of terms

AAV = adeno-associated virus; C/EBPβ = CCAAT/enhancer binding protein beta; HSV = herpes simplex virus; IKK = IκB kinase; IKKβ = inhibitor of NF-κB kinase beta; IL-1Ra = interleukin-1 receptor antagonist; LTβR = lymphotoxin beta-receptor; NIK = NF-κB-inducing kinase.

References
1. Darnay BG, Aggarwal BB: **Signal transduction by tumour necrosis factor and tumour necrosis factor related ligands and their receptors.** *Ann Rheum Dis* 1999, **58 (Suppl 1)**:I2-I13. [key review]
2. Li S, Wu SP, Whitmore M, Loeffert EJ, Wang L, Watkins SC, Pitt BR, Huang L: **Effect of immune response on gene transfer to the lung via systemic administration of cationic lipidic vectors.** *Am J Physiol* 1999, **276**:L796-L804. [general reference]
3. Norman J, Denham W, Denham D, Yang J, Carter G, Abouhamze A, Tannahill CL, MacKay SL, Moldawer LL: **Liposome-mediated, nonviral gene transfer induces a systemic inflammatory response which can exacerbate pre-existing inflammation.** *Gene Ther* 2000, **7**:1425-1430. [general reference]
4. Yew NS, Zhao H, Wu IH, Song A, Tousignant JD, Przybylska M, Cheng SH: **Reduced inflammatory response to plasmid DNA vectors by elimination and inhibition of immunostimulatory CpG motifs.** *Mol Ther* 2000, **1**:255-262. [general reference]
5. Wolff JA, Malone RW, Williams P, Chong W, Acsadi G, Jani A, Felgner PL: **Direct gene transfer into mouse muscle in vivo.** *Science* 1990, **247**:1465-1468. [archival research]
6. Mahato RI, Kawabata K, Takakura Y, Hashida M: **In vivo disposition characteristics of plasmid DNA complexed with cationic liposomes.** *J Drug Target* 1995, **3**:149-157. [archival research]
7. Liu F, Song Y, Liu D: **Hydrodynamics-based transfection in animals by systemic administration of plasmid DNA.** *Gene Ther* 1999, **6**:1258-1266. [general reference]
8. Yang NS, Burkholder J, Roberts B, Martinell B, McCabe D: **In vivo and in vitro gene transfer to mammalian somatic cells by particle bombardment.** *Proc Natl Acad Sci USA* 1990, **87**:9568-9672. [archival research]
9. Mumper RJ, Ledebur HC Jr: **Dendritic cell delivery of plasmid DNA. Applications for controlled genetic immunization.** *Mol Biotechnol* 2001, **19**:79-95. [general reference]
10. Hashida M, Nishikawa M, Yamashita F, Takakura Y: **Cell-specific delivery of genes with glycosylated carriers.** *Adv Drug Deliv Rev* 2001, **52**: 87-196. [key review]
11. Douar AM, Poulard K, Stockholm D, Danos O: **Intracellular trafficking of adeno-associated virus vectors: routing to the late endosomal compartment and proteasome degradation.** *J Virol* 2001, **75**:1824-1833. [general reference]
12. Ponnazhagan S, Erikson D, Kearns WG, Zhou SZ, Nahreini P, Wang XS, Srivastava A: **Lack of site-specific integration of the recombinant adeno-associated virus 2 genomes in human cells.** *Hum Gene Ther* 1997, **8**:275-284. [general reference]

13. Watanabe S, Imagawa T, Boivin GP, Gao G, Wilson JM, Hirsch R: **Adeno-associated virus mediates long-term gene transfer and delivery of chondroprotective IL-4 to murine synovium.** *Mol Ther* 2000, **2**:147-152. [general reference]

14. Cottard V, Mulleman D, Bouille P, Mezzina M, Boissier MC, Bessis N: **Adeno-associated virus-mediated delivery of IL-4 prevents collagen-induced arthritis.** *Gene Ther* 2000, **7**:1930-1939. [general reference]

15. Zhang HG, Xie J, Yang P, Wang Y, Xu L, Liu D, Hsu HC, Zhou T, Edwards CK 3rd, Mountz JD: **Adeno-associated virus production of soluble tumor necrosis factor receptor neutralizes tumor necrosis factor alpha and reduces arthritis.** *Hum Gene Ther* 2000, **11**:2431-2442. [general reference]

16. Latchman DS: **Gene delivery and gene therapy with herpes simplex virus-based vectors.** *Gene* 2001, **264**:1-9. [key review]

17. Fu X, Zhang X: **Delivery of herpes simplex virus vectors through liposome formulation.** *Mol Ther* 2001, **4**:447-453. [general reference]

18. Oligino T, Ghivizzani S, Wolfe D, Lechman E, Krisky D, Mi Z, Evans C, Robbins P, Glorioso J: **Intra-articular delivery of a herpes simplex virus IL-1Ra gene vector reduces inflammation in a rabbit model of arthritis.** *Gene Ther* 1999, **6**:1713-1720. [general reference]

19. Cavazzana-Calvo M, Hacein-Bey S, de Saint Basile G, Gross F, Yvon E, Nusbaum P, Selz F, Hue C, Certain S, Casanova JL, Bousso P, Deist FL, Fischer A: **Gene therapy of human severe combined immunodeficiency (SCID)-X1 disease.** *Science* 2000, **288**:669-672. [general reference]

20. Weber E, Anderson WF, Kasahara N: **Recent advances in retrovirus vector-mediated gene therapy: teaching an old vector new tricks.** *Curr Opin Mol Ther* 2001, **3**:439-453. [key review].

21. Triantaphyllopoulos KA, Williams RO, Tailor H, Chernajovsky Y: **Amelioration of collagen-induced arthritis and suppression of interferon-gamma, interleukin-12, and tumor necrosis factor alpha production by interferon-beta gene therapy.** *Arthritis Rheum* 1999, **42**:90-99. [general reference]

22. Croxford JL, Feldmann M, Chernajovsky Y, Baker D: **Different therapeutic outcomes in experimental allergic encephalomyelitis dependent upon the mode of delivery of IL-10: a comparison of the effects of protein, adenoviral or retroviral IL-10 delivery into the central nervous system.** *J Immunol* 2001, **166**:4124-4130. [general reference]

23. Ghivizzani SC, Lechman ER, Tio C, Mehle KM, Chada S, McCormack JE, Evans CH, Robbins PD: **Direct retrovirus-mediated gene transfer to the synovium of the rabbit knee: implications for arthritis gene therapy.** *Gene Ther* 1997, **4**:977-982. [general reference]

24. Nguyen KH, Boyle DL, McCormack JE, Chada S, Jolly DJ, Firestein GS: **Direct synovial gene transfer with retroviral vectors in rat adjuvant arthritis.** *J Rheumatol* 1998, **25**:1118-1125. [general reference]

25. Evans C, Robbins P, Ghivizzani S: **Results of the first human clinical trial of gene therapy for arthritis [abstract].** *Arthritis Rheum* 1999, **42**:S170. [general reference]

26. Hitt M, Bett AJ, Prevec L, Graham FL: **Construction and propagation of human adenovirus vectors.** In *Cell Biology: A Laboratory Handbook*, Volume 1. Edited by Celis JE. San Diego, CA: Academic Press; 1994:479-490. [general reference]

27. He TC, Zhou S, da Costa LT, Yu J, Kinzler KW, Vogelstein B: **A simplified system for generating recombinant adenoviruses.** *Proc Natl Acad Sci USA* 1998, **95**:2509-2514. [general reference]

28. Bergelson JM, Cunningham JA, Droguett G, Kurt-Jones EA, Krithivas A, Hong JS, Horwitz MS, Crowell RL, Finberg RW: **Isolation of a common receptor for Coxsackie B viruses and adenoviruses 2 and 5.** *Science* 1997, **275**:1320-1323. [general reference]

29. Bondeson J, Browne KA, Brennan FM, Foxwell BM, Feldmann M: **Selective regulation of cytokine induction by adenoviral gene transfer of IkappaBalpha into human macrophages: lipopolysaccharide-induced, but not zymosan-induced, proinflammatory cytokines are inhibited, but IL-10 is nuclear factor-kappaB independent.** *J Immunol* 1999, **162**:2939-2945. [general reference]

30. Brennan FM, Foey AD: **Cytokine regulation in RA synovial tissue: role of T cell/macrophage contact-dependent interactions.** *Arthritis Res* 2002, **4(suppl 3)**:S177-S182.

31. Foxwell B, Browne K, Bondeson J, Clarke C, de Martin R, Brennan F, Feldmann M: **Efficient adenoviral infection with IkappaB alpha reveals that macrophage tumor necrosis factor alpha production in rheumatoid arthritis is NF-kappaB dependent.** *Proc Natl Acad Sci USA* 1998, **95**:8211-8215. [general reference]

32. Pope R, Mungre S, Liu H, Thimmapaya B: **Regulation of TNF-alpha expression in normal macrophages: the role of C/EBPbeta.** *Cytokine* 2000, **12**:1171-1181. [general reference]

33. Malinin NL, Boldin MP, Kovalenko AV, Wallach D: **MAP3K-related kinase involved in NF-kappaB induction by TNF, CD95 and IL-1.** *Nature* 1997, **385**:540-544. [general reference]

34. Song HY, Regnier CH, Kirschning CJ, Goeddel DV, Rothe M: **Tumor necrosis factor (TNF)-mediated kinase cascades: bifurcation of nuclear factor-kappaB and c-jun N-terminal kinase (JNK/SAPK) pathways at TNF receptor-associated factor 2.** *Proc Natl Acad Sci USA* 1997, **94**:9792-9796. [general reference]

35. Woronicz JD, Gao X, Cao Z, Rothe M, Goeddel DV: **IkappaB kinase-beta: NF-kappaB activation and complex formation with IkappaB kinase-alpha and NIK.** *Science* 1997, **278**:866-869. [general reference]

36. Smith C, Andreakos E, Crawley JB, Brennan FM, Feldmann M, Foxwell BM: **NF-kappaB-inducing kinase is dispensable for activation of NF-kappaB in inflammatory settings but essential for lymphotoxin beta receptor activation of NF-kappaB in primary human fibroblasts.** *J Immunol* 2001, **167**:5895-5903. [general reference]

37. Shinkura R, Kitada K, Matsuda F, Tashiro K, Ikuta K, Suzuki M, Kogishi K, Serikawa T, Honjo T: **Alymphoplasia is caused by a point mutation in the mouse gene encoding Nf-kappa b-inducing kinase.** *Nat Genet* 1999, **22**:74-77. [general reference]

38. Bondeson J, Foxwell B, Brennan F, Feldmann M: **Defining therapeutic targets by using adenovirus: blocking NF-kappaB inhibits both inflammatory and destructive mechanisms in rheumatoid synovium but spares anti-inflammatory mediators.** *Proc Natl Acad Sci USA* 1999, **96**:5668-5673. [general reference]

39. Georganas C, Liu H, Perlman H, Hoffmann A, Thimmapaya B, Pope RM: **Regulation of IL-6 and IL-8 expression in rheumatoid arthritis synovial fibroblasts: the dominant role for NF-kappa B but not C/EBP beta or c-Jun.** *J Immunol* 2000, **165**:7199-7206. [general reference]

40. Quattrocchi E, Dallman MJ, Dhillon AP, Quaglia A, Bagnato G, Feldmann M: **Murine IL-10 gene transfer inhibits established collagen-induced arthritis and reduces adenovirus-mediated inflammatory responses in mouse liver.** *J Immunol* 2001, **166**:5970-5978. [general reference]

41. Quattrocchi E, Dallman MJ, Feldmann M: **Adenovirus-mediated gene transfer of CTLA-4Ig fusion protein in the suppression of experimental autoimmune arthritis.** *Arthritis Rheum* 2000, **43**:1688-1697. [general reference]

42. Kim SH, Evans CH, Kim S, Oligino T, Ghivizzani SC, Robbins PD: **Gene therapy for established murine collagen-induced arthritis by local and systemic adenovirus-mediated delivery of interleukin-4.** *Arthritis Res* 2000, **2**:293-302. [general reference]

43. Woods JM, Katschke KJ, Volin MV, Ruth JH, Woodruff DC, Amin MA, Connors MA, Kurata H, Arai K, Haines GK, Kumar P, Koch AE: **IL-4 adenoviral gene therapy reduces inflammation, proinflammatory cytokines, vascularization, and bony destruction in rat adjuvant-induced arthritis.** *J Immunol* 2001, **166**:1214-1222. [general reference]

44. Yao Q, Wang S, Glorioso JC, Evans CH, Robbins PD, Ghivizzani SC, Oligino TJ: **Gene transfer of p53 to arthritic joints stimulates synovial apoptosis and inhibits inflammation.** *Mol Ther* 2001, **3**:901-910. [general reference]

45. Makarov SS, Johnston WN, Olsen JC, Watson JM, Mondal. K, Rinehart C, Haskill JS: **NF-kappa B as a target for anti-inflammatory gene therapy: suppression of inflammatory responses in monocytic and stromal cells by stable gene transfer of I kappa B alpha cDNA.** *Gene Ther* 1997, **4**:846-852. [general reference]

46. Tak PP, Gerlag DM, Aupperle KR, van de Geest DA, Overbeek M, Bennett BL, Boyle DL, Manning AM, Firestein GS: **Inhibitor of nuclear factor kappaB kinase beta is a key regulator of synovial inflammation.** *Arthritis Rheum* 2001, **44**:1897-1907. [general reference]

47. Daly G, Chernajovsky Y: **Recent developments in retroviral-mediated gene transduction.** *Mol Ther* 2000, **2**:423-434. [general reference]

48. Chen Z, Ahonen M, Hamalainen H, Bergelson JM, Kahari VM, Lahesmaa R: **High-efficiency gene transfer to primary T lymphocytes by recombinant adenovirus vectors.** *J Immunol Methods* 2002, **260**:79-89. [general reference]

49. Toyoda K, Nakane H, Heistad DD: **Cationic polymer and lipids augment adenovirus-mediated gene transfer to cerebral arteries in vivo.** *J Cereb Blood Flow Metab* 2001, **21**:1125-1131. [general reference]

50. Juillard V, Villefroy P, Godfrin D, Pavirani A, Venet A, Guillet JG: **Long-term humoral and cellular immunity induced by a single immunization with replication-defective adenovirus recombinant vector.** *Eur J Immunol* 1995, **25**:3467-3473. [general reference]

51. Christ M, Lusky M, Stoeckel F, Dreyer D, Dieterle A, Michou AI, Pavirani A, Mehtali M: **Gene therapy with recombinant adenovirus vectors: evaluation of the host immune response.** *Immunol Lett* 1997, **57**:19-25. [general reference]

52. Zou L, Zhou H, Pastore L, Yang K: **Prolonged transgene expression mediated by a helper-dependent adenoviral vector (hdAd) in the central nervous system.** *Mol Ther* 2000, **2**:105-113. [general reference]

53. Maione D, Rocca CD, Giannetti P, D'Arrigo R, Liberatoscioli L, Franlin LL, Sandig V, Ciliberto G, La Monica N, Savino R: **An improved helper-dependent adenoviral vector allows persistent gene expression after intramuscular delivery and overcomes preexisting immunity to adenovirus.** *Proc Natl Acad Sci USA* 2001, **98**:5986-5991. [general reference]

Supplement Review

Signaling crosstalk between RANKL and interferons in osteoclast differentiation

Hiroshi Takayanagi, Sunhwa Kim and Tadatsugu Taniguchi

Department of Immunology, Faculty of Medicine and Graduate School of Medicine, University of Tokyo, Tokyo, Japan

Correspondence: Tadatsugu Taniguchi, Department of Immunology, Faculty of Medicine and Graduate School of Medicine, University of Tokyo, 7-3-1, Hongo, Bunkyo-ku, Tokyo 113-0033, Japan. Tel: +81 3 5841 3375; fax: +81 3 5841 3450; e-mail: tada@m.u-tokyo.ac.jp

Received: 26 February 2002
Accepted: 20 March 2002
Published: 9 May 2002

Arthritis Res 2002, **4 (suppl 3)**:S227-S232

This article may contain supplementary data which can only be found online at http://arthritis-research.com/content/4/S3/S227

© 2002 BioMed Central Ltd
(Print ISSN 1465-9905; Online ISSN 1465-9913)

Chapter summary

Regulation of osteoclast differentiation is an aspect central to the understanding of the pathogenesis and the treatment of bone diseases such as autoimmune arthritis and osteoporosis. In fact, excessive signaling by RANKL (receptor activator of nuclear factor κB ligand), a member of the tumor necrosis factor (TNF) family essential for osteoclastogenesis, may contribute to such pathological conditions. Here we summarize our current work on the negative regulation of osteoclastogenesis by unique signaling crosstalk between RANKL and interferons (IFNs). First, activated T cells maintain bone homeostasis by counterbalancing the action of RANKL through production of IFN-γ. This cytokine induces rapid degradation of the RANK (receptor activator of nuclear factor κB) adapter protein TRAF6 (TNF-receptor-associated factor 6), resulting in strong inhibition of the RANKL-induced activation of NF-κB and JNK (c-Jun N-terminal kinase). Second, RANKL induces the IFN-β gene but not IFN-α genes, in osteoclast precursor cells, and that IFN-β strongly inhibits the osteoclast differentiation by interfering with the RANKL-induced expression of c-Fos. The series of *in vivo* experiments revealed that these two distinct IFN-mediated regulatory mechanisms are both important to maintain homeostasis of bone resorption. Collectively, these studies revealed novel aspects of the two types of IFN, beyond their original roles in the immune response, and may offer a molecular basis for the treatment of bone diseases.

Keywords: arthritis, interferon, osteoclast, osteoporosis, RANKL

Historical background

A delicate balance between bone resorption and bone formation is critical for the maintenance of bone strength and integrity, wherein bone-resorbing osteoclasts and bone-forming osteoblasts play central roles [1]. In fact, this physiologic process, termed bone remodeling, must be regulated strictly, and tipping the balance in favor of osteoclasts causes bone destruction observed in pathological conditions such as autoimmune arthritis, perio-

dontitis, postmenopausal osteoporosis, Paget's disease and bone tumors [2,3].

RANKL (receptor activator of nuclear factor κB ligand), a member of the TNF (tumor necrosis factor) family, is an essential cytokine for the differentiation of monocyte/macrophage precursors to osteoclasts [4–6]. Briefly, binding of RANKL to its receptor, RANK (receptor activator of nuclear factor κB), results in the recruitment of

---

A glossary of specialist terms used in this chapter appears at the end of the text section. A list of common abbreviations used in this issue appears just before the indexes.

proteins of the TRAF (TNF-receptor-associated factor) family, such as TRAF6, which activates NF-κB and JNK (c-Jun N-terminal kinase) pathways [7–9]. By a yet unknown mechanism, RANKL also induces expression of c-Fos [10,11]. The essential role of these TRAF6 and c-Fos pathways in osteoclastogenesis has been well documented by gene disruption studies [12–15]. To maintain normal bone homeostasis, this RANKL signaling must be properly regulated. In this context, osteoprotegerin (OPG), a soluble 'decoy' receptor for RANKL, is known as a negative regulator of osteoclastogenesis [16]. In fact, mice lacking OPG develop osteoporosis, suggesting that the balance between RANKL and OPG dictates the levels of bone resorption [17].

It has been reported that prolonged or aberrant activation of the immune system in certain autoimmune conditions often results in tissue destruction mediated by effector cells. In fact, enhanced osteoclastic bone resorption causes severe bone damage leading to progressive joint destruction in autoimmune arthritis [18,19], wherein T-cell expression of RANKL may play a critical role. In this context, it has been reported that activated T cells promote osteoclastogenesis through expression of RANKL *in vitro* [18,20]. However, it is not known whether activated T cells maintain bone homeostasis by counterbalancing the action of RANKL.

One may infer that the process of osteolastogenesis is under negative regulation by factors in addition to OPG, at multiple levels, in order to maintain bone homeostasis.

Regulation of osteoclastogenesis by T cells via IFN-γ

Involvement of the T-cell-produced IFN-γ in negative regulation of osteoclastogenesis

To study whether activated T cells contribute in the regulation of osteoclastogenesis, we used a well-established model of endotoxin-induced bone resorption, in which the essential involvement of T cells has been documented [21,22]. A notable exacerbation of osteoclast formation and bone destruction was observed in mice lacking IFNGR1, one of the components of IFN-γ receptor (IFNGR) (IFN-γR$^{-/-}$ mice) [8]. This observation is also consistent with an enhanced severity in the T-cell-mediated collagen-induced model of autoimmune arthritis observed in IFN-γR$^{-/-}$ mice [23,24]. When the effect of IFN-γ-producing T cells on osteoclastogenesis was examined *in vitro,* osteoclast formation from RANKL-stimulated bone-marrow-derived monocyte/macrophage precursor cells (BMMs) was strongly inhibited by the coculture with T cells activated with the anti-CD3 antibody but not with resting T cells. When activated T cells were cocultured with IFN-γR$^{-/-}$ BMMs, however, the inhibitory effect of activated T cells was completely abrogated. These IFN-γR$^{-/-}$ BMMs differentiated into osteoclasts, albeit with low effi-

ciency, when cocultured with activated T cells, even in the absence of recombinant RANKL, suggesting that the effect of T cells on osteoclastogenesis depends on the balance between RANKL and IFN-γ. Activated T-cell supernatant also suppressed osteoclastogenesis induced by recombinant RANKL, and this suppressive activity was inhibited by a neutralizing antibody against IFN-γ. These results collectively indicate that IFN-γ is critical for T-cell suppression of RANKL-induced osteoclastogenesis.

Mechanism of action of IFN-γ

A marked inhibitory effect of IFN-γ was observed by an *in vitro* assay for osteoclast formation in RANKL-stimulated BMMs, and a very low level of IFN-γ strongly inhibited osteoclast formation even in the presence of an excess amount of RANKL. The cytokine signals the cell through activation of the transcription factor STAT1 (signal transducer and activator of transcription 1) [25]. The active form of this transcription factor, termed IFN-γ-activated factor (GAF), induces target genes of IFN-γ either directly or through the induction of the transcription factor IRF-1 (interferon regulatory factor 1) [26]. The inhibitory effect of IFN-γ on osteoclastogenesis was completely abrogated in STAT1$^{-/-}$ mice but not in IRF-1$^{-/-}$ mice. Thus, the STAT1 (GAF)-mediated, IRF-1-independent gene induction pathway is critical for interfering with the RANKL signaling pathway.

To investigate the target of IFN-γ inhibition of osteoclastogenesis, RANKL-induced activation of NF-κB and JNK was examined in IFN-γ-treated BMMs. It was found that RANKL-induced activation of NF-κB and JNK was markedly inhibited in IFN-γ-treated BMMs and that this inhibition was accompanied by strong suppression of TRAF6 expression. Notably, overexpression of TRAF6 in BMMs by retrovirus-mediated gene transfer rendered them resistant to IFN-γ-mediated inhibition of osteoclastogenesis. In these cells, RANKL-induced activation of NF-κB and JNK was also restored, indicating further that TRAF6 is the critical target of the action of IFN-γ. Thus, downregulation of TRAF6 expression accounts, at least in part, for the IFN-γ inhibition of osteoclastogenesis.

The mechanism by which TRAF6 expression is downregulated by IFN-γ was investigated further. It was found that TRAF6 protein levels, rather than its mRNA levels, were suppressed after RANKL stimulation in the presence of IFN-γ. Interestingly, stimulation by RANKL per se promoted TRAF6 degradation, which was markedly accelerated by IFN-γ. Since the TRAF6 level is upregulated during stimulation by RANKL, the equilibrium of TRAF6 protein is apparently shifted toward its synthesis rather than its degradation in the absence of IFN-γ, but the addition of IFN-γ reverses the equilibrium. Notably, IFN-γ alone had no effect on TRAF6 expression, suggesting that accelerated TRAF6 degradation by IFN-γ requires RANKL signaling.

Figure 1

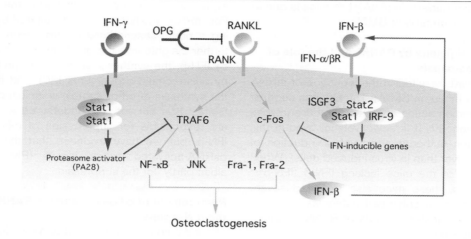

Signaling crosstalk between RANKL and IFNs. IFN-γ and IFN-β inhibit RANKL signaling by downregulating essential mediators of osteoclastogenesis (TRAF6 and c-Fos, respectively). (See [8,30], and text for the details). Fra, fos-related antigen; IRF, interferon regulatory factor; ISGF3, interferon-stimulated gene factor-3; JNK, c-Jun N-terminal kinase; NF-κB, nuclear factor κB; OPG, osteoprotegerin; RANK, receptor activator of nuclear factor κB; Stat, signal transducer and activator of transcription; TRAF, TNF receptor-associated factor.

Further studies revealed that TRAF6 is a direct target for the ubiquitin–proteasome system, which is enhanced by IFN-γ [8] (Fig. 1).

Physiological significance of the IFN-γ-mediated regulation of RANKL signaling

It has recently been found that activated T cells promote osteoclastogenesis through expression of RANKL and regulate bone loss in autoimmune arthritis [18]. The results presented above revealed that activated T cells can also negatively affect osteoclastogenesis through IFN-γ production. It is likely that the balance between the actions of RANKL and of IFN-γ may regulate osteoclast formation. For example, during acute immune reactions, an enhanced production of IFN-γ counterbalances the augmentation of RANKL expression and reduces aberrant formation of osteoclasts. On the other hand, in chronic synovitis of rheumatoid arthritis, this balance may be skewed in favor of RANKL expression. In this context, it is noteworthy that expression of IFN-γ is suppressed, despite a significant infiltration of T cells [27,28], in the arthritic joints in which RANKL expression is enhanced. Thus, the paucity of IFN-γ and the enhanced expression of RANKL may contribute to the activation of osteoclastogenesis in arthritis. It is clear that other factors must be taken into consideration in the control of osteoclastogenesis in arthritis, e.g. RANKL induction in IL-1-stimulated or TNF-α-stimulated synovial fibroblasts [3,29], and local cytokine production pattern regulated by differentiation status of T cells into Th1 or Th2 type.

Autoregulation of RANKL signaling by IFN-β induction and the critical role of IFN-β in bone metabolism

Involvement of the IFN-γ system in the regulation of bone remodeling

During our study to analyze genes induced by RANKL, we noted induction of mRNAs known to be commonly induced by IFN-α/β. Although the integral role of the IFN-α/β system in the immune system has been extensively documented, it was unknown whether this system is linked to RANKL signaling. To investigate the physiological role of the IFN system in the control of bone homeostasis, we studied the skeletal system of mice deficient in one of the IFN receptor components, IFNAR1 (IFNAR1$^{-/-}$ mice) [30]. Surprisingly, a notable reduction of trabecular bone mass, a characteristic feature of osteoporosis, was observed in the mutant mice. Concomitantly, the number of osteoclasts was notably greater in the bone of the IFNAR1$^{-/-}$ mice than in the wild-type mice. Quantitative bone morphometric analyses further revealed a significant decrease in the trabecular bone volume, a feature that is diagnostic for enhanced osteoclastic bone resorption, without any remarkable difference in the markers of osteoblastic bone formation, indicating that the IFN-α/β signaling is physiologically critical for maintaining the normal bone mass by regulating osteoclastic bone resorption. RANKL-induced osteoclast formation in vitro is remarkably enhanced in BMMs from IFNAR1$^{-/-}$ mice, whereas no difference was seen in the osteoblast differentiation between cultured calvarial cells from wild-type mice and those from IFNAR1$^{-/-}$ mice. We deduce that the enhanced osteoclastogenesis in IFNAR1$^{-/-}$ mice is due to a cell-autonomous abnormality of BMMs.

Induction of the IFN-β gene by RANKL and the role of IFN-β in bone homeostasis

Stimulation by RANKL resulted in the induction of mRNA of IFN-β, but not of IFN-α, in BMMs. The findings suggest that, unlike the common action of these two IFN subtypes against viral infection, IFN-β is selectively involved in this osteoclast regulation (although the level of induction of mRNA was much lower than in virus-induced cells). When the skeletal system of the mice lacking IFN-β (IFN-β$^{-/-}$ mice) was examined, these mice also exhibited severe osteopenia resulting from enhanced osteoclastogenesis, an observation that indicates the role of RANKL-induced IFN-β in bone homeostasis.

Recombinant mouse IFN-β has a remarkably strong inhibitory effect on osteoclastogenesis induced by RANKL in combination with macrophage-colony-stimulating factor: the effect was observed at a concentration as low as one unit ml^{-1}. IFN-β (as well as IFN-α) invokes cellular responses through activation/induction of transcription factors; these include ISGF3 [a heteromeric complex consisting of signal transducer and activator of transcription 1 (STAT1), STAT2 and interferon regulatory factor 9 (IRF-9)], STAT1 homodimer and IRF-1 [25,26]. It was found that the inhibitory action of IFN-β is abrogated in BMMs from mice lacking STAT1 or IRF-9, indicating that the inhibitory action is linked to the ISGF3-mediated gene induction pathway (see Fig. 1).

To assess the efficacy of IFN-β for the suppression of osteoclast-mediated pathological conditions, an endo-toxin-induced model of inflammatory bone destruction in mice was used [30]. Daily administration of IFN-β into the inflamed site markedly inhibited the osteoclast formation and bone resorption, indicating that IFN-β does indeed have a beneficial effect on bone destruction, most likely by downregulating osteoclastogenesis.

Signaling crosstalk between RANKL and IFN-β vying for c-Fos

To identify the downstream effector(s) of RANKL signaling affected by the IFN-β signaling, we first carried out immunoblot analysis of the effector molecules of RANKL signaling in IFN-β-treated BMMs and found that expression of c-Fos was selectively and dramatically downregulated. To examine further whether the inhibitory action of IFN-β is mediated through downregulation of c-Fos expression, c-Fos was artificially expressed by retrovirus-mediated gene transfer in BMMs. More than 50% of the virus-infected cells underwent differentiation in the presence of IFN-β, under condition in which fewer than 5% of cells did so when infected by either the control virus or virus expressing c-Jun.

What is the mechanism underlying the inhibition of c-Fos expression by IFN-β? Interestingly, the RANKL-induced Fos mRNA was not significantly altered by IFN-β, suggesting a post-transcriptional control mechanism(s). To gain further insights into the mechanism of c-Fos suppression by IFN-β, the synthesis of the c-Fos protein was studied by pulse–chase experiments [30], and it was found that the synthesis of c-Fos protein is inhibited in IFN-β-treated BMMs. It is not yet fully understood which target genes are responsible for suppression of c-Fos expression by IFN-β, but we have evidence that the ISGF3-inducible dsRNA-activated protein kinase (PKR) is responsible, albeit partly, for the suppression.

Requirement of c-Fos itself in the RANKL induction of the *IFN-β* gene

The induction of the *IFN-α/β* gene in virally infected cells requires two IRF transcription factors, IRF-3 and IRF-7 [31]. In the case of IFN-β, induction has also been known to depend on NF-κB (which is also activated by RANKL) [32]. Interestingly, when RANKL-induced expression of IFN-β mRNA was studied in BMMs from mice lacking c-Fos, or both IRF-3 and IRF-9, expression of this mRNA was no longer observed in the absence of c-Fos but was still detected in the absence of the IRFs critical for the virus-mediated induction. Furthermore, stimulation with RANKL induced a significant activation of the IFN-β promoter, as revealed by a reporter-gene transfection assay, and this activation was abrogated in cells from c-Fos-deficient mice. Thus, the RANKL-induced c-Fos per se induces its own inhibitor gene, *IFN-β*.

Conclusions and future prospects

Immune response is essential for host defense, but its prolonged or aberrant activation under certain autoimmune conditions often results in tissue destruction mediated by effector cells. As described here, a new biological function of IFN-γ was discovered: to protect against destruction of calcified tissue on T-cell activation [8]. The disease-limiting effect of IFN-γ in autoimmune arthritis may be explained, at least in part, by its potent suppressive effect on osteoclast development. Although the clinical application of IFN-γ has been difficult, probably because of its disease-promoting effect at the onset phase of autoimmunity [33], our results suggest that TRAF6, the critical target of IFN-γ-mediated suppression of osteoclastogenesis, could be a possible molecular target of pharmacological intervention in inflammatory bone diseases.

Our study also revealed a hitherto unknown signaling crosstalk between RANKL and IFN-β system, which is critical for bone homeostasis [30]. This crosstalk is unique in that RANKL signaling per se is responsible for the induction of *IFN-β*, and that c-Fos, the positive regulator of RANKL signaling, is required for the induction of its own inhibitor (see Fig. 1). In view of the osteoporotic phenotype found in mice lacking IFN-β or its receptor, we believe that this novel, negative-feedback regulation mechanism is physiologically important for maintaining bone mass. In this context, it would be interesting to find out if the negative regulation of osteoclastogenesis by IFN-β is modulated in osteopenic disease conditions.

Although further study is needed, the series of observations on the novel role of IFN-β may offer new therapeutic approaches to bone diseases such as inflammation-induced bone destruction and osteoporosis. In fact, exogenous application of IFN-β indeed has a beneficial effect against bone destruction in the lipopolysaccharide-induced model, most likely by downregulation of osteoclastogenesis. Our preliminary results also suggest that the systemic administration of IFN-β can reverse bone loss in an osteoporosis model of ovariectomized mice. In addition, identification of the critical target gene(s) of IFN-β responsible for the suppression of osteoclastogenesis may provide further insights into the regulation of bone remodeling.

Glossary of terms

BMM = bone-marrow-derived monocyte/macrophage precursor cell; GAF = IFN-γ-activated factor; IFNAR = interferon-α/β receptor; IFNGR = interferon-γ receptor; IRF = interferon regulatory factor; ISGF3 = interferon-stimulated gene factor 3; JNK = c-Jun N-terminal kinase; OPG = osteoprotegerin; RANK = receptor activator of nuclear factor κB; RANKL = receptor activator of nuclear factor κB ligand; TRAF = TNF receptor-associated factor.

References

1. Manolagas SC: **Birth and death of bone cells: basic regulatory mechanisms and implications for the pathogenesis and treatment of osteoporosis.** Endocr Rev 2000, **21**:115-137. [general reference]
2. Rodan GA, Martin TJ: **Therapeutic approaches to bone diseases.** Science 2000, **289**:1508-1514. [general reference]
3. Takayanagi H, Iizuka H, Juji T, Nakagawa T, Yamamoto A, Miyazaki T, Koshihara Y, Oda H, Nakamura K, Tanaka S: **Involvement of receptor activator of nuclear factor κB ligand/osteoclast differentiation factor in osteoclastogenesis from synoviocytes in rheumatoid arthritis.** Arthritis Rheum 2000, **43**:259-269. [general reference]
4. Yasuda H, Shima N, Nakagawa N, Yamaguchi K, Kinosaki M, Mochizuki S, Tomoyasu A, Yano K, Goto M, Murakami A, Tsuda E, Morinaga T, Higashio K, Udagawa N, Takahashi N, Suda T: **Osteoclast differentiation factor is a ligand for osteoprotegerin/osteoclastogenesis-inhibitory factor and is identical to TRANCE/RANKL.** Proc Natl Acad Sci U S A 1998, **95**:3597-3602. [general reference]
5. Lacey DL, Timms E, Tan HL, Kelley MJ, Dunstan CR, Burgess T, Elliott R, Colombero A, Elliott G, Scully S, Hsu H, Sullivan J, Hawkins N, Davy E, Capparelli C, Eli A, Qian YX, Kaufman S, Sarosi I, Shalhoub V, Senaldi G, Guo J, Delaney J, Boyle WJ: **Osteoprotegerin ligand is a cytokine that regulates osteoclast differentiation and activation.** Cell 1998, **93**:165-176. [general reference]
6. Kong YY, Yoshida H, Sarosi I, Tan HL, Timms E, Capparelli C, Morony S, Oliveira-dos-Santos AJ, Van G, Itie A, Khoo W, Wakeham A, Dunstan CR, Lacey DL, Mak TW, Boyle WJ, Penninger JM: **OPGL is a key regulator of osteoclastogenesis, lymphocyte development and lymph-node organogenesis.** Nature 1999, **397**:315-323. [general reference]
7. Wong BR, Josien R, Lee SY, Vologodskaia M, Steinman RM, Choi Y: **The TRAF family of signal transducers mediates NF-κB activation by the TRANCE receptor.** J Biol Chem 1998, **273**:28355-28359. [general reference]
8. Takayanagi H, Ogasawara K, Hida S, Chiba T, Murata S, Sato K, Akinori T, Yokochi T, Oda H, Tanaka K, Nakamura K, Taniguchi T: **T cell-mediated regulation of osteoclastogenesis by signalling cross-talk between RANKL and IFN-γ.** Nature 2000, **408**:600-605. [general reference]
9. Kobayashi N, Kadono Y, Naito A, Matsumoto K, Yamamoto T, Tanaka S, Inoue J: **Segregation of TRAF6-mediated signaling pathways clarifies its role in osteoclastogenesis.** EMBO J 2001, **20**:1271-1280. [general reference]
10. Matsuo K, Owens JM, Tonko M, Elliott C, Chambers TJ, Wagner EF: **Fosl1 is a transcriptional target of c-Fos during osteoclast differentiation.** Nat Genet 2000, **24**:184-187. [general reference]
11. Wagner EF, Karsenty G: **Genetic control of skeletal development.** Curr Opin Genet Dev 2001, **11**:527-532. [general reference]
12. Lomaga MA, Yeh WC, Sarosi I, Duncan GS, Furlonger C, Ho A, Morony S, Capparelli C, Van G, Kaufman S, van der Heiden A, Itie A, Wakeham A, Khoo W, Sasaki T, Cao Z, Penninger JM, Paige CJ, Lacey DL, Dunstan CR, Boyle WJ, Goeddel DV, Mak TW: **TRAF6 deficiency results in osteopetrosis and defective interleukin-1, CD40, and LPS signaling.** Genes Dev 1999, **13**:1015-1024. [general reference]
13. Naito A, Azuma S, Tanaka S, Miyazaki T, Takaki S, Takatsu K, Nakao K, Nakamura K, Katsuki M, Yamamoto T, Inoue J: **Severe osteopetrosis, defective interleukin-1 signalling and lymph node organogenesis in TRAF6-deficient mice.** Genes Cells 1999, **4**:353-362. [general reference]
14. Wang ZQ, Ovitt C, Grigoriadis AE, Mohle-Steinlein U, Ruther U, Wagner EF: **Bone and haematopoietic defects in mice lacking c-fos.** Nature 1992, **360**:741-745. [general reference]
15. Grigoriadis AE, Wang ZQ, Cecchini MG, Hofstetter W, Felix R, Fleisch HA, Wagner EF: **c-Fos: a key regulator of osteoclast-macrophage lineage determination and bone remodeling.** Science 1994, **266**:443-448. [general reference]
16. Simonet WS, Lacey DL, Dunstan CR, Kelley M, Chang MS, Luthy R, Nguyen HQ, Wooden S, Bennett L, Boone T, Shimamoto G, DeRose M, Elliott R, Colombero A, Tan HL, Trail G, Sullivan J, Davy E, Bucay N, Renshaw-Gegg L, Hughes TM, Hill D, Pattison W, Campbell P, Sander S, Van G, Tarpley J, Derby P, Lee R, Boyle WJ: **Osteoprotegerin: a novel secreted protein involved in the regulation of bone density.** Cell 1997, **89**:309-319. [general reference]
17. Bucay N, Sarosi I, Dunstan CR, Morony S, Tarpley J, Capparelli C, Scully S, Tan HL, Xu W, Lacey DL, Boyle WJ, Simonet WS: **Osteoprotegerin-deficient mice develop early onset osteoporosis and arterial calcification.** Genes Dev 1998, **12**:1260-1268. [general reference]
18. Kong YY, Feige U, Sarosi I, Bolon B, Tafuri A, Morony S, Capparelli C, Li J, Elliott R, McCabe S, Wong T, Campagnuolo G, Moran E, Bogoch ER, Van G, Nguyen LT, Ohashi PS, Lacey DL, Fish E, Boyle WJ, Penninger JM: **Activated T cells regulate bone loss and joint destruction in adjuvant arthritis through osteoprotegerin ligand.** Nature 1999, **402**:304-309. [general reference]
19. Takayanagi H, Juji T, Miyazaki T, Iizuka H, Takahashi T, Isshiki M, Okada M, Tanaka Y, Koshihara Y, Oda H, Kurokawa T, Nakamura K, Tanaka S: **Suppression of arthritic bone destruction by adenovirus-mediated csk gene transfer to synoviocytes and osteoclasts.** J Clin Invest 1999, **104**:137-146. [general reference]
20. Horwood NJ, Kartsogiannis V, Quinn JM, Romas E, Martin TJ, Gillespie MT: **Activated T lymphocytes support osteoclast formation in vitro.** Biochem Biophys Res Commun 1999, **265**:144-150. [general reference]
21. Ukai T, Hara Y, Kato I: **Effects of T cell adoptive transfer into nude mice on alveolar bone resorption induced by endotoxin.** J Periodont Res 1996, **31**:414-422. [general reference]
22. Chiang CY, Kyritsis G, Graves DT, Amar S: **Interleukin-1 and tumor necrosis factor activities partially account for calvarial bone resorption induced by local injection of lipopolysaccharide.** Infect Immun 1999, **67**:4231-4236. [general reference]
23. Manoury-Schwartz B, Chiocchia G, Bessis N, Abehsira-Amar O, Batteux F, Muller S, Huang S, Boissier MC, Fournier C: **High susceptibility to collagen-induced arthritis in mice lacking IFN-γ receptors.** J Immunol 1997, **158**:5501-5506. [general reference]

24. Vermeire K, Heremans H, Vandeputte M, Huang S, Billiau A, Matthys P: **Accelerated collagen-induced arthritis in IFN-γ receptor-deficient mice**. *J Immunol* 1997, **158**:5507-5513. [general reference]

25. Stark GR, Kerr IM, Williams BR, Silverman RH, Schreiber RD: **How cells respond to interferons**. *Annu Rev Biochem* 1998, **67**:227-264. [general reference]

26. Taniguchi T, Ogasawara K, Takaoka A, Tanaka N: **IRF family of transcription factors as regulators of host defense**. *Annu Rev Immunol* 2001, **19**:623-655. [general reference]

27. Firestein GS, Zvaifler NJ: **How important are T cells in chronic rheumatoid synovitis?** *Arthritis Rheum* 1990, **33**:768-773. [general reference]

28. Kinne RW, Palombo-Kinne E, Emmrich F: **T-cells in the pathogenesis of rheumatoid arthritis: villains or accomplices?** *Biochim Biophys Acta* 1997, **1360**:109-141. [general reference]

29. Takayanagi H, Oda H, Yamamoto S, Kawaguchi H, Tanaka S, Nishikawa T, Koshihara Y: **A new mechanism of bone destruction in rheumatoid arthritis: synovial fibroblasts induce osteoclastogenesis**. *Biochem Biophys Res Commun* 1997, **240**: 279-286. [general reference]

30. Takayanagi H, Kim S, Mastuo K, H. S, T. S, Sato K, Yokochi T, Oda H, Tanaka K, Nakamura K, Ida N, Wagner EF, Taniguchi T: **RANKL maintains bone homeostasis through c-Fos-dependent induction of IFN-β**. *Nature* 2002, **416**:744-749. [general reference]

31. Sato M, Suemori H, Hata N, Asagiri M, Ogasawara K, Nakao K, Nakaya T, Katsuki M, Noguchi S, Tanaka N, Taniguchi T: **Distinct and essential roles of transcription factors IRF-3 and IRF-7 in response to viruses for IFN-α/β gene induction**. *Immunity* 2000, **13**:539-548. [general reference]

32. Wathelet MG, Lin CH, Parekh BS, Ronco LV, Howley PM, Maniatis T: **Virus infection induces the assembly of coordinately activated transcription factors on the IFN-β enhancer in vivo**. *Mol Cell* 1998, **1**:507-518. [general reference]

33. Billiau A: **Interferon-γ: biology and role in pathogenesis**. *Adv Immunol* 1996, **62**:61-130. [general reference]

Supplement Review

The paradigm of IL-6: from basic science to medicine

Tetsuji Naka*, Norihiro Nishimoto† and Tadamitsu Kishimoto‡

*Department of Molecular Medicine, Osaka University Graduate School of Medicine, Osaka, Japan
†Department of Medical Science I, School of Health and Sport Sciences, Osaka University, Japan
‡Osaka University, Japan

Correspondence: Tetsuji Naka, Department of Molecular Medicine, Osaka University Graduate School of Medicine, 2-2, Yamadaoka Suita City, Osaka, 560-0871 Japan. Tel: +81 6 6879 4143; fax: +81 6 6879 4143; e-mail: naka@imed3.med.osaka-u.ac.jp

Received: 12 February 2002
Revisions requested: 13 February 2002
Revisions received: 1 March 2002
Accepted: 6 March 2002
Published: 9 May 2002

Arthritis Res 2002, **4 (suppl 3)**:S233-S242

This article may contain supplementary data which can only be found online at http://arthritis-research.com/content/4/S3/S233

© 2002 BioMed Central Ltd
(Print ISSN 1465-9905; Online ISSN 1465-9913)

Chapter summary

IL-6 is a pleiotropic cytokine with a wide range of biological activities in immune regulation, hematopoiesis, inflammation, and oncogenesis. Its activities are shared by IL-6-related cytokines such as leukemia inhibitory factor and oncostatin M. The pleiotropy and redundancy of IL-6 functions have been identified by using a unique receptor system comprising two functional proteins: an IL-6 receptor (IL-6R) and gp130, the common signal transducer of cytokines related to IL-6. Signal transduction through gp130 is mediated by two pathways: the JAK–STAT (Janus family tyrosine kinase–signal transducer and activator of transcription) pathway and the Ras mitogen-activated protein kinase pathway. The negative regulators of IL-6 signaling have also been identified, although the physiological roles of the molecules are not yet fully understood. The pathological roles of IL-6 have also been clarified in various disease conditions, such as inflammatory, autoimmune, and malignant diseases. On the basis of the findings, a new therapeutic approach to block the IL-6 signal using humanized anti-IL-6R antibody for rheumatoid arthritis, Castleman's disease, and multiple myeloma has been attempted.

Keywords: cytokines, gp130, interleukin-6, SOCS, rheumatoid arthritis

Identification of IL-6 and its pleiotropic functions

IL-6 was originally identified as an antigen-nonspecific B-cell differentiation factor in the culture supernatants of mitogen- or antigen-stimulated peripheral blood mononuclear cells that induced B cells to produce immunoglobulins [1,2], and was named B-cell stimulatory factor 2 (BSF-2). The cDNA encoding human BSF-2 was cloned in 1986 [3]. Simultaneously, IFN-β2 [4,5] and a 26-kDa protein [6] in fibroblasts were independently cloned by different groups and found to be identical to BSF-2. Later, a hybridoma/plasmacytoma growth factor [7–10] and a hepatocyte-stimulating factor [11–13] were also proven to be the same molecule as BSF-2. Although various names

have been used for this molecule because of its multiple biological activities, it is now known as IL-6.

A pleiotropic cytokine with a wide range of biological activities (Fig. 1), IL-6 is produced by various types of lymphoid and nonlymphoid cells, such as T cells, B cells, monocytes, fibroblasts, keratinocytes, endothelial cells, mesangial cells, and several tumor cells [14]. It induces growth of T cells and differentiation of cytotoxic T cells [15–19] by augmenting the expression of IL-2 receptor [15] and the production of IL-2 [20]. IL-6 acts synergistically with IL-3 to support the formation of multilineage blast cell colonies in hematopoiesis [21–25]. IL-6 also induces differentiation of macrophages [26], megakaryocytes [27–29], and

---

A glossary of specialist terms used in this chapter appears at the end of the text section. A list of common abbreviations used in this issue appears just before the indexes.

Figure 1

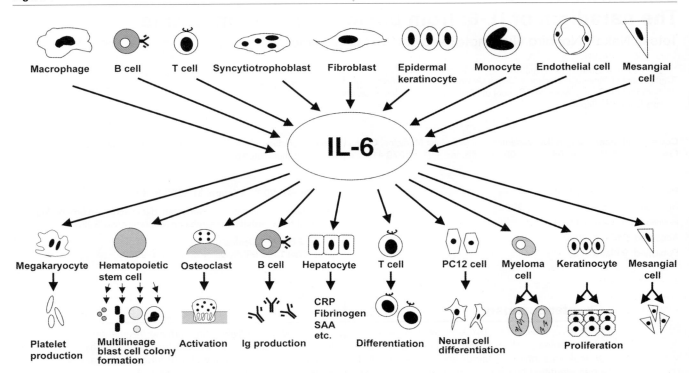

IL-6-producing cells and biological activities of IL-6. IL-6 is produced by lymphoid and nonlymphoid cells, such as T cells, B cells, monocytes, fibroblasts, keratinocytes, endothelial cells, mesangial cells, and several kinds of tumor cell (top of figure). IL-6 also has a wide range of biological activities on various target cells (bottom of figure).

osteoclasts [30]. In the acute-phase reaction, this cytokine stimulates hepatocytes to produce acute-phase proteins such as C-reactive protein (CRP), fibrinogen, α_1-antitrypsin, and serum amyloid A [12,13], and it simultaneously suppresses albumin production [11]. It causes leukocytosis and fever when administered *in vivo* [31] and also acts as a growth factor for renal mesangial cells [32], epidermal keratinocytes [33,34], and various types of tumor cells, for example, in plasmacytoma [8], multiple myeloma [35], and renal cell carcinoma [36].

Although IL-6 has pleiotropic effects on various target cells, some of the biological activities are also mediated by other cytokines, such as leukemia inhibitory factor (LIF) and oncostatin M (OSM). The pleiotropy and redundancy of IL-6 functions can be identified by using a unique receptor system of cytokines [14].

Identification and characterization of IL-6R as the specific receptor of IL-6, and of gp130 as the common signal transducer of the IL-6 superfamily

We and our colleagues identified the two components of IL-6 receptor (IL-6R), an 80-kDa IL-6-binding protein (α chain) and a 130-kDa signal transducer known as gp130

(β chain), in 1988 and 1990 [37–39], respectively. Although IL-6 cannot directly bind to gp130, it can bind to IL-6R to generate the high-affinity complex of IL-6/IL-6R/gp130. Furthermore, the complex of IL-6 and soluble IL-6R can generate IL-6-mediated signal transduction [38,39]. Another feature of cytokines is the redundancy of their functions. For example, IL-6, LIF, and OSM all induce macrophage differentiation in the myeloid leukemia cell line M1 [40–43] and acute-phase protein synthesis in hepatocytes [11,12,44–46]. An important finding as regards cytokine receptors is that one constituent of a given cytokine receptor is shared by several other cytokine receptors [47]. For example, gp130 is in fact shared by the receptors for such cytokines of the IL-6 superfamily as ciliary neurotrophic factor (CNTF), LIF, OSM, IL-11, and cardiotrophin-1 [14,48,49]. Thus, the molecular mechanisms of redundancy in functions of cytokines of the IL-6 superfamily can be explained at least in part by the sharing of gp130 among their receptors.

Investigations of the IL-6R system have provided evidence that the combination of IL-6 and soluble IL-6R can act on cells that express gp130 but not IL-6R [48]. A complex consisting of a soluble cytokine receptor and its corresponding cytokine acquires different target specificity from the original cytokine and should therefore express different functions from those of the original cytokine. In fact, we found that doubly transgenic mice expressing human IL-6 and IL-6R showed myocardial hypertrophy [50], indicating that the combination of IL-6 and soluble IL-6R acts on heart muscle cells that express gp130, an action that IL-6 cannot exert by itself. The action leads to the induction of cardiac hypertrophy, so that the effect is similar to that of cardiotrophin-1. This combination of cytokine and its soluble receptor may contribute to the generation of the functional diversity of cytokines in a wide range of other receptor systems and may also play a pathological role in various diseases in which an increase in the serum-soluble form of various cytokine receptors has been reported.

Clarification of multiple signal cascades in IL-6 signal

As the cytoplasmic domain of most cytokine receptors, including gp130, does not have an intrinsic catalytic domain, one of the most controversial issues before 1993 was the identification of catalytic molecules that associate with cytokine receptors. This issue was resolved by the discovery of several Janus family tyrosine kinases (JAK1, JAK2, JAK3, Tyk-2), which are involved in the transduction of cytokine and hormone signals [51–53]. Furthermore, the signal transducer and activator of transcription (STAT) was found to play a central role in a variety of cytokine signal cascades. Our group and others found that JAK1, JAK2, and Tky-2 are activated and are tyrosine-phosphorylated in response to IL-6, CNTF, LIF, and OSM [14], and also identified and characterized STAT3 [54]. IL-6 activates STAT1 and STAT5 in addition to STAT3. In the absence of JAK1, the activation of transcriptional factor STATs following stimulation by IL-6 is not effective as long as both JAK2 and Tky-2 are activated. This finding suggests that there is a hierarchy among gp130-associated JAKs [55].

Several research groups, including ours, have identified two types of IL-6 response element (IL-6RE) in the genes encoding acute-phase proteins. The presence of type I IL-6RE, which is a binding site for NF-IL-6 (nuclear factor for IL-6 expression), IL-6DBP (IL-6 vitamin-D-binding protein), and C/EBPβ [56–59], has been confirmed in the genes for CRP, hemopexin A, and haptoglobin. The binding activity of NF-IL-6 is probably induced by IL-6 through the increased expression of the NF-IL-6 gene rather than through its post-translational modification. Type II IL-6RE is contained in the fibrinogen, α_2-macroglobin, α_1-acid glycoprotein, and haptoglobin genes. IL-6 triggers the rapid activation of a nuclear factor, known as the acute-phase response factor, which binds to type II IL-6RE [60]. Purification and molecular cloning of this factor revealed that it is identical to STAT3 [54,61].

We clarified that human gp130 has 277 amino acid residues in its cytoplasmic domain, which contains two motifs, Box1 and Box2, conserved among the cytokine receptor family (Fig. 2) [39,62,63]. The membrane-proximal region containing Box1 and Box2 was found to be sufficient for the activation of JAK through gp130 [64]. Furthermore, human gp130 has six tyrosine residues in its cytoplasmic domain. Finally, the tyrosine phosphorylation of Src homology protein 2 tyrosine phosphatase-2 (SHP-2), a phosphotyrosine phosphatase, and that of STAT3 depend on the second tyrosine residue (Y2) from the membrane, and on any one of the four tyrosine residues (Y3, Y4, Y5, Y6) in the carboxy terminus that have a glutamine residue at the third position behind tyrosine (Y-X-X-Q) (see Fig. 2) [65,66].

It is known that IL-6 induces growth arrest and macrophage differentiation in the murine myeloid leukemic cell line M1. The essential role of STAT3 in the IL-6-induced macrophage differentiation of M1 cells was demonstrated by using dominant negative forms of STAT3 [67], which inhibit both IL-6-induced growth arrest and macrophage differentiation in M1 transformants. Blocking STAT3 activation inhibits IL-6-induced repression of c-Myb and c-Myc, but not EGR-1 induction [68], while IL-6 enhances the growth of M1 cells when STAT3 is suppressed. Thus, IL-6 simultaneously generates growth-enhancing signals as well as growth-arrest and differentiation-inducing signals, but the former are apparent only when STAT3 activation is suppressed. As for the growth signals, a 65-amino-acid region proximal to the transmembrane domain was found to be sufficient for generating a growth response by using gp130 transfectants of an IL-3-dependent proB-cell line BAF/BO3 [14,63]. However, the membrane-proximal region of 68 amino acids is not sufficient for the induction of tritium thymidine (^{3}H-Tdr) uptake when cells are starved of IL-3. For cell growth, the membrane-proximal region containing 133 amino acid residues is both required and sufficient [69]. Furthermore, at least two distinct signals are required for gp130-induced cell growth: a cell cycle progression signal dependent on the second tyrosine residue, Y2, and possibly mediated by SHP-2, and an antiapoptotic signal dependent on the third tyrosine residue, Y3, and mediated by STAT3 through induction of BCL-2. However, our recent study using mice with STAT3 deficiency in a T-cell-specific manner has revealed that STAT3 activation is involved in IL-6-dependent T cell proliferation through prevention of apoptosis without the need for BCL-2 induction [70]. Thus, STAT3 plays pivotal roles in gp130-mediated signal transduction regulating cell growth, differentiation, and survival. In addition to the JAK–STAT signal transduction pathway, it is known that the Ras mitogen-activated protein (MAP) kinase pathway is also activated through SHP-2 [69] or Shc [71]. Furthermore, nonreceptor tyrosine kinases, such as Btk, Tec, Fes, and Hck [72,73] are activated through the IL-6 receptor, as well as through a variety of other cytokine receptors [74], although the biological significance of these signal transduction pathways remains to be

Figure 2

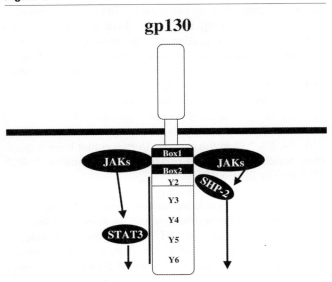

Schematic structure of gp130. Binding of IL-6 to IL-6R induces homodimerization of gp130, activating JAK associating with gp130 at Box1. This is followed by the tyrosine phosphorylation of the distal part of gp130 and recruitment of STAT3. STAT3 is then tyrosine-phosphorylated by JAK. SHP-2 on the second tyrosine (Y2) residue of gp130 activates the MAP kinase pathway. JAK, Janus family tyrosine kinase; SHP-2, Src homology protein 2 tyrosine phosphatase-2; STAT, signal transducer and activator of transcription; Y(2,3, etc.), (second, third, etc.) tyrosine residue (from the membrane).

clarified. Several distinct signal transduction pathways are generated through different regions of the cytoplasmic domain of gp130. The expression pattern of these signaling molecules determines which set of signaling pathways is activated in a given cell. Furthermore, these signaling pathways may interact with each other and contribute to a variety of biological activities. In fact, a recent study reported that knock-in mutation mice lacking SHP-2 signal showed sustained gp130-induced STAT3 activation; this finding indicates a negative regulatory role of SHP-2 for STAT3 activation [75]. These knock-in mice also displayed splenomegaly and lymphadenopathy and an acute-phase reaction. In contrast, all known mice deficient in the STAT3 binding site, such as the gp130-deficient mouse, died perinatally [75]. However, it has also been reported that mice deficient in STAT3 signal displayed a severe joint disease in association with mitogenic hyper-responsiveness of the synovial cells to the IL-6-family cytokines. This hyper-responsiveness was the result of sustained gp130-mediated SHP-2 activation due to a lack of the SHP-2 inhibitor induced by STAT3 [76].

Identification of new inhibitors of IL-6 signaling

Cytokine signaling, including that of IL-6, is negatively regulated with respect to both magnitude and duration. Recently, it has been found that at least two new families

of inhibitors contribute to the negative regulation of cytokine signaling: the suppressor of cytokine signaling (SOCS) and the protein inhibitors of activated STATs (PIAS) (Fig. 3). In 1997, two other groups and ours identified SOCS-1, also known as SSI-1 (STAT-induced STAT inhibitor 1) or JAB-1 (JAK-binding protein 1), as a negative regulatory molecule of IL-6 signaling on the basis of its binding to JAK [77–79]. Subsequently, database searches have shown that the SOCS family now includes eight members (CIS and SOCS1–SOCS7), all of which are characterized by a central SH2 domain flanked by an N-terminal region containing a conserved motif known as the SOCS box [77,80–82]. mRNA of SOCS-1, SOCS-2, and SOCS-3 is induced by cytokines such as IL-6, IFN-γ, IL-4, and granulocyte-colony-stimulating factor and several other members, and they inhibit cytokine-activated JAK–STAT signal pathways [83–85]. However, the factors that induce mRNA of the other SOCS families, such as SOCS-4–7, have not been clarified and their functions have not been thoroughly characterized.

SOCS-1 and SOCS-3 are especially well known as inhibitors of cytokine signaling [86], acting through different mechanisms. SOCS-1 directly interacts with JAKs, and thus inhibits their catalytic activity. SOCS-3 also inhibits JAK activity (but only partially in comparison with SOCS-1) although the augmentation of its effect in the presence of receptors suggests that SOCS-3 inhibits cytokine signaling by binding to the receptor complex. In the IL-6 signal cascade, the SHP-2 interaction site of gp130 has also been shown to be a SOCS-3 contact site, so that SOCS-3 may compete for the SHP-2–gp130 interaction site [86,87]. Gene-targeting mice of the SOCS family were used to show that SOCS-2 and SOCS-3 are critical molecules for, respectively, GH/IGF-1 and EPO signaling *in vivo* [88,89]. In particular, mice deficient in SOCS-2 exhibit giantism, reduced production of major urinary proteins, increased local production of IGF-1, and accumulation of collagen in the dermis, while SOCS-3-deficient mice die at 12–16 days of age because of erythrocytosis by deregulation of fetal liver hematopoiesis. However, a recent study of SOCS-3-deficient mice showed that SOCS-3 was required for placental development but not for normal hematopoiesis in the mouse embryo [90].

Two groups of researchers, including ours, initially reported that SOCS-1-deficient mice are born healthy but with growth disclose various kinds of abnormalities, including stunted growth, fulminant hepatitis with serious fatty degradation, and mononuclear cell infiltration of several organs, and die within 3 weeks after birth [91,92]. Subsequently, it was reported that SOCS-1 is a key molecule for IFN-γ actions *in vivo* as seen in SOCS-1-deficient mice that also lack the IFN-γ gene (SOCS-1/IFN-γ doubly deficient mice) [93,94]. However, it was also found that

Figure 3

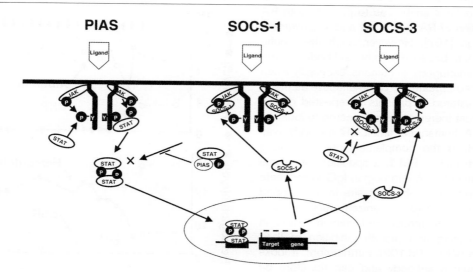

Molecular mechanism of inhibition by new cytokine inhibitors. **(Left)** PIAS inhibits DNA-binding activity of STATs through association with activated them. **(Center)** SOCS-1 inhibits catalytic activity of JAKs by direct interaction with them. **(Right)** SOCS-3 inhibits catalytic activity of JAKs by binding to receptor complex. JAK, Janus family tyrosine kinases; P, phosphorylation; PIAS, protein inhibitors of activated STATs; SOCS, suppressor of cytokine signaling; STAT, signal transducer and activator of transcription; Y, tyrosine residue.

SOCS-1 *in vitro* inhibits activation of STAT6 by IL-4 stimulation [92], and that SOCS-1 *in vivo* inhibits TNF-α and insulin signaling [95,96]. In a recent study of SOCS-1/STAT1 and SOCS-1/STAT6 doubly deficient mice, we found that the physiological role of SOCS-1 is essential for inhibition of crosstalk in cytokine signaling, particularly for IFN-γ-induced inhibition of STAT6 [97]. SOCS-1-deficient mice feature an intact IL-6 signaling pathway, suggesting that SOCS-3 may act as a crucial inhibitor of IL-6 signaling *in vivo*.

Unlike the SOCS family, PIAS proteins constitute a family of constitutively expressed negative regulators of STATs. Five members of this family have been identified with the yeast two-hybrid method and by a search of the expressed sequence tag database: PIAS-1, PIAS-3, PIAS-Xα, PIAS-Xβ, and PIAS-Y [98,99]. They all share homology and contain several highly conserved domains, including a putative zinc-binding motif and a highly acidic region. PIAS-1 and PIAS-3 have been identified as specific inhibitors of STAT signal pathways [98,99]. Overexpression studies have shown that PIAS-1 associates only with activated STAT1 dimers and inhibits their DNA-binding activity, but that no monomeric forms of STAT1 are present [99]. Similarly, PIAS-3 associates specifically with activated STAT3 but not with STAT1, resulting in the blocking of all STAT3-mediated gene transcriptions, and is especially well known as an inhibitor of IL-6 signaling in M1 cell lines [98]. The constitutive expression of PIAS proteins implies that their physiological role differs from that of SOCS proteins, which are induced by cytokine stimulation. So far, however, the differences in the physiological roles of these two families of proteins are not well known.

Application of anti-IL-6R antibody to clinical medicine

Rheumatoid arthritis (RA) is a systemic inflammatory disease characterized by destructive changes in bone and cartilage of affected joints as well as the emergence of rheumatoid factors. Although the exact causes of RA remain unknown, immunological dysregulation by inflammatory cytokines has been shown to be involved in its development [100]. IL-6 is one of these cytokines and uncontrolled IL-6 overproduction appears to be responsible for the clinical symptoms and abnormal laboratory findings in RA [101]. Because of the B-cell differentiation factor activity of IL-6, overproduction of IL-6 is responsible for the increase in serum γ-globulin and the emergence of rheumatoid factors. IL-6 as a hepatocyte-stimulating factor causes an increase in CRP, serum amyloid A, and erythrocyte sedimentation rate and a decrease in serum albumin [11–13]. On the other hand, IL-6 as a megakaryocyte differentiation factor causes thrombocytosis [22,27,28]. Since IL-6 in the presence of soluble IL-6R activates osteoclasts to induce bone absorption [30], IL-6 may be involved in the osteoporosis [102] and destruction of bone and cartilage associated with RA. In fact, a large amount of IL-6 has been observed in both sera and synovial fluids from the affected joints of patients with RA [103–106]. Blockade of the IL-6 signal may thus constitute a new therapeutic strategy for RA.

Wendling *et al.* reported that the administration of mouse antihuman IL-6 monoclonal antibodies to patients with RA resulted in amelioration of RA symptoms and improvement of laboratory findings [107]. However, such therapeutic effects were transient, because murine antibodies were found to be highly immunogenic in humans, especially when they were administered repeatedly. To be effective as therapeutic agents administered to patients in repeated doses, mouse antibodies must therefore be engineered to look like human antibodies. A humanized anti-IL-6R antibody was constructed by grafting the complementarity-determining regions (CDRs) from mouse PM-1, a specific monoclonal antibody against human IL-6R, into human IgG to re-create a properly functioning antigen-binding site in a reshaped human antibody [108]. *In vitro*, humanized anti-IL-6R antibody is equivalent to both mouse and chimeric PM-1 in terms of antigen binding and growth inhibition of IL-6-dependent myeloma cells [108,109]. Furthermore, it looks very much like a human antibody and can therefore be expected to be a poor immunogen in human patients [110].

The *in vivo* effect of humanized anti-IL-6R antibody on the development of collagen-induced arthritis was examined in cynomolgus monkeys because it cross-reacts with the monkey IL-6R [111]. Intravenous administration of humanized anti-IL-6R antibody (10 mg/kg once a week) significantly inhibited the onset of joint inflammation and the elevation of serum CRP and fibrinogen levels and erythrocyte sedimentation rate that were induced by immunization with bovine type II collagen with a complete adjuvant.

On the basis of the above findings, we administered humanized anti-IL-6R antibody to RA patients whose active disease was resistant to conventional therapy using methotrexate, various disease-modifying antirheumatic drugs, and corticosteroids, with the permission of the Ethical Committee of Osaka University Medical School. Low-grade fever and fatigue disappeared and CRP and fibrinogen levels were normalized within 2 weeks after the start of humanized anti-IL-6R antibody treatment (50 mg twice a week) (Fig. 4). This was followed by reduction of morning stiffness, improvement of the swollen-joint score and the pain and tenderness score, and reduction of anemia, thrombocytosis, and hypoalbuminemia. A score of ACR20 on the American College of Rheumatology scale was achieved in 7 of 8 patients after 8 weeks of treatment and ACR50 in 4 of 8 patients after 8 weeks. The treatment was well tolerated and no major side effects were observed. These data indicate that humanized anti-IL-6R antibody is useful for the treatment of RA. Phase I clinical trials in the United Kingdom and a phase I/II study in Japan also proved the safety and the efficacy of humanized anti-IL-6R antibody [112,113]. Double-blind, randomized, placebo-controlled phase II studies for the use of the antibody to treat RA are now in the progress both in Europe and in Japan. In addition to RA, various other IL-6-related

Figure 4

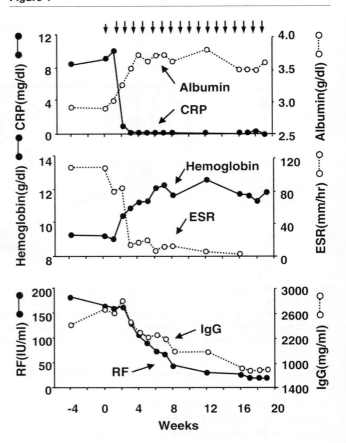

Representative clinical course of an RA patient treated with humanized anti-IL-6R antibody. A 51-year-old woman with RA was given humanized anti-IL-6R antibody intravenously (50 mg twice a week). Although she had active disease refractory to conventional treatment with drugs including methotrexate and prednisolone, treatment with humanized anti-IL-6R remarkably improved her condition. CRP, C-reactive protein; ESR, erythrocyte sedimentation rate; RF, rheumatoid factor.

diseases such as Castleman's disease, multiple myeloma, mesangial proliferative glomerulonephritis, psoriasis, and Kaposi's sarcoma are possible targets of humanized anti-IL-6R antibody.

Conclusion

IL-6 participates in immune response, hematopoiesis, and acute-phase reactions. On the other hand, deregulation of IL-6 production has been implicated in the pathogenesis of a variety of diseases, including plasmacytoma/myeloma and several chronic inflammatory proliferative diseases. Future studies on the regulation of IL-6 expression and clarification of the molecular mechanisms of IL-6 functions, as well as of inhibitors of IL-6 signal, should provide information critical to a better understanding of the molecular mechanisms of these diseases and the development of new therapeutic methods such as antibody therapy.

Glossary of terms

BSF = B-cell stimulatory factor; CNTF = ciliary neuro-trophic factor; IL-6RE = IL-6 response element; LIF = leukemia inhibitory factor; NF-IL-6 = nuclear factor for IL-6 expression; OSM = oncostatin M; PIAS = protein inhibitors of activated STATs; SHP-2 = SH2-containing protein tyrosine phosphatase-2; SOCS = suppressor of cytokine signaling; Y(2,3, etc.) = (second, third, etc.) tyrosine residue (from the membrane).

References

1. Muraguchi A, KishimotoT, Miki T, Kuritani T, Kaieda T, Yoshizaki K, Yamamura Y: **T cell-replacing factor (TRF)-induced IgG secretion in human B blastoid cell line and demonstration of acceptors for TRF.** *J Immunol* 1981, **127**:412-416. [archival reference]
2. Yoshizaki K, Nakagawa T, Kaieda T, Muraguchi A, Yamamura Y, Kishimoto T: **Induction of proliferation and Ig production in human B leukemic cells by anti-immunoglobulins and T cell factors.** *J Immunol* 1982, **128**: 1296-1301. [archival reference]
3. Hirano T, Yasukawa K, Harada H, Taga T, Watanabe Y, Matsuda T, Kashiwamura S, Nakajima K, Koyama K, Iwamatsu A, Tsunasawa S, Sakiyama F, Matsui H, Takahara Y, Taniguchi T, Kishimoto T: **Complementary DNA for a novel human interleukin (BSF-2) that induces B cell lymphocytes to produce immunoglobulin.** *Nature* 1986, **324**:73-76. [archival reference]
4. Zilberstein A, Ruggieri R, Korn JH, Revel M: **Structure and expression of cDNA and genes for human interferon-β2, a distinct species inducible by growth-stimulatory cytokines.** *EMBO J* 1986, **5**:2529-2537. [archival reference]
5. Sehgal PB, Walther Z, Tamm I: **Rapid enhancement of b2-interferon/B-cell differentiation factor BSF-2 gene expression in human fibroblasts by diacylglycerols and calcium ionophore A23187.** *Proc Natl Acad Sci USA* 1987, **84**:3663-3667. [archival reference]
6. Haegeman G, Content J, Volckaert, G, Derynck R, Taverneir J, Fires W: **Structural analysis of the sequence encoding for an inducible 26-kDa protein in human fibroblasts.** *Eur J Biochem* 1986, **159**:625-632. [archival reference]
7. Van Damme J, Opdenakker G, Simpson RJ, Rubira MR, Cayphas S, Vink A, Billiau A, Van Snick JV: **Identification of the human 26-kDa protein, interferon β2 (IFN-β2), as a B cell hybridoma/plasmacytoma growth factor induced by interleukin-1 and tumor necrosis factor.** *J Exp Med* 1987, **165**:914-919. [archival reference]
8. Nordan RP, Pumphrey JG, Rudikoff S: **Purification and NH2-terminal sequence of a plasmacytoma growth factor derived from the murine macrophage cell line P388D1.** *J Immunol* 1987, **139**:813-817. [archival reference]
9. Uyttenhove C, Coulie PG, Van Snick JV: **T cell growth and differntiation induced by interleukin-HP1/IL-6, the murine hybridoma/plasmacytoma growth factor.** *J Exp Med* 1988, **167**:1417-1427. [archival reference]
10. Van Snick JV, Cayphas S, Szikora J-P, Renauld J-C, Van Roost E, Boon T, Simpson RJ: **cDNA cloning of murine interleukin-HP1: homology with human interleukin 6.** *Eur J Immunol* 1988, **18**: 193-197. [archival reference]
11. Andus T, Geiger T, Hirano T, Northoff H. Ganter, U, Bauer J, Kishimoto T, Heinrich PC: **Recombinant human B cell stimulatory factor 2 (BSF-2/ IFNβ2) regulates β-fibrinogen and albumin mRNA levels in Fao-9 cells.** *FEBS Lett* 1987, **221**:18-22. [archival reference]
12. Gauldie J, Richards C, Harnish D, Landsdorp P, Baumann H: **Interferon-β2/ B cell-stimulatory factor type 2 shares identity with monocyte-derived hepatocyte-stimulating factor and regulates the major acute phase protein response in liver cells.** *Proc Natl Acad Sci USA* 1987, **84**:7251-7255. [archival reference]
13. Castell JV, Gomez-Lechon MJ, David M, Hirano T, Kishimoto T, Heinrich PC: **Recombinant human interleukin-6 (IL-6/BSF-2/ HSF) regulates the synthesis of acute phase proteins in human hepatocytes.** *FEBS Lett* 1988, **232**:347-350. [archival reference]
14. Kishimoto T, Akira S, Narazaki M, Taga T: **Interleukin-6 family of cytokines and gp130.** *Blood* 1995, **86**:1243-1254. [general reference]
15. Noma T, Mizuta T, Rosen A, Hirano T, Kishimoto T, Honjo T: **Enhancement of the interleukin-2 receptor expression on T cells by multiple B-lymphotropic lymphokines.** *Immunol Lett* 1987, **15**:249-253. [archival reference]
16. Okada M, Kitahara M, Kishimoto S, Matsuda T, Hirano T, Kishimoto T: **BSF-2/IL-6 functions as killer helper factor in the in vitro induction of cytotoxic T cells.** *J Immunol* 1988, **141**:1543-1549. [archival reference]
17. Ceuppens JL, Baroja ML, Lorre K, Van Damme J, Billiau A: **Human T cell activation with phytohemagglutinin: the function of IL-6 as an accessory signal.** *J Immunol* 1988, **141**:3868-3874. [archival reference]
18. Le J, Fredrickson G, Reis L, Diamantsein T, Hirano T, Kishimoto T, Vilcek J: **Interleukin-2-dependent and interleukin-2-independent pathways of regulation of thymocyte function by interleukin-6.** *Proc Natl Acad Sci USA* 1988, **85**:8643-8647. [archival reference]
19. Lotz M, Jirik F, Kabouridis R, Tsoukas C, Hirano T, Kishimoto T, Carson DA: **BSF-2/IL-6 is costimulant for human thymocytes and T lymphocytes.** *J Exp Med* 1988, **167**:1253-1258. [archival reference]
20. Garman RD, Jacobs KA, Clark SC, Raulet DH: **B cell-stimulatory factor 2 (β2 interferon) functions as a second signal for interleukin 2 production by mature murine T cells.** *Proc Natl Acad Sci USA* 1987, **84**:7629-7633. [archival reference]
21. Ikebuchi K, Wong GG, Clark. SC, Ihle JN, Hirai Y, Ogawa M: **Interleukin-6 enhancement of interleukin-3-dependent proliferation of multipotential hemopoietic progenitors.** *Proc Natl Acad Sci USA* 1987, **84**:9035-9039. [archival reference]
22. Koike K, Nakahata T, Takagi M, Kobayashi T, Ishiguro A, Tsujii K, Naganuma K, Okano A, Akiyama Y, Akabane T: **Synergism of BSF2/interleukin-6 and interleukin-3 on development of multipotential hemopoietic progenitors in serum free culture.** *J Exp Med* 1988, **168**:879-890. [archival reference]
23. Leary A, Ikebuchi K, Hirai Y, Wong G, Yang Y-C, Clark SC, Ogawa M: **Synergism between interleukin-6 and interleukin-3 in supporting proliferation of human hematopoietic stem cells: comparison with interleukin-1a.** *Blood* 1988, **71**:1759-1763. [archival reference]
24. Ogawa M: **Differentiation and proliferation of hematopoietic stem cells.** *Blood* 1993, **81**:2844-2853. [archival reference]
25. Stanley ER, Bartocci A, Patinkin D, Rosendaal M, Bradley TR: **Regulation of very primitive, multipotent, hemopoietic cells by hemopoietin-1.** *Cell* 1986, **45**:667-674. [archival reference]
26. Nicola NA. Metcalf, D, Matsumoto M, Johnson GR: **Purification of a factor inducing differentiation in murine myelomonocytic leukemia cells. Identification as granulocyte colony-stimulating factor.** *J Biol Chem* 1983, **258**:9017-9023. [archival reference]
27. Ishibashi T, Kimura H, Uchida T, Kariyone S, Friese P, Burstein SA: **Human interleukin6 is a direct promoter of maturation of megakaryocytes in vitro.** *Proc Natl Acad Sci USA* 1987, **86**: 5953-5957. [archival reference]
28. Ishibashi T, Kimura H, Shikama Y, Uchida T, Kariyone S, Hirano T, Kishimoto T, Takatsuki F, Akiyama Y: **Interleukin-6 is a potent thrombopoietic factor in vivo in mice.** *Blood* 1989, **74**:1241-1244. [archival reference]
29. Koike K, Nakahata T, Kubo T, Kikuchi T, Takagi M, Ishiguro A, Tsuji K, Naganuma K, Okano A, Akiyama Y, Akabane T: **Interleukin-6 enhances murine megakariocytopoiesis in serum-free culture.** *Blood* 1990, **75**:2286-2291. [archival reference]
30. Tamura T, Udagawa N, Takahashi N, Miyaura C, Tanaka S, Yamada Y, Koishihara Y, Ohsugi Y, Kumaki K, Taga T, Kishimoto T, Suda T: **Soluble interleukin-6 receptor triggers osteoclast formation by interleukin 6.** *Proc Natl Acad Sci USA* 1993, **90**: 11924-11928. [archival reference]
31. Ulich TR, del Castillo J, Guo KZ: **In vivo hematologic effects of recombinant interleukin-6 on hematopoiesis and circulating numbers of RBCs and WBCs.** *Blood* 1989, **73**:108-110. [archival reference]
32. Horii Y, Muraguchi A, Iwano M, Matsuda T, Hirayama T, Yamada H, Fujii Y, Dohi K, Ishikawa H, Ohmoto Y, Yoshizaki K, Hirano T, Kishimoto T: **Involvement of interleukin-6 in mesangial proliferation of glomerulonephritis.** *J Immunol* 1989, **143**:3949-3955. [archival reference]
33. Grossman RM, Krueger J, Yourish D, Granelli-Piperno A, Murphy DP, May LT, Kupper TS, Sehgal PB, Gottlieb AB: **Interleukin 6 is**

expressed in high levels in psoriasis skin and stimulates proliferation of cultured human keratinocytes. *Proc Natl Acad Sci USA* 1989, **86**:6367-6371. [archival reference]

34. Yoshizaki K, Nishimoto N, Matsumoto K, Tagoh H, Taga T, Deguchi Y, Kuritani T, Hirano T, Kishimoto T: **Interleukin-6 and its receptor expression on the epidermal keratinocytes.** *Cytokine* 1990, **2**:381-387. [archival reference]

35. Kawano M, Hirano T, Matsuda T, Taga T, Horii Y, Iwato K, Asaoku H, Tang B, Tanabe O, Tanaka H, Kuramoto A, Kishimoto T: **Autocrine generation and requirement of BSF-2/IL-6 for human multiple myelomas.** *Nature* 1988, **332**:83-85. [archival reference]

36. Miki S, Iwano M, Miki Y, Yamamoto M, Tang B, Yokokawa K, Sonoda T, Hirano T, Kishimoto T: **Interleukin-6 (IL-6) functions as an in vitro autocrine growth factor in renal cell carcinomas.** *FEBS Lett* 1989, **250**:607-610. [archival reference]

37. Yamasaki K, Taga T, Hirata Y, Yawata H, Kawanishi Y, Seed B, Taniguchi T, Hirano T, Kishimoto T: **Cloning and expression of the human interleukin-6 (BSF-2/INF b2) receptor.** *Science* 1988, **241**:825-828. [archival reference]

38. Taga T, Hibi M, Hirata Y, Yamasaki K, Yasukawa K, Matsuda T, Hirano T, Kishimoto T: **Interleukin-6 triggers the association of its receptor with a possible signal transducer, gp130.** *Cell* 1989, **58**:573-581. [archival reference]

39. Hibi M, Murakami M, Saito M, Hirano T, Taga T, Kishimoto T: **Molecular cloning and expression of an IL-6 signal transducer, gp130.** *Cell* 1990, **63**:1149-1157. [archival reference]

40. Miyaura C, Onozaki K, Akiyama Y, Taniyama T, Hirano T, Kishimoto T, Suda T: **Recombinant human interleukin 6 (B-cell stimulatory factor 2) is a potent inducer of differentiation of mouse myeloid leukemia cells (M1).** *FEBS Lett* 1988, **234**:17-21. [archival reference]

41. Shabo Y, Lotem J, Rubinstein M, Revel M, Clark SC, Wolf SF, Kamen R, Sachs L: **The myeloid blood cell differentiation-inducing protein MGI-2A is interleukin-6.** *Blood* 1988, **72**:2070-2073. [archival reference]

42. Metcalf D: **Actions and interactions of G-CSF, LIF, and IL-6 on normal and leukemic murine cells.** *Leukemia* 1989, **3**:349-355. [archival reference]

43. Rose TM, Bruce AG: **Oncostatin M is a member of a cytokine family which includes leukemia inhibitory factor, granulocyte colony-stimulating factor and interleukin-6.** *Proc Natl Acad Sci USA* 1991, **88**:8641-8645. [archival reference]

44. Baumann H, Onorato V, Gauldie J, Jahreis GP: **Distinct sets of acute phase plasma proteins are stimulated by separate human hepatocyte-stimulating factors and monokines in rat hepatoma cells.** *J Biol Chem* 1987, **262**:9756-9768. [archival reference]

45. Baumann H, Wong GG: **Hepatocyte-stimulatory factor III shares structural and functional identity with leukemia inhibitory factor.** *J Immunol* 1989, **143**:1163-1167. [archival reference]

46. Richards CD. Brown, TJ. Shoyab, M, Baumann H, Gauldie J: **Recombinant oncostatin M stimulates the production of acute phase protein in HepG2 cells and rat primary hepatocytes in vitro.** *J Immunol* 1992, **148**:1731-1736. [archival reference]

47. Miyajima A, Kitamura T, Harada N, Yokota T, Arai K: **Cytokine receptors and signal transduction.** *Annu Rev Immunol* 1992, **10**:295-331. [key review]

48. Hirano T, Matsuda T, Nakajima K: **Signal transduction through gp130 that is shared among the receptors for the interleukin 6 related cytokine subfamily.** *Stem Cells* 1994, **12**:262-277. [archival reference]

49. Hibi M, Nakajima K, Hirano H: **IL-6 cytokine family and signal transduction: a model of the cytokine system.** *J Mol Med* 1996, **74**:1-12. [archival reference]

50. Hirota H, Yoshida K, Kishimoto T, Taga T: **Continuous activation of gp130, a signal-transducing receptor component for interleukin 6-related cytokines, causes myocardial hypertrophy in mice.** *Proc Natl Acad Sci USA* 1995, **92**:4862-4866. [archival reference]

51. Darnell JE Jr, Kerr IM, Stark GR: **Jak-STAT pathways and transcriptional activation in response to IFNs and other extracellular signaling proteins.** *Science* 1994, **264**:1415-1421. [archival reference]

52. Ihle JN, Witthuhn BA, Quelle FW, Yamamoto K, Thierfelder WE, Kreider B, Silvennoinen O: **Signaling by the cytokine receptor superfamily: JAKs and STATs.** *Trends Biochem Sci* 1994, **19**:222-227. [archival reference]

53. Schindler C, Darnell JE Jr: **Transcriptional responses to polypeptide ligands: the JAK-STAT pathway.** *Annu Rev Biochem* 1995, **64**:621-651. [key review]

54. Akira S, Nishio Y, Inoue M, Wang XJ. Wei, S, Matsusaka T, Yoshida K, Sudo T, Naruto M, Kishimoto T: **Molecular cloning of APRF, a novel IFN-stimulated gene factor 3 p91-related transcription factor involved in the gp130-mediated signaling pathway.** *Cell* 1994, **77**:63-71. [archival reference]

55. Guschin D, Rogers N, Briscoe J, Witthuhn BA, Wathing D, Horn F, Pellegrini S, Yasukawa K, Heinrich P, Stark GR, Ihle JN, Kerr IM: **A major role for the protein kinase JAK1 in the JAK/STAT signal transduction pathway in response to the interleukin-6.** *EMBO J* 1995, **14**:1421-1429. [archival reference]

56. Akira S, Isshiki H, Sugita T, Tanabe O, Kinoshita S, Nishio Y, Nakajima T, Hirano T, Kishimoto T: **A nuclear factor for IL-6 expression (NF-IL6) is a member of a C/EBP family.** *EMBO J* 1990, **9**:1897-1906. [archival reference]

57. Poli V, Mancini FP, Cortese R: **IL-6DBP, a nuclear protein involved in interleukin-6 signal transduction, defines a new family of leucine zipper proteins related to C/EBP.** *Cell* 1990, **63**:643-653. [archival reference]

58. Cao Z, Umkek RM, McKnight SL: **Regulated expression of three C/EBP isoforms during adipose conversion of 3T3-L1 cells.** *Genes Dev* 1991, **5**:1538-1552. [archival reference]

59. De Groot RP, Auwerx J, Karperien M, Staels B, Kruijer W: **Activation of junB by PKC and PKA signal transduction through a novel cis-acting element.** *Nucleic Acids Res* 1991, **19**:775-781. [archival reference]

60. Wegenka UM, Buschmann J, Lutticken C, Heinrich PC, Horn F: **Acute-phase response factor, a nuclear factor binding to acute-phase response elements, is rapidly activated by interleukin-6 at the posttranslational level.** *Mol Cell Biol* 1993, **13**:276-288. [archival reference]

61. Zhong Z, Wen Z, Darnell JE Jr: **Stat3: a STAT family member activated by tyrosine phosphorylation in response to epidermal growth factor and interleukin-6.** *Science* 1994, **264**:95-98. [archival reference]

62. Fukunaga R, Ishizaka Ikeda E, Pan CX, Seto Y, Nagata S: **Functional domains of the granulocyte colony-stimulating factor receptor.** *EMBO J* 1991, **10**:2855-2865 [archival reference]

63. Murakami M, Narazaki M, Hibi M, Yawata H, Yasukawa K, Hamaguchi M, Taga T, Kishimoto T: **Critical cytoplasmic region of the interleukin 6 signal transducer gp130 is conserved in the cytokine receptor family.** *Proc Natl Acad Sci USA* 1991, **88**:11349-11353. [archival reference]

64. Narazaki M, Witthuhn BA, Yoshida K, Silvennoinen O, Yasukawa K, Ihle JN, Kishimoto T, Taga T: **Activation of JAK2 kinase mediated by the interleukin 6 signal transducer gp130.** *Proc Natl Acad Sci USA* 1994, **91**:2285-2289. [archival reference]

65. Stahl N, Farruggella TJ, Boulton TG, Zhong Z, Darnell JJ, Yancopoulos GD: **Choice of STATs and other substrates specified by modular tyrosine-based motifs in cytokine receptors.** *Science* 1995, **267**:1349-1353. [archival reference]

66. Yamanaka Y, Nakajima K, Fukada T, Hibi M, Hirano T: **Differentiation and growth arrest signals are generated through the cytoplamic region of gp130 that is essential for Stat3 activation.** *EMBO J* 1996, **15**:1557-1565. [archival reference]

67. Minami M, Inoue M, Wei S, Takeda K, Matsumoto M, Kishimoto T, Akira S: **STAT3 activation is a critical step in gp130-mediated terminal differentiation and growth arrest of a myeloid cell line.** *Proc Natl Acad Sci USA* 1996, **93**:3963-3966. [archival reference]

68. Nakajima K, Yamanaka Y, Nakae K, Kojima H, Kiuchi N, Ichiba M, Kitaoka T, Fukada T, Hibi M, Hirano T: **A central role for Stat3 in IL-6-induced regulation of growth and differentiation in M1 leukemia cells.** *EMBO J* 1996, **15**:3651-3658. [archival reference]

69. Fukada T, Hibi M, Yamanaka Y, Takahashi-Tezuka M, Fijitani Y, Yamaguchi T, Nakajima K, Hirano T: **Two signals are necessary for cell proliferation induced by a cytokine receptor gp130: involvement of STAT3 in anti-apoptosis.** *Immunity* 1996, **5**:449-460. [archival reference]

70. Takeda K, Kaisho T, Yoshida N, Takeda J, Kishimoto T, Akira S: **Stat3 activation is irresponsible for IL-6-dependent T cell proliferation through preventing apoptosis: generation and characterization of T cell-specific Stat3-deficient mice.** *J Immunol* 1998, **161**:4652-4660. [general reference]

71. Kumar G, Gupta S, Wang S, Nel AE: **Involvement of Janus kinases, p52shc, Raf-1, and MEK-1 in the IL-6-induced mitogen-activated protein kinase cascade of a growth-responsive B cell line.** *J Immunol* 1994, **153**:4436-4447. [archival reference]

72. Ernst M, Gearing DP, Dunn AR: **Functional and biochemical association of Hck with the LIF/IL-6 receptor signal transducting subunit gp130 in embryonic stem cells.** *EMBO J* 1994, **13**: 1574-1584. [archival reference]

73. Matsuda T, Fukada T, Takahashi-Tezuka M, Okuyama Y, Fujitani Y, Hanazono Y, Hirai H, Hirano T: **Association and activation of Btk and Tec tyrosine kinases by gp130, a signal transducer of the interleukin-6 family of cytokines.** *J Biol Chem* 1995, **270**: 11037-11039. [archival reference]

74. Taniguchi T: **Cytokine signaling through nonreceptor protein tyrosine kinase.** *Science* 1995, **268**:251-255. [archival reference]

75. Ohtani T, Ishihara K, Atsumi T, Nishida K, Kaneko Y, Miyata H, Itoh T, Narimatsu M, Maeda H, Fukada T, Itoh M, Okano H, Hibi M, Hirano T: **Dissection of signaling cascades through gp130 in vivo: reciprocal roles for STAT3- and SHP2-mediated signals in immune responses.** *Immunity* 2000, **12**:95-105. [general reference]

76. Ernst M, Inglese M, Waring P, Cambell IK, Bao S, Clay FJ, Alexander WS, Wicks IP, Tarlinton DM, Novak U, Heath JK, Dunn AR: **Defective gp130-mediated signal transducer and activator of transcription (STAT) signaling results in degenerative joint disease, gastrointestinal ulceration, and failure of uterine implantation.** *J Exp Med* 2001, **194**:189-203. [general reference]

77. Starr R, Willson TA, Viney EM, Murray LJL, Rayner JR, Jenkis BJ, Gonda TJ, Alexander WS, Metcalf D, Nicola NA, Hilton DJ: **A family of cytokine-inducible inhibitors of signaling.** *Nature* 1997, **387**:917-921. [general reference]

78. Naka T, Narazaki M, Hirata M, Matsumoto T, Minamoto S, Aono A, Nishimoto N, Kajita T, Taga T, Yoshizaki K, Akira S, Kishimoto T: **Structure and function of a new STAT-induced STAT inhibitor.** *Nature* 1997, **387**:924-929. [general reference]

79. Endo TA, Masuhara M, Yokouchi M, Suzuki R, Sakamoto H, Mitsui K, Matsumoto A, Tanimura S, Ohtsubo M, Misawa H, Miyazaki T, Leonor N, Taniguchi T, Fujita T, Kanakura Y, Komiya S, Yoshimura A: **A new protein containing an SH2 domain that inhibits JAK kinase.** *Nature* 1997, **387**:921-924. [general reference]

80. Minamoto.S. Ikegame, K, Ueno K, Narazaki M, Naka T, Yamamoto H, Matsumoto T, Saito H, Hosoe S, Kishimoto T: **Cloning and functional analysis of new members of STAT induced STAT inhibitor (SSI) family: SSI-2 and SSI-3.** *Biochem Biophys Res Commun* 1997, **237**:79-83. [general reference]

81. Masuhara M, Sakamoto H, Matsumoto A, Suzuki R, Yasukawa H, Mitsui K, Wakioka T, Tanimura S, Sasaki A, Misawa H, Yokouchi M, Ohtsubo M, Yoshimura A: **Cloning and characterization of novel CIS family genes.** *Biochem Biophys Res Commun* 1997, **239**:436-446. [general reference]

82. Hilton DJ, Richardson RT, Alexander WS, Viney EM, Sprigg NS, Nicholson SE, Metcalf D, Nicola NA: **Twenty proteins containing C-terminal SOCS-box form five structural classes.** *Proc Natl Acad Sci USA* 1998, **95**:114-119. [general reference]

83. Naka T, Fujimoto M, Kishimoto T: **Negative regulation of cytokine signaling: STAT-induced STAT inhibitor.** *Trends Biochem Sci* 1999, **24**:394-398. [general reference]

84. Yasukawa H, Sasaki A, Yoshimura A: **Negative regulation of cytokine signaling pathways.** *Annu Rev Immunol* 2000, **18**: 143-164. [key review]

85. Krebs DL, Hilton DJ: **SOCS proteins: negative regulators of cytokine signaling.** *Stem Cells* 2001, **19**:378-387. [general reference]

86. Nicholson SE, Willson TA, Farley A, Starr R, Zhang JG, Baca M, Alexander WS, Metcalf D, Hilton DJ, Nicola NA: **Mutational analyses of the SOCS proteins suggest a dual domain requirement but distinct mechanisms for inhibition of LIF and IL-6 signal transduction.** *EMBO J* 1999, **18**:375-385. [general reference]

87. Schmitz J, Weissenbach M, Haan S, Heinrich PC, Schaper F: **SOCS-3 exerts its inhibitory function on interleukin-6 signal transduction through the SHP-2 recruitment site of gp130.** *J Biol Chem* 2000, **275**:12848-12856. [general reference]

88. Metcalf D, Greenhalgh CJ, Viney E, Willson TA. Starr R, Nicola NA, Hilton DJ, Alexander WS: **Giantism in mice lacking sup-**

89. Marine JC, Topham DJ, McKay C, Wang D, Parganas E, Nakajima H, Pendeville H, Yasukawa H, Sasaki A. Yoshimura, A, Ihle JN: **SOCS3 is essential in the regulation of fetal liver erythropoiesis.** *Cell* 1999, **98**:617-627. [general reference]

90. Robert AW, Robb L, Rakar S, Hartley L, Nicola NA, Metcalf D, Hilton DJ, Alexander WS: **Placental defects and embryonic lethality in mice lacking suppressor of cytokine signaling 3.** *Proc Natl Acad Sci USA* 2001, **98**:9324-9329. [general reference]

91. Starr R, Metcalf D, Elefanty AG, Brysha M, Willson TA, Nicola NA, Hilton DJ, Alexander WS: **Liver degeneration and lymphoid deficiencies in mice lacking suppressor of cytokine signaling-1.** *Proc Natl Acad Sci USA* 1998, **95**:14395-14399. [general reference]

92. Naka T, Matsumoto T, Narazaki M, Fujimoto M, Morita Y, Ohsawa Y, Saito H, Nagasawa T, Uchiyama Y, Kishimoto T: **Accelerated apoptosis of lymphocytes by augmented induction of Bax in SSI-1(STAT-induced STAT inhibitor) deficient mice.** *Proc Natl Acad Sci USA* 1998, **95**:15575-15582. [general reference]

93. Alexander WA, Starr R, Fenner JE, Scott CL, Handman E, Springg NS, Corbin JE, Cornish AL, Darwiche R, Owczarek CM, Kay TWH, Nicola NA, Hertzog PJ, Metcalf D, Hilton DJ: **SOCS1 is critical inhibitor of interferon γ signaling and prevents the potentially fatal neonatal actions of this cytokine.** *Cell* 1999, **98**:597-608. [general reference]

94. Marine JC, Topham DJ, McKay C, Wang D, Parganas E, Stravopodis D, Yoshimura A, Ihle JN: **SOCS1 deficiency causes a lymphocyte-dependent perinatal lethality.** *Cell* 1999, **98**:609-616. [general reference]

95. Morita Y, Naka, T, Kawazoe Y, Fujimoto M, Narazaki M, Nakagawa R, Fukuyama H, Nagata S, Kishimoto T: **SSI/SOCS-1 suppresses TNF α-induced cell death by regulation of p38 MAP kinase signal in fibroblast.** *Proc Natl Acad Sci USA* 2000, **97**: 5405-5410. [general reference]

96. Kawazoe Y, Naka T, Fujimoto M, Kohzaki H, Morita Y, Narazaki M, Okumura K, Saitoh H, Nakagawa R, Uchiyama Y, Akira S, Kishimoto T: **SSI-1/SOCS-1 family proteins inhibit insulin signal transduction pathway through modulating IRS-1 phosphorylation.** *J Exp Med* 2001, **193**:263-269. [general reference]

97. Naka T, Tsutsui H, Fujimoto M, Kawazoe Y, Kohzaki H, Morita Y, Nakagawa R, Narazaki M, Adachi K, Yoshimoto T, Nakanishi K, Kishimoto T: **SOCS-1/SSI-1-deficient NKT cells participate in severe hepatitis through dysregulated cross-talk inhibition of IFN-γ and IL-4 signaling in vivo.** *Immunity* 2001, **14**:535-545. [general reference]

98. Chung CD, Liao J, Lui B, Rao X, Jay P, Berta P, Shuai K: **Specific inhibiton of Stat3 signal transduction by PIAS3.** *Science* 1997, **278**:1803-1805. [general reference]

99. Liu B, Liao J, Rao X, Kushner SA, Chung CD, Chang DD, Shuai K: **Inhibition of Stat-1 mediated gene activation by PIAS1.** *Proc Natl Acad Sci USA* 1998, **95**:10626-10631. [general reference]

100. Feldmann M, Elliott MJ, Woody JN, Maini RN: **Anti-tumor necrosis factor-α therapy of rheumatoid arthritis.** *Adv Immunol* 1997, **64**:283-350. [general reference]

101. Yoshizaki K, Nishimoto N, Mihara M, Kishimoto T: **Therapy of RA by blocking IL-6 signal transduction with humanized anti-IL-6 receptor antibody.** *Springer Semin Immunopathol* 1998, **20**: 247-259. [general reference]

102. Jilka RH, Hangoc G, Girasole G, Passeri G, Williams DC, Abrams JS, Boice B, Broxmeyer H, Manolagas SC: **Increased osteoclast development after estrogen loss: Mediation by interleukin-6.** *Science* 1992, **257**:88-91. [archival reference]

103. Hirano T, Matsuda T, Turner M, Miyasaka N, Buchan G, Tang B, Sato K, Shimizu M, Maini R, Feldman M, Kishimoto T: **Excessive production of interleukin 6/B cell stimulatory factor-2 in rheumatoid arthritis.** *Eur J Immunol* 1988, **18**:1797-1801. [archival reference]

104. Houssiau FA, Devogelaer JP, Van Damme J, De Deuxchaisies CN, Van Snick J: **Interleukin-6 in synovial fluid and serum of patients with rheumatoid arthritis and other inflammatory arthritis.** *Arthritis Rheum* 1988, **31**:784-788. [archival reference]

105. Sack U, Kinne R, Marx T, Heppt P, Bender S, Emmrich F: **Interleukin-6 in synovial fluid is closely associated with chronic synovitis in rheumatoid arthritis.** *Rheumatol Int* 1993, **13**:45-51. [archival reference]

106. Madhok R, Crilly A, Watson J, Capell HA: **Serum interleukin 6 levels in rheumatoid arthritis: correlation with clinical and laboratory indices of disease activity.** *Ann Rheum Dis* 1993, **52**: 232-234. [archival reference]

107. Wendling D, Racadot E, Wijdenes J: **Treatment of severe rheumatoid arthritis by anti-interleukin 6 monoclonal antibody.** *J Rheumatol* 1993, **20**:259-262. [archival reference]

108. Sato K, Tsuchiya M, Saldanha J, Koishihara Y, Ohsugi Y, Kishimoto T, Bendig MM: **Reshaping a human antibody to inhibit the interleukin-6-dependent tumor cell growth.** *Cancer Res* 1993, **53**:851-856. [archival reference]

109. Nishimoto N, Sasai M, Shima Y, Nakagawa M, Matsumoto T, Shirai T, Kishimoto T, Yoshizaki Y: **Improvement in Castleman's disease by humanized anti-IL-6 receptor antibody therapy.** *Blood* 2000, **95**:56-61. [general reference]

110. Nishimoto N, Maeda K, Kuritani T, Deguchi H, Sato B, Imai N, Kakehi T, Suemura M, Kishimoto T, Yoshizaki K: **Safety and efficacy of repetitive treatment with humanized anti-interleukin-6 receptor antibody (MRA) in rheumatoid arthritis (RA) [abstract].** *Arthritis Rheum* 2001, **44**:S84. [abstract]

111. Mihara M, Kotoh M, Nishimoto N, Oda Y, Kumagai E, Takagi N, Tsunemi K, Ohsugi Y, Kishimoto T, Yoshizaki Y, Takeda Y: **Humanized antibody to human interleukin-6 receptor inhibits the development of collagen arthritis in cynomolgus monkeys.** *Clin Immunol* 2001, **98**:319-326. [general reference]

112. Choy EH, Isenberg DA, Farrow S, Garrood T, Ioannou Y, Bird H, Cheung N, Williams BD, Hazlemau B, Price R, Kishimoto T, Panayi GS: **A double-blind, randomized, placebo-controlled trial of anti-interleukin-6 (IL-6) receptor monoclonal antibody in rheumatoid arthritis (RA) [abstract].** *Arthritis Rheum* 2001, **44**:S84. [abstract]

113. Nishimoto N, Ogata A, Shima Y, Tani Y, Ogawa H, Nakagawa M, Sugiyama H, Yoshizaki K, Kishimoto T: **Oncostatin M, leukemia inhibitory factor, and interleukin 6 induce the proliferation of human plasmacytoma cells via the common signal transducer, gp130 [abstract].** *J Exp Med* 1994, **179**:1343-1347. [archival reference]

Supplement Review
Signaling for survival and apoptosis in the immune system
Tak W Mak and Wen-Chen Yeh

Ontario Cancer Institute and Department of Medical Biophysics, University of Toronto, Toronto, Ontario, Canada

Correspondence: Tak W Mak, Ontario Cancer Institute and Department of Medical Biophysics, University of Toronto, 620 University Avenue, Suite 706, Toronto, Ontario, Canada M5G 2C1. Tel: +1 416 204 2236; fax: +1 416 204 5300; e-mail: tmak@oci.utoronto.ca

Received: 11 March 2002
Revisions requested: 12 March 2002
Revisions received: 13 March 2002
Accepted: 26 March 2002
Published: 9 May 2002

Arthritis Res 2002, **4 (suppl 3)**:S243-S252

This article may contain supplementary data which can only be found online at http://arthritis-research.com/content/4/S3/S243

© 2002 BioMed Central Ltd
(Print ISSN 1465-9905; Online ISSN 1465-9913)

Chapter summary

Signal transduction induced by tumor necrosis factor (TNF) family members and their receptors has been an intensive area of research for several years. The major impact of these studies has been the delineation of apoptotic and cell survival signaling pathways. These discoveries, coupled with major advances in the study of mammalian apoptotic machinery, constitute a promising blueprint of the molecular network governing the fate of all living cells. In this review, we concentrate on the fate of cells in the immune system, where regulation of cell death and cell survival is a frequent and important exercise. A small imbalance in favor of either fate can result in disastrous pathological outcomes, such as cancer, autoimmunity or immune deficiency. It is an insurmountable task to discuss all molecules reported in the literature that are implicated in lymphocyte death or survival. We have therefore focused on discoveries made by mouse gene targeting, as these studies provide the most physiologically relevant information on each molecule. We begin with a description of signaling channels initiated by TNF receptor type 1 engagement, which can lead to either cell survival or to cell death. The point of bifurcation of this pathway and the decision-making molecules FADD, TRAF2 and RIP are discussed. We then follow apoptotic and survival pathways from upstream to downstream, describing many important players involved in signal transduction. Molecules important for NF-κB and JNK/stress-activated protein kinase activation such as IKKβ, NEMO, MAP3K and TRAF6 are discussed, as is the impact of BAFF and its receptors on B-cell survival. Mouse mutants that have helped to define the mammalian apoptosis execution machinery, including animals lacking Apaf-1, caspase-3 and caspase-9, are also described. We conclude with a brief analysis of the potential therapeutic options arising from this body of work.

Keywords: apoptosis, inflammation, mutant mice, signal transduction

Introduction

Homeostasis is an essential aspect of the mammalian immune system [1,2]. The majority of lymphocytes that expand and proliferate in response to antigens *in vivo* has to subsequently die to maintain a constant number of these cells between immune responses. During the initial expansion phase of an immune response, T cells and B cells are induced to divide by antigens, growth factors and cytokines. These agents trigger cellular signals that sustain lymphocyte growth and survival. During the eclipse phase of an immune response, however, apoptosis (programmed cell death [PCD]) must occur to reduce the number of accumulated cells and to restore homeostasis. These survival and apoptotic signals are highly regulated

---

A glossary of specialist terms used in this chapter appears at the end of the text section. A list of common abbreviations used in this issue appears just before the indexes.

[3,4], and the understanding of the processes mediating these cellular decisions should aid in the design of rational therapeutics for autoimmune diseases, inflammation and infections.

For the immune system, many apoptotic signals and survival signals are mediated via receptors present on the surfaces of lymphocytes and other hemopoietic cells. The most prominent of these receptors belong to a group of structurally related signaling proteins called the TNF receptor (TNFR) superfamily [5–7]. Over the past decade, many TNFRs and their ligands have been molecularly cloned and characterized.

Even more exciting is the identification of the myriad of downstream effector proteins involved in coordinating and controlling various signaling cascades. Both apoptotic signals and survival signals in lymphocytes are primarily mediated by various members of the TNFR superfamily. Intriguingly, in some cases, signals associated with PCD or survival can be transmitted through the same receptor in response to the same ligand. Understanding how such signal transduction is executed is a key goal for the many laboratories studying immune and inflammatory responses.

In the present review, we shall concentrate on information gained from studies of gene-targeted mutant mice deficient in the expression of proteins involved in apoptotic and survival signaling pathways in lymphocytes. We shall focus particularly on signal mediators and effectors that act in the TNFR pathways and on the common apoptosis execution machinery. For a more in-depth survey of work in this area, please refer to other recent comprehensive reviews [2–11].

TNFR superfamily
The most important members of the TNFR superfamily involved in lymphocyte signal transduction are TNF receptor-associated factor type 1 (TNFR1), TNF receptor-associated factor type 2 (TNFR2) and Fas (CD95). TNFR1 and TNFR2, which both bind to the cytokine TNF, were the first members of the TNFR family to be identified.

Studies of gene-targeted mice lacking expression of TNFR1 demonstrated that this receptor is involved in signaling leading to inflammation and cell survival [12]. Paradoxically, however, PCD was also found to be impaired in TNFR1$^{-/-}$ mutants [13]. In response to a single ligand (TNF), TNFR1 thus mediates not only survival and inflammatory signaling, but also apoptotic signaling. In contrast, in response to TNF binding, TNFR2 transduces signals principally for survival and inflammation [8]. The Fas (CD95) receptor, which was originally discovered as the product of the mutated gene in MRL/lpr mice [14], mediates mainly signals for apoptosis in response to the binding of its ligand FasL. Mice deficient for Fas or FasL

show massive lymphoadenopathy and disruption of lymphocyte homeostasis due to a lack of PCD.

How is the signaling initiated by engagement of TNFR superfamily members transduced within the cell? In response to ligand binding, various proteins are recruited to specific domains in the cytoplasmic tails of the receptors. It is these downstream effectors, which vary in structure and function, that determine signaling outcomes. Some effectors are enzymes, such as kinases, phosphatases and proteases, some are adaptor proteins that serve to recruit still more signaling intermediaries, and some are regulatory proteins. Understanding the nature and functions of these downstream effectors will allow us to explain how particular cellular outcomes result from signaling through a limited number of receptors.

TNFR superfamily members are categorized into two classes based on the effectors recruited to their cytoplasmic domains. In the first class, which includes TNFR1, Fas, death receptor (DR)3, DR4, DR5 and DR6, the cytoplasmic tail contains a 'death domain' (DD) [6,15]. The DDs may vary slightly in sequence between receptors but all are highly homologous and provide the capacity for protein–protein interaction. The DD in a receptor tail recruits intracellular adaptor proteins that also contain a DD. For example, TNFR1 contains a DD that binds to the TNF receptor-associated death domain protein (TRADD), and Fas contains a DD that binds to both Fas-associated death domain protein (FADD) and receptor-interacting protein (RIP) [5,9] (Fig. 1).

The second class of TNFR superfamily receptors includes TNFR2, CD30, CD40, lymphotoxin receptor, the osteoprotegerin ligand (OPGL) receptor activator of NF-κB (RANK), and B-lymphocyte activating factor (BAFF) receptors [6,16]. The cytoplasmic tails of these receptors do not contain DDs. Instead, they have sequences allowing them to associate with a different set of intracellular adaptors called TNF receptor-associated factors (TRAFs) [17,18]. Although six TRAF proteins (TRAF1–TRAF6) have been identified to date, only five (TRAF1, TRAF2, TRAF3, TRAF5 and TRAF6) actually bind to the cytoplasmic tails of the second class of TNFR superfamily receptors.

Other groups and ourselves have generated gene-targeted 'knockout mice' for several signaling proteins downstream of these receptors, and have been able to gain insights into their functions and regulation from examining the phenotypes of these animals and their cells. In the present review, we discuss the receptor-proximal signaling adaptors and their key functions in deciding whether a cell will survive or will undergo apoptosis. We also examine the successive molecular events that make up the initial phase of the cascade of apoptosis, and its terminal execution machinery.

Figure 1

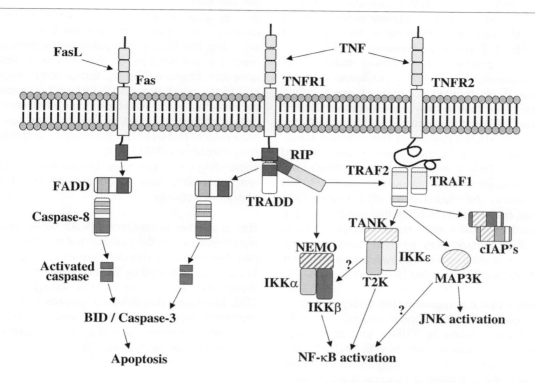

Intracellular signaling pathways downstream of tumor necrosis factor (TNF) receptor superfamily receptors. The Fas, tumor necrosis factor receptor type 1 (TNFR1) and tumor necrosis factor receptor type 2 (TNFR2) receptors are shown extending through the cell membrane with their extracellular domains projecting into the extracellular space. Various adaptor proteins and signal transducing molecules that convey signals initiated by the binding of the ligands Fas ligand (FasL) to Fas and TNF to TNFR1 and TNFR2, respectively, are shown, as is the crosstalk between various molecules and pathways. Functional domains within a protein are shown as colored blocks. Recruitment of one protein to another is indicated by the juxtaposition of like-colored and like-shaped domain blocks. BID, beta interaction domain; cIAPs, cellular inhibitors of apoptosis; FADD, Fas-associated death domain protein; IKK, IκB kinase; JNK, c-Jun N-terminal kinase; MAP3K, mitogen-activated protein 3 kinase; NEMO, NF-κB essential modulator protein; RIP, receptor-interacting protein; T2K, TRAF2-associated kinase; TANK, TRAF family member associated NF-κB activator; TRADD, TNF receptor-associated death domain protein; TRAF, TNF receptor-associated factor. See Colour figure section.

FADD, TRAF2 and RIP

It is now well established that TNFR1 can mediate signals for either apoptosis or cell survival. Which signaling path is triggered following receptor aggregation appears to be a function of the recruitment of the different adaptor proteins appropriate for each path. Indeed, Hsu *et al.* showed that when TRADD binds to TNFR1, TRADD can then associate with either FADD or TRAF2 and with RIP [19] (Fig. 1). This observation led to the hypothesis that recruitment of FADD to the TNFR1 complex would lead to PCD, while recruitment of TRAF2 and RIP would signal for survival. We tested this hypothesis by generating gene-targeted mutant mice deficient for expression of either FADD or TRAF2.

FADD-deficient mice do not survive beyond day 11.5 of embryogenesis [20,21], indicating that FADD is essential for embryonic development. *In situ* hybridization studies confirmed that FADD is expressed widely during embryo-

genesis, consistent with its role in fundamental developmental processes. Most FADD−/− embryos have thin ventricular myocardium, poorly developed inner trabeculation, and abdominal hemorrhage.

The precise function of FADD in embryonic development is not clearly understood at this time. Using cells derived from FADD−/− embryos, however, we have demonstrated the importance of FADD in apoptotic signaling initiated by TNFR superfamily receptors. Following engagement of Fas, TNFR1 or DR3, apoptosis was dramatically reduced in FADD−/− cells compared with in controls. However, levels of PCD in response to viral oncogene overexpression or chemotherapeutic drug administration were normal in FADD−/− cells [20], indicating that not all agents inducing apoptosis transduce their signals through FADD. Interestingly, FADD-deficient T cells, in addition to being resistant to Fas-induced apoptosis, showed a defect in activation-induced proliferation [21].

In contrast, TRAF2$^{-/-}$ cells showed increased levels of PCD on stimulation by TNF [22], consistent with a scenario in which cell survival depends on the recruitment of TRAF2 to TNFR1. Surprisingly, however, TRAF2$^{-/-}$ cells were still able to activate the transcription factor NF-κB following engagement of TNFR1. The activation of NF-κB had previously been thought to depend on signaling through TRAF2, in that a dominant negative TRAF2 protein blocked TNF-mediated activation of NF-κB. Rather than effects on NF-κB, we found that TNF-induced activation of the Jun kinase (JNK) pathway was greatly impaired in the absence of TRAF2. Interestingly, cells deficient in RIP, another adaptor protein associated with TRADD, show a reduction in TNF-mediated NF-κB activation [23]. Taken together, these results indicate that cell survival signaling mediated by TRAF2 does more than just activate NF-κB. The JNK pathway and perhaps other proteins, such as the cellular inhibitors of apoptosis, may also contribute to TNF-induced cell survival [24].

Caspase-8 and c-FLICE (caspase-8) inhibitory protein

Caspase-8 is the key initiator caspase downstream of the apoptosis pathway induced by TNFR1 and other death receptors (Fig. 1). Caspase-8 interacts with FADD through homologous death effector domains. Aggregation and close proximity result in the activation of caspase-8 such that its caspase domain is processed into two active subunits.

c-FLICE (caspase-8) inhibitory protein (c-FLIP), a cellular homolog of viral FLICE (caspase-8) inhibitory protein, is structurally similar to caspase-8 in that it possesses death effector domains and a caspase-like domain. However, c-FLIP lacks caspase enzymatic activity. It is thought that c-FLIP recruited by FADD to the receptor complex in the place of caspase-8 impedes the progression of apoptotic signals. Caspase-8 and c-FLIP thus appear to play critical, but opposite, roles in regulating DR signaling.

Mice lacking caspase-8 are phenotypically similar to FADD-deficient mice [25]. Caspase-8$^{-/-}$ mice die at approximately day 12.5 of embryogenesis with apparent hyperemia and heart defects. Caspase-8$^{-/-}$ cells, like FADD$^{-/-}$ cells, are specifically resistant to DR-induced apoptosis. Surprisingly, c-FLIP$^{-/-}$ mice show a very similar embryonic phenotype to FADD$^{-/-}$ mice and caspase-8$^{-/-}$ mice [26]. The ventricular myocardium and trabeculae are poorly developed in day 10.5 of embryogenesis c-FLIP$^{-/-}$ embryos.

Like FADD-deficient embryos, embryos lacking c-FLIP do not show signs of increased or decreased cell death, suggesting that the developmental defects in these mutant mice may be independent of apoptosis. In contrast, cells lacking c-FLIP are highly sensitive to apoptotic stimuli that trigger death receptors [26]. This result is consistent with the predicted role of c-FLIP to counteract FADD and caspase-8 in the regulation of DR-induced apoptosis.

Bid and Bim

Bid is a proapoptotic Bcl-2 family member that is cleaved and activated by caspase-8 in response to DR signaling. Bid then translocates to the mitochondria and mediates the release of cytochrome c that leads to apoptotic changes (Fig. 2). Bid-deficient mice are resistant to the anti-Fas antibody-induced apoptosis of hepatocytes that kills wild-type mice. However, a milder defect of FasL-induced or TNF-induced apoptosis was observed in Bid-deficient thymocytes and mouse embryonic fibroblasts (MEF) [27]. These results suggest that, depending on tissue type, DR-induced apoptosis does not necessarily have to go through Bid and the mitochondrial pathway.

Bim is another proapoptotic Bcl-2 family member that is not involved in the DR pathway but is critical for thymocyte negative selection. Bim-deficient thymocytes are refractory to apoptosis induced by TCR stimulation, and autoreactive thymocytes accumulate in TCR transgenic Bim$^{-/-}$ mice [28]. Moreover, Bim-deficient lymphocytes accumulate in peripheral blood and in the spleen, and these cells are resistant to apoptotic stimuli such as cytokine deprivation and microtubule perturbation [29].

Mitogen-activated protein 3 kinases

During the induction of cell survival by TNFR1 engagement, a number of mitogen-activated protein 3 kinase (MAP3K) family members has been shown to associate with TRAF2 or RIP (Fig. 1). NF-κB inducing kinase (NIK) was initially proposed to be the downstream target of TRAF2 in mediating TNF-induced NF-κB activation leading to survival [30]. However, NIK-deficient mice show a specific defect in lymph node development and in lymphotoxin-β-receptor signaling [31,32], and cells lacking NIK respond normally to TNF in activating NF-κB.

Instead, the mitogen-activated protein extracellular signal regulated kinase kinase (MEKK)-1 was implicated in this NF-κB activation pathway [33]. In addition, MEKK-1 and apoptosis signal-regulating kinase 1 (ASK-1) were reported to mediate TRAF2-triggered JNK activation [34–36]. From studies of knockout mice, however, it seems that MEKK-1 is required for TNF-induced JNK activation only in embryonic stem cells and not in fibroblasts or T cells [37–39]. Similarly, ASK-1 is not required for early phase TNF-induced JNK activation, and ASK-1$^{-/-}$ cells exhibit only a partial defect in sustained stress kinase activation [40]. A new member of the MEKK family (MEKK-3) has recently been found to associate with RIP, meaning that it could potentially play a role in downstream survival signaling. Indeed, disruption of MEKK-3 severely impairs the activation of NF-κB induced by TNF, and MEKK-3$^{-/-}$ cells are highly sensitive to TNF-induced apoptosis [41].

Figure 2

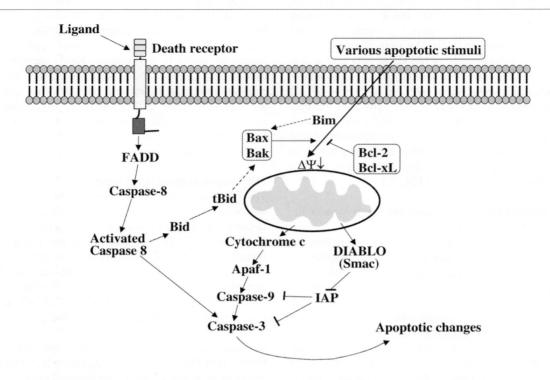

Intrinsic and extrinsic pathways of apoptosis. The extrinsic pathway is triggered by death receptor engagement, which initiates a signaling cascade mediated by caspase-8 activation. Caspase-8 both feeds directly into caspase-3 activation and stimulates the release of cytochrome c by the mitochondria. Caspase-3 activation leads to the degradation of cellular proteins necessary to maintain cell survival and integrity. The intrinsic pathway occurs when various apoptotic stimuli trigger the release of cytochrome c from the mitochondria (independently of caspase-8 activation). Cytochrome c interacts with Apaf-1 and caspase-9 to promote the activation of caspase-3. Various intermediary signaling molecules (many of whose functions are not completely defined) and proteins inhibiting the apoptotic cascade are also shown. Apaf-1, apoptosis-activating factor 1; Bak, bacille Calmette–Guérin; Bax, BCL-2-associated x protein; Bid, proapoptotic Bcl-2 family member; Bim, proapoptotic Bcl-2 family member; DIABLO, direct IAP binding protein with low PI; FADD, Fas-associated death domain protein; IAP, inhibitors of apoptosis; Smac, second mitochondria-derived activator of caspase; tBid, truncated beta interaction domain. See Colour figure section.

The IκB kinase complex

NF-κB is a key transcription factor whose activation generally promotes cell survival. Mice lacking RelA (p65), a principal subunit of NF-κB, die during embryogenesis due to massive liver apoptosis [42]. NF-κB is normally held inactive in the cytoplasm by its association with the inhibitor of NF-κB protein, IκB. To activate NF-κB, IκB must be removed via phosphorylation followed by ubiquitination and proteasomal degradation. Phosphorylation of IκB is mediated primarily by the IκB kinase (IKK) complex containing the proteins IKKα, IKKβ and NF-κB essential modulator (NEMO) (also known as IKKγ) [10]. IKKα and IKKβ are active kinases, while NEMO is a regulatory protein that binds tightly to both kinases.

Deficiency for IKKβ is embryonic lethal, with the mice displaying a liver apoptosis phenotype similar to that of the RelA knockout [43–45]. In addition, the activation of NF-κB by TNF or IL-1 is defective in IKKβ$^{-/-}$ cells. Reconstitution of lethally irradiated hosts with IKKβ-deficient fetal liver cells revealed a defect in T-lymphocyte survival [46].

The absence of T cells in the IKKβ-deficient fetal liver chimerae was due to the activity of circulating TNF, and normal development of T cells was restored in mice lacking both IKKβ and TNFR1.

NEMO-deficient mice also display a phenotype of fetal liver apoptosis and embryonic lethality, consistent with an essential role for NEMO in the central pathway mediating NF-κB activation [47]. Like RelA$^{-/-}$ cells and IKKβ$^{-/-}$ cells, NEMO$^{-/-}$ cells show an increased susceptibility to TNF-induced apoptosis. NEMO is an X-linked gene, and female NEMO$^{+/-}$ mice develop a self-limiting inflammatory skin disorder characterized by hyperkeratosis and increased apoptosis. This phenotype is presumably dependent on X-chromosome inactivation [48,49]. Importantly, these symptoms are reminiscent of incontinentia pigmenti, an X-linked dominant hereditary disease in humans. Indeed, genetic studies of incontinentia pigmenti patients have revealed mutations in the NEMO gene and defects in NF-κB activation in the majority of cases [50].

Interestingly, IKKα-deficient mice do not exhibit a fetal liver defect like IKKβ−/− mice. Instead, IKKα−/− mice display abnormal limb and skeletal patterns and display defective epidermal differentiation [51,52]. The defect in skin formation seems to be independent of NF-κB activity and is due instead to failed secretion of a keratinocyte differentiation-inducing factor [53]. IKKα is not required for IKK or NF-κB activation in response to inflammatory cytokines. Further studies have revealed that IKKα is required for B-cell maturation and secondary lymphoid organogenesis. Most recently, it has been found that IKKα does play a role in NF-κB activation by mediating the processing of the NF-κB2 (p100) precursor protein [54,55].

TRAF2-associated kinase, glycogen synthase kinase 3β and atypical protein kinase C

NF-κB activation can occur via signaling pathways that are independent of the IKK complex. TRAF2-associated kinase (T2K) (also called TBK and NAK) associates with TRAF2 through an intermediary protein, TRAF family member associated NF-κB activator (TANK) [56–58]. TANK is a serine threonine kinase that is distantly related to IKKα and IKKβ. TANK phosphorylates serine 36 on the IκBα subunit of IκB, but this partial phosphorylation is not sufficient to trigger degradation of IκB. T2K−/− cells show normal IκB phosphorylation and degradation, normal NF-κB translocation into the nucleus, and normal NF-κB binding to target DNA sequences in response to TNF and IL-1. However, NF-κB transactivation activity is affected in cells lacking T2K [58]. This phenomenon is validated by the phenotype of T2K−/− mice, which show liver apoptosis and embryonic lethality similar to that in mice lacking RelA, IKKβ or NEMO. Furthermore, elimination of TNFR1 rescues T2K-deficient mice from embryonic lethality, and the double-knockout animals survive for extended periods with no gross abnormalities [58].

The kinases glycogen synthase kinase (GSK3)α and GSK3β act as inhibitory components of the Wnt signaling pathway important for embryonic development. In frogs and zebrafish, GSK3 is required for the definition of the embryonic axes [59]. However, analysis of GSK3β-deficient mice revealed a surprisingly specific and limited phenotype of fetal liver apoptosis similar to that in mice with NF-κB activation defects [60]. GSK3β−/− MEF were highly susceptible to TNF killing, much like wild-type fibroblasts treated with TNF in the presence of the documented GSK3 inhibitor lithium. Interestingly, TNF-induced IκB phosphorylation and degradation were normal in GSK3β−/− cells, but NF-κB activation was diminished due to reduced DNA binding activity and due to severely impaired transcriptional activation of a target reporter gene [60].

Another molecule implicated in TNF-induced NF-κB activation is atypical protein kinase C (ζPKC). ζPKC associates with RIP through the adapter protein p62 [61]. A lack of ζPKC severely impairs cellular responses to TNF that depend on the transcriptional activity of NF-κB [62]. However, IKK activation is normal in ζPKC-deficient MEF, and NF-κB DNA binding is only mildly reduced in response to TNF. Intriguingly, RelA phosphorylation is defective in ζPKC−/− cells, suggesting that an alternative pathway may exist to activate NF-κB. While ζPKC−/− cells are hypersensitive to TNF-induced apoptosis, ζPKC−/− mice do not exhibit fetal liver apoptosis or embryonic lethality [62]. These mutant mice are viable but display a reduced number of Peyer's patches.

TNF receptor-associated factor 6

TRAF6 is emerging as one of the key players in survival signaling. TRAF6 binds to the cytoplasmic tails of both the B-cell costimulatory molecule CD40 and the inflammatory IL-1 receptor [17]. In response to the binding of CD40 ligand and IL-1 to CD40 and IL-1 receptor, respectively, TRAF6 mediates the activation of NF-κB and JNK/stress-activated protein kinase. Study of TRAF6−/− cells confirmed the importance of TRAF6 in NF-κB activation in response to CD40 or IL-1 signaling [63].

Interestingly, lipopolysaccharide signaling was also impaired in TRAF6−/− cells, suggesting that TRAF6 may be involved in signal transduction downstream of the Toll-like receptors, particularly Toll-like receptor 4. A most unexpected finding was that TRAF6−/− mice suffered from severe osteopetrosis, showing defects in tooth eruption and bone remodeling due to impaired osteoclast function [63]. Interestingly, mice lacking expression of OPGL [64], the ligand for RANK, also exhibited osteopetrosis, strongly suggesting that TRAF6 may act downstream of RANK. OPGL−/− mice also show defects in T-cell and B-cell homeostasis [64].

BAFF and its receptors

BAFF (also called BlyS, TALL-1 or zTNF4) is a new TNF family member that has been implicated in promoting B-cell survival [16]. Mice overexpressing BAFF display mature B-cell hyperplasia and systemic lupus erythematosus-like symptoms. Conversely, BAFF-deficient mice show a complete loss of follicular and marginal-zone B lymphocytes [65]. Moreover, both T-cell-dependent and T-cell-independent antibody responses are impaired in mice lacking BAFF.

BAFF can bind to three receptors on the cell surface, B-cell maturation antigen (BCMA), transmembrane activator and calcium modulator and cyclophilin ligand interactor (TACI) and BAFF-R. Studies of knockout mice have shown that these molecules are not directly equivalent in function [66,67]. Mice lacking BCMA show normal B-cell development and antibody responses [68], while TACI-deficient mice are deficient only in T-cell-independent antibody responses [69,70]. Paradoxically, mice lacking

TACI show increased B-cell proliferation and accumulation, suggesting an inhibitory role for TACI in B-cell homeostasis. Gene-targeted mice lacking BAFF-R have yet to be reported, but the natural mouse mutant A/WySnJ has a disruption of the intracellular domain of BAFF-R. A/WySnJ mice display a phenotype that is similar to BAFF$^{-/-}$ mice, although follicular and marginal-zone B cells are not completely abolished [65]. In addition, A/WySnJ mice are impaired only in T-cell-dependent antibody responses, unlike the more comprehensive defect observed in BAFF-deficient mice. These results suggest that, while BAFF-R may be the major receptor relaying BAFF-mediated signals for B-cell survival, some redundancy in function may be provided by the other two receptors, particularly TACI.

Apoptosis execution machinery

In mammals, apoptosis depends on the actions of a family of cysteine proteases called caspases. Two classes of caspases exist: the executioner caspases, which initiate the apoptotic cascade in response to extracellular signals transduced by cell surface receptors such as TNFR1; and the effector caspases, which are activated by the executioner caspases.

In a resting cell, caspases are present as proenzymes containing prodomains. The prodomains must be cleaved off to activate caspase activity. Cleavage of caspases is an element of the two pathways of apoptosis operating in mammalian cells: the 'intrinsic' pathway, which depends on mitochondrial involvement; and the 'extrinsic' pathway, which is independent of the mitochondria. The extrinsic pathway is initiated by the binding of a ligand to a DR as already described. In the intrinsic pathway, the mitochondria in a stimulated cell make the critical decision whether to initiate PCD [71]. In so doing, the mitochondria evaluate the balance of apoptotic signals with other signals promoting survival. If the net result favors the triggering of apoptosis, cytochrome c is released from the mitochondria at a level sufficient to initiate the activation of executioner caspases.

Specifically, cytochrome c in conjunction with dATP promotes the association of procaspase-9 with apoptosis-activating factor 1 (Apaf-1) [72]. This recruitment activates caspase-9 through an unknown mechanism. Activated caspase-9 in turn removes the prodomain of procaspase-3, resulting in the activation of this critical effector caspase (Fig. 2). Activated caspase-3 drives the apoptotic process by degrading a panel of cellular proteins crucial for cell survival

We have taken a genetic approach to dissecting apoptotic pathways in various cell types. The evidence shows, perhaps surprisingly, that not all elements are required in all cell types or in response to all apoptotic agents.

Apoptosis-activating factor 1

Deficiency for Apaf-1 is embryonic lethal [73,74]. The mutant embryos show dramatically reduced levels of apoptosis in the brain, and hyperproliferation of neuronal cells that leads to striking craniofacial deformities [73]. Analysis of various cell types lacking Apaf-1 confirmed the vital role of this protein in the induction of apoptosis by a range of stimuli. However, we were surprised to observe that Fas-induced cell death of thymocytes and T cells was normal in the absence of Apaf-1. This was the first clue that, at least in some cell types, Fas-mediated apoptosis occurs by mechanism that can bypass Apaf-1.

Caspase-3

Most caspase 3$^{-/-}$ mice die at or before birth [75,76]. The few survivors are smaller than their littermates and have visible masses in their heads. These masses are ectopic protrusions of supernumerary cells that accumulate in place of the pyknotic clusters usually derived from apoptosis during normal brain development [75,76]. Caspase-3 is thus crucial for normal embryonic development.

Deficiency for caspase-3 also dramatically reduces the ability of many different cell types to undergo apoptosis in different settings. For example, PCD of oncogenically transformed MEF induced by a chemotherapeutic agent is greatly compromised in the absence of caspase-3. Activation-induced cell death of peripheral T cells is also dramatically reduced. However, while caspase-3 is necessary for efficient apoptosis of embryonic stem cells following UV irradiation, it is not required for PCD induced by γ-irradiation [76]. In addition, the requirement for caspase-3 in PCD induced by a given stimulus can be tissue specific. For example, while TNF induces the apoptosis of caspase-3$^{-/-}$ thymocytes, transformed caspase-3$^{-/-}$ MEFs are resistant to this stimulus.

Finally, caspase-3 is required for certain events transpiring during PCD but is not required for other events. In response to certain stimuli, caspase-3$^{-/-}$ cells fail to display DNA degradation or chromatin condensation but still exhibit other physical signs characteristic of apoptosis [76]. Thus, while caspase-3 is an important player in many instances of PCD, it is dispensable in certain apoptotic settings.

Caspase-9

Caspase-9 deficiency also results in embryonic lethality due to defective brain development [77,78]. Analysis of neuronal tissues of these mutant embryos again revealed decreased apoptosis. Determination of the PCD of several caspase-9$^{-/-}$ cell types showed that, like caspase-3, caspase-9 is not required in all cell types for all apoptotic events. Caspase-9 is necessary for the PCD of embryonic stem cells and MEFs induced by UV irradiation or γ-irradiation, and for PCD of thymocytes exposed to dexamethasone or γ-irradiation. However, caspase-9$^{-/-}$ thymocytes readily undergo apoptosis in response to UV irradiation or engagement of Fas [78].

Future prospects and concluding remarks

Over the past decade, the understanding of the molecular pathways leading to activation of apoptosis and cell survival has increased substantially. This knowledge is an essential prerequisite to our contemplating the design of therapeutics to combat diseases. It is now clear that in addition to autoimmune diseases, this understanding will help in the development of drugs that may have an impact on the treatment of cancer and degenerative diseases.

Glossary of terms

Apaf-1 = apoptosis-activating factor 1; ASK-1 = apoptosis signal-regulating kinase 1; BAFF = B-lymphocyte activating factor; BAFF-R = BAFF receptor; BCMA = B-cell maturation antigen; Bid = proapoptotic Bcl-2 family member; Bim = proapoptotic Bcl-2 family member; DD = death domain; DR = death receptor; FADD = Fas-associated death domain protein; c-FLIP = cellular homologue of FLICE (caspase-8) inhibitory protein; GSK3 = glycogen synthase kinase 3; IKK = IκB kinase; JNK = Jun kinase; MAP3K = mitogen-activated protein 3 kinase; MEF = mouse embryonic fibroblasts; MEKK = mitogen-activated protein extracellular signal regulated kinase; NEMO = NF-κB essential modulator protein; NIK = NF-κB inducing kinase; OPGL = osteoproteregin ligand; PCD = programmed cell death; ζPKC = atypical protein kinase C; RANK = receptor activator of NF-κB; RIP = receptor-interacting protein; T2K = TRAF2-associated kinase; TACI = transmembrane activator and calcium modulator and cyclophilin ligand interactor; TANK = TRAF family member associated NF-κB activator; TRADD = TNF receptor-associated death domain protein; TRAF = TNF receptor-associated factor; TNFR1 = TNF receptor-associated factor type 1; TNFR2 = TNF receptor-associated factor type 2.

Funds for research

Funds for research in this field may be obtained from CANVAC (contact: Rafic Sekaly, 500 Sherbrooke Street West, Suite 800, Montreal, Quebec, Canada H3A 3C6), by the National Cancer Institute Of Canada (10 Alcorn Avenue, Suite 200, Toronto, Ontario, Canada M4V 3B1), and by Canadian Institutes of Health Research (formerly the Medical Research Council of Canada; 410 Laurier Avenue West, 9th Floor, Address Locator 4209A, Ottawa, Ontario, Canada K1A 0W9).

References

1. Debatin KM: **Cell death in T- and B-cell development.** *Ann Hematol* 2001, **80**:B29-B31. [key review]
2. Pinkoski MJ, Green DR: **Lymphocyte apoptosis: refining the paths to perdition.** *Curr Opin Hematol* 2002, **9**:43-49. [key review]
3. Kaufmann SH, Hengartner MO: **Programmed cell death: alive and well in the new millennium.** *Trends Cell Biol* 2001, **11**:526-534. [key review]
4. Meier P, Finch A, Evan G: **Apoptosis in development.** *Nature* 2000, **407**:796-801. [key review]
5. Baud V, Karin M: **Signal transduction by tumor necrosis factor and its relatives.** *Trends Cell Biol* 2001, **11**:372-377. [key review]
6. Locksley RM, Killeen N, Lenardo MJ: **The TNF and TNF receptor superfamilies: integrating mammalian biology.** *Cell* 2001, **104**:487-501. [key review]
7. Chan KF, Siegel MR, Lenardo JM: **Signaling by the TNF receptor superfamily and T cell homeostasis.** *Immunity* 2000, **13**:419-422. [key review]
8. Yeh WC, Hakem R, Woo M, Mak TW: **Gene targeting in the analysis of mammalian apoptosis and TNF receptor superfamily signaling.** *Immunol Rev* 1999, **169**:283-302. [key review]
9. Strasser A, O'Connor L, Dixit VM: **Apoptosis signaling.** *Annu Rev Biochem* 2000, **69**:217-245. [key review]
10. Senftleben U, Karin M: **The IKK/NF-kappa B pathway.** *Crit Care Med* 2002, **30**:S18-S26. [key review]
11. Karin M, Ben-Neriah Y: **Phosphorylation meets ubiquitination: the control of NF-[kappa]B activity.** *Annu Rev Immunol* 2000, **18**:621-663. [key review]
12. Pfeffer K, Matsuyama T, Kundig TM, Wakeham A, Kishihara K, Shahinian A, Wiegmann K, Ohashi PS, Kronke M, Mak TW: **Mice deficient for the 55 kd tumor necrosis factor receptor are resistant to endotoxic shock, yet succumb to *L. monocytogenes* infection.** *Cell* 1993, **73**:457-467. [general reference]
13. Zheng L, Fisher G, Miller RE, Peschon J, Lynch DH, Lenardo MJ: **Induction of apoptosis in mature T cells by tumour necrosis factor.** *Nature* 1995, **377**:348-351. [general reference]
14. Watanabe-Fukunaga R, Brannan CI, Copeland NG, Jenkins NA, Nagata S: **Lymphoproliferation disorder in mice explained by defects in Fas antigen that mediates apoptosis.** *Nature* 1992, **356**:314-317. [general reference]
15. Tartaglia LA, Ayres TM, Wong GH, Goeddel DV: **A novel domain within the 55 kd TNF receptor signals cell death.** *Cell* 1993, **74**:845-853. [general reference]
16. Laabi Y, Egle A, Strasser A: **TNF cytokine family: More BAFF-ling complexities.** *Curr Biol* 2001, **11**:R1013-R1016. [key review]
17. Bradley JR, Pober JS: **Tumor necrosis factor receptor-associated factors (TRAFs).** *Oncogene* 2001, **20**:6482-6491. [key review]
18. Wajant H, Henkler F, Scheurich P: **The TNF-receptor-associated factor family: scaffold molecules for cytokine receptors, kinases and their regulators.** *Cell Signal* 2001, **13**:389-400. [key review]
19. Hsu H, Shu HB, Pan MG, Goeddel DV: **TRADD–TRAF2 and TRADD–FADD interactions define two distinct TNF receptor 1 signal transduction pathways.** *Cell* 1996, **84**:299-308. [general reference]
20. Yeh WC, de la Pompa JL, McCurrach ME, Shu HB, Elia AJ, Shahinian A, Ng M, Wakeham A, Khoo W, Mitchell K, El-Deiry WS, Lowe SW, Goeddel DV, Mak TW: **FADD: essential for embryo development and signaling from some, but not all, inducers of apoptosis.** *Science* 1998, **279**:1954-1958. [general reference]
21. Zhang J, Cado D, Chen A, Kabra NH, Winoto A: **Fas-mediated apoptosis and activation-induced T-cell proliferation are defective in mice lacking FADD/Mort1.** *Nature* 1998, **392**:296-300. [general reference]
22. Yeh WC, Shahinian A, Speiser D, Kraunus J, Billia F, Wakeham A, de la Pompa JL, Ferrick D, Hum B, Iscove N, Ohashi P, Rothe M Goeddel DV, Mak TW: **Early lethality, functional NF-kappaB activation, and increased sensitivity to TNF-induced cell death in TRAF2-deficient mice.** *Immunity* 1997, **7**:715-725. [general reference]
23. Kelliher MA, Grimm S, Ishida Y, Kuo F, Stanger BZ, Leder P: **The death domain kinase RIP mediates the TNF-induced NF-kappaB signal.** *Immunity* 1998, **8**:297-303. [general reference]
24. Wang CY, Mayo MW, Korneluk RG, Goeddel DV, Baldwin AS Jr: **NF-kappaB antiapoptosis: induction of TRAF1 and TRAF2 and c-IAP1 and c-IAP2 to suppress caspase-8 activation.** *Science* 1998, **281**:1680-1683. [general reference]
25. Varfolomeev EE, Schuchmann M, Luria V, Chiannilkulchai N, Beckmann JS, Mett IL, Rebrikov D, Brodianski VM, Kemper OC, Kollet O, Lapidot T, Soffer D, Sobe T, Avraham KB, Goncharov T, Holtmann H, Lonai P, Wallach D: **Targeted disruption of the mouse caspase 8 gene ablates cell death induction by the TNF receptors, Fas/Apo1, and DR3 and is lethal prenatally.** *Immunity* 1998, **9**:267-276. [general reference]
26. Yeh WC, Itie A, Elia AJ, Ng M, Shu HB, Wakeham A, Mirtsos C, Suzuki N, Bonnard M, Goeddel DV, Mak TW: **Requirement for**

Casper (c-FLIP) in regulation of death receptor-induced apoptosis and embryonic development. *Immunity* 2000, **12**:633-642. [general reference]

27. Yin XM, Wang K, Gross A, Zhao Y, Zinkel S, Klocke B, Roth KA, Korsmeyer SJ: **Bid-deficient mice are resistant to Fas-induced hepatocellular apoptosis.** *Nature* 1999, **400**:886-891. [general reference]

28. Bouillet P, Purton JF, Godfrey DI, Zhang LC, Coultas L, Puthalakath H, Pellegrini M, Cory S, Adams JM, Strasser A: **BH3-only Bcl-2 family member Bim is required for apoptosis of autoreactive thymocytes.** *Nature* 2002, **415**:922-926. [general reference]

29. Bouillet P, Metcalf D, Huang DC, Tarlinton DM, Kay TW, Kontgen F, Adams JM, Strasser A: **Proapoptotic Bcl-2 relative Bim required for certain apoptotic responses, leukocyte homeostasis, and to preclude autoimmunity.** *Science* 1999, **286**:1735-1738. [general reference]

30. Malinin NL, Boldin MP, Kovalenko AV, Wallach D: **MAP3K-related kinase involved in NF-kappaB induction by TNF, CD95 and IL-1.** *Nature* 1997, **385**:540-544. [general reference]

31. Shinkura R, Kitada K, Matsuda F, Tashiro K, Ikuta K, Suzuki M, Kogishi K, Serikawa T, Honjo T: **Alymphoplasia is caused by a point mutation in the mouse gene encoding Nf-kappa b-inducing kinase.** *Nat Genet* 1999, **22**:74-77. [general reference]

32. Yin L, Wu L, Wesche H, Arthur CD, White JM, Goeddel DV, Schreiber RD: **Defective lymphotoxin-beta receptor-induced NF-kappaB transcriptional activity in NIK-deficient mice.** *Science* 2001, **291**:2162-2165. [general reference]

33. Lee FS, Hagler J, Chen ZJ, Maniatis T: **Activation of the IkappaB alpha kinase complex by MEKK1, a kinase of the JNK pathway.** *Cell* 1997, **88**:213-222. [general reference]

34. Baud V, Liu ZG, Bennett B, Suzuki N, Xia Y, Karin M: **Signaling by proinflammatory cytokines: oligomerization of TRAF2 and TRAF6 is sufficient for JNK and IKK activation and target gene induction via an amino-terminal effector domain.** *Genes Dev* 1999, **13**:1297-1308. [general reference]

35. Nishitoh H, Saitoh M, Mochida Y, Takeda K, Nakano H, Rothe M, Miyazono K, Ichijo H: **ASK1 is essential for JNK/SAPK activation by TRAF2.** *Mol Cell* 1998, **2**:389-395. [general reference]

36. Hoeflich KP, Yeh WC, Yao Z, Mak TW, Woodgett JR: **Mediation of TNF receptor-associated factor effector functions by apoptosis signal-regulating kinase-1 (ASK1).** *Oncogene* 1999, **18**:5814-5820. [general reference]

37. Yujiri T, Ware M, Widmann C, Oyer R, Russell D, Chan E, Zaitsu Y, Clarke P, Tyler K, Oka Y, Fanger GR, Henson P, Johnson GL: **MEK kinase 1 gene disruption alters cell migration and c-Jun NH2-terminal kinase regulation but does not cause a measurable defect in NF-kappa B activation.** *Proc Natl Acad Sci USA* 2000, **97**:7272-7277. [general reference]

38. Xia Y, Makris C, Su B, Li E, Yang J, Nemerow GR, Karin M: **MEK kinase 1 is critically required for c-Jun N-terminal kinase activation by proinflammatory stimuli and growth factor-induced cell migration.** *Proc Natl Acad Sci USA* 2000, **97**:5243-5248. [general reference]

39. Yujiri T, Sather S, Fanger GR, Johnson GL: **Role of MEKK1 in cell survival and activation of JNK and ERK pathways defined by targeted gene disruption.** *Science* 1998, **282**:1911-1914. [general reference]

40. Tobiume K, Matsuzawa A, Takahashi T, Nishitoh H, Morita K, Takeda K, Minowa O, Miyazono K, Noda T, Ichijo H: **ASK1 is required for sustained activations of JNK/p38 MAP kinases and apoptosis.** *EMBO Rep* 2001, **2**:222-228. [general reference]

41. Yang J, Lin Y, Guo Z, Cheng J, Huang J, Deng L, Liao W, Chen Z, Liu Z, Su B: **The essential role of MEKK3 in TNF-induced NF-kappaB activation.** *Nat Immunol* 2001, **2**:620-624. [general reference]

42. Beg AA, Sha WC, Bronson RT, Ghosh S, Baltimore D: **Embryonic lethality and liver degeneration in mice lacking the RelA component of NF-kB.** *Nature* 1995, **376**:167-170. [general reference]

43. Li Q, Van Antwerp D, Mercurio F, Lee KF, Verma IM: **Severe liver degeneration in mice lacking the IkappaB kinase 2 gene.** *Science* 1999, **284**:321-325. [general reference]

44. Tanaka M, Fuentes ME, Yamaguchi K, Durnin MH, Dalrymple SA, Hardy KL, Goeddel DV: **Embryonic lethality, liver degeneration, and impaired NF-kappa B activation in IKK-beta-deficient mice.** *Immunity* 1999, **10**:421-429. [general reference]

45. Li ZW, Chu W, Hu Y, Delhase M, Deerinck T, Ellisman M, Johnson R, Karin M: **The IKKbeta subunit of IkappaB kinase (IKK) is essential for nuclear factor kappaB activation and prevention of apoptosis.** *J Exp Med* 1999, **189**:1839-1845. [general reference]

46. Senftleben U, Li ZW, Baud V, Karin M: **IKKbeta is essential for protecting T cells from TNFalpha-induced apoptosis.** *Immunity* 2001, **14**:217-230. [general reference]

47. Rudolph D, Yeh WC, Wakeham A, Rudolph B, Nallainathan D, Potter J, Elia AJ, Mak TW: **Severe liver degeneration and lack of NF-kappaB activation in NEMO/IKKgamma-deficient mice.** *Genes Dev* 2000, **14**:854-862. [general reference]

48. Makris C, Godfrey VL, Krahn-Senftleben G, Takahashi T, Roberts JL, Schwarz T, Feng L, Johnson RS, Karin M: **Female mice heterozygous for IKK gamma/NEMO deficiencies develop a dermatopathy similar to the human X-linked disorder incontinentia pigmenti.** *Mol Cell* 2000, **5**:969-979. [general reference]

49. Schmidt-Supprian M, Bloch W, Courtois G, Addicks K, Israel A, Rajewsky K, Pasparakis M: **NEMO/IKK gamma-deficient mice model incontinentia pigmenti.** *Mol Cell* 2000, **5**:981-992. [general reference]

50. Smahi A, Courtois G, Vabres P, Yamaoka S, Heuertz S, Munnich A, Israel A, Heiss NS, Klauck SM, Kioschis P, Wiemann S, Poustka A, Esposito T, Bardaro T, Gianfrancesco F, Ciccodicola A, D'Urso M, Woffendin H, Jakins T, Donnai D, Stewart H, Kenwrick SJ, Aradhya S, Yamagata T, Levy M, Lewis RA, Nelson DL: **Genomic rearrangement in NEMO impairs NF-kappaB activation and is a cause of incontinentia pigmenti. The International Incontinentia Pigmenti (IP) Consortium.** *Nature* 2000, **405**:466-472. [general reference]

51. Hu Y, Baud V, Delhase M, Zhang P, Deerinck T, Ellisman M, Johnson R, Karin M: **Abnormal morphogenesis but intact IKK activation in mice lacking the IKKalpha subunit of IkappaB kinase.** *Science* 1999, **284**:316-320. [general reference]

52. Li Q, Lu Q, Hwang JY, Buscher D, Lee KF, Izpisua-Belmonte JC, Verma IM: **IKK1-deficient mice exhibit abnormal development of skin and skeleton.** *Genes Dev* 1999, **13**:1322-1328. [general reference]

53. Hu Y, Baud V, Oga T, Kim KI, Yoshida K, Karin M: **IKKalpha controls formation of the epidermis independently of NF-kappaB.** *Nature* 2001, **410**:710-714. [general reference]

54. Senftleben U, Cao Y, Xiao G, Greten FR, Krahn G, Bonizzi G, Chen Y, Hu Y, Fong A, Sun SC, Karin M: **Activation by IKKalpha of a second, evolutionary conserved, NF-kappa B signaling pathway.** *Science* 2001, **293**:1495-1499. [general reference]

55. Kaisho T, Takeda K, Tsujimura T, Kawai T, Nomura F, Terada N, Akira S: **IkappaB kinase alpha is essential for mature B cell development and function.** *J Exp Med* 2001, **193**:417-426. [general reference]

56. Pomerantz JL, Baltimore D: **NF-kappaB activation by a signaling complex containing TRAF2, TANK and TBK1, a novel IKK-related kinase.** *Embo J* 1999, **18**:6694-6704. [general reference]

57. Tojima Y, Fujimoto A, Delhase M, Chen Y, Hatakeyama S, Nakayama K, Kaneko Y, Nimura Y, Motoyama N, Ikeda K, Karin M, Nakanishi M: **NAK is an IkappaB kinase-activating kinase.** *Nature* 2000, **404**:778-782. [general reference]

58. Bonnard M, Mirtsos C, Suzuki S, Graham K, Huang J, Ng M, Itie A, Wakeham A, Shahinian A, Henzel WJ, Elia AJ, Shillinglaw W, Mak TW, Cao Z, Yeh W-C: **Deficiency of T2K leads to apoptotic liver degeneration and impaired NF-kappaB-dependent gene transcription.** *Embo J* 2000, **19**:4976-4985. [general reference]

59. He X, Saint-Jeannet JP, Woodgett JR, Varmus HE, Dawid IB: **Glycogen synthase kinase-3 and dorsoventral patterning in Xenopus embryos.** *Nature* 1995, **374**:617-622. [general reference]

60. Hoeflich KP, Luo J, Rubie EA, Tsao MS, Jin O, Woodgett JR: **Requirement for glycogen synthase kinase-3beta in cell survival and NF-kappaB activation.** *Nature* 2000, **406**:86-90. [general reference]

61. Sanz L, Sanchez P, Lallena MJ, Diaz-Meco MT, Moscat J: **The interaction of p62 with RIP links the atypical PKCs to NF-kappaB activation.** *Embo J* 1999, **18**:3044-3053. [general reference]

62. Leitges M, Sanz L, Martin P, Duran A, Braun U, Garcia JF, Camacho F, Diaz-Meco MT, Rennert PD, Moscat J: **Targeted dis-**

ruption of the zetaPKC gene results in the impairment of the NF-kappaB pathway. *Mol Cell* 2001, **8**:771-780. [general reference]

63. Lomaga MA, Yeh WC, Sarosi I, Duncan GS, Furlonger C, Ho A, Morony S, Capparelli C, Van G, Kaufman S, van der Heiden A, Itie A, Wakeham A, Khoo W, Sasaki T, Cao Z, Penninger JM, Paige CJ, Lacey DL, Dunstan CR, Boyle WJ, Goeddel DV, Mak TW: **TRAF6 deficiency results in osteopetrosis and defective interleukin-1, CD40, and LPS signaling.** *Genes Dev* 1999, **13**:1015-1024. [general reference]

64. Kong YY, Yoshida H, Sarosi I, Tan HL, Timms E, Capparelli C, Morony S, Oliveira-dos-Santos AJ, Van G, Itie A, Khoo W, Wakeham A, Dunstan CR, Lacey DL, Mak TW, Boyle WJ, Penninger JM: **OPGL is a key regulator of osteoclastogenesis, lymphocyte development and lymph-node organogenesis.** *Nature* 1999, **397**:315-323. [general reference]

65. Schiemann B, Gommerman JL, Vora K, Cachero TG, Shulga-Morskaya S, Dobles M, Frew E, Scott ML: **An essential role for BAFF in the normal development of B cells through a BCMA-independent pathway.** *Science* 2001, **293**:2111-2114. [general reference]

66. Gross JA, Johnston J, Mudri S, Enselman R, Dillon SR, Madden K, Xu W, Parrish-Novak J, Foster D, Lofton-Day C, Moore M, Littau A, Grossman A, Haugen H, Foley K, Blumberg H, Harrison K, Kindsvogel W, Clegg CH: **TACI and BCMA are receptors for a TNF homologue implicated in B-cell autoimmune disease.** *Nature* 2000, **404**:995-999. [general reference]

67. Thompson JS, Bixler SA, Qian F, Vora K, Scott ML, Cachero TG, Hession C, Schneider P, Sizing ID, Mullen C, Strauch K, Zafari M, Benjamin CD, Tschopp J, Browning JL, Ambrose C: **BAFF-R, a newly identified TNF receptor that specifically interacts with BAFF.** *Science* 2001, **293**:2108-2111. [general reference]

68. Xu S, Lam KP: **B-cell maturation protein, which binds the tumor necrosis factor family members BAFF and APRIL, is dispensable for humoral immune responses.** *Mol Cell Biol* 2001, **21**:4067-4074. [general reference]

69. Yan M, Wang H, Chan B, Roose-Girma M, Erickson S, Baker T, Tumas D, Grewal IS, Dixit VM: **Activation and accumulation of B cells in TACI-deficient mice.** *Nat Immunol* 2001, **2**:638-643. [general reference]

70. von Bulow GU, van Deursen JM, Bram RJ: **Regulation of the T-independent humoral response by TACI.** *Immunity* 2001, **14**:573-582. [general reference]

71. Green DR, Reed JC: **Mitochondria and apoptosis.** *Science* 1998, **281**:1309-1312. [key review]

72. Li P, Nijhawan D, Budihardjo I, Srinivasula SM, Ahmad M, Alnemri ES, Wang X: **Cytochrome c and dATP-dependent formation of Apaf-1/caspase-9 complex initiates an apoptotic protease cascade.** *Cell* 1997, **91**:479-489. [general reference]

73. Yoshida H, Kong YY, Yoshida R, Elia AJ, Hakem A, Hakem R, Penninger JM, Mak TW: **Apaf1 is required for mitochondrial pathways of apoptosis and brain development.** *Cell* 1998, **94**:739-750. [general reference]

74. Cecconi F, Alvarez-Bolado G, Meyer BI, Roth KA, Gruss P: **Apaf1 (CED-4 homolog) regulates programmed cell death in mammalian development.** *Cell* 1998, **94**:727-737. [general reference]

75. Kuida K, Zheng TS, Na S, Kuan C, Yang D, Karasuyama H, Rakic P, Flavell RA: **Decreased apoptosis in the brain and premature lethality in CPP32-deficient mice.** *Nature* 1996, **384**:368-372. [general reference]

76. Woo M, Hakem R, Soengas MS, Duncan GS, Shahinian A, Kagi D, Hakem A, McCurrach M, Khoo W, Kaufman SA, Senaldi G, Howard T, Lowe SW, Mak TW: **Essential contribution of caspase 3/CPP32 to apoptosis and its associated nuclear changes.** *Genes Dev* 1998, **12**:806-819. [general reference]

77. Kuida K, Haydar TF, Kuan CY, Gu Y, Taya C, Karasuyama H, Su MSS, Rakic P, Flavell RA: **Reduced apoptosis and cytochrome c-mediated caspase activation in mice lacking caspase 9.** *Cell* 1998, **94**:325-337. [general reference]

78. Hakem R, Hakem A, Duncan GS, Henderson JT, Woo M, Soengas MS, Elia A, de la Pompa JL, Kagi D, Khoo W, Potter J, Yoshida R, Kaufman SA, Lowe SW, Penninger JM, Mak TW: **Differential requirement for caspase 9 in apoptotic pathways in vivo.** *Cell* 1998, **94**:339-352. [general reference]

Genetics and Therapeutics

Supplement Review
Susceptibility genes in the pathogenesis of murine lupus
Charles Nguyen, Nisha Limaye and Edward K Wakeland

Center for Immunology, University of Texas Southwestern Medical Center, Dallas, Texas, USA

Correspondence: Dr Ward Wakeland, Center for Immunology, University of Texas Southwestern Medical Center, Dallas, TX 75290-9093, USA.
Tel: +1 214 648 7334; fax: +1 214 648 7331; e-mail: edward.wakeland@UTSouthwestern.edu

Received: 4 March 2002
Accepted: 13 March 2002
Published: 9 May 2002

Arthritis Res 2002, **4 (suppl 3)**:S255-S263

This article may contain supplementary data which can only be found online at http://arthritis-research.com/content/4/S3/S255

Chapter summary

Systemic lupus erythematosus (SLE) is the paradigm of a multisystem autoimmune disease in which genetic factors strongly influence susceptibility. Through genome scans and congenic dissection, numerous loci associated with lupus susceptibility have been defined and the complexity of the inheritance of this disease has been revealed. In this review, we provide a brief description of animal models of SLE, both spontaneous models and synthetic models, with an emphasis on the B6 congenic model derived from analyses of the NZM2410 strain. A hypothetical model of disease progression that organizes many of the identified SLE susceptibility loci in three distinct biological pathways that interact to mediate disease pathogenesis is also described. We finally discuss our recent fine mapping analysis, which revealed a cluster of loci that actually comprise the *Sle1* locus.

Keywords: antinuclear autoantibodies, autoimmunity, congenic dissection, murine lupus, SLE

Introduction
SLE is a complex autoimmune disease of unknown etiology. It is estimated to affect about 1 in 2000 people, and the clinical presentation is highly variable and can sometimes be fatal, with a 10-year mortality rate of 28%. There is a strong gender bias, with a female : male ratio of about 9 : 1 between the ages of 15 and 50 years. Ethnicity also influences the incidence of the disease: African-Americans and Hispanics are approximately two to four times more likely to contract the disease than Caucasians [1,2].

SLE is primarily characterized by the production of autoantibodies directed against nuclear antigens such as double-stranded DNA and chromatin. These antinuclear autoantibodies (ANAs) cause end-organ damage by a variety of mechanisms, notably via immune-complex-mediated inflammation, which can result in glomerulonephritis (GN), arthritis, rashes, serositis, and vasculitis. At the molecular level, defects in both immune complex clear-

ance and in B-cell and T-cell tolerance and function have been implicated in the pathogenesis of this disease [3].

A great deal of evidence supports a genetic basis for susceptibility to SLE. Estimates of the concordance rates in monozygotic twins range between 25% and 69%, while the rate is only 1–2% in dizygotic twins. The concordance rate for the presence of ANAs in serum is as high as 92% in monozygotic twins, and 10–12% of SLE patients have first-degree or second-degree relatives with the disease [4]. Stochastic processes and environmental influences clearly also play a significant role in disease development and exacerbation. These can include stress, bacterial and viral infections, sun exposure, exogenous hormones and certain drugs [2].

SLE rarely occurs as a result of a single gene mutation. However, deficiencies in the early components of the complement cascade can cause the phenotype: 95% of

A glossary of specialist terms used in this chapter appears at the end of the text section. A list of common abbreviations used in this issue appears just before the indexes.

Table 1

Synthetic murine models of lupus

Model [reference]	Affected function
Fas [42], FasL [43], *Bcl2* [44]	Regulation of apoptosis
Sap [25], C1q [26], C4 [27], DNAse [28]	Clearance of antigen, such as apoptotic bodies and DNA
Ctla-4 [30], p21 [32], PD-1 [33], Lyn [38–40], Fyn [41]	Activation and regulation of T cells
BLyS [35–37], PD-1 [33], Lyn [38–40], Fyn [41], FcγRIIB [51]	Activation and regulation of B cells
FcγRIII [53], ICAM-1 [46]	Proinflammatory mechanisms

BLyS, B-lymphocyte stimulator; FasL, Fas ligand; ICAM-1, intracellular adhesion molecule-1.

Table 2

Spontaneous murine models of lupus

Model [reference]	Properties
(NZB × NZW)F1, NZM2410, (SWR × NZB)F1	Develops antinuclear autoantibodies and glomerulonephritis that resembles human lupus; exhibits a complex inheritance
MRL/*lpr* [42], MRL/*gld* [43]	Contains a single-gene mutation (Fas or Fas ligand) that leads to autoimmunity when expressed in MRL background
BXSB/*yaa*	Contains the Y-linked autoimmune accelerator gene that causes a more severe disease in BXSB males

C1-deficient and C4-deficient people develop lupus, as do 30% of people with C2 deficiency. In animal models, disruption of Fas and Fas ligand (FasL) also has major effects in disease susceptibility [5,6]. SLE more commonly occurs as a complex, polygenic disease, with many MHC and nonMHC genes interacting with each other and with the environment to create the varied disease phenotypes [5,6].

No single gene has been found to be necessary or sufficient to cause the disease. As with any multifactorial disease, this complicates the identification of disease genes. There is a low degree of penetrance associated with individual susceptibility loci, and different combinations of genes may be associated with disease development in different families. In addition, the lack of any strong selection against the susceptibility loci makes them fairly common in the general population. This makes their detection by linkage analysis difficult in human populations, which have a high degree of genetic variability. Nonetheless, several SLE susceptibility intervals have been identified in the human genome [7–9].

Animal models

A useful alternative strategy when dealing with genetically complex diseases like SLE is the elucidation of disease mechanisms in suitable animal models. These studies often yield valuable insights that can then be applied to human studies [10,11].

There are numerous synthetic murine models and spontaneous murine models of lupus (see Tables 1 and 2). The synthetic models include transgenics and targeted gene disruptions in which candidate disease genes that are involved in a variety of lymphocytic interactions, apoptosis, or antigen clearance are silenced or overexpressed [12–14]. As might be expected, disrupting or enhancing pathways involved in normal immune surveillance and reactivity often results in autoimmunity.

In addition to synthetic mouse models, there are also classic spontaneous models, including the (NZB × NZW)F1 (or NZB/W) mouse and the congenic recombinant NZM2410 strain derived from this cross, the MRL/*lpr* mouse, and the BXSB/*yaa* mouse. NZB/W mice develop systemic autoimmunity with ANA production and immune-complex-mediated GN, much like that seen in humans. There is also a strong female gender bias in disease susceptibility, which is not seen in the NZM2410 strain. It is thought that this may be due to the presence of very strong susceptibility alleles in the NZM2410 strain, which cause a phenotype severe enough to mask the effects of sex hormones [15]. The *lpr* mutation of the Fas gene, which is involved in apoptosis, is a strongly potentiating factor for autoimmunity. In combination with a susceptible genome, it causes systemic disease in MRL/*lpr* mice. In the case of BXSB mice, the Y-linked autoimmune accelerator gene causes severe disease in males when expressed in the susceptible BXSB genome.

Figure 1

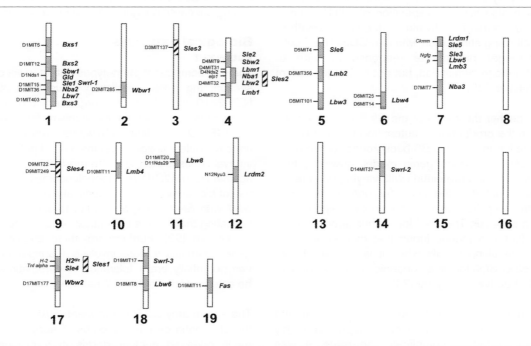

Genomic distribution of susceptibility intervals identified in linkage analysis on murine test crosses involving BSXB, MRL/lpr, PL/J, SWR, NZB, NZW, and NZM2410 strains [14,60,62,63]. See Colour figure section.

Numerous linkage analyses have been carried out in each of these strains to identify the chromosomal regions responsible for mediating susceptibility to various component phenotypes such as ANA production, splenomegaly, and GN [14]. In each study, three or more loci were linked to disease susceptibility. This holds true in the case of the (SWR × NZB)F1 strain. Mice of this strain also develop disease very similar to that seen in NZB/W mice, and linkage analysis has recently been carried out to understand the contribution of the SWR genome to disease susceptibility [16].

More than 50 loci have been found to affect susceptibility to lupus or one of its component phenotypes [13,14], pointing to the complexity and the polygenic nature of this disease. Loci on chromosomes 1, 4, 7 and 17 have been identified in multiple studies, which indicates that genes in these regions may be important in immune regulation and function, and may play a role in mediating disease in a nonstrain-specific manner (Fig. 1). Many mapped loci co-localize with regions linked to other autoimmune diseases like insulin-dependent diabetes, experimental autoimmune encephalomyelitis, and experimental induced arthritis in various murine models [17]. This makes it probable that certain loci affect autoimmune susceptibility in general by modulating processes such as immune reactivity or apoptosis, while other genes play a role in determining the specific target organ and antigens involved in disease pathogenesis.

Linkage analysis followed by congenic dissection is a powerful strategy that is used to narrow identified regions showing linkage to susceptibility, down to a point where physical mapping and candidate gene analysis can be meaningfully carried out. In congenic dissection, the various genomic regions are moved individually onto a resistant genome or *vice versa*, allowing one to see the effects of each individual locus. Using this technique, significant advances have been made towards identifying genes that may be involved in the loss of tolerance to nuclear antigens in the spontaneous models of murine lupus. Linkage analysis of susceptibility to GN and ANA production in the NZM2410 strain by Morel and Wakeland identified three prominent loci [18], and congenic strains were then made by moving each locus onto the lupus-resistant C57Bl/6J (B6) background [19].

The B6.*Sle1* congenic carries the *Sle1* interval, found on chromosome 1. The congenic is associated with the production of autoantibodies against H2A/H2B/DNA subnucleosomes and with the elevated expression of the activation markers B7.2 on B cells and CD69 on CD4+ T cells [20]. B6.*Sle2* harbors the *Sle2* interval on chromosome 4 and shows a reduction in the threshold for activation of B cells, leading to the production of polyclonal IgM and increased numbers of peritoneal and splenic B1 cells when present on the B6 genetic background [21]. B6.*Sle3*, whose congenic interval lies on chromosome 7, possesses an affected T-cell compartment, as well as the production of polyclonal IgG by B cells. These B6.*Sle3* congenic mice also have an expansion of CD4+ T cells, along with a decrease in activation-induced cell death of these cells following stimulation with anti-CD3. The T cells exhibit a stronger proliferative response *in vitro* to T-dependent antigen stimulation, but not to T-independent antigen stimulation [22].

Significantly, neither the *Sle2* nor the *Sle3* interval is sufficient to cause the production of autoantibodies and kidney disease on the lupus-resistant B6 background. When combined with *Sle1* as a bicongenic model, however, they cause renal lesions and proteinuria with varying penetrance [23]. This demonstrates the need for both an initiating factor and the amplification of the immune response for pathogenesis to occur. The *Sle1* locus thus appears to be an initiating factor in murine lupus that causes systemic autoimmunity, resulting in GN when it is combined with either the *Sle2* or *Sle3* loci in bicongenic strains of mice, or with the BXSB-derived *yaa* gene [23].

Given the multiple loci that were identified in the NZM2410 strain, the susceptibility to lupus is highly complex. But to further complicate the issue, it was recently discovered that there existed epistatic modifiers or genes that suppress autoimmunity. Most of the *Sle* intervals were derived from the NZW strain, which does not have the significant autoimmune phenotype seen in the NZM2410 strain [24].

Linkage analysis then confirmed that there existed four suppressive loci, labeled '*Sles*' (SLE suppressor), in the NZW genome. The *Sles1* locus, which is a specific suppressor of *Sle1*, can in fact completely suppress the entire autoimmune cascade that is caused by *Sle1* on a B6/NZW heterozygous background. This includes a powerful humoral autoimmune response, and a high penetrance of fatal lupus nephritis (> 75%). *Sles1* is located on chromosome 17, in the complement region of the murine MHC. B6 mice congenic for both the *Sle1* and the *Sles1* intervals are phenotypically indistinguishable from B6 mice. Heterozygosity at the H2 locus has previously been linked to lupus susceptibility in mouse models as well as human lupus [12].

Sles2 is located on a region on chromosome 4 that was previously shown to contain NZB-derived susceptibility loci, and is linked to suppression of autoantibody production. *Sles3* on chromosome 3 is located near Il2, a region that has been linked to diabetes and experimental autoimmune encephalomyelitis susceptibility in murine models. It is linked with humoral autoimmunity and, more weakly, nephritis suppression. *Sles4* on chromosome 9 is linked with protection from nephritis but not humoral autoimmunity, and its effect is entirely male specific [24]. These four suppressive loci, along with the *Sle* loci, help illustrate the com-

plexity of SLE and the importance of epistatic interactions among susceptibility genes in leading to autoimmunity.

Biological pathways
Pathway 1
Through component phenotypes detected via congenic dissection, the genes mediating lupus susceptibility in the NZM2410 model can be organized into a hypothetical pathway that provides the mechanisms for disease development (Fig. 2). The first pathway requires a breach in tolerance to nuclear antigens. As mentioned previously, the *Sle1* interval is associated with the production of autoantibodies against H2A/H2B/DNA subnucleosomes [20]. Through the use of bicogenic and tricongenic strains, the combination of *Sle1* with *Sle2*, *Sle3*, or *yaa* led to severe lupus nephritis, indicating that *Sle1* is the critical factor in the pathogenesis of disease [23]. Furthermore, there are other numerous genes, particularly those involved in antigen clearance, that can potentially break tolerance to chromatin and can thus be categorized into this first pathway.

The serum amyloid P component (SAP) is known to bind the chromatin on surface blebs of apoptotic cells as well as in released nuclear debris in a calcium-dependent manner. Bickerstaff *et al.* have shown that the targeted disruption of SAP in mice leads to an accelerated rate of chromatin degradation when compared with SAP-sufficient mice [25]. The SAP-deficient mice spontaneously developed high titers of ANAs and severe GN. It has been suggested that SAP seems to prevent the production of autoantibodies against chromatin by binding to it and regulating its degradation and/or by sequestering it from antigen receptors [25].

Early components of complement phenotypes are also strongly associated with SLE. The first component of the complement pathway, C1q, leads to the development of autoimmunity when it is disrupted in the mouse. C1q-deficient mice show high levels of ANAs as well as increased numbers of apoptotic bodies in their glomeruli. This accumulation of apoptotic bodies suggests that there is a defect in the clearance of apoptotic debris [26]. C4 deficiency in mice has similarly been demonstrated to cause high titers of ANAs, GN and splenomegaly. In addition, these mice accumulate activated T cells and B cells, and there is impaired immune complex clearance [27].

DNase I is a major nuclease that may be involved in removing DNA from apoptotic debris. Napirei *et al.* constructed a knockout model, and demonstrated ANA production and GN [28]. DNase I is expressed at sites of high cellular turnover such as the skin and gastrointestinal tract. It is hypothesized that defective or decreased expression of the enzyme may cause a buildup of DNA antigen, leading to an increased risk of autoantibody formation. Treatment of NZB/W mice with DNase I results in a

Figure 2

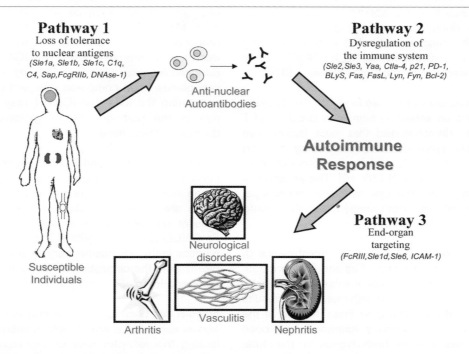

Hypothetical pathways involved in the pathogenesis of SLE. See Colour figure section.

decrease in the level of anti-DNA IgG, supporting such a role for the molecule [29].

Pathway 2

The autoimmune response initiated by a breach in tolerance to self-antigen can be amplified by genes in the second pathway that cause a dysregulation of the immune response. Both *Sle2* and *Sle3*, mediating the abnormal phenotypes in B cells and T cells, respectively, belong in this second pathway. The B6.*Sle1* congenic mouse does not develop GN, and only when either *Sle2* or *Sle3* is combined with the *Sle1* loci in the bicongenic strain does one see evidence of renal disease [23]. This vividly illustrates the notion that the breach in tolerance to nuclear antigen does not lead to disease unless there is an amplification of the autoimmune response, mediated by a dysregulated immune system.

In addition to *Sle2* and *Sle3*, there are other molecules that belong in the second pathway and that play important roles in the activation or inhibition of lymphocytes. CTLA4 is a cell-surface molecule that, on binding to its ligand B7, inhibits the CD28 costimulation of T cells. Mice that are deficient in CTLA4 have been shown to have hyperproliferative T cells and increased titers of serum antibodies [30]. When anti-CTLA4 antibodies are administered to NZB/W mice, the production of autoantibodies is inhibited [31]. Another gene that regulates T-cell proliferation (and, potentially, tolerance to self-antigen) is p21, a cyclin-

dependent kinase that is involved in the inhibition of cell-cycle progression. p21-deficient mice were generated, and they displayed T cells that had a hyperproliferative response to sustained stimulation *in vitro*. Furthermore, these mice developed a lupus-like syndrome with the presence of ANAs as well as GN [32].

Another gene that may play a role in amplifying an autoimmune response is PD-1, a cell-surface receptor that belongs to the immunoglobulin superfamily and contains an immunoreceptor tyrosine-based inhibitory motif. Mice deficient in PD-1 develop an autoimmune phenotype characterized by GN, which is further accelerated by the presence of the *lpr* mutation in the Fas gene. Although expressed on a small percentage of cells in the thymus, PD-1 becomes highly expressed on activated T cells and B cells, and has been shown to inhibit the proliferative response of primed T cells. It has been suggested that this molecule may therefore play a role in maintaining peripheral self-tolerance [33].

B-lymphocyte stimulator (BLyS), a member of the tumor necrosis factor family of ligands, also plays an important role in the immune system. It has been demonstrated to enhance B-cell responses both *in vitro* and *in vivo* [34]. When overexpressed in transgenic mice, BLyS causes an increase in the number of peripheral B cells and of autoantibodies directed against nuclear antigens, as well as in GN and lymphadenopathy [35–37]. Furthermore, BLys has been directly linked to murine lupus. Levels of circulating BLyS are elevated in the autoimmune NZB/W and MRL-*lpr/lpr* mice during the onset and progression of disease. When the mice were treated with an antibody directed against one of the receptors for BLyS, kidney disease was inhibited and mortality was reduced [37].

Lyn and Fyn are members of the *src* family protein tyrosine kinases that transduce activating signals in B cells and T cells. It has been demonstrated that mice lacking Lyn develop a lupus-like syndrome, characterized by elevated serum immunoglobulin levels and by the production of autoantibodies that lead to GN [38–40]. The absence of Fyn seems to accelerate the Lyn deficiency phenotype, with mice deficient for both molecules developing extremely severe lupus GN [41].

Apoptosis is an important process in the maintenance of homeostasis in the immune system. Fas and FasL are both cell-surface proteins that play critical roles in the regulation of cell death. Their interaction with one another results in rapid apoptosis of cells that bear Fas. The role of the apoptotic process in maintaining tolerance has been demonstrated in mice that are homozygous for the mutations *lpr* [42] and *gld* [43] in the Fas and FasL genes, respectively. These mice spontaneously develop severe lymphadenopathy and produce T-cell-dependent autoantibodies, indicating that Fas and FasL are important in regulating T-cell tolerance.

A member of a family of anti-apoptotic genes, *Bcl2*, may also be involved in autoimmunity through its role in B-cell tolerance. Strasser *et al.* studied mice carrying a transgene for *Bcl2*, and they demonstrated that the mice have a large expansion of the B-cell compartment and spontaneously produce ANAs. A large percentage of them also develop lupus-like GN. It was determined through FACS analysis that this phenotype is not caused by the increased proliferation of B cells, but by their prolonged life spans [44].

Pathway 3

A third pathway in the development of lupus nephritis is comprised of genes that potentiate end-organ damage. When the loss of tolerance to chromatin and the continued production of autoantibodies due to a dysregulated immune system occurs, genes such as *Sle6* on chromosome 5 [24] and intracellular adhesion molecule-1 (ICAM-1) can target end-organ damage by the deposition of immune complexes and the subsequent recruitment of inflammatory mediators.

ICAM-1 is a member of the immunoglobulin superfamily of adhesion receptors and, through its interaction with the β_2 integrin LFA-1, it is believed to be involved in the recruitment of lymphocytes to the kidney. It has been demonstrated that ICAM-1 is upregulated in the kidneys from MRL/*lpr* and NZB/W mice when compared with normal mice [45]. MRL/*lpr* mice deficient in ICAM-1 show a reduction in renal disease, as well as a remarkable decrease in mortality [46]. The ICAM-1-deficient mice exhibited less vasculitis in the kidney, lung, skin, and salivary glands when compared with wild-type MRL/*lpr* mice, supporting the idea that ICAM-1 may play an important role in the pathogenesis of glomerular and vascular damage in these mice.

In addition to *Sle6* and ICAM-1, receptors for the IgG class of antibodies, which play a variety of complex roles in the immune system, also belong in the third pathway. There are three major classes of Fc gamma receptors present on cells of the immune system: FcγRI(CD64), FcγRII(CD32), and FcγRIII(CD16). Fc gamma receptors function in the noninflammatory clearance of immune complexes from the circulation by mononuclear phagocytes in the liver and spleen.

FcγRIIB has been found to be crucial to this process [47] and, in accordance with its role in antigen clearance, mice lacking this receptor have an increased susceptibility to collagen-induced arthritis and Goodpasture's syndrome, which are both immune complex mediated [48–50]. FcγRIIB-deficient mice spontaneously develop autoantibodies and GN in a strain-dependent manner [51]. Homotypic ligation of FcγRIIB on B cells sends a proapoptotic signal, and this process has been postulated to help in the maintenance of peripheral tolerance of B cells that have undergone somatic hypermutation. Follicular dendritic cells in germinal centers retain antigen in immune complexes through FcγRIIB. B cells that interact with the immune complex through both the B-cell receptor and FcγRIIB survive, whereas those that do not see the antigen through the B-cell receptor apoptose. This enables selection against those B cells that bear very low affinity, and therefore against potentially crossreactive antigen receptors, pointing to a protective regulatory role for FcγRIIB [52].

In contrast, FcγRIII seems to be more proinflammatory in function. It can cause degranulation, phagocytosis, antibody-dependent, cell-mediated cytotoxicity, and cytokine release on engagement, and it has been observed that the deletion of FcγRIII actually has a protective effect on end-organ damage in the autoimmune NZB/W strain. Mice lacking these FcγIII receptors still produce autoantibodies, deposit immune complexes, and activate complement, but do not develop lupus nephritis [53].

Given the large number of susceptibility loci detected by genome scans across various mouse strains, these three pathways help define a mechanistic order with which the pathogenesis of lupus occurs. Furthermore, identifying how a given disease gene functions via knockout and transgenic technology provides a better understanding of how the gene contributes to lupus and provides a better approach for therapeutic intervention.

Fine mapping of *Sle1* susceptibility loci

Linkage studies have provided a large collection of loci linked to susceptibility to lupus. It is also notable from Figure 1 that, although over 50 loci have been identified, there appears to be multiple loci on chromosomes 1, 4, 7, and 17 that have been identified in multiple studies. As mentioned previously, many of the loci colocalize to regions associated with other autoimmune diseases, strongly indicating that a certain locus is involved in autoimmunity. Furthermore, it is also becoming evident that an individual locus may actually be a cluster of loci that are associated with a spectrum of phenotypes, as in the case with the *Sle1* locus. Fine mapping of the NZW-derived *Sle1* locus revealed that it consists of at least four closely linked, functionally related genes that can each cause a break in tolerance to chromatin: *Sle1a*, *Sle1b*, *Sle1c*, and *Sle1d*. Analysis of recombinant mice carrying the first three of these loci showed that these subcongenic intervals are associated with phenotypes that are very similar to each other and to the overall *Sle1* phenotype, but are subtly different from one another [54].

Sle1a is an approximately 1 cM interval that is associated with the production of ANAs specific for H2A/H2B/DNA, but is not associated with increased CD69 or B7.2 expression. Mice of this strain have reduced numbers of T cells, and a moderate increase in B220+ cells. The CD4+ T cells have a more activated phenotype than in B6 mice, and there is a higher proportion of cells with a memory phenotype. There is an increased IgG, but not IgM, response to ovalbumin immunization. Thus, when isolated from the other subcongenic loci, *Sle1a* was found to have phenotypes that were masked in the entire *Sle1* interval.

The 0.4 cM *Sle1b* locus has the highest penetrance of ANA production of the three subcongenic mouse strains, with the same subnucleosomal specificity as that of the entire interval. It also has the earliest age of onset of autoantibody production. *Sle1b* is the only subinterval to exhibit the female gender bias seen in *Sle1* and to have an increase in total IgM and IgG levels over B6. It also shows the increased expression of CD69 and B7.2 seen in *Sle1*, suggesting that it is the strongest contributor to the overall phenotype of the chromosome 1 interval. The combination of *Sle1a* with *Sle1b* was equivalent to the entire *Sle1* interval with respect to ANA production, whereas the region between the two loci by itself did not produce an autoimmune phenotype above background levels. This would indicate that the two loci together have a synergistic effect, which is not caused by a gene that lies in the interval between them [54].

The *Sle1c* locus is an approximately 3 cM interval. Unlike *Sle1a* and *Sle1b*, *Sle1c* does not show specificity for any one component of chromatin and shows no difference from B6 in IgM response or IgG response to ovalbumin immunization. *Sle1c* does not have an increased level of activation markers CD69 and B7.2, but it has an increased proportion of CD4+ T cells with a memory phenotype.

It has been shown that B6 mice and NZW mice have different alleles of the *Cr2* gene, which lies within the *Sle1c* locus. This gene encodes the complement receptors 1 and 2 as separate splice variants. Complement receptors 1 and 2 bind antigen-bound degradation products of the complement components C3 and C4. SLE patients have lower levels of these receptors on their B cells [55], as do MRL/*lpr* mice, prior to disease onset [56]. This indicates that lowered expression of these receptors may play a role in pathogenesis. One of the single nucleotide polymorphisms between the B6 and NZW alleles of Cr2 occurs in the ligand-binding domain and introduces a novel glycosylation site in the NZW allele. This results in lower ligand-binding affinity, probably by interfering with receptor dimerization. Complement receptor 1/complement receptor 2-mediated signaling is lower in B cells carrying this allele, and cells are also impaired in their response to T-dependent antigens [57]. It has been shown that complement receptors may play an important role in maintaining both central and peripheral B-cell tolerance [58]. Hence, the lowered functioning of these receptors may allow autoreactive B cells to escape tolerance, leading to the ANA production phenotype.

Congenic dissection has also been applied to the *Nba2* locus, which maps to the same region on chromosome 1 as does *Sle1*. This NZB-derived region of about 8 cM is contained in the 30 cM congenic interval in the B6.*Nba2* congenic strain. Females of this strain develop IgG antibodies to chromatin, to double-stranded DNA, and to total histones. When crossed with NZW, female (B6.*Nba2*X-NZW)F1 mice develop ANAs and proteinuria, and they die from nephritis with a high frequency. This again points to the possibility that the loss of tolerance to the chromatin pathway may be an initiating factor in overall disease development. Microarray analysis carried out on spleen cells of preautoimmune mice of the congenic strain showed that, of 11,000 genes analyzed, two interferon-responsive genes belonging to the Ifi200 gene cluster showed a highly significant difference in expression from B6 spleen cells. Both of these genes mapped within the *Nba2* locus. Ifi202, which inhibits apoptosis when overexpressed and may play a role in transcriptional regulation [36], was expressed at much higher levels in B6.*Nba2* spleens, while Ifi203 was expressed at lower levels. It has been postulated that either molecule could underlie the *Nba2* phenotype, which may be found to correlate with additional genes within the same locus as well, as in the case of *Sle1* [59].

The region of mouse chromosome 1 that contains *Sle1* and *Nba2* has consistently been implicated in studies of murine models of systemic autoimmunity [12,60]. Other loci that map here include NZB-derived *Lbw7* and SWR-derived *Swrl-1*. Significantly, the human region syntenic to the telomeric region of chromosome 1 where this cluster of murine susceptibility loci lies (1q22–1q44) has also been linked to lupus susceptibility in genome wide scans using a variety of ethnic groups [7–9,61]. Advances made in identifying the susceptibility genes in this region could yield valuable insights into the checks and balances that usually operate in the immune system, which when they fail can result in a breach in tolerance to self-antigens, initiating an autoimmune cascade.

Concluding remarks

The inheritance of lupus susceptibility is undoubtedly complex and, although numerous susceptibility loci have so far been identified, piecing them together into a meaningful pathway that illustrates the pathogenesis of the disease is very difficult. It is becoming evident through congenic dissection that there is a strong genetic interaction among multiple loci that leads to the expression of disease. A hypothetical model, containing three biologically distinct pathways, has been constructed that outlines these genetic interactions and illustrates the progression of lupus. The mechanisms within these pathways are still poorly understood, however, and further work remains to fully elucidate the pathogenesis of SLE.

Glossary of terms

ANA = antinuclear autoantibody; BLyS = B-lymphocyte stimulator; FasL = Fas ligand; GN = glomerulonephritis; SAP = serum amyloid P component; SLE = systemic lupus erythematosus; *Sles* = SLE suppressor.

Funds for research

Organizations that provide funding for research in this field include the Alliance for Lupus Research, the SLE Foundation, the Arthritis Foundation, and the National Institutes of Health.

References

1. Blatt NB, Glick GD: **Anti-DNA autoantibodies and systemic lupus erythematosus.** *Pharmacol Ther* 1999, **33**:125-139. [general reference]
2. Kotzin BL: **Systemic lupus erythematosus.** *Cell* 1996, **85**:303-306. [general reference]
3. Sullivan KE: **Genetics of systemic lupus erythematosus. Clinical implications.** *Rheum Dis Clin North Am* 2000, **26**:229. [general reference]
4. Kotzin BL, O'Dell JR: **Systemic lupus erythematosus.** In *Samter's Immunologic Diseases.* Edited by Frank MM, Austen KF, Claman HN, Unanue ER. Boston, MA: Little, Brown & Co; 1995:667-697. [general reference]
5. Johnson GC, Todd JA: **Strategies in complex disease mapping.** *Curr Opin Genet Dev* 2000, **10**:330-334. [general reference]
6. Lindqvist AK, Alarcon-Riquelme ME: **The genetics of systemic lupus erythematosus.** *Scand J Immunol* 1999, **50**:562-571. [key review]
7. Gaffney PM, Kearns GM, Shark KB, Ortmann WA, Selby SA, Malmgren ML, Rohlf KE, Ockenden TC, Messner RP, Rich S, Behrens TW: **A genome-wide search for susceptibility genes in human systemic lupus erythematosus sib-pair families.** *Proc Natl Acad Sci USA* 1998, **95**:14875-14879. [general reference]
8. Moser KL, Neas BR, Salmon JE, Yu H, Gray-McGuire C, Asundi N, Bruner GR, Fox J, Kelly J, Henshall S, Bacino D, Dietz M, Hogue R, Koelsch G, Nightingale L, Shayer T, Abdou NI, Albert A, Carson C, Petri M, Treadwell EL, James JA, Harley JB: **Genome scan of human systemic lupus erythematosus: evidence for linkage on chromosome 1q in African-American pedigrees.** *Proc Natl Acad Sci USA* 1998, **95**:14869-14874. [general reference]
9. Shai R, Quismorio F Jr, Li L, Kwon O-J, Morrison J, Wallace D, Neuwelt C, Brautbar C, Gauderman W, Jacob CO: **Genome-wide screen for systemic lupus erythematosus susceptibility genes in multiplex families.** *Hum Mol Genet* 1999, **8**:639-644. [general reference]
10. Vyse TJ, Rozzo SJ, Drake CG, Izui S, Kotzin BL: **Control of multiple autoantibodies linked with a lupus nephritis susceptibility locus in New Zealand black mice.** *J Immunol* 1997, **158**:5566-5574. [general reference]
11. Risch N: **Searching for genes in complex diseases: lessons from systemic lupus erythematosus [comment].** *J Clin Invest* 2000, **105**:1503-1506. [general reference]
12. Vyse TJ, Kotzin BL: **Genetic susceptibility to systemic lupus erythematosus.** *Annu Rev Immunol* 1998, **16**:261-292. [key review]
13. Wakeland EK, Liu K, Graham RR, Behrens TW: **Delineating the genetic basis of systemic lupus erythematosus.** *Immunity* 2001; **15**:397-408. [key review]
14. Mohan C: **Murine lupus genetics: lessons learned.** *Curr Opin Rheumatol* 2001, **13**:352-360. [key review]
15. Morel L, Wakeland EK: **Susceptibility to lupus nephritis in the NZB/W model system.** *Curr Opin Immunol* 1998, **10**:718-725. [key review]
16. Xie S, Chang SH, Yang P, Jacob C, Kaliyaperumal A, Datta SK, Mohan C: **Genetic contributions of nonautoimmune SWR mice to lupus nephritis.** *J Immunol* 2001, **167**:7141-7149. [general reference]
17. Marrack P, Kappler J, Kotzin BL: **Autoimmune disease: why and where it occurs.** *Nat Med* 2001, **7**:899-905. [general reference]
18. Morel L, Wakeland EK: **Lessons from the NZM2410 model and related strains.** *Int Rev Immunol* 2000, **19**:423-446. [key review]
19. Morel L, Mohan C, Croker BP, Tian X-H, Wakeland EK: **Functional dissection of systemic lupus erythematosus using congenic mouse strains.** *J Immunol* 1997, **158**:6019-6028. [general reference]
20. Mohan C, Alas E, Morel L, Yang P, Wakeland EK: **Genetic dissection of SLE pathogenesis: *Sle1* on murine chromosome 1 leads to a selective loss of tolerance to H2A/H2B/DNA subnucelosomes.** *J Clin Invest* 1998, **101**:1362-1372. [general reference]
21. Mohan C, Morel L, Yang P, Wakeland EK: **Genetic dissection of SLE pathogenesis: *Sle2* on murine chromosome 4 leads to B-cell hyperactivity.** *J Immunol* 1997, **159**:454-465. [general reference]
22. Mohan C, Yu Y, Morel L, Yang P, Wakeland EK: **Genetic dissection of SLE pathogenicity: *Sle3* on murine chromosome 7 impacts T cell activation, differentiation, and cell death.** *J Immunol* 1999, **162**:6492-6502. [general reference]
23. Morel L, Croker BP, Blenman KR, Mohan C, Huang G, Gilkeson G, Wakeland EK: **Genetic reconstitution of systemic lupus erythematosus immunopathology with polycongenic murine strains.** *Proc Natl Acad Sci USA* 2000, **97**:6670-6675. [general reference]
24. Morel L, Tian X-H, Croker BP, Wakeland EK: **Epistatic modifiers of autoimmunity in a murine model of lupus nephritis.** *Immunity* 1999, **11**:131-139. [general reference]
25. Bickerstaff MC, Botto M, Hutchinson WL, Herbert J, Tennent GA, Bybee A, Mitchell DA, Cook HT, Butler PJ, Walport MJ, Pepys MB: **Serum amyloid P component controls chromatin degradation and prevents antinuclear autoimmunity.** *Nat Med* 1999, **5**:694-697. [general reference]
26. Botto M, Dell'Agnola C, Bygrave AE, Thompson EM, Cook HT, Petry F, Loos M, Pandolfi P, Walport MJ: **Homozygous C1q deficiency causes glomerulonephritis associated with multiple apoptotic bodies.** *Nat Genet* 1998, **19**:56-59. [general reference]
27. Chen Z, Koralov SB, Kelsoe G: **Complement C4 inhibits systemic autoimmunity through a mechanism independent of

complement receptors CR1 and CR2. *J Exp Med* 2000, **192:**1339-1351. [general reference]

28. Napirei M, Karsunky H, Zevnik B, Stephan H, Mannherz HG, Moroy T: **Features of systemic lupus erythematosus in Dnase1-deficient mice.** *Nat Genet* 2000, **25:**177-181. [general reference]

29. Macanovic M, Sinicropi D, Shak S, Baughman S, Thiru S, Lachmann PJ: **The treatment of systemic lupus erythematosus (SLE) in NZB/W F1 hybrid mice; studies with recombinant murine DNase and with dexamethasone.** *Clin Exp Immunol* 1996, **106:**243-252. [general reference]

30. Waterhouse P, Penninger JM, Timms E, Wakeham A, Shahinian A, Lee KP, Thompson CB, Griesser H, Mak TW: **Lymphoproliferative disorders with early lethality in mice deficient in Ctla-4.** *Science* 2002, **270:**985-988. [general reference]

31. Finck BK, Linsley PS, Wofsy D: **Treatment of murine lupus with CTLA4Ig.** *Science* 1994, **265:**1225-1227. [general reference]

32. Balomenos D, Martin-Caballero J, Garcia MI, Prieto I, Flores JM, Serrano M, Martinez A: **The cell cycle inhibitor p21 controls T-cell proliferation and sex-linked lupus development.** *Nat Med* 2000, **6:**171-176. [general reference]

33. Nishimura H, Nose M, Hiai H, Minato N, Honjo T: **Development of lupus-like autoimmune diseases by disruption of the PD-1 gene encoding an ITIM motif-carrying immunoreceptor.** *Immunity* 1999, **11:**141-151. [general reference]

34. Do RK, Chen-Kiang S: **Mechanism of BLyS action in B cell immunity.** *Cytokin Growth Factor Rev* 2002, **1:**19-25. [general reference]

35. Mackay F, Woodcock SA, Lawton P, Ambrose C, Baetscher M, Schneider P, Tschopp J, Browning JL: **Mice transgenic for BAFF develop lymphocytic disorders along with autoimmune manifestations.** *J Exp Med* 1999, **190:**1697-1710. [general reference]

36. Khare SD, Sarosi I, Xia XZ, McCabe S, Miner K, Solovyev I, Hawkins N, Kelley M, Chang D, Van G, Ross L, Delaney J, Wang L, Lacey D, Boyle WJ, Hsu H: **Severe B cell hyperplasia and autoimmune disease in TALL-1 transgenic mice.** *Proc Natl Acad Sci USA* 2000, **97:**3370-3375. [general reference]

37. Gross JA, Johnston J, Mudri S, Enselman R, Dillon SR, Madden K, Xu W, Parrish-Novak J, Foster D, Lofton-Day C, Moore M, Littau A, Grossman A, Haugen H, Foley K, Blumberg H, Harrison K, Kindsvogel W, Clegg CH: **TACI and BCMA are receptors for a TNF homologue implicated in B-cell autoimmune disease.** *Nature* 2000, **404:**995-999. [general reference]

38. Chan VW, Meng F, Soriano P, DeFranco AL, Lowell CA: **Characterization of the B lymphocyte populations in Lyn-deficient mice and the role of Lyn in signal initiation and down-regulation.** *Immunity* 1997, **7:**69-81. [general reference]

39. Hibbs ML, Tarlinton DM, Armes J, Grail D, Hodgson G, Maglitto R, Stacker SA, Dunn AR: **Multiple defects in the immune system of Lyn-deficient mice, culminating in autoimmune disease.** *Cell* 1995, **83:**301-311. [general reference]

40. Nishizumi H, Taniuchi I, Yamanashi Y, Kitamura D, Ilic D, Mori S, Watanabe T, Yamamoto T: **Impaired proliferation of peripheral B cells and indication of autoimmune disease in lyn-deficient mice.** *Immunity* 1995, **3:**549-560. [general reference]

41. Yu CC, Yen TS, Lowell CA, DeFranco AL: **Lupus-like kidney disease in mice deficient in the Src family tyrosine kinases Lyn and Fyn.** *Curr Biol* 2001, **11:**34-38. [general reference]

42. Watanabe-Fukunaga R, Brannan CI, Copeland NG, Jenkins NA, Nagata S: **Lymphoproliferation disorder in mice explained by defects in Fas antigen that mediates apoptosis.** *Nature* 1992, **356:**314-317. [general reference]

43. Takahashi T, Tanaka M, Brannan CI, Jenkins NA, Copeland NG, Suda T, Nagata S: **Generalized lymphoproliferative disease in mice, caused by a point mutation in the Fas ligand.** *Cell* 1994, **76:**969-976. [general reference]

44. Strasser A, Whittingham S, Vaux DL, Bath ML, Adams JM, Cory S, Harris AW: **Enforced BCL2 expression in B-lymphoid cells prolongs antibody responses and elicits autoimmune disease.** *Proc Natl Acad Sci* 1991, **88:**8661-8665. [general reference]

45. Wuthrich RP, Jevnikar AM, Takei F, Glimcher LH, Kelley VE: **Inter-cellular adhesion molecule-1 (ICAM-1) expression is upregulated in autoimmune murine lupus nephritis.** *Am J Pathol* 1990, **136:**441-450. [general reference]

46. Bullard DC, King PD, Hicks MJ, Dupont B, Beaudet AL, Elkon KB: **Intercellular adhesion molecule-1 deficiency protects**

MRL/MpJ-Fas(lpr) mice from early lethality. *J Immunol* 1997, **159:**2058-2067. [general reference]

47. Dijstelbloem HM, van de Winkel J, Kallenberg CG: **Inflammation in autoimmunity: receptors for IgG revisited.** *Trends Immunol* 2001, **22:**510-516. [general reference]

48. Yuasa T, Kubo S, Yoshino T, Ujike A, Matsumura K, Ono M, Ravetch JV, Takai T: **Deletion of fcgamma receptor IIB renders H-2(b) mice susceptible to collagen-induced arthritis.** *J Exp Med* 1999, **189:**187-194. [general reference]

49. Kleinau S, Martinsson P, Heyman B: **Induction and suppression of collagen-induced arthritis is dependent on distinct fcgamma receptors.** *J Exp Med* 2000, **191:**1611-1616. [general reference]

50. Qu WM, Miyazaki T, Terada M, Lu LM, Nishihara M, Yamada A, Mori S, Nakamura Y, Ogasawara H, Yazawa C, Nakatsuru S, Nose M: **Genetic dissection of vasculitis in MRL/lpr lupus mice: a novel susceptibility locus involving the CD72c allele.** *Eur J Immunol* 2000, **30:**2027-2037. [general reference]

51. Bolland S, Ravetch JV: **Spontaneous autoimmune disease in Fc(gamma)RIIB-deficient mice results from strain-specific epistasis.** *Immunity* 2000, **13:**277-285. [general reference]

52. Ravetch JV, Lanier LL: **Immune inhibitory receptors.** *Science* 2000, **290:**84-89. [key review]

53. Clynes R, Dumitru C, Ravetch JV: **Uncoupling of immune complex formation and kidney damage in autoimmune glomerulonephritis.** *Science* 1998, **279:**1052-1054. [general reference]

54. Morel L, Blenman KR, Croker BP, Wakeland EK: **The major murine systemic lupus erythematosus susceptibility locus, Sle1, is a cluster of functionally related genes.** *Proc Natl Acad Sci USA* 2001, **98:**1787-1792. [general reference]

55. Wilson JG, Ratnoff WD, Schur PH, Fearon DT: **Decreased expression of the C3b/C4b receptor (CR1) and the C3d receptor (CR2) on B lymphocytes and of CR1 on neutrophils of patients with systemic lupus erythematosus.** *Arthritis Rheum* 1986, **29:**739-747. [general reference]

56. Takahashi K, Kozono Y, Waldschmidt TJ, Quigg RJ, Baron A, Holers VM: **Mouse complement receptors type 1 (CR1;CD35) and type 2 (CR2;CD21): expression on normal B cell subpopulations and decreased levels during the development of autoimmunity in MRL/lpr mice.** *J Immunol* 1997, **159:**1557-1569. [general reference]

57. Boackle SA, Holers VM, Chen X, Szakonyi G, Karp D, Wakeland EK, Morel L: **Cr2, a candidate gene in the murine Sle1c lupus susceptibility locus, encodes a dysfunctional protein.** *Immunity* 2002, **15:**785. [general reference]

58. Prodeus AP, Goerg S, Shen LM, Pozdnyakova OO, Chu L, Alicot EM, Goodnow CC, Carroll MC: **A critical role for complement in maintenance of self-tolerance.** *Immunity* 1998, **9:**721-731. [general reference]

59. Rozzo SJ, Allard JD, Choubey D, Vyse TJ, Izui S, Peltz G, Kotzin BL: **Evidence for an interferon-inducible gene, Ifi202, in the susceptibility to systemic lupus.** *Immunity* 2001, **15:**435-443. [general reference]

60. Wakeland EK, Wandstrat AE, Liu K, Morel L: **Genetic dissection of systemic lupus erythematosus.** *Curr Opin Immunol* 1999, **11:**701-707. [key review]

61. Tsao BP, Cantor RM, Kalunian C, Chen C-J, Badsha H, Singh R, Wallace DJ, Kitridou RC, Chen S, Shen N, Song YW, Isenberg DA, Yu C-L, Hahn BH, Rotter JI: **Evidence for linkage of a candidate chromosome 1 region to human systemic lupus erythematosus.** *J Clin Invest* 1997, **99:**725-731. [general reference]

62. Rahman ZS, Tin SK, Buenaventura PN, Ho CH, Yap EP, Yong RY, Koh DR: **A novel susceptibility locus on chromosome 2 in the (New Zealand Black x New Zealand White)F1 hybrid mouse model of systemic lupus erythematosus.** *J Immunol* 2002, **168:**3042-3049. [general reference]

63. Xie S, Chang S, Yang P, Jacob C, Kaliyaperumal A, Datta SK, Mohan C: **Genetic contributions of nonautoimmune SWR mice toward lupus nephritis.** *J Immunol* 2001, **167:**7141-7149. [general reference]

Supplement Review
Epidemiology and genetics of rheumatoid arthritis
Alan J Silman and Jacqueline E Pearson

ARC Epidemiology Unit, School of Epidemiology & Health Sciences, University of Manchester, Manchester, UK

Correspondence: Alan J Silman, ARC Epidemiology Unit, School of Epidemiology & Health Sciences, University of Manchester, Room 2.514, Stopford Building, Oxford Road, Manchester M13 9PT, UK. Tel: +44 161 275 5041; fax: +44 161 275 5043; e-mail: alan.silman@man.ac.uk; departmental website: http://www.arc.man.ac.uk

Received: 27 February 2002
Accepted: 13 March 2002
Published: 9 May 2002

Arthritis Res 2002, **4 (suppl 3)**:S265-S272

This article may contain supplementary data which can only be found online at http://arthritis-research.com/content/4/S3/S265

© 2002 BioMed Central Ltd
(Print ISSN 1465-9905; Online ISSN 1465-9913)

Chapter summary

The prevalence of rheumatoid arthritis (RA) is relatively constant in many populations, at 0.5–1.0%. However, a high prevalence of RA has been reported in the Pima Indians (5.3%) and in the Chippewa Indians (6.8%). In contrast, low occurrences have been reported in populations from China and Japan. These data support a genetic role in disease risk. Studies have so far shown that the familial recurrence risk in RA is small compared with other autoimmune diseases. The main genetic risk factor of RA is the HLA DRB1 alleles, and this has consistently been shown in many populations throughout the world. The strongest susceptibility factor so far has been the HLA DRB1*0404 allele. Tumour necrosis factor alleles have also been linked with RA. However, it is estimated that these genes can explain only 50% of the genetic effect. A number of other non-MHC genes have thus been investigated and linked with RA (e.g. corticotrophin releasing hormone, oestrogen synthase, IFN-γ and other cytokines). Environmental factors have also been studied in relation to RA. Female sex hormones may play a protective role in RA; for example, the use of the oral contraceptive pill and pregnancy are both associated with a decreased risk. However, the postpartum period has been highlighted as a risk period for the development of RA. Furthermore, breastfeeding after a first pregnancy poses the greatest risk. Exposure to infection may act as a trigger for RA, and a number of agents have been implicated (e.g. Epstein–Barr virus, parvovirus and some bacteria such as *Proteus* and *Mycoplasma*). However, the epidemiological data so far are inconclusive. There has recently been renewed interest in the link between cigarette smoking and RA, and the data presented so far are consistent with and suggestive of an increased risk.

Keywords: environment, family studies, HLA, occurrence, rheumatoid arthritis

Introduction
This chapter reviews recent epidemiological data on the relative contributions of genetic and environmental risk factors for the development of RA. It considers and proposes the direct and indirect evidence to the contribution of various risk factors for disease susceptibility. The quality of the evidence varies and, where appropriate, this is highlighted.

Genetic factors
Descriptive epidemiology of RA
The descriptive epidemiology of RA is suggestive of a genetic effect. The occurrence of RA is relatively constant with a prevalence of between 0.5 and 1.0%, a frequency that has been reported from several European [1–8] and North-American populations [9,10]. However, there are some interesting exceptions (Fig. 1).

A list of common abbreviations used in this issue appears just before the indexes.

Figure 1

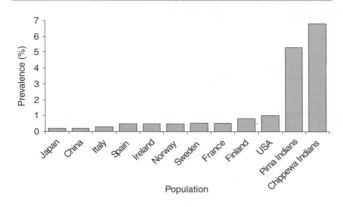

Prevalence of rheumatoid arthritis in various populations. Data from [1–4,6–9,11,12,16,17].

Specifically, native American-Indian populations have the highest recorded occurrence of RA, with a prevalence of 5.3% noted for the Pima Indians [11] and of 6.8% for the Chippewa Indians [12]. By contrast, there are a number of groups with a very low occurrence. Studies in rural African populations, both in South Africa [13] and in Nigeria [14], failed to find any RA cases in studies of 500 and 2000 adults, respectively. Studies in populations from Southeast Asia [15], including China and Japan [16,17], have similarly shown very low occurrences (0.2–0.3%).

'Migrant' studies

It is clearly difficult from a review of the descriptive epidemiological data to know whether environmental or genetic effects explain the differences between countries. One handle on this is to consider the occurrence in populations presumed to be of the same genetic origin but living in different environments. Such a situation arises by studying populations that have moved from one environment to another.

There are a few studies addressing this with respect to RA. A low occurrence of disease was found in one study of a Caribbean population of African origin living in Manchester, UK, suggesting that the protection to this group was indeed genetically determined [18]. Similarly, the investigation of a Chinese population living in an urban environment in Hong Kong showed the same consistent low frequency [19]. Recent data have shown, however, that Pakistanis living in England had a higher prevalence than those in Pakistan, but it is not as high as the prevalence in ethnic English populations [20]. In general, the data on the geographical occurrence of RA would support the existence of genetic factors being important and explaining differences in disease risk.

Familial clustering

The next stage in accruing evidence for genetic risk is to document an increased occurrence of disease in relatives of probands compared with the background population prevalence, so-called familial recurrence risk. Studies of hospital attendees are subject to bias as there may be a selection process whereby individuals would more probably be referred to hospital if they have an affected family member. Furthermore, several studies rely on family history as elicited by the proband, which again is subject to bias.

Few studies have been performed comparing familial recurrence risk in relatives of cases derived from population samples with those of controls. Indeed, such studies have only shown a modest increased risk [21,22]. For example, a study from the Norfolk Arthritis Register in England showed only a twofold increased risk [23]. Such an observation does not negate the role of genetic factors, but underscores that their contribution to explain disease susceptibility may be modest. This is important as the familial recurrence risk is a key factor in determining the power of genetic linkage studies within affected family pairs. Indeed, in contrast to other autoimmune diseases such as insulin-dependent diabetes and multiple sclerosis, the familial recurrence risk in RA is certainly smaller, thereby making it harder for studies to identify new genetic factors.

Twin studies

A variant of studies of familial recurrence risk is the comparison of disease risk in the initially unaffected co-twin of monozygotic probands compared with dizygotic probands. The assumption is that the environmental sharing between these different twin pair types is the same and thus any increased disease concordance in the monozygotic twins confirms the genetic effect. It is important in such studies to ensure that it is only like-sexed dizygotic twin pairs that are compared with the monozygotic twin pairs. However, there may be a greater environmental concordance in monozygotic twins due, for example, to psychological and other factors.

Twin studies have consistently showed a fourfold increased concordance in monozygotic twins compared with dizygotic twins [24]. This increased risk, however, is of little value in attempting to quantify the genetic contribution to disease risk. The concordance between twins is dependent on the prevalence of disease. As the population prevalence approaches 100%, the concordance will increase accordingly, independent of the true genetic effect. The appropriate way of quantifying genetic risk is to assess the heritability based on a series of assumptions of environmental sharing and genetic sharing between twin types. Such a study has recently been attempted using data from both Finnish and English twins [24]. The results suggest that approximately 50–60% of the occurrence of disease in the twins is explained by shared genetic effects.

Table 1

Phenotype frequencies of HLA DRB1

HLA DRB1 phenotype	Controls ($n = 286$)	Cases ($n = 680$)	Odds ratio (95% confidence interval)
*0101/2	62	155	1.0 (0.8–1.5)
*04	100	306	1.5 (1.1–2.0)
*0401	63	204	1.5 (1.1–2.1)
*0404	10	77	3.5 (1.8–6.8)
*0405/8/9	5	19	1.6 (0.6–4.3)
*1001	3	17	2.4 (0.8–7.8)
SE+	127	400	1.8 (1.4–2.4)

SE+, shared epitope positive. Data from [32].

Genetic susceptibility factors: human leukocyte antigen

The role of HLA DRB1 alleles as a risk factor of RA has been known for 25 years. Associations between different HLA DRB1 alleles have been demonstrated in several populations across the world [25–31]. Indeed, there have been few populations where associations have not been demonstrated.

Interestingly, there do appear to be differences in the strength of association between different alleles. For example, HLA DRB1*0404 is a much stronger susceptibility factor than HLA DRB1*0101 [32] (Table 1). Although it has been suggested that the susceptibility alleles all share a single epitope [33], it is difficult to explain the variable risk under this model. Furthermore, the risk of disease is related not only to the presence of one single allele, but also to the full HLA DRB1 genotype [34]. Individuals who carry the so-called 'compound heterozygote' genotype HLA DRB*0401/*0404 thus have a substantially greater risk than, for example, individuals who carry single HLA DRB*0101 alleles.

There is some suggestion that the relationship between human leukocyte antigen (HLA) and RA may be more related to the severity of disease, and that the development of arthritis *per se* is only weakly related. Support for this comes from studies from the Norfolk Arthritis Register population-based study of inflammatory joint disease in England [32]. Data from this study show only a weak relationship between susceptibility to the disease and the HLA DRB1 genotype (Table 1). The association is fairly strong in those individuals who satisfy the criteria for RA. The data show there is an influence of genotype, with some genotypes having a stronger association as shown.

The HLA region on the short arm of chromosome 6 is a gene-rich area including several candidate genes that have an influence on the immune process. One of the most highly investigated is tumour necrosis factor (TNF). Studies have shown associations between TNF alleles and RA [35,36], although one explanation may be linkage disequilibrium with HLA DRB1. Studies have also suggested, however, that the associations between HLA and TNF-c1 and TNF-b3 are independent of associations between HLA and the shared epitope [37]. Other studies have shown an extended haplotype stretching from HLA through to TNF that has been implicated in disease [38].

Genetic susceptibility factors: non-MHC genes

Data from twin studies in the HLA association and sharing studies have been used to estimate that only 50% of the genetic contribution to RA can be explained by HLA [24]. This has sparked a search for non-MHC genes.

The largest effort has been expanded in some whole genome screens on affected sibling pair families. Four such screens have now been undertaken in Europe [39], the United States [33], Japan [40] and the United Kingdom [41]. A number of markers emerge from these studies suggestive of a linkage with RA, although the linkage with HLA is by far the strongest. One problem is that such studies often have only a weak power to detect defects. By contrast, because such studies may be simultaneously testing the possibility that any one of 200 regions may be linked with disease, the likelihood of a false-positive result is also very high. It is for this reason that it is not surprising studies often fail to replicate results both between themselves and on further samples within the population. It is therefore necessary to undertake further validation studies and more in-depth investigations, using more closely spaced markers.

An alternative approach is to use a candidate gene screen where there is no prior reason for looking at a particular region. Such an approach has been productive, and evidence has shown that corticotrophin releasing hormone [42], CYP19 (oestrogen synthase) [43], IFN-γ [44–46] and other cytokines [47–49] are linked to RA. Other approaches have addressed the possibility that genetic regions linked to other autoimmune diseases, such as insulin-dependent diabetes [50], may also be linked to RA. Indeed, linkage to a locus on chromosome X was shown in one study [51]. A further strategy has been to use results and genome screens on animal models of arthritis to see whether syntenic regions are also linked to RA in humans. Such studies have suggested linkage to 17q22 [52].

Whether any of these positive findings discussed will result in the identification of a true disease susceptibility mutation remains to be seen. However, one clear problem is that RA itself is probably heterogeneous and studies that fail to take notice of this heterogeneity may make it possible to find a positive result.

Figure 2

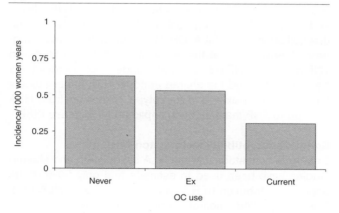

The incidence of rheumatoid arthritis in relation to use of the oral contraceptive pill (OC). Data from the Royal College of General Practioners' oral contraception study [54].

Figure 3

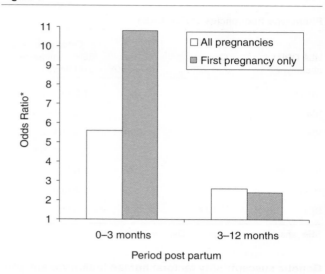

Increased risk of rheumatoid arthritis onset in the postpartum period. * Relative to nonpregnant periods. Data from [59].

Environmental factors

The term 'environment' is frequently used to describe all those susceptibility factors leading to disease that are not explicable on the basis of an identifiable genetic marker. In a strict sense, however, environment could be taken to refer to those factors external to the individual; for example, factors associated with diet, water or air-borne exposures. It is also important to consider factors implicated with diseases that are internal to the subject without an obvious genetic basis. An appropriate term for this group of factors is 'nongenetic host factors'.

Nongenetic host factors: hormonal and pregnancy factors

The increased risk of RA in females has lead to considerable effort in examining the role of hormonal and pregnancy factors in disease occurrence. In general, male sex hormones, particularly testosterone, are lower in men who have RA [25]. By contrast, levels of female sex hormones are not different between RA cases and controls [53].

Interestingly, exogenous hormonal influences are implicated in disease risk. The most widely studied of these is exposure to the oral contraceptive pill, based on an observation made over 20 years ago [54] (Fig. 2). There have been several studies [55] confirming that women who take the oral contraceptive pill are at reduced risk of developing RA [25]. There is no clear explanation for this and the association exists despite the formulation of the oral contraceptive pill varying enormously both between populations and over time. A follow-up of the original study was undertaken that suggested the oral contraceptive pill was protective. This showed that the initial protection was lost on follow-up [56]. One conclusion might therefore be that oral contraceptive use may postpone, rather than totally protect against, the development of RA.

Pregnancy itself has been investigated as a risk factor in RA development. Studies on the influence of pregnancy on RA have produced conflicting results. A number of studies [25] have suggested that women who are nulliparous are at increased risk of developing the disease, although there is no increased risk in women who are single [57]. It would thus appear that subfertility highlights a group at higher risk.

Recent studies have suggested that pregnancy might also be important with the interesting observation that the postpartum period, particularly after the first pregnancy, represents a strong risk period of disease development [58,59] (Fig. 3). Subsequent investigations showed that much of this increased risk could be explained by exposure to breastfeeding and it is women who breastfeed after their first pregnancy who are at the greatest risk [60]. The suggestion then arose linking breastfeeding with subfertility in so far as RA may be related to either increased prolactin or abnormal response to prolactin, this latter hormone being proinflammatory [61].

Nongenetic host factors: other

There have been a number of studies looking at other comorbidities that have an increased frequency in both subjects with RA and in their families. The most widely investigated has been the occurrence of other autoimmune diseases, particularly type 1 or insulin-dependent diabetes and autoimmune thyroid disease [62]. Other diseases, for example schizophrenia, have been shown to be negatively associated with RA development [63–65]. The significance of these findings is unclear.

There have been relatively few studies on anthropometric factors associated with RA, although one recent case–control study suggested that people who were obese were at higher risk [66]. The reason for this is unclear, and it is not certain whether this may represent a confounding factor of another exposure or whether people who are obese have, for example, increased production of oestrogens, which might pose a risk. A more recent case–control study found, however, after adjusting for age, smoking and marital status, that a link with obesity was nonsignificant [67].

Environmental factors: infection
Indirect evidence
There is much indirect evidence suggesting that exposure to infectious agents may be the trigger for RA. First, epidemiological data come from the observation of a decline in the incidence of RA in several populations [9,16]. Many studies have indeed shown a halving in incidence over the past 30 years [68]. Given the genetically stable population, the most probable explanation is that of a decline in an infectious trigger. This effect of time on occurrence might also be related to the period of birth as well as to the current year of observations. The Pima Indians, for example, showed a decline in occurrence of disease, and an in-depth study based on analysis of birth cohorts has shown a decline in the population occurrence of rheumatoid factor with increasingly recent birth cohorts [69].

There have been a few studies looking at clustering of RA in time and space, although there have been reports of nonrandom clusters occurring within the Norfolk Arthritis Register population [70]. Other indirect evidence regarding the role of an infectious agent has arisen from case–control studies suggesting that people who have had a blood transfusion, even some years prior to disease onset, may be at an increased risk of disease [66]. Recent practice has been to screen blood for a number of agents such as hepatitis, but the increased reporting of blood transfusion in older cohorts may indeed be explained by the increased likelihood of infection.

Possible infectious agents
There have been a large number of infectious agents that have been implicated in RA, including Epstein–Barr virus and parvovirus, as well as other agents, including bacteria such as *Proteus* and *Mycoplasma*. The epidemiological studies supporting or refuting these possible links are reviewed elsewhere [25] but, in general, such studies have been disappointing. One problem for the epidemiologist is that if RA represents the final common pathway of exposure to one of several different potential susceptibility organisms, many of which are also frequently observed in the general (i.e. nonarthritic population), it makes it more difficult to confirm a relationship with epidemiological studies.

Table 2

Summary of recent epidemiological studies showing the association between rheumatoid arthritis and cigarette smoking

Study	Cases (n)	Controls (n)	Smoking group	Odds ratio (95% confidence interval)
[78]	239	239	41–50 pack years	13.5 (2.9–63.4)
			Ever	1.8 (1.2–2.2)
			Never	1.0
[66]	165	178	Current	0.95 (0.6–1.6)
			Ex	1.7 (0.95–3.1)
			Never	1.0
[79]	7697	370,000	Current	1.2 (1.1–1.3)
			Ex	1.0 (0.95–1.1)
			Never	1.0
[67]	361	5851	Current (males)	2.4 (1.5–3.9)
			Current (females)	1.1 (0.8–1.6)
			Never	1.0

Noninfectious environmental factors
There have been remarkably few studies on factors such as diet, although there is a theoretical basis for investigating the role of omega-3 fatty acids [71,72]. Randomised trials suggest that diets high in eicosapentaenoic acid have a favourable effect on the outcome of RA [73–75]. This might be because such fatty acids compete with arachidonic acids, the latter of which are involved in inflammation. Whether such dietary factors have a role in RA onset is much less clear.

It is perhaps surprising, given how much this exposure has been investigated in other chronic diseases, that very little attention has been given to cigarette smoking until recently. However, findings from a number of recent studies showed that cigarette smoking is associated with an increased risk of RA [66,67,76–79] (Table 2). Studies have also suggested that smoking is related to development of rheumatoid factor independent of RA. Indeed, in many of the epidemiological studies showing a relationship between smoking and RA, the positive findings have been restricted to those with rheumatoid factor.

Future prospects
There has been considerable recent interest in understanding the epidemiology of RA. There have been several population studies in many different countries around the world, and observations of differential occurrence (with time, between populations and between the genders) has stimulated a number of analytical studies looking for both

genetic and environmental risk factors. Future studies will benefit from advances in molecular biology techniques to aid with the identification and characterisation of potential new genes for RA susceptibility. These studies, as already described, have revealed some tantalising clues that will require further follow-up in years to come.

Concluding remarks

RA presents an epidemiological challenge and further elucidation of both genetic and environmental factors, together with interactions between them, are likely to be revealed.

Organisations supplying funds for research

Funds can be obtained from the Arthritis Research Campaign [http://www.arc.org.uk] and the Arthritis Foundation [http://www.arthritis.org].

References

1. Carmona L, Villaverde V, Hernandez-Garcia C, Ballina J, Gabriel R, Laffon A: **The prevalence of rheumatoid arthritis in the general population of Spain.** Rheumatology 2002, **41**:88-95. [general reference]
2. Riise T, Jacobsen BK, Gran JT: **Incidence and prevalence of rheumatoid arthritis in the county of Troms, northern Norway.** J Rheumatol 2000, **27**:1386-1389. [general reference]
3. Aho K, Kaipiainen-Seppanen O, Heliovaara M, Klaukka T: **Epidemiology of rheumatoid arthritis in Finland.** Semin Arthritis Rheum 1998, **27**:325-334. [key review]
4. Cimmino MA, Parisi M, Moggiana G, Mela GS, Accardo S: **Prevalence of rheumatoid arthritis in Italy: the Chiavari study.** Ann Rheum Dis 1998, **57**:315-318. [general reference]
5. Kvien TK, Glennas A, Knudsrod OG, Smedstad LM, Mowinckel P, Forre O: **The prevalence and severity of rheumatoid arthritis in Oslo: results from a county register and a population survey.** Scand J Rheumatol 1997, **26**:412-418. [general reference]
6. Power D, Codd M, Ivers L, Sant S, Barry M: **Prevalence of rheumatoid arthritis in Dublin, Ireland: a population based survey.** Ir J Med Sci 1999, **168**:197-200. [general reference]
7. Saraux A, Guedes C, Allain J, Devauchelle V, Valls I, Lamour A, Guillemin F, Youinou P, Le Goff P: **Prevalence of rheumatoid arthritis and spondyloarthropathy in Brittany, France.** J Rheumatol 1999, **26**:2622-2627. [general reference]
8. Simonsson M, Bergman S, Jacobsson LT, Petersson IF, Svensson B: **The prevalence of rheumatoid arthritis in Sweden.** Scand J Rheumatol 1999, **28**:340-343. [general reference]
9. Gabriel SE, Crowson CS, O'Fallon WM: **The epidemiology of rheumatoid arthritis in Rochester, Minnesota, 1955–1985.** Arthritis Rheum 1999, **42**:415-420. [general reference]
10. Gabriel SE: **The epidemiology of rheumatoid arthritis.** Rheum Dis Clin North Am 2001, **27**:269-281. [key review]
11. del Puente A, Knowler WC, Pettit DJ, Bennett PH: **High incidence and prevalence of rheumatoid arthritis in Pima Indians.** Am J Epidemiol 1989, **129**:1170-1178. [archival research]
12. Harvey J, Lotze M, Stevens MB, Lambert G, Jacobson D: **Rheumatoid arthritis in a Chippewa band. I. Pilot screening study of disease prevalence.** Arthritis Rheum 1981, **24**:717-721. [archival research]
13. Brighton SW, de la Harpe AL, van Staden DJ, Badenhorst JH, Myers OL: **The prevalence of rheumatoid arthritis in a rural African population.** J Rheumatol 1988, **15**:405-408. [archival research]
14. Silman AJ, Ollier W, Holligan S, Birrell F, Adebajo A, Asuzu MC, Thomson W, Pepper L: **Absence of rheumatoid arthritis in a rural Nigerian population.** J Rheumatol 1993, **20**:618-622. [archival research]
15. Dans LF, TankehTorres S, Amante CM, Penserga EG: **The prevalence of rheumatic diseases in a Filipino urban population: a WHO-ILAR COPCORD study.** J Rheumatol 1997, **24**:1814-1819. [general reference]
16. Shichikawa K, Inoue K, Hirota S, Maeda A, Ota H, Kimura M, Ushiyama T, Tsujimoto M: **Changes in the incidence and prevalence of rheumatoid arthritis in Kamitonda, Wakayama, Japan, 1965–1996.** Ann Rheum Dis 1999, **58**:751-756. [general reference]
17. Zeng Q, Huang S, Chen R: **10-year epidemiological study on rheumatic diseases in Shantou area.** Zhonghua Nei Ke Za Zhi 1997, **36**:193-197. [general reference]
18. MacGregor AJ, Riste LK, Hazes JMW, Silman AJ: **Low prevalence of rheumatoid arthritis in black-Caribbeans compared with whites in inner city Manchester.** Ann Rheum Dis 1994, **53**:293-297. [archival research]
19. Lau E, Symmons D, Bankhead C, MacGregor A, Donnan S, Silman A: **Low prevalence of rheumatoid arthritis in the urbanized Chinese of Hong Kong.** J Rheumatol 1993, **20**:1133-1137. [archival research]
20. Hameed K, Gibson T: **A comparison of the prevalence of rheumatoid arthritis and other rheumatic diseases amongst Pakistanis living in England and Pakistan.** Br J Rheumatol 1997, **36**:781-785. [general reference]
21. Lawrence JS, Ball J: **Genetic studies on rheumatoid arthritis.** Ann Rheum Dis 1958, **17**:160-168. [archival research]
22. Lawrence JS: **Heberden oration, 1969. Rheumatoid arthritis — nature or nurture?** Ann Rheum Dis 1970, **29**:357-379. [key review]
23. Jones MA, Silman AJ, Whiting S, Barrett EM, Symmons DPM: **Occurrence of rheumatoid arthritis is not increased in the first degree relatives of a population based inception cohort of inflammatory polyarthritis.** Ann Rheum Dis 1996, **55**:89-93. [general reference]
24. MacGregor AJ, Snieder H, Rigby AS, Koskenvuo M, Kaprio J, Aho K, Silman AJ: **Characterizing the quantitative genetic contribution to rheumatoid arthritis using data from twins.** Arthritis Rheum 2000, **43**:30-37. [general reference]
25. Silman AJ, Hochberg MC: **Rheumatoid arthritis.** In Epidemiology of the Rheumatic Diseases. Edited by AJ Silman, MC Hochberg. Oxford: Oxford University Press; 2001:31-71. [key review]
26. Pascual M, Nieto A, Lopez-Nevot MA, Ramal L, Mataran L, Caballero A, Alonso A, Martin J, Zanelli E: **Rheumatoid arthritis in southern Spain — toward elucidation of a unifying role of the HLA class II region in disease predisposition.** Arthritis Rheum 2001, **44**:307-314. [general reference]
27. Citera G, Padulo LA, Fernandez G, Lazaro MA, Rosemffet MG, Cocco JAM: **Influence of HLA-DR alleles on rheumatoid arthritis: susceptibility and severity in Argentine patients.** J Rheumatol 2001, **28**:1486-1491. [general reference]
28. Zanelli E, Breedveld FC, de Vries RRP: **HLA class II association with rheumatoid arthritis — facts and interpretations.** Hum Immunol 2000, **61**:1254-1261. [key review]
29. Balsa A, Minaur NJ, Pascual-Salcedo D, McCabe C, Balas A, Fiddament B, Vicario JL, Cox NL, Martin-Mola E, Hall ND: **Class II MHC antigens in early rheumatoid arthritis in Bath (UK) and Madrid (Spain).** Rheumatology 2000, **39**:844-849. [general reference]
30. del Rincon I, Escalante A: **HLA-DRB1 alleles associated with susceptibility or resistance to rheumatoid arthritis, articular deformities, and disability in Mexican Americans.** Arthritis Rheum 1999, **42**:1329-1338. [general reference]
31. Wakitani S, Murata N, Toda Y, Ogawa R, Kaneshige T, Nishimura Y, Ochi T: **The relationship between HLA-DRB1 alleles and disease subsets of rheumatoid arthritis in Japanese.** Br J Rheumatol 1997, **36**:630-636. [general reference]
32. Thomson W, Harrison B, Ollier B, Wiles N, Payton T, Barrett J, Symmons D, Silman A: **Quantifying the exact role of HLA-DRB1 alleles in susceptibility to inflammatory polyarthritis: results from a large, population-based study.** Arthritis Rheum 1999, **42**:757-762. [general reference]
33. Gregersen PK: **The North American Rheumatoid Arthritis Consortium — bringing genetic analysis to bear on disease susceptibility, severity, and outcome.** Arthritis Care Res 1998, **11**:1-2. [general reference]
34. Meyer JM, Evans TI, Small RE, Redford TW, Han JF, Singh R, Moxley G: **HLA-DRB1 genotype influences risk for and severity of rheumatoid arthritis.** J Rheumatol 1999, **26**:1024-1034. [general reference]
35. Mattey DL, Hassell AB, Dawes PT, Ollier WE, Hajeer A: **Interaction between tumor necrosis factor microsatellite polymor-**

phisms and the HLA-DRB1 shared epitope in rheumatoid arthritis: influence on disease outcome. *Arthritis Rheum* 1999, **42**:2698-2704. [general reference]

36. Barton A, John S, Ollier WER, Silman A, Worthington J: **Association between rheumatoid arthritis and polymorphism of tumor necrosis factor receptor II, but not tumor necrosis factor receptor I, in Caucasians.** *Arthritis Rheum* 2001, **44**:61-65. [general reference]

37. Hajeer AH, Dababneh A, Makki RF, Thomson W, Poulton K, Gay MA, Garcia-Porrua C, Mattey DL, Ollier WE: **Different gene loci within the HLA-DR and TNF regions are independently associated with susceptibility and severity in Spanish rheumatoid arthritis patients.** *Tissue Antigens* 2000, **55**:319-325. [general reference]

38. Hajeer AH, Worthington J, Silman AJ, Ollier WER: **Association of tumor necrosis factor microsatellite polymorphisms with HLA-DRB1(*)04-bearing haplotypes in rheumatoid arthritis patients.** *Arthritis Rheum* 1996, **39**:1109-1114. [general reference]

39. Cornelis F, Faure S, Martinez M, Prudhomme JF, Fritz P, Dib C, Alves H, Barrera P, de Vries N, Balsa A, Pascual-Salcedo D, Maenaut K, Westhovens R, Migliorini P, Tran TH, Delaye A, Prince N, Lefevre C, Thomas G, Poirier M, Soubigou S, Alibert O, Lasbleiz S, Fouix S, Bouchier C, Liote F, Loste MN, Lepage V, Charron D, Gyapay G, Lopes-Vaz A, Kuntz D, Bardin T, Weissenbach J: **New susceptibility locus for rheumatoid arthritis suggested by a genome-wide linkage study.** *Proc Natl Acad Sci USA* 1998, **95**:10746-10750. [general reference]

40. Shiozawa S, Hayashi S, Tsukamoto Y, Goko H, Kawasaki H, Wada T, Shimizu K, Yasuda N, Kamatani N, Takasugi K, Tanaka Y, Shiozawa K, Imura S: **Identification of the gene loci that predispose to rheumatoid arthritis.** *Int Immunol* 1998, **10**:1891-1895. [general reference]

41. Worthington J, Ollier WE, Leach MK, Smith I, Hay EM, Thomson W, Pepper L, Carthy D, Farhan A, Martin S, Dyer P, Davison J, Bamber S, Silman AJ: **The Arthritis and Rheumatism Council's National Repository of Family Material: pedigrees from the first 100 rheumatoid arthritis families containing affected sibling pairs.** *Br J Rheumatol* 1994, **33**:970-976. [archival research]

42. Fife MS, Fisher SA, John S, Worthington J, Shah CJ, Ollier WER, Panayi GS, Lewis CM, Lanchbury JS: **Multipoint linkage analysis of a candidate gene locus in rheumatoid arthritis demonstrates significant evidence of linkage and association with the corticotropin-releasing hormone genomic region.** *Arthritis Rheum* 2000, **43**:1673-1678. [general reference]

43. John S, Myerscough A, Eyre S, Roby P, Hajeer A, Silman AJ, Ollier WE, Worthington J: **Linkage of a marker in intron D of the estrogen synthase locus to rheumatoid arthritis.** *Arthritis Rheum* 1999, **42**:1617-1620. [general reference]

44. Khani-Hanjani A, Lacaille D, Hoar D, Chalmers A, Horsman D, Anderson M, Balshaw R, Keown PA: **Association between dinucleotide repeat in non-coding region of interferon-gamma gene and susceptibility to, and severity of, rheumatoid arthritis.** *Lancet* 2000, **356**:820-825. [general reference]

45. Ollier WE: **Role of interferon-gamma gene in rheumatoid arthritis?** *Lancet* 2000, **356**:783-784. [general reference]

46. Pokorny V, McLean L, McQueen F, Abu-Maree M, Yeoman S: **Interferon-gamma microsatellite and rheumatoid arthritis.** *Lancet* 2001, **358**:122-123. [general reference]

47. Hajeer AH, Lazarus M, Turner D, Mageed RA, Vencovsky J, Sinnott P, Hutchinson IV, Ollier WER: **IL-10 gene promoter polymorphisms in rheumatoid arthritis.** *Scand J Rheumatol* 1998, **27**:142-145. [general reference]

48. John S, Myerscough A, Marlow A, Hajeer A, Silman A, Ollier W, Worthington J: **Linkage of cytokine genes to rheumatoid arthritis. Evidence of genetic heterogeneity.** *Ann Rheum Dis* 1998, **57**:361-365. [general reference]

49. John S, Eyre S, Myerscough A, Barrett J, Silman A, Ollier W, Worthington J: **Linkage and association analysis of candidate genes in rheumatoid arthritis.** *J Rheumatol* 2001, **28**:1752-1755. [general reference]

50. Myerscough A, John S, Barrett JH, Ollier WE, Worthington J: **Linkage of rheumatoid arthritis to insulin-dependent diabetes mellitus loci: evidence supporting a hypothesis for the existence of common autoimmune susceptibility loci.** *Arthritis Rheum* 2000, **43**:2771-2775. [general reference]

51. Myerscough A, John S, Barrett JH, Eyre S, Barton A, Brintnell B, Ollier WER, Worthington J: **Linkage and linkage disequilibrium analysis of chromosome Xp11-p21 microsatellite markers with rheumatoid arthritis (RA) [abstract].** *Arthritis Rheum* 2001, **44 (Suppl)**:1299. [general reference]

52. Barton A, Eyre S, Myerscough A, Brintnell B, Ward D, Ollier WE, Lorentzen JC, Klareskog L, Silman A, John S, Worthington J: **High resolution linkage and association mapping identifies a novel rheumatoid arthritis susceptibility locus homologous to one linked to two rat models of inflammatory arthritis.** *Hum Mol Genet* 2001, **10**:1901-1906. [general reference]

53. Heikkila R, Aho K, Heliövaara M, Knekt P, Reunanen A, Aromaa A, Leino A, Palosuo T: **Serum androgen-anabolic hormones and the risk of rheumatoid arthritis.** *Ann Rheum Dis* 1998, **57**:281-285. [general reference]

54. Anonymous: **Reduction in incidence of rheumatoid arthritis associated with oral contraceptives. Royal College of General Practitioners' oral contraception study.** *Lancet* 1978, **1**:569-571. [archival research]

55. Brennan P, Bankhead C, Silman A, Symmons D: **Oral contraceptives and rheumatoid arthritis: results from primary care-based incident case–control study.** *Semin Arthritis Rheum* 1997, **26**:817-823. [general reference]

56. Hannaford PC, Kay CR, Hirsch S: **Oral contraceptives and rheumatoid arthritis: new data from the Royal College of General Practitioners' oral contraception study.** *Ann Rheum Dis* 1990, **49**:744-746. [archival research]

57. Silman AJ: **Epidemiology of rheumatoid arthritis.** *APMIS* 1994, **102**:721-728. [archival research]

58. Nelson JL, Ostensen M: **Pregnancy and rheumatoid arthritis.** *Rheum Dis Clin North Am* 1997, **23**:195-212. [key review]

59. Silman AJ, Kay A, Brennan P: **Timing of pregnancy in relation to the onset of rheumatoid arthritis.** *Arthritis Rheum* 1992, **35**:152-155. [archival research]

60. Brennan P, Silman A: **Breast-feeding and the onset of rheumatoid arthritis.** *Arthritis Rheum* 1994, **37**:808-813. [archival research]

61. Brennan P, Hajeer A, Ong KR, Worthington J, John S, Thomson W, Silman A, Ollier B: **Allelic markers close to prolactin are associated with HLA-DRB1 susceptibility alleles among women with rheumatoid arthritis and systemic lupus erythematosus.** *Arthritis Rheum* 1997, **40**:1383-1386. [general reference]

62. Silman AJ, Ollier WER, Bubel MA: **Autoimmune thyroid disease and thyroid autoantibodies in rheumatoid arthritis patients and their families.** *Br J Rheumatol* 1989, **28**:18-21. [archival research]

63. Oken RJ, Schulzer M: **At issue: schizophrenia and rheumatoid arthritis: the negative association revisited.** *Schizophr Bull* 1999, **25**:625-638. [general reference]

64. Mors O, Mortensen PB, Ewald H: **A population-based register study of the association between schizophrenia and rheumatoid arthritis.** *Schizophr Res* 1999, **40**:67-74. [general reference]

65. Rubinstein G: **Schizophrenia, rheumatoid arthritis and natural resistance genes.** *Schizophr Res* 1997, **25**:177-181. [general reference]

66. Symmons DPM, Bankhead CR, Harrison BJ, Brennan P, Barrett EM, Scott DGI, Silman AJ: **Blood transfusion, smoking, and obesity as risk factors for the development of rheumatoid arthritis: results from a primary care-based incident case–control study in Norfolk, England.** *Arthritis Rheum* 1997, **40**:1955-1961. [general reference]

67. Uhlig T, Hagen KB, Kvien TK: **Current tobacco smoking, formal education, and the risk of rheumatoid arthritis.** *J Rheumatol* 1999, **26**:47-54. [general reference]

68. Jacobsson LT, Hanson RL, Knowler WC, Pillemer S, Pettitt DJ, McCance DR, Bennett PH: **Decreasing incidence and prevalence of rheumatoid arthritis in Pima Indians over a 25 year period.** *Arthritis Rheum* 1994, **37**:1158-1165. [archival research]

69. Silman AJ, Enzer I, Knowler W, Dunn G, Jacobsson L: **Strong influence of period of birth on the occurrence of rheumatoid factor: results from a 30 year follow-up study on Pima Indians [abstract].** *Arthritis Rheum* 2000, **43 (Suppl)**:605. [general reference]

70. Silman AJ, Bankhead C, Rowlingson B, Brennan P, Symmons D, Gatrell A: **Do new cases of rheumatoid arthritis cluster in time or in space?** *Int J Epidemiol* 1997, **26**:628-634. [general reference]

71. Ariza-Ariza R, Mestanza-Peralta M, Cardiel MH: **Omega-3 fatty acids in rheumatoid arthritis: an overview.** *Semin Arthritis Rheum* 1998, **27**:366-370. [key review]

72. James MJ, Cleland LG: **Dietary n-3 fatty acids and therapy for rheumatoid arthritis.** *Semin Arthritis Rheum* 1997, **27**:85-97. [key review]

73. Volker D, Fitzgerald P, Major G, Garg M: **Efficacy of fish oil concentrate in the treatment of rheumatoid arthritis.** *J Rheumatol* 2000, **27**:2343-2346. [general reference]

74. Kremer JM: **n-3 fatty acid supplements in rheumatoid arthritis.** *Am J Clin Nutr* 2000, **71 (Suppl)**:349S-351S. [general reference]

75. Hernandez-Cruz B, Alcocer-Varela J, Cardiel MH: **Omega-3 fatty acids supplementation in Mexican patients with rheumatoid arthritis with standard treatment. A blinded, randomized, placebo controlled, one year, clinical trial [abstract].** *Arthritis Rheum* 1998, **41 (Suppl)**:738. [general reference]

76. Albano SA, Santana-Sahagun E, Weisman MH: **Cigarette smoking and rheumatoid arthritis.** *Semin Arthritis Rheum* 2001, **31**:146-159. [key review]

77. Harrison BJ, Silman AJ, Wiles NJ, Scott DG, Symmons DP: **The association of cigarette smoking with disease outcome in patients with early inflammatory polyarthritis.** *Arthritis Rheum* 2001, **44**:323-330. [general reference]

78. Hutchinson D, Shepstone L, Moots R, Lear JT, Lynch MP: **Heavy cigarette smoking is strongly associated with rheumatoid arthritis (RA), particularly in patients without a family history of RA.** *Ann Rheum Dis* 2001, **60**:223-227. [general reference]

79. Karlson EW, Min Lee I, Cook NR, Manson JE, Buring JE, Hennekens CH: **A retrospective cohort study of cigarette smoking and risk of rheumatoid arthritis in female health professionals.** *Arthritis Rheum* 1999, **42**:910-917. [general reference]

Supplement Review
Single nucleotide polymorphisms and disease gene mapping
John I Bell

Nuffield Department of Clinical Medicine, John Radcliffe Hospital, Oxford, UK

Correspondence: John I Bell, Nuffield Department of Clinical Medicine, John Radcliffe Hospital, Oxford OX3 9DU, UK. Tel: +44 (0)1865 221340; fax: +44 (0)1865 220993; e-mail: john.bell@ndm.ox.ac.uk

Received: 27 February 2002
Accepted: 3 March 2002
Published: 9 May 2002

Arthritis Res 2002, **4 (suppl 3)**:S273-S278

This article may contain supplementary data which can only be found online at http://arthritis-research.com/content/4/S3/S273

© 2002 BioMed Central Ltd
(Print ISSN 1465-9905; Online ISSN 1465-9913)

Chapter summary

Single nucleotide polymorphisms are the most important and basic form of variation in the genome, and they are responsible for genetic effects that produce susceptibility to most autoimmune diseases. The rapid development of databases containing very large numbers of single nucleotide polymorphisms, and the characterization of haplotypes and patterns of linkage disequilibrium throughout the genome, provide a unique opportunity to advance association strategies in common disease rapidly over the next few years. Only the careful use of these strategies and a clear understanding of their statistical limits will allow novel genetic determinants for many of the common autoimmune diseases to be determined.

Keywords: disease association, genetics, HLA, linkage disequilibrium, SNP

Introduction

Advances in human molecular genetics have greatly enhanced our ability to identify the genetic basis for many human diseases, including the autoimmune diseases. Characterization of the genetic determinants requires the evaluation of polymorphism in families and populations to detect the relationship between individual variants and disease phenotypes. Such activities originally relied on measuring polymorphism at the protein level. The extensive literature on human leukocyte antigen (HLA) and disease began with antibodies that defined allelic variation with sera that recognized individual polymorphisms, now understood to be expressed in a host of HLA molecules that regulate the immune response.

This approach has recently become more general as DNA variants can be characterized systematically and can be correlated with disease. The first sets of polymorphisms available for such studies were variable repeats spread throughout the genome. Typing polymorphisms in DNA has always been a limiting factor in such studies and, for the first time, the identification of variable number of tandem repeat sequences allowed highly variable repeat sequences to be readily typed using Southern blots [1]. However, the infrequency of such complex repeats limited their utility and, although they have been informative in terms of describing individual genetic diversity, their role in identifying disease-related genetic variation has been limited.

The next revolution in genetic variation scoring arose directly from the introduction of another methodology; the polymerase chain reaction. This methodology allowed the systematic characterization of smaller dinucleotide and trinucleotide repeats throughout the genome. These could be easily identified, were highly polymorphic, and could be readily mapped at high density throughout the human genome. These repeats provided the first mechanism for searching genome wide for evidence of genetic linkage and disease. Their frequency was not sufficiently high, however, to allow their application in population-based studies of human disease that had proved so productive

A list of common abbreviations used in this issue appears just before the indexes.

S273

when the HLA region had been studied using antibodies. Despite this, the application of these markers became the basis for whole genome linkage studies that have provided information, in family samples, of the localization of a large number of disease genes in autoimmune disease and other complex traits [2].

The most significant development to date in the molecular study of disease genetics has emerged from the availability of the human genome sequence. This data provided the template from which to generate extensive amounts of information on single nucleotide variants. Several important advantages emerge from the availability of such single nucleotide polymorphisms (SNPs). These are by far the commonest form of polymorphism within the genome. These variants will account for the vast majority of polymorphism responsible for human disease. The variation occurs in both coding and noncoding sequences at a frequency of approximately 1 per 1000 base pairs. The extent of variation is limited, however, by the complex relationship between these variants, reflecting population history, recombination hot spots, and selection.

Although large numbers of such polymorphisms had been previously described, both within genes and in intervening sequences, the systematic generation of very large numbers of such variants at high density throughout the genome was necessary if these variants were to be used to look systematically for disease-related genetic variation. The generation of this large set of SNPs has been accompanied by methodology for typing such variation efficiently. The binary nature of these polymorphisms makes them much easier to type in an automated fashion. As this methodology becomes more inexpensive and efficient, it should be possible to catalogue the polymorphisms that exist at a very large number of sites in individuals with and without disease, and hence should be possible to derive information about the genetic susceptibility factors that contribute to many human diseases.

This review will consider the role of these SNPs in mapping human disease related to DNA variation; in particular, the use of SNP typing to characterize haplotypes throughout the genome, and the use of linkage disequilibrium (LD) patterns to find changes that relate to phenotypes. It will also consider how such information should be used to study disease in association strategies and will highlight the basis for current failings of this approach.

The SNP map of the human genome
Although there is extensive data to suggest that single nucleotide variation exists within the human genome at a frequency of approximately 1 per 1000 base pairs [3], only recently has extensive sequencing and resequencing of the genome provided large sets of SNPs to study [4–6]. The publication reporting the identification of 1.42 million SNPs

in 2001 provided the necessary information to study their relationship to each other across the genome [4].

The SNP Consortium (TSC) has contributed the largest set of SNPs identified by shotgun sequencing of genomic fragments [4]. These were obtained using an ethnically diverse panel of 24 individuals. Other large sets of SNPs have been derived from analysis of overlap regions of the human genome sequence derived from bacterial artificial chromosome-derived and P1-derived artificial chromosome sequences obtained during the human genome project. The allele frequency of these SNPs suggests that 82% are polymorphic at frequencies of 10% or greater in at least one ethnic population. Twenty-seven percent had an allele frequency >20% in the three ethnic groups studied (European, African-American and Chinese).

On average, the TSC SNPs were most evenly distributed and were found every 3.05 kb. The SNP density was found to be relatively even across most chromosomes except for the X and Y chromosomes, where there were lower rates of heterozygosity. This was explained by the lower effective population size associated with the X chromosome (hemizygosity in males means that the effective population is three-quarters that of the autosomes) and with the Y chromosome, which has a lower effective population size but a higher mutation rate at male meiosis. The pseudoautosomal region of the Y chromosome known to recombine with the X chromosome shows very high levels of heterozygosity as expected, while the nonrecombining region shows very low levels.

The extent of polymorphism is potentially driven by a number of factors. The population history would undoubtedly be important, in particular the timing of individual mutations, the population admixture and recombination rates, as will balancing selection in some cases. Regions of very high heterozygosity were also detected, including the HLA region on chromosome 6. We already know a great deal about this region and the role of balancing selection in establishing and maintaining polymorphisms in the HLA loci. It will be interesting to see whether other regions of high heterozygosity relate to genomic regions where selection and or recombination rates have played a dominant role.

LD patterns and haplotypes
With the availability of genome wide sets of SNPs, it becomes possible to search the genome for genetic variation that accounts for human disease and other traits [7,8]. No technology is currently available to type the full set of SNPs in population samples, nor indeed is such a comprehensive set of markers available. Of the marker sets available of polymorphic sequences, only a fraction of functional disease-related SNPs are currently available.

If each genetic polymorphism added independently to the variation, then the total set of variable chromosomes would be huge and the prospect of defining disease-related changes in the short term would be small. Fortunately, not all genetic variants operate independently. Alleles that lie close to each other on the chromosome are often found together more often than one would predict if they were segregating independently. This results from a variety of mechanisms but is most commonly the result of the historical development of mutations on a haplotype. New variants always occur in the context of already existing variants. These allelic associations will break down over time but that will depend on recombination between adjacent polymorphisms and, in some cases, selection. Because of the time frame necessary to separate these associations, many ancestral haplotypes exist widely throughout the genome. The relationship between polymorphic markers on the chromosome is referred to as linkage disequilibrium (LD) [9].

Those interested in the genetics of autoimmune disease will be familiar with the concept of LD as it exists within the HLA complex. The earliest studies of the relationship between autoimmune disease and HLA alleles suggested associations with HLA class I loci. As typing improved, it became evident that many of these associations related instead to class II alleles that reside several hundreds of kilobases away from the class I region. Fortunately for those using the HLA as a locus for disease genetics, the level of polymorphism in this region is extraordinarily high and there is extensive LD across the region. So, for example, the original association between HLA B8 and type I diabetes has now been shown to reflect the causative mutations within the HLA DQ region [10].

Some of the ancestral haplotypes extend over the entire region and show very high levels of conservation (i.e. A1, B8, DR3). This LD allowed the region to be associated with a large number of autoimmune diseases and, in some cases, even diseases that are nonimmune in nature but where genetic variation occurred on top of the existing ancestral haplotype. The association of the mutation in the HFE protein responsible for haemochromatosis with the HLA A3 haplotype is a clear example of this pattern of LD [11]. The rich disease gene mining that occurred by studying the HLA succeeded only because of the strong LD in the region, because none of the polymorphisms serologically studied initially were the variants responsible for disease.

Little is known about the mechanisms responsible for the persistent and strong LD in the HLA region. We do know that the alleles in the region are the subject of strong balancing selection. Clear evidence now exists for the role of these alleles in determining the response to infectious pathogens that have exerted powerful selective forces on human populations. For example, the severity of malaria infection seems to be determined by the presence of alleles of the HLA loci [12]. Recombination in this HLA region, detected in family studies, suggests that crossovers occur at a rate (2 cM/Mb) that is somewhat higher than the average around the genome.

Recent studies have attempted to study in detail the pattern of LD within a small portion of the MHC region [13]. In the region between DNA and TAP2, a region of approximately 200 kb, there are three regions of very strong LD that are broken up into discreet regions where LD is broken down. Sperm typing has been used to define the precise regions of meiotic recombination, and this revealed that such crossovers are highly clustered into five recombinational hot spots [14]. One of these hot spots (DNA 3) has a recombination frequency of 140 cM/Mb. In total, 94% of the crossovers recorded occurred within hot spots, although no sequence motifs defining such regions were recognized. Detailed analysis of this region by several groups has therefore defined regions of LD extending across distances of up to 100 kb that are interrupted by short recombinational hot spots [15,16].

Although much is known about patterns of LD within the MHC, the important outstanding question for human genetics is whether the same pattern of LD exists elsewhere in the genome. The large, dense set of SNPs now available is the resource necessary to undertake such studies. Predictions of LD across the genome have been unhelpful, largely because it is widely recognized that the patterns are heterogeneous. Studies of individual regions have suggested that, typically, LD often extends 60 kb from common alleles when tested with islands of sequences leading out from such common SNPs. In characterizing 19 such regions [14], the pattern of LD was greater than expected and there was evidence of significant variation from region to region. LD declined as distance grew from the central allele. Interestingly, this study established a correlation between the recombination rate within a genomic segment and the extent of LD in that region.

Although such studies provide some indication of what may be evident on a genome wide basis, more robust data comes from systematic approaches to haplotype mapping using large sets of markers across whole chromosomes. Such marker sets are widely available as a result of the SNP map. The first of these to be systematically tested covers chromosome 22 with a set of 1504 SNPs studied in the CEPH reference families (Dawson E et al., manuscript submitted). Again, significant heterogeneity in levels of LD were seen, with large regions >700 kb showing extensive LD while other regions revealed little evidence of LD, even between adjacent high-frequency alleles. Systematic study of LD on chromosome 21 has similarly been performed using radiation hybrids and oligonucleotide arrays, and it has revealed similar areas of limited haplotype diversity [17].

It would appear, therefore, that the situation seen in the MHC region with regard to LD is not unique and that extensive regions of LD exist throughout the genome, but that significant heterogeneity also exists between regions. A central, remaining question is how such regions occur and are maintained. Population history remains important and large areas of LD may reflect the lack of opportunity for recombination because the time frame has been short since the founder haplotype occurred or since an evolutionary bottleneck occurred. As in the MHC, the role of recombination rates and sites of recombinational activity may also be important. Selection also cannot be discounted in this process. Particularly in regions where gene products are heavily selected and potentially interactive, this may determine the coexistence of neighbouring alleles. Little is known about the sequences associated with high recombination rates, nor is there any good data on the sequences most associated with high LD.

Importantly, these data suggest that haplotypes are widespread throughout the genome and, whatever their mechanisms, may be valuable tools for moving into association studies in common disease. By carefully choosing markers from regions where LD is strong, it should be possible to undertake anonymous association strategies with the minimal number of SNPs. This approach should make non-hypothesis-based association strategies viable in the short term, allowing genetic effects such as those seen in the HLA region to be readily recognized and validated.

The use of such SNP tools holds great promise, but is not without its own complications. Disease-related genomic regions will be easier to detect in regions of strong and extensive LD. Once detected, however, it becomes challenging to detect the exact locus and polymorphism that accounts for disease susceptibility. This obstacle remains an issue for most HLA disease associations because the strong LD makes difficult the characterization of the role of any single polymorphism in the region where multiple variants contribute identical genetic information. This problem has arisen repeatedly in the HLA and has also been seen in other regions, such as the region around the insulin locus on chromosome 11 in the study of type I diabetes [18] and, more recently, in the study of the role of the cytokine cluster on 5q21 in Crohn's disease [19]. So although the presence of strong LD facilitates the identification of disease-associated regions, it makes the characterization of disease mutations or polymorphisms more difficult.

Another important issue to consider is that patterns of LD vary significantly between different population groups. This is potentially a mechanism whereby LD can be broken down to allow disease polymorphisms to be mapped. Such an approach was used to describe the role of individual loci in type I diabetes susceptibility utilizing the differential HLA haplotypes seen in Africa and Western Europe [20].

Ethnic heterogeneity in LD, however, also proves challenging in interpreting disease association data. Any bias in ethnic sampling between patients and controls can give rise to inappropriate assumptions about responsible loci and levels of risk that they confer.

The pattern of LD that is determined by population history can also be seriously influenced by the use of founder populations. The advantages of such approaches have been emphasized for studying complex traits. Populations with strong founder effects have obvious advantages in that they share significant genetic determinants and hence the locus and allelic heterogeneity that complicate the study of these diseases are reduced.

Population history determined the benefits derived from LD. When Eaves et al. characterized Finnish and Sardinian isolates, and compared their LD pattern in a region of chromosome 18 with Western European mixed populations, the levels of LD were not significantly different [21]. They suggest that this may reflect the entry of individual polymorphisms into the population through a number of different founders. The history of genetic isolates is therefore crucial for understanding the LD achieved.

Rare polymorphisms are likely to have arisen recently or from a single founder. If the variant is recent then the LD is probably strong and will represent the relatively short recombinational history of the haplotype. When the polymorphism is found at a higher frequency, it may have arisen from multiple founders and one would not expect the LD to be dramatically increased. The LD around a common variant will be increased only if it has arisen on a founder haplotype from a limited number of individuals, and hence this is likely to arise only in a small, isolated population. Overall, therefore, the role of founder populations in facilitating the search for common disease genes and polymorphisms is complex and the utility relates as much to the population history and age of the variants as it does to the presence of the concept of founders in the population.

Association strategies using SNPs in common disease

One of the most important applications that will arise from the availability of a large number of SNPs and LD on haplotype maps around the genome is the ability to systematically undertake association studies directed at identifying genetic determinants for common disease [22]. Association studies have been enormously successful at identifying some of the major loci involved in common disease. Associations between HLA alleles, first determined by serology and more recently by DNA typing, have identified a role for HLA gene products in determining susceptibility to a range of autoimmune diseases, including type I diabetes, rheumatoid arthritis, coeliac disease, multiple sclerosis and ulcerative colitis.

The success of these studies has, however, provided a false sense of security around the use of association strategies in mapping disease genes. The history of association studies in autoimmune disease since the identification of HLA associations has been limited. Many associations have been identified and then proven not to be reproducible in subsequent studies. Association strategies have therefore developed a bad reputation for producing false-positive results. Nevertheless, it is clear that, when properly applied, association strategies have potentially much greater power to detect genetic contributions to common complex diseases than that available using linkage studies. Not only is the statistical power to detect the genetic contribution to disease greater in association studies [23], it is also an essential component of the proof necessary to implicate a DNA variant within a linkage region as mediating disease susceptibility or pathogenesis.

An analysis of the potential pitfalls linked with association strategies is helpful, particularly at this time when they are likely to be more widely applied with the increasingly available SNP resources. First and foremost among the problems surrounding association strategy is the failure to have a sufficiently large sample size to produce convincing statistical support for a hypothesis. Few, if any, genetic loci yet to be identified in autoimmune disease will have the strength of HLA associations. Many of the genetic determinants of autoimmune disease will be contributing relative risks of between 2 and 4; as a result, large numbers of patients will need to be studied to identify these effects. These effects will also be diluted by the considerable heterogeneity that may underlie these diseases and by the fact that most genetic associations originally described are unlikely to be primary associations, but simply represent LD with the functional DNA variant responsible for disease. Both locus and allelic heterogeneity may add complexity to this formula. Together these confounding factors mean that large sample sizes (many hundreds of cases and controls) need to be studied to detect significant effects.

Population stratification is often identified as a cause for false-positive association studies. Although this has often been suggested, it has seldom been documented with any degree of rigour. Nevertheless, it is important to identify control populations that most properly represent samples for comparison with the disease group. Several strategies can be applied for identifying control populations [22]. Age-matched and sex-matched controls from similar ethnic backgrounds will provide some degree of confidence in variation in allele frequencies between patients and controls. Alternatively, sampling widely from diverse ethnic populations may provide information on the normal range of allele frequencies in diverse population groups.

Family-based controls provide an opportunity to reduce population stratification [24]. Should the disease popula-tion vary substantially from these, it provides confidence that the allele may be genuinely contributing to the disease state. Multiple testing and repeated subgroup analysis are conventional errors in methodology often seen in association strategies in human disease. Such strategies have proved to be misleading in epidemiological studies of all kinds and, increasingly, have proved to be the cause of false-positive data in genetic association studies. Any analysis of subsets of the disease population gives rise to serious statistical problems and can only be corrected by large and robust replicated studies, where the hypothesis is defined before the study is undertaken.

The availability of a large number of SNPs has also given rise to a problem associated with multiple testing of different allelic variants in case and control populations. At its worst, this problem is seen in 'whole genome association' strategies whereby very large numbers of SNPs are typed in disease and control populations. For example, if 1000 random SNPs are utilized for such association studies, one would expect 50 associations to be found at a significance level of $P < 0.05$. Given the issues of power already discussed, this strategy on its own is clearly fraught with difficulties. The significance of an association is obviously enhanced by the characterization biologically of an important candidate in disease pathogenesis or by the availability of previous data that points to a role for a specific polymorphism or gene in disease. Again, however, *post hoc* identification of candidates (e.g. in the region of linkage) can be a misleading approach, which carries with it risks of data overinterpretation.

The availability of haplotype maps around the genome provides perhaps the best opportunity for large-scale association strategies in autoimmune disease and other common disorders [25–27]. Based on currently available data, it would appear that some significant component of the genome can be analysed by the relatively small number of markers covering the areas where LD is strong and the number of haplotypes is limited. Within carefully controlled studies it may therefore be possible to eliminate, by association strategies, large segments of the genome from contributing any significant degree of risk to complex diseases, while other regions, where strong disequilibrium exists, may be identified for future analysis.

While this strategy has the potential of ruling in or ruling out very large segments of the genome for genetic analysis, the regions that have been identified through LD mapping as having a role in common disease provide significant challenges for the characterization of individual disease variants. Regions where LD is strong are extremely difficult to break down to the level of single DNA variants. This is particularly evident in regions such as the HLA, where the search for individual DNA variants responsible for disease associations continues to challenge immunogeneticists. Nevertheless, this appears to be a strategy that will yield important association data, at least in the short term.

Concluding remarks

The availability of a large number of SNPs widely dispersed throughout the genome is likely to greatly accelerate disease gene hunting in autoimmunity. SNPs are thus not always independent, and the use of LD may facilitate the systematic search for associations. Before this happens, however, it is important to be clear about the methodological issues that have limited the effectiveness of previous simple association strategies. Only then will definitive genetic association data emerge.

References

1. Nakamura Y, Koyama K, Matsushima M: **VNTR (variable number of tandem repeat) sequences as transcriptional, translational or functional regulators.** *J Hum Genet (Jpn)* 1998, **43**:149-152. [general reference]
2. Altmüller J, Palmer LJ, Fischer G, Scherb H, Wjst M: **Genomewide scans of complex human diseases: true linkage is hard to find.** *Am J Hum Genet* 2001, **69**:936-950. [key review]
3. Mullikin JC, Hunt SE, Cole CG, Mortimore BJ, Rice CM, Burton J, Matthews LH, Pavitt R, Plumb RW, Sims SK, Ainscough RM, Attwood J, Bailey JM, Barlow K, Bruskiewich RM, Butcher PN, Carter NP, Chen Y, Clee CM, Coggill PC, Davies J, Davies RM, Dawson E, Francis MD, Joy AA, Lamble RG, Langford CF, Macarthy J, Mall V, Moreland A, Overton-Larty EK, Ross MT, Smith LC, Steward CA, Sulston JE, Tinsley EJ, Turney KJ, Willey DL, Wilson GD, McMurray AA, Dunham I, Rogers J, Bentley DR: **An SNP map of human chromsome 22.** *Nature* 2000, **407**:516-520. [general reference]
4. Sachidanandam R, Weissman D, Schmidt SC, Kakol JM, Stein LD, Marth G, Sherry S, Mullikin JC, Mortimore BJ, Willey DL, Hunt SE, Cole CG, Coggill PC, Rice CM, Ning Z, Rogers J, Bentley DR, Kwok PY, Mardis ER, Yeh RT, Schultz B, Cook L, Davenport R, Dante M, Fulton L, Hillier L, Waterston RH, McPherson JD, Gilman B, Schaffner S, Van Etten WJ, Reich D, Higgins J, Daly MJ, Blumenstiel B, Baldwin J, Stange-Thomann N, Zody MC, Linton L, Lander ES, Altshuler D: **A map of human genome sequence variation containing 1.42 single nucleotide polymorphisms.** *Nature* 2001, **409**:928-933. [general reference]
5. Altshuler D, Pollara VJ, Cowles CR, Van Etten WJ, Baldwin J, Linton L, Lander ES: **An SNP map of the human genome generated by reduced representation shotgun sequencing.** *Nature* 2000, **407**:513-516. [general reference]
6. Wang DG, Fan JB, Siao CJ, Berno A, Young P, Sapolsky R, Ghandour G, Perkins N, Winchester E, Spencer J, Kruglyak L, Stein L, Hsie L, Topaloglou T, Hubbell E, Robinson E, Mittmann M, Morris MS, Shen N, Kilburn D, Rioux J, Nusbaum C, Rozen S, Hudson TJ, Lander ES: **Large-scale identification, mapping, and genotyping of single-nucleotide polymorphisms in the human genome.** *Science* 1998, **280**:1077-1082. [general reference]
7. Kruglyak L: **Prospects for whole-genome linkage disequilibrium mapping of common disease genes.** *Nat Genet* 1999, **22**:139-144. [key review]
8. Risch N, Merikangas K: **The future of genetic studies of complex human diseases.** *Science* 1996, **273**:1516-1517. [key review]
9. Hartl DL, Clark AG: *Principles of Population Genetics.* Sunderland, MA: Sinauer Associates; 1997. [book]
10. She JX: **Susceptibility to type I diabetes: HLA-DQ and DR revisited.** *Immunol Today* 1996, **17**:323-329. [key review]
11. Cullen LM, Anderson GJ, Ramm GA, Jawinska EC, Powell LW: **Genetics of hemochromatosis.** *Annu Rev Med* 1999, **50**:87-98. [key review]
12. Hill AV: **Genetic susceptibility to malaria and other infectious diseases: from the MHC to the whole genome.** *Parasitology* 1996, **112**:S75-S84. [general reference]
13. Jeffreys AJ, Kauppi L, Neumann R: **Intensely punctate meiotic recombination in the class II region of the major histocompatibility complex.** *Nat Genet* 2002, **29**:217-222. [general reference]
14. Reich DE, Cargill M, Bolk S, Ireland J, Sabeti PC, Richter DJ, Lavery T, Kouyoumjian R, Farhadian SF, Ward R, Lander ES: **Linkage Disequilibrium in the human genome.** *Nature* 2001, **411**:199-204. [general reference]
15. Abecasis GR, Noguchi E, Heinzmann A, Traherne JA, Bhattacharyya S, Leaves NI, Anderson GG, Zhang Y, Lench NJ, Carey A, Cardon LR, Moffatt MF, Cookson WO: **Extent and distribution of linkage disequilibrium in three genomic regions.** *Am J Hum Genet* 2001, **68**:191-197. [general reference]
16. Stephens JC, Schneider JA, Tanguay DA, Choi J, Acharya T, Stanley SE, Jiang R, Messer CJ, Chew A, Han JH, Duan J, Carr JL, Lee MS, Koshy B, Kumar AM, Zhang G, Newell WR, Windemuth A, Xu C, Kalbfleisch TS, Shaner SL, Arnold K, Schulz V, Drysdale CM, Nandabalan K, Judson RS, Ruano G, Vovis GF: **Haplotype variation and linkage disequilibrium in 313 human genes.** *Science* 2001, **293**:489-493. [general reference]
17. Patil N, Berno AJ, Hinds DA, Barrett WA, Doshi JM, Hacker CR, Kautzer CR, Lee DH, Marjoribanks C, McDonough DP, Nguyen BT, Norris MC, Sheehan JB, Shen N, Stern D, Stokowski RP, Thomas DJ, Trulson MO, Vyas KR, Frazer KA, Fodor SP, Cox DR: **Blocks of limited haplotype diversity revealed by high-resolution scanning of human chromosome 21.** *Science* 2001, **294**:1719-1723. [general reference]
18. Bennett ST, Lucassen AM, Gough SC, Powell EE, Undlien DE, Pritchard LE, Merriman ME, Kawaguchi Y, Dronsfield MJ, Pociot F, Nerup J, Bouzekri N, Cambon-Thomsen A, Rønningen KS, Barnett AH, Bain SC, Todd JA: **Susceptibility to human type 1 diabetes at IDDM2 is determined by tandem repeat variation at the insulin gene minisatellite locus.** *Nat Genet* 1995, **10**:378-380. [general reference]
19. Rioux JD, Daly MJ, Silverberg MS, Lindblad K, Steinhart H, Cohen Z, Delmonte T, Kocher K, Miller K, Guschwan S, Kulbokas EJ, O'Leary S, Winchester E, Dewar K, Green T, Stone V, Chow C, Cohen A, Langelier D, Lapointe G, Gaudet D, Faith J, Branco N, Bull SB, McLeod RS, Griffiths AM, Bitton A, Greenberg GR, Lander ES, Siminovitch KA, Hudson TJ: **Genetic variation in the 5q31 cytokine gene cluster confers susceptibility to Crohn disease.** *Nat Genet* 2001, **29**:223-228. [general reference]
20. Lampis R, Morelli L, Congia M, Macis MD, Mulargia A, Loddo M, De Virgiliis S, Marrosu MG, Todd JA, Cucca F: **The inter-regional distribution of HLA class II haplotypes indicates the suitability of the Sardinian population for case–control association studies in complex diseases.** *Hum Mol Genet* 2000, **9**:2959-2965. [general reference]
21. Eaves IA, Merriman TR, Barber RA, Nutland S, Tuomilehto-Wolf E, Tuomilehto J, Cucca F, Todd JA: **The genetically isolated populations of Finland and Sardinia may not be a panacea for linkage disequilibrium mapping of common disease genes.** *Nat Genet* 2000, **25**:320-323. [general reference]
22. Cardon LR, Bell JI: **Association study designs for complex diseases.** *Nat Rev Genet* 2001, **2**:91-99.[key review]
23. Risch NJ: **Searching for genetic determinants in the new millennium.** *Nature* 2000, **405**:847-856.[key review]
24. Spielman RS, McGinnis RE, Ewens WJ: **Transmission test for linkage disequilibrium: the insulin gene region and insulin-dependent diabetes mellitus.** *Am J Hum Genet* 1993, **52**:506-516. [general reference]
25. Jorde LB: **Linkage disequilibrium and the search for complex disease genes.** *Genome Res* 2000, **10**:1435-1444. [general reference]
26. Xiong M, Guo SW: **Fine-scale genetic mapping based on linkage disequilibrium: theory and applications.** *Am J Hum Genet* 1997, **60**:1513-1531. [general reference]
27. Freimer NB, Reus VI, Escamilla MA, McInnes LA, Spesny M, Leon P, Service SK, Smith LB, Silva S, Rojas E, Gallegos A, Meza L, Fournier E, Baharloo S, Blankenship K, Tyler DJ, Batki S, Vinogradov S, Weissenbach J, Barondes SH, Sandkuijl LA: **Genetic mapping using haplotype, association and linkage methods suggests a locus for severe bipolar disorder (BPI) at 18q22-q23.** *Nat Genet* 1996, **12**:436-441. [general reference]

Supplement Review
Complement and systemic lupus erythematosus
Mark J Walport

Division of Medicine, Imperial College of Science, Technology and Medicine, London, UK

Correspondence: Mark J Walport, MA, PhD, FRCP, FRCPath, FMedSci, Rheumatology Section, Division of Medicine, Imperial College of Science, Technology and Medicine, Hammersmith Campus, Du Cane Road, London, W12 0NN, UK. Tel: +44 (0)208 383 3299; fax +44 (0)208 383 2024; e-mail m.walport@ic.ac.uk

Received: 28 February 2002
Accepted: 4 March 2002
Published: 9 May 2002

Arthritis Res 2002, **4 (suppl 3)**:S279-S293

This article may contain supplementary data which can only be found online at http://arthritis-research.com/content/4/S3/S279

© 2002 BioMed Central Ltd
(Print ISSN 1465-9905; Online ISSN 1465-9913)

Chapter summary

Complement is implicated in the pathogenesis of systemic lupus erythematosus (SLE) in several ways and may act as both friend and foe. Homozygous deficiency of any of the proteins of the classical pathway is causally associated with susceptibility to the development of SLE, especially deficiency of the earliest proteins of the activation pathway. However, complement is also implicated in the effector inflammatory phase of the autoimmune response that characterizes the disease. Complement proteins are deposited in inflamed tissues and, in experimental models, inhibition of C5 ameliorates disease in a murine model. As a further twist to the associations between the complement system and SLE, autoantibodies to some complement proteins, especially to C1q, develop as part of the autoantibody response. The presence of anti-C1q autoantibodies is associated with severe illness, including glomerulonephritis. In this chapter the role of the complement system in SLE is reviewed and hypotheses are advanced to explain the complex relationships between complement and lupus.

Keywords: C1q, complement, glomerulonephritis, lupus, SLE

Introduction

The major discoveries that led to the modern era of work on systemic lupus erythematosus (SLE) were those of Hargraves *et al.* in 1947 of the lupus erythematosus (or 'LE') cell phenomenon [1], followed by the discovery of autoreactivity to nuclei [2,3] and to nucleoprotein [4]. Contemporaneous with these findings came the discovery that complement levels were abnormal in patients with SLE [5,6] and the discovery a few years later that complement was deposited in inflammatory lesions in tissues [7]. These findings led to a model for the pathogenesis of SLE in which autoantibodies formed immune complexes with their autoantigens, the resulting immune complexes activated complement, and the products of complement activation caused tissue injury and disease.

Subsequent findings have shown that the associations of complement with SLE are much more complex and it is now clear that complement may be friend as well as foe. The first finding was of a rare subgroup of patients with SLE with inherited homozygous deficiencies of certain complement proteins, particularly proteins of the early part of the classical pathway of complement activation. Subsequently it was discovered that up to a third of patients with SLE had high levels of autoantibodies to some complement proteins, especially to C1q, the very first protein in the classical pathway of complement.

These data allowed three deductions to be made about the association of complement with SLE. The first is that SLE is associated with complement activation, which may

---

A glossary of specialist terms used in this chapter appears at the end of the text section. A list of common abbreviations used in this issue appears just before the indexes.

cause tissue injury. The second is that hereditary complement deficiency may cause SLE. The third is that the disease processes in SLE cause the development of autoantibodies to certain complement proteins. At first sight these statements appear to be mutually contradictory and difficult to reconcile one with the other.

In this chapter I will illustrate the evidence in support of these three deductions and develop some hypotheses that may explain these complex abnormalities of the complement system found in association with SLE.

The first section of this review will first describe the clinical associations of complement abnormalities with SLE, followed by the mechanisms of these associations. Finally a hypothesis will be proposed to explain the associations and consider the therapeutic implications.

Complement and SLE: the clinical observations
Complement is activated in SLE
Complement activation is easy to demonstrate in the plasma and tissues of patients with SLE. Indeed measures of complement activation are part of the standard repertoire of laboratory tests to which most patients with SLE are subjected on a regular basis. In this section I will describe the evidence for complement activation in plasma, on cells and in tissues. I will also discuss abnormalities that have been discovered in an important complement receptor, complement receptor type 1 (CR1), expressed on erythrocytes and cells of the immune system. I will review the evidence that measurements of complement activation correlate with disease activity, and the value of such measurements in the assessment and management of patients with SLE.

Complement activation in plasma
Assays of complement levels in serum are one of the standard assays used to assist the clinical management of patients with SLE [8]. The majority of laboratories measure antigenic concentrations of C3 and C4. A smaller number of laboratories also routinely provide a functional measurement of the activity of the whole complement pathway from classical pathway activation through to formation of the membrane attack complex, such as the CH50 (complement haemolysis 50%) test.

The dominant pathway for complement activation in SLE is the classical pathway, triggered by the interaction of C1q with immune complexes. Classical pathway complement protein levels are reduced in association with active disease, especially C1, C4 and C2 levels. Levels of C3 are typically at the lower end of the normal range and only occasionally severely depressed. Levels of C3 are maintained because of the regulatory mechanisms that control classical pathway complement activation *in vivo*, espe-

cially the activity of C4 binding protein that inhibits classical pathway activation [9]. When C3 levels are reduced, this is usually associated with reduced levels of factor B, indicating amplification of C3 turnover *in vivo* by the amplification loop of the alternative pathway [10,11].

Complement levels, however, provide a rather poor surrogate of clinical disease activity [12–14] for four reasons. Firstly, there is wide variation in normal complement protein levels between different individuals, partly due to genetic polymorphisms and partly for unknown reasons. The second reason is that protein levels are controlled by the balance of protein synthesis and catabolism, and the increase in catabolism of complement proteins caused by immune complexes in SLE is balanced by a variable response in complement protein synthetic rates between individuals [15–17]. As an additional factor that affects protein synthetic rates, many complement proteins are acute phase reactants, including C3 and C4. Such proteins display an increase in synthetic rate in response to inflammatory stimuli, which may compensate for the hypercatabolism of complement secondary to complement activation [18]. Thirdly, measurement of complement levels in serum may not reflect accurately what is occurring in tissues. This can be illustrated by diseases such as myasthenia gravis in which complement activation occurs at the motor neurone end plate [19,20], or membranous nephritis in which complement activation occurs at the subendothelial surface of the glomerular basement membrane [21,22]. Experimental models show that, in these diseases, complement activation is a key part of the inflammatory injury, but complement activation is virtually undetectable in peripheral blood. By contrast, when complement activation occurs in peripheral blood, for example in autoimmune haemolytic anaemia, then serum levels of C4 and C3 may be severely reduced. The fourth reason why complement levels are a poor surrogate of disease activity is that autoantibodies to complement proteins, especially to C1q, may be associated with profound activation of the complement pathway *in vivo*, and the level of complement activation may be associated with the levels of these autoantibodies rather than by disease per se. Autoantibodies to C1q are reviewed later in this chapter.

In patients with established disease, regular measurement of complement activity is a helpful guide to disease activity [23], though only as one of a series of assessments, of which the most important relate to clinical symptoms and signs of disease. In an attempt to improve the value of complement measurements in the assessment of disease activity, investigators have measured the levels of serum markers of complement activation, such as anaphylatoxin levels [24], C1r-C1s-C1 inhibitor complexes [18], C4d levels [25], iC3b or C3dg levels [26,27] and membrane attack complex levels [28,29]. Although there is evidence that measurement of these complement activation products correlates somewhat better with disease activity than measurement of total C4 and C3 levels [30–32], none of these assays has been widely adopted in clinical practice. There are two reasons for this: each of these complement activation products is highly unstable *in vivo* and therefore difficult to measure with any useful reliability outside a research setting; and the plethora of different causes of complement activation in lupus, which were discussed earlier.

In spite of all of these caveats it is worthwhile to measure complement activity in patients with SLE. At the onset of disease, complement measurements may have diagnostic value. Evidence of complement activation is a marker of the family of diseases in which immune-complex-mediated pathology is prominent. Although a rare finding, it is also important to consider whether a patient might have an inherited complement deficiency underlying the disease. Assay of C4 and C3 levels alone may not alert the practitioner to the presence of complement deficiency. Indeed in the case of C1 deficiency, C4 and C3 levels may be high because of reduced consumption of classical pathway proteins [33]. For this reason, a functional assay of the pathway, such as a CH50, should be considered in all patients with suspected SLE.

The second diagnostic value of complement measurement in SLE is that evidence of marked complement activation should alert the clinician to one of three possibilities. The first is the presence of anti-C1q antibodies, which I will discuss below. The second is the presence of haemolytic anaemia; a Coombs' test should be performed in patients in whom this possibility is suspected. The third is the presence of active disease with the presence of glomerulonephritis. Finally, regular measurements of complement may disclose changes in complement levels that, when considered with the clinical findings and the results of other serological assays, may point towards changes in disease activity. There is a series of studies (reviewed in [34]) that show that changes in complement, anti-double-stranded (ds) DNA and anti-C1q antibody levels may predict the onset of disease flares [23,35–39].

Complement activation on cells and in tissues
Many tissues from patients with SLE show deposits of antibodies and complement proteins [7,40]. The demonstration of these in biopsies can be of diagnostic value, for example as part of the characterization of the histology of renal biopsies, or at the dermo-epidermal junction in the skin.

There is usually a correlation between the presence of antibody deposits and the presence of complement proteins. However, there is no simple correlation between the presence of antibody or complement deposits and the presence of tissue inflammation. For example, biopsies of clinically normal skin typically show deposits of antibody

and complement at the basement membrane at the dermo-epidermal junction, and this has some diagnostic value for SLE, known as the 'lupus band' test. Attempts have been made to identify markers of complement activation in tissues that correlate better with the presence of inflammation. One such marker is the presence of the membrane attack complex, which is more prominent in inflamed tissues compared with clinically normal tissues from patients with SLE [41–44]. Complement may also be detected on the cellular elements in blood and this is especially prominent in patients with autoimmune haemolytic anaemia or thrombocytopenia as part of the spectrum of disease.

Red cells and CR1
Erythrocytes in primates bear a complement receptor known as complement receptor type 1, usually abbreviated as CR1 (reviewed by [45]). Alternative names for this protein include the immune adherence receptor and CD35. The receptor has specificity for C3b, C4b and iC3b, in order of binding strength (C3b highest). On erythrocytes CR1 is present at low copy number (between 70 and 700 molecules per cell) but is organized in clusters that allow high avidity binding. Erythrocyte CR1 levels in patients with SLE are reduced, and before discussing the explanation and possible significance of this finding, a brief preamble will be given describing the biology of this interesting molecule.

Complement receptor type 1 has several biological activities. It acts as a binding and transport molecule for particles in the circulation bearing C3b clusters, for example parasites and bacteria. Red cells are thought to act as particulate carriers of pathogens bearing C3b and C4b in the circulation, transporting them to the fixed mononuclear phagocytic system in the liver, spleen and bone marrow.

Complement also has a biochemical activity as a cofactor to the serine esterase factor I in the cleavage of C3b to inactive products. Factor I cleaves C3 sequentially to iC3b, then to C3dg plus C3c. Factor I may use one of several cofactors for the first cleavage reaction, including the plasma protein, factor H, and the cell membrane proteins CR1 or membrane cofactor protein (also known as CD46). However, CR1 is the sole known cofactor for the second cleavage reaction by factor I of iC3b to C3dg and C3c.

Complement receptor type 1 is also present on other cell types, including B cells (on which ligation of complement receptors modulates the threshold for B cell activation), neutrophils and other phagocytic cells on which CR1 contributes to the recognition, uptake and destruction of particles such as pathogens or immune complexes carrying C3 and C4 split products. Finally CR1 is present on antigen-presenting cells and reservoirs of antigen such as follicular dendritic cells that act as a long-lived 'sump' of foreign antigens, preserving immunological memory.

It had been known since the 1930s that there was variation between normal humans in the expression of CR1 levels on erythrocytes [46], and a study in the 1960s provided evidence that this variation was inherited [47]. These studies were lost in the pre-Medline mists but interest in CR1 in SLE was aroused when it was discovered that erythrocyte CR1 levels were reduced on the erythrocytes of patients with SLE [48] and evidence emerged that inherited factors might contribute to this reduction [49,50]. However, there is now a large body of evidence (reviewed in [51]) that shows that CR1 levels on erythrocytes from patients with SLE are reduced as a consequence of disease activity [52]. In addition, although there is a genetic polymorphism that determines CR1 levels on normal erythrocytes [53], the distribution of the allele of CR1 associated with reduced CR1 expression shows no increase in frequency amongst patients with SLE [54,55].

Most data now point to low levels of CR1 in SLE being caused by the removal of the receptor from the cell. This is associated with evidence of complement activation in the vicinity of red cells with low CR1 numbers (i.e. a correlation has been found between raised levels of C3dg deposited on erythrocytes and reduced CR1 numbers [56]). Erythrocytes that were transfused into patients with SLE rapidly lost CR1 expression from the cell surface [57]. Similarly, when the formation of immune complexes *in vivo* was monitored in humans, clearance of immune complexes was accompanied by deposition of C4 and C3 on erythrocytes and loss of CR1 from these cells [58]. Proteolysis of the receptor, which is highly susceptible to cleavage by trypsin-like enzymes [59], is the most likely mechanism for loss of the receptor from erythrocytes [60,61]. Studies in nonhuman primates have shown that when erythrocytes are infused bearing immune complexes ligated to CR1 there is concerted removal of immune complexes from erythrocytes together with a reduction in CR1 levels [62–64]. This reaction, including the loss of CR1, has been modeled *in vitro* by studying the transfer of immune complexes from erythrocytes to macrophages [65]. Indeed, loss of erythrocyte CR1 may be a physiological release mechanism that facilitates the transfer of opsonised immune complexes and pathogens from red cells to tissue macrophages.

CR1 levels are also low on certain other cell types in SLE, most notably on glomerular epithelial cells [66,67]. Soluble CR1 was detected in the urine of patients with SLE on microvesicles that were derived from kidney tissue, most probably from glomerular podocytes [68]. Both enhanced microvesiculation and proteolytic cleavage are candidates for the mechanism of removal of CR1 from podocytes in SLE [69,70].

Autoantibodies to complement proteins in patients with SLE

A series of autoantibodies have been described that bind with high affinity to complement proteins. The majority of these are directed to 'neoepitopes'. These are defined as epitopes that are not expressed in the native protein and are only exposed in protein that has been modified by a change in structure. Such a change in structure to reveal a neoepitope may follow proteolytic cleavage, a conformational change following activation or following binding of the protein to another protein. Amongst the earliest autoantibodies to complement proteins to be identified were immunoconglutinins and these have been found in the sera of patients with SLE [71,72]. These autoantibodies bind to an activation product of C3 known as iC3b and are something of an esoteric curiosity since, although quite common, they have never been shown to play any direct role in disease.

In contrast, subsequently identified autoantibodies to complement proteins are more malign. They include C3 nephritic factor, associated with partial lipodystrophy, and a form of mesangiocapillary glomerulonephritis with electron dense deposits in glomerular basement membranes. A small number of patients with C3 nephritic factor and SLE have been identified [73]. Another important, albeit rare, autoantibody to a complement protein is anti-C1 inhibitor autoantibody [74,75], occurring particularly in some patients with lymphoma [76–78].

In SLE, the most important autoantibody to a complement protein is anti-C1q, which is found in approximately a third of patients with SLE. In the next few paragraphs I will review the nature and significance of anti-C1q autoantibodies. Before doing so I should note that other autoantibodies to complement proteins that have been described in a small number of patients with SLE are against CR1 [79,80] and against the C4b2a C3 classical pathway convertase enzyme [81]. These antibodies are similar to immunoconglutinins in being of doubtful pathological significance.

Autoantibodies to C1q in hypocomplementaemic urticarial vasculitis

The major clinical features of the clinical syndrome hypocomplementaemic urticarial vasculitis (HUVS) are well encompassed by its cumbersome name. This syndrome is associated with evidence of intense activation of the classical pathway, with very low levels of C1q, C4 and C2, and moderately reduced levels of C3, in serum samples from patients. This syndrome is defined serologically by the presence of very high titres of autoantibodies to C1q [82], which were identified originally as C1q precipitins [83]. These autoantibodies react with a neoepitope in the collagenous region of C1q that is not exposed in the C1 complex, comprising one molecule of C1q combined with two C1r and two C1s molecules. The epitope is only exposed when the C1 complex is activated with the removal of the C1r and C1s molecules in combination with C1 inhibitor.

In addition to chronic urticaria, with its accompanying cutaneous leukocytoclastic vasculitis, other clinical features of the disease can include angioedema, glomerulonephritis, neuropathy and airways obstruction [84]. No other autoantibodies have been identified in HUVS but some of the features of this syndrome may be found in patients with 'full-blown' SLE who also have anti-C1q autoantibodies. The relationship between HUVS and SLE is analogous to that between the primary antiphospholipid syndrome and SLE. In the case of the latter association, patients with the primary antiphospholipid syndrome have a clinical syndrome of recurrent thromboses and abortions in the presence of autoantibodies to cardiolipin and to β2-glycoprotein-I. Approximately a third of patients with SLE also have these autoantibodies as part of their autoantibody spectrum and may also have some of the clinical features of the antiphospholipid syndrome.

Anti-C1q autoantibodies in SLE

During the 1970s and 1980s there was a great deal of interest in trying to measure pathogenic immune complexes in those diseases that were thought to be mediated by immune complexes (reviewed in [85]). Very many assays were devised, including two based on the capacity of immune complexes to activate complement by the binding of C1q. These assays were the fluid phase and solid phase C1q-binding assays. The fluid phase assay was conducted by adding radiolabelled C1q to serum; some of this bound to immune complexes and the bound material could be measured as a coprecipitate with the immune complexes by addition of polyethylene glycol [86,87]. The solid phase C1q-binding assay was conducted by incubating serum samples in microtitre plates coated with C1q [88]. Immune complexes were thought to bind to the C1q and could be detected using labelled antiglobulins that bound to the antibodies within the immune complexes. Positive results for 'immune complexes' using both of these assays were found in patients with SLE and correlated with the presence of active disease, the presence of hypocomplementemia and elevated titres of anti-DNA antibodies [86,87,89,90]. There was a poor correlation, however, between results obtained using the fluid phase and solid phase C1q-binding assays [91]. It was subsequently discovered that the explanation for this discrepancy was that the solid phase C1q-binding assay is mainly a measure of autoantibodies to C1q rather than of immune complexes. This was discovered in the following way.

Agnello and colleagues [83] had observed that C1q precipitins could be characterized in a small number of patients with SLE and some of these sedimented at 7S,

the sedimentation constant of monomeric IgG. These observations were confirmed in two further studies of the size of 'immune complexes' in the sera of patients with SLE [92,93]. These results raised the possibility that the C1q binding activity was attributable to an autoantibody rather than to circulating immune complexes that could bind C1q. This was found to be the case [94–96] and it was shown that the majority of IgG binding to C1q in solid phase assays was attributable to autoantibodies reacting with a neoepitope in the collagenous portion of C1q [97].

The assay has now been adapted to provide a specific measurement of anti-C1q autoantibodies. The adaptation to give this specificity is simply the addition of sodium chloride (1M) during the incubation step of serum with the C1q-coated plates. This high ionic strength prevents the binding of immune complexes to C1q but is insufficient to prevent high affinity binding of antibody to antigen [98].

The ready availability of simple quantitative assays for autoantibodies to C1q has allowed many studies of the prevalence and clinical association of C1q autoantibodies in patients with SLE (reviewed in [99]). The main conclusions of these are as follows. Approximately a third of patients with SLE have elevated levels of anti-C1q antibodies and these patients often have severe disease [100]. Several studies have shown an association between the presence of anti-C1q autoantibodies and glomerulonephritis [39,101–105]. There is usually evidence of intense activation of the classical pathway of complement, with very low C1q and C4 levels. A small number of patients with high titres of anti-C1q autoantibodies have been described with angioedema, resembling that of hereditary angioedema. These patients have low levels of C1 inhibitor and of classical pathway complement proteins [106]. Levels of C3, which tend to be well maintained in patients with SLE, probably because of effective regulation of classical pathway activation by C4 binding protein, may be substantially below the normal range in patients with anti-C1q autoantibodies [107]. Autoantibodies to C1q have been described in mice with lupus-like disease as well as in humans [108,109].

The association between the presence of anti-C1q autoantibodies and classical pathway, both in HUVS and SLE, leads to the obvious question, which is whether the C1q autoantibodies cause or amplify the classical pathway activation. There is not a certain answer to this. Simply adding anti-C1q antibodies to normal serum does not cause complement activation [110], which may reflect the fact that these autoantibodies are to a neoepitope of C1q not expressed in the intact C1q complex. A more likely explanation is that anti-C1q antibodies fix to C1q that is bound to immune complexes on cells and within tissues and that this causes the amplification of the complement activation by immune complexes. There is some experimental evidence in support of this hypothesis [111]. An alternative theory is that anti-C1q antibodies arise in response to intense activation of the classical pathway with large-scale exposure of an autoantigenic neoepitope in C1q, and that the anti-C1q antibodies are a consequence and not a cause of the complement activation. As I will discuss below, the correct answer may be a combination of these hypotheses.

Complement deficiency is associated with the development of SLE

Homozygous hereditary deficiency of each of the early proteins of the classical pathway of complement activation is very strongly associated with the development of SLE [112]. Indeed such deficiencies are the strongest disease susceptibility genes for the development of this disease that have been characterised in humans. The association shows a hierarchy of prevalence and disease severity according to the position of the protein in the activation pathway. The most prevalent and most severe disease is associated with deficiency of the proteins of the C1 complex and with total C4 deficiency. More than 75% of all individuals with deficiency of one of these proteins have SLE, which is commonly severe. By contrast, C2 deficiency is associated with a much lower prevalence of disease, estimated at approximately 10%. Deficiency of C3 is only very uncommonly associated with the development of SLE, but because of the rarity of homozygous C3 deficiency, only limited data exist [113].

These clinical data suggest that there is an activity of the early part of the classical pathway of complement that is protective in normal individuals against the development of SLE. Deficiency of this activity predisposes very strongly to the development of disease, as shown by the observation that almost every human, so far identified, who lacks C1q has developed SLE.

It is always a concern that a reported disease association is due to an ascertainment artefact rather than due to a true causal association. In the case of complement and SLE, it could be argued that because complement is frequently measured in patients with SLE, it is not surprising that complement deficiency turns up in these patients.

There is a group of arguments that militate against this artefactual explanation for the association. Complement deficiency has been sought in large normal populations, but no classical pathway deficiencies have been identified. The clearest example is the enormous study of Japanese blood donors, amongst whom no hereditary classical pathway deficiency states were found [114,115]. There is a reported Japanese patient, however, with C1q deficiency and SLE [116]. Another argument is that the observed intrafamilial disease concordance for SLE in combination with complement deficiency is extremely high.

In the case of C1q deficiency it is more than 90%, a figure that far exceeds the observed concordance of SLE between siblings in monozygotic twin pairs (24%) [117]. The third argument is that disease associated with hereditary complement deficiency tends to be of early onset and the male to female ratio approximates to unity, unlike the high female preponderance amongst the majority of SLE patients without complement deficiency.

Each of these observations illustrates the strength of the disease association and provides evidence that the association between complement deficiency and SLE is not likely to be explained by ascertainment artefact. A further argument for a causal link is the finding that acquired complement deficiency states also predispose to the development of SLE. There is an increased prevalence of SLE amongst patients with hereditary angioedema who, because of inherited partial deficiency of C1 inhibitor, fail to regulate classical pathway complement activation [118–120] and amongst patients with C3 nephritic factor [73].

This evidence leaves no doubt that homozygous classical pathway protein deficiencies are causally associated with the development of SLE. There is less certainty in the case of partial inherited complement deficiencies. There has been particular interest in the associations between partial deficiencies of C4 and SLE. In humans, C4 is encoded by two tandemly duplicated genes within the major histocompatibility complex (MHC), encoding respectively isotypes known as C4A and C4B [121]. In common with other MHC genes, each of the C4 genes is highly polymorphic and, included in the polymorphisms, are null alleles from which no protein is produced. These null alleles are very common and approximately 6% of most populations have homozygous deficiency of either C4A or C4B. It should be noted that total C4 deficiency is exceptionally rare because haplotypes encoding null alleles at both the C4A and C4B loci are very rare. The functions of the two C4 isotypes differ slightly. The internal thioester bond of C4A shows preferential binding to amino groups with the formation of covalent amide bonds between C4A and proteins. Preferential binding to hydroxyl groups is shown by C4B, typically in carbohydrates, forming ester linkages [122].

There are disease susceptibility genes for SLE in the MHC (reviewed in [123,124]). Following the discovery of the two isotypes of C4 and the existence of null alleles at both loci there have been many studies to attempt to determine whether null alleles of C4 might play a role in determining disease susceptibility. Initial studies showed an increased prevalence of C4A null alleles in Caucasoid patients with SLE [125,126]. However, null alleles for C4A are found commonly in a particular MHC haplotype, HLA-A1, B8, C4AQ0, C4B1, DR3, and it is exceptionally difficult to determine which is the real susceptibility gene or genes for SLE and which are the 'passengers'. The literature abounds with case-control and family studies either confirming or refuting associations between C4 null alleles and SLE. A definitive answer is likely to emerge in the next few years as large scale genotyping methods are applied to the very large family collections of patients with SLE that are being formed around the world.

What is the explanation for these clinical findings?

The role of complement in the pathogenesis of inflammatory lesions in SLE

The traditional view of the pathogenesis of SLE is that immune complexes containing autoantigens and autoantibodies activate complement, and that this causes inflammatory injury to tissues. Although this model is biologically plausible, it cannot account for all of the clinical observations that link the complement system and SLE. In particular, the observation that complement deficiency causes lupus is hard to reconcile with the concept that complement activation products are the major cause of inflammatory injury in the disease.

The development of gene-targeted strains of mice that lack individual protein constituents of inflammatory pathways has led to a plethora of apparently inconsistent findings on mechanisms of immune-complex-mediated inflammation. There is a large array of mice lacking complement proteins and Fc receptors, and an equally large array of studies of these mice. In this section the mechanisms of complement activation in SLE will be reviewed briefly and the pathogenesis of inflammation caused by immune complexes will be considered.

How is complement activated in SLE?
The cause of complement activation in SLE is the formation of immune complexes, which in turn activate complement, predominantly by means of the classical pathway. Complement activation is normally measured in clinical practice by estimation of antigenic levels of both C3 and C4, and measured functionally using the CH50 assay. In the majority of patients with moderate or active SLE, reduced levels of C4 are detected, with the level of C3 varying between normal to slightly reduced. The CH50 is typically below normal.

Up to 25% of patients with SLE, however, may have much more dramatic reductions in C4 levels, typically associated with significantly subnormal C3 levels and CH50. Three subsets of patients make up the majority of these individuals. There are those subjects who have evidence of autoimmunity to red blood cells. This may manifest as overt autoimmune haemolytic anaemia, but it may be more subtle and be detectable only by means of direct antiglobulin test (Coombs' test) positivity for IgG, C3 and C4 deposition on red cells. Some of these patients also have

antiphospholipid (also known as anticardiolipin) autoantibodies. A study in a murine model of the antiphospholipid syndrome has recently shown that antiphospholipid antibodies cause foetal resorption by means of complement activation in the decidua in the pregnant uterus [127]. The complement activation at this site was shown to cause inflammatory injury, which appeared to be responsible for the foetal death and resorption.

Another subset comprises patients with very systemic disease, typically associated with high levels of anti-dsDNA autoantibodies and, sometimes, with the presence of type III cryoglobulins [128] in serum containing polyclonal IgG and C3.

The third group of patients comprises those individuals who have anti-C1q autoantibodies. These subjects often have the most severe evidence of classical pathway complement activation, with profoundly reduced C4 levels and moderate to substantial reductions in C3 levels. It is thought that anti-C1q autoantibodies are the cause and not the consequence of the complement activation measured in serum, and possible mechanisms were reviewed above.

Mechanisms of immune-complex-mediated injury
Until very recently it was believed that tissue injury in SLE was caused by the formation of immune complexes that caused complement activation, which in turn caused inflammatory injury. Tissue injury was thought to be mediated by the direct effects of activation of the triggered enzyme cascades of complement, coagulation and kinin pathways, coupled with an influx of inflammatory cells, including polymorphonuclear leukocytes and monocytes. The activities of complement in the mediation of inflammation include the ligation of complement receptors for the opsonic components of complement subcomponents C3b and C4b, the effects of the anaphylatoxins C5a and C3a, and the effects of insertion of sublethal amounts of the membrane attack complex into cell membranes.

The development of mice with null mutations in selected proteins of inflammatory pathways has enabled the precise dissection of their role in both host defence and the causation of inflammatory injury. There are many experimental models of injury caused by immune complexes and the use of these in gene-targeted mice has led to a reappraisal of the role of complement and Fc receptors in inflammatory responses to immune complexes. The major conclusions from these experiments are as follows. Firstly, it is clear that all immune complexes are not equal in the manner in which they cause tissue injury. The site of immune complex formation [129], the species [130] and strain [131] of animal, and the nature of the antigen [132], as well as the antibody, may affect the inflammatory response. Secondly, in many models it has been found that the ligation of Fc receptors by immune complexes is the dominant cause of tissue injury, and complement plays no important role in the induction of tissue injury [133]. Indeed, in experimental models of complement deficiency, it has been shown that immune-complex-mediated glomerulonephritis can develop spontaneously in the presence of genetic deficiency of the complement activation pathways [134,135]. In other experimental models, however, complement activation, and in particular C5a production, have been found to be essential for the full expression of tissue injury [136]; inhibition of C5a activity is therapeutic [137]. Thirdly, it has been found that complement may provide some degree of protection against inflammatory injury induced by immune complexes in some models of experimental glomerulonephritis [138]. We will consider possible mechanisms for this in a subsequent section of this chapter. Finally, it is clear that in mice and humans, inflammatory pathways that operate downstream from the activation of complement, and the ligation of Fc and complement receptors play crucial roles in the expression of inflammation that is mediated by immune complexes [139].

Complement deficiency and SLE

The associations of complement deficiency with SLE have been reviewed in the Introduction. Here we shall consider three hypotheses that have been advanced to explain the mechanism of the association. The first two of these are closely related, proposing mechanisms that could operate in tandem. These hypotheses are that complement prevents the development of SLE through a role in the processing and clearance from the body of immune complexes, and dying and dead cells. In the absence of these activities, autoantigens may be presented to the immune system in the context of inflammatory injury and this may drive the development of autoimmunity. The third hypothesis invokes a role for complement in the development of self-tolerance to the autoantigens of SLE, and proposes that B cells with specificity for lupus autoantigens are not effectively silenced or eliminated in the absence of complement. Each of these hypotheses will be explored briefly in this section.

Complement and immune complex processing
Michael Heidelberger in the 1940s demonstrated a role for complement in the modification of immune complex lattices [140]. Since then there have been many studies that showed that complement promotes the inactivation and clearance of immune complexes by two main mechanisms. One of these is the reduction in the size of immune complex lattices (reviewed in [141,142]). This is achieved by the interaction of C1q with immune complexes, which interferes with Fc–Fc interactions that stabilize immune complexes, and by the covalent binding of C4b and C3b to antigens within the immune complexes. This binding interferes with the binding of antigen to antibody by effectively reducing the valency of antigen for antibody. As well as reducing the size of immune complexes, complement provides additional ligands within the immune complex, promoting the clearance of immune complexes by complement as well as Fc receptors. As discussed in earlier in this chapter, immune complexes that have bound C4b and C3b can bind to CR1 on erythrocytes in the circulation that promote the clearance of immune complexes to the fixed mononuclear phagocytic system.

These observations led to the hypothesis that complement deficiency may promote the development of SLE by impairment of the normal mechanisms for clearance and processing of immune complexes. These could cause inflammatory injury in tissues, resulting in the release of autoantigens in an inflammatory context, promoting the development of an autoimmune response [143]. There is abundant evidence that immune complex processing in SLE is abnormal and related to abnormal complement function [144–146]. Both the discovery that complement deficiency is compatible with the normal spontaneous development of glomerulonephritis in murine models of SLE [134,135] and the surprising finding that induced glomerulonephritis may be exacerbated in the presence of complement deficiency [147] are compatible with this proposed role for complement in protection against immune-complex-mediated injury.

This hypothesis is complementary to and was the precursor of the 'waste disposal' hypothesis, developed in the next section, which advances the hypothesis that complement provides protection against the development of SLE by impairment of the physiological waste disposal of autoantigens released by dying and dead cells.

Complement and the clearance of apoptotic cells
A central question about the aetiology of SLE is to understand how an autoimmune response develops to autoantigens that are found ubiquitously in cells of the body. There is abundant evidence that the established autoantibody response in SLE is driven by the actual autoantigens (as opposed to being part of a polyclonal antibody response or driven by cross-reacting antigens). What is the source of these autoantigens? Cell death is an obvious potential source of autoantigens that are otherwise hidden from immune receptors in the heart of living cells. However, cell death is a highly regulated process and the normal mechanisms of apoptosis ensure that dying cells are cleared without the induction of tissue inflammatory responses [148]. One possible source is dead or dying cells from sites of inflammation and tissue injury. A possible connection between apoptotic cells and the autoantibody response of SLE was established by Rosen and his colleagues, who showed that a number of lupus autoantigens were located at the surface of apoptotic bodies and on apoptotic blebs [149].

These observations have been followed by a series of studies of the mechanisms of apoptotic cell clearance in SLE. It was shown that macrophages derived from peripheral blood of patients with SLE showed defective uptake of apoptotic cells [150]. The idea that complement might play a role in the clearance of apoptotic cells came from the observation that C1q bound to apoptotic keratinocytes [151]. An excess of apoptotic cells was observed in kidneys from C1q-deficient mice [152]. It was later shown that elicited peritoneal macrophages from C1q-deficient mice showed defective clearance of injected apoptotic thymocytes and the human lymphocyte cell lines known as Jurkat cells [153]. Similarly, monocyte-derived macrophages from a small number of C1q-deficient humans showed defective clearance of apoptotic cells, a defect that could be reversed by the addition of purified C1q. It was also found that the clearance of apoptotic cells could be mediated by bound C3 [154], although there may be an additional role for earlier proteins of the classical pathway in mediating and/or augmenting apoptotic cell clearance. This work has led to the hypothesis that complement plays a role in the prevention of autoimmunity through a role in the disposal of dying and dead cells. Absence of this activity, possibly occurring in the context of an inflammatory environment, may promote the development of an autoantigen-driven autoimmune response [155,156]. It has also been shown that C4-deficient mice are prone to the development of lupus-like autoimmunity [157,158], which provides further evidence that complement-deficient mice are a useful model to study the association between complement deficiency and SLE, first described in humans.

The steps from defective clearance of apoptotic cells to the development of an autoimmune response remain unknown. At least in mice, there is evidence that other genes contribute to the autoimmune phenotype in the context of C1q deficiency, which is associated with lupus in mice on a hybrid (129 strain × C57/BL6 strain) background. It also causes disease acceleration in the lupus prone MRL.mp mouse. However, no autoimmunity is seen in C1q-deficient mice on 129 and C57/BL6 inbred strains [152,159]. These data show the necessity for the presence of other disease-modifying genes that enable the potential autoimmune consequences of C1q deficiency to be expressed in mice. In humans, the strength of the contribution of C1q deficiency to disease appears higher than in mice, as the majority of humans with C1q deficiency express some manifestations of SLE [112]. However, only approximately a third of patients develop glomerulonephritis, again indicating that C1q deficiency is not sufficient for the development of glomerular inflammation. Lupus in humans and mice is subject to the influence of multiple genetic and, probably also environmental, factors.

Complement and the induction of tolerance
An alternative hypothesis to explain the link between complement deficiency and SLE is that complement plays a role in the induction of tolerance to autoantigens [160]. Deficiency of this activity disturbs the normal tolerance mechanisms of lymphocytes leading to the induction of SLE. This hypothesis is difficult to reconcile with the observations that the complement system plays a physiological role in the augmentation of antibody responses. Pepys showed many years ago that depletion of complement C3 was associated with reduced primary and secondary antibody responses to T-cell-dependent antigens [161], a finding that has subsequently been reproduced in complement genetically-deficient mice and guinea pigs [162,163]. The corollary of these observations was the engineering of complement as an adjuvant by the covalent attachment of oligomers of C3d to an experimental antigen [164].

Using a transgenic model to study tolerance to hen egg lysozyme, expressed as an autoantigen, it was found that tolerance was disturbed in C4-deficient, but not C3-deficient, mice [165]. In similar experiments with C1q-deficient mice, however, tolerance induction to hen egg lysozyme as an autoantigen was normal [166]. This model of tolerance induction has important limitations as a model for exploring SLE, as in this disease, the majority of the autoantigens are cell-associated, as will be reviewed in the next section. Experimental studies are underway exploring the role of complement deficiency in tolerance induction in experimental animals expressing transgenic lupus autoantibodies, which may provide a clearer test of the hypothesis that complement is involved in the induction of tolerance.

A unifying hypothesis that links C1q deficiency, C1q autoantibodies and SLE

A prominent feature of the autoantibody response in SLE is that it is directed not against isolated proteins but typically against whole complexes of proteins and nucleic acids [167–169]. Autoantibodies are found in clusters reactive against the different protein, nucleic acid and phospholipid components of these complexes. For example anti-dsDNA autoantibodies are usually associated with antihistone autoantibodies and antibodies reacting with conformational determinants of chromatin. The autoantigens in this case are thought to be nucleosomes. Anti-Sm and antiribonucleoprotein specificities are directed against different proteins in the spliceosome complex. Anti-Ro and anti-La are directed against the major protein component of a small cytoplasmic ribonucleoprotein complex. These clinical findings point to actual autoantigenic particles in lupus being these large complexes and there is evidence that B cells play a key role as antigen-presenting cells in lupus [170–172]. A B cell bearing an antigen receptor for a component of one of these complexes can internalize the complex and then act as antigen-presenting cell for other peptides within the complex. In this way it is likely that the autoantibody response in SLE is diversified and amplified.

How do these data explain how on the one hand C1q deficiency causes SLE and on the other that SLE causes an autoantibody response to C1q? The hypothesis has been reviewed above that C1q and other complement proteins prevent lupus by binding to apoptotic and necrotic cells and promoting their clearance. The absence of C1q promotes autoimmunity by allowing these autoantigens to drive an autoimmune response.

This hypothesis implies that C1q binds to the autoantigens of SLE. In doing so, it may itself become part of the autoantigenic complexes that characterize the disease. Although it is unusual for plasma proteins to be targets for the autoimmune response in SLE, there is an important and informative analogy. Approximately a third of patients with SLE develop antiphospholipid autoantibodies. These are directed against negatively charged phospholipids, especially phosphatidylserine, which normally reside on the inner lamella of cell membranes. However, they are translocated to the outer lamella of apoptotic cells, which reinforces the possible role of these cells as the source of the autoantigens that drive SLE [173,174]. Antiphospholipid autoantibodies in SLE are typically associated with an autoantibody response to the plasma proteins β2-glycoprotein-I and annexin V, that binds to negatively-charged phospholipids [175,176].

Thus, the observation that C1q is itself an autoantigen in many patients with SLE reinforces the hypothesis that C1q and the complement system may prevent disease by binding to and promoting the clearance of autoantigens.

Complement and the treatment of disease

It is not straightforward to treat SLE by the manipulation of the complement system. On the one hand complement deficiency, as we have seen, is a powerful cause of SLE and this provides arguments for increasing complement activity by repletion of classical pathway proteins, at least in the case of the rare hereditary deficiencies. On the other hand, there is evidence that complement, especially the anaphylatoxins and the membrane attack complex, may be a cause of tissue injury and this raises the possibility of the treatment of SLE by therapeutic inhibition of the complement system. Both approaches to therapy have been attempted in different contexts in SLE and will be reviewed in the next few paragraphs.

Complement is a potent cause of tissue injury in ischaemia-reperfusion injury and therefore is a therapeutic target in patients with myocardial infarction and stroke. Because these are highly prevalent and disabling diseases

there have been many studies that have validated the potential importance of complement inhibition as a treatment for them. There are several reviews that illustrate the range of diseases that are under investigation and the many approaches to treatment by inhibition of the complement system [177–182].

Anti-C5 therapy

There is increasing evidence that the key mediators of injury induced by the complement system are the anaphylatoxins, especially C5a, and the membrane attack complex. An anti-C5 monoclonal antibody reduced the expression of glomerulonephritis and increased the lifespan of NZB/W F1 hybrid mice [183]. Similar anti-C5 antibodies have also been found to be therapeutically effective in other disease models where complement is thought to play an important role, such as ischaemia-reperfusion injury in the heart [184] and hyperacute xenograft rejection [185]. There have been preliminary studies of this approach to treatment in humans undergoing coronary artery bypass surgery on cardiopulmonary bypass, which is known to be a potent means of activating the complement system [186].

These studies, however, have to be balanced against the findings that lupus nephritis may develop in humans lacking classical pathway proteins and in mice which are either unable to activate C3 [134] or genetically deficient in this protein [135]. Trials have been proposed of anti-C5 therapy in patients with SLE and nephritis.

Complement repletion therapy

Given that deficiency of classical pathway complement proteins is a potent cause for the development of SLE, one obvious approach to therapy is replacement of the missing protein. However, there are potential pitfalls to this approach. Purified or engineered complement proteins are not available for treatment purposes. Therefore, whole plasma preparations have to be used, which entail all of the complications of plasma treatment, including hypersensitivity reactions and the potential for transmitted viral infections. Another pitfall is the possibility that replacement of a missing complement protein in a patient with months or years of accumulated immune complexes in tissues may be followed by complement activation in tissues causing inflammatory injury. A further issue is that, following exposure to a protein that is genetically deficient and therefore 'foreign', antibodies may develop, preventing treatment by replenishment.

There are several anecdotal reports of the treatment of complement-deficient patients with plasma; benefit has been reported in two patients with C2 deficiency [187,188]. There was no significant clinical response in a patient with C1q deficiency who had received briefly fresh-frozen plasma, but antibodies developed to C1q [189].

Treatment with plasma of two dogs with hereditary C3 deficiency and mesangiocapillary glomerulonephritis was not successful and led to a worsening of disease [190].

Many tissues synthesize complement proteins. The bone marrow is the major source of C1q [191] and this raises the possibility that C1q replenishment in patients with C1q deficiency and severe SLE might be achieved by bone marrow transplantation.

C1q absorption
Another approach that is undergoing experimental evaluation in small numbers of patients with SLE is immunoabsorption by perfusion of plasma over columns coupled with C1q [192,193]. These columns can remove anti-C1q autoantibodies from serum and may also be capable of extracting immune complexes from the circulation. This is an interesting approach, particularly in the light of the evidence discussed above that anti-C1q antibodies may play a pathogenic role in disease. It is too early to know whether this approach will have any important role to play in the management of SLE.

Glossary of terms
C = complement component; CH50 = complement haemolysis 50% test; CR = complement receptor; HUVS = hypocomplementaemic urticarial vasculitis.

Acknowledgments
I would like to acknowledge the support of my colleagues, Drs Marina Botto, Kevin Davies, Bernard Morley and Tim Vyse, and of my teacher and mentor Prof Peter Lachmann. The work of the Rheumatology Section at Imperial College has been supported for many years by programme grants from the Arthritis Research Campaign and the Wellcome Trust.

References
1. Hargraves MM, Richmond H, Morton R: **Presentation of two bone marrow elements: the "tart" cell and the "L.E." cell.** *Proc Staff Meetings Mayo Clinic* 1948, **23**:25-28.
2. Miescher P, Fauconnet M, Beraud TH: **L'absorption du facteur (L.E.) par des noyaux cellulaires isolés.** *Experientia* 1954, **10**:252-254.
3. Friou GJ: **Identification of the nuclear component of the interaction of lupus erythematosus globulin and nuclei.** *J Immunol* 1958, **80**:476-480.
4. Holman HR, Kunkel HG: **Affinity between the lupus erythematosus serum factor and cell nuclei and nucleoprotein.** *Science* 1957, **126**:162-163.
5. Wedgwood RJP, Janeway CA: **Serum complement in children with "collagen diseases".** *Pediatrics* 1953, **11**:569-581.
6. Elliott JA, Mathieson DR: **Complement in disseminated (systemic) lupus erythematosus.** *AMA Arch Dermat Syphilol* 1953, **68**:119-128.
7. Lachmann PJ, Muller-Eberhard HJ, Kunkel HG, Paronetto F: **The localization of in vivo bound complement in tissue sections.** *J Exp Med* 1962, **115**:63-115.
8. Schur PH, Sandson J: **Immunologic factors and clinical activity in systemic lupus erythematosus.** *N Engl J Med* 1968, **278**:533-538.
9. Daha MR, Hazevoet HM, Hermans J, van Es LA, Cats A: **Relative importance of C4 binding protein in the modulation of the classical pathway C3 convertase in patients with systemic lupus erythematosus.** *Clin Exp Immunol* 1983, **54**:248-252.
10. Perrin LH, Lambert PH, Nydegger UE, Miescher PA: **Quantitation of C3PA (properdin factor B) and other complement components in diseases associated with a low C3 level.** *N Engl J Med* 1973, **2**:16-27.
11. Mayes JT, Schreiber RD, Cooper NR: **Development and application of an enzyme-linked immunosorbent assay for the quantitation of alternative complement pathway activation in human serum.** *J Clin Invest* 1984, **73**:160-170.
12. Valentijn RM, van Overhagen H, Hazevoet HM, Hermans J, Cats A, Daha MR, van Es LA: **The value of complement and immune complex determinations in monitoring disease activity in patients with systemic lupus erythematosus.** *Arthritis Rheum* 1985, **28**:904-913.
13. Smeenk RJ, Aarden LA, Swaak TJ: **Laboratory tests as predictors of disease exacerbations in systemic lupus erythematosus: comment on the article by Esdaile et al.** *Arthritis Rheum* 1996, **39**:2083-2085.
14. Esdaile JM, Joseph L, Abrahamowicz M, Li Y, Danoff D, Clarke AE: **Routine immunologic tests in systemic lupus erythematosus: is there a need for more studies?** *J Rheumatol* 1996, **23**:1891-1896.
15. Alper CA, Rosen FS: **Studies of the in vivo behavior of human C'3 in normal subjects and patients.** *J Clin Invest* 1967, **46**:2021-2034.
16. Hunsicker LG, Ruddy S, Carpenter CB, Schur PH, Merrill JP, Muller-Eberhard HJ, Austen KF: **Metabolism of third complement component (C3) in nephritis. Involvement of the classic and alternate (properdin) pathways for complement activation.** *N Engl J Med* 1972, **287**:835-840.
17. Sliwinski AJ, Zvaifler NJ: **Decreased synthesis of the third component of complement (C3) in hypocomplementemic systemic lupus erythematosus.** *Clin Exp Immunol* 1972, **11**:21-29.
18. Sturfelt G, Sjoholm AG: **Complement components, complement activation, and acute phase response in systemic lupus erythematosus.** *Int Arch Allergy Appl Immunol* 1984, **75**:75-83.
19. Mendell JR, Garcha TS, Kissel JT: **The immunopathogenic role of complement in human muscle disease.** *Curr Opin Neurol* 1996, **9**:226-234. [key review]
20. Ashizawa T, Appel SH: **Immunopathologic events at the endplate in myasthenia gravis.** *Springer Semin Immunopathol* 1985, **8**:177-196. [key review]
21. Couser WG: **Glomerulonephritis.** *Lancet* 1999, **353**:1509-1515. [key review]
22. Cavallo T: **Membranous nephropathy. Insights from Heymann nephritis.** *Am J Pathol* 1994, **144**:651-658. [key review]
23. Lloyd W, Schur PH: **Immune complexes, complement, and anti-DNA in exacerbations of systemic lupus erythematosus (SLE).** *Medicine (Baltimore)* 1981, **60**:208-217.
24. Hopkins P, Belmont HM, Buyon J, Philips M, Weissmann G, Abramson SB: **Increased levels of plasma anaphylatoxins in systemic lupus erythematosus predict flares of the disease and may elicit vascular injury in lupus cerebritis.** *Arthritis Rheum* 1988, **31**:632-641.
25. Senaldi G, Makinde VA, Vergani D, Isenberg DA: **Correlation of the activation of the fourth component of complement (C4) with disease activity in systemic lupus erythematosus.** *Ann Rheum Dis* 1988, **47**:913-917.
26. Perrin LH, Lambert PH, Miescher PA: **Complement breakdown products in plasma from patients with systemic lupus erythematosus and patients with membranoproliferative or other glomerulonephritis.** *J Clin Invest* 1975, **56**:165-176.
27. Negoro N, Okamura M, Takeda T, Koda S, Amatsu K, Inoue T, Curd JG, Kanayama Y: **The clinical significance of iC3b neoantigen expression in plasma from patients with systemic lupus erythematosus.** *Arthritis Rheum* 1989, **32**:1233-1242.
28. Falk RJ, Dalmasso AP, Kim Y, Lam S, Michael A: **Radioimmunoassay of the attack complex of complement in serum from patients with systemic lupus erythematosus.** *N Engl J Med* 1985, **312**:1594-1599.
29. Gawryl MS, Chudwin DS, Langlois PF, Lint TF: **The terminal complement complex, C5b-9, a marker of disease activity in patients with systemic lupus erythematosus.** *Arthritis Rheum* 1988, **31**:188-195.
30. Buyon JP, Tamerius J, Belmont HM, Abramson SB: **Assessment of disease activity and impending flare in patients with systemic lupus erythematosus. Comparison of the use of complement split products and conventional measurements of complement.** *Arthritis Rheum* 1992, **35**:1028-1037.

31. Manzi S, Rairie JE, Carpenter AB, Kelly RH, Jagarlapudi SP, Sereika SM, Medsger TA Jr, Ramsey-Goldman R: **Sensitivity and specificity of plasma and urine complement split products as indicators of lupus disease activity.** *Arthritis Rheum* 1996, **39**: 1178-1188.

32. Porcel JM, Ordi J, Castro-Salomo A, Vilardell M, Rodrigo MJ, Gene T, Warburton F, Kraus M, Vergani D: **The value of complement activation products in the assessment of systemic lupus erythematosus flares.** *N Engl J Med* 1995, **74**:283-288.

33. Manderson AP, Pickering MC, Botto M, Walport MJ, Parish CR: **Continual low-level activation of the classical complement pathway.** *J Exp Med* 2001, **194**:747-756.

34. Swaak AJ, Smeenk RJ: **Following the disease course in systemic lupus erythematosus: are serologic variables of any use?** *J Rheumatol* 1996, **23**:1842-1844.

35. Sjoholm AG, Martensson U, Sturfelt G: **Serial analysis of autoantibody responses to the collagen-like region of C1q, collagen type II, and double stranded DNA in patients with systemic lupus erythematosus.** *J Rheumatol* 1997, **24**:871-878.

36. Jonsson H, Sturfelt G, Martensson U, Truedsson L, Sjoholm AG: **Prospective analysis of C1 dissociation and complement activation in patients with systemic lupus erythematosus.** *Clin Exp Rheumatol* 1995, **13**:573-580.

37. Swaak AJ, Groenwold J, Bronsveld W: **Predictive value of complement profiles and anti-dsDNA in systemic lupus erythematosus.** *Ann Rheum Dis* 1986, **45**:359-366.

38. Swaak AJ, Aarden LA, Statius van Eps LW, Feltkamp TE: **Anti-dsDNA and complement profiles as prognostic guides in systemic lupus erythematosus.** *Arthritis Rheum* 1979, **22**:226-235.

39. Coremans IE, Spronk PE, Bootsma H, Daha MR, van der Voort EA, Kater L, Breedveld FC, Kallenberg CG: **Changes in antibodies to C1q predict renal relapses in systemic lupus erythematosus.** *Am J Kidney Dis* 1995, **26**:595-601.

40. Paronetto F, Koffler D: **Immunofluorescent localization of immunoglobulins, complement, and fibrinogen in human diseases. I. Systemic lupus erythematosus.** *J Clin Invest* 1965, **44**:1657-1664.

41. Biesecker G, Katz S, Koffler D: **Renal localization of the membrane attack complex in systemic lupus erythematosus nephritis.** *J Exp Med* 1981, **154**:1779-1794.

42. Biesecker G, Lavin L, Ziskind M, Koffler D: **Cutaneous localization of the membrane attack complex in discoid and systemic lupus erythematosus.** *N Engl J Med* 1982, **306**:264-270.

43. Helm KF, Peters MS: **Deposition of membrane attack complex in cutaneous lesions of lupus erythematosus.** *J Am Acad Dermatol* 1993, **28**:687-691.

44. French LE, Tschopp J, Schifferli JA: **Clusterin in renal tissue: preferential localization with the terminal complement complex and immunoglobulin deposits in glomeruli [see comments].** *Clin Exp Immunol* 1992, **88**:389-393.

45. Ahearn JM, Fearon DT: **Structure and function of the complement receptors, CR1 (CD35) and CR2 (CD21).** *Adv Immunol* 1989, **46**:183-219. [key review]

46. Brown HC, Broom JC: **Studies in trypanosomiasis. II Observations on the red cell adhesion test.** *Trans R Soc Trop Med Hyg* 1938, **32**:209-222.

47. Klopstock A, Schartz J, Bleiberg Y, Adam A, Szeinberg A, Schlomo J: **Hereditary nature of the behavious of erythrocytes in immune adherence - haemagglutination phenomenon.** *Vox Sang* 1965, **10**:177-187.

48. Miyakawa Y, Yamada A, Kosaka K, Tsuda F, Kosugi E, Mayumi M: **Defective immune-adherence (C3b) receptor on erythrocytes from patients with systemic lupus erythematosus.** *Lancet* 1981, **2**:493-497.

49. Iida K, Mornaghi R, Nussenzweig V: **Complement receptor (CR1) deficiency in erythrocytes from patients with systemic lupus erythematosus.** *J Exp Med* 1982, **155**:1427-1438.

50. Wilson JG, Wong WW, Schur PH, Fearon DT: **Mode of inheritance of decreased C3b receptors on erythrocytes of patients with systemic lupus erythematosus.** *N Engl J Med* 1982, **307**: 981-986.

51. Walport MJ, Lachmann PJ: **Erythrocyte complement receptor type 1, immune complexes, and the rheumatic diseases.** *Arthritis Rheum* 1988, **31**:153-158. [key review]

52. Ross GD, Yount WJ, Walport MJ, Winfield JB, Parker CJ, Fuller CR, Taylor RP, Myones BL, Lachmann PJ: **Disease-associated loss of erythrocyte complement receptors (CR1, C3b receptors) in patients with systemic lupus erythematosus and other diseases involving autoantibodies and/or complement activation.** *J Immunol* 1985, **135**:2005-2014.

53. Wilson JG, Wong WW, Murphy EE, III, Schur PH, Fearon DT: **Deficiency of the C3b/C4b receptor (CR1) of erythrocytes in systemic lupus erythematosus: analysis of the stability of the defect and of a restriction fragment length polymorphism of the CR1 gene.** *J Immunol* 1987, **138**:2708-2710.

54. Moldenhauer F, David J, Fielder AH, Lachmann PJ, Walport MJ: **Inherited deficiency of erythrocyte complement receptor type 1 does not cause susceptibility to systemic lupus erythematosus.** *Arthritis Rheum* 1987, **30**:961-966.

55. Cohen JH, Caudwell V, Levi-Strauss M, Bourgeois P, Kazatchkine MD: **Genetic analysis of CR1 expression on erythrocytes of patients with systemic lupus erythematosus.** *Arthritis Rheum* 1989, **32**:393-397.

56. Hammond A, Rudge AC, Loizou S, Bowcock SJ, Walport MJ: **Reduced numbers of complement receptor type 1 on erythrocytes are associated with increased levels of anticardiolipin antibodies. Findings in patients with systemic lupus erythematosus and the antiphospholipid syndrome.** *Arthritis Rheum* 1989, **32**:259-264.

57. Walport M, Ng YC, Lachmann PJ: **Erythrocytes transfused into patients with SLE and haemolytic anaemia lose complement receptor type 1 from their cell surface.** *Clin Exp Immunol* 1987, **69**:501-507.

58. Davies KA, Hird V, Stewart S, Sivolapenko GB, Jose P, Epenetos AA, Walport MJ: **A study of in vivo immune complex formation and clearance in man.** *J Immunol* 1990, **144**:4613-4620.

59. Ripoche J, Sim RB: **Loss of complement receptor type 1 (CR1) on ageing of erythrocytes. Studies of proteolytic release of the receptor.** *Biochem J* 1986, **235**:815-821.

60. Pascual M, Danielsson C, Steiger G, Schifferli JA: **Proteolytic cleavage of CR1 on human erythrocytes in vivo: evidence for enhanced cleavage in AIDS.** *Eur J Immunol* 1994, **24**:702-708.

61. Moldenhauer F, Botto M, Walport MJ: **The rate of loss of CR1 from ageing erythrocytes in vivo in normal subjects and SLE patients: no correlation with structural or numerical polymorphisms.** *Clin Exp Immunol* 1988, **72**:74-78.

62. Taylor RP, Ferguson PJ, Martin EN, Cooke J, Greene KL, Grinspun K, Guttman M, Kuhn S: **Immune complexes bound to the primate erythrocyte complement receptor (CR1) via anti-CR1 mAbs are cleared simultaneously with loss of CR1 in a concerted reaction in a rhesus monkey model.** *N Engl J Med* 1997, **82**:49-59.

63. Cosio FG, Shen XP, Birmingham DJ, Van Aman M, Hebert LA: **Evaluation of the mechanisms responsible for the reduction in erythrocyte complement receptors when immune complexes form in vivo in primates.** *J Immunol* 1990, **145**:4198-4206.

64. Birmingham DJ, Hebert LA, Cosio FG, VanAman ME: **Immune complex erythrocyte complement receptor interactions in vivo during induction of glomerulonephritis in nonhuman primates.** *J Lab Clin Med* 1990, **116**:242-252.

65. Reinagel ML, Taylor RP: **Transfer of immune complexes from erythrocyte CR1 to mouse macrophages.** *J Immunol* 2000, **164**: 1977-1985.

66. Emancipator SN, Iida K, Nussenzweig V, Gallo GR: **Monoclonal antibodies to human complement receptor (CR1) detect defects in glomerular diseases.** *N Engl J Med* 1983, **27**:170-175.

67. Kazatchkine MD, Fearon DT, Appay MD, Mandet C, Bariety J: **Immunohistochemical study of the human glomerular C3b receptor in normal kidney and in seventy-five cases of renal diseases: loss of C3b receptor antigen in focal hyalinosis and in proliferative nephritis of systemic lupus erythematosus.** *J Clin Invest* 1982, **69**:900-912.

68. Pascual M, Steiger G, Sadallah S, Paccaud JP, Carpentier JL, James R, Schifferli JA: **Identification of membrane-bound CR1 (CD35) in human urine: evidence for its release by glomerular podocytes.** *J Exp Med* 1994, **179**:889-899.

69. Teixeira JE, Costa RS, Lachmann PJ, Wurzner R, Barbosa JE: **CR1 stump peptide and terminal complement complexes are found in the glomeruli of lupus nephritis patients.** *Clin Exp Immunol* 1996, **105**:497-503.

70. Moll S, Miot S, Sadallah S, Gudat F, Mihatsch MJ, Schifferli JA: **No complement receptor 1 stumps on podocytes in human glomerulopathies.** *Kidney Int* 2001, **59**:160-168.

71. Bienenstock J, Bloch KJ: **Immunoconglutinin in various rheumatic diseases and certain diseases suspected of an autoimmune pathogenesis.** Arthritis Rheum 1967, **10**:187-198.

72. Nilsson B, Ekdahl KN, Svarvare M, Bjelle A, Nilsson UR: **Purification and characterization of IgG immunoconglutinins from patients with systemic lupus erythematosus: implications for a regulatory function.** Clin Exp Immunol 1990, **82**:262-267.

73. Walport MJ, Davies KA, Botto M, Naughton MA, Isenberg DA, Biasi D, Powell RJ, Cheung NT, Struthers GR: **C3 nephritic factor and SLE: report of four cases and review of the literature.** QJM 1994, **87**:609-615.

74. Jackson J, Sim RB, Whelan A, Feighery C: **An IgG autoantibody which inactivates C1-inhibitor.** Nature 1986, **323**:722-724.

75. Alsenz J, Bork K, Loos M: **Autoantibody-mediated acquired deficiency of C1 inhibitor.** N Engl J Med 1987, **316**:1360-1366.

76. Cicardi M, Beretta A, Colombo M, Gioffre D, Cugno M, Agostoni A: **Relevance of lymphoproliferative disorders and of anti-C1 inhibitor autoantibodies in acquired angio-oedema.** Clin Exp Immunol 1996, **106**:475-480.

77. Cicardi M, Bisiani G, Cugno M, Spath P, Agostoni A: **Autoimmune C1 inhibitor deficiency: report of eight patients.** Am J Med 1993, **95**:169-175.

78. Gelfand JA, Boss GR, Conley CL, Reinhart R, Frank MM: **Acquired C1 esterase inhibitor deficiency and angioedema: a review.** Medicine (Baltimore) 1979, **58**:321-328. [key review]

79. Wilson JG, Jack RM, Wong WW, Schur PH, Fearon DT: **Autoantibody to the C3b/C4b receptor and absence of this receptor from erythrocytes of a patient with systemic lupus erythematosus.** J Clin Invest 1985, **76**:182-190.

80. Cook JM, Kazatchkine MD, Bourgeois P, Mignon F, Mery JP, Kahn MF: **Anti-C3b-receptor (CR1) antibodies in patients with systemic lupus erythematosus.** N Engl J Med 1986, **38**:135-138.

81. Daha MR, Hazevoet HM, Vanes LA: **Regulation of immune complex-mediated complement activation by autoantibodies (F-42) isolated from sera of patients with systemic lupus erythematosus.** Clin Exp Immunol 1983, **53**:541-546.

82. Wisnieski JJ, Naff GB: **Serum IgG antibodies to C1q in hypocomplementemic urticarial vasculitis syndrome.** Arthritis Rheum 1989, **32**:1119-1127.

83. Agnello V, Koffler D, Eisenberg JW, Winchester RJ, Kunkel HG: **C1q precipitins in the sera of patients with systemic lupus erythematosus and other hypocomplementemic states: characterization of high and low molecular weight types.** J Exp Med 1971, **134 (Suppl)**: 228-241.

84. Wisnieski JJ, Baer AN, Christensen J, Cupps TR, Flagg DN, Jones JV, Katzenstein PL, McFadden ER, McMillen JJ, Pick MA: **Hypocomplementemic urticarial vasculitis syndrome. Clinical and serologic findings in 18 patients.** Medicine (Baltimore) 1995, **74**:24-41.

85. Theofilopoulos AN, Dixon FJ: **The biology and detection of immune complexes.** Adv Immunol 1979, **28**:89-220. [key review]

86. Nydegger UE, Lambert PH, Gerber H, Miescher PA: **Circulating immune complexes in the serum in systemic lupus erythematosus and in carriers of hepatitis B antigen. Quantitation by binding to radiolabeled C1q.** J Clin Invest 1974, **54**:297-309.

87. Zubler RH, Lange G, Lambert PH, Miescher PA: **Detection of immune complexes in unheated sera by modified 125I-Clq binding test. Effect of heating on the binding of Clq by immune complexes and application of the test to systemic lupus erythematosus.** J Immunol 1976, **116**:232-235.

88. Hay FC, Nineham LJ, Roitt IM: **Routine assay for the detection of immune complexes of known immunoglobulin class using solid phase C1q.** Clin Exp Immunol 1976, **24**:396-400.

89. Hay FC, Nineham LJ, Roitt IM: **Routine assay for the detection of immune complexes of known immunoglobulin class using solid phase C1q.** Clin Exp Immunol 1976, **24**:396-400.

90. Tung KS, DeHoratius RJ, Williams RC: **Study of circulating immune complex size in systemic lupus erythematosus.** Clin Exp Immunol 1981, **43**:615-625.

91. Abrass CK, Nies KM, Louie JS, Border WA, Glassock RJ: **Correlation and predictive accuracy of circulating immune complexes with disease activity in patients with systemic lupus erythematosus.** Arthritis Rheum 1980, **23**:273-282.

92. Robinson MF, Roberts JL, Jones JV, Lewis EJ: **Circulating immune complex assays in patients with lupus and membranous glomerulonephritis.** N Engl J Med 1979, **14**:348-360.

93. Tung KS, DeHoratius RJ, Williams RC: **Study of circulating immune complex size in systemic lupus erythematosus.** Clin Exp Immunol 1981, **43**:615-625.

94. Uwatoko S, Aotsuka S, Okawa M, Egusa Y, Yokohari R, Aizawa C, Suzuki K: **C1q solid-phase radioimmunoassay: evidence for detection of antibody directed against the collagen-like region of C1q in sera from patients with systemic lupus erythematosus.** Clin Exp Immunol 1987, **69**:98-106.

95. Antes U, Heinz HP, Loos M: **Evidence for the presence of autoantibodies to the collagen-like portion of C1q in systemic lupus erythematosus.** Arthritis Rheum 1988, **31** :457-464.

96. Uwatoko S, Mannik M: **Low-molecular weight C1q-binding immunoglobulin G in patients with systemic lupus erythematosus consists of autoantibodies to the collagen-like region of C1q.** J Clin Invest 1988, **82**:816-824.

97. Wener MH, Uwatoko S, Mannik M: **Antibodies to the collagen-like region of C1q in sera of patients with autoimmune rheumatic diseases.** Arthritis Rheum 1989, **32**:544-551.

98. Kohro-Kawata J, Wener MH, Mannik M: **The effect of high salt concentration on detection of serum immune complexes and autoantibodies to C1q in patients with systemic lupus erythematosus.** J Rheumatol 2002, **29**:84-89.

99. Siegert CE, Kazatchkine MD, Sjoholm A, Wurzner R, Loos M, Daha MR: **Autoantibodies against C1q: view on clinical relevance and pathogenic role.** Clin Exp Immunol 1999, **116**:4-8. [key review]

100. Siegert CE, Breedveld FC, Daha MR: **Autoantibodies against C1q in systemic lupus erythematosus.** Behring Inst Mitt 1993, 279-286. [key review]

101. Trendelenburg M, Marfurt J, Gerber I, Tyndall A, Schifferli JA: **Lack of occurrence of severe lupus nephritis among anti-C1q autoantibody-negative patients.** Arthritis Rheum 1999, **42**:187-188.

102. Gunnarsson I, Ronnelid J, Huang YH, Rogberg S, Nilsson B, Lundberg I, Klareskog L: **Association between ongoing anti-C1q antibody production in peripheral blood and proliferative nephritis in patients with active systemic lupus erythematosus.** Br J Rheumatol 1997, **36**:32-37.

103. Siegert CE, Daha MR, Tseng CM, Coremans IE, van Es LA, Breedveld FC: **Predictive value of IgG autoantibodies against C1q for nephritis in systemic lupus erythematosus.** Ann Rheum Dis 1993, **52**:851-856.

104. Norsworthy P, Theodoridis E, Botto M, Athanassiou P, Beynon H, Gordon C, Isenberg D, Walport MJ, Davies KA: **Overrepresentation of the Fcgamma receptor type IIA R131/R131 genotype in caucasoid systemic lupus erythematosus patients with autoantibodies to C1q and glomerulonephritis.** Arthritis Rheum 1999, **42**:1828-1832.

105. Moroni G, Trendelenburg M, Del Papa N, Quaglini S, Raschi E, Panzeri P, Testoni C, Tincani A, Banfi G, Balestrieri G, Schifferli JA, Meroni PL, Ponticelli C: **Anti-C1q antibodies may help in diagnosing a renal flare in lupus nephritis.** Am J Kidney Dis 2001, **37**:490-498.

106. Cacoub P, Fremeaux-Bacchi V, De L, I, Guillien F, Kahn MF, Kazatchkine MD, Godeau P, Piette JC: **A new type of acquired C1 inhibitor deficiency associated with systemic lupus erythematosus.** Arthritis Rheum 2001, **44**:1836-1840.

107. Fremeaux-Bacchi V, Weiss L, Demouchy C, Blouin J, Kazatchkine MD: **Autoantibodies to the collagen-like region of C1q are strongly associated with classical pathway-mediated hypocomplementemia in systemic lupus erythematosus.** Lupus 1996, **5**:216-220.

108. Hogarth MB, Norsworthy PJ, Allen PJ, Trinder PK, Loos M, Morley BJ, Walport MJ, Davies KA: **Autoantibodies to the collagenous region of C1q occur in three strains of lupus-prone mice.** Clin Exp Immunol 1996, **104**:241-246.

109. Trinder PK, Maeurer MJ, Schorlemmer HU, Loos M: **Autoreactivity to mouse C1q in a murine model of SLE.** Rheumatol Int 1995, **15**:117-120.

110. Siegert CE, Daha MR, Lobatto S, van der Voort EA, Breedveld FC: **IgG autoantibodies to C1q do not detectably influence complement activation in vivo and in vitro in systemic lupus erythematosus.** Immunol Res 1992, **11**:91-97.

111. Uwatoko S, Gauthier VJ, Mannik M: **Autoantibodies to the collagen-like region of C1Q deposit in glomeruli via C1Q in immune deposits.** N Engl J Med 1991, **61**:268-273.

112. Pickering MC, Botto M, Taylor PR, Lachmann PJ, Walport MJ: **Systemic lupus erythematosus, complement deficiency, and apoptosis.** Adv Immunol 2000, **76**:227-324. [key review]

113. Botto M, Walport MJ: **Hereditary deficiency of C3 in animals and humans.** Int Rev Immunol 1993, **10**:37-50. [key review]

114. Inai S, Akagaki Y, Moriyama T, Fukumori Y, Yoshimura K, Ohnoki S, Yamaguchi H: **Inherited deficiencies of the late-acting complement components other than C9 found among healthy blood donors.** Int Arch Allergy Appl Immunol 1989, **90**:274-279.

115. Fukumori Y, Yoshimura K, Ohnoki S, Yamaguchi H, Akagaki Y, Inai S: **A high incidence of C9 deficiency among healthy blood donors in Osaka, Japan.** Int Immunol 1989, **1**:85-89.

116. Nishino H, Shibuya K, Nishida Y, Mushimoto M: **Lupus erythematosus-like syndrome with selective complete deficiency of C1q.** Ann Intern Med 1981, **95**:322-324.

117. Deapen D, Escalante A, Weinrib L, Horwitz D, Bachman B, Roy-Burman P, Walker A, Mack TM: **A revised estimate of twin concordance in systemic lupus erythematosus [see comments].** Arthritis Rheum 1992, **35**:311-318.

118. Brickman CM, Tsokos GC, Balow JE, Lawley TJ, Santaella M, Hammer CH, Frank MM: **Immunoregulatory disorders associated with hereditary angioedema. I. Clinical manifestations of autoimmune disease.** J.Allergy Clin.Immunol. 1986, **77**:749-757.

119. Donaldson VH, Hess EV, McAdams AJ: **Lupus-erythematosus-like disease in three unrelated women with hereditary angioneurotic edema [letter].** Ann Intern Med 1977, **86**:312-313.

120. Kohler PF, Percy J, Campion WM, Smyth CJ: **Hereditary angioedema and "familial" lupus erythematosus in identical twin boys.** Am J Med 1974, **56**:406-411.

121. Yu CY, Belt KT, Giles CM, Campbell RD, Porter RR: **Structural basis of the polymorphism of human complement components C4A and C4B: gene size, reactivity and antigenicity.** EMBO J 1986, **5**:2873-2881.

122. Law SK, Dodds AW, Porter RR: **A comparison of the properties of two classes, C4A and C4B, of the human complement component C4.** EMBO J 1984, **3**:1819-1823.

123. Wakeland EK, Liu K, Graham RR, Behrens TW: **Delineating the genetic basis of systemic lupus erythematosus.** Immunity. 2001, **15**:397-408. [key review]

124. Gaffney PM, Moser KL, Graham RR, Behrens TW: **Recent advances in the genetics of systemic lupus erythematosus.** Rheum Dis Clin North Am 2002, **28**:111-126. [key review]

125. Christiansen FT, Dawkins RL, Uko G, McCluskey J, Kay PH, Zilko PJ: **Complement allotyping in SLE: association with C4A null.** Aust N Z J Med 1983, **13**:483-488.

126. Fielder AH, Walport MJ, Batchelor JR, Rynes RI, Black CM, Dodi IA, Hughes GR: **Family study of the major histocompatibility complex in patients with systemic lupus erythematosus: importance of null alleles of C4A and C4B in determining disease susceptibility.** Br Med J (Clin Res Ed) 1983, **286**:425-428.

127. Holers VM, Girardi G, Mo L, Guthridge JM, Molina H, Pierangeli SS, Espinola R, Xiaowei LE, Mao D, Vialpando CG, Salmon JE: **Complement C3 activation is required for antiphospholipid antibody-induced fetal loss.** J Exp Med 2002, **195**:211-220.

128. Brouet JC, Clauvel JP, Danon F, Klein M, Seligmann M: **Biologic and clinical significance of cryoglobulins. A report of 86 cases.** Am J Med 1974, **57**:775-788.

129. Kohl J, Gessner JE: **On the role of complement and Fc gamma-receptors in the Arthus reaction.** Mol Immunol 1999, **36**:893-903. [key review]

130. Szalai AJ, Digerness SB, Agrawal A, Kearney JF, Bucy RP, Niwas S, Kilpatrick JM, Babu YS, Volanakis JE: **The Arthus reaction in rodents: species-specific requirement of complement.** J Immunol 2000, **164**:463-468.

131. Heller T, Gessner JE, Schmidt RE, Klos A, Bautsch W, Kohl J: **Cutting edge: Fc receptor type I for IgG on macrophages and complement mediate the inflammatory response in immune complex peritonitis.** J Immunol 1999, **162**:5657-5661.

132. Rifai A, Finbloom DS, Magilavy DB, Plotz PH: **Modulation of the circulation and hepatic uptake of immune complexes by carbohydrate recognition systems.** J Immunol 1982, **128**:2269-2275.

133. Ravetch JV, Clynes RA: **Divergent roles for Fc receptors and complement in vivo.** Annu Rev Immunol. 1998, **16**:421-432. [key review]

134. Mitchell DA, Taylor PR, Cook HT, Moss J, Bygrave AE, Walport MJ, Botto M: **Cutting edge: C1q protects against the develop-**

ment of glomerulonephritis independently of C3 activation. J Immunol 1999, **162**:5676-5679.

135. Sekine H, Reilly CM, Molano ID, Garnier G, Circolo A, Ruiz P, Holers VM, Boackle SA, Gilkeson GS: **Complement component C3 is not required for full expression of immune complex glomerulonephritis in MRL/lpr mice.** J Immunol 2001, **166**:6444-6451.

136. Hopken UE, Lu B, Gerard NP, Gerard C: **Impaired inflammatory responses in the reverse arthus reaction through genetic deletion of the C5a receptor.** J Exp Med 1997, **186**:749-756.

137. Strachan AJ, Woodruff TM, Haaima G, Fairlie DP, Taylor SM: **A new small molecule C5a receptor antagonist inhibits the reverse-passive Arthus reaction and endotoxic shock in rats.** J Immunol 2000, **164**:6560-6565.

138. Robson MG, Cook HT, Botto M, Taylor PR, Busso N, Salvi R, Pusey CD, Walport MJ, Davies KA: **Accelerated nephrotoxic nephritis is exacerbated in C1q-deficient mice.** J Immunol 2001, **166**:6820-6828.

139. Bozic CR, Lu B, Hopken UE, Gerard C, Gerard NP: **Neurogenic amplification of immune complex inflammation.** Science 1996, **273**:1722-1725.

140. Heidelberger M: **Quantitative chemical studies on complement or alexin. I A method.** J Exp Med 1941, **73**:691-694.

141. Schifferli JA, Ng YC, Peters DK: **The role of complement and its receptor in the elimination of immune complexes.** N Engl J Med 1986, **315**:488-495. [key review]

142. Schifferli JA: **Complement and immune complexes.** Res Immunol 1996, **147**:109-110. [key review]

143. Lachmann PJ, Walport MJ: **Deficiency of the effector mechanisms of the immune response and autoimmunity.** Ciba Found Symp 1987, **129**:149-171. [key review]

144. Walport MJ, Davies KA: **Complement and immune complexes.** Res Immunol 1996, **147**:103-109. [key review]

145. Hebert LA, Cosio G: **The erythrocyte-immune complex-glomerulonephritis connection in man.** Kidney Int 1987, **31**:877-885. [key review]

146. Walport MJ, Davies KA: **Immune complexes.** In Samter's Immunologic Diseases. Edited by Austen KF, Frank MM, Atkinson JP, Cantor H. Philadelphia: Lippincott Williams and Wilkins; 2001:270-281. [key review]

147. Robson MG, Cook HT, Botto M, Taylor PR, Busso N, Salvi R, Pusey CD, Walport MJ, Davies KA: **Accelerated nephrotoxic nephritis is exacerbated in C1q-deficient mice.** J Immunol 2001, **166**:6820-6828.

148. Savill J, Fadok V: **Corpse clearance defines the meaning of cell death.** Nature 2000, **407**:784-788. [key review]

149. Casciola-Rosen LA, Anhalt G, Rosen A: **Autoantigens targeted in systemic lupus erythematosus are clustered in two populations of surface structures on apoptotic keratinocytes [see comments].** J Exp Med 1994, **179**:1317-1330.

150. Herrmann M, Voll RE, Zoller OM, Hagenhofer M, Ponner BB, Kalden JR: **Impaired phagocytosis of apoptotic cell material by monocyte-derived macrophages from patients with systemic lupus erythematosus.** Arthritis Rheum 1998, **41**:1241-1250.

151. Korb LC, Ahearn JM: **C1q binds directly and specifically to surface blebs of apoptotic human keratinocytes: complement deficiency and systemic lupus erythematosus revisited.** J Immunol 1997, **158**:4525-4528.

152. Botto M, Dell'Agnola C, Bygrave AE, Thompson EM, Cook HT, Petry F, Loos M, Pandolfi PP, Walport MJ: **Homozygous C1q deficiency causes glomerulonephritis associated with multiple apoptotic bodies [see comments].** Nat Genet 1998, **19**:56-59.

153. Taylor PR, Carugati A, Fadok VA, Cook HT, Andrews M, Carroll MC, Savill JS, Henson PM, Botto M, Walport MJ: **A hierarchical role for classical pathway complement proteins in the clearance of apoptotic cells in vivo.** J Exp Med 2000, **192**:359-366.

154. Mevorach D, Mascarenhas JO, Gershov D, Elkon KB: **Complement-dependent clearance of apoptotic cells by human macrophages.** J Exp Med 1998, **188**:2313-2320.

155. Walport MJ: **Complement. First of two parts.** N Engl J Med 2001, **344**:1058-1066. [key review]

156. Walport MJ: **Complement. Second of two parts.** N Engl J Med 2001, **344**:1140-1144. [key review]

157. Einav S, Pozdnyakova OO, Ma M, Carroll MC: **Complement C4 is protective for lupus disease independent of C3.** J Immunol 2002, **168**:1036-1041.

158. Chen Z, Koralov SB, Kelsoe G: **Complement C4 inhibits systemic autoimmunity through a mechanism independent of complement receptors CR1 and CR2.** *J Exp Med* 2000, **192**:1339-1352.

159. Mitchell DA, Pickering MC, Warren J, Fossati-Jimack L, Cortes-Hernandez J, Cook HT, Botto M, Walport MJ: **C1q deficiency and autoimmunity: the effects of genetic background on disease expression.** *J Immunol* 2002, **168**:2538-2543.

160. Carroll MC: **The role of complement in B cell activation and tolerance.** *Adv Immunol* 2000, **74**:61-88. [key review]

161. Pepys MB: **Role of complement in induction of the allergic response.** *Nat New Biol* 1972, **237**:157-159.

162. Carroll MC: **The role of complement and complement receptors in induction and regulation of immunity.** *Annu.Rev.Immunol.* 1998, **16**:545-568. [key review]

163. Pickering MC, Botto M, Taylor PR, Lachmann PJ, Walport MJ: **Systemic lupus, complement deficiency and apoptosis.** *Adv Immunol* 2000, **76**:227-324. [key review]

164. Dempsey PW, Allison ME, Akkaraju S, Goodnow CC, Fearon DT: **C3d of complement as a molecular adjuvant: bridging innate and acquired immunity.** *Science* 1996, **271**:348-350.

165. Prodeus AP, Goerg S, Shen LM, Pozdnyakova OO, Chu L, Alicot EM, Goodnow CC, Carroll MC: **A critical role for complement in maintenance of self-tolerance.** *Immunity.* 1998, **9**:721-731.

166. Cutler AJ, Cornall RJ, Ferry H, Manderson AP, Botto M, Walport MJ: **Intact B cell tolerance in the absence of the first component of the classical complement pathway.** *Eur J Immunol* 2001, **31**:2087-2093.

167. Tan EM: **Autoantibodies and autoimmunity: a three-decade perspective. A tribute to Henry G. Kunkel.** *Ann N Y Acad Sci* 1997, **815**:1-14. [key review]

168. Hardin JA, Craft JE: **Patterns of autoimmunity to nucleoproteins in patients with systemic lupus erythematosus.** *Rheum Dis Clin North Am* 1987, **13**:37-46. [key review]

169. Doyle HA, Yan J, Liang B, Mamula MJ: **Lupus autoantigens: their origins, forms, and presentation.** *Immunol Res* 2001, **24**:131-147. [key review]

170. Chan OT, Madaio MP, Shlomchik MJ: **The central and multiple roles of B cells in lupus pathogenesis.** *Immonol Rev* 1999, **169**:107-121. [key review]

171. Mamula MJ: **Epitope spreading: the role of self peptides and autoantigen processing by B lymphocytes.** *Immonol Rev* 1998, **164**:231-239. [key review]

172. Lin RH, Mamula MJ, Hardin JA, Janeway CA Jr: **Induction of autoreactive B cells allows priming of autoreactive T cells.** *J Exp Med* 1991, **173**:1433-1439.

173. Casciola-Rosen L, Rosen A, Petri M, Schlissel M: **Surface blebs on apoptotic cells are sites of enhanced procoagulant activity: implications for coagulation events and antigenic spread in systemic lupus erythematosus.** *Proc Natl Acad Sci U S A* 1996, **93**:1624-1629.

174. Levine JS, Koh JS, Subang R, Rauch J: **Apoptotic cells as immunogen and antigen in the antiphospholipid syndrome.** *Exp Mol Pathol* 1999, **66**:82-98.

175. Matsuda J, Saitoh N, Gohchi K, Gotoh M, Tsukamoto M: **Anti-annexin V antibody in systemic lupus erythematosus patients with lupus anticoagulant and/or anticardiolipin antibody.** *Am J Hematol* 1994, **47**:56-58.

176. Rauch J: **Lupus anticoagulant antibodies: recognition of phospholipid-binding protein complexes.** *Lupus* 1998, **7 (Suppl 2)**:S29-S31.

177. Kirschfink M: **Targeting complement in therapy.** *Immonol Rev* 2001, **180**:177-189. [key review]

178. Smith GP, Smith RA: **Membrane-targeted complement inhibitors.** *Mol Immunol* 2001, **38**:249-255. [key review]

179. D'Ambrosio AL, Pinsky DJ, Connolly ES: **The role of the complement cascade in ischemia/reperfusion injury: implications for neuroprotection.** *Mol Med* 2001, **7**:367-382. [key review]

180. Makrides SC: **Therapeutic inhibition of the complement system.** *Pharmacol Rev* 1998, **50**:59-87. [key review]

181. Sheerin NS, Sacks SH: **Complement and complement inhibitors: their role in autoimmune and inflammatory diseases.** *Curr Opin Nephrol Hypertens* 1998;**7**:305-310. [key review]

182. Caliezi C, Wuillemin WA, Zeerleder S, Redondo M, Eisele B, Hack CE: **C1-esterase inhibitor: an anti-inflammatory agent and its potential use in the treatment of diseases other than hereditary angioedema.** *Pharmacol Rev* 2000, **52**:91-112. [key review]

183. Wang Y, Hu Q, Madri JA, Rollins SA, Chodera A, Matis LA: **Amelioration of lupus-like autoimmune disease in NZB/WF1 mice after treatment with a blocking monoclonal antibody specific for complement component C5.** *Proc Natl Acad Sci U S A* 1996, **93**:8563-8568.

184. Vakeva AP, Agah A, Rollins SA, Matis LA, Li L, Stahl GL: **Myocardial infarction and apoptosis after myocardial ischemia and reperfusion: role of the terminal complement components and inhibition by anti-C5 therapy.** *Circulation* 1998, **97**:2259-2267.

185. Wang H, Rollins SA, Gao Z, Garcia B, Zhang Z, Xing J, Li L, Kellersmann R, Matis LA, Zhong R: **Complement inhibition with an anti-C5 monoclonal antibody prevents hyperacute rejection in a xenograft heart transplantation model.** *Transplantation* 1999, **68**:1643-1651.

186. Fitch JC, Rollins S, Matis L, Alford B, Aranki S, Collard CD, Dewar M, Elefteriades J, Hines R, Kopf G, Kraker P, Li L, O'Hara R, Rinder C, Rinder H, Shaw R, Smith B, Stahl G, Shernan SK: **Pharmacology and biological efficacy of a recombinant, humanized, single-chain antibody C5 complement inhibitor in patients undergoing coronary artery bypass graft surgery with cardiopulmonary bypass.** *Circulation* 1999, **100**:2499-2506.

187. Steinsson K, Erlendsson K, Valdimarsson H: **Successful plasma infusion treatment of a patient with C2 deficiency and systemic lupus erythematosus: clinical experience over forty-five months.** *Arthritis Rheum* 1989, **32**:906-913.

188. Hudson-Peacock MJ, Joseph SA, Cox J, Munro CS, Simpson NB: **Systemic lupus erythematosus complicating complement type 2 deficiency: successful treatment with fresh frozen plasma.** *Br J Dermatol* 1997, **136**:388-392.

189. Bowness P, Davies KA, Norsworthy PJ, Athanassiou P, Taylor-Wiedeman J, Borysiewicz LK, Meyer PA, Walport MJ: **Hereditary C1q deficiency and systemic lupus erythematosus.** *QJM* 1994, **87**:455-464.

190. Cork LC, Morris JM, Olson JL, Krakowka S, Swift AJ, Winkelstein JA: Membranoproliferative glomerulonephritis in dogs with a genetically determined **deficiency of the third component of complement.** *N Engl J Med* 1991, **60**:455-470.

191. Petry F, Botto M, Holtappels R, Walport MJ, Loos M: **Reconstitution of the complement function in c1q-deficient (c1qa(-/-)) mice with wild-type bone marrow cells.** *J Immunol* 2001, **167**:4033-4037.

192. Berner B, Scheel AK, Schettler V, Hummel KM, Reuss-Borst MA, Muller GA, Oestmann E, Leinenbach HP, Hepper M: **Rapid improvement of SLE-specific cutaneous lesions by C1q immunoadsorption.** *Ann Rheum Dis* 2001, **60**:898-899.

193. Pfueller B, Wolbart K, Bruns A, Burmester GR, Hiepe F: **Successful treatment of patients with systemic lupus erythematosus by immunoadsorption with a C1q column: a pilot study.** *Arthritis Rheum* 2001, **44**:1962-1963.

Future directions

Supplement Review
Why do we not have a cure for rheumatoid arthritis?

Hani S El-Gabalawy* and Peter E Lipsky†

*Arthritis Centre, University of Manitoba, Winnipeg, Manitoba, Canada
†Intramural Research Program, National Institute of Arthritis and Musculoskeletal and Skin Diseases, Bethesda, MD, USA

Correspondence: Peter E Lipsky, Intramural Research Program, National Institute of Arthritis and Musculoskeletal and Skin Diseases, 9000 Rockville Pike, Building 10, Room 9N228, Bethesda, MD 20892-1820, USA. Tel: +1 301 496 2612; fax: +1 301 402 0012; e-mail: LipskyP@mail.nih.gov

Received: 18 April 2002
Accepted: 22 April 2002
Published: 9 May 2002

Arthritis Res 2002, 4 (suppl 3):S297-S301

This article may contain supplementary data which can only be found online at http://arthritis-research.com/content/4/S3/S297

Chapter summary

There are currently unprecedented opportunities to treat rheumatoid arthritis using well-designed, highly effective, targeted therapies. This will result in a substantial improvement in the outcome of this disorder for most affected individuals, if they can afford these therapies. Yet our lack of understanding of the basic mechanisms that initiate and sustain this disease remains a major obstacle in the search for a definitive cure. It is possible, if not likely, that our best approach will be to identify individuals at risk and devise reliable, safe methods of preventing the disease before it occurs. The means to do this are currently unknown but should serve as a major focus of research.

Keywords: etiology, prevention, rheumatoid arthritis, therapy

Introduction

New therapies have dramatically changed the way both clinicians and patients think about treatment of rheumatoid arthritis (RA). Indeed, it has become realistic to think about improvement defined by the ACR70 (reduction by 70% in the American College of Rheumatology composite response criteria) as the standard of care, and even to consider the possibility of remission and prevention of long-term disability. However, the possibility of cure remains remote. Why we do not have a cure for RA is a question that patients around the world continue to ask their physicians daily but, unfortunately, is no better answered in this millennium than it was in the last. Rheumatologists, the eternal optimists, can now offer their patients confident reassurance that the tragic outcomes of past decades are largely preventable, albeit at considerable ongoing expense. Yet the very fact that chronic, and generally uninterrupted, therapy is needed to suppress the manifestations of this disease is perhaps the clearest indication that a cure is nowhere in sight. Indeed, finding a cure for established RA is possibly no more likely than finding a cure for hypertension, where control of organ damage is the only realistic goal of therapy. The impediments we currently face in finding a cure for RA are numerous and are considered here. They are summarized in Table 1. In addition, the possibility that RA can be prevented is explored.

Is there a well-defined etiology for RA?

It is hard to find a cure for RA when the cause is unknown. Considerable attention has focused on the possibility that there is an infectious etiology of RA. Most would, however, agree that the possibility of finding a single infectious etiology for this disorder has been all but eliminated. Yet the modest success achieved by the use of minocycline in the treatment of RA continues to be interpreted by some as being indicative of a bacterial etiology that has completely eluded detection by the scientific community. Proponents of this hypothesis have been particularly vocal and visible to the lay community at large. A viral etiology has been

A list of common abbreviations used in this issue appears just before the indexes.

S297

Table 1

Obstacles to curing RA

Lack of knowledge of etiology

Incomplete understanding of pathogenesis

Lack of means to intervene in most of the relevant processes

Disease heterogeneity

Inability to make an early diagnosis

Limited ability to recognize those at risk

Figure 1

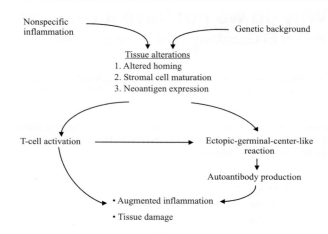

A current paradigm for the pathogenesis of rheumatoid arthritis that does not require an immune-recognition event of arthritogenic antigens at the induction phase. In this paradigm, nonspecific inflammation from a variety of causes precipitates an aberrant synovial response in a genetically susceptible individual. Subsequent recruitment of immune cells, including B cells, T cells, and dendritic cells, establishes an ectopic lymphoid organ in the synovium that facilitates the local production of autoantibodies to synovial constituents. Autoantibodies, along with activated T cells, serve to amplify the inflammation and the consequent tissue damage. Such a nonspecific onset for the disease is in keeping with the observed heterogeneity in clinical, pathological, and immunological features of RA.

even more difficult to disprove. Perhaps the strongest case has been made for parvovirus B19 and retroviruses. However, recent findings identifying parvovirus-B19 nucleic acid and antigens in a high proportion of RA synovial tissue samples and not in samples of non-RA synovium have not been replicated [1]. The synovial detection of this ubiquitous agent is probably related to the presence of inflammation rather than the cause of it. The RA-like lentivirus arthropathy that affects goats has stimulated interest in a retroviral etiology for the human disease. Studies demonstrating the presence of unique retroviral sequences in genomic material from RA synovial tissues and cells have also been difficult to reproduce [2,3]. Even if a retroviral etiology were to be discovered, the lessons learned from HIV would suggest that the discovery would be unlikely to lead to a cure or a vaccine in the foreseeable future.

If microorganisms are involved in the pathogenesis of at least some cases of RA, it is more likely in an indirect role, such as contributing to the development of autoimmunity through mechanisms such as molecular mimicry. A persuasive case has been made for immune responses to endogenous heat shock proteins that have been shown to share sequences with those of a number of microorganisms [4]. One of the microorganisms incriminated is *Escherichia coli*, a ubiquitous part of the gastrointestinal flora. Intriguingly, these sequences are also present in the HLA-DR4 alleles that are associated with RA [5]. If gut bacteria are indeed involved in precipitating immune responses to endogenous antigens, the elimination of such etiologic agents is obviously not a realistic goal. More viable approaches might be specific immunomodulation using strategies such as oral tolerization, induction of T-regulatory cells, or redirection of T-cell function.

It is now widely believed that the first event in RA may be nonspecific inflammation, which leads to T-cell priming in genetically susceptible individuals as a secondary event, this serving to accentuate and amplify the inflammation. This paradigm is shown in Fig. 1. An alternative hypothesis suggests that autoimmunity is primary in RA, and that autoimmune mechanisms precipitate and sustain the disease. Yet the identification of RA specific autoantigens has been elusive. The most logical place to look for autoantigens is in the joint itself. Antigens derived from cartilage are particularly intriguing candidates. Because of its established role in precipitating a destructive, RA-like arthropathy in susceptible mice, type II collagen has been the most thoroughly studied antigen. The adoptive transfer of murine collagen-induced arthritis using T cells and antibodies has suggested that immune responses to this articular antigen are likely to be of relevance in human RA. Yet extensive studies in RA patients have failed to confirm this hypothesis. Indeed, detailed analyses of T-cell receptor repertoire in RA do not consistently demonstrate evidence of any oligoclonal bias, and when present, the patterns differ from patient to patient. It has been suggested that there may be a global defect in generating a diverse T-cell repertoire in patients with RA, and that this may be a primary defect rather than a result of the disease [6].

Recently, there has been a resurgence of interest in the potential role of autoantibodies in the pathogenesis of RA. Although rheumatoid factor has long been the hallmark of this disease, it has been difficult to incriminate this autoantibody directly in the pathogenesis of either the synovitis or the resultant articular damage. The demonstration that there are other autoantibodies with a higher degree of specificity for RA than that of rheumatoid factor has given new impetus to the attempts to identify their corresponding autoantigens [7]. In particular, it has been shown that reactivity to citrulline, a residue generated by the post-translational modification of arginine, is critical to a number of the autoantibody responses specific to RA [8]. Whether these antibodies are directed towards a specific articular antigen remains to be seen. In contrast, the need to implicate an antigen specific to joints has recently been challenged by a murine serum-transfer model, in which a ubiquitous cytoplasmic protein, glucose-6-phosphate isomerase (GPI), is the target antigen [9]. Very recent studies suggest that this enzyme of the Krebs cycle is abundant on the surface of the articular cartilage in affected animals [10]. Although anti-GPI antibodies have been detected in patients with inflammatory arthritis, RA specificity remains controversial.

Another issue that may influence the capacity to induce remission in RA patients is the considerable heterogeneity of the disease. The clinical, pathological, and immunological heterogeneity seen in this disorder has been well documented. Yet the underlying basis of this heterogeneity is not well understood. This may well be indicative of the presence of multiple pathogenic factors, operating individually or in combination, in genetically susceptible individuals. Moreover, it is clear that the underlying genetic susceptibility itself may be heterogeneous in different populations. Thus, RA may not be a single disease entity with a well-defined etiology that has yet to be identified, but rather a characteristic clinical syndrome resulting from a complex, and possibly cumulative, interaction of multiple environmental and genetic factors.

Can RA be 'cured' once persistent synovitis is established?

There are now highly effective therapies for RA. Control of systemic and articular inflammation, along with significant retardation of articular damage, are becoming the norm in all but the most resistant patients. This will almost certainly translate into long-term prevention of disability as patients are aggressively treated early in their disease course. Yet the available arsenal of RA therapies rarely, if ever, induces a lasting, drug-free remission in the disease, in other words something akin to a cure. Indeed, there is an almost predictable, often severe, relapse associated with the withdrawal of most of the 'disease-modifying' antirheumatic drugs currently used in clinical practice, including biologic agents that target tumor necrosis factor (TNF)-α and IL-1. The exceptions to this phenomenon, observed occasionally in some individuals having taken antimalarials and injectable gold salts, most likely relate to the long tissue half-life of these agents rather than an intrinsic ability to induce sustained remissions.

The most plausible explanation for the phenomenon of relapse after withdrawal of antirheumatic drugs is that these therapies are collectively aimed at suppressing relatively peripheral pathways of inflammation and not central abnormalities in cell function that underlie the disease. What are some potential candidates for such central abnormalities? There is clearly a wide divergence of opinion regarding the answer to this question. Proponents of the central and primary role of autoimmunity in the pathogenesis of RA conclude that autoantigens, either in intra-articular or extra-articular locations, will invariably reignite inflammation when the effects of suppressive therapy are withdrawn. Even a relatively complete 'overhaul' of the immune system, as achieved by bone marrow transplantation, has been associated with recurrence of disease, albeit in milder form, presumably because disease-specific memory cells are not adequately deleted by these procedures. Proponents of an occult infectious etiology conclude that recurrence of disease is inevitable if the offending agent is not specifically eradicated. Finally, mechanical abnormalities in the joints induced by antecedent inflammation may predispose to subsequent inflammation whenever anti-inflammatory treatments are withdrawn.

A hypothesis that is currently gaining momentum suggests that RA patients may have intrinsic abnormalities in their synovial responses to inflammation and injury, irrespective of the cause. The inability to bring these responses to resolution effectively may lead to the persistence of an aggressive, angiogenic granulation tissue that is highly equipped to reinduce inflammation and remodel the surrounding articular structures. It has been suggested that the primary effectors of this aberrant response are macrophages, osteoclasts, and fibroblasts.

Macrophages and their products, particularly TNF-α, are responsible for many of the inflammatory manifestations of the synovial lesion, including the activation of the synovial endothelium, which results in the ongoing recruitment of other classes of leukocytes. The dramatic and rapid anti-inflammatory effect associated with the inhibition of TNF-α is compelling evidence for its central role in regulating this inflammatory process. Yet, as mentioned above, the almost predictable recurrence of the inflammation with the withdrawal of this therapy clearly indicates that this effector pathway is rapidly reinitiated by more central mechanisms.

Recent evidence suggests that osteoclasts are likely to be the primary effectors of the bone erosions that are typical of RA [11]. Osteoclastogenesis and bone resorption occur from the outside in, i.e. from the synovial pannus into the marginal bone, and from the inside out, i.e. from the subchondral bone out to the bone surface. The importance of the subchondral bone and bone marrow in the pathogenesis of rheumatoid articular damage is becoming increasingly recognized. Strategies targeting osteoclasts and osteoclastogenesis are quite promising as regards preventing erosive damage, even in the absence of associated anti-inflammatory effects [12]. Indeed, the impressive effects of anti-TNF agents in retarding the progression of erosive damage may well be related to their direct effects on osteoclast formation and/or function rather than their effects on inflammation [13]. Is this bringing us closer to a cure? Most would agree that effective prevention of tissue damage is a major step forward, but that the need to sustain therapy to achieve this cannot be equated with a cure, in which the entire inflammatory/proliferative/ destructive process is brought to a complete and sustained resolution. In this latter scenario, although a relapse may still be possible, as it is in the case of tumors and chronic infections, there would be no need for ongoing therapy unless such a relapse did indeed occur.

In contrast to the erosive bone damage, damage to the articular cartilage in RA appears to be mediated by synovial fibroblast-like cells and chondrocytes. 'Transformed' synovial fibroblasts invade articular cartilage by degrading the extracellular matrix of the cartilage through the production of a variety of proteases. Additionally, under the influence of proinflammatory cytokines, particularly IL-1, chondrocytes become major participants in the degradation of the surrounding cartilage matrix, while losing their capacity to repair the damage by synthesizing new matrix components. Inhibiting the effects of IL-1 by changing the balance between this cytokine and its physiological inhibitor IL-1Ra has proven to be an effective strategy in preventing articular damage. Ultimately, because of the avascular nature of cartilage, once damage has occurred, it cannot be repaired, thus making a cure essentially impossible.

It appears that once the inflammatory rheumatoid synovial organ has formed in a specific joint, it is unlikely that this tissue can be brought back to 'normal'. Moreover, the process almost certainly begins before there are clinical signs, and by the time the disease becomes clinically evident, in most cases the synovitis is capable of autonomous perpetuation. Therefore, by the time clinicians perceive that the disease is even present, a cure may have already become very difficult to achieve.

Can RA be prevented before synovitis becomes clinically evident?

One of the major impediments to the development of definitive treatment for RA is the inability to detect, and in turn study, the earliest events that predictably lead to the development of persistent, destructive synovitis. There are virtually no data, epidemiologic or otherwise, regarding the premorbid status of individuals destined to develop RA. It can reasonably be asked: can anyone develop RA given the right circumstances? The available data indicate that a typical high-risk individual would be a perimenopausal woman with a family history of RA or a related autoimmune disease, who is a smoker, who is positive for rheumatoid factor, and who carries at least one HLA-DR4 allele. The risk of such an individual developing clinically detectable

disease, say, within 5 years, has not been established. A conservative estimate would be at least 5% and the actual risk could be substantially higher. Assembling and longitudinally studying a cohort of such individuals would afford the best opportunity to understand how RA starts and, ultimately, how it can be prevented.

If such a 'pre-RA' cohort were to be assembled, early indicators of impending clinical disease would need to be sought in a longitudinal study. Particular attention would be paid to aspects such as the development of specific autoantibodies. Such a strategy has been used effectively to predict the onset of autoimmune diabetes in genetically susceptible children [14]. Although this latter disorder has a more predictable age of onset, thus lending itself better to this type of strategy, a similar approach might be adopted with certain populations of individuals that are at high risk for developing RA. Longitudinal analysis of serum to detect the development of specific autoantibodies may ultimately be too restrictive an approach, and the application of broad-based proteomic approaches may be necessary to identify novel and unsuspected markers.

An important aspect of studying the early stages of RA would be the longitudinal examination of typical 'RA joints' such as the knees and MCPs using sensitive imaging modalities such as MRI, PET, or spectroscopy. The available histopathologic studies of clinically uninvolved joints have demonstrated the presence of subclinical synovitis in affected individuals [15,16]. This can broadly be taken to imply that there is likely an early, subclinical stage in the history of each RA patient in which the synovium becomes abnormal without actually being clinically inflamed. During this initiation stage, it may be possible to prevent the trafficking of specific cells into the synovial microevironment, thereby averting the deleterious downstream events that result once these cells provoke aberrant synovial responses. In particular, inhibiting the recruitment of T cells and dendritic cells would be a logical objective. A potentially appealing strategy involves the use of chemokine inhibitors. The inhibition of candidate chemokines such as stromal derived factor-1 (CXCL12), which is an important mechanism by which stromal cells recruit lymphocytes, has been shown to be quite effective in animal models [17]. Alternatively, strategies that serve to bias the immune system away from Th1 responses towards Th2 responses may also prove to be effective in preventing the disease, although there has been a suggestion that patients with RA may have defects in Th2 differentiation [18]. The key would be the detection of early events, before the establishment of the chronic inflammatory synovial organ.

References
1. Takahashi Y, Murai C, Shibata S, Munakata Y, Ishii T, Ishii K, Saitoh T, Sawai T, Sugamura K, Sasaki T: **Human parvovirus B19 as a causative agent for rheumatoid arthritis.** *Proc Natl Acad Sci USA* 1998, **95**:8227-8232. [general reference]

2. Neidhart M, Rethage J, Kuchen S, Kunzler P, Crowl RM, Billingham ME, Gay RE, Gay S: **Retrotransposable L1 elements expressed in rheumatoid arthritis synovial tissue: association with genomic DNA hypomethylation and influence on gene expression.** *Arthritis Rheum* 2000, **43**:2634-2647. [general reference]

3. Griffiths DJ, Cooke SP, Herve C, Rigby SP, Mallon E, Hajeer A, Lock M, Emery V, Taylor P, Pantelidis P, Bunker CB, du Bois R, Weiss RA, Venables PJ: **Detection of human retrovirus 5 in patients with arthritis and systemic lupus erythematosus.** *Arthritis Rheum* 1999, **42**:448-454. [general reference]

4. Albani S, Keystone EC, Nelson JL, Ollier WE, La Cava A, Montemayor AC, Weber DA, Montecucco C, Martini A, Carson DA: **Positive selection in autoimmunity: abnormal immune responses to a bacterial dnaJ antigenic determinant in patients with early rheumatoid arthritis.** *Nat Med* 1995, **1**:448-452. [archival research]

5. La Cava A, Nelson JL, Ollier WE, MacGregor A, Keystone EC, Thorne JC, Scavulli JF, Berry CC, Carson DA, Albani S: **Genetic bias in immune responses to a cassette shared by different microorganisms in patients with rheumatoid arthritis.** *J Clin Invest* 1997, **100**:658-663. [archival research]

6. Wagner UG, Koetz K, Weyand CM, Goronzy JJ: **Perturbation of the T cell repertoire in rheumatoid arthritis.** *Proc Natl Acad Sci USA* 1998, **95**:14447-14452. [general reference]

7. Goldbach-Mansky R, Lee J, McCoy A, Hoxworth J, Yarboro C, Smolen JS, Steiner G, Rosen A, Zhang C, Menard HA, Zhou ZJ, Palosuo T, Van Venrooij WJ, Wilder RL, Klippel JH, Schumacher HR Jr, El-Gabalawy HS: **Rheumatoid arthritis associated autoantibodies in patients with synovitis of recent onset.** *Arthritis Res* 2000, **2**:236-243. [general reference]

8. Schellekens GA, de Jong BA, van den Hoogen FH, van de Putte LB, van Venrooij WJ: **Citrulline is an essential constituent of antigenic determinants recognized by rheumatoid arthritis-specific autoantibodies.** *J Clin Invest* 1998, **101**:273-281. [general reference]

9. Matsumoto I, Staub A, Benoist C, Mathis D: **Arthritis provoked by linked T and B cell recognition of a glycolytic enzyme.** *Science* 1999, **286**:1732-1735. [general reference]

10. Matsumoto I, Maccioni M, Lee DM, Maurice M, Simmons B, Brenner M, Mathis D, Benoist C: **How antibodies to a ubiquitous cytoplasmic enzyme may provoke joint-specific autoimmune disease.** *Nat Immunol* 2002, **3**:360-365. [general reference]

11. Gravallese EM, Harada Y, Wang JT, Gorn AH, Thornhill TS, Goldring SR: **Identification of cell types responsible for bone resorption in rheumatoid arthritis and juvenile rheumatoid arthritis.** *Am J Pathol* 1998, **152**:943-951. [general reference]

12. Pettit AR, Ji H, von Stechow D, Muller R, Goldring SR, Choi Y, Benoist C, Gravallese EM: **TRANCE/RANKL knockout mice are protected from bone erosion in a serum transfer model of arthritis.** *Am J Pathol* 2001, **159**:1689-1699. [general reference]

13. Lipsky PE, van der Heijde DM, St Clair EW, Furst DE, Breedveld FC, Kalden JR, Smolen JS, Weisman M, Emery P, Feldmann M, Harriman GR, Maini RN: **Infliximab and methotrexate in the treatment of rheumatoid arthritis. Anti-Tumor Necrosis Factor Trial in Rheumatoid Arthritis with Concomitant Therapy Study Group.** *N Engl J Med* 2000, **343**:1594-1602. [general reference]

14. Kulmala P, Savola K, Petersen JS, Vahasalo P, Karjalainen J, Lopponen T, Dyrberg T, Akerblom HK, Knip M: **Prediction of insulin-dependent diabetes mellitus in siblings of children with diabetes. A population-based study. The Childhood Diabetes in Finland Study Group.** *J Clin Invest* 1998, **101**:327-336. [general reference]

15. Soden M, Rooney M, Cullen A, Whelan A, Feighery C, Bresnihan B: **Immunohistological features in the synovium obtained from clinically uninvolved knee joints of patients with rheumatoid arthritis.** *Br J Rheumatol* 1989, **28**:287-292. [archival research]

16. Kraan MC, Versendaal H, Jonker M, Bresnihan B, Post WJ, 't Hart BA, Breedveld FC, Tak PP: **Asymptomatic synovitis precedes clinically manifest arthritis.** *Arthritis Rheum* 1998, **41**:1481-1488.

17. Matthys P, Hatse S, Vermeire K, Wuyts A, Bridger G, Henson GW, De Clercq E, Billiau A, Schols D: **Amd3100, a potent and specific antagonist of the stromal cell-derived factor-1 chemokine receptor cxcr4, inhibits autoimmune joint inflammation in IFN-gamma receptor-deficient mice.** *J Immunol* 2001, **167**:4686-4692. [general reference]

18. Skapenko A, Wendler J, Lipsky PE, Kalden JR, Schulze-Koops H: **Altered memory T cell differentiation in patients with early rheumatoid arthritis.** *J Immunol* 1999, **163**:491-499. [general reference]

Colour figure section

This section contains the colour figures which are shown in black and white within the individual articles.

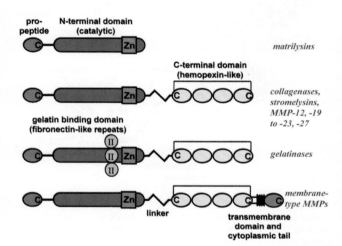

Basic domain structures of the matrix metalloproteinases (MMPs). MMPs consist of: a propeptide (grey), which maintains the enzymes in a latent state; a catalytic domain (blue) with the active site and the catalytic zinc (Zn) (red); and, with the exception of the matrilysins, a COOH-terminal domain (C) (yellow) with homology to the serum protein hemopexin. The latter two domains are connected by a linker peptide. Gelatinases have an insert of three fibronectin type II repeats (turquoise) in the catalytic domain, which is involved in substrate recognition. Membrane-type MMPs contain a transmembrane domain (black) and a cytoplasmic tail (green) at the COOH terminus, which anchors these enzymes in the cell membrane. Figure 1 from Murphy *et al.*, page S42.

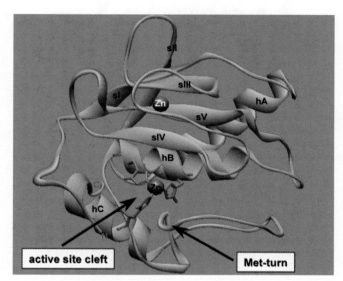

Structure of the catalytic domain of the matrix metalloproteinase MMP-3. The ribbon diagram was created using WebLab Viewer software based on a crystal structure analysis by Gomis-Rüth *et al.* [61]. Strands (sI–sV) and helices (hA–hC) are labelled in black; the catalytic zinc (centre), coordinated by three histidine residues (pink), and the structural zinc (Zn) (top) are labelled in black and white, respectively; and the NH$_2$ terminus (N) and COOH terminus (C) are labelled in red. The active site cleft and the characteristic methionine (Met) turn are indicated with arrows. Figure 2 from Murphy *et al.*, page S43.

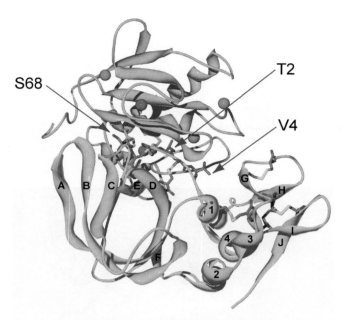

A ribbon diagram of tissue inhibitor of metalloproteinases 1 (TIMP-1) bound to the catalytic domain of matrix metalloproteinase 3 [MMP-3 (ΔC)]. TIMP-1 is shown in green and MMP-3 (ΔC) is shown in light brown. Cystines, Thr2, Val4 and Ser68 in TIMP-1 are indicated: N, blue; O, red; C, grey; and disulfide bonds, yellow. Strands and helices in TIMP-1 are labelled A–J and 1–4, respectively. The catalytic and structural zinc ions are shown in purple, and calcium ions are shown in orange. The image was prepared from the Brookhaven Protein Data Bank entry (1UEA) using the Swiss PDB viewer [91]. Figure 1 from Nagase and Brew, page S55.

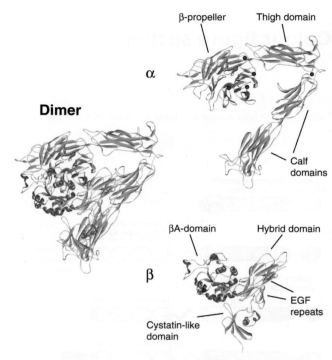

Crystal structure of integrin αVβ3 showing the dimer and individual subunits [1]. The domains that make up each integrin subunit are shown. Secondary structure elements are shown as red α-helices or cyan β-strands/ribbons. Blue circles represent the six cation-binding sites. The plexin–semaphorin–integrin domain and two of the four epidermal growth factor (EGF) repeats in the β-subunit are not visible in the structure. Figure 1 from Humphries, page S70.

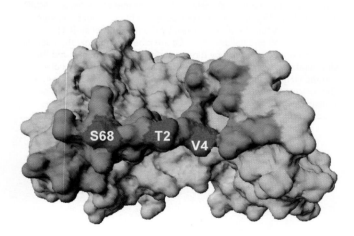

The surface structure of tissue inhibitor of metalloproteinases 1 (TIMP-1). The N-terminal domain and the C-terminal domain are shown in light red and green, respectively. The region within 4 Å contact with the matrix metalloproteinase (MMP) catalytic domain is shown in blue. Mutation sites coloured red modulate the selectivity of N-TIMP-1 against different MMPs. The image was prepared from the Brookhaven Protein Data Bank entry (1UEA) using the Swiss PDB viewer [91]. Figure 4 from Nagase and Brew, page S58.

(a)

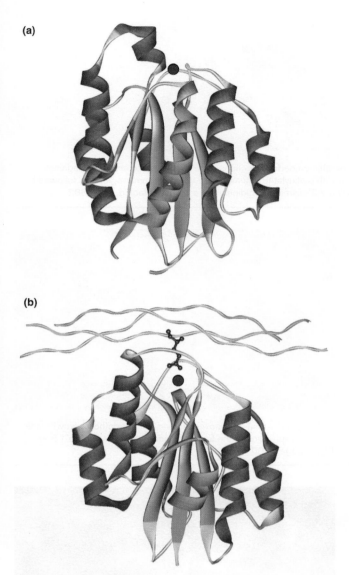

(b)

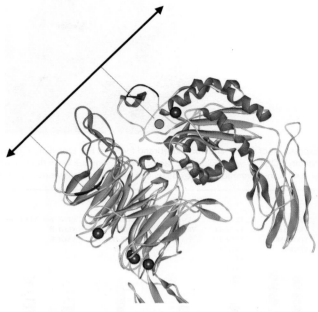

Enlarged view of the potential ligand-binding pocket of integrin αVβ3. The loops on the top of the α-subunit β-propeller implicated in ligand binding are coloured: purple, the 4–1 loop connecting repeats 1–2; orange, the 4–1 loop connecting repeats 2–3; pink, the 4–1 loop connecting repeats 3–4; green, the 2–3 loop in repeat 2; yellow, the 2–3 loop in repeat 3. The potential site for binding the fibronectin synergy sequence in α5β1, the β-strand 4 in repeat 3, is coloured blue (left side of β-propeller). The CYDMKTTC peptide sequence determining ligand specificity in β3 is coloured blue (top of βA-domain). Cations in the αVβ3 crystal structure are shown as blue spheres. The potential site of the metal ion-dependent adhesion site (MIDAS) cation is shown as a green circle. The site of insertion of an αA-domain would be in the orange loop of the β-propeller. The solid double arrow shows the possible orientation of ligand relative to the integrin, with dashed lines indicating speculative contacts with the MIDAS cation and β-strand 4 in repeat 3. Figure 3 from Humphries, page S72.

Comparison of the crystal structure of the α2 A-domain either **(a)** free or **(b)** complexed with a collagenous peptide [41,47]. Secondary structure elements are shown as red α-helices or cyan β-strands/ribbons. Spheres represent the divalent cation coordinated by the metal ion-dependent adhesion site (MIDAS) motif. The α7 helix is shown in pink. Note the difference in position of α7 in the two structures and the fact that the construct used in (b) contained a truncated α7 helix. The collagen glutamate residue that coordinates the MIDAS cation is shown in green. The MIDAS cation is shown as a blue circle. Figure 2 from Humphries, page S71.

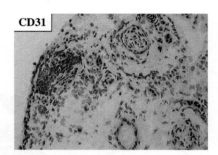
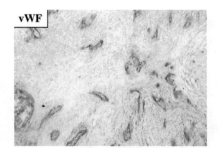

Expression of CD31 and von Willebrand factor in RA synovium. Frozen or paraffin-embedded sections were stained using antibodies against human CD31 or von Willebrand factor (vWf). Samples were then incubated with biotinylated anti-mouse or anti-goat immunoglobulin, followed by streptavidin–horseradish peroxidase. Immune complexes were detected using 3,3′-diaminobenzidine. Figure 1 from Paleolog, page S82.

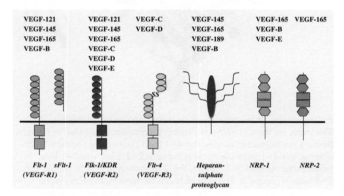

The VEGF family. The binding of VEGF ligands and their splice variants to cell-surface receptors. Figure 3 from Paleolog, page S84.

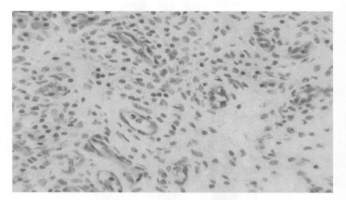

Staining of rheumatoid synovium for vascular endothelial growth factor, showing expression of the factor in endothelial cells. Figure 1 from Taylor, page S100.

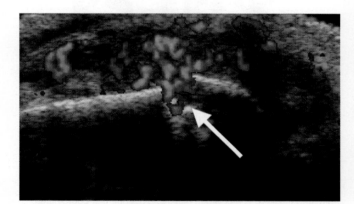

Combined high-resolution ultrasound and power Doppler imaging of a metacarpophalangeal joint in RA, seen in longitudinal section. The red colouring represents vascular signal and the arrow indicates a vascularised erosion. Figure 3 from Taylor, page S102.

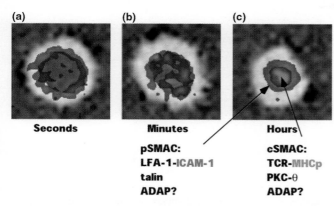

Seconds | **Minutes** | **Hours**

pSMAC:
LFA-1-ICAM-1
talin
ADAP?

cSMAC:
TCR-MHCp
PKC-θ
ADAP?

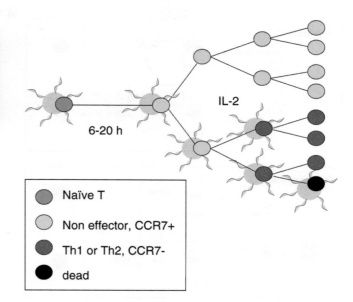

IL-2

6–20 h

	Naïve T
	Non effector, CCR7+
	Th1 or Th2, CCR7-
	dead

The development of the immunological synapse. Images adapted from [2] based on fluorescence microscope images of T-cell interaction with agonist MHC–peptide complexes (green) and ICAM-1 (red) in a supported planar bilayer with a T cell. The accumulation of fluorescence represents interactions in different time frames. **(a)** Within seconds, the T cell attaches to the substrate using LFA-1/ICAM-1 interactions in the center based on TCR signaling triggered at the periphery of the contact area. **(b)** Over a period of minutes, the engaged TCRs are translocated to the center of the contact area. **(c)** The final pattern, with a central cluster of engaged TCRs surrounded by a ring of engaged LFA-1, is stable for hours. Molecular markers for the cSMAC and pSMAC are indicated. For scale, the pSMAC is ~5 μm across. ADAP, adhesion and degranulation adapter protein; cSMAC, central supramolecular activation cluster; ICAM, intercellular adhesion molecule; LFA, lymphocyte-function-associated antigen; MHCp, major histocompatibility complex protein complexed to a foreign or self-peptide; PKC-θ, a protein kinase C isoform that is activated by DAG but not Ca^{2+}; pSMAC, peripheral supramolecular activation cluster – the ring of LFA-1 and talin on the T cell and ICAM-1 on the antigen-presenting cell in the mature immunological synapse; TCR, T-cell antigen receptor. Figure 1 from Dustin, page S120.

Stochastic stimulation of proliferating T cells leads to intraclonal functional diversification. By establishing immunological synapses with dendritic cells (DCs), naïve T cells (green) achieve stimulation and become committed to proliferate in response to autocrine or paracrine IL-2. T-cell receptor stimulation is sustained by serial encounters with DCs and, in the presence of polarizing cytokines (IL-12 and IL-4, not shown), drives T-cell differentiation to Th1 or Th2 effector cells that have lost CCR7 expression (red). T cells receiving a shorter stimulation do not acquire effector function and do retain lymph-node homing capacity (yellow). An excessive stimulation leads to activation-induced cell death (black). Figure 1 from Sallusto and Lanzavecchia, page S128.

monocyte — GM-CSF + IL-4 → immature DC — LPS, dsRNA − IL1, TNFα T cells → — → mature DC

		monocyte	immature DC		mature DC
Antigen capture	macropinocytosis		++	+	-
	Mannose R++			+	-
	FcR		++	+	-
Antigen presentation	Class II synthesis		+	++	-
	Class II halflife		10 h	>>	>100 h
	Class I synthesis		+	++	++
Costimulation	ICAM-1		-	+	+
	B7		-	+	+
Migration	CCR5		+	-	-
	MIP-1β		-	++	-
	CCR7		-	+	+
	ELC, TARC		-	-	+
Cytokines	TNF-α		-	2-6 h	-
	IL-6		-	2-6 h	-
	IL-10		-	8-24 h	-
	IL-12		-	8-16 h	-

The maturation programme studied in monocyte-derived dendritic cells. DC, dendritic cells; ELC, endothelial-like cells; FcR, receptors for crystallizable fragment [of antibody]; GM-CSF, granulocyte/macrophage-colony-stimulating factor; ICAM-1, intracellular adhesion molecule-1; LPS, lipopolysaccharide; MIP, macrophage inflammatory protein; TARC, thymus- and activation-regulated chemokine. Figure 2 from Sallusto and Lanzavecchia, page S129.

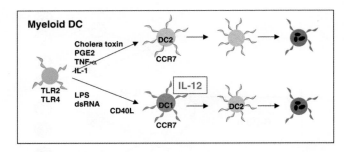

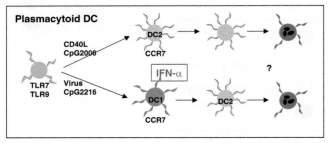

Reactivity, flexibility, kinetics and exhaustion in myeloid and plasmacytoid dendritic cells (DCs). The figure summarizes the properties of immature myeloid and plasmacytoid DCs. Indicated are the most relevant Toll-like receptors (TLR) and chemokine receptors, and the response to various maturation stimuli. DC1 and DC2 refer to the capacity of the cells to induce Th1 and Th2 responses, respectively. CD40L, CD40 ligand; LPS, lipopolysaccharide; PGE2, prostaglandin E$_2$. Figure 3 from Sallusto and Lanzavecchia, page S130.

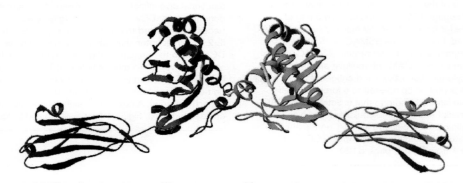

Hypothetical molecular model of the HLA-B27 heavy chain homodimer structure. The alpha 1, 2, and 3 domains of two HLA-B27 molecules are shown in ribbon form, bound peptide shown. Orientation: cell surface at bottom of picture. Figure 2 from McMichael and Bowness, page S156.

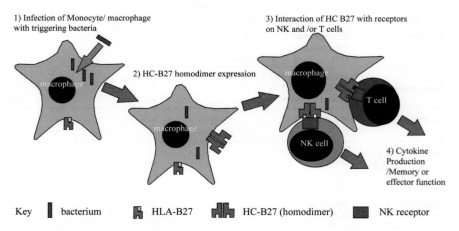

Hypothetical model for the role of HLA-B27 homodimers in the pathogenesis of spondyloarthritis. NK, natural killer. Figure 3 from McMichael and Bowness, page S157.

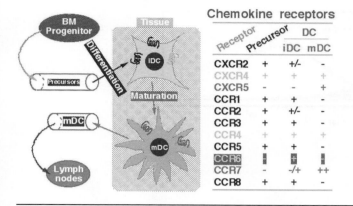

Chemokine receptors

Receptor	Precursor	DC	
		iDC	mDC
CXCR2	+	+/-	-
CXCR4	+	+	+
CXCR5	-	-	+
CCR1	+	+	-
CCR2	+	+/-	-
CCR3	+	+	-
CCR4	+	+	+
CCR5	+	+	-
CCR6	▮	+	▮
CCR7	-	-/+	++
CCR8	+	+	-

Changes in chemokine receptor expression in the course of maturation of dendritic cells. The *in vivo* traffic route of dendritic cells as they mature is depicted, along with the changes in the expression of chemokine receptors. BM, bone marrow; CC indicates the presence of adjoining cysteines in sequence; DC, dendritic cell; iDC, immature dendritic cell; mDC, mature dendritic cell. Figure 2 from Oppenheim *et al.*, page S185.

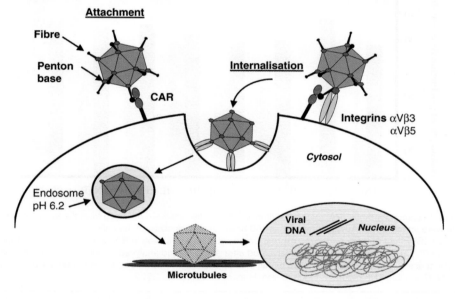

Schematic representation of the adenoviral attachment and internalisation. CAR, Coxsackievirus and adenovirus receptor. Figure 1 from Horwood *et al.*, page S218.

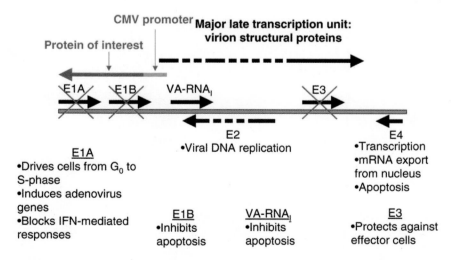

Schematic diagram of the adenoviral genome. In the first generation of adenoviral vectors, the E1A, E1B and E3 regions have been deleted to allow for insertion of your gene of interest. CMV, cytomegalovirus. Figure 2 from Horwood *et al.*, page S219.

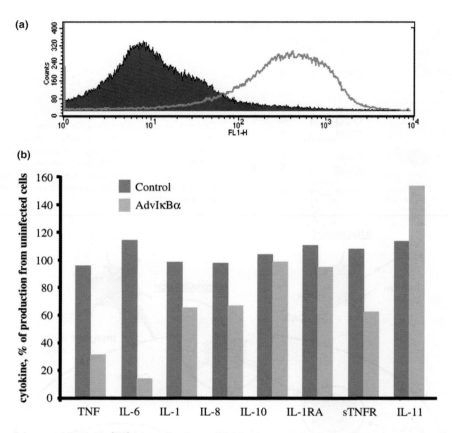

(a) Efficiency of infection of rheumatoid arthritis (RA) joint cell cultures. RA joint tissues were obtained from the synovium from patients with RA undergoing surgery. Cells were infected with Advβgal (moi 40) for 48 hours prior to analysis of the cells for βgal expression by fluorescence activated cell sorting (FACS). (B) Effect of IκBα transgene expression on cytokine expression in RA joint cell cultures. RA joint cells were infected with AdvIκBα or AdvO (moi 40). Culture supernatants were harvested after 48 hours and analysed for the expression of various cytokines by enzyme-linked immunosorbent assay. Data are representative of samples from at least five patients. IL-1RA, interleukin-1 receptor antagonist; TNF, tumour necrosis factor; sTNFR, soluble TNF receptor. Figure 5 from Horwood *et al.*, page S222.

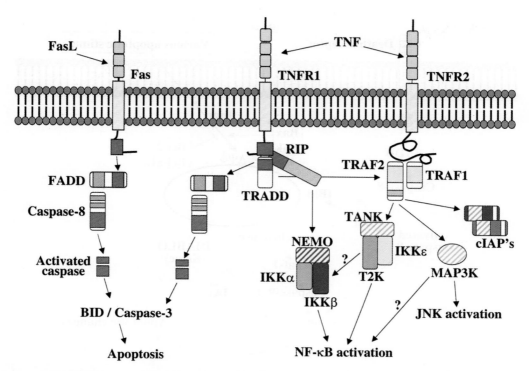

Intracellular signaling pathways downstream of tumor necrosis factor (TNF) receptor superfamily receptors. The Fas, tumor necrosis factor receptor type 1 (TNFR1) and tumor necrosis factor receptor type 2 (TNFR2) receptors are shown extending through the cell membrane with their extracellular domains projecting into the extracellular space. Various adaptor proteins and signal transducing molecules that convey signals initiated by the binding of the ligands Fas ligand (FasL) to Fas and TNF to TNFR1 and TNFR2, respectively, are shown, as is the crosstalk between various molecules and pathways. Functional domains within a protein are shown as colored blocks. Recruitment of one protein to another is indicated by the juxtaposition of like-colored and like-shaped domain blocks. BID, beta interaction domain; cIAPs, cellular inhibitors of apoptosis; FADD, Fas-associated death domain protein; IKK, IκB kinase; JNK, c-Jun N-terminal kinase; MAP3K, mitogen-activated protein 3 kinase; NEMO, NF-κB essential modulator protein; RIP, receptor-interacting protein; T2K, TRAF2-associated kinase; TANK, TRAF family member associated NF-κB activator; TRADD, TNF receptor-associated death domain protein; TRAF, TNF receptor-associated factor. Figure 1 from Mak and Yeh, page S245.

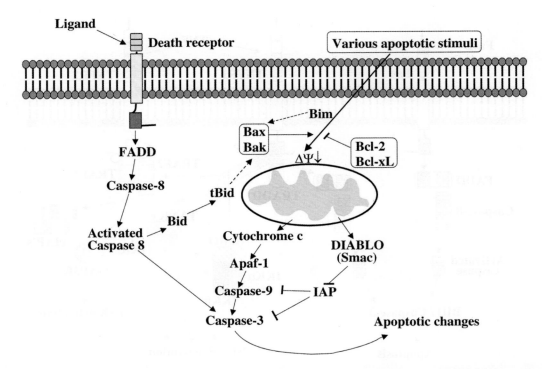

Intrinsic and extrinsic pathways of apoptosis. The extrinsic pathway is triggered by death receptor engagement, which initiates a signaling cascade mediated by caspase-8 activation. Caspase-8 both feeds directly into caspase-3 activation and stimulates the release of cytochrome c by the mitochondria. Caspase-3 activation leads to the degradation of cellular proteins necessary to maintain cell survival and integrity. The intrinsic pathway occurs when various apoptotic stimuli trigger the release of cytochrome c from the mitochondria (independently of caspase-8 activation). Cytochrome c interacts with Apaf-1 and caspase-9 to promote the activation of caspase-3. Various intermediary signaling molecules (many of whose functions are not completely defined) and proteins inhibiting the apoptotic cascade are also shown. Apaf-1, apoptosis-activating factor 1; Bak, bacille Calmette–Guérin; Bax, BCL-2-associated x protein; Bid, proapoptotic Bcl-2 family member; Bim, proapoptotic Bcl-2 family member; DIABLO, direct IAP binding protein with low PI; FADD, Fas-associated death domain protein; IAP, inhibitors of apoptosis; Smac, second mitochondria-derived activator of caspase; tBid, truncated beta interaction domain. Figure 2 from Mak and Yeh, page S247.

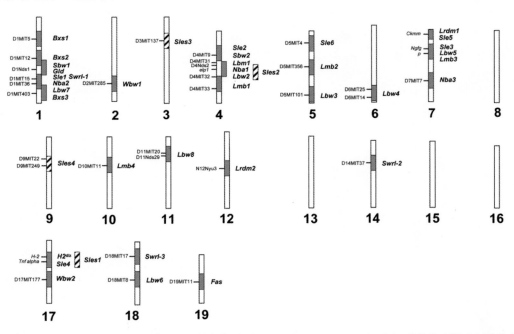

Genomic distribution of susceptibility intervals identified in linkage analysis on murine test crosses involving BSXB, MRL/*lpr*, PL/J, SWR, NZB, NZW, and NZM2410 strains [14,60,62,63]. Figure 1 from Nguyen *et al.*, page S257.

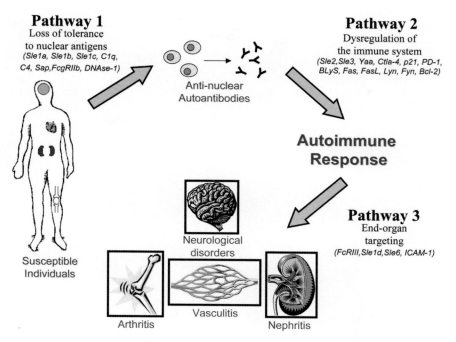

Hypothetical pathways involved in the pathogenesis of SLE. Figure 2 from Nguyen *et al.*, page S259.

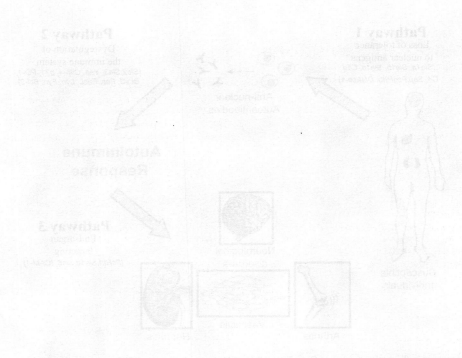

List of common abbreviations

AP-1	=	activating protein-1
APC	=	antigen-presenting cell
CIA	=	collagen-induced arthritis
CRP	=	C-reactive protein
CTL	=	cytotoxic T lymphocytes
DC	=	dendritic cell
DMARD	=	disease-modifying antirheumatic drug
EBV	=	Epstein–Barr virus
EC	=	endothelial cell
ECM	=	extracellular matrix
ELISA	=	enzyme-linked immunosorbent assay
EMSA	=	electrophoretic mobility shift assay
ERK	=	extracellular signal-regulated kinase
ESR	=	erythrocyte sedimentation rate
FACS	=	fluorescence-activating cell sorting
FADD	=	Fas-associated death-domain protein
FasL	=	Fas ligand
Fc	=	crystallizable fragment (of an antibody)
FcγR	=	Fc gamma receptor
FGF	=	fibroblast growth factor
G-CSF	=	granulocyte-colony-stimulating factor
GM-CSF	=	granulocyte/macrophage-colony-stimulating factor
HDL	=	high-density lipoprotein
HLA	=	human leukocyte antigen
hsp	=	heat shock protein
HTLV	=	human T-cell lymphotropic virus
IκB	=	inhibitor of kappa B
IκBα	=	inhibitor of kappa B alpha
ICAM	=	intracellular adhesion molecule
IDDM	=	insulin-dependent diabetes mellitus
IFN	=	interferon
IFN-γ	=	interferon gamma
IFN-α/β	=	interferon alpha/beta
IL	=	interleukin
IL-6R	=	interleukin-6 receptor
JAK	=	Janus kinase
JNK	=	c-Jun N-terminal kinase
k_{cat}	=	catalytic rate constant
K_i	=	inhibition constant
K_m	=	Michaelis–Menten equilibrium constant
LAT	=	linker for activation of T cells
LD	=	linkage disequilibrium
LFA	=	lymphocyte-function-associated antigen
LPS	=	lipopolysaccharide
Mϕ	=	monocyte–macrophage(s)
mAb	=	monoclonal antibody
MAPK	=	mitogen-activated protein kinase
MHC	=	major histocompatibility complex
MMP	=	matrix metalloproteinase
MRI	=	magnetic resonance imaging
MTX	=	methotrexate
NF	=	nuclear factor
NF-κB	=	nuclear factor kappa B
NFAT	=	nuclear factor of activated T cells
NGF	=	nerve growth factor
NK	=	natural killer (cell)
NMR	=	nuclear magnetic resonance
NSAID	=	nonsteroidal anti-inflammatory drug
OA	=	osteoarthritis
OPG	=	osteoprotegerin

PBMC	=	peripheral blood mononuclear cells
PDGF	=	platelet-derived growth factor
PGE$_2$	=	prostaglandin E$_2$
PMA	=	phorbol 12-myristate 13-acetate
RA	=	rheumatoid arthritis
RANK	=	receptor activator of nuclear factor kappa B
RANKL	=	receptor activator of nuclear factor kappa B ligand
RF	=	rheumatoid factor
RT-PCR	=	reverse transcriptase polymerase chain reaction
SLE	=	systemic lupus erythematosus
SNP	=	single nucleotide polymorphism
STAT	=	signal transducer and activator of transcription
TCR	=	T-cell receptor
TGF-β	=	transforming growth factor beta
Th	=	T helper (cell)
TIMP	=	tissue inhibitor of metalloproteinases
TNF	=	tumor necrosis factor
TNF-α	=	tumor necrosis factor alpha
TNFR	=	tumor necrosis factor receptor
TRADD	=	TNF-receptor-associated death-domain protein
TRAF	=	TNF-receptor-associated factor
TRIM	=	T-cell-receptor-interacting molecule
VCAM	=	vascular cell adhesion molecule
VEGF	=	vascular endothelial growth factor

Author index

Subject index